BEGINNING
SHAREPOINT 2010 DEVELOPMENT

BEGINNING

SharePoint® 2010 Development

BEGINNING

SharePoint® 2010 Development

Steve Fox

WILEY

Wiley Publishing, Inc.

Beginning SharePoint® 2010 Development

Published by
Wiley Publishing, Inc.
10475 Crosspoint Boulevard
Indianapolis, IN 46256
www.wiley.com

Copyright © 2010 by Wiley Publishing, Inc., Indianapolis, Indiana

Published simultaneously in Canada

ISBN: 978-0-470-58463-7
ISBN: 978-0-470-88182-8 (ebk)
ISBN: 978-0-470-88183-5 (ebk)
ISBN: 978-0-470-90477-0 (ebk)

Manufactured in the United States of America

10 9 8 7 6 5 4 3 2 1

For general information on our other products and services please contact our Customer Care Department within the United States at (877) 762-2974, outside the United States at (317) 572-3993 or fax (317) 572-4002.

Wiley also publishes its books in a variety of electronic formats. Some content that appears in print may not be available in electronic books.

Library of Congress Control Number: 2010926824

For my wife

ABOUT THE AUTHOR

STEVE FOX of Redmond, WA, is a Senior Technical Evangelist in the Developer Platform Evangelism group at Microsoft. He's worked in the IT industry for more than 15 years, and has worked in the areas of natural language, search, developer tools, and, more recently, Office Business Application and SharePoint development. Fox also presents at both domestic and international conferences (such as TechEd, PDC, DevConnections, and SAP TechEd, among others), and has written a number of books such as *Professional SharePoint 2007 Development using Silverlight 2* (Indianapolis: Wiley, 2009) and *Microsoft .NET and SAP* (Redmond, WA: Microsoft Press, 2009), as well as articles for *MSDN Magazine* and other technical magazines.

ABOUT THE TECHNICAL EDITORS

DARRIN BISHOP is a speaker, author, and developer focusing on Microsoft SharePoint Technologies. He is the president and lead developer for Darrin Bishop Group, Inc., a Midwest-based Microsoft Partner focusing on SharePoint Technologies, portals, and collaboration. He is the author of *The Rational Guide to Building SharePoint Web Parts* (Greenland, N.H: Rational Press, 2008), as well as several articles in various magazines. Bishop is an international speaker and speaks at many SharePoint conferences, SharePoint Saturdays, MOSS Camps, and User Groups. He has been working with SharePoint Technologies since the release of SharePoint Portal Server 2001.

ELI ROBILLARD designs and guides the delivery of global SharePoint solutions as a Principal Architect at Infusion Development Corporation. He is a SharePoint Server MVP, a co-author of *Professional SharePoint 2007 Development* (Indianapolis: Wiley, 2007), founder of the Toronto SharePoint Users Group, co-chair of the Toronto SharePoint Camp, and past chair of a group of high-profile industry influencers and early-adopters known as the ASPInsiders. Robillard lives in Toronto, Ontario, Canada where he also plays music and goes on adventures with Dawn, Irina, and their dog, Dakota.

KENNETH SCHAEFER is an independent developer and designer focusing on SharePoint and Web-based solutions.

BRENDON SCHWARTZ has worked in the Atlanta area User Group scene, and is known around town as one of the Atlanta .NET Regular Guys (www.devcow.com). He is currently on the INETA Board of Directors as the Vice President of Technology, and is a Microsoft MVP for ASP.NET. Today, Brendon works to solve real-world business problems with Microsoft technologies, such as SharePoint, Office, BizTalk, VSTS, and .NET technologies. In addition to presenting at local User Groups, he helped create the "Free Training 1,2,3!" series (www.freetraining123.com) to help developers learn Microsoft technologies. He presented material at the first SharePoint 1,2,3! event (www.sharepoint123.com), along with other members of the Atlanta Microsoft Professionals. Schwartz has helped on the leadership teams of five different User Groups. At the first Atlanta Code Camp in 2005, he presented material on ASP.NET mobile controls.

CREDITS

ACQUISITIONS EDITOR
Paul Reese

PROJECT EDITOR
Kevin Shafer

TECHNICAL EDITORS
Darrin Bishop
Eli Robillard
Ken Schaefer
Brendon Schwartz

PRODUCTION EDITOR
Eric Charbonneau

COPY EDITOR
Foxxe Editorial

EDITORIAL DIRECTOR
Robyn B. Siesky

EDITORIAL MANAGER
Mary Beth Wakefield

ASSOCIATE DIRECTOR OF MARKETING
David Mayhew

PRODUCTION MANAGER
Tim Tate

VICE PRESIDENT AND EXECUTIVE GROUP PUBLISHER
Richard Swadley

VICE PRESIDENT AND EXECUTIVE PUBLISHER
Barry Pruett

ASSOCIATE PUBLISHER
Jim Minatel

PROJECT COORDINATOR, COVER
Lynsey Stanford

COMPOSITOR
Jeff Lytle, Happenstance Type-O-Rama

PROOFREADER
Beth Prouty, Word One

INDEXER
Johnna VanHoose Dinse

COVER DESIGNER
Michael E. Trent

COVER IMAGE
© Slobo Mitic/istockphoto

ACKNOWLEDGMENTS

WHEN IT COMES TO WRITING A BOOK, no man is an island. It takes countless hours and resources to compile a book of this nature. That said, I'd like to thank Jim Minatel and Paul Reese for taking on the project, and to Kevin Shafer for marshaling the book through the editorial and review process.

A number of technical editors helped review chapters, so a big thanks to Darrin, Eli, Ken, and Brendan. The comments were great and helped create a better end product. They also taught me a few things along the way.

I'd also like to say a blanket thanks to all of the content and production editors. All of you made the book possible and, at the end of the day, a much better product for the beginning SharePoint developer.

On a personal note, I'd like to thank my wife who put up with me locking myself away for hours at a time. Nicole, you are ever-tolerant and I'm deeply indebted to you.

CONTENTS

INTRODUCTION

MY FIRST EXPERIENCE WITH SHAREPOINT was the task of integrating multiple SharePoint 2003 sites into one all-up organizational portal — a fairly straightforward project that integrated four sites into one. This one project got me curious, and, in the process, not only exposed me to the inner workings of SharePoint, but also got me hooked on the technology.

As I learned more about SharePoint, I realized the path was longer than I had originally thought. Since that time, I've seen the platform mature quite a bit, and interest from developers like yourself swell to what is now a very high rate of growth and adoption. And the market for SharePoint is also growing at a very rapid pace — one that is currently outpacing the growth of the SharePoint developer community.

What you'll learn in this book is that SharePoint 2010 has a lot to offer the developer. You can move from the small-scale development project where you're building custom Web parts, to the larger, enterprise-grade solution that leverages Web services and integrates with other Microsoft and non-Microsoft technologies. This is the incredible part about SharePoint — it is a platform with huge potential in multiple directions. And, as a beginning SharePoint developer, you should strap yourself in, because you're in for a great ride.

WHO THIS BOOK IS FOR

Simply put, this book is aimed at the developer who is new to SharePoint. The book assumes that you have some programming experience and a passion to learn how to develop for SharePoint. But this book does not assume that you've programmed against SharePoint before. If this somewhat fits with you, then this book is absolutely for you.

With regard to your general development background, the two assumptions in this book are that you have some familiarity with Web development, and you have an understanding of .NET programming. With regard to Web development, this book assumes that you understand HTML, and may have an understanding of Cascading Style Sheets (CSS), Extensible Markup Language/Extensible Stylesheet Language (XML/XSL), and dynamic languages such as JavaScript. You may have a light understanding of ASP.NET and are looking to apply this knowledge to the SharePoint space. In any case, you have some understanding of the fundamentals of Web and .NET development, and are looking to apply those to the SharePoint space.

WHAT THIS BOOK COVERS

SharePoint 2010 is a significant leap forward from the 2007 release, and you will find that there are a ton of features built into the platform for you to leverage in your solution development. Because SharePoint is a broad platform that covers a lot, this book also covers quite a bit of ground surface. As a *Wrox Beginning* book, the goal of the book is to get you started with many of the fundamentals so that you can continue on to advanced programming beyond this book.

In this book, you can expect to see coverage of the following:

➤ Getting started with development for SharePoint 2010

➤ Becoming familiar with tools that you will use to develop for SharePoint

➤ Becoming familiar with common SharePoint development tasks

➤ Programming against lists and developing custom Web parts

➤ Integrating line-of-business (LOB) data with SharePoint and Microsoft Office

➤ Integrating Silverlight and SharePoint

➤ Creating service-oriented solutions for SharePoint

➤ Integrating SharePoint and Microsoft Office

➤ Security fundamentals in SharePoint

This book will not cover SharePoint 2007, but will cover areas that span SharePoint Foundation 2010 and SharePoint Server 2010. You can also expect to find references to other resources as you work through the book — resources such as blogs, Microsoft Developer Network (MSDN) articles, C9 training modules, and source code — all of the things that you need to get started developing for SharePoint.

HOW THIS BOOK IS STRUCTURED

This book is structured in four parts:

➤ *Part I: Welcome to SharePoint 2010* — This includes the following:

  ➤ Chapter 1, "Introduction to SharePoint"

  ➤ Chapter 2, "Getting Started with SharePoint Development"

➤ *Part II: Getting Started with SharePoint 2010 Development* — This includes the following:

  ➤ Chapter 3, "SharePoint 2010 Developer Tools"

  ➤ Chapter 4, "Common Developer Tasks in SharePoint 2010"

  ➤ Chapter 5, "Programming Against SharePoint 2010 Lists"

  ➤ Chapter 6, "Building and Deploying SharePoint Web Parts"

  ➤ Chapter 7, "Creating Your First SharePoint 2010 Application"

➤ *Part III: Advanced Topics for SharePoint 2010 Development* — This includes the following:

  ➤ Chapter 8, "Integrating Line-of-Business Data Using Business Connectivity Services"

  ➤ Chapter 9, "Creating Enhanced User Experiences for SharePoint with Silverlight"

  ➤ Chapter 10, "Developing Service-Oriented Applications for SharePoint 2010"

➤   Chapter 11, "Integrating SharePoint with Microsoft Office"

➤   Chapter 12, "Securing Your SharePoint 2010 Applications"

➤ *Part IV: Appendix* — This includes the following:

➤   Appendix, "Where to Go from Here"

The goal is to quickly take you from the basics of SharePoint, to installing and configuring a development environment, and then into how you can develop for SharePoint. The book is heavy on coding exercises, but tries to stick to a common set of .NET patterns to ensure you walk away understanding the different ways in which you can code for SharePoint. Moving from beginning to advanced means that you can expect the walkthroughs and chapters to become increasingly more complex within each chapter and throughout the book. The walkthroughs have been created to be concise and to guide you through all of the steps you must accomplish to complete a coding task.

The structure of the book mimics the development ramp-up cycle for SharePoint. That is, you must first understand the breadth of the SharePoint platform. You then install it and the development environment; and then you begin to code — simple at first, but tasks that grow increasingly more complex. You will find that when coding against SharePoint, you may do certain things more (such as programming against lists and creating custom Web parts). As such, these topics are covered in Part II of the book. Also, you may find that, as you advance in your SharePoint development, you will need to incorporate either Silverlight or Web services in your SharePoint solutions. Because you would likely combine these types of tasks inside of a custom Web part, list-based application, or event receiver, these were placed in Part III of the book.

To help you along, this book has source code samples you can download at the Wrox Web site (http://www.wrox.com). You'll also find some video screencasts here to accompany some of the more challenging developer tasks to provide you with more insight on how to walk through the exercises.

WHAT YOU NEED TO USE THIS BOOK

To use this book, the following hardware is recommended:

➤ 64-bit compliant hardware

➤ 8 GB RAM

➤ 150 GB hard drive space

➤ Dual processor (or reasonably close)

And the following software is recommended:

➤ Windows operating system, specifically the following:

➤   Windows Server 2008 or 2008 R2 (for installation or Hyper-V)

➤   Windows 7 (for installation)

➤ SharePoint Server 2010

➤ SQL Server 2008 (Express or above)

➤ Visual Studio 2010 (Professional)

➤ Silverlight Tools and SDK

➤ SharePoint Designer 2010

➤ Office 2010 (Professional Plus)

➤ Expression Blend (Optional)

> **NOTE** *You can download a virtual machine that has all of the necessary software on it. It runs in Hyper-V and can be downloaded from* `http://www .microsoft.com/downloads/details.aspx?FamilyID=0c51819b-3d40-435c- a103-a5481fe0a0d2&displaylang=en`. *Chapter 2 discusses this in more depth.*

CONVENTIONS

To help you get the most from the text and keep track of what's happening, we've used a number of conventions throughout the book.

Examples that you can download and try out for yourself generally appear in a box like this:

TRY IT OUT

The *Try It Out* is an exercise you should work through, following the text in the book.

1. They usually consist of a set of steps.

2. Each step has a number.

3. Follow the steps through with your copy of the database.

How It Works

After each *Try It Out*, the code you've typed will be explained in detail.

> **WARNING** *Boxes like this one hold important, not-to-be forgotten information that is directly relevant to the surrounding text.*

> **NOTE** *Tips, hints, tricks, and asides to the current discussion are offset and placed in italics like this.*

As for styles in the text:

➤ We *highlight* new terms and important words when we introduce them.

➤ We show keyboard strokes like this: Ctrl+A.

➤ We show filenames, URLs, and code within the text like so: `persistence.properties`.

➤ We present code in two different ways:

```
In code examples, we highlight new and important code with a boldface font.
The boldfacing is not used for code that's less important in the present context,
    or has been shown before.
```

SOURCE CODE

As you work through the examples in this book, you may choose either to type in all the code manually, or to use the source code files that accompany the book. All of the source code used in this book is available for download at `http://www.wrox.com`. Once at the site, simply locate the book's title (either by using the Search box, or by using one of the title lists) and click the Download Code link on the book's detail page to obtain all the source code for the book.

> **NOTE** *Because many books have similar titles, you may find it easiest to search by ISBN. This book's ISBN is 978-0-470-58463-7.*

Once you download the code, just decompress it with your favorite compression tool. Alternately, you can go to the main Wrox code download page at `http://www.wrox.com/dynamic/books/download.aspx` to see the code available for this book and all other Wrox books.

> **NOTE** *This book provides a lot of code samples — you'll see many of the code samples focus on the core processing code for a specific API or feature. When you leverage what you learn from this code in your production coding, you will, of course, want to apply proper coding practices, such as error trapping and exception handling. For more information on coding best practices, visit the MSDN Patterns and Practices site at* `http://msdn.microsoft.com/en-us/practices/default.aspx`*.*

ERRATA

We make every effort to ensure that there are no errors in the text or in the code. However, no one is perfect, and mistakes do occur. If you find an error in one of our books (such as a spelling mistake or faulty piece of code), we would be very grateful for your feedback. By sending in errata, you may save another reader hours of frustration and, at the same time, you will be helping us provide even higher-quality information.

To find the errata page for this book, go to `http://www.wrox.com` and locate the title using the Search box or one of the title lists. Then, on the book details page, click the Book Errata link. On this page you can view all errata that has been submitted for this book and posted by Wrox editors. A complete book list including links to each book's errata is also available at `www.wrox.com/misc-pages/booklist.shtml`.

If you don't spot "your" error on the Book Errata page, go to `www.wrox.com/contact/techsupport.shtml` and complete the form there to send us the error you have found. We'll check the information and, if appropriate, post a message to the book's errata page and fix the problem in subsequent editions of the book.

P2P.WROX.COM

For author and peer discussion, join the P2P forums at `p2p.wrox.com`. The forums are a Web-based system for you to post messages relating to Wrox books and related technologies, and to interact with other readers and technology users. The forums offer a subscription feature to email you topics of interest of your choosing when new posts are made to the forums. Wrox authors, editors, other industry experts, and your fellow readers are present on these forums.

At `http://p2p.wrox.com` you will find a number of different forums that will help you not only as you read this book, but also as you develop your own applications. To join the forums, just follow these steps:

1. Go to `p2p.wrox.com` and click the Register link.
2. Read the terms of use and click Agree.
3. Complete the required information to join, as well as any optional information you wish to provide, and click Submit.
4. You will receive an email with information describing how to verify your account and complete the joining process.

> **NOTE** *You can read messages in the forums without joining P2P, but, in order to post your own messages, you must join.*

Once you join, you can post new messages and respond to messages other users post. You can read messages at any time on the Web. If you would like to have new messages from a particular forum emailed to you, click the "Subscribe to this Forum" icon by the forum name in the forum listing.

For more information about how to use the Wrox P2P, be sure to read the P2P FAQs for answers to questions about how the forum software works, as well as many common questions specific to P2P and Wrox books. To read the FAQs, click the FAQ link on any P2P page.

PART I
Welcome to SharePoint 2010

1

Introduction to SharePoint 2010

WHAT YOU'LL LEARN IN THIS CHAPTER:

➤ Getting familiar with the core functionality and features of SharePoint

➤ Understanding the basics of SharePoint architecture

➤ What's available to developers in SharePoint 2010

SharePoint is an exciting Web-based technology. In its fourth version, SharePoint has undergone quite an evolution since the 2003 release, and the types of things you can do with SharePoint run far and wide. Those who have had the chance to see the product grow up will be surprised and happy with many of the changes that are now built into the platform. In fact, existing SharePoint developers will witness what arguably is a significant change in the features and functionality that SharePoint provides, as well as an evolution in the tools supported and the developer community that rallies around the technology. Aspiring SharePoint developers will realize there is quite a bit of power in the platform that you should be able to put into practice by the end of this book.

SharePoint has matured into a first-class *platform* that will enable you to build and deploy a wide array of solutions, as well as take advantage of the build-and-publish model that SharePoint users and developers have come to enjoy. In fact, SharePoint 2010 offers such a wide array of features that it is challenging for any one person to claim to be an expert across all of the SharePoint workloads. You will need to dedicate some time to becoming an expert, but the journey will be worth it.

With that in mind, this chapter introduces you to what SharePoint is and examines some of the high-level features for the developer. This chapter will also describe the capabilities that make SharePoint a platform that is interesting and compelling for you, the developer, to learn. Specific topics include the types of platform services to expect, data programmability, and the ways in which you can build and deploy a SharePoint solution. Toward the end of this chapter, you'll be introduced to Central Administration, where you'll find an array of administrative capabilities for SharePoint.

GETTING TO KNOW SHAREPOINT

Microsoft describes SharePoint 2010 as the *business productivity platform for the enterprise and the Internet.* To provide you with an idea of the types of things that you can do with SharePoint, Figure 1-1 breaks down SharePoint into three separate areas:

➤ *Collaborate* — As you move throughout this book, you'll see the notion of *collaboration* is a very strong theme for SharePoint. This is because SharePoint is about bringing people together through different types of collaboration, such as enterprise content management (ECM), Web content management (WCM), social computing through the use of wikis or blogs, creating dashboards to fulfill your business intelligence (BI) needs, and so on.

➤ *Interoperability* — SharePoint is also about bringing this collaboration together through *interoperability.* This means Office client and Web-based document integration, and the capability to build and deploy Office business applications (OBAs) — custom solutions that integrate line-of-business (LOB) data with SharePoint and Office, integrating with Web 2.0 technologies, or deploying applications to the cloud. It also means enhanced security through an evolved security model called Claims-Based Authentication that helps facilitate integration with other line-of-business (LOB) systems.

➤ *Platform* — As you'll see, SharePoint is a *platform* that supports not only interoperability and collaboration but also extensibility, through a rich object model, a solid set of developer tools, and a growing developer community.

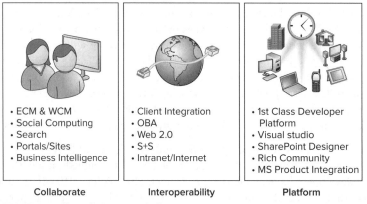

Collaborate	Interoperability	Platform
• ECM & WCM • Social Computing • Search • Portals/Sites • Business Intelligence	• Client Integration • OBA • Web 2.0 • S+S • Intranet/Internet	• 1st Class Developer Platform • Visual studio • SharePoint Designer • Rich Community • MS Product Integration

FIGURE 1-1 SharePoint as a platform

These are three key themes that you will find crop up throughout most discussions of SharePoint and implicitly through many of the capabilities you'll get to explore throughout this book.

At its essence, SharePoint is a Web-based platform that provides the following:

➤ A set of native capabilities to support productivity and collaboration

➤ An extensible set of APIs and services

➤ A configuration engine that provides rich administrative abilities

However, depending on the role of the person who is using SharePoint (for example, the end user versus the developer versus the IT professional), the stated definition may take on a slightly different hue.

For example, for the end user, SharePoint enhances productivity by providing a core set of connected applications that essentially act as the Web-based application platform. The applications enable people to connect using wiki sites, workspaces, lists, document libraries, and integration with Microsoft Office applications, such as Outlook, Excel, and Word 2010.

From an organizational point of view, the unified infrastructure enables the organization to rally around a central point of collaboration — be it through an organizational portal, a team site, or a personal My Site. It also enables organizations to integrate LOB systems, such as SAP, Siebel, PeopleSoft, and Microsoft Dynamics, into the information worker experience through SharePoint.

The response to business needs arrives through the capability to use SharePoint as a toolset in the everyday work lives of an organization's employees — for example routing documents through managed processes, providing BI dashboards, or supplying audit tracking for documents in the Record Center. In essence, SharePoint 2010 represents a platform that offers the organization a lot of functionality to do many different things, with collaboration lying at the heart of them.

By stating that SharePoint is the platform for the enterprise and the Internet, Microsoft is implying that SharePoint has predominantly excelled in two spaces.

The first (and historically predominant) is the enterprise, which means that many large companies are attracted by what SharePoint offers, and are attracted to its lower cost compared to competitive products or technologies. This is because, for example, the platform is tightly integrated with Office, other Microsoft technologies (such as SQL Server and Silverlight), and external technologies and LOB systems.

While the enterprise has been an historical stronghold for SharePoint, there have been some interesting movements into the small and medium-sized business (SMB) space for SharePoint as well. This is evidenced by the fact that SharePoint comes in a variety of flavors and editions, as shown in Figure 1-2, and some of these can be leveraged by SMB developers to deliver some great experiences for SharePoint consumers. (Note that these were the editions as of this writing, and may be subject to change. For the latest editions, see `http://sharepoint2010.microsoft.com`.)

For example, among the different SharePoint editions shown in Figure 1-2 is SharePoint Foundation 2010. SharePoint Foundation (roughly equivalent to *Windows SharePoint Services 3.0* in the 2007 release) is a free version of SharePoint and offers a baseline set of capabilities such as a set of site templates, security and administration, and web collaboration capabilities. Further, SharePoint Server 2010 (which is roughly equivalent to Microsoft Office SharePoint Server (MOSS) in 2007) is an edition that provides richer capabilities built into the platform such as a wider array of server-side services and collaboration options. You need to pay for SharePoint Server 2010, but the key is that these different editions offer you some choice as to where you want to start and the types of solutions you can build. Thus, companies have great flexibility when deciding upon what flavor of SharePoint to implement.

Because SharePoint is essentially a Web-based technology, you interact with SharePoint from your Internet browser. The Web-based experience is managed through an intranet, an extranet, or the Internet. For example, Figure 1-3 shows the SharePoint 2010 interface invoked from the Internet Explorer browser. (SharePoint is cross-browser, so you can use other Internet browsers such as

Safari or Firefox with SharePoint.) This view is the default Team Site template (one of the site templates that ships with SharePoint) that is typical of a SharePoint intranet site.

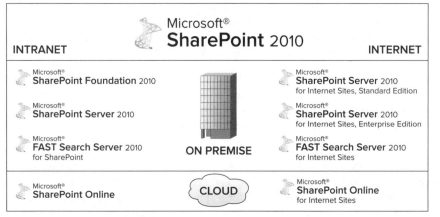

FIGURE 1-2 SharePoint 2010 Editions

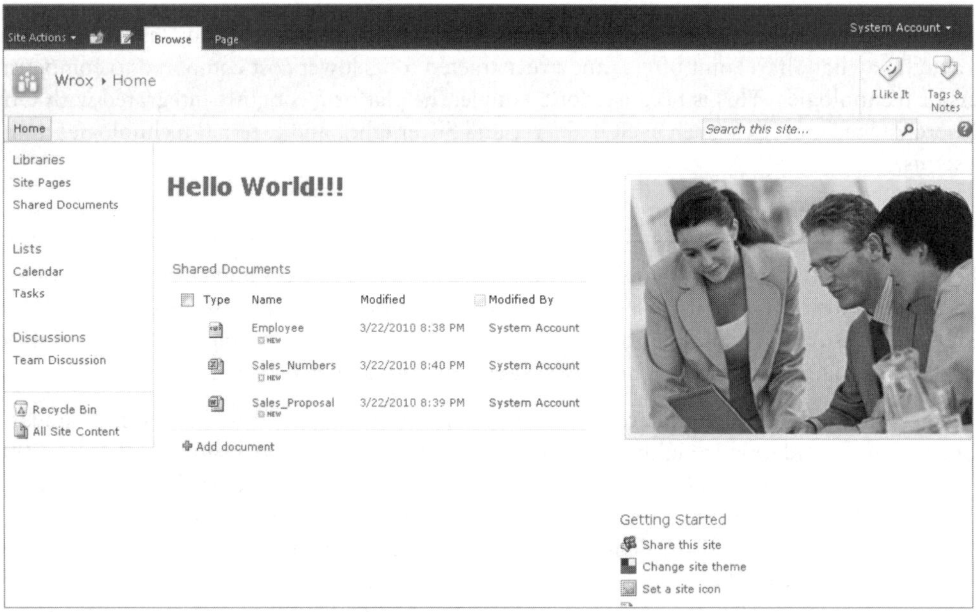

FIGURE 1-3 SharePoint, Hello World!

As you can see in Figure 1-3, the main portion of the page consists of three different components:

➤ Some text ("Hello World!!!"),

➤ A link to Microsoft Office documents

➤ A default image

Also note that, down the left-hand side of the page, you have the Quick Launch navigation pane, which enables you to link to other functionality and sites within the SharePoint site. A ribbon at the top (very similar to the Office 2007 and 2010 Office client ribbon) provides centralized groups of elements that also load different functionality into the main content window. There is also a search option that connects you to other core SharePoint sites, functionality, and content within the site located in the top right of the page. And, lastly, you also have a set of other links, such as one to your My Site on this Web site, located in the upper right-hand corner of the page. As you'll find out throughout this book, SharePoint is very user-friendly. The view you see in Figure 1-3 can be edited and customized by the user, it can be integrated with Office documents, and it can be branded with a specific theme.

Thus, the Web-based experience that SharePoint provides intrinsically facilitates an out-of-the-box experience and integrates core (as well as external) applications and functionality that end users can employ during their daily work lives.

In Figure 1-4, you'll note that the default view has changed. This is because the site is now in Edit mode, which enables you to customize the SharePoint site. In this view, you can see that the user has clicked a part of the SharePoint page, and is now trying to insert an instance of the Content Editor Web part (which provides HTML and source-code editing capabilities) from the Authoring Web part category. The fact that you can quickly put a site into Edit mode, make some changes, and then save those changes back to the server is one of the great advantages of SharePoint.

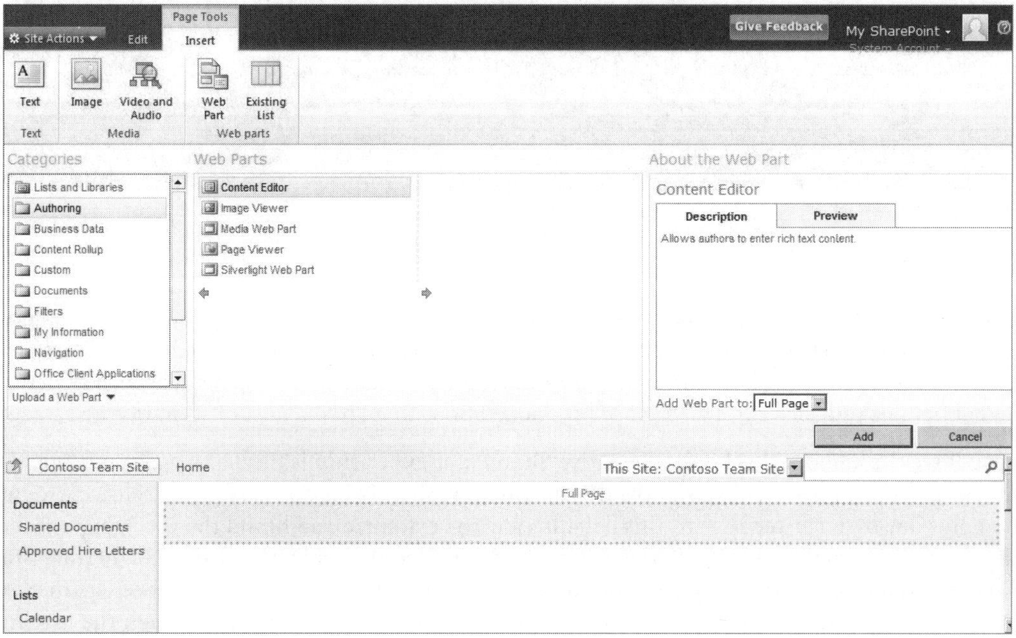

FIGURE 1-4 Editing a SharePoint site

While the experiences in Figure 1-3 and Figure 1-4 are the out-of-the-box default intranet site experiences (for viewing and editing), SharePoint also offers a full publishing-to-the-Web experience. This manifests in a special publishing template to meet your WCM needs, and provides you with templates, theming, a default site experience, workflow, and so on, so that you can create and publish content to your Internet Web sites.

You may be surprised to learn that innumerable companies are using SharePoint for their Internet-facing Web sites. For example, Figure 1-5 shows the Ferrari Internet Web site that is built using SharePoint. You'll also note that the site is rendered in Firefox.

FIGURE 1-5 Ferrari Web site built using SharePoint

For organizations, this can provide a one-stop shop for leveraging the SharePoint infrastructure both for internal sites, to manage your day-to-day project needs, and as an external publishing workflow and infrastructure to manage your publicly facing sites as well. The key point is that SharePoint provides the infrastructure for both intranet *and* Internet publishing and development, as well as many different options provided through a set of product editions to map to a host of scenarios and budgets.

As you'll see throughout this book, the native SharePoint experience is, in many ways, customizable. For example, Figure 1-4 shows the default site that SharePoint creates for you. However, you can apply your own master page to this default view to customize and brand the user's experience. This could be as simple as changing the colors, or it could be as deeply branded as the Ferrari site. You could even reconstruct the navigation through the use of Silverlight to simply leverage the SharePoint infrastructure and re-create your own customized user experience through the user interface (UI). And this is just the tip of the iceberg.

ADDRESSING THE NEEDS OF THE DEVELOPER

If you define SharePoint as a *business productivity platform*, you may be wondering exactly where the developer fits into this description. Although it seems like a convenient and common-sense way of viewing SharePoint from an end-user perspective, what about the needs of the developer? To understand how SharePoint applies to the developer, you must get past the surface definition and drive toward the platform capabilities. Here, you'll begin to see some interesting and compelling pivots for the developer.

Let's look at a practical example. As you have seen, a *business productivity platform* implies having a platform for end users to make them more productive in their day-to-day work lives — and SharePoint can certainly do that. In short order, it can be used as an application for end users. For example, a Human Resources (HR) department might use SharePoint to manage employee reviews, or a sales team might use it to manage a monthly sales-forecasting dashboard for BI.

In both of these scenarios, SharePoint represents an end-user application (or *bundle* of applications), but developers are not necessarily called out at this level. However, because SharePoint represents a platform, you know that you can build on this platform, or extend its capabilities.

So, when your HR manager comes to you and asks you to design a SharePoint site collection that integrates data from SQL Server or SAP, you get excited. When that same HR manager asks you to map a custom document template to a SharePoint 2010 content type (that also pulls data in from PeopleSoft), you become equally excited. And when the sales manager asks you to get data from an Excel 2010 worksheet and then render that data inside of a Silverlight application in SharePoint, you really start to jump up and down.

Extension and Enrichment for Developers

While SharePoint 2010 represents a set of connected applications (such as dashboards, document libraries, and the like), it still has a vast array of opportunities for developers to extend and enrich that end-user experience at multiple levels. This experience is obviously important when you think about SharePoint in the context of the enterprise developer. However, when the independent software vendors (ISVs) begin to think about that custom experience they want to deploy to their customers, it becomes vital that they have a reliable platform beneath their feet that they can deploy to and use to customize their SharePoint solutions. Their business depends on this stability and predictability. Thus, SharePoint 2010 has done a very good job of providing a scalable platform that supports multiple types of developers and their nd design ambitions.

So, SharePoint pplications that make up SharePoint serve the ne here developers can develop on top of SharePoint

In a paper a om/rb/Research/now_is_time_to_determine_snarepoints_place/q/id/45560/t/2) entitled "Now Is the Time to Determine SharePoint's Place in Your Application Development Strategy," John R. Rymer and Rob Koplowitz reinforce this model. The two authors propose that SharePoint has an application level, where end users integrate with the out-of-the-box collaboration and productivity applications. They then add a customization layer, where either power users or developers can begin to customize the SharePoint experience for the end user. And lastly, they have a third layer, which is the application development layer.

It is at this application development layer where things get very interesting for developers. Here is where you'll find the solution developer who builds and deploys (or integrates through existing SharePoint artifacts) applications or business solutions — such as creating a SharePoint list that is capable of reading and writing data into an external LOB system, such as SAP or Siebel, or a Silverlight-enabled business application that is deployed as a Web part into your SharePoint infrastructure.

Breaking It Down for Developers

What you may have gathered so far in this chapter is that SharePoint development can, indeed, mean a number of things. For example, if you want to simply customize SharePoint, you may only have to interact with page layouts or master pages (that is, the way in which you structure content in SharePoint). This type of work would entail a baseline understanding of HTML editing, CSS, and some understanding of how ASP.NET master pages work. However, if you want to do deeper-level solution development, you may be interacting with the SharePoint object model, and leveraging .NET and Web services to do this. This type of development would entail using managed-code (that is, C# and Visual Basic, or VB.NET) solutions that are built and deployed into SharePoint — a potentially more complex type of coding experience for the developer.

You could argue that the people performing both tasks are equally identified as developers on the SharePoint platform, but what this brings to bear is the fact that actual development can range from HTML/XHTML, AJAX, and XSLT to .NET and service-based development — and a few things in between. So, what you might find are *both* developers and power users of SharePoint operating at this level. However, this is not only symptomatic of SharePoint being a broad platform but also a symptom of the different standards, applications, and interoperability that SharePoint must support as a good citizen of the Web.

Thus, if you break down the use of SharePoint across the three levels shown in Figure 1-6, you'll find the largest population of SharePoint consumers interacting with the Applications level. These are the end users, and they represent your core audience when building and deploying your custom applications to SharePoint. Next, you may also operate at the

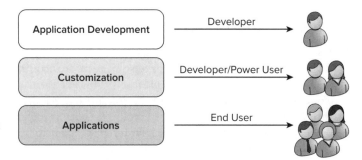

FIGURE 1-6 Three levels of SharePoint

Customization level, where power users possess a high degree of SharePoint knowledge. In some cases, you may work with these people, and in others you will work independently of one another.

Lastly, there is you: the developer. You are, in many cases, the person who is developing those custom applications for SharePoint. You are the one who is developing that next killer app in the ISV ecosystem. And you are the one for whom this book has been written.

Therefore, while the original definition of SharePoint highlights Microsoft's core messaging for the SharePoint 2010 platform, it may not necessarily strike a deep chord with the developer. To capture this, let's expand the original definition and re-frame the context for you, the developer:

> *SharePoint 2010 is about developer productivity, the availability of rich platform services, and the capability to manage and deploy your applications with maximum flexibility.*

With regard to developer productivity, this means that you can use either Visual Studio 2010 or SharePoint Designer (SPD) 2010 as your core set of developer tools. As a professional developer, you'll likely use Visual Studio 2010 as your core toolset — especially if you're a .NET programmer looking to get into the SharePoint space. As for SPD, you're more than likely going to use it to edit master pages and page layouts, as well as to build declarative or rules-based workflows using a visual rules approach (for example, using Visio 2010 and SPD 2010). And as a complement to these tools, you may also use Expression Blend — either as a way to build more advanced and interactive UIs (through Expression Blend) or through Expression Web for baseline Web sites.

> **NOTE** *Chapter 3 explores developer tools in more detail.*

In terms of rich platform services, SharePoint 2010 offers the developer much more in the way of getting, managing, and updating objects and data within a SharePoint site. In this book, you'll learn about new application programming interfaces (APIs) and services that will allow you to do this, and you'll also learn about how to enable LOB system integration to bring external data into your SharePoint applications. You'll see many of the new and still-supported APIs and services throughout the entire book.

You obviously have a number of deployment options at your fingertips. For example, you can import a standard Windows SharePoint Services Solution Package (WSP) into your SharePoint farm. You can build and deploy a solution to a SharePoint instance within the corporate firewall, and you can also build and deploy solutions to a SharePoint site hosted on the wider Internet. What the latter looks like is very similar to the on-premises version of SharePoint; what is different is the fact that you don't need to worry about management of that SharePoint server.

Figure 1-7 shows these as the three core pillars that map to the SharePoint developer experience.

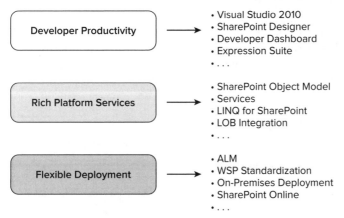

FIGURE 1-7 Developer tenets in SharePoint 2010

You should keep in mind a number of key points with regard to these three core pillars of the developer experience within SharePoint:

➤ SharePoint 2010 has a rich object model, as well as a set of services and APIs that can be leveraged when developing custom solutions.

➤ Visual Studio 2010 now has an out-of-the-box experience for building and deploying SharePoint solutions.

➤ You have a number of ways available to interact with the SharePoint object model using Web services, Windows Communication Foundation (WCF), REST, and the SharePoint Client Object Model.

➤ Data programmability using Language Integrated Query (LINQ) for SharePoint, Business Connectivity Services (BCS) and External Lists makes SharePoint 2010 a first-class platform to extend LOB applications.

➤ There are multiple integration points across other Microsoft and third-party applications (such as Office 2010, SAP, PeopleSoft, Microsoft Dynamics, Microsoft Silverlight, and so on).

➤ A standard deployment methodology now exists for SharePoint 2010 that is defined using the WSP standard deployment method.

➤ You can deploy SharePoint 2010 solutions on premises or to the cloud (that is, SharePoint Online).

These points represent just a sampling of what you can do with SharePoint, and the goal of this book is to show you how you can get started with all of these and more. Keep in mind that, when SharePoint references business productivity, it not only means the applications that you'll be building and customizing for your end users, but it also means for the developers themselves through all of the enhancements in SharePoint 2010.

Now, let's take a closer look at SharePoint at the platform level.

SHAREPOINT 2010: THE PLATFORM

SharePoint 2010 is a rich platform on which you can build and deploy your applications. And it is also an environment that can be customized for your audience or end user. This much you know. What hasn't been discussed yet, though, is what exactly this platform looks like. For example, what is the architecture of SharePoint? What are the specific capabilities of SharePoint? What are the objects and APIs that you, as a developer, have access to?

The first thing to understand is the architecture of SharePoint 2010. Figure 1-8 provides a high-level overview of the technology stack for SharePoint 2010. From the bottom up, note first that SharePoint 2010 runs on the Windows operating system (OS), namely Windows Server 2008 or 2008 R2.

When you install SharePoint, there is also a dependence on SQL Server and ASP.NET. SharePoint is built on the ASP.NET foundation. Thus, if you're familiar with ASP.NET, many of the foundational programming concepts will be familiar to you, such as Web parts or master pages, both in the architecture and programmatically.

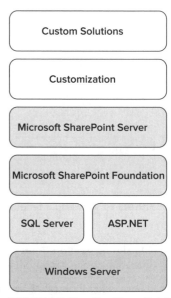

FIGURE 1-8 Baseline SharePoint architecture

In SharePoint 2010, you have two main pieces that make up SharePoint: SharePoint Foundation 2010 and SharePoint Server 2010. While these essentially represent two different editions of SharePoint, SharePoint Server 2010 is built on top of SharePoint Foundation 2010.

> **NOTE** *You can also install SharePoint on Windows 7 (64 bit), Windows Vista SP1 (64 bit), or Windows Vista SP2 (64 bit).*

> **NOTE** *When this book refers to SharePoint 2010 (or just SharePoint), both SharePoint Foundation 2010 and SharePoint Server 2010 are included in this reference.*

SharePoint Foundation ships as a free, downloadable install on the Windows OS, and represents a core part of SharePoint. It includes a number of features such as security and administration, user and team site collaboration, and document libraries and lists. In essence, it provides a baseline set of features that will enable you to get started with both using SharePoint and developing for SharePoint.

While the functionality that ships in SharePoint Foundation is less broad than that which ships in SharePoint 2010, it costs you nothing to download and install SharePoint Foundation. You can get up and running very quickly with this version and begin your development work using it.

However, SharePoint Server 2010 offers a wealth of features that make the leap to buy worth it. For example, you get additional features such as additional Web parts, Office server-side services such as Word and Excel Services, enhanced search versions, enhanced BI, and much, much more. You can also choose to purchase the Internet-specific edition (SharePoint 2010 For Internet Sites), which will provide you with the rich publishing templates and workflow that you can use to create and deploy SharePoint sites to the wider Web (for example, building a scalable SharePoint site for public, anonymous access).

As a developer, you have the capability to customize any of the SharePoint editions — you just have more to customize and leverage with the SharePoint Server 2010 edition. For example, you could create a custom master page and apply it to a team site using SharePoint Foundation, or you can do the same thing in SharePoint Server 2010 and apply it to, for example, a publishing site (a specific type of site that you can use to build and deploy externally facing Web sites).

Beyond thematic or branding customizations, you can also develop and deploy custom solutions. These are, for example, .NET applications that you build using C# or Visual Basic, and then deploy into SharePoint as solutions comprising one or more features. Further, with the full version of SharePoint, you'll have a wider array of services, APIs, and objects that you can either code against, or leverage. This will ultimately make the development experience much richer for you.

If you drill into the SharePoint part of the architecture (that is, the Microsoft SharePoint Server and SharePoint Foundation boxes), you'll find additional functionality within the SharePoint platform that you can leverage. Figure 1-9 shows a high-level overview of the components of the platform.

In this diagram, SharePoint is broken out across a number of areas, including a core set of capabilities, site collection and sites, server APIs and client APIs, and data modeling and programmability.

The "SharePoint Capabilities" provide a convenient way for Microsoft to break out the core competencies of SharePoint. You can consider these the topmost way of breaking out the feature areas of SharePoint. Because SharePoint exists as a Web-based solution, you'll note that the next level down is called "Site Collection and Sites," which is how SharePoint organizes itself as a set of related sites within a site hierarchy. The "Server APIs" and "Client APIs" essentially represent the different ways in which you can interact with the SharePoint objects, such as data in a list or document libraries. And, finally, "Data Modeling & Programmability" represents the ways in which developers can program against the different data objects within SharePoint (for example, list data).

Let's look at each of these in greater detail.

SharePoint 2010 Capabilities

At the top of Figure 1-9, you see the "SharePoint Capabilities." These are the core ways in which SharePoint partitions itself into its respective and related parts. You may also hear Microsoft refer to these capabilities as *workloads*. These workloads (which are shown in Figure 1-10) provide a way to talk about the different capabilities of SharePoint coming together, and you should see these workloads as not only representing a core set of related applications but also as opportunities for your application development.

Within each of the capabilities, you'll find many different development opportunities. For example, the Table 1-1 shows the capabilities in the left-hand column, describes the out-of-the-box features in the next column, and then lists out some examples of extensibility for SharePoint in the third column.

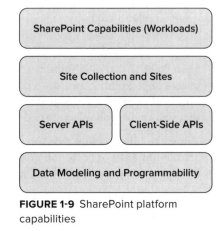

FIGURE 1-9 SharePoint platform capabilities

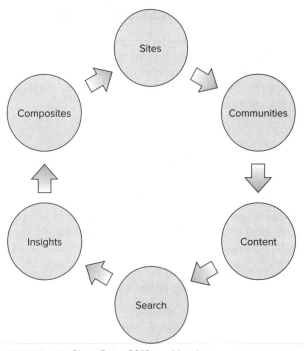

FIGURE 1-10 SharePoint 2010 workloads

TABLE 1-1 Key SharePoint Capabilities

CAPABILITY	NATIVE FEATURES	EXAMPLE EXTENSIBILITY
Sites	Sites is where you'll predominantly find the collaborative aspects of SharePoint. Sites contain an abundance of features, including the capability to create, store, and retrieve list data and document content. You also have connectivity into the Microsoft Office 2010 client applications through the list and document library.	Web parts, workflow, master pages, site pages, Office Web parts
Communities	Provides social APIs and networking capabilities, along with the capability to search against profiles and locate and interact with people through their profile metadata, relationships, tagging, and rating of content.	Search customization, rating and tagging capabilities, blogs, wikis
Content	The capability to collaboratively manage content using Web pages, document libraries, workflow, or content types.	Field controls, content types, workflows, Word or Excel Services
Search	The power to search content inside and outside of SharePoint, including information in structured database systems and external LOB systems such as SAP, Siebel, and Microsoft Dynamics.	Search customization, Business Connectivity Services (BCS), FAST for SharePoint
Insights	Predominantly about BI that supports, for example, the capability to integrate Microsoft Access into SharePoint, leverage Excel and SQL Server to access and display data on a Web page, dashboards, and key performance indicators (KPIs) to transform raw data into actionable information.	Excel Services, Access Services, dashboards, BCS, PerformancePoint Services
Composites	The capability for business users to create their own BI solutions through connection, InfoPath, and Access Data Services integration, customization, and business process management.	Web parts, external lists, workflows , BCS

Site Collection and Sites

Site collection and sites represent the site hierarchy when you create a new site or extend an existing one. As shown in Figure 1-11, a SharePoint server farm (which can comprise one or more physical servers), can be broken out into three major parts:

➤ The Web application that lives in Internet Information Services (IIS)

➤ The site collection, which represents the root SharePoint site

➤ The individual sites that live under the site collection

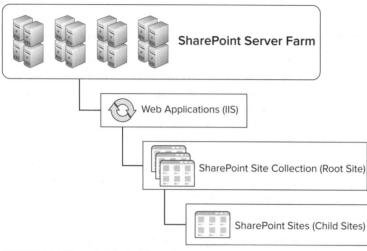

FIGURE 1-11 SharePoint site hierarchy

SharePoint uses IIS as its Web server. So, when you install it and open IIS, you'll see an entry for SharePoint that uses the standard port 80 in IIS. If you open IIS, you should also see a separate Web application entry in IIS for the SharePoint Central Administration site collection. This will be located on a separate port.

If you set up a standalone instance of SharePoint (which you'll do in Chapter 2), you should note that the default site created for you is a *site collection*. The site collection is the uppermost, root site that you'll work from within SharePoint. The site collection is also a site that you can customize and interact with. You grow your SharePoint site collection by adding additional Web sites to it. Any site you create underneath the site collection is called a *site* (and is sometimes referred to as a *Web*). Furthermore, any site you create within that site is a *subsite*. This may seem confusing, but just think of the site collection being the parent and the sites within that collection being children sites.

Within the site, you will predominantly create subsites and interact with lists and list items, document libraries, and a host of other, more discrete features of SharePoint. However, you can also develop against many of the UI-level features that are new to SharePoint 2010. For example, key functionality includes features such as site pages that can be customized and stored in a pages library, the capability to edit text inline (with HTML source or rich text) and more easily add images to a Web part, to utilize Silverlight applications to improve the look, feel, and experience of a user, to transform your pages from XML to HTML using XSLT, and much more. Each of these activities can be accomplished at the site level through the page interface (and, of course, through the developer tools). You should think of each of these as part of a cadre of opportunities for your SharePoint development.

One of the core parts of the SharePoint 2010 UI that is customizable is the *ribbon*, which integrates JavaScript with XML to provide developers with a way to deploy customized elements. You can see in Figure 1-12 that there are tabs with controls on them. The tabs are contextually driven and change depending on what you're doing within SharePoint.

The ribbon is a significant change from earlier versions of SharePoint. The reason that Microsoft changed the ribbon was to make the functions available to the user more central, and to create an experience similar to that of the Office 2010 UI client ribbon. As a developer, you're probably already asking yourself how you can build a custom ribbon. You can do this using XML (that represents the structure of the ribbon), and then mapping JavaScript to that XML document.

As you can see in Figure 1-13, outside of the ribbon, the page structure of a SharePoint Web page is similar to one in SharePoint 2007. There is an area where you add content to the page and an area for your navigation links. The content essentially means anything that you create for the SharePoint site (for example, wiki text, photos, and Web parts). The area that surrounds the content within SharePoint is called the *chrome*.

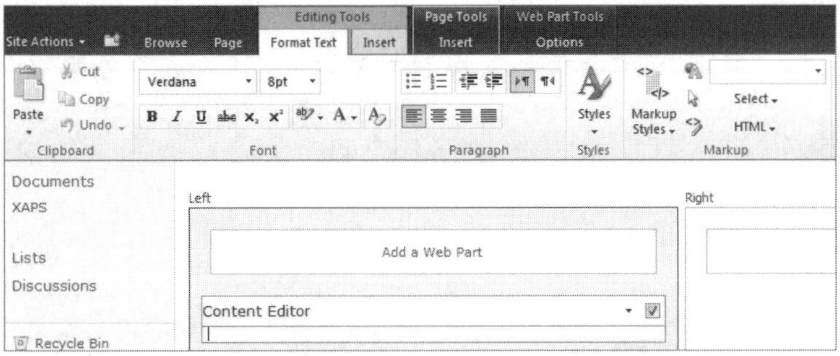

FIGURE 1-12 SharePoint ribbon

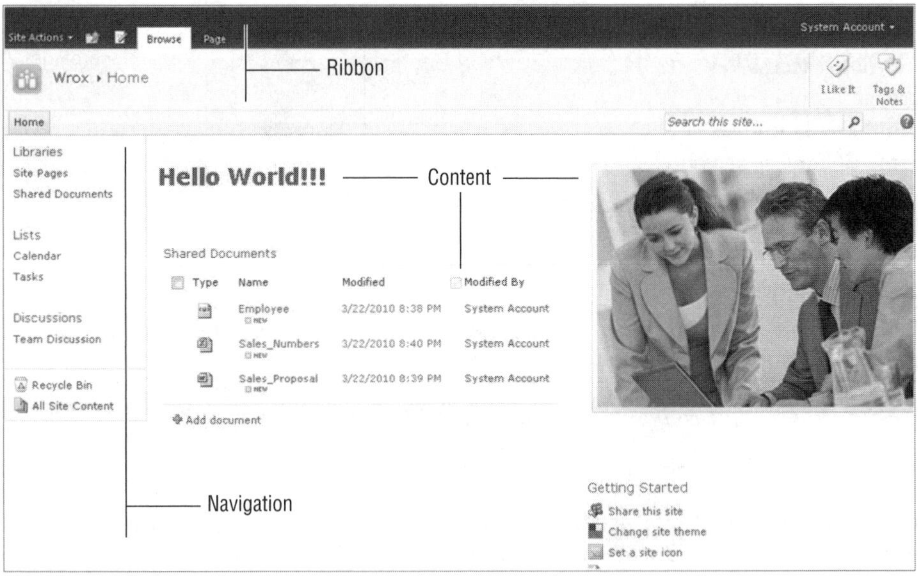

FIGURE 1-13 SharePoint 2010 ribbon and page structure

Server APIs and Client APIs

At some point, you will integrate your solution at some level with the SharePoint object model. For example, you may want to get data out of, or put it into, a SharePoint list, and this will require you to have a "mediation" point to integrate with SharePoint.

In previous versions of SharePoint, you could interact with the SharePoint object model in a couple of different ways (such as through ASP.NET Web services, or by using a server-side reference, and coding directly against the object model). SharePoint 2007 supported ASP.NET Web services out of the box, so you could create and deploy Web services with some degree of ease to either the SharePoint "hive" (that is, the _vti_bin folder within the SharePoint folder hierarchy), or you could create and deploy a Web service to IIS. WCF services were also supported by way of IIS deployment, but were not supported out-of-the-box when deploying to the SharePoint file system — you needed to create a special `VirtualPathProvider` object to handle the `.svc` extension on the WCF service.

SharePoint 2010, however, has made a significant advancement in supporting services. SharePoint 2010 supports interacting with SharePoint through multiple service endpoints. Specifically, it supports the ASP.NET (`.asmx`) Web service standard, WCF services, and RESTful services. It also supports the server-side object model, which enables you to access key SharePoint artifacts from server-deployed assemblies. This gives you a wide array of choices as you embark on your solution development, which, in some way, involves a service-based approach. Figure 1-14 provides an overview of these options.

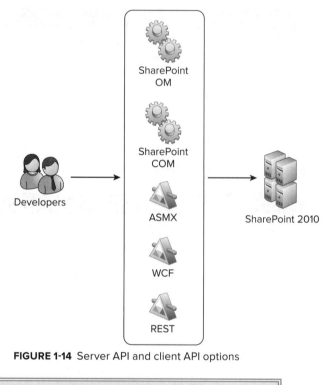

FIGURE 1-14 Server API and client API options

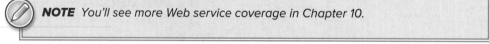

> **NOTE** *You'll see more Web service coverage in Chapter 10.*

Furthermore, SharePoint 2010 also provides you with a client object model, which means that you can program against SharePoint from Silverlight, JavaScript, or Windows Presentation Foundation (WPF) clients (or, more generally, .NET applications) simply by adding a DLL reference to your application and leveraging a new set of APIs. This eliminates the need to use a Web service reference whenever you want to interact with, for example, a SharePoint list, and allows you to have an API that you can use to directly interact with the list and its properties without a service connection.

Data Modeling and Programmability

Within each SharePoint site that you create, you're going to find many different opportunities to program against data. In fact, you'll very often start off with your data and design around it.

In the world of SharePoint, *data* can mean many different things. For example, it might mean connecting a Microsoft Access 2010 database to SharePoint by way of Access Data Services by creating a database in Access and then publishing it to SharePoint. It might also mean interacting with SQL Server data, or interacting with service endpoints through BCS to integrate with LOB and non-Microsoft systems. Further, it might also mean leveraging SQL Server Reporting Services or PerformancePoint Server to bring enhanced BI into your solutions. And, lastly, the data might actually come from a SharePoint list (where users manually enter the list data, and you programmatically code against it).

Each of these examples will require different ways of interacting with data within SharePoint. However, each of them will have different implications for you. For example, you'll find it very easy to create read/write SharePoint lists that connect to SQL Server using a connection string. However, you'll need to think more deeply about authentication to an outside LOB system when connecting using the BCS. Also, you could leverage the SharePoint client object model or an out-of-the-box Web service to interact with SharePoint list data, so you'll need to understand how you design your application to work with that data.

You should be interested not only in how you connect to your data sources but also in how you interact with them. For example, in many cases, you will want to query data when you have created a connection to it from within your SharePoint site. This may mean creating SQL queries or, more optimally, it may mean leveraging LINQ in your applications. Because SharePoint 2010 has the capability to abstract objects such as list data into strongly typed data objects, you can use LINQ to query that data within your applications, making interacting and managing your data a much more efficient process.

In a nutshell, those who are new to SharePoint will find a myriad of opportunities to select when interacting with data. And those who were familiar with SharePoint 2007 will be extremely happy to discover many advancements in SharePoint 2010.

SHAREPOINT CENTRAL ADMINISTRATION

While this is not a book on administration, this section provides a high-level introduction to the topic. As a developer, there may be cases where you want to leverage the capabilities built into SharePoint Central Administration.

After you install SharePoint 2010, a separate site collection is created for your use in performing the different administrative functions that you might do on a daily basis. This site collection is called the *Central Administration* site. This site collection is run as its own Web application in IIS and is separate from the site collections you create. But it is still the central point of administration for your SharePoint site. All farm server administrators can access this site, and, much like your regular SharePoint sites, you can edit and customize the Central Administration site.

Many of you who will develop for SharePoint 2010 will also be the person who administers certain aspects of your SharePoint site. For example, this might mean that you would have to install and configure SharePoint, understand how to upgrade some of your solutions from SharePoint 2007 to 2010, or even create new Web applications or sites using the Central Administration functions. And, while this book is not necessarily meant to be a comprehensive overview of SharePoint 2010 Central Administration, it does provide an introduction.

With this in mind, Figure 1-15 shows the SharePoint 2010 Central Administration site that lists the core administration features. Within the Central Administration site, you can manage a number of activities, which are broken out into the following eight areas:

➤ Application management

➤ Monitoring

➤ Security

➤ General application settings

➤ System settings

➤ Backup and restore

➤ Upgrade and migration

➤ Configuration wizards

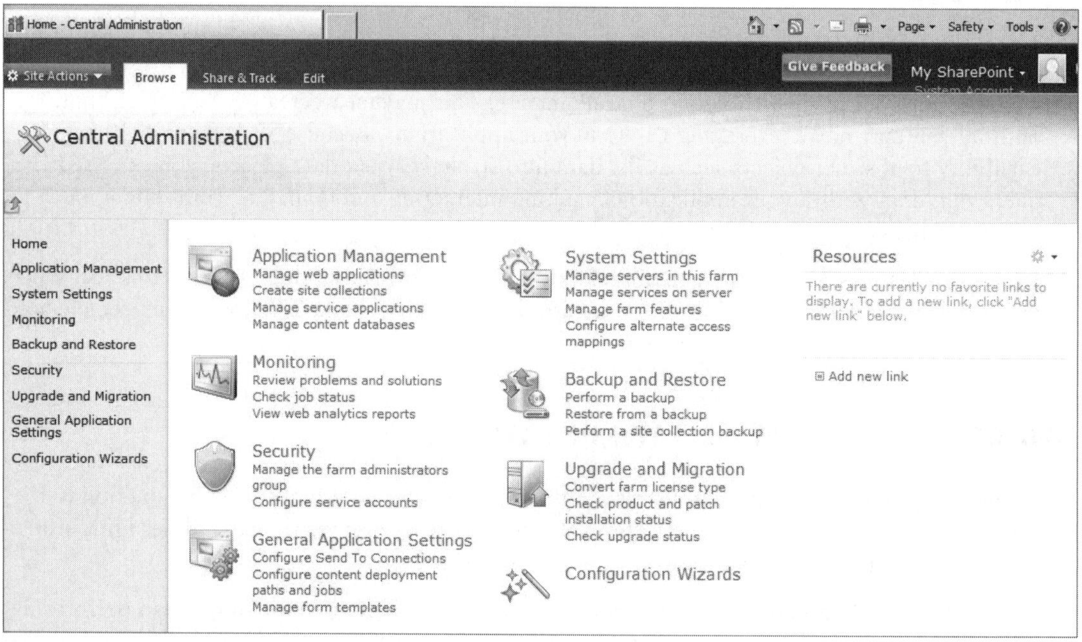

FIGURE 1-15 SharePoint 2010 Central Administration

Application Management

Application Management is the place where you can, for example, create new Web applications and site collections, and, more generally, manage the services that are installed on your SharePoint site (for example, Excel Services or BCS) and manage your content database. (The content database stores SharePoint data, and is the reason why SharePoint takes a dependency on SQL Server upon installation.) Using the application management options, you can accomplish tasks such as modifying the properties of the content database, activating features, creating new site collections, and so on.

Monitoring

Monitoring is the central place within Central Administration to manage reporting, monitoring, and the status of your SharePoint site. The Monitoring site is broken down into three areas:

➤ *Health status* — Health status provides a place for you to manage the status of different services on your SharePoint server (such as Visio services or farm-level services). You can see which services are failing, for example, through reports that are surfaced here. Health status also enables you to define rules (such as the scheduling of application pool recycles).

➤ *Timer jobs* — Timer jobs enable you to define specific jobs to run, and when to run them (such as search crawl log cleanup or audit log trimming jobs).

➤ *Reporting* — Reporting provides you with a set of tools that enables you to create and manage reports, run diagnostic logging, and view reports on various server-side activities.

Security

Security covers a number of areas, including the management of administrator accounts, the configuration and management of service accounts, the management of password change settings and policies, and the specification of authentication providers, trusted identity providers, antivirus settings, blocked file types, Web part security, self-service security, and secure token services. The security settings here supplement the security in the main browser UI, where users and site administrators can assess specific permissions that relate to users for their sites.

General Application Settings

The General Application Settings site is where you configure a number of general options for your SharePoint site collections and sites. For example, you'll often find that you'll want to have the capability for your SharePoint site to send mail to users. You configure these options from within this part of the site.

Also, in the context of WCM, you may want to manage a number of deployment and approval options (such as content deployment location and approvers of that content). You also manage that type of activity from within the General Application Settings.

In general, think of this site as the generic settings for your SharePoint sites.

System Settings

Conversely to using the SharePoint site settings, you may also want to configure more server-centric settings such as farm-level or access features, or even manage the services (for example, Excel Services) that are available to users of the site collection. You manage these types of settings from within the System Settings site.

Backup and Restore

At some point, you may find that you must back up and restore your SharePoint site. The "Backup and Restore" features within Central Administration enable you to create and schedule regular backups for your SharePoint, perform ad hoc backups, restore from a previously backed-up SharePoint site, and so on. Essentially, this is your point of entry if you want to ensure that you have a failover plan for backing up a site.

While you think you may never need this, there is sometimes the convergence of heightened permissions settings with user error, which can result in new users deleting parts of a site by accident — which may include something you've created as a developer.

Upgrade and Migration

At some point, you may find yourself wanting to upgrade from one version of SharePoint to another — for example, moving from SharePoint Standard to SharePoint Enterprise. This requires a license and a server-driven process to upgrade one version of SharePoint to another.

You can do this type of action from within the "Upgrade and Migration" part of the Central Administration site. Note that you can also install service patches and check on installation and upgrade progress from within this part of the administration toolset.

Configuration Wizards

The Configuration Wizard is simply a step-by-step wizard that configures your SharePoint server for you. You should have seen this wizard when you first installed SharePoint. However, if you want to run it again after installation to change some of the configurations on your SharePoint server, you can do so.

SUMMARY

This chapter provided a first look at SharePoint — both for those who have never seen it and for those who are returning SharePoint developers — and answered the question of what it is and what the high-level architectural pieces and capabilities of SharePoint are.

In this chapter, SharePoint was broadly defined as a business productivity platform for the enterprise and the Internet. More specifically, for the developer (and in the context of this book), this definition was recast as a *platform that supports developer productivity, has extensive platform services, and can support multiple deployment options.*

One of the key takeaways from this chapter should be that SharePoint is a rich developer platform. There are an abundance of APIs, an object model, and a powerful set of services that can be leveraged to create some very compelling applications. There is also a great set of tools that will support your efforts at evolving or improving your SharePoint development skills.

In Chapter 2, you will begin to work through a number of exercises that cover installation, configuration, and development.

EXERCISES

1. Define what SharePoint is for both the end user and the developer.

2. What are the three ways in which you can look at SharePoint from a developer's perspective?

3. What are some of the key developer features in SharePoint 2010?

4. What are some of the key administrative features in SharePoint 2010?

▶ **WHAT YOU LEARNED IN THIS CHAPTER**

ITEM	DESCRIPTION
SharePoint	Business productivity platform for the enterprise and the Internet.
SharePoint for the Developer	SharePoint 2010 is about developer productivity, the availability of rich platform services, and the capability to manage and deploy your applications with maximum flexibility.
SharePoint Foundation	Core edition for SharePoint 2010. It ships as a free download. (This was called Windows SharePoint Services 3.0 in SharePoint 2007.)
SharePoint Server 2010	Enterprise edition that is covered in this book, and will be referred to as SharePoint throughout the book. (This was called Microsoft Office SharePoint Server (MOSS) in the 2007 release.)
SharePoint Architecture	SharePoint is built on ASP.NET and installs on a number of 64-bit Windows operating systems.
SharePoint Online	Hosted version of SharePoint that is managed by Microsoft for you in the cloud.
SharePoint Central Administration	The site collection that you use to administer your SharePoint site.

RECOMMENDED READING

There is a vast array of resources out there to get you started on developing for SharePoint 2010. Following are some key resources:

➤ MSDN SharePoint Developer Center at `http://msdn.microsoft.com/en-us/sharepoint/default.aspx`

➤ Channel 9 SharePoint Developer Learning Center at `http://channel9.msdn.com/learn/courses/SharePoint2010Developer/`

➤ SharePoint 2010 SDK at `http://msdn.microsoft.com/en-us/library/ee557253%28office.14%29.aspx`

2

Getting Started with SharePoint 2010 Development

WHAT YOU'LL LEARN IN THIS CHAPTER:

➤ Getting to know the core developer pillars in SharePoint 2010 (including tools, platform services, and deployment options)

➤ Becoming familiar with the primary tools to develop and deploy SharePoint solutions

➤ Performing a number of installation, configuration, and simple development tasks

➤ Understanding site-level security settings within SharePoint

In Chapter 1, you learned about some of the basics of SharePoint 2010, including *what it is* and *some of the high-level features for developers*. You also became familiar with some of the basic architectural concepts, as well as the overall look and feel of a SharePoint site — both the SharePoint site you would interact with on a daily basis and the Central Administration site.

This chapter dives deeper into the developer features of SharePoint 2010, building on the discussion from Chapter 1. This chapter also walks you through some how-to examples that show you some basic Web-based actions, and then progresses into some more in-depth development samples. This chapter addresses some of the technical skills that you can expect to learn and hone as you get more involved with SharePoint development.

Thus, the goals of this chapter are twofold:

➤ To get you more familiar and comfortable with some of the core developer features of SharePoint

➤ To begin to show how you can programmatically interact with SharePoint

So, let's jump in and get started by talking about some of the core developer features for SharePoint.

CORE DEVELOPER FEATURES FOR SHAREPOINT 2010

As mentioned in Chapter 1, the major features for the SharePoint developer can be broken down into three main categories:

➤   Developer productivity

➤   Rich platform services

➤   Flexible deployment

These three areas, in turn, can be broken down into greater detail. By doing so, you'll see that there exist a number of developer-centric features you can take advantage of.

Developer Productivity

For developer productivity, a significant advance for SharePoint 2010 is the tooling support that ships with Visual Studio 2010. Included with Visual Studio are a number of project-level templates and item-level templates that you can use to create and deploy a wide array of features and solutions to SharePoint. For example, Figure 2-1 shows the different templates available to you, which are described in the following list:

➤   *Import SharePoint Solution Package* — This option imports a SharePoint Solution Package (a file with a `.WSP` extension), the standard way of building and deploying SharePoint solutions into your current project that can be redeployed into another SharePoint instance of your choice.

➤   *State Machine Workflow* — This represents a workflow that is based on the system or application state and can be deployed to SharePoint. It leverages Windows Workflow and is a special template that enables automated deployment to SharePoint.

➤   *Event Receiver* — This allows you to create server-side code that can be called and executed by a feature or solution. Event receivers are often created to respond to a user action (for example, when a user adds an item to a list, an event is triggered to update a log entry).

➤   *Empty Project* — An empty SharePoint project can be used as a blank starting point for project development. You can add lists, Web parts, event receivers, and so on, to an empty project, and then deploy it to SharePoint.

➤   *Module* — This provides a way to deploy a specific file to a SharePoint site. It allows for the bundling and provisioning of files for a feature. So, when the feature is activated, the files are deployed to the specified file location.

➤   *Business Data Catalog Model* — This is used to create connections to line-of-business (LOB) systems. This is similar to what is created by SharePoint Designer 2010 (see Chapter 8), but Visual Studio uses a more code-centric approach for more advanced and complex connectivity scenarios.

➤ *Content Type* — A custom content type (for example, a template, document, list column, and so on) can be repurposed across SharePoint.

➤ *Sequential Workflow* — This represents a workflow that works in a sequential manner through a set of activities and can be deployed to SharePoint. It also leverages Windows Workflow and is a specific template that enables automated deployment to SharePoint.

➤ *List Definition* — This is used to define and deploy a list to a SharePoint site. For example, you can define fields or columns when you create the list definition.

➤ *Import Reusable Workflow* — This is used to import a declarative workflow (only the XML part of the declarative workflow) that has been created by SharePoint Designer 2010, and converts it into a code workflow that a developer can then further customize.

➤ *Site Definition* — This is used to define and deploy a site into a site collection. Your site can also contain elements such as lists or Web parts — items that are available from the Project Item templates.

➤ *Visual Web part* — This is an ASP.NET-based Web part that you can use to build and deploy Web parts using drag-and-drop controls. You can then write ASP.NET event handlers for those controls.

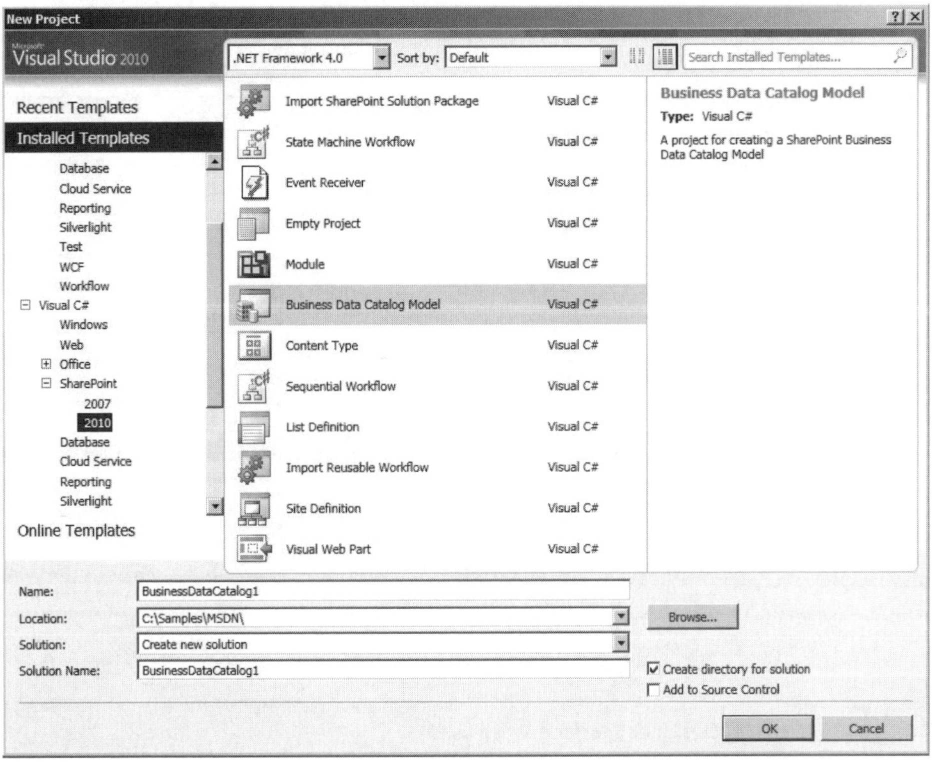

FIGURE 2-1 Visual Studio 2010 project templates

> **NOTE** *You can also add item-level templates after you create a Visual Studio project, but that will be examined in greater detail in Chapter 4. Of note is the fact that you can also extend Visual Studio 2010 SharePoint templates to create more custom project-level or item-level templates. For example, one interesting community example is the creation of a Visual Web part project template that can be deployed to SharePoint Online via a sandboxed solution.*

For your SharePoint development, you may find yourself using not only Visual Studio 2010 but also SharePoint Designer 2010, which is particularly useful for a number of key developer tasks (for example, building rules-based or declarative workflows, creating and editing master pages and page layouts, and creating connections to LOB systems via an ADO.NET or Web service connection). Figure 2-2 illustrates the new SharePoint Designer 2010 interface, and, in this particular instance, shows the creation of an external content type that maps data sources to a SharePoint list (which is called an *external list*).

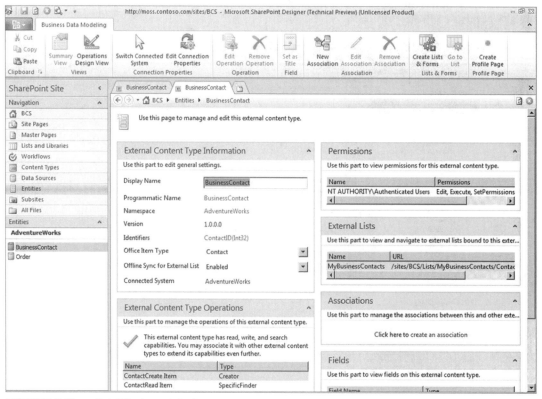

FIGURE 2-2 SharePoint Designer interface

Interestingly, professional developers historically shied away from SharePoint Designer because it was mainly used for page layout and design. However, because the 2010 version offers more ease of use for building workflow (that builds out in a format that is interchangeable with Visual Studio 2010) and LOB connectivity features, developers most likely will be returning to this tool. SharePoint Designer has made tremendous strides in the 2010 release, and it's also free — two reasons why this should be a part of your developer toolkit.

Another key productivity advance for SharePoint 2010 is the operating system support for developers. With SharePoint 2007, developers were required to use a Windows Server operating system (OS), such as Windows Server 2003 or 2008, to host and develop for SharePoint. However, with SharePoint 2010, you can now develop on a client OS like Windows 7. The flip side to this, though, is that SharePoint 2010 requires a 64-bit machine on which to run.

Another developer-centric feature in SharePoint 2010 is the developer dashboard, which provides statistics and reports about code that is executed against your SharePoint site. Those who have coded against SharePoint in the past may have used tools like Fiddler to understand how custom code was executing against SharePoint. The developer dashboard now tracks how your custom code interacts with SharePoint to show where performance bottlenecks or exceptions may occur. Figure 2-3 shows a SharePoint command that turns on the developer dashboard in the SharePoint site in ondemand view — meaning you can toggle the view on and off as you wish.

FIGURE 2-3 PowerShell command

You get a variety of performance and query details for the objects on a given SharePoint page with the developer dashboard, so you can troubleshoot potential problem areas in your custom code. For example, you can expect information such as request/response times for your operations, Web part load times, and database response times.

The developer dashboard is accessible through PowerShell commands, an object model, or through stsadm commands. Figure 2-3 showed you the command using the ondemand parameter, but you could also replace the same command with on or off to either have the developer dashboard turned on (and have it on all the time), or turned off. Figure 2-4 shows the developer dashboard.

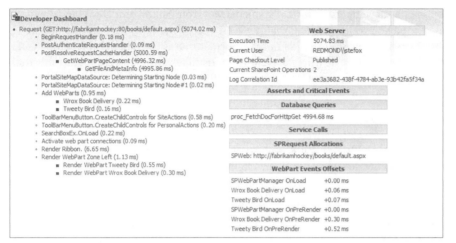

FIGURE 2-4 Developer dashboard

There are other features that you'll see throughout this book within the area of developer productivity. But, from a high level, you can expect to see great opportunities to build your SharePoint applications using Visual Studio 2010 or SharePoint Designer 2010. Many of the examples throughout this book will leverage these two tools.

Through template-specific discussions and coverage of Visual Studio 2010, you'll also learn about some of the application lifecycle management (ALM) capabilities. Examples of ALM include having the capability to import existing .WSP packages and using the Team Foundation Server features of Visual Studio for your SharePoint 2010 development.

> **NOTE** *While Visual Studio 2010 and SharePoint Designer 2010 should be treated as your primary ways of developing for SharePoint, the Expression Blend Suite also offers some value for the developer when building advanced user interfaces (UI) for SharePoint, such as a Silverlight-based UI.*

Rich Platform Services

In terms of rich platform services, SharePoint has evolved quite a bit from SharePoint 2007. For example, you have a rich set of UI objects that you can develop against (such as the SharePoint ribbon), and you have a core set of SharePoint artifacts that can be used to build out your SharePoint site (such as Web parts and lists), which you'll get a chance to test out later in this chapter.

Beyond these core SharePoint artifacts, you also have a set of services you can leverage in your SharePoint development and client-side application programming interfaces (APIs) that can be used in your application development. As discussed in Chapter 1, these services range from ASP.NET (for example, Lists.asmx) to native and custom Windows Communication Foundation (WCF) support (for example, myCustomService.svc) to RESTful services (for example, ListData.svc). SharePoint 2010 also supports the capability to build and deploy custom services into the SharePoint 2010 folder hierarchy (now referred to as the *SharePoint root*), or you can deploy ASP.NET and WCF services to Internet Information Server (IIS) — you'll see this in detail in Chapter 10.

> **NOTE** In SharePoint 2007, the server file system was often called the "SharePoint hive." In SharePoint 2010, it is now referred to as the "SharePoint root." However, you may hear developers refer to either of these terms, which mean the same thing: the SharePoint file system (`<drive>:\Program Files\ Common Files\Microsoft Shared\Web Server Extensions\14`).

Beyond the core support for services, SharePoint 2010 also ships with a number of services out of the box that are extensible and can be used in a variety of ways. For example, one of the services that really accelerates SharePoint 2010 development for the beginning professional is the use of the Business Connectivity Services (BCS), which is discussed more in Chapter 8. In essence, BCS enables you to quickly integrate LOB system data with SharePoint and Office 2010.

Another set of server-side services that extend the capabilities of the Office client technologies to SharePoint is Excel services and Word services, which are server-side ways of interacting with your Microsoft Office documents. For example, you can use Word Services to batch process the translation of `.docx` files (the standard format of documents created with newer versions of Word) into PDF or XPS files on the server — which provides a huge cost savings when manipulating data into documents and then processing those documents for mass distribution to your customers. You'll also see coverage of other server-side services in this book, including Visio services (which provide diagramming and workflow capabilities for SharePoint) and Access services (which enable publishing of Access data to SharePoint).

Data programmability capabilities represent another significant advancement in SharePoint 2010. Key to any application design is knowing what data source or service you're programming against. SharePoint development is no different. If you understand the data source or the Web methods that connect into that data source, you can design your middle-tier and UI experience from there.

In SharePoint development, your data could be represented as a SharePoint list or derive from external data sources that are either ADO.NET-based or integrated using a service-based architecture. This data programmability will become especially apparent in the way in which you connect lists to back-end data sources, and the ways in which you can query and filter that data once you've successfully created a connection to it through, for example, Language Integrated Query (LINQ) for SharePoint (which applies the principles of LINQ to data that resides in SharePoint).

The following code snippet shows the capability to retrieve data from a SharePoint list and then treat that list as a strongly typed object by using LINQ (shown in boldface). The query enables you to filter the data and then bind it to the data-display object, which, in this case, is a datagrid called `myGrid`. This represents a great way to query and filter with data that is being retrieved from SharePoint.

```
protected void Page_Load(object sender, EventArgs e)
{
    ProjectsDataContext dataContext = new ProjectsDataContext
        ("http://stefoxdemosvr/customers);
    EntityList<MyCustomers> Customers = dataContext.GetList<MyCustomers>
```

```
                     ("Customers");

        var custQuery = from customer in Customers
                        where cust.Sales >= 3000000
                        orderby cust.Name
                        select new { cust.Name, cust.Sales };

        myGrid.DataSource =  custQuery;
        myGrid.DataBind();
    }
```

Another major investment in SharePoint 2010 is the capability to support Silverlight applications out of the box. You will see that just this one feature alone will open up quite a few opportunities for you to really begin to explore and build exciting and dynamic experiences for your users using Silverlight support.

This support comes in two primary ways:

➤ You can use the Silverlight Web part as a container for your Silverlight application, as shown in Figure 2-5.

➤ Silverlight development on SharePoint 2010 comes already configured and supported — so, for example, you have no additional server-side configuration you must do to prepare your environment. (In SharePoint 2007, there were a number of configuration steps you needed to undertake to get Silverlight to work.)

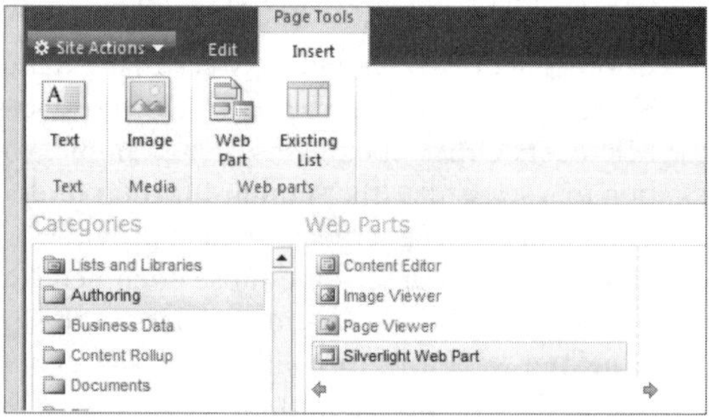

FIGURE 2-5 Silverlight Web part

There are many, many more platform services (such as list lookups and relationships, workflow enhancements, site theming with live preview, XLST-supported customization, and so on), some of which are explored throughout this book and others that you'll discover as you get more deeply entrenched in SharePoint development. In fact, there are too many to fully articulate in one chapter. However, your key takeaway should be that there are a ton of great platform services you can leverage to get started developing for SharePoint 2010.

Flexible Deployment

With SharePoint 2010, you have two primary deployment options:

➤ *On-premises* — The on-premises version of SharePoint is where you or your company own the assets on which the instance of SharePoint runs. For example, you deploy it on your corporate network behind the firewall, you manage the hardware and updates to that hardware, and you manage the administration of the site. Subsequently, you absorb the costs of running SharePoint for your organization.

➤ *SharePoint Online* — SharePoint Online is a hosted version of SharePoint that Microsoft runs for you out of its data centers. In SharePoint Online, you build and deploy your

SharePoint solutions to a sandboxed environment — a ring-fenced environment that runs in the cloud within the purview of a site collection. For example, you can build a solution that reads and writes to a contact list within a site collection. This works on-premises, and can equally work in SharePoint Online.

The functionality of the two is very similar. However, following are a couple of major differences:

➤ When you navigate to SharePoint Online, you are accessing an instance of SharePoint in the cloud (so you are accessing it from the Web, as opposed to behind a corporate firewall or private network).

➤ As a developer, you have some restrictions because you are primarily deploying custom solutions into a managed environment within the site collection. This environment is managed by Microsoft's IT staff.

However, the latter notwithstanding, if you combine a new feature in SharePoint 2010 called *sandboxed solutions* with SharePoint Online, you can maintain a very comfortable price point for SharePoint and still reach many development goals. For enterprise-level deployments of SharePoint, you will more than likely deploy to the on-premises version of SharePoint, and sandboxed solutions can also be used here. However, small and medium-sized businesses may find that SharePoint Online is the way to go. Either way, you should know that there is a good developer story, and if you want to have symmetry across both on-premises and SharePoint Online, then sandboxed solutions are one of the ways in which you can achieve that.

Sandboxed solutions also enable developers to have more control over their site collections. This frees up the farm-level administrators from the developers/site collection administrators, and enables both to have a tighter level of management over their environments, as well as the code running in that environment. The challenge was creating and deploying solutions you could trust not to do bad things to the SharePoint farm. With sandboxed solutions, site collection administrators have the authority to manage the applications (or delegate that authority to others) in their site collection. And developers have more flexibility, at the cost of using a limited subset of SharePoint, to create solutions they know will be deployed in a safe and rapid manner.

In essence, what you're deploying to SharePoint is a partially trusted application that runs in a special "sandbox." This sandbox runs at the site-collection or site level, as opposed to the farm level, and gives you more flexibility for building custom solutions for a surface area in which you have a vested interest and potential site ownership. What runs within a sandboxed solution is a subset of the SharePoint object model. For example, using sandboxed solutions, you can build and deploy list definitions and instances, content types, customize navigation, create and deploy modules or custom files, a limited set of event receivers, Web parts, custom actions, and workflows.

For example, let's say you want to build a custom ASP.NET application and deploy it as a Web part to a site within a site collection. You create the Web part as a partial trust application, so, when it comes time to deploy that application, Visual Studio knows where to deploy it — that is, in the Sandboxed Solutions Gallery, where you can activate or de-activate it. With this model, this type of solution development will broaden the pipeline and really open up SharePoint development opportunities. Figure 2-6 shows the Solutions Gallery, where you upload and activate your custom solution.

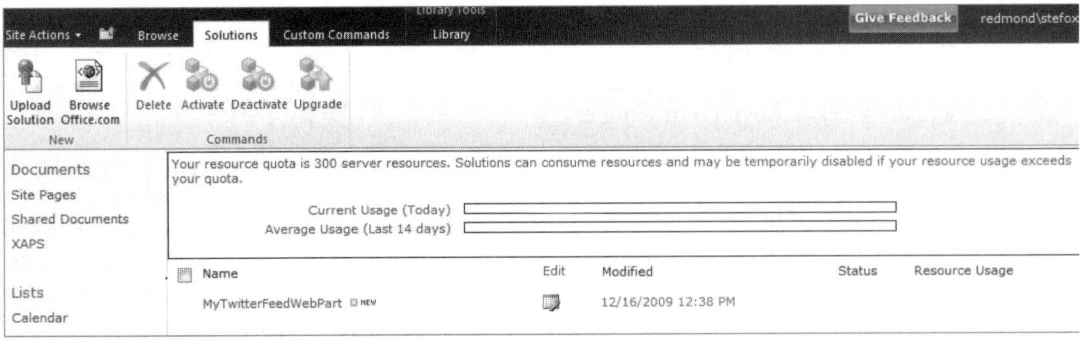

FIGURE 2-6 Sandboxed Solutions Gallery

KEY SKILLS FOR THE SHAREPOINT DEVELOPER

There are a number of skills that are important to learn before you can become proficient at developing SharePoint 2010 applications. Admittedly, there are many different types of development that you can accomplish with SharePoint 2010 and still call yourself a SharePoint developer. However, there is a set of core skills you'll want to have in your back pocket.

The first is a baseline understanding of how Web pages are structured and rendered using Hypertext Markup Language (HTML) standards. SharePoint 2010 is a Web-based technology and is built on ASP.NET. Thus, it is rendered as pages with an `.aspx` extension (for example, `foo.aspx`). This means that if you have a baseline understanding of how `.aspx` pages are structured and where HTML meets ASP.NET, then you can get up and running very quickly in terms of creating and customizing SharePoint site pages.

One example of how you might edit the content on a SharePoint Web page is using the inline HTML editing capabilities, where you can edit HTML within an editor and then save the HTML code to render on the SharePoint page. For example, Figure 2-7 illustrates the new wiki experience in SharePoint, and shows how you can edit the HTML source when the page is in Edit mode through the HTML Source editor (select Site Actions ➪ Edit, click on the top region of the actual wiki page (in the content area of the page), and then choose "Markup and Edit HTML Source"). When you save, SharePoint saves your HTML changes to the wiki page, and renders the content. Note that this method of HTML source injection into the page also supports other mark-up standards and syntax (for example, JavaScript or CSS).

Another example of how you might edit your SharePoint site pages is with your page design and layouts from within SharePoint Designer 2010. SharePoint Designer is a much richer development environment than the inline HTML editors that you use in the browser. It enables you to drag and drop controls onto a page, view design-time changes that you're making to the page, create data views, explore the files and folders that live on your SharePoint site through a site hierarchy, and so on. If you contrast this with the HTML Source editor (which only provides page content saving and rendering), SharePoint Designer is a more feature-rich experience, enabling you to create, edit, and manage content across the entire SharePoint site.

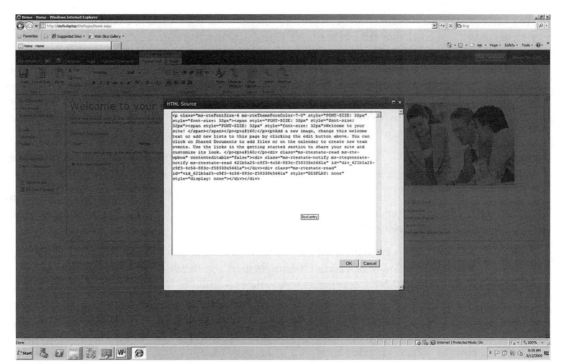

FIGURE 2-7 HTML editing on a SharePoint page

If you're using SharePoint Designer, you may want to use Cascading Style Sheets (CSS), which is a way of providing custom formatting and structure to your Web pages. (You can apply the CSS transformations at design-time with SharePoint Designer to see the changes.) And you may also want to include JavaScript functions, which you can also use in SharePoint Designer.

Thus far, you've seen three technologies about which you may want to have some level of understanding — HTML, CSS, and JavaScript. One that has not been mentioned but that you'll come across in your SharePoint development is Extensible Markup Language (XML). SharePoint makes good use of XML throughout its architecture and programming model, and you'll see references to it throughout this book. Further, to translate XML into styled or structured HTML pages, you may need to leverage Extensible Stylesheet Language (XSL) and XSL Transformations (XSLT).

These are the baseline languages you want to be sure that you have some familiarity with, and there's no reason why you couldn't exist solely in this space and become a proficient SharePoint developer. Several people who focus their time on this type of SharePoint customization make a good living doing so.

However, if you want to move into the solution-development aspect of SharePoint (which is what this book drives you toward), you must jump into the world of .NET development. SharePoint 2010 is built on ASP.NET as a foundational technology, so, by virtue of this architecture, you can build and deploy ASP.NET applications to SharePoint with relative ease.

An example of this is building and deploying a Web part that uses ASP.NET controls and events. Further, when you enter into the world of .NET (if you're not there already), you'll begin to realize that there are a lot of things that you can do with SharePoint within the wider scope of .NET. This is because you can deploy custom assemblies (that is, compiled applications using C# or Visual Basic) that you create using the .NET Framework and install those as solutions on top of SharePoint. These solutions can run the gamut; they could be simple .NET applications that leverage a small set of ASP.NET controls, or they could be more complex Silverlight applications that are still based on .NET but are more centric to an advanced UI design and experience.

So, as a recommendation for the skills you'll want to develop as you embark on your SharePoint development career, the following is a list you might think about working down as you learn SharePoint:

➤ The first item is an understanding of HTML, XML/XSL, and CSS as a structural baseline to understand page rendering in SharePoint. Having some dynamic Web language experience would also be good (such as JavaScript).

➤ The second item is an understanding of ASP.NET. If you don't have skills in these first two items out of the gate, you'll certainly gain them as you develop more with SharePoint. For those who are ASP.NET developers today, the transition to SharePoint development will be much easier.

➤ The third item is a baseline understanding of one of the managed code languages — that is, C# or Visual Basic (VB.NET). These are object-oriented languages that fully leverage the .NET Framework, and both are supported within Visual Studio 2010 for SharePoint 2010 development.

➤ The last is a wider understanding of the .NET Framework such as Windows Workflow Foundation or WCF. Again, this is something that will come with experience, but be open to learning .NET because you'll begin to understand elements you can apply to your SharePoint development efforts.

This book presupposes that you have a baseline understanding of building Web sites and some baseline knowledge of how .NET works.

You may discover along the way that there are other languages that you want to learn — for example, you may be interested in integrating dynamic languages such as Ruby, Python, or PhP into SharePoint — and this is possible but out of scope of this book. This book is about the basics of professional development, which targets the technologies described previously.

With all this talk of development, it's time to put this theory to practice. In the next section, you'll get a standalone version of SharePoint 2010 up and running and set up your development environment so that you can get started with a couple of end-user and developer-oriented walkthroughs.

YOUR DEVELOPMENT ENVIRONMENT

Now that you understand some of the core developer features of SharePoint, as well as some of the key developer skills you'll need, you're probably eager to get started developing. Before you can start developing, though, you must set up your development environment. Let's first tackle the baseline software requirements and then examine the different options you have in setting up your environment.

Following is the baseline software you need to set up your development environment:

➤ A Windows 64-bit-compliant operating system (for example, Windows Server 2008 R2 or Windows 7)

➤ SharePoint Foundation 2010 and SharePoint Server 2010

➤ SharePoint Designer 2010

➤ Microsoft Office (Professional Plus) 2010

➤ Visual Studio 2010

➤ .NET Framework 4.0

➤ Microsoft Expression Blend (optional, but recommended for Silverlight programming)

➤ SQL Server (Express) 2008

Not only will having this software enable you to follow along with the coding examples used throughout this book, but you will also find that these are the baseline requirements to get yourself up and running for SharePoint 2010 development in your organization.

However, you do have a choice as to whether you should build this out "on the metal" (that is, install all of the software on the hard drive of your development machine) or create a virtual image and install all of the software on that image. Many developers prefer to build out a virtual environment to host all of the bits that they need to code against and then use that as the development environment.

For example, for SharePoint 2007, many developers used Virtual PC or Virtual Server (virtualization technologies) to create a virtual hard disk so that they could then rebuild that environment on a regular basis without having to disrupt their primary working environment. Further, they could keep the environment isolated and then, when finished with the development within the virtual environment, move the code into a production environment. Virtualized environments are also useful if you require a more portable environment, such as demo or prototype environments.

> **NOTE** *You can download a preconfigured virtual machine from Microsoft's Download Center at* `www.microsoft.com/downloads/details.aspx?FamilyID=0c51819b-3d40-435c-a103-a5481fe0a0d2&displaylang=en`. *You will also find instructions on the Download Center page to add the virtual machine to an instance of Hyper-V.*

Installing and Configuring Windows Server Hyper-V

In Windows 2008 R2 (64 bit), you can use the Hyper-V Manager to manage and run your virtual machines. The environment is a role you set up when configuring your Windows operating system. For example, after you install Windows Server 2008 R2, you can add the Hyper-V role through the Server Manager.

Figure 2-8 shows an example of the Add Roles Wizard at the Server Roles step in the wizard. You can see that, when you invoke the wizard, you have a place where you can click the checkbox beside the Hyper-V role, and then Windows installs it for you. Note that in this figure, the Hyper-V role has been added to the machine.

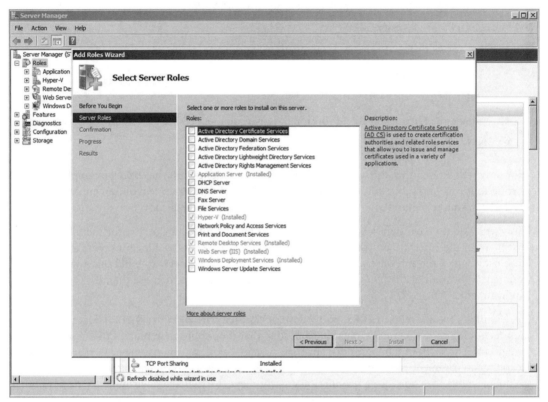

FIGURE 2-8 Hyper-V role

Assuming that you already have your Windows operating system in place, let's walk through the process of installing the Hyper-V role.

TRY IT OUT Installing Hyper-V

Installing Hyper-V is an alternative to setting up an "on-the-metal" development environment. To install Hyper-V, follow these steps:

1. Click Start ➪ Administrative Tools ➪ Server Manager.

2. In the Server Manager, scroll to the Roles Summary, and then click Add Roles. Select Hyper-V from the list.

3. Server Manager takes you through a number of steps. Accept the default options, and click Next until the Install button is enabled.

4. Click Install to complete the Hyper-V installation. Note that Windows will prompt you for a system restart. Restart your computer to complete the Hyper-V installation.

5. After you have Hyper-V installed, you can then add a Hyper-V compliant .vhd file if your team has already prepared one (see the download location noted previously), or you can go about creating one from scratch.

6. To add an existing image, open the Hyper-V snap-in by clicking Start ⇨ Administrative Tools ⇨ Hyper-V Manager.

7. Under Actions, click New ⇨ Virtual Machine. Specify a Name and Location for the image, and click Next.

8. You'll then need to assign a level of RAM to the image. Specify 6,500 MB or more.

9. Accept the default option for Configure Networking and click Next.

10. Click the radio button beside "Use an Existing Hard Disk," and then browse to that disk and click Finish.

> **NOTE** *If you want to create an image from scratch, you can select the first option ("Create a Virtual Hard Disk") and then select one of the options for how you want to install the operating system on the new image. An easy way to install the image is to have the Windows DVD in your machine's CD/DVD drive and select the second option. Associate a specific drive with the installation process (the drive that contains the Windows Installation DVD). When the wizard completes, it will automatically begin installing the OS from that drive, after which you can install all of the software needed for your development.*

Once you've completed the process of installing Hyper-V and adding a (or creating a new) virtual hard disk, the last (and optional) step is to set up a network switch with your Hyper-V instance. This will make it easy for you to both remotely access your Hyper-V development environment and create a network share on your virtual hard disk where you can move software to be installed on your virtual hard disk.

TRY IT OUT Creating a Network Switch

The network switch enables you to remote into your virtual machine. To configure the network switch with Hyper-V, follow these steps:

1. In your Hyper-V Manager, click Virtual Network Manage from the Actions pane.

2. Select New virtual network and Internal, then click Add. Provide a name for the network, select Internal Only, and click OK, as shown in Figure 2-9.

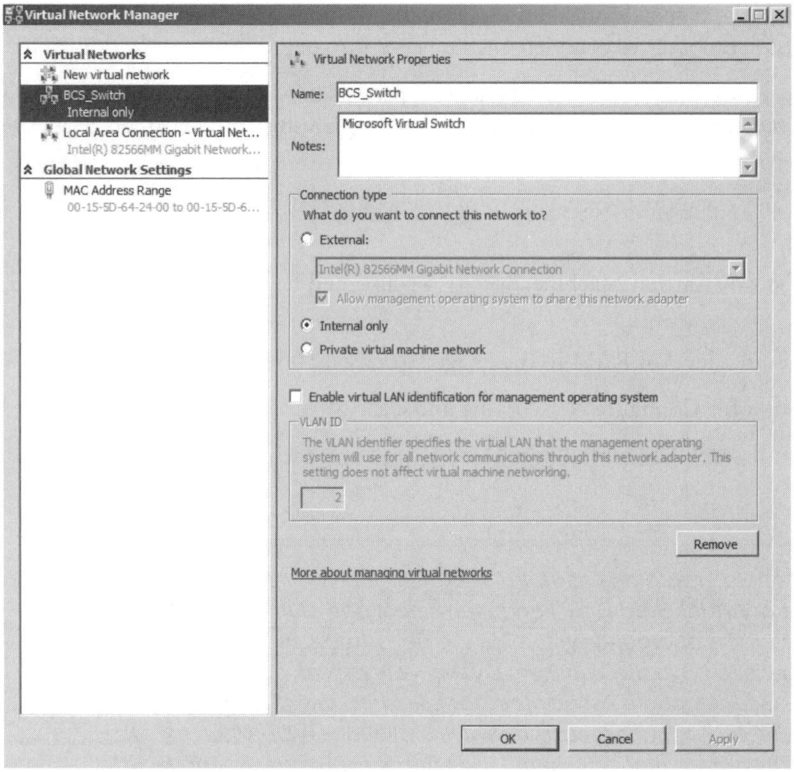

FIGURE 2-9 Adding a network adapter

3. On the host machine, click Start ⇨ Control Panel ⇨ Network and Internet ⇨ Network and Sharing Center.

4. Click Change Adapter Settings, and right-click the network adapter you just added. Select Properties.

5. Select Internet Protocol Version 4 (TCP/IPv4), and click Properties.

6. Click "Use the following IP Address," add a unique IP address in the IP address field (for example, 192.168.1.1), and click the Subnet mask field to have one automatically generated for you, as shown in Figure 2-10.

7. The last step is to configure the network adapter on the virtual hard disk. To do this, start the image by clicking Start ⇨ Connect in the Hyper-V Manager.

8. Log in to your virtual image, and then click Start ⇨ Control Panel ⇨ Network and Internet ⇨ Network and Sharing Center.

9. Click Change Adapter Settings.

10. Configure the network adapter properties as you did earlier by right-clicking the network adapter that is present by default on the image. Select Properties ⇨ Internet Protocol Version 4 (TCP/IPv4), and then change the IP address to be something unique (for example, 192.168.1.50). Lastly, tab to the Subnet mask to have one automatically generated for you.

11. Click OK to complete the process.

12. To test the remote desktop, click Start ⇨ All Programs ⇨ Accessories ⇨ Remote Desktop Connection. Type the IP address you configured within the virtual hard disk, and then click Connect. Windows will connect you to your development environment via Remote Desktop.

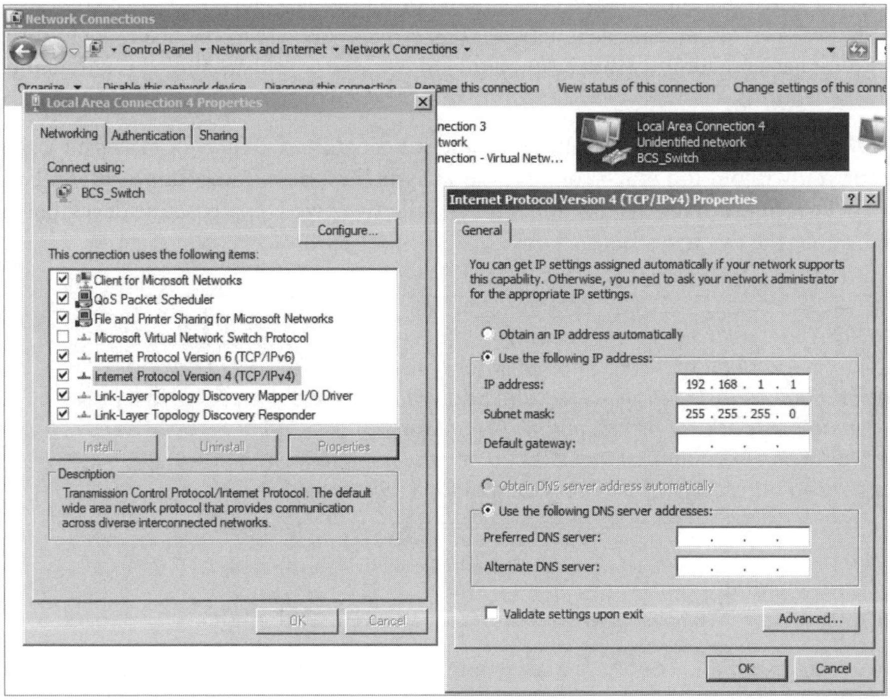

FIGURE 2-10 IP properties

How It Works

Using these instructions, you now have an environment that leverages the Hyper-V role within Windows Server 2008 R2. What this means is that you can have a virtualized instance of SharePoint on a virtual image (that is, a .vhd file) that you can start, save, and stop using the features of Hyper-V. It works by virtue of the Hyper-V role hosting the images and running them in what effectively becomes a separate environment. The separate (or virtualized) environment can be integrated with the host or parent environment through the network switch that you set up to open up the resources available to the virtual image.

Installing SharePoint Server 2010

At this point, you should have successfully created and mounted a virtual machine, and you should have configured the network switch so that you can remote into your development environment. You can continue to work with this virtual machine and install all of the software, or if you want to install all of the software on your machine, you can do that as well. While this chapter won't cover all of the software prerequisites, it will briefly walk you through the SharePoint 2010 installation procedures.

There are a number of different ways of installing SharePoint within an environment. A SharePoint server farm may consist of one or more servers providing various services to the farm. You can also configure SQL Server when installing SharePoint. (SharePoint uses SQL Server to store all of its content.) All of the services can be balanced between one or more servers in the farm. A multi-server farm is typically a higher-end administrative function and one that, at this point, should remain a goal for your future learning.

For now, install the *standalone* SharePoint 2010 instance to get started. This will provision a single-server instance for you without too much configuration hassle, but, more importantly, it will be simple to set up and configure. This installation method will also give you a baseline development environment to test out the examples in this book.

> **WARNING** *This would not be the option you choose when deploying a SharePoint 2010 server to production. There are a number or restrictions that come along with the standalone installation — for example, content database size restrictions. When you do get ready for production-ready SharePoint development, build a replicated production environment that sits in a development (and staging) environment before you drop your code into a production environment.*

TRY IT OUT Installing a Standalone Instance of SharePoint 2010

There are various ways to install and configure SharePoint 2010, one of which is a standalone server installation. To install a standalone instance of SharePoint, follow these steps:

1. Click the Setup.exe file on your SharePoint 2010 installation DVD (or from your installation location).

2. You'll be prompted to "Agree to the License Terms." Click the "I accept the terms of this agreement" checkbox and click Continue, as shown in Figure 2-11.

3. At the next step, you have the opportunity to select different installation options. Click the Standalone button to invoke the standalone installation.

4. SharePoint will then work through the installation process.

5. When it has completed the installation process, you will be prompted with a dialog where you can choose to run the Configuration Wizard, which configures things like the services, content database, and so on, for first-time use, as shown in Figure 2-12. Click the "Run the SharePoint Products and Technologies Configuration Wizard now" checkbox and click Close. The Configuration Wizard is automatically invoked upon closing this dialog.

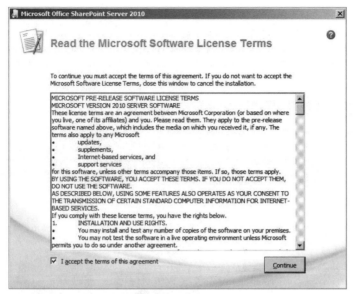

FIGURE 2-11 SharePoint 2010 license terms

FIGURE 2-12 Configuration Wizard

6. SharePoint works through a series of 10 configuration steps to complete the installation process.

7. When complete, it will prompt you with a Configuration Successful dialog. Click Finish to complete the process.

8. SharePoint should automatically prompt you with the standalone SharePoint instance you created. Upon first opening, it will ask you to select a type of site. Explore the different site templates that are available to you, but choose Team Site and click OK. Leave the default security options and click OK. Your site will then be created and will open at the default landing page, as shown in Figure 2-13.

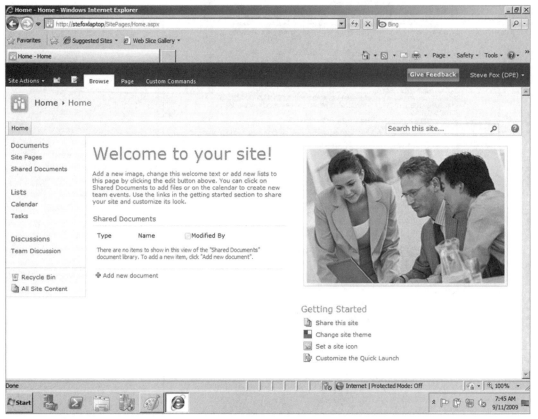

FIGURE 2-13 Default site

How It Works

The installation process installs all of the SharePoint server files on your local development machine. Since you opted to do a standalone installation, SharePoint uses the name of your server as the default name for your base SharePoint site collection that is created during the installation process. When it is installed, you can navigate to the SharePoint root to explore the files and folders that were installed as a part of the SharePoint installation (`../Program Files/Common Files/Microsoft Shared/Web Server Extensions/14`).

At this point, you now either have a site collection up and running through a virtual hard disk, or you have a site that is running "on the metal" on your development machine. If you've opted to install on the metal, remember that you would now install the other products listed as prerequisites for the development environment (for example, Visual Studio 2010, .NET, Microsoft Office, SharePoint Designer 2010, and, optionally, Expression Blend). You may also want to upgrade the default SQL Server Express edition to the SQL Server Standard edition. From here on out, this chapter will not provide guidance on what specific environment you should use. Rather, it will walk you through the examples assuming that you are comfortable in whatever environment you have created for yourself.

Now, let's move on to getting you more familiar with the SharePoint UI, from the perspectives of both an end user and a future SharePoint developer.

GETTING FAMILIAR WITH SHAREPOINT 2010

As discussed in Chapter 1, the architecture of SharePoint extends from an entry in IIS as a Web application through to site collections, sites (and subsites), and, of course, all of the elements that make up a site (such as lists, document libraries, content types, and so on). During the installation process, SharePoint created a default site collection, and, as you configured the site for first use, the walkthrough instructed you to create a Team Site, which is a specific site template.

SharePoint has a number of different site templates that you can use when creating new sites such as Team site, Blank site, Meeting Space, Wiki, Blog, and so on. You likely explored these as you completed the installation process. You could think of the site template as simply providing you with a predefined structure for your SharePoint site, that includes items such as an Announcements or Calendar list, or specific Web parts that may be pertinent to the type of site you're trying to create (for example, business intelligence Web parts for a Reports Center site).

You can use the out-of-the-box templates that ship with SharePoint to begin crafting your site, and then use that as your foundation for customization, or you can completely build a site template from scratch and build on that. Get familiar with each of the site templates first, to understand their functionality and their points of extensibility, before moving on to the custom site templates (which take a little more effort and understanding to build). SharePoint provides you with a lot of infrastructure for sites out of the box, so you won't be short on functionality for a site within your development efforts.

The URL of my root site collection is `http://fabrikamhockey`, which was essentially created by using the name of my server. The Team site (which is the default site template for a new SharePoint site) is a straightforward template and includes a number of default options.

For example, in Figure 2-13, on the Quick Launch Toolbar, you can see that the Team site was created with Site Pages and Shared Documents libraries, which represent special lists where you can store Web pages and documents, respectively. You'll also notice that there is a Calendar list and a Tasks list, along with a Team Discussion. Within the content portion of the site collection, you have a welcome message with some text and a couple of Web parts that display a default image and surface the Shared Documents on the landing page of the site collection.

To get you more familiar with SharePoint 2010, let's walk through a few exercises.

Working with SharePoint Sites

While this book is about development, you will want to learn some of the fundamental aspects of SharePoint administration. Having some knowledge in this space will help you quite a bit in your development efforts.

For administration, there are a few things that you'll need to do as a developer. For example, you may need to create a site collection within which you can create and add SharePoint sites. You may also need to configure email to be sent from that site, or ensure that specific SharePoint services (such as Excel Services or BCS) are configured with the appropriate security configurations.

One common activity you (or your farm administrator) will use SharePoint Central Administration for is the provisioning of a new SharePoint site collection (which SharePoint did for you already through the installation process you walked through earlier in this chapter). Let's tackle that now.

TRY IT OUT   Creating a Site Collection in Central Administration

Site collections are the main point of entry for you when you are interacting with SharePoint. To create a site collection using the Central Administration features, follow these steps:

1.   Click Start ➪ All Programs ➪ Microsoft SharePoint 2010 Products. Select SharePoint 4.0 Central Administration. This will open your browser and load the SharePoint Central Administration home page.

2.   After Central Administration has loaded, click Create Site Collections.

3.   On the Create Site Collection page shown in Figure 2-14, add a Title, Description, and URL. Select the type of template you want to use for the site (for this example, choose Team Site). Add the primary and secondary site administrators, and leave the Quota Template set to its default (No Quota).

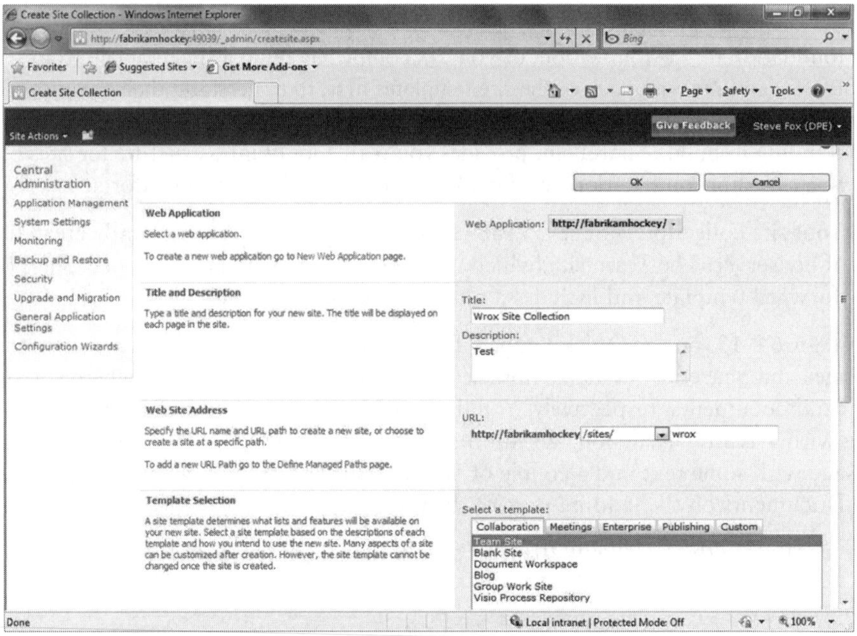

FIGURE 2-14 Central Administration Create Site Collection page

4. After you click OK, SharePoint will provision a new SharePoint site collection based on the information you provided. You will also be taken to the Top-Level Site Successfully Created page, shown in Figure 2-15, where you can then click the link to your new site collection to load it.

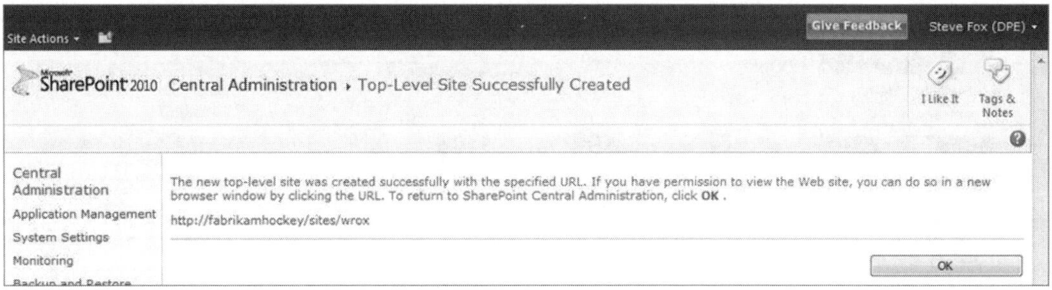

FIGURE 2-15 Top-Level Site Successfully Created page

How It Works

Central Administration is the place where you create new site collections. In this walkthrough, SharePoint used your selection (that is, the Team Site template) to structure a site for you. The Central Administration process amended the IIS Web application to include any newly generated files, which were also added to your SharePoint file system. Any new sites or subsites you add to the site collection will further amend the file system hierarchy.

With your top-level site collection created, you can now create and add a site. In the next exercise, you create a new site within your site collection.

> **NOTE** If you're using the virtual machine from the Microsoft Download Center, then the appropriate trust and application settings should already be set for you in your Internet browser. However, if you've set up your environment on the metal, then you may need to set your intranet site as trusted, enable script, and so on. For Internet Explorer, this can be done from the Security tab (click Tools ⇨ Internet Options).

TRY IT OUT Creating a Site within a Site Collection

Site collections can include multiple sites and/or subsites. To create a site within the site collection, follow these steps:

1. Navigate to the home page of your SharePoint site by opening Internet Explorer and entering in the SharePoint URL (for example, `http://fabrikamhockey.com`).

2. Click Site Actions ⇨ View All Site Content.

3. Click Create. This launches a Silverlight-enabled Create gallery.

4.   Click Site ➾ Team Site.

5.   Enter some text for the Title, Description (optional), and the URL name (for example, `sprocks`) for your Web site address, as shown in Figure 2-16.

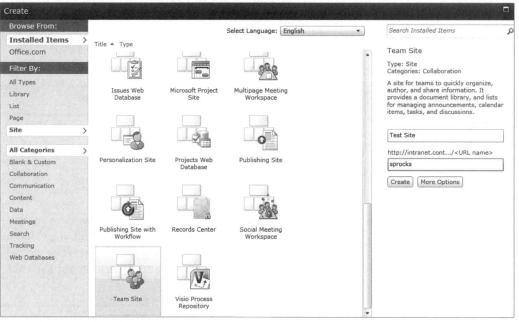

FIGURE 2-16 Creating your first team site

6.   Click Create to complete the process of creating the new team site.

SharePoint creates a new site, with all of the basic plumbing, that maps to the specific SharePoint template you selected (the Team site). The result of this quick walkthrough should be a number of default navigation options down the left-hand side, a standard ribbon structure, and some default content in the main content portion of the page.

If you disable Silverlight in your browser, this will disable the Silverlight-enabled Create view that you used in the previous walkthrough. To disable (or enable) Silverlight in your browser, click Tools ➾ Internet Options ➾ Programs ➾ Manage add-ons. You then find Silverlight in the list and either click Enable or Disable. If you disable, an HTML view of the Create page will be displayed instead of the Silverlight-enabled view.

Let's now perform a couple of editing functions against this page. Follow these steps:

1.   Click Site Actions ➾ Edit Page. This opens the page in Edit mode.

2.   Write some text in the wiki content by clicking in the top part of the content window and typing some text. Note that there are formatting options available to you, so you can resize and format text for a specific size and look.

3.   To exit the site, click Save and Close.

4. After your team site exits Edit mode, under the "Getting Started links on the Home Page for a Team Site," click "Change site theme" and change the theme. Click Apply.

If you don't want to commit to the theme you selected, then you can click Preview and SharePoint will display your SharePoint site in Preview mode. You may need to allow pop-ups from your site to view the preview.

How It Works

With the site collection acting as the parent Web site, the site creation process again leverages the Team Site template to build a new team site and deploy it to the site hierarchy. Here again, the SharePoint file system and IIS settings are amended to handle the new site that was added.

Although using Central Administration is one way to create a site, another way is to programmatically create a site using the SharePoint project templates within Visual Studio 2010. This is useful when you want to create site templates that can be used within your team or across the organization with specific customizations in place.

TRY IT OUT Create a Simple SharePoint Site Programmatically

You have the option to create a site through the Web-based features in SharePoint or to use Visual Studio 2010. To create a simple site programmatically using Visual Studio 2010, follow these steps:

1. Open Visual Studio 2010 and click File ➪ New ➪ Project. Select the Site Definition project template under the SharePoint 2010 templates folder.

2. Provide a name and location for your project, and click OK.

3. Specify the site and click Validate to test the connection to the site. By default, sites can only be deployed as full-trust solutions (that is, farm solutions), so you do not have the option to deploy the site as a sandboxed solution. Select "Deploy as a farm solution" and then click Finish to create the project, as shown in Figure 2-17.

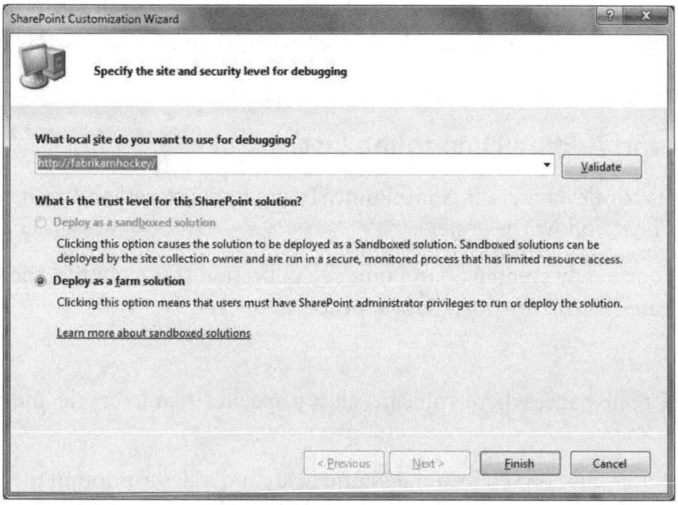

FIGURE 2-17 Site and security level dialog

4. If you didn't change anything within the project, you could right-click the project and select Deploy. SharePoint would then deploy the new site template within the specified site collection. However, the site would essentially be a blank site template with no other objects (such as lists, document templates, or features) associated with it. Thus, you'd likely want to add some sort of customization to the site. You can do this, for example, by editing the `onet.xml` file (which Visual Studio opens by default) and the `default.aspx` files that are created as a part of the solution.

5. When your site has successfully deployed, it is now available as a site template — similar to the Team Site template or Blank template.

6. To use your template, navigate to your site collection landing page and click All Site Content. Click Create and select "Sites and Workspaces."

7. Provide a name, description, and URL for your site, and, in the SharePoint Customization tab, select the site template you deployed to SharePoint. Click Create.

How It Works

Similar to using the SharePoint administrative and site-creation functionality to create a new site, Visual Studio can programmatically create and deploy the site template and site to SharePoint. Whereas SharePoint provides you with some limited metadata (such as template, name and URL), the programmatic way of building out a site provides you access to an underlying XML layer where you can customize the site with more options. Further, you can use Visual Studio to add other artifacts to your site (for example, Web parts, list definitions and instances, content types, and so on). So, when users provision a site using your custom template, all of these options will be available to them after the site is created.

WORKING WITH SHAREPOINT LISTS

Now that you have a site collection up and running, let's jump in and look at some of the things that you can do with the site. The first exercise you'll walk through is creating a list in SharePoint and manually adding some data to that list. While you can programmatically add data to and remove it from a list, this exercise will help you understand what the end user would go through when interacting with the list. For this exercise, disable the Silverlight add-on so you can also see the HTML view that SharePoint provides.

TRY IT OUT Creating a List and Adding Data to the List

Lists are one of the major entry points for developers in SharePoint. To create a list and add some data to that list using the Web-based interface, follow these steps:

1. Navigate to the home page of your newly created SharePoint site collection (for example, the home site collection page that was created during the installation process).

2. Click All Site Content.

3. Click Create. This invokes the Create page, where you can select a specific item to create and provide a name for that item.

4. Select the Custom List option. Enter **Customers** into the Name field, and a description in the Description field. Leave the Quick Launch navigation setting on Yes, and Click Create.

This will create a new custom list for you; however, there will only be one column in the list. Let's add three columns, called Region, Size, and Sales.

1. To add the Region column, click the Create Column button on the SharePoint ribbon. This will invoke the Create Column form. Enter **Region** in the Name field, and select Choice as the type of field. Then, add four choices in the choices settings: **East, West, North,** and **South.** Leave all other default selections and click OK.

2. To add the Size column, click the Create Column button. Add **Size** to the Name field, and select Choice as the type of field. Then, add three choices: **Small, Medium,** and **Enterprise.** Click OK.

3. To add the Sales column, click the Create Column button. Add **Sales** to the Name field, and select the "Single line of text" field. Click OK.

4. Lastly, change the name of the default Title field (the one field that is created by default when you create a custom list). To do this, click the List Settings button on the SharePoint ribbon. Click the Title link, and then change the name of the column from "Title" to "Name." Click OK.

5. Even though you changed the display name of the default column name from "Title" to "Name," programmatically, in some cases, you'll still need to develop using the Title string. To test this out, click the List Settings button and then mouse over the Name field. Take note of the Field=Title in the URL, as shown in see Figure 2-18.

http://fabrikamhockey/_layouts/FldEdit.aspx?List=%7B1B7851DA%2DEB6F%2D4638%2DA921%2D6253E01FB451%7D&Field=Title

FIGURE 2-18 Field=Title

6. To add some items to the list, click the Customers link to the list in the Quick Launch, and then click the Add New Item link. Enter data into the New Item form, and then repeat to add a few records into the list. When complete, your list entries should look something like Figure 2-19.

Customers

Name	Region	Size	Sales
Trey Research ☑ NEW	East	Small	$1,300,000.00
Contoso ☑ NEW	West	Medium	$2,900,049.00
Fabrikam ☑ NEW	North	Enterprise	$1,309,200,099.00
AdventureWorks ☑ NEW	North	Small	$900,878.00
Wingtip Toys ☑ NEW	South	Medium	$3,890,283.00
Blue Yonder ☑ NEW	East	Enterprise	$2,090,899,000.00
Acme Industries ☑ NEW	South	Small	$3,000,910

FIGURE 2-19 Completed Customer list

How It Works

When you create a list, you create a structure that has columns and rows, and represents an object within SharePoint that can not only be populated by end users but can also be programmed against by you. This process simply generated a default list, which has some hidden properties and some properties that can be edited by the user.

If you are new to SharePoint, you've created your first SharePoint list — and this is something that you (and all of your end users) will do on a regular basis. Lists are one of the most commonly used objects in SharePoint. As you'll see in Chapter 5, you can program against lists in many different ways. However, in this chapter, you'll complete a simple programming exercise to kick-start your application development. So, now that you've created a simple list in SharePoint, let's write a little code that does something with that Customers list.

The next example walks you through how to programmatically establish a connection to a SharePoint list and update the data in that list using the Lists ASP.NET Web service that ships with SharePoint 2010. For those that are new to SharePoint, you won't have seen the Lists Web service. It is one of the native ways in which you can interact with SharePoint. For those who have developed against SharePoint, you'll recognize this service as an API that has persisted forward.

There are a number of ways to interact with a list; this example uses the native Lists Web service that enables you to interact with SharePoint lists. However, to showcase that you can leverage SharePoint data from applications that don't necessarily live inside SharePoint, you'll create a WPF-based application that adds data to a SharePoint list from a WPF application. The application is simple, but it is illustrative of the following:

➤ The connectivity to SharePoint

➤ Interacting with the list

➤ Accomplishing this from an application outside of the SharePoint domain

TRY IT OUT **Programming Against a List Using the Lists Web Service**

Code file [WPFSPListApp.zip] available for download at Wrox.com.

You can also program against lists in SharePoint 2010, which enables you to manage, create, read, update, and delete (CRUD) operations against the list. To program against a list, follow these steps:

1. Open Visual Studio 2010 and click File ➪ New ➪ Project. In the New Project dialog, navigate to the Windows templates under the Installed Templates gallery and select "WPF application."

2. Provide a name for your application (for example, WPFSPListApp) and a location, and then click OK. Visual Studio 2010 will create a new solution for you that includes a number of files. Right-click the MainWindow.xaml file, and select View Designer (if the view is not already open).

3. Add five labels, four textboxes, and three buttons to your Designer from the Toolbox so that the UI looks similar to Figure 2-20.

Table 2-1 provides a summary of the control types and names that you will add to the WPF application.

FIGURE 2-20 SharePoint List app UI

TABLE 2-1 Control Types and Names

CONTROL TYPE	CONTROL NAME
Label	lblTitle, lblCompanyName, lblRegion, lblSize, lblSales
Textbox	txtbxCompanyName, txtbxSize, txtbxSales
Button	btnUpdate, btnClear, btnExit

4. The UI uses a type of XML syntax called Extended Application Markup Language (XAML), which is specific to Windows WPF and Silverlight applications. The XML must be well formed, and, when you drag and drop controls from the Toolbox onto the designer surface, the XAML will automatically be generated for you. You'll need to add a couple of event handlers to the button controls to manage the loading of the SharePoint list data into the application. So, after you add the button controls to the Designer, go to the XAML code view, click your mouse within the button element, and press the spacebar. This will trigger IntelliSense, allowing you to select the Click event. Accept the default event handler name, and Visual Studio will add a method for your buttons in the code behind. The XAML for your application should look something like the following:

```
<Window x:Class="WPFListApp.MainWindow"
        xmlns="http://schemas.microsoft.com/winfx/2006/xaml/presentation"
        xmlns:x="http://schemas.microsoft.com/winfx/2006/xaml"
        Title="MainWindow" Height="300" Width="500">
    <Grid Height="270">
        <Label Content="SharePoint List Data"
               Height="28"
               HorizontalAlignment="Left"
               Margin="21,14,0,0"
               Name="lblTitle"
               VerticalAlignment="Top"
               Width="162"
               FontWeight="Bold"
               FontSize="13" />
        <Label Content="Company Name:"
               Height="28"
               HorizontalAlignment="Left"
               Margin="21,56,0,0"
               Name="lblCompanyName"
               VerticalAlignment="Top"
               Width="120" />
        <Label Content="Region:"
               Height="28"
               HorizontalAlignment="Left"
               Margin="21,90,0,0"
               Name="lblRegion"
               VerticalAlignment="Top"
               Width="120" />
        <Label Content="Size:"
               Height="28"
               HorizontalAlignment="Left"
               Margin="21,124,0,0"
               Name="lblSize"
               VerticalAlignment="Top"
```

```
                     Width="120" />
        <Label Content="Sales:"
               Height="28"
               HorizontalAlignment="Left"
               Margin="21,158,0,0"
               Name="lblSales"
               VerticalAlignment="Top"
               Width="120" />
        <TextBox Height="23"
                 HorizontalAlignment="Left"
                 Margin="119,56,0,0"
                 Name="txtbxCompanyName"
                 VerticalAlignment="Top"
                 Width="245" />
        <TextBox Height="23"
                 HorizontalAlignment="Left"
                 Margin="119,90,0,0"
                 Name="txtbxRegion"
                 VerticalAlignment="Top"
                 Width="245" />
        <TextBox Height="23"
                 HorizontalAlignment="Left"
                 Margin="119,124,0,0"
                 Name="txtbxSize"
                 VerticalAlignment="Top"
                 Width="245" />
        <TextBox Height="23"
                 HorizontalAlignment="Left"
                 Margin="119,158,0,0"
                 Name="txtbxSales"
                 VerticalAlignment="Top"
                 Width="245" />
        <Button Content="Update"
                Height="23"
                HorizontalAlignment="Left"
                Margin="29,218,0,0"
                Name="btnUpdate"
                VerticalAlignment="Top"
                Width="75"
                Click="btnUpdate_Click" />
        <Button Content="Clear"
                Height="23"
                HorizontalAlignment="Left"
                Margin="119,218,0,0"
                Name="btnClear"
                VerticalAlignment="Top"
                Width="75"
                Click="btnClear_Click" />
        <Button Content="Exit"
                Height="23"
                HorizontalAlignment="Left"
                Margin="210,218,0,0"
                Name="btnExit"
                VerticalAlignment="Top"
                Width="75"
                Click="btnExit_Click" />
```

```
        </Grid>
</Window>
```

5. Right-click the `MainWindow.xaml` file, and then click View Code. This will open up the code view.

6. Right-click the References project node, and select Add Service Reference. On the Add Service Reference dialog, click the Advanced button and then click Add Web Reference on the Service Reference Settings dialog.

7. In the Add Web Reference dialog, click the Web services on the local machine link. This will search for and display all of the Web services that are located on your developer machine, which will include the SharePoint Web services, as shown in Figure 2-21.

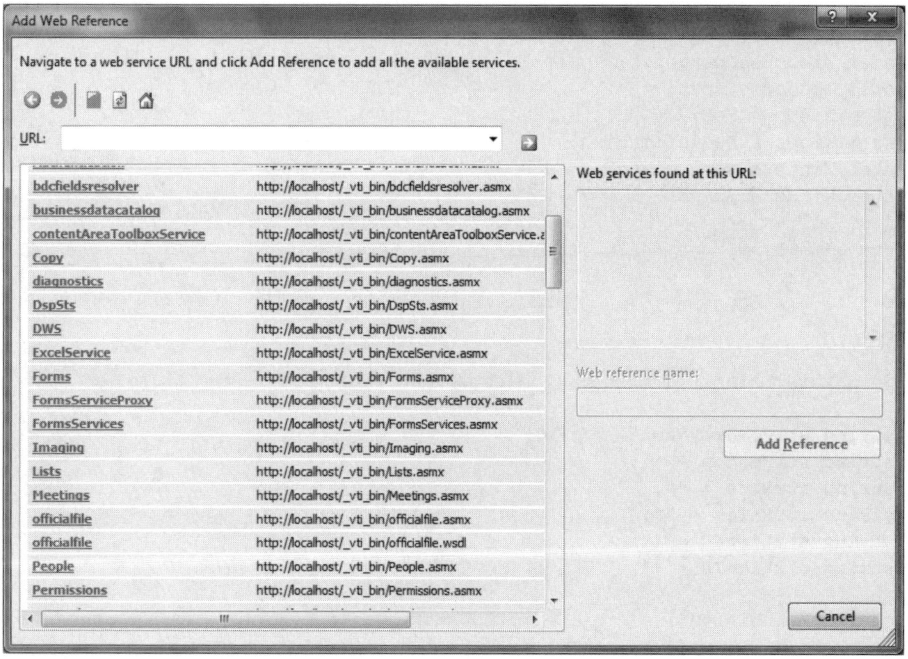

FIGURE 2-21 SharePoint Web service

8. One of the Web services is the Lists service (with the endpoint listed as `http://<server name>/_ vti_bin/Lists.asmx`). Select this service. Note that you may need to change the Web service URL to reflect your local server, for example `http://fabrikamhockey/_vti_bin/Lists.asmx`. Provide a name for the service (for example, `MySPWebService`) and click Add Reference. (You can also explore the Web methods that are a part of that service before you click Add Reference.)

9. At this point, you can add an event handler for each of the buttons in your WPF UI (which should already be stubbed out for you). The Update button is the one button that will leverage the Web service connection to SharePoint. You'll also require a set of class-level variables to get the user input and pass that into the Lists Web service. When you call the Lists Web service, you'll also need to create an XML construct that passes the data from your WPF application to your SharePoint list. This XML is called the *Collaborative Application Markup Language* (CAML).

10. The following code snippet illustrates the three event handlers, one for each of the buttons. The bolded code is what you will need to add to the default code that is created for you by Visual Studio. If you use the accompanying source code, you'll need to ensure that you update the Web service reference (by re-adding the service to the Visual Studio project), and update any URL references in the code. For example, you would need to update the following line of code:

```
            myListService.Url =
                "http://<your server name>/_vti_bin/Lists.asmx";
using System;
using System.Collections.Generic;
using System.Linq;
using System.Text;
using System.Windows;
using System.Windows.Controls;
using System.Windows.Data;
using System.Windows.Documents;
using System.Windows.Input;
using System.Windows.Media;
using System.Windows.Media.Imaging;
using System.Windows.Navigation;
using System.Windows.Shapes;
using System.Xml;
using System.Xml.Linq;

namespace WPFSPListApp
{

    public partial class MainWindow : Window
    {
        string strCompanyName = "";
        string strRegion = "";
        string strSize = "";
        string strSales = "";
        string strListID = "";
        string strViewID = "";

        public MainWindow()
        {
            InitializeComponent();
    }

        private void btnUpdate_Click(object sender, RoutedEventArgs e)
        {

            strCompanyName = txtbxCompanyName.Text;
            strRegion = txtbxRegion.Text;
            strSize = txtbxSize.Text;
            strSales = "$" + txtbxSales.Text;

            WPFSPListApp.MySPWebService.Lists myListService =
                new MySPWebService.Lists();
            myListService.Credentials =
                System.Net.CredentialCache.DefaultCredentials;
            myListService.Url =
                "http://fabrikamhockey/_vti_bin/Lists.asmx";

            XmlNode myListView = myListService.GetListAndView("Customers", "");
```

```
            strListID = myListView.ChildNodes[0].Attributes["Name"].Value;
            strViewID = myListView.ChildNodes[1].Attributes["Name"].Value;

            XmlDocument myListDoc = new XmlDocument();
            XmlElement batchXML = myListDoc.CreateElement("Batch");

            batchXML.InnerXml = "<Method ID = '1' Cmd='New'><Field Name='Title'>" +
                strCompanyName + "</Field><Field Name='Region'>" + strRegion +
                "</Field><Field Name='Size'>" + strSize +
                "</Field><Field Name='Sales'>" + strSales +
                "</Field>" + "</Method>";

            XmlNode myListReturn = myListService.
                UpdateListItems(strListID, batchXML);
            MessageBox.Show("SharePoint List was updated!");
        }

        private void btnClear_Click(object sender, RoutedEventArgs e)
        {
            txtbxCompanyName.Text = "";
            txtbxRegion.Text = "";
            txtbxSales.Text = "";
            txtbxSize.Text = "";
        }

        private void btnExit_Click(object sender, RoutedEventArgs e)
        {
            Application.Current.Shutdown();
        }
    }
}
```

11. Assuming that your code reflects what is shown here, you should now be able to press F5 and run the application in Debug mode, add some string entries to the WPF application, and click Update to add the record to your SharePoint list, as shown in Figure 2-22.

Customers			
☐ 📄 Name	Region	Size	Sales
Trey Research 🔲NEW	East	Small	$1,300,000.00
Contoso 🔲NEW	West	Medium	$2,900,049.00
Fabrikam 🔲NEW	North	Enterprise	$1,309,200,099.00
AdventureWorks 🔲NEW	North	Small	$900,878.00
Wingtip Toys 🔲NEW	South	Medium	$3,890,283.00
Blue Yonder 🔲NEW	East	Enterprise	$2,090,899,000.00

FIGURE 2-22 Updated list

How It Works

The SharePoint Web services offer quite a range of functionality for the developer and should be one of your first stops when developing for SharePoint (to leverage what already ships with SharePoint). Many of these are services that were available in SharePoint 2007 and have evolved to be supported in SharePoint 2010. For those who used them in production code in 2007, this is good news, because upgrading your 2007 code should not prove too difficult.

For this example, you used the Lists Web service, which provides a number of different ways to interact with a list — for example, you can add or delete a list, add an attachment to a list, get the list, and so on. In this example, you used the `GetListAndView` Web method, which returns a schema for a list that you pass in as a parameter to the `GetListAndView` method call. Note that, in this call, you passed the name of the list, `Customers`, and mapped the return value to an `XMLNode` object.

```
XmlNode myListView = myListService.GetListAndView("Customers", "");
```

The example also used CAML to insert data back into the SharePoint list. Admittedly, CAML is a little verbose, as you can see from the following line of code. (You'll see different ways to interact with a list in Chapter 5, ones that are less syntactically verbose and more lightweight to code.)

```
batchXML.InnerXml = "<Method ID = '1' Cmd='New'><Field Name='Title'>" +
    strCompanyName + "</Field><Field Name='Region'>" + strRegion +
    "</Field><Field Name='Size'>" + strSize + "</Field><Field Name='Sales'>"
    + strSales + "</Field>" + "</Method>";
```

The last key piece in this example was the `UpdateListItems` method, which passed the list ID (that is, the name of the list) and the list schema that was mapped to the CAML construct (which was further tied to the data in the WPF client).

```
XmlNode myListReturn = myListService.UpdateListItems(strListID, batchXML);
```

While this method leverages native Web services, there are both pros and cons to using them. Pros include ease of use and service plumbing that exists, as opposed to your having to create a custom Web service. Cons include potential performance hits with service integration and syntax verbosity with the CAML construct.

If you followed along with this example and successfully updated your SharePoint list, then congratulations! You just wrote your first application against SharePoint 2010 that interacts with a SharePoint list.

Now, let's take a look at Web parts.

WORKING WITH SHAREPOINT WEB PARTS

Web parts are also very common artifacts in SharePoint. In fact, you'll find that the Web part is one of the most commonly customized objects for SharePoint developers because it represents a core building block for SharePoint and can be customized to do many different things.

You add a Web part from the Web Part Gallery, which provides you with categories that help classify Web parts. To add a Web part to a SharePoint wiki page, you click Site Actions ➪ Edit Page ➪ Insert and select Web Part from the ribbon menu. If you create a Web part page (which is a site page with a predefined structure), you can also add a Web part, but the steps to do it are a little different. You click Site Actions ➪ Edit Page ➪ "Insert a web part." Then select the type of Web part you want to add from the Web Part Gallery and click Add. The Web Part Gallery exposes the Web parts that are available as either part of the SharePoint installation, or those custom Web parts that have been deployed to your SharePoint server.

Web parts can act as containers for your custom functionality (for example, a custom ASP.NET application), and they can also act as a container for a list or document library. For example, let's add the `Customers` list you created in the last section of the chapter to the home page of your new site collection as a Web part.

TRY IT OUT — Add the Customers List as a Web Part

Web parts are very important building blocks, and you will use them often. To add a list as a Web part to a page, follow these steps:

1. Click Site Actions ⇨ Edit Page ⇨ Insert ⇨ Web Part.

2. Click Web Part to load the Web Part Gallery options.

3. Click "Lists and Libraries" and select the `Customers` list.

4. Click Add. SharePoint loads the list within a Web part at the top of the page.

> **NOTE** *You could continue to run your WPF application against the list, and the changes would be reflected in this list. This is because this list is a view of the actual data that is rendered within a Web part.*

Figure 2-23 shows the `Customers` list rendered within the Web part. Test out the WPF application again, and add some data to the list to test the rendering of that data within the Web part.

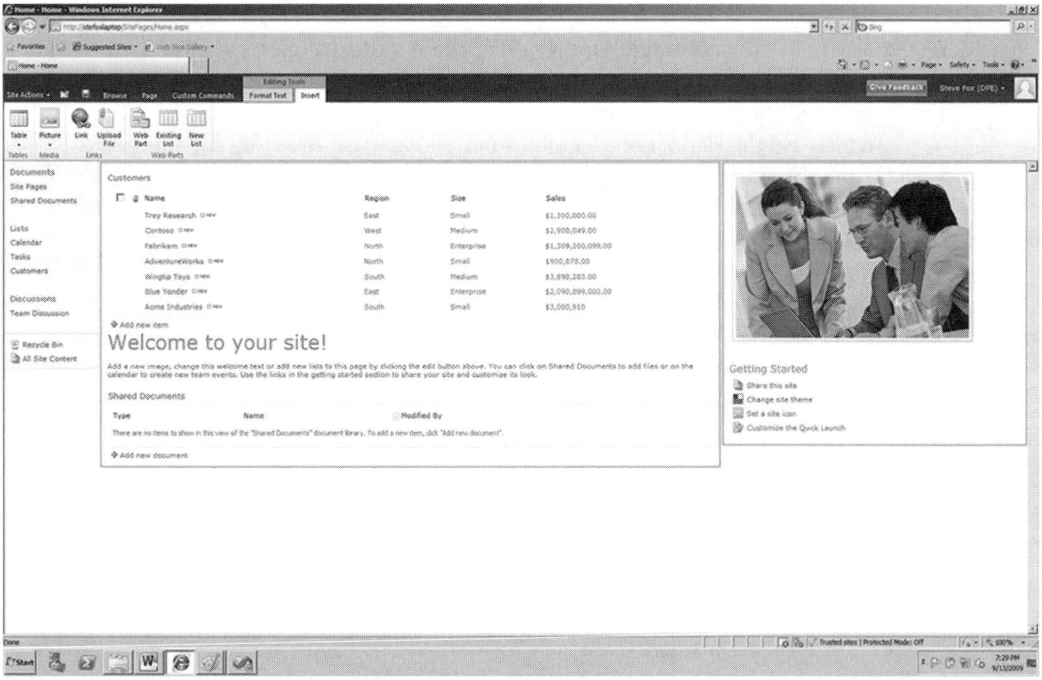

FIGURE 2-23 Customer list as a Web part

Web parts are very customizable. In fact, you'll see a number of ways in which you can interact with Web parts programmatically within this book, ranging from visual Web parts to Silverlight applications embedded within Web parts.

In this next exercise, you'll create your first Web part. It won't be pretty, but it'll be simple and illustrative of how you can apply your ASP.NET coding skills to a custom SharePoint object.

TRY IT OUT **Create a Custom Web Part Programmatically**

Code file [MyFirstWebPart.zip] available for download at Wrox.com.

You can programmatically customize Web parts using Visual Studio 2010. To customize and deploy a Web part, follow these steps:

1. Open Visual Studio 2010 and click File ➪ New ➪ Project. Navigate to the SharePoint 2010 template folder, and select Empty SharePoint Project. Give your project a name (for example, `MyFirstWebPart`) and location. Click OK.

2. In the Project Wizard, ensure that the site URL is pointing to your local SharePoint site. Click Validate to test the connection to the site. You can select either deployment method (that is, as Sandboxed Solution or Farm Solution).

3. After Visual Studio creates the project for you, right-click the project and select Add ➪ New Item. In the SharePoint 2010 folder, select Web Part.

4. Navigate to the Web part code file (for example, `MyFirstWebPart.cs`) and add the bolded code in the following code listing to this project file.

> 🖉 **NOTE** If you use the accompanying source code, be sure to open the code and then change the Site URL property to point to your local SharePoint site. Click the project and then, in the Properties window, change the Site URL property. You can also use the Import SharePoint Solution Package (the `.wsp` file that ships with the accompanying source code) project template.

```
using System;
using System.ComponentModel;
using System.Runtime.InteropServices;
using System.Web.UI;
using System.Web.UI.WebControls;
using System.Web.UI.WebControls.WebParts;
using Microsoft.SharePoint;
using Microsoft.SharePoint.WebControls;

namespace MyFirstWebPart.MyFirstWebPart
{
    [ToolboxItemAttribute(false)]
    public class MyFirstWebPart : WebPart
    {
        Label lblUserEntry = new Label();
```

```
TextBox txtbxUserEntry = new TextBox();
Label lblFinalCost = new Label();
TextBox txtbxFinalCost = new TextBox();
Button btnCalcTax = new Button();
double totalTax = 0.00;
double prodTax = 0.11;

public MyFirstWebPart()
{
}

protected override void CreateChildControls()
{
    lblUserEntry.Text = "Cost of Widget:";
    lblFinalCost.Text = "Final Cost:    ";
    btnCalcTax.Text = "Calc.";
    txtbxUserEntry.Text = "59.30";
    this.Controls.Add(lblUserEntry);
    this.Controls.Add(txtbxUserEntry);
    this.Controls.Add(new LiteralControl("<p>"));
    this.Controls.Add(lblFinalCost);
    this.Controls.Add(txtbxFinalCost);
    this.Controls.Add(new LiteralControl("<p>"));
    this.Controls.Add(btnCalcTax);
    btnCalcTax.Click +=
        new EventHandler(btnCalcTax_Click);

    base.CreateChildControls();
}

void btnCalcTax_Click(object sender, EventArgs e)
{
    double prodCost = Convert.ToDouble
        (txtbxUserEntry.Text);
    totalTax = Math.Round(prodCost -
        (prodCost * prodTax),2) *100/100;
    txtbxFinalCost.Text = totalTax.ToString();
}

protected override void RenderContents
    (HtmlTextWriter writer)
{
    base.RenderContents(writer);
}
    }
}
```

5. Press F6 to test to see if the project builds successfully.

6. After it builds successfully, press F5 to test the Web part deployment in Debug mode. (You can optionally set a breakpoint at the `btnCalcTax_Click` event.)

7. On your SharePoint site, select Site Actions ⇨ Edit Page. Then, click to activate the content portion of the SharePoint site — that is, the area beneath one of the other SharePoint Web parts.

8. Select Insert on the SharePoint ribbon and select Web Part. In the Custom category, you'll find the Web part that you just built and deployed, as shown in Figure 2-24. Select the Web part and click Add.

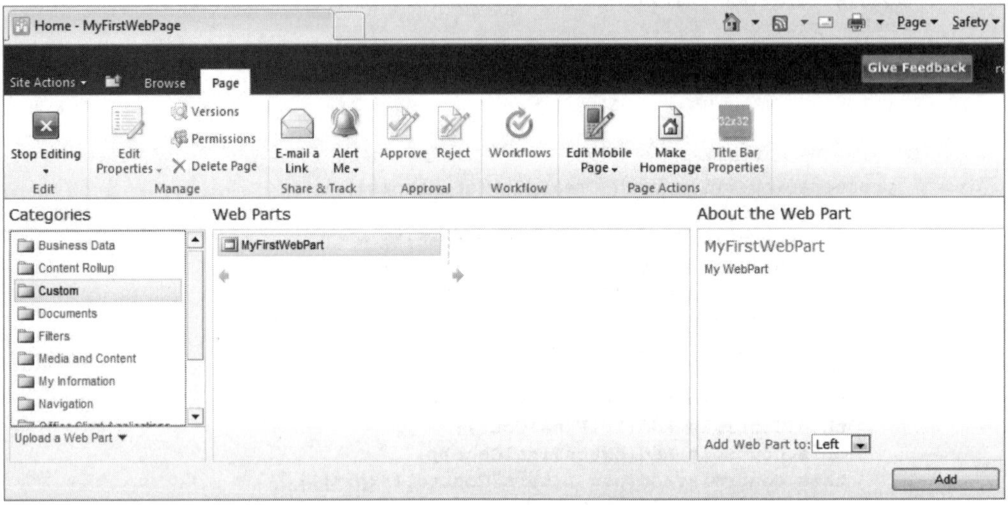

FIGURE 2-24 Custom Web part

9. This adds the Web part to your SharePoint site, as shown in Figure 2-25. You can test the Web part by adding a decimal currency value in the Cost of Widget field and clicking the Calc. button. This executes the `btnCalcTax_Click` event, and then adds the final cost of the Widget to the Final Cost field.

FIGURE 2-25 Deployed Web part

And there you go! You just built your first custom Web part. It was simple, and, yes, used absolutely no design skills at all. But it did illustrate the use of pure ASP.NET code for a Web part.

How It Works

SharePoint is built on top of ASP.NET. So, when you create Web parts for SharePoint, you are leveraging the members and classes of the ASP.NET namespaces. This was evident in the `MyFirstWebPart` class declaration, which derives from the `System.Web.UI.WebControls` namespace.

```
public class MyFirstWebPart : WebPart
```

When you derive from `WebPart`, this provides a set of controls that you can use to build out your UI. For example, in this exercise, you used `Label`, `Button`, and `Textbox` controls. In this case, these controls were hand-coded, but if you're not familiar with all of the available controls, an easy way to learn about them is to first create the Visual Web part project and then use the Designer to drag and drop the available controls.

```
Label lblUserEntry = new Label();
TextBox txtbxUserEntry = new TextBox();
```

```
Label lblFinalCost = new Label();
TextBox txtbxFinalCost = new TextBox();
Button btnCalcTax = new Button();
```

Each of the controls that you instantiate must be added to the `Controls` collection, which is the way in which the Web part displays the controls. This was done by calling the `Controls.Add` method and then passing in the name of the control to add to the Web part.

Lastly, the event for the button was created simply by typing `btnCalcTax.Click+=` and then pressing the Tab key twice, which auto-generates a stubbed method for you to use. In this example, the code converted the user entry into a value it could handle, calculated the final cost of the widget, and displayed that cost in the `txtbxFinalCost` textbox control.

```
void btnCalcTax_Click(object sender, EventArgs e)
    {
        double prodCost = Convert.ToDouble(txtbxUserEntry.Text);
        totalTax = prodCost - (prodCost * prodTax);
        txtbxFinalCost.Text = totalTax.ToString();
    }
```

If you're already familiar with ASP.NET, this is great; you'll be able to apply a wealth of your knowledge within the SharePoint space. If you're not, have no fear, because you'll surely pick some up along the way as you move through the book. You'll also learn about some more advanced UI experiences using Silverlight. You'll get a sense for how this is done in Chapter 9.

Setting Permissions for a SharePoint Site

One key aspect of SharePoint is the different security permissions you'll need to provision for a given site. This is important more from an end-user perspective, but for those of you who are new to SharePoint, what's key here is that you, as the owner of a SharePoint site (or other object within SharePoint), can assess certain levels of security.

TRY IT OUT   Edit Permissions for a SharePoint Site

Security is very important in SharePoint. You must understand how you can control the different levels of permission that are available to you in SharePoint 2010. To edit permissions for a SharePoint site, follow these steps:

1. Navigate to the home page of the site you created in the last exercise (for example, `http://fabrikamhockey/sprocks`).

2. Click Site Actions ➪ Site Permissions. This opens the Permissions page, which displays the different options available to you, as shown in Figure 2-26.

3. To provide a particular person with specific permissions, click on one of the permission types (for example, Team Site Members) and then click New ➪ Add Users. Add the user (or the group) to the Users/Groups field. You can also optionally send a welcome email to the individual (or group) by checking the "Send welcome email to the new users" checkbox and adding a title and some welcome text for the mail.

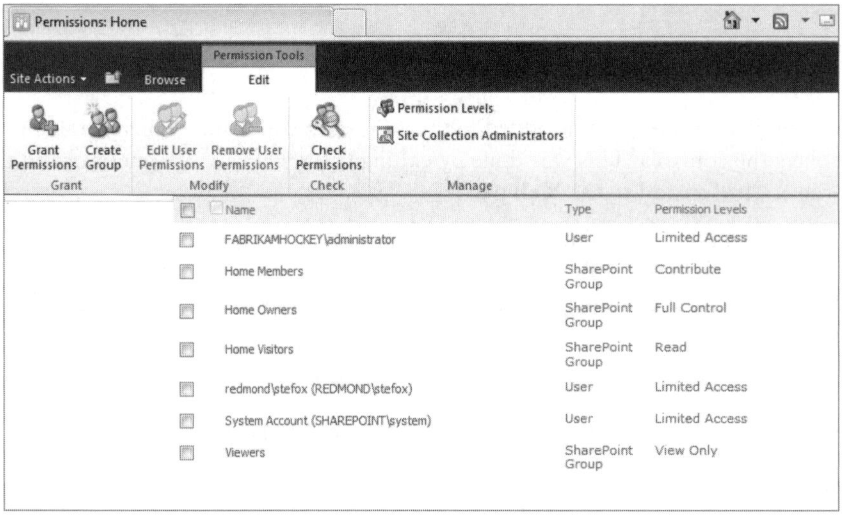

FIGURE 2-26 Permissions

How It Works

SharePoint uses Active Directory, so when users are added (or sites are provisioned by an administrator), an Active Directory identity is associated with the users. Further, those users who are added to the site can be given specific levels of permission (such as Viewer, Member, Administrator, and so on). You can also create security groups for SharePoint to create custom security groups for specific sites or objects within sites. The groups are simply aggregations of individual entries in Active Directory. This walkthrough simply enabled you to provision access for a specific Active Directory entry that existed in the context of your SharePoint server. Chapter 12 provides more information about security in SharePoint.

SUMMARY

This chapter discussed the types of skills that you (as an aspiring SharePoint developer) should know or learn as you embark on your journey. Key to these skills, though, is the understanding that different meanings are associated with SharePoint development. For example, if you simply want to play in the content and page customization space, then perhaps ASP.NET, HTML, and CSS are all you will need (and perhaps JavaScript). However, if you want to get deeper into building managed code solutions for SharePoint 2010, then you'll want to learn more about C# and VB.NET, and, more generally, the .NET Framework.

This chapter also provided an introduction to the Visual Studio 2010 templates, and introduced you to SharePoint Designer 2010. Both of these applications should definitely be an important part of your development toolkit, which is explored in greater detail in Chapter 3. This chapter also discussed the skills you'd need to get started as a SharePoint developer, specifically calling out HTML, XML, XSL, JavaScript, CSS, and one of C# or VB.NET as your managed code languages.

This chapter also walked you through a number of examples that enabled you to get a hands-on understanding not only of the SharePoint interface but also of some of the more basic ways to program against SharePoint. The rest of the book will continue to build these basic examples into more advanced examples of programming against SharePoint.

EXERCISES

1. What are the different ways of setting up and configuring SharePoint for development?

2. How is using Hyper-V better or worse than installing SharePoint "on the metal"?

3. What are some of the common project templates you'll find in Visual Studio 2010?

4. What are the different levels of security that can be assessed against an individual in SharePoint 2010?

▶ **WHAT YOU LEARNED IN THIS CHAPTER**

ITEM	DESCRIPTION
Developer Tools	High-level feature descriptions of Visual Studio 2010 and SharePoint Designer 2010, and how they can be used.
SharePoint 2010 Platform Services	The different services and APIs that make up the SharePoint 2010 plat-form, such as enhanced Web services (for example, support for WCF and ASP.NET); improved data programmability; REST and ADO.NET Data Services, and LINQ support; and LOB integration using BCS.
SharePoint 2010 Deployment Options	The capability to deploy SharePoint solutions on-premises or to a hosted SharePoint instance online (called SharePoint Online) using sandboxed solutions.

RECOMMENDED READING

➤ SharePoint virtual machine download at `http://www.microsoft.com/downloads/details.aspx?FamilyID=0c51819b-3d40-435c-a103-a5481fe0a0d2&displaylang=en`

➤ SharePoint Development Center on MSDN at `http://msdn.microsoft.com/en-us/sharepoint/default.aspx`

➤ Channel 9 SharePoint Developer Learning Center at `http://channel9.msdn.com/learn/courses/SharePoint2010Developer/`

PART II
Getting Started with SharePoint 2010 Development

3

SharePoint 2010 Developer Tools

WHAT YOU'LL LEARN IN THIS CHAPTER:

➤ Understanding the different ways of developing for SharePoint

➤ Getting to know the primary developer tools and environments for SharePoint 2010

➤ Using Visual Studio 2010, SharePoint Designer 2010 and Expression Blend when developing for SharePoint

At this stage in the book, you've been introduced to what SharePoint is. You've learned how to set up a development environment (either virtualized or on the metal), and you've read about some of the developer features in SharePoint 2010. From here on out, you will become more practical in your interaction with this book, and you will begin to write applications for SharePoint 2010.

In this chapter, you learn about the different tools that you will want to have in your developer toolkit. You may have more or less than what is described in this chapter, but ultimately this chapter is about the core developer tools you should either use or be aware of when embarking on your SharePoint development projects.

This chapter examines the following four main developer tools/environments:

➤ Browser-based development

➤ SharePoint Designer 2010

➤ Visual Studio 2010

➤ Expression Blend

Depending on your skills and design goals, you may use these environments or tools in different ways. So, this chapter introduces you to these different possibilities and walks you through some practical examples.

SHAREPOINT DEVELOPMENT ACROSS DEVELOPER SEGMENTS

In Chapter 1, you saw the different types of users that interact with SharePoint, as well as the different ways in which they use SharePoint. If you remember that discussion, there are end users who use SharePoint as an application platform, and then there are power users, designers, and developers who, in some way, engage in administration, configuration, or development against SharePoint. Thinking about a development lifecycle for each of these types of users, you can imagine that there are ways in which these people might work together, or they may act independently with something that was created specifically for them.

For example, the end user is the ultimate consumer of the product, while the power user configures it. Thus, they are downstream from the development process. Further upstream, you have the developer and the designer, who may work together to deliver both the code and the user experience (branded or otherwise) to the power user and, ultimately, to the end user. The point is that there is a range of people interacting with SharePoint — from the developer all the way downstream to the end user. Figure 3-1 illustrates the range of these types of users.

FIGURE 3-1 Who interacts with SharePoint 2010

With this in mind, users require different ways to develop for SharePoint — and, in this case, users would primarily include developers, designers, and power users. That is what this chapter is all about — talking about the different tools that these various types of users can use to develop for SharePoint.

Figure 3-2 shows an interesting way to divide up what have traditionally been associated with SharePoint development — namely, Visual Studio and SharePoint Designer. This chapter proposes the Web interface as an end-user and power-user "tool," SharePoint Designer as a Web developer tool, and Expression Blend as more of a designer tool for the development experience. Visual Studio, then, would be for a more managed-code development experience.

On the designer/power-user side, you will invariably use the Web-based interface as a user with augmented permissions — for example, full control — so you could perform the duties of a site administrator. What this means is that you may be creating artifacts like custom lists, inserting Web parts, editing content, creating master pages, and the like. You may get into coding here, and more than likely that will involve HTML, XML, CSS, ASP.NET, JavaScript, and other dynamic languages. You may also get into some integration with Silverlight, as you will see in an example where a Silverlight banner ad is integrated with an ASP.NET master page.

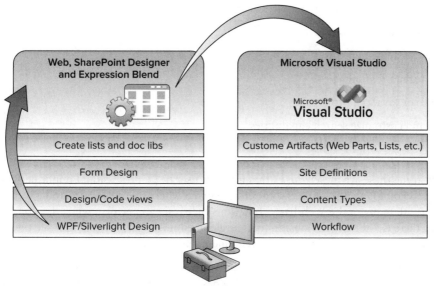

FIGURE 3-2 Range of tools for users

On the managed side of the house, you will find development that is more centric to C# or VB.NET (managed-code languages), and you may also find scripted languages here. Using Visual Studio, you will also find that development efforts may be managed as a part of an application lifecycle, which is more broadly called *application lifecycle management (ALM)*. During ALM, source code is checked into team folders (in Team Foundation Server, for example). You can add SharePoint development projects to those folders and centrally manage them. You'll also find custom solutions that leverage other parts of the .NET Framework, such as solutions based on Windows Workflow (WF), or service-based applications built and deployed as Web parts or event receivers.

Ultimately for you, the benefits of these two development paradigms are choices offered along the spectrum of SharePoint development. Depending on what you're trying to develop for SharePoint, each of these tools (or interfaces) will have pros and cons for the task at hand.

Let's walk through each of these development experiences so that you can get a better sense for how you might leverage each of them in different ways.

WEB-BASED DEVELOPMENT IN SHAREPOINT

As mentioned, SharePoint development can be defined in a number of ways. A light developer (or *power user*) may leverage more of the native SharePoint features to do development through the Web-based environment. This type of user will require escalated permissions on a SharePoint site, and, thus, will be able to accomplish tasks such as the following:

➤ Configure a new theme to the site

➤ Add a new Web part to the site

➤ Create and deploy multimedia for sitewide consumption

➤ Manage sandboxed solutions

➤ Activate and deactivate features

➤ Write and format text inline

➤ Add HTML or JavaScript to a page

➤ Configure and customize search capabilities

➤ Map master pages to sites

While some might argue these are merely *tasks* that a power user or IT professional might perform, one thing about SharePoint is that the line is sometimes blurred where one role starts and another ends. For example, with many of the Web-based functions that you can perform when developing for SharePoint, there is a direct relationship to a development task. Thus, you might see the SharePoint Web interface as an *endpoint* to the development experience.

For example, if you create a custom Web part, you must load that Web part into a SharePoint site using the Web Part Gallery. Or, if you're working with a designer to create a new master page, you must associate that new master page with a specific site through the Site Settings of that SharePoint site. The types of Web-based tasks that you can perform go on and on.

The key take-away from this is that, as a SharePoint solution developer, you will be interacting with the Web-based features in SharePoint, as well as potentially leveraging other tools that will be examined in this chapter.

Site Settings

An important part of SharePoint to be familiar with is the Site Settings page. You'll find most configuration options for your site here, so it's a good place to start when trying to understand where you can, for example, change the theme of your site, activate features, upload sandboxed solutions, and so on.

Figure 3-3 shows the Site Settings page. Note that the core features of the Site Settings page are split up into major categories. For example, most of your security settings are available to you in the "Users and Permissions" category.

The features that you develop and deploy to SharePoint will appear in the Feature Gallery. To see the Feature Gallery, locate the Site Actions area and click "Manage site features." Note that the Feature Gallery also indicates which features are active or deactivated. When you develop and deploy a feature to SharePoint, this is where you will activate and deactivate it.

Farm or site administrators can use the Feature Gallery as a place where they can activate and deactivate the features in a SharePoint site collection. In Figure 3-4, notice that at the top of the Feature Gallery is a feature called the `AnnouncementListEvent Feature1`. This is an example of a custom feature built and deployed to SharePoint, and it can be activated or deactivated at any time by the person with the appropriate permissions.

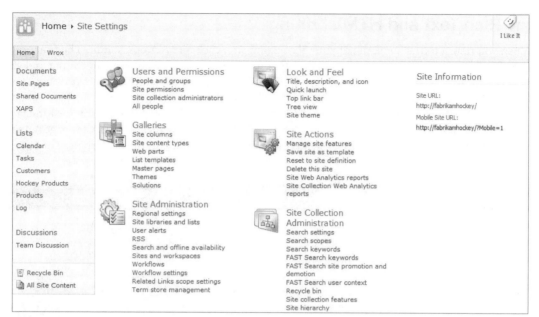

FIGURE 3-3 Site Settings page

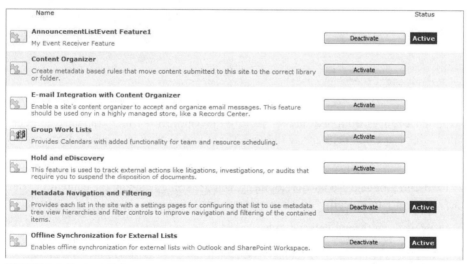

FIGURE 3-4 Feature Gallery

Take some time to explore the different parts of the Site Settings page to become familiar with all it offers for configuring SharePoint sites.

Inline Rich Text and HTML Editing

When you return to the home site of your SharePoint site, click Site Actions ⇨ Edit. The functions available to you at this point range from inserting native and custom Web parts, to editing and generating custom lists. If you click inside the top-level Web part to expose the in-context ribbon, you will see that you can now edit the page using the ribbon controls. Thus, while the Site Settings provide you with configurable settings for the applications that you deploy to SharePoint (or for changing the configuration of the site that hosts your applications, such as themes or master pages), the Edit mode enables those who have elevated permissions to contribute to the development of content on the site, as shown in Figure 3-5.

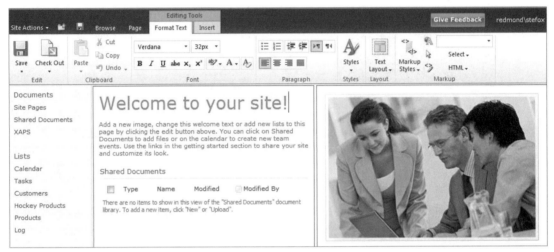

FIGURE 3-5 Inline HTML and text editing

The editing experience ranges from text, HTML, and JavaScript formatting to the inclusion of images or multimedia. For example, let's say that you've created a training video, and you now want to embed that video in a Web part on a page. You can use the Site Actions ⇨ Edit menu to open the Insert Web part, where you can then insert a Web part that supports multimedia. While this may not constitute hard-core, managed-code development, you are still advancing the content of your site, so, in a sense, you are technically "developing" your site.

Let's try this out by walking through an example.

TRY IT OUT   Testing Out the Inline Editing Experience

The new SharePoint ribbon experience enables you to quickly customize and edit SharePoint pages. To edit a SharePoint page inline, follow these steps:

1.   Open your SharePoint site.

2.   Navigate to the home page of your site, and click All Site Content.

3.   Click Create.

4. On the Create Gallery page, click Page ➪ Web Part Page, and click Create.

5. Provide a name for the new Web part page (for example, `WroxWPP`), as shown in Figure 3-6. Leave the default options and click Create.

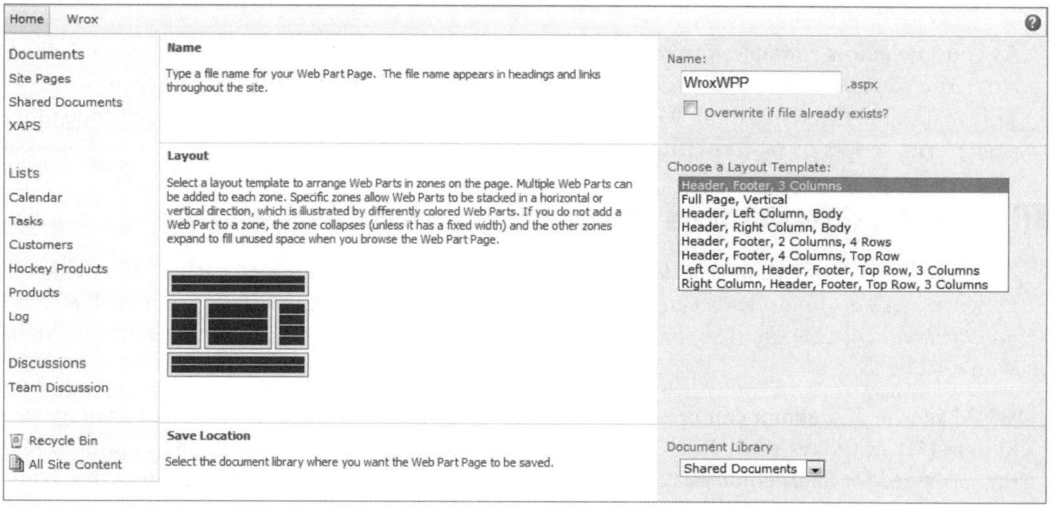

FIGURE 3-6 Creating a new Web part page

6. By default, SharePoint should open the page in Edit mode. If it doesn't, click Site Actions ➪ Edit Page, which will open the page in Edit mode.

7. Click the top Web part Zone, and click "Add a web part."

8. Select the "Media and Content" category, and then select Content Editor. SharePoint adds a Content Editor Web part for you in the top zone, and you can now add and edit text and images using the contextual ribbon.

9. Add some text and format it. When you have finished, click the Page tab on the ribbon and click Stop Editing to save your changes to the Web part.

How It Works

This initial example was a simple illustration of using the Site Actions menu to open up Edit options. Essentially, when you have a SharePoint page in Edit mode, it exposes a set of features to you, depending on your permissions level for the site.

For example, if you had only read permissions, then you would not have the same functionality available to you as you would if you had full control rights to the SharePoint site. What it did do, though, was expose the functionality of the new SharePoint ribbon. The ribbon is a major leap forward in SharePoint 2010 and provides you with a number of different contextually driven capabilities across SharePoint.

The Content Editor Web part represents a way for you to add rich text or HTML source to the page (beyond the default behavior of a wiki page). When the site is loaded, text or source in this Web part is treated as part of the page and is rendered. So, for example if you were to click View Source on your browser, you'd see that the simple content you just added to your Content Editor Web part in this exercise would be rendered as HTML as a part of the page.

As you saw in this example, you're not limited to only rich text when using the Content Editor Web part. You can add source code (such as HTML or JavaScript) that will also run when the page loads. This makes the Content Editor Web part a versatile way to inject rich text or source code into the page to run scripts or set formatting at page load.

Adding Multimedia to a Site

Let's move on to something a little different and add the video mentioned earlier in the chapter. However, let's do so inside of a new wiki site, which, in SharePoint 2010, is a type of *Web content management* (WCM) site that enables authors to contribute rich text and multimedia to a shared Web experience.

WCM sites in SharePoint can be traced back historically to the *Microsoft Content Management System* (MCMS) days when Microsoft acquired CMS and integrated it with SharePoint 2003. What this provided for SharePoint was a way to have a managed workflow around content that could be published to the Web. Originally, the publishing framework targeted more Internet-facing sites, so developers and designers could build and deploy a controlled and managed publishing environment to get Web content out to these Internet-facing sites. In SharePoint 2007, you found the WCM templates under the Publishing tab when creating a new site collection.

In SharePoint 2010, you have a Publishing template called the Enterprise Wiki, which allows you to build a rich wiki experience — quite a leap from the simpler, one-dimensional wiki site that was available in SharePoint 2007. The template is here because, in SharePoint 2010, the wiki is part of the WCM offerings for SharePoint, and, thus, it represents an enterprise-wide publishing portal. Also, wiki sites now support a wider array of features, including tagging, author attribution, and multimedia content. To create one, you will need to start out in Central Administration.

Let's first create an enterprise wiki, and then use the Web-based features in SharePoint to develop some content for the wiki site. Note that, for this exercise, you will need a sample video file (that is, a .wmv file). It could be any file you have handy, but you will upload the video file as a part of this walkthrough.

TRY IT OUT   Creating and Editing a Wiki Site

Wiki sites provide a way to enable informal social networking across a community. To create and edit a wiki site, follow these steps:

1. Click Start ➪ All Programs ➪ Microsoft SharePoint 2010 Products ➪ SharePoint Central Administration.

2. Under Application Management, click Create Site Collections.

3. Provide a name for the new site (for example, MyWroxWiki), a description, and a URL (for example, wroxwiki). Then, using the template selector, click the Publishing tab and select Enterprise Wiki, as shown in Figure 3-7.

4. Provide an administrator for the site. Leave the other default options, and then click OK.

5. After SharePoint finishes creating the new site collection, it will provide a link that you can click to navigate to the new site collection you have created. Click that link to navigate to your new wiki site.

6. After you've landed on the home page of the wiki site, click Site Actions ⇨ Edit Page.

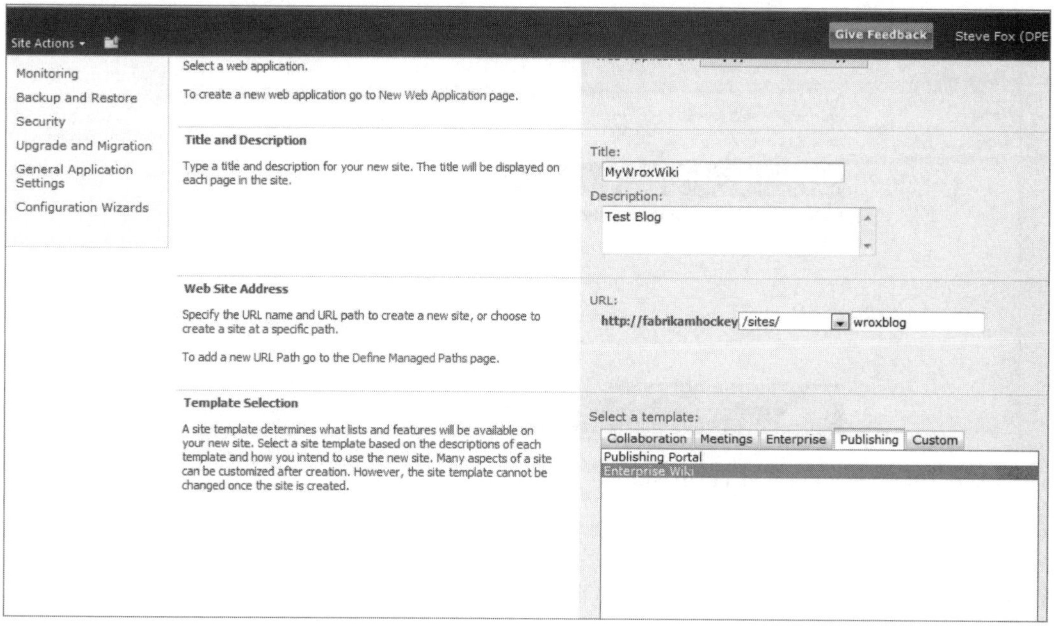

FIGURE 3-7 New wiki site

7. Click the Insert page, and then select "Video and Audio." This automatically adds a special Silverlight control into the wiki page. Click that control to expose more options on the contextual ribbon menu.

8. In the Options tab, click the Change Media button and select From Computer.

9. Upload to SharePoint a sample .wmv file that you have, to test the video. Complete the fields during the uploading process to complete uploading the video to SharePoint.

10. After you've uploaded the .wmv file, click the small Save icon beside the Site Actions menu to save the page and exit Edit mode.

11. You should now see the video embedded into the Wiki page, as shown in Figure 3-8, and you should now be able to click the Play button to play the video.

How It Works

SharePoint 2010 natively supports Silverlight, which, as you will see in this chapter and in later chapters in the book, makes integrating Silverlight with SharePoint a lot easier. There are two out-of-the-box Web parts intended to support Silverlight.

The first is the generic Silverlight Web part, which represents a "host container" for Silverlight applications. The second is the Multimedia Web part, which is, in essence, a Silverlight Web part that supports and serves the multimedia that is associated with the Web part.

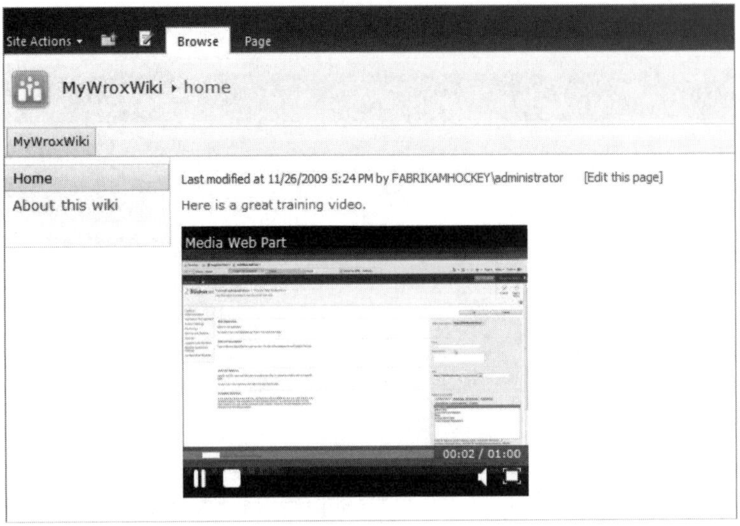

FIGURE 3-8 Completed media Web part

So, in the previous example, you "mapped" a video with the Multimedia Web part, which further enabled you to view the video when you clicked the Play button. The generic Multimedia control is nice in that it provides a set of controls to play, pause, and stop the video, as well as increase the volume, or toggle between thumbnail and full-screen views. The mapping of the video essentially represents a source property that is being set behind the scenes, so that the `MediaElement` object (a native part of the Silverlight video-playing capabilities) understands where to find and play the video.

The previous examples reinforce the fact that development for SharePoint can go beyond perhaps what many feel is typical development, and reinforce the whole spectrum of development from Web to design to managed code.

So, let's move on to the second environment in which you may find yourselves doing SharePoint development: SharePoint Designer 2010.

DEVELOPING SHAREPOINT APPLICATIONS USING SHAREPOINT DESIGNER 2010

SharePoint Designer 2010 is a great tool to have in your development toolkit because you will discover some new features in SharePoint Designer 2010 that will make some of what you do as a developer much easier. You'll also find that SharePoint Designer integrates really well with SharePoint 2010.

Chapter 2 provided you with a glimpse of the new SharePoint Designer 2010 UI, so you saw that it leverages the ribbon and has a new navigation pane with the common site objects you will interact with as a SharePoint developer. Also, similar to the other Office 2010 applications, you have the Backstage feature, which provides more generic features and shortcuts (such as Open Site, New, and so on).

One of the core features that you will use quite frequently within SharePoint Designer is the navigation pane, which is shown in Figure 3-9.

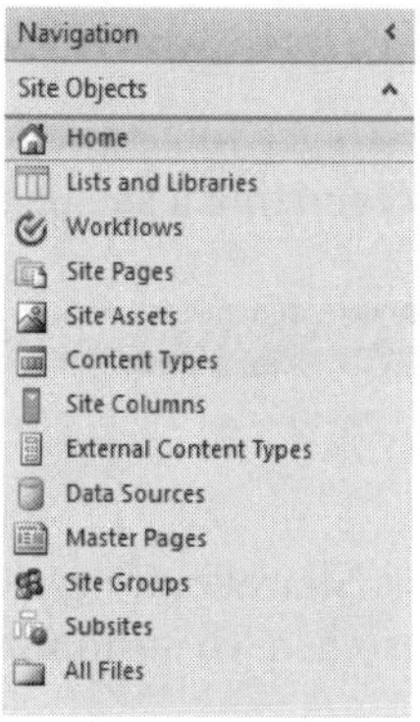

The navigation pane provides a way for you to navigate across the major functional areas of SharePoint Designer to quickly get to the things that you need to do. The navigation pane provides links to the following functionality:

➤ *Lists and Libraries* — Allows you to create, edit, and manage lists and libraries.

➤ *Workflows* — Facilitates the creation of rules-based, declarative workflow (that can be imported into Visual Studio and extended).

➤ *Site Pages* — Provides the capability to create, customize, and edit site-level Web pages, or edit existing SharePoint site pages.

FIGURE 3-9 SharePoint Designer Navigation options

➤ *Site Assets* — Provides a listing for different types of resources (for example, JavaScript files that you want to globally reference across a SharePoint site).

➤ *Content Types* — Provides the capability to create, edit, and manage content types. (Content types are reusable objects and metadata, such as columns, custom documents, and site columns.)

➤ *Site Columns* — Supports the creation, editing, and management of site columns. (Site columns are reusable columns that can be repurposed across a SharePoint site collection.)

➤ *External Content Types* — Enables you to create ADO.NET or Web service-based external content types for deployment using the new Business Connectivity Services (BCS) functionality.

➤ *Data Sources* — Enables you to create and manage data source connections to a SharePoint site.

➤ *Master Pages* — Enables you to create, edit, and manage the master pages mapped to a specific SharePoint site. (Master pages provide a way to structure and brand your site.)

➤ *Site Groups* — Displays the groups of sites within your SharePoint site.

➤ *Subsites* — Shows the subsites within the site collection.

➤ *All Files* — Displays all files in the SharePoint site.

Depending on your level of permission to a given site, some of these features may be hidden to you from within the SharePoint Designer IDE. For example, without administrator privileges, you will not see the Master Pages link in the navigation pane, so you will not be able to build and deploy master pages to that SharePoint site.

Customizing a Site Page

There are some very useful features in SharePoint Designer, and to cover them all would take a separate book. However, let's at least take a look at a few to get you started and get you familiar with SharePoint Designer. In this chapter, you will use SharePoint Designer to create site pages and master pages. In later chapters, you will also use SharePoint Designer to create external content types and workflow.

To get you started, let's walk through some of the functionality associated with creating and customizing a site page.

TRY IT OUT Customizing a Site Page

Code file [XMLEmployee.zip] available for download at Wrox.com.

As a SharePoint developer, you will be asked to customize many sites, which is a strength of SharePoint Designer. To customize a site, follow these steps:

1. Open SharePoint Designer 2010.
2. On the left-hand navigation list, click Site Pages. This opens the default Site Pages page in the IDE (see Figure 3-10), which enables you to manage permissions for specific sites, preview the page in a browser, check in and check out the site page for editing, and so on.

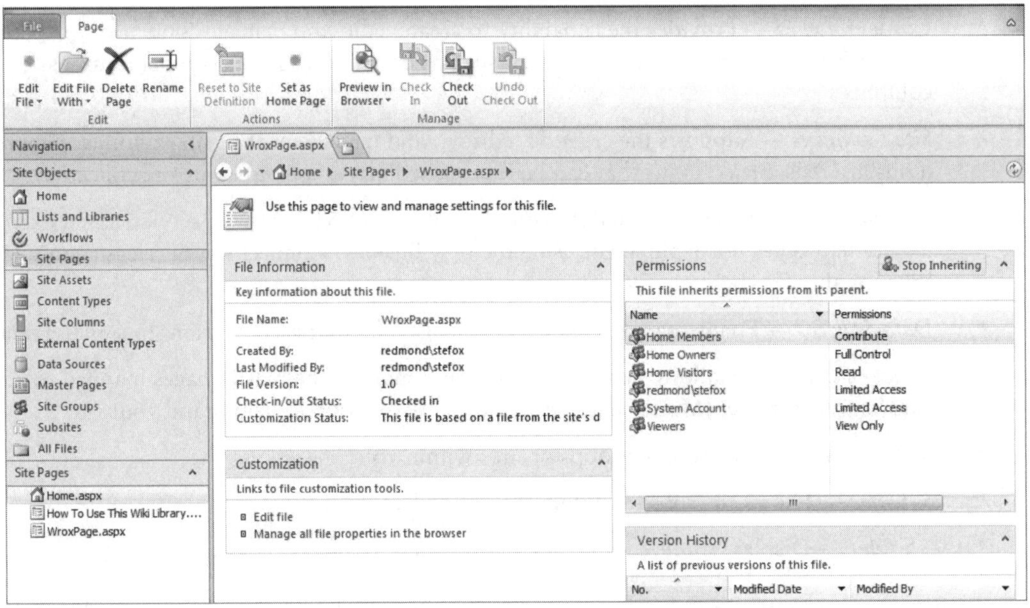

FIGURE 3-10 Properties view for site page

3. On the ribbon, click Web Part Page to create a new Web part page. Rename the new page that is created for you to `Employee.aspx`.
4. Right-click `Employees.aspx`, and select Check Out. This marks the file as locked exclusively by you for editing.

5. After you check out the file, click the link to open the Properties pane.

6. Under Customization, click Edit File.

7. Click Code to change the view to code view.

8. Add a set of `<div>` tags within which you will add an ASP.NET control.

9. In the Toolbox, under the Standard ASP.NET controls, drag and drop the XML control to the Site Page Designer between the `<div>` tags you just added and rename the default ID to `xmlEmployee`. The code should now look similar to the boldfaced code that follows:

```
...
<WebPartPages:WikiContentWebpart frametype="none" runat="server" partorder="1"
    __WebPartId="{B33365D3-49F7-43F6-B833-B06139DB7AD4}"
    id="g_b33365d3_49f7_43f6_b833_b06139db7ad4">
    <content>
        <div>
            <asp:Xml runat="server" id="xmlEmployee"></asp:Xml>
        </div>
    </content>
</WebPartPages:WikiContentWebpart>
...
```

10. Click Design to change the view to design view.

11. Click the new XML control you added to the page, and then click the Tag Properties tab.

12. Under Behavior, you can upload a `DocumentSource` (an XML file that contains the data) and a `TransformSource` (XSLT that formats the XML data), as shown in Figure 3-11.

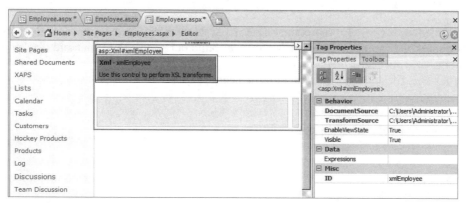

FIGURE 3-11 XML control

13. Upload your own XML file and a corresponding XLST file. If you don't have anything handy, some sample XML code follows that you can use for this walkthrough.

The first file (`Employee.xml`) represents the data file. This well-formed XML document is composed of multiple employees, as is denoted by the `Employee` element that is the child element of the `Employees` element. Each employee record comprises a `Name` element and an `EmpID` (or employee ID) element.

```
<?xml version="1.0" encoding="ISO-8859-1"?>
<Employees>
     <Employee>
          <Name>John Doe</Name>
          <EmpID>77804</EmpID>
     </Employee>
     <Employee>
          <Name>Jane Doe</Name>
          <EmpID>09029</EmpID>
     </Employee>
     <Employee>
          <Name>Ken Smith</Name>
          <EmpID>10290</EmpID>
     </Employee>
     <Employee>
          <Name>Kendra LaMont</Name>
          <EmpID>76802</EmpID>
     </Employee>
     <Employee>
          <Name>Ahmed Banerjee</Name>
          <EmpID>89300</EmpID>
     </Employee>
     <Employee>
          <Name>Pierre LaCroix</Name>
          <EmpID>00918</EmpID>
     </Employee>
</Employees>
```

The second file (`Employee.xls`) represents the XSLT style sheet that formats the data. Note that, in the style sheet, Cascading Style Sheets (CSS) styles build out a table to format and display the data from the `Employee.xml` file. Also note that `for-each` and `select` statements iterate through the `Employee.xml` file and load the data into the page.

```
<?xml version="1.0" encoding="ISO-8859-1"?>
<xsl:stylesheet version="1.0"
xmlns:xsl="http://www.w3.org/1999/XSL/Transform">
<xsl:template match="/">
<html>
<head>
<title>Employee</title>
<style type="text/css">
.style2 {
     border-collapse: collapse;
     font-size: 6.0pt;
     font-family: Calibri, sans-serif;
     color: #376092;
     border-left-style: none;
     border-left-color: inherit;
     border-left-width: medium;
     border-right-style: none;
```

```
        border-right-color: inherit;
        border-right-width: medium;
        border-top: 1.0pt solid #4F81BD;
        border-bottom: 1.0pt solid #4F81BD;
}
</style>
</head>
<body bgcolor="#8FACC7" text="#ffffff" link="#808040">
<h1>
<left>Employee Information</left>
</h1>
<table border="0" cellpadding="0" cellspacing="0" class="style2"
      style="mso-border-top-alt: solid #4F81BD 1.0pt;
      mso-border-top-themecolor: accent1; mso-border-bottom-alt:
            solid #4F81BD 1.0pt;
      mso-border-bottom-themecolor: accent1; mso-yfti-tbllook: 1184;
      mso-padding-alt: 0in 5.4pt 0in 5.4pt">
  <thead>
      <tr style="mso-yfti-irow:-1;mso-yfti-firstrow:yes">

    <th align="left">
     <font face="arial" color="purple">Emp. Name</font>
    </th>
    <th align="left">
     <font face="arial" color="purple">Emp. ID</font>
    </th>
   </tr>
</thead>
<tbody>
<xsl:for-each select="Employees/Employee">
  <tr style="mso-yfti-irow:0">
          <td style="width:159.6pt;border-top:solid #4F81BD 1.0pt;
  mso-border-top-themecolor:accent1;border-left:
      none;border-bottom:solid #4F81BD 1.0pt;
  mso-border-bottom-themecolor:accent1;border-right:none;
      padding:0in 5.4pt 0in 5.4pt" valign="top" width="213">
          <p class="MsoNormal">
<xsl:value-of select="Name" />
          <span style="color:#376092;mso-themecolor:accent1;
  mso-themeshade:191"></span></p>
          </td>
          <td style="width:159.6pt;border-top:solid #4F81BD 1.0pt;
  mso-border-top-themecolor:accent1;border-left:none;
      border-bottom:solid #4F81BD 1.0pt;
      mso-border-bottom-themecolor:accent1;border-right:none;
      padding:0in 5.4pt 0in 5.4pt" valign="top" width="213">
          <p class="MsoNormal">
<xsl:value-of select="EmpID" />
          <span style="color:#376092;mso-themecolor:accent1;
  mso-themeshade:191"></span></p>
          </td>
  </tr>
</xsl:for-each>
```

```
</tbody>
</table>
</body>
</html>
</xsl:template>
</xsl:stylesheet>
```

14. After you've uploaded the two files, click the Preview in Browser button to test out the look and feel of the XML file and style sheet formatting. If you used the XML and XLST that has been provided here, the data that is displayed in your browser should look similar to Figure 3-12.

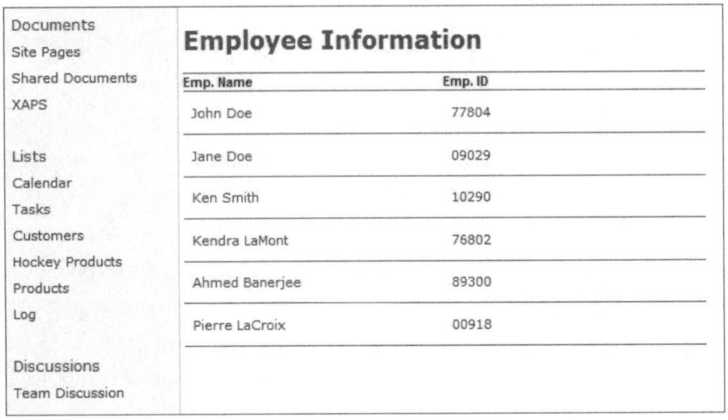

FIGURE 3-12 Transformed and rendered XML object

How It Works

When you create a style sheet, you leverage a set of commands that enable you to load specific parts of the XML data, and then decorate that data with HTML. Using this method, you can create relatively simple articulations of the XML data by using HTML only, or you can get complex by leveraging CSS. In this example's style sheet, you can see that there is a simple CSS style at work that is defined as `.style2`.

```
...
<style type="text/css">
.style2 {
    border-collapse: collapse;
    font-size: 6.0pt;
    font-family: Calibri, sans-serif;
    color: #376092;
    border-left-style: none;
    border-left-color: inherit;
    border-left-width: medium;
    border-right-style: none;
    border-right-color: inherit;
    border-right-width: medium;
    border-top: 1.0pt solid #4F81BD;
```

```
        border-bottom: 1.0pt solid #4F81BD;
    }
    </style>
    ...
```

style2 is then used in the styling of the table, as you can see in the following bolded code.

```
    ...
    <table border="0" cellpadding="0" cellspacing="0" class="style2"
        style="mso-border-top-alt: solid #4F81BD 1.0pt;
        mso-border-top-themecolor:
        accent1; mso-border-bottom-alt: solid #4F81BD 1.0pt;
        mso-border-bottom-themecolor:
        accent1; mso-yfti-tbllook: 1184; mso-padding-alt: 0in 5.4pt 0in 5.4pt">
    ...
```

With the CSS styling, and some inline styling as well, SharePoint Designer loads the two files and then maps them, so when the XML Web part loads into the page, it merges the XML data file with the XSLT style sheet.

Managing Other Data Sources in SharePoint Designer

XML is not the only data source you tap into to create data-based custom site pages with SharePoint Designer. You can also leverage other data connections such as Access or SQL Server databases, or even Web services. For example, you can create simple data connections in SharePoint Designer that can be subsequently used when building out custom site pages or Web parts from within SharePoint Designer.

To add a data source, you click the Data Sources link in the navigation pane. You then click the appropriate button on the ribbon to select which data source you want to connect. To create a database connection, click the Database Connection button, and then work through the wizard to configure the database. Or, you can create the database connection when creating the actual custom Web part page.

For example, click Site Pages in the navigation pane and then click Web Part Page ⇨ Edit File. You can now add data sources to the page by clicking Data Sources on the ribbon and then selecting from existing SharePoint data sources (for example, lists). If you insert controls into the Web part zones on the custom page, such as an ASP.NET GridView, you can associate database connections with that GridView, as shown in Figure 3-13. 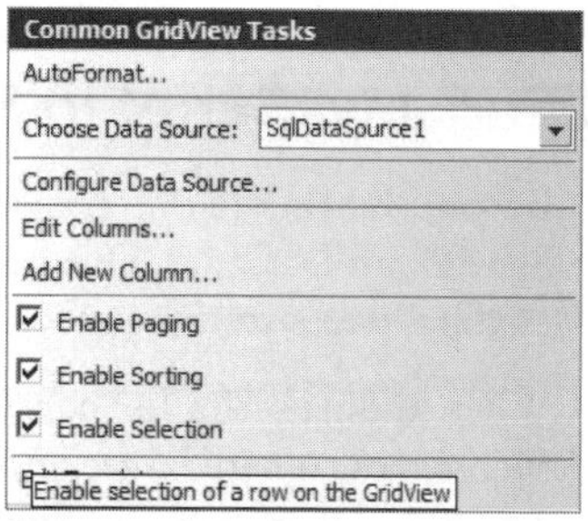

You can create new connections using this entry point as well. For example, after you add the GridView, in the Common GridView Tasks menu, select New Data Source in Choose Data Source. Click Database, provide a name for your connection, and then connect to a database you have on your machine by configuring a new connection to that

FIGURE 3-13 Adding SQL data sources to site page

database. As shown in Figure 3-14, you can select which columns you want to expose from your database, and you can test the connection from within SharePoint Designer by clicking Test Query.

After you've created the connection, you have a connection between the database and your data grid in the SharePoint Designer IDE, as shown in Figure 3-15.

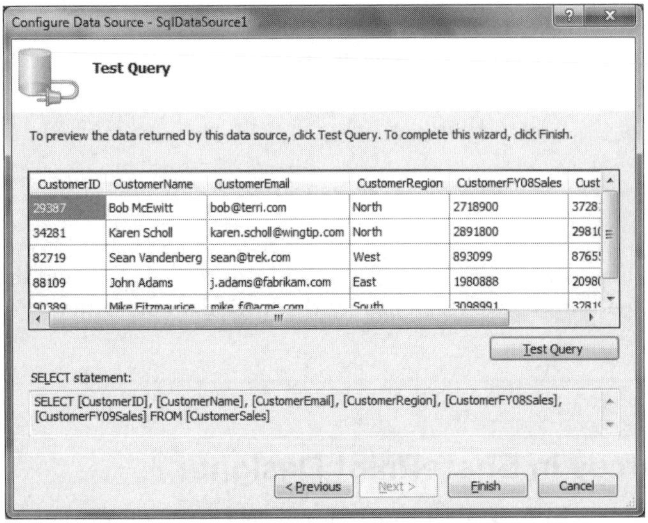

FIGURE 3-14 Configuring Data Source page of the wizard

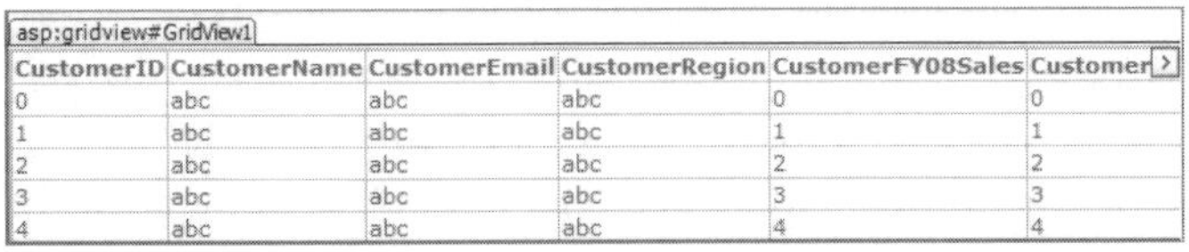

FIGURE 3-15 Data view in SharePoint Designer

Using JavaScript in SharePoint Designer

Beyond XML and database connectivity, there are many other useful developer features within SharePoint Designer. One key feature that you will likely use is the capability to create JavaScript-enabled pages so that you can insert dynamic scripting when loading specific pages.

When adding script to SharePoint pages, many developers opt to insert smaller sets of code into their Web pages. Where larger, more complex code is required, developers often build out managed-code assemblies that then get deployed to the global assembly cache (GAC). Site pages are one such example of where you can deploy JavaScript to add dynamic capabilities to your SharePoint Web page.

Let's try this out now.

TRY IT OUT   Integrating JavaScript with a Custom Site Page

Dynamic script languages like JavaScript can provide some powerful augmentations to your page. To add JavaScript to a custom site page, follow these steps:

1. Open SharePoint Designer 2010. Open a specific SharePoint site and click Site Pages.

2. Click Web Part Page on the ribbon to create a new page. Right-click the default site that is created for you and click Rename. Provide a name for the Site page (for example, `WroxPage.aspx`), and then click the link to open the Properties page for the new page. To edit the new Web part page, click Edit File.

3. You can toggle between different views, which include a code view, design view, and a split view. Open the Toolbox to see the different controls that are available for use.

4. Open the page in code view. You'll notice that there are some shaded and unshaded portions of the page. The unshaded portions of the page are where you can edit. Use the following sample code to build out your custom Web part, adding the bolded code between the `Content` tags within your Web part.

```
...
<WebPartPages:WikiContentWebpart runat="server" AllowEdit="True"
    AllowConnect="True" ConnectionID="00000000-0000-0000-0000-000000000000"
    Title=""        IsIncluded="True" Dir="Default"
    IsVisible="True" AllowMinimize="True"
    ExportControlledProperties="True" ID="g_086fe54d_7b3b_464b_aa61_f2cbe884276d"
    PartImageSmall="" FrameType="None" FrameState="Normal" ExportMode="All"
    AllowHide="True" SuppressWebPartChrome="False" DetailLink="" ChromeType="None"
    HelpLink="" MissingAssembly="Cannot import this Web part." AllowRemove="True"
    HelpMode="Modeless" Directive="&lt;%@ Register
    TagPrefix=&quot;SharePoint&quot;
    Namespace=&quot;Microsoft.Sharepoint.WebControls&quot;
    Assembly=&quot;Microsoft.SharePoint, Version=14.0.0.0, Culture=neutral,
    PublicKeyToken=71e9bce111e9429c&quot; %&gt;"
    AllowZoneChange="True" PartOrder="1"
    Description="" PartImageLarge="" IsIncludedFilter=""
    __MarkupType="vsattributemarkup" __WebPartId="{086FE54D-7B3B-464B-AA61-
    F2CBE884276D}" WebPart="true" Height="" Width="">
<Content>

<div>
    <asp:Label runat="server" Text="Developer Book Info" id="Label1"
        Font-Bold="True" Font-Size="Medium"></asp:Label>
        <br /><br /></div><div>
    <asp:Image runat="server" id="Image1" Width="413px" Height="55px"
        ImageUrl="http://fabrikamhockey/Shared%20Documents/WroxLogo.jpg" />
        <br /></div><div>
    <asp:Table runat="server" id="customTable">
    <asp:TableHeaderRow></asp:TableHeaderRow>
      <asp:TableRow>
        <asp:TableCell>
        <asp:Label runat="server" Text="Books:" Font-Bold="True"
            id="lblBooks2"></asp:Label>
```

```
            </asp:TableCell>
            <asp:TableCell>
<select id='dropdiv' onchange="getBookInfo(this)">
              <option value='1'>Professional SharePoint 2007
                Development</option>
              <option value='2'>Beginning ASP.NET 3.5</option>
              <option value='3'>Professional SharePoint Development using
                  Silverlight</option>
            </select>

<script language="javascript" type="text/javascript">
function getBookInfo(object)
{
var selected = object.options[object.selectedIndex].value;
var ISBN;
var Price;
var Message;

if (selected == '1')
{
    ISBN = "091283900129";
    Price = "$39.99";
    Message = "Book Info: " + ISBN + " | " + Price;
    alert(Message);
}
else if (selected == '2')
{
    ISBN = "298734689102";
    Price = "$42.99";
    Message = "Book Info: " + ISBN + " | " + Price;
    alert(Message);
}

else if (selected == '3')
{
    ISBN = "948302381002";
    Price = "$36.99";
    Message = "Book Info: " + ISBN + " | " + Price;
    alert(Message);
}
}

            </script>
            </asp:TableCell>
</asp:TableRow>
    </asp:Table>
  </div>
</Content>
</WebPartPages:WikiContentWebpart>
...
```

5. Once you've added the code to the Web part
   page, your custom Web part should look
   similar to Figure 3-16.

FIGURE 3-16 Custom Web part page in SharePoint Designer

6. Click Preview in Browser to ensure that the custom Web part loads as you've designed it.

7. Now that you've completed the design, click the drop-down box and change the selection. You should see an alert message pop-up with some additional information about that book, as shown in Figure 3-17.

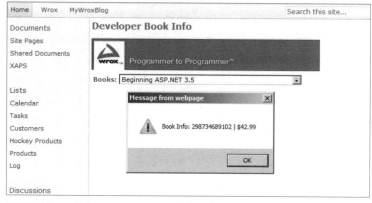

FIGURE 3-17 Web part page running JavaScript

How It Works

This is a straightforward example, but it illustrates the marriage of ASP.NET controls with dynamic scripting languages such as JavaScript.

JavaScript is a dynamic language that runs on the client. What that means is when the client loads the browser and subsequently the page, it runs the script that you've embedded within the page. However, one of the key things you must be aware of when using JavaScript for developing for SharePoint is that it doesn't maintain state natively, so you have to incorporate this into the design of your applications.

You'll note that there are a number of things happening in the code shown in this exercise. For example, you have an ASP `Label` control and an ASP `Image` control — which are controls that run on the server when the page loads. You also have a `select` HTML object that provides you with a type of HTML listbox with three options — different books that have been added as selections. You also have a JavaScript function called `getBookInfo()` that is called every time you change your selection in the drop-down box. What is more important in this example code, however, is that you're adding the code inline to the ASPX page. Alternatively, you could add the JavaScript code to the Content Editor Web part or to the master page of the SharePoint site.

As you can see from the following code, JavaScript events are encapsulated within the `script` tag. In this example, the events live on the page within which they are called. This is not the only way to call JavaScript code, however. You can also store the code in a separate file (for example, `foo.js`) that can be stored within SharePoint as a site asset. If you were to store the JavaScript separately, you would not encapsulate the script in script tags. You would merely add the methods and any helper functions to that `.js` file so that it is executed when called from the page.

```
...
<script language="javascript" type="text/javascript">
function foo()
```

```
{
...

}
 </script>
...
```

With the previous example using in-line JavaScript, the `getBookInfo` method call is triggered when the user changes his or her selection within the `ListBox`. You can see that the event that is triggered is the `onChange` event.

```
...
<select id='dropdiv' onchange="getBookInfo(this)">
 <option value='1'>
Professional SharePoint 2007 Development
 </option>
 <option value='2'>
Beginning ASP.NET 3.5
 </option>
 <option value='3'>
Professional SharePoint Development using Silverlight
 </option>
</select>
...
```

Depending on what the user selects, you can see that the object (that is, the selected item) is passed with the call to `getBookInfo`. The variable called `selected` then gets the value of the selected item, which further enables the code to run a conditional check against the selected item. So, if the selected item is the first item, other variables are set and then subsequently concatenated and pushed out in an `alert` event to the user.

> **NOTE** *One item worth mentioning is that, when you're integrating script within a SharePoint page, you can use the* `ClientScriptManager` *object to add and manage scripts within a Web application. For example, the following code snippet shows a simple method that ensures only one instance of each script is added to a page:*
>
> ```
> public static void RegisterScript
>     (ref ClientScriptManager csm,
>     string key, string url)
>  {
>      if (!csm.IsClientScriptBlockRegistered(key))
>          csm.RegisterClientScriptInclude(key, url);
>  }
> ```
>
> *For more information on the* `ClientScriptManager`, *see* http://msdn.microsoft .com/en-us/library/system.web.ui.clientscriptmanager.aspx.

Master Pages

The example you just saw was a SharePoint site page, which could exist on any site. Interestingly, when the site page loads, however, it does not just appear without some help. Behind the scenes, it leverages what is called a *master page*, which provides some structure and styling for the SharePoint page. Master pages can be a little tricky, so before you jump into editing them, you will want to understand a little bit about their structure and purpose.

SharePoint is built on ASP.NET, so many of the artifacts that are core to SharePoint extend from ASP.NET. Master pages are an ASP.NET concept leveraged in SharePoint. However, the master pages in SharePoint are a little different, because they involve having multiple core `ContentPlaceHolder` controls that must exist within a master page for those site pages within a SharePoint site to be displayed correctly.

For example, earlier in this chapter, you saw that one of the new features of SharePoint is the ribbon, and the master page provides a content placeholder object on the page to handle the rendering of the ribbon. Likewise, there are other objects that require the ASP `ContentPlaceHolder` object as well, such as the navigation bars.

The following code snippet shows a set of ASP `ContentPlaceHolder` objects within a `div` tag that support navigation functionality:

```
...
<div style="display:none;">
<asp:ContentPlaceHolder id="PlaceHolderLeftNavBar" runat="server" />
<asp:ContentPlaceHolder id="PlaceHolderNavSpacer" runat="server" />
<asp:ContentPlaceHolder id="PlaceHolderBodyLeftBorder" runat="server" />
<asp:ContentPlaceHolder id="PlaceHolderPageImage" runat="server" />
<asp:ContentPlaceHolder id="PlaceHolderTitleLeftBorder" runat="server" />
<asp:ContentPlaceHolder id="PlaceHolderSearchArea" runat="server" />
<asp:ContentPlaceHolder id="PlaceHolderTitleAreaClass" runat="server" />
<asp:ContentPlaceHolder id="PlaceHolderTitleAreaSeparator" runat="server" />
</div>
...
```

While SharePoint requires a specific set of these content placeholders to be present (being without them would break the page), you can also create very powerful branding experiences through the master page. This can be done by using any number of techniques.

For example, in the last exercise, you customized a site page using JavaScript. You could equally add JavaScript into a master page to render a specific script at page load time. Or, you could have a specific object (such as an image or even a compiled Silverlight application) that equally appears each time you leverage the master page.

What this means, though, is that for each page that uses the master page, the object or code that you add to that master page (or the way in which you style that master page using HTML or CSS) will also equally apply to that site page. This is an important point to remember, but, at the same time, it can strengthen the case for using master pages to provide branding and structure for your sites.

Let's look at an example.

> *📝* **NOTE** *For this exercise, you will use a community-created minimal master page. You can download the master page from Codeplex at* `http://startermasterpages.codeplex.com/`. *For this exercise, some small adjustments were made to the minimal master page. The amended master page* (`Wrox_Master_Page.master`) *is available as part of the code that accompanies this book, which you may find at* `www.wrox.com`.

TRY IT OUT Customizing a Master Page

Code files [Wrox_Master_Page.master and MyBannerAd.zip] available for download at Wrox.com.

Master pages are files that provide structure and branding across a SharePoint site. To customize a master page, follow these steps:

1. Open SharePoint Designer and open your SharePoint site.

2. In the navigation pane, click Master Pages.

3. Click Blank Master Page, and provide a name for your master page (for example, `SharePoint_2010_Master.master`).

4. Open the Foundation Starter master page in Notepad. Copy and replace the code from the downloaded master page to your new master page while in code view.

5. Toggle to design view to see the master page as it would look in the browser (see Figure 3-18).

6. To set this master page as the default master page for your SharePoint site, click Master Pages in the navigation pane. Right-click the master page and select Set as Default Master Page.

7. Browse to your SharePoint site to test the look and feel of your new master page.

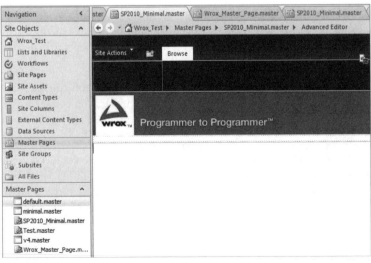

FIGURE 3-18 Minimal master page in SharePoint Designer

At this point, the master page renders the site in a fairly vanilla way — with only the minimal number of controls showing on the page. In the SharePoint site shown in Figure 3-19, a number of controls (for example, sidebar navigation) have been commented out to remove many of the active placeholder controls beneath the ribbon. This is because, as a part of this exercise, you will add a Silverlight application in the master page to show that you can brand a SharePoint site with a master page in combination with other .NET technologies.

FIGURE 3-19 Minimal master page rendered in browser

First, though, let's change the brand of the site to be a little different from the brand shown in Figure 3-19. To do this, follow these steps:

1. Upload a new image and add it to a custom directory you will need to create in the `_layouts/images` directory within the SharePoint 14 root (for example, `_layouts/images/WroxImages`). The direct path to this directory is: `...\Program Files\Common Files\Microsoft Shared\Web Server Extensions\14\TEMPLATE\IMAGES`.

2. Change the following code to include this new image:

```
...
<SharePoint:SiteLogoImage id="onetidHeadbnnr0"
    LogoImageUrl="/_layouts/images/WroxImages/FictionalCompanyLogo.jpg"
        runat="server"/></td>
...
```

3. Save the new master page and then switch to your browser and refresh the page. Your new SharePoint site should now look similar to Figure 3-20 (at least in terms of your image showing up in the master page).

FIGURE 3-20 Minimal master page customized using an image

Using images is an easy way to quickly customize and brand a SharePoint site by using a minimal master page with minimal changes. However, you're probably already wondering how you can do something more advanced.

So, what if you want to add an additional branding element, such as a banner ad, to your master page that you want available to all of the sites that leverage this master page? You could create a simple banner ad using Photoshop, or, as many companies are doing nowadays, you could build a more dynamic banner ad using Silverlight.

Let's build a simple Silverlight application and then incorporate that into the new branded master page. This will do a couple of things. First, it will introduce you to Silverlight if you haven't previously used this technology. It will also show you one way to incorporate Silverlight into SharePoint. And, lastly, it will show you how to integrate a managed-code application such as Silverlight with a master page to change the look and feel of all site pages that leverage that master page.

Follow these steps:

1. Open Visual Studio and select File ➪ New ➪ Project ➪ Silverlight.

2. Provide a name for your project (for example, `MyBannerAd`), and click OK.

3. Uncheck the "Host the Silverlight app in a new Web site" checkbox.

4. When the new solution is created, right-click the project and select Add New Folder. Name the folder `Images`. Right-click the new `Images` folder, and then select Add Existing. Add two images: one called `gear.png`, and the other called `branded.png`. The two images are provided for you in a zipped file called `Images.zip` in the companion download site. Note that these images are to be used only for learning purposes, and are not licensed for reuse in any production or public code.

5. Right-click the `MainPage.xaml` file and select View in Designer. Replace the default code that exists between the `UserControl` elements with the following code:

```
<UserControl x:Class="MyBannerAd.MainPage"
    xmlns="http://schemas.microsoft.com/winfx/2006/xaml/presentation"
    xmlns:x="http://schemas.microsoft.com/winfx/2006/xaml"
    xmlns:d="http://schemas.microsoft.com/expression/blend/2008"
    xmlns:mc="http://schemas.openxmlformats.org/markup-compatibility/2006"
    mc:Ignorable="d"
    d:DesignHeight="700" d:DesignWidth="400">
    <Grid x:Name="LayoutRoot" Height="700" Width="400">
        <Rectangle
Margin="66,42,152,20"
Stroke="#FF000000"
RadiusX="0"
RadiusY="0">
            <Rectangle.Fill>
                <LinearGradientBrush
x:Name="MRGB"
EndPoint="0.5,1"
StartPoint="0.5,0">
                    <GradientStop Color="#FF000000" Offset="0"/>
                    <GradientStop Color="#FF5E0805" Offset="0.478"/>
```

```xml
                        </LinearGradientBrush>
                    </Rectangle.Fill>
                </Rectangle>
                <Image Margin="48,49,128,20"
                        x:Name="brandedImage"
                        Source="Images/brand.png"/>
                <TextBlock x:Name="titleTextBlock"
                            Margin="75,59,161,0"
                            FontFamily="Arial"
                            FontSize="24"
                            FontWeight="Bold"
                            TextWrapping="Wrap"
                            Foreground="#FFF9F4F4"
                            TextAlignment="Center"
                            Height="56"
                            VerticalAlignment="Top"
                            Text="Life Without Borders">
                </TextBlock>
                <TextBlock x:Name="footerTextBlock"
                            Margin="75,564,161,0"
                            FontFamily="Arial"
                            FontSize="16"
                            FontWeight="Bold"
                            TextWrapping="Wrap"
                            Foreground="#FFF9F4F4"
                            TextAlignment="Center"
                            Height="56"
                            VerticalAlignment="Top"
                            Text="Fabrikam, Inc.">
                </TextBlock>
                <Image Margin="121,559,216,14"
                        x:Name="gearImage"
                        Source="Images/gear.png"/>
            </Grid>
</UserControl>
```

6. When finished, your Silverlight application in Visual Studio should look like Figure 3-21.

7. When it is complete, press F5 to build and test the application to make sure it works. This will invoke an instance of your default browser and instantiate the banner ad.

8. Next, go to your SharePoint site and create a new Document library called XAPS. When it's complete, navigate to the bin\debug directory of the solution you just created in Visual Studio (for example, …\Source\CSharp\MyBannerAd\MyBannerAd\Bin\Debug) and upload the .xap file (for example, MyBannerAd.xap) to the XAPS document library.

Now, this banner ad is fairly simple, but you could get creative and add animations and additional graphics, swap out videos to play every few seconds, and so on using Silverlight (which is discussed in more detail later in this book). In this sense, Silverlight is a very powerful option for you to use to brand your sites.

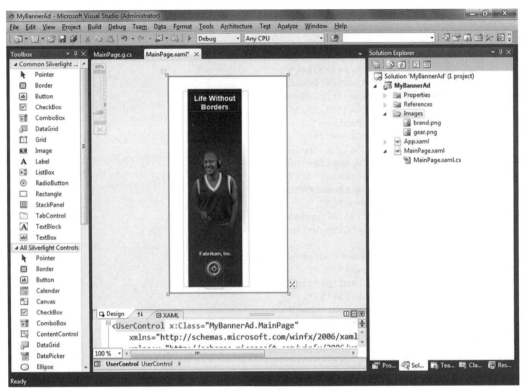

FIGURE 3-21 Silverlight application in Visual Studio 2010 IDE

With the XAP file in the XAPS document library, you can now reference and load that Silverlight application within SharePoint in different ways. For this example, let's embed some code within the master page so that when the page renders, it displays the Silverlight application by default. Follow these steps:

1. Go back to SharePoint Designer and open your master page. Click Master Pages in the Navigation list and select the new master page (for example, SharePoint_2010_Master.master). Click Edit File to open the master page in Edit mode.

2. Add the following JavaScript script into your master page near the bottom of the file. If you used the master page from the code download, you will see a commented out ContentPlaceHolder object called PlaceHolderUtilityContent. Uncomment this code and add the following bolded code to your master page. Save the file when complete, and then return to the browser and refresh the browser. (Note that you will need to update the server reference in the value variable to point to your SharePoint server and .xap file URL.)

```
…
<asp:ContentPlaceHolder id="PlaceHolderUtilityContent" runat="server">

<div id="silverlightBannerAd" />

<script language="JavaScript" type="text/javascript">
var slDIV = document.getElementById('silverlightBannerAd');
slDIV.appendChild(slDIV);
```

```
slDIV.innerHTML = '<object data="data:application/x-silverlight,"
    type="application/x-silverlight" width="400" height="800">
    <param name="source" value="http://fabrikamhockey/XAPS/MyBannerAd.xap"
    /></object>';
</script>

</asp:ContentPlaceHolder>
...
```

3. You will now see a SharePoint site that uses a custom, minimal master page using an image and a Silverlight application — see Figure 3-22. You may want to add additional CSS styling or position the banner (and most definitely improve the look and feel of the banner). But, at the end of the day, any time you build out a site using this as the default master page, this would be the baseline template you would start from.

FIGURE 3-22 Master page rendered in browser with image and Silverlight application

How It Works

As a SharePoint developer, you should take an interest in Silverlight. This is one of the key directions that Microsoft is taking when it comes to building out Rich Internet Applications (RIAs). And, for SharePoint, Silverlight offers some amazing potential not only for building out some simple branding customizations as shown here, but also because of its great potential to build out hard-core business applications that have dynamic user experiences. (Some of these will be explored later in the book.)

With SharePoint 2010 arrives the native support for Silverlight capabilities. This is contrary to SharePoint 2007, where there were a number of required configurations within the `web.config` file, for example, just to get up and running. So, this one version represents a huge leap for SharePoint.

It is the out-of-the-box support for Silverlight in SharePoint 2010 that provides a lot of the behind-the-scenes support for this "Try It Out" example. By using JavaScript within the master page, you can create a reference to the Silverlight application through the `slDIV var` object, and then set the inner HTML of the `var` to further set the properties of an HTML `object` to render the Silverlight application.

As you can see from the discussion thus far on SharePoint Designer, quite a bit is possible. In some cases, absolutely no code was required to get started with your development process (which is why you will see SharePoint Designer being picked up and used by those with a variety of skills and backgrounds). In other cases, you saw the combination of JavaScript with HTML, and then the integration of Silverlight (using Visual Studio 2010 to build the `.xap` files) with master pages through JavaScript.

Your key takeaway from this discussion so far, then, should be threefold:

➤ SharePoint Designer is a versatile tool and should absolutely be a part of your developer toolkit.

➤ There are many things you can do with SharePoint Designer, ranging from no-code to code.

➤ In some cases, SharePoint Designer has a great hand-in-glove relationship with Visual Studio 2010.

However, many developers live and breathe Visual Studio, so let's move on to examine SharePoint development using Visual Studio 2010.

DEVELOPING SHAREPOINT APPLICATIONS USING VISUAL STUDIO 2010

Visual Studio 2010 now ships with a standard set of project-level and item-level templates that make SharePoint development much, much easier (and more accessible) than in previous versions. It's not that development wasn't possible before; it's just that there were many ways to skin the cat, so to speak. And this lack of consistency across the development tools caused disconnects in the developer community over the best way to productively and consistently develop for SharePoint.

Microsoft settled on shipping standard project templates out of the box with an additional set of project item templates. For example, if you create an Empty SharePoint Project, you have the option of building out that empty SharePoint project using a number of different item-level templates. These templates were described to you in Chapter 2, and you will see most (if not all) of them in use throughout this book in some capacity. In this chapter, you will walk through a couple of examples to get used to developing in Visual Studio so that you can be prepared to tackle the many other examples you will come across throughout the book.

Beyond the wealth of templates available to you, there are also some other great features that Visual Studio supports. For example, the Server Explorer lets you see the components of your SharePoint site. Figure 3-23 shows an abbreviated view of the different objects found in a demo SharePoint site (`http://fabrikamhockey`). The great thing about this view is that it shows both custom and native objects, so if you create a custom workflow and deploy it to your SharePoint site, it will appear in the Server Explorer.

Another great feature of Visual Studio 2010 is the way in which it structures a new SharePoint project. For example, a SharePoint Visual Studio solution contains SharePoint Features, each containing one or more SharePoint elements (for example, Web parts or List Templates). These Features are then packaged for release as a SharePoint Solution Package (WSP). The WSP is the standard way of building a SharePoint solution — one that SharePoint natively understands. A SharePoint feature contains items (which are represented through XML files that live on the server file system) that are deployed into your SharePoint site for activation and use.

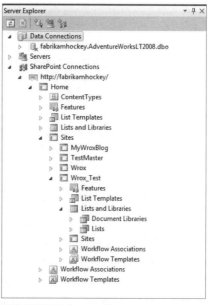

FIGURE 3-23 Server Explorer

Each feature is deployed into a specific folder in the SharePoint root (`...\Program Files\Common Files\ Microsoft Shared\Web Server Extensions\14\ Template\Features`). Within the `Features` directory, you will note that each feature is created and deployed within its own folder. The folder for a feature contains XML configuration files that leverage the Collaborative Application Markup Language (CAML), a standard XML syntax you will see throughout this book that SharePoint natively understands. A manifest file lives in each folder, which provides feature-specific information such as GUIDs, version info, and any dependencies that are required by the feature.

For example, following is an example of a `feature.xml` file for the `PPSSiteMaster` feature (a PerformancePoint Server feature). You can see that this feature has multiple dependencies listed.

```
<Feature Id="0B07A7F4-8BB8-4ec0-A31B-115732B9584D"
         Title="$Resources:ppsma,SiteMaster_ContentType_Title"
         Description="$Resources:ppsma,SiteMaster_ContentType_Description"
         Version="14.0.0.0"
         Scope="Web"
         SolutionId="7ED6CD55-B479-4EB7-A529-E99A24C10BD3"
         Hidden="FALSE"
         DefaultResourceFile="core"
         xmlns="http://schemas.microsoft.com/sharepoint/">
  <ElementManifests/>
  <ActivationDependencies>
    <!-- PPS Site Collection Feature -->
    <ActivationDependency FeatureId="A1CB5B7F-E5E9-421B-915F-BF519B0760EF" />
    <!--  PPS content List -->
    <ActivationDependency FeatureId="481333E1-A246-4D89-AFAB-D18C6FE344CE" />
    <!-- Bi Center DataConnections library template -->
    <ActivationDependency FeatureId="26676156-91A0-49F7-87AA-37B1D5F0C4D0" />
    <!-- Bi Center Dashboards library template -->
    <ActivationDependency FeatureId="F979E4DC-1852-4F26-AB92-D1B2A190AFC9" />
```

```
        <!-- Status Lists template -->
        <ActivationDependency FeatureId="065C78BE-5231-477e-A972-14177CC5B3C7" />
        <!-- DocumentLibrary Feature -->
        <ActivationDependency FeatureId="00BFEA71-E717-4E80-AA17-D0C71B360101"/>
        <!-- CustomList Feature -->
        <ActivationDependency FeatureId="00BFEA71-DE22-43B2-A848-C05709900100"/>
    </ActivationDependencies>
  </Feature>
```

While the packaging and deployment of features in SharePoint 2010 is mostly automated, it is still useful to understand how it works for the times you need more than what automation provides. For example, in previous versions of SharePoint, you may have had to hand-code the aforementioned `feature.xml` file, or edit it using Visual Studio. However, with Visual Studio 2010, this file is somewhat obfuscated from your view, leaving you to focus on the fun part of development — building the code for the custom solutions. You still could edit the file, but Visual Studio abstracts the XML configuration away from your view so that you can focus on core development tasks. As you work through the example in this section of the chapter, you will eventually see where the feature file is built and deployed in SharePoint, but you don't necessarily need to interact with it during the development process.

Beyond the `feature.xml` file (which you could think of as the core file that defines the feature), you will also have other XML configuration files (for example, an `elements.xml` file), code-behind files, and any dependencies files or assemblies. All applications and solutions are built using a standard packaging and deployment method with the feature framework lying at the heart of this package.

While this is often taken for granted by .NET developers, the SharePoint tools also facilitate a great F5 experience (for example, connection to worker processes, landing on key SharePoint pages to kick off the debug process, and so on), as well as some additional capabilities for tasks that were previously difficult to do, such as deployment and retraction. For example, retraction often meant either issuing commands through a command-line tool or, in some cases, going into the SharePoint file system and deleting folders.

In Visual Studio 2010, you can build and deploy applications through the Build menu, and then right-click your project to retract it from the server. You can also select Retract from the Build menu. Visual Studio does all the cleanup for you — exactly what you'd expect when cleaning your solutions from your local development machines.

Figure 3-24 shows the options that are now available to you from within your SharePoint Build menu. You can see your Build and Rebuild solutions, but then you also see the Deploy (which deploys the solution to SharePoint) and Clean Solution functionality, as well as many other features.

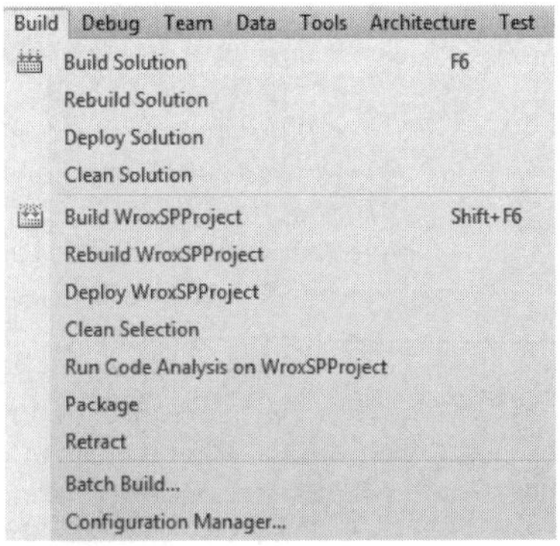

Another work item that was difficult to accomplish with previous versions of SharePoint was source-code control. There existed no native project templates in Visual Studio, which made it difficult (or near impossible) to team-track source-code projects. However, with the ALM features built into Team Foundation Server, you can now manage your source code in a streamlined way. For example, when you create

FIGURE 3-24 Build Menu in Visual Studio 2010 SharePoint project

a new project, as
Figure 3-25 shows,
you can click "Add to
source control" to add
your project to a Team
Foundation Server
instance.

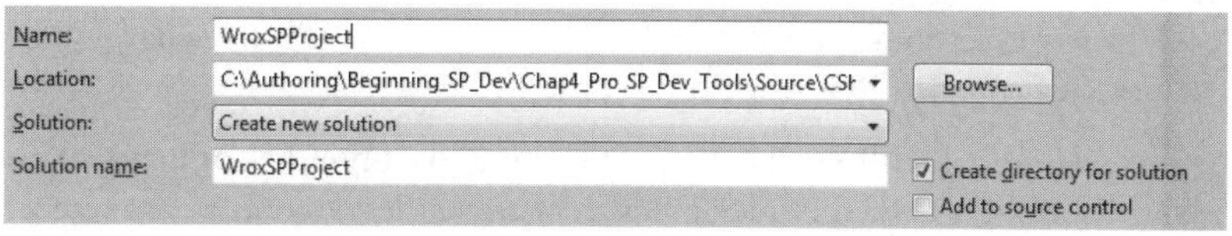

Name:	WroxSPProject
Location:	C:\Authoring\Beginning_SP_Dev\Chap4_Pro_SP_Dev_Tools\Source\CSI ▼
Solution:	Create new solution
Solution name:	WroxSPProject

☑ Create directory for solution
☐ Add to source control

Browse...

FIGURE 3-25 ALM in Visual Studio 2010

Let's walk through a couple of examples to explore some of the Visual Studio 2010 features. In the first
walkthrough, you will create an empty SharePoint project and then add a new Web part to that project.

TRY IT OUT   Creating a New Web Part Project

Code file [WroxSPProject.zip] available for download at Wrox.com.

A Web part is one of the most common objects you will create for SharePoint. It is a core building block
of the platform. To create a new Web part project, follow these steps:

1.   Open Visual Studio and click File ⇨ New ⇨ Project ⇨ Empty SharePoint Project in the `SharePoint
2010` templates directory. Provide a name for the project (for example, `WroxSPProject`), and click
OK. When prompted, select "Deploy as farm solution" and click Finish.

2.   After Visual Studio sets up your project, right-click the project and select Add ⇨ New Item. In the
`SharePoint 2010` templates directory, choose Web Part, as shown in Figure 3-26. Provide a name
(for example, `SimpleWebPart`), and click Add.

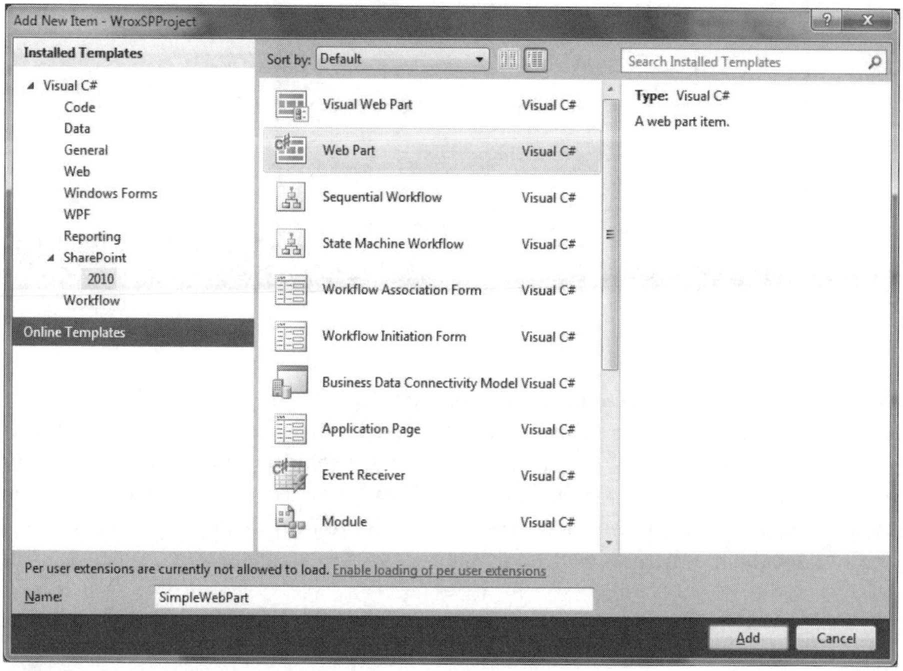

FIGURE 3-26 Web Part item template

3. Before you go any further, click Build ➪ Deploy Solution. Don't switch to SharePoint in your browser yet to inspect the deployed Web part. You'll see what you built a little later in the walkthrough.

At this point, you will see that Visual Studio adds a number of items to your solution. For example, as shown in Figure 3-27, it adds a new feature (called `Feature1.feature`). A new node called `SimpleWebPart` is added that contains a number of files within it as well. Although you can't see it, some of the configuration XML behind the scenes is also updated.

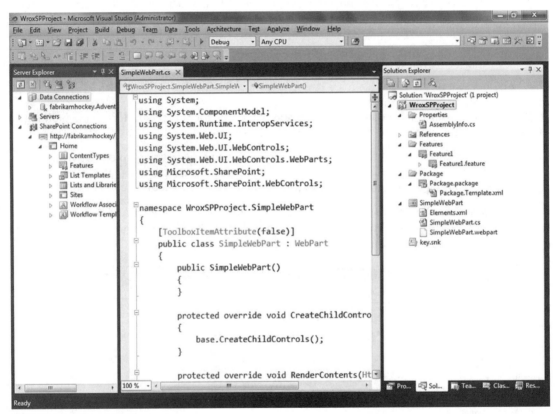

FIGURE 3-27 SharePoint project

If you double-click the `Feature1.feature` node, this will open another new part of the SharePoint feature set in Visual Studio, called the Feature Designer. This designer provides you with a graphical view of the features that make up the current WSP package within your solution. It also provides you with the capability to set the deployment level for the feature (for example, site or farm). You can add and remove features from the package from this view. You can configure your deployment options, and you can even edit the XML for the files here as well.

Given that you only have one feature (that is, the Web part) added to this project, you only have one feature shown in Figure 3-28.

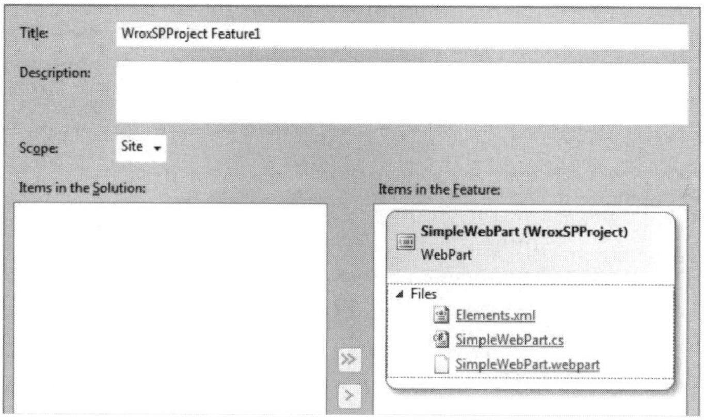

FIGURE 3-28 Visual Studio 2010 SharePoint Feature Designer

You can also see the core files that are associated with the feature:

➤ Elements.xml

➤ SimpleWebPart.cs

➤ SimpleWebPart.webpart

Each one of these files has a specific function in the context of the feature. For example, the Elements.xml file provides some basic configuration options for the feature. The SimpleWebPart.cs file contains the core code behind, and the SimpleWebPart.webpart file is an XML file that represents the metadata for the Web part project.

If you open up each of the three core files that make up the SimpleWebPart feature, you will find a number of things going on. For example, the following code snippet shows the Elements.xml file, which defines the elements that make up the feature. Here you can see that, because you only have a Web part currently in your feature, this is the only module that is listed in the Elements.xml file.

```xml
<?xml version="1.0" encoding="utf-8"?>
<Elements xmlns="http://schemas.microsoft.com/sharepoint/" >
  <Module Name="SimpleWebPart" List="113" Url="_catalogs/wp">
    <File Path="SimpleWebPart\SimpleWebPart.webpart" Url="SimpleWebPart.webpart"
        Type="GhostableInLibrary">
      <Property Name="Group" Value="Custom" />
    </File>
  </Module>
</Elements>
```

If you open the SimpleWebPart.cs file, you will see that Visual Studio has generated some default code for you that you can extend to, in this case, build out a custom Web part. Here, the code has created an instance of the `SimpleWebPart` object and contains two override methods that will be used when building out the Web part functionality later on in this walkthrough.

```
using System;
using System.ComponentModel;
using System.Runtime.InteropServices;
using System.Web.UI;
using System.Web.UI.WebControls;
using System.Web.UI.WebControls.WebParts;
using Microsoft.SharePoint;
using Microsoft.SharePoint.WebControls;

namespace WroxSPProject.SimpleWebPart
{
    [ToolboxItemAttribute(false)]
    public class SimpleWebPart : WebPart
    {
        public SimpleWebPart()
        {
        }

        protected override void CreateChildControls()
        {
            base.CreateChildControls();
        }

        protected override void RenderContents(HtmlTextWriter writer)
        {
            base.RenderContents(writer);
        }
    }
}
```

The last major file of concern here is the `SimpleWebPart.webpart` file, which contains metadata about the simple Web part you're about to build out. You have, for example, editable properties such as `Title` and `Description` that can actually make it more intuitive for a user to interact with your custom Web part within SharePoint.

```
<?xml version="1.0" encoding="utf-8"?>
<webParts>
  <webPart xmlns="http://schemas.microsoft.com/WebPart/v3">
    <metaData>
      <type name="WroxSPProject.SimpleWebPart.SimpleWebPart,
          $SharePoint.Project.AssemblyFullName$" />
      <importErrorMessage>$Resources:core,ImportErrorMessage;</importErrorMessage>
    </metaData>
    <data>
      <properties>
        <property name="Title" type="string">SimpleWebPart</property>
        <property name="Description" type="string">My WebPart</property>
      </properties>
    </data>
  </webPart>
</webParts>
```

Now, follow these steps:

1. Navigate to the `SimpleWebPart.webpart` file and double-click it to open it in the code view. Within the properties element, amend the `Title` and `Description` to be more descriptive, similar to the following:

...

```
<properties>
  <property name="Title" type="string">Wrox Book Delivery</property>
  <property name="Description" type="string">Web part that
      calculates cost for delivery on Wrox developer books. </property>
</properties>
```

...

2. Open the `SimpleWebPart.cs` file and amend the code, adding the following bolded code:

```
using System;
using System.ComponentModel;
using System.Runtime.InteropServices;
using System.Web.UI;
using System.Web.UI.WebControls;
using System.Web.UI.WebControls.WebParts;
using Microsoft.SharePoint;
using Microsoft.SharePoint.WebControls;
using System.Text;

namespace WroxSPProject.SimpleWebPart
{
    [ToolboxItemAttribute(false)]
    public class SimpleWebPart : WebPart
    {
        Label lblBook = new Label();
        ListBox lstbxBooks = new ListBox();
        Label lblDelMethods = new Label();
        ListBox lstbxDeliveryMethods = new ListBox();
        Label lblDelDate = new Label();
        TextBox txtbxDelDate = new TextBox();
        Label lblFinalPrice = new Label();
        TextBox txtbxFinalPrice = new TextBox();
        Button btnCalc = new Button();

        public SimpleWebPart()
        {
        }

        protected override void CreateChildControls()
        {
            lblBook.Text = "Book Name:";
            lblFinalPrice.Text = "Final Cost:";
            lblDelDate.Text = "Del Date:";
            lblDelMethods.Text = "Del Methods:";
            btnCalc.Text = "Calc.";

            lstbxBooks.Items.Add("Professional SharePoint 2007 Development");
```

```
        lstbxBooks.Items.Add("Beginning ASP.NET Development");
        lstbxBooks.Items.Add("WPF Programming");

        lstbxDeliveryMethods.Items.Add("Ground");
        lstbxDeliveryMethods.Items.Add("Express");
        lstbxDeliveryMethods.Items.Add("Overnight");

        txtbxDelDate.Enabled = false;
        txtbxFinalPrice.Enabled = false;

        StringBuilder sb1 = new StringBuilder();
        sb1.AppendLine("<table border='0'><tr><td>");
        StringBuilder sb2 = new StringBuilder();
        sb2.AppendLine("</td><td>");
        StringBuilder sb3 = new StringBuilder();
        sb3.AppendLine("</td></tr><tr><td>");
        StringBuilder sb4 = new StringBuilder();
        sb4.AppendLine("</td><td></td></tr></table>");

        this.Controls.Add(new LiteralControl(sb1.ToString()));
        this.Controls.Add(lblBook);
        this.Controls.Add(new LiteralControl(sb2.ToString()));
        this.Controls.Add(lstbxBooks);
        this.Controls.Add(new LiteralControl(sb3.ToString()));
        this.Controls.Add(lblDelMethods);
        this.Controls.Add(new LiteralControl(sb2.ToString()));
        this.Controls.Add(lstbxDeliveryMethods);
        this.Controls.Add(new LiteralControl(sb3.ToString()));
        this.Controls.Add(lblDelDate);
        this.Controls.Add(new LiteralControl(sb2.ToString()));
        this.Controls.Add(txtbxDelDate);
        this.Controls.Add(new LiteralControl(sb3.ToString()));
        this.Controls.Add(lblFinalPrice);
        this.Controls.Add(new LiteralControl(sb2.ToString()));
        this.Controls.Add(txtbxFinalPrice);
        this.Controls.Add(new LiteralControl(sb3.ToString()));
        this.Controls.Add(btnCalc);
        this.Controls.Add(new LiteralControl(sb4.ToString()));

        btnCalc.Click += new EventHandler(btnCalc_Click);

        base.CreateChildControls();

    }

    void btnCalc_Click(object sender, EventArgs e)
    {
        double finalCost = 0.00;
        double costOfDel = 0.00;
        double costOfBook = 0.00;
        double salesTax = .08;
        double numOfDays = 0;
        DateTime today = DateTime.Now;
        DateTime delDate;
        string strBook = lstbxBooks.SelectedItem.ToString();
```

```
string delMethod = lstbxDeliveryMethods.SelectedItem.ToString();

if (strBook == "Professional SharePoint 2007 Development")
{
    costOfBook = 39.99;
}
else if (strBook == "Beginning ASP.NET Development")
{
    costOfBook = 42.99;
}
else if (strBook == "WPF Programming")
{
    costOfBook = 28.99;
}

if (delMethod == "Ground")
{
    costOfDel = 3.99;
    numOfDays = 5;
}
else if (delMethod == "Express")
{
    costOfDel = 7.99;
    numOfDays = 3;
}
else if (delMethod == "Overnight")
{
    costOfDel = 11.99;
    numOfDays = 1;
}

finalCost = costOfDel + costOfBook;
finalCost = Math.Round(finalCost + (finalCost * salesTax), 2)/100*100;
txtbxFinalPrice.Text = "$" + finalCost.ToString();
delDate = today.AddDays(numOfDays);
txtbxDelDate.Text = delDate.ToShortDateString();
        }

    }
}
```

3. When you've completed the addition of this code to your Web part (and amended the SimpleWebPart.webpart), click Build ➪ Deploy Solution. This builds the solution and runs through a number of steps to deploy it to your SharePoint site — the site that was validated and associated with the project when you first created your project.

4. As your project builds, click View ➪ Output. In the Output window, you will see the processing of the default build and deploy steps that Visual Studio runs through as it builds out your project.

If you followed along with the instructions and built the project once already, you will see something similar to the following. Note that Visual Studio has discovered the fact that you already deployed this solution once and is now retracting it and removing all conflicts, as shown in the following bolded output:

```
------ Build started: Project: WroxSPProject, Configuration: Debug Any CPU ------
  WroxSPProject -> C:\Authoring\Beginning_SP_Dev\Chap4_Pro_SP_Dev_Tools\
```

```
                Source\CSharp\WroxSPProject\WroxSPProject\bin\Debug\WroxSPProject.dll
        Successfully created package at:
                C:\Authoring\Beginning_SP_Dev\Chap4_Pro_SP_Dev_Tools\Source\
                CSharp\WroxSPProject\WroxSPProject\bin\Debug\WroxSPProject.wsp
------ Deploy started: Project: WroxSPProject, Configuration: Debug Any CPU ------
Active Deployment Configuration: Default
Run Pre-Deployment Command:
        Skipping deployment step because a pre-deployment command is not specified.
Recycle IIS Application Pool:
        Recycling IIS application pool 'SharePoint - 80'...
Retract Solution:
        Deactivating feature 'WroxSPProject_Feature1' ...
        Retracting solution 'wroxspproject.wsp'...
        Deleting solution 'wroxspproject.wsp'...
Add Solution:
        Found 1 deployment conflict(s).  Resolving conflicts ...
        Deleted file 'http://fabrikamhockey/_catalogs/wp/
                SimpleWebPart.webpart' from server.
        Adding solution 'WroxSPProject.wsp'...
        Deploying solution 'WroxSPProject.wsp'...
Activate Features:
        Activating feature 'Feature1' ...
Run Post-Deployment Command:
        Skipping deployment step because a post-deployment command is not specified.
========== Build: 1 succeeded or up-to-date, 0 failed, 0 skipped ==========
========== Deploy: 1 succeeded, 0 failed, 0 skipped ==========
```

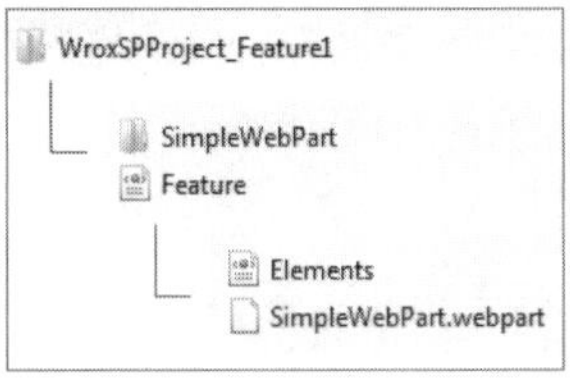

After you've deployed the SharePoint project, a new folder is created in the `Features` directory. For example, if you browse to the `Features` directory, this project has created the subdirectory structure shown in Figure 3-29.

If you open the `Feature.xml` file, you will see that it refers to an `ElementManifest` object that corresponds to the folder struc- ture within the `WroxSPProject_Feature1` folder (that is, the

FIGURE 3-29 Feature directory

`SimpleWebPart` folder, which contains the `Elements.xml` file and the `SimpleWebPart.webpart` file). Thus, you can see how your project is packaged and deployed. The appropriate assemblies are built and deployed to the GAC (because you built this as a farm-level solution), and the XML configuration files live in the `Features` directory.

```xml
<?xml version="1.0" encoding="utf-8"?>
<Feature xmlns="http://schemas.microsoft.com/sharepoint/"
        Id="e9577309-e63d-482a-8815-6b17916f2bfd" Scope="Site"
        Title="WroxSPProject Feature1">
    <ElementManifests>
        <ElementManifest Location="SimpleWebPart\Elements.xml" />
        <ElementFile Location="SimpleWebPart\SimpleWebPart.webpart" />
    </ElementManifests>
</Feature>
```

Now that you have an understanding of where the glue and the bits are deployed to, follow these steps:

1. Open your SharePoint site. (Note that you will walk through some long-hand steps in this walk-through that will be shortened in the next walkthrough by using the F5 debug function.)

2. Click All Site Content and click Create.

3. Click Sites in the left-hand pane and select Blank Site Template. Provide a name and URL, and click Create.

4. When the new site is created, click Site Actions ➪ Edit Page.

5. While in Edit mode, click "Add a web part." This displays the Web Part Gallery.

6. Navigate to the Custom category, and you will find the Web part that you just deployed to SharePoint. Note that the title and the description that you provided in the `.webpart` file are displayed in the appropriate places, as shown in Figure 3-30.

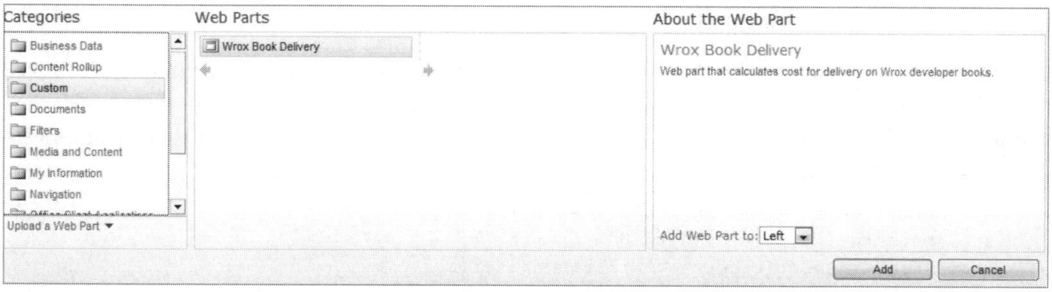

FIGURE 3-30 Adding a Web part to a page

7. Click Add. This will add the Web part you just created in your SharePoint project to the Web part page, as shown in Figure 3-31. You can test out the functionality of the Web part by selecting entries in the listbox and clicking the Calc. button. The appropriate delivery date and final cost are calculated for you and displayed in the (disabled) textboxes.

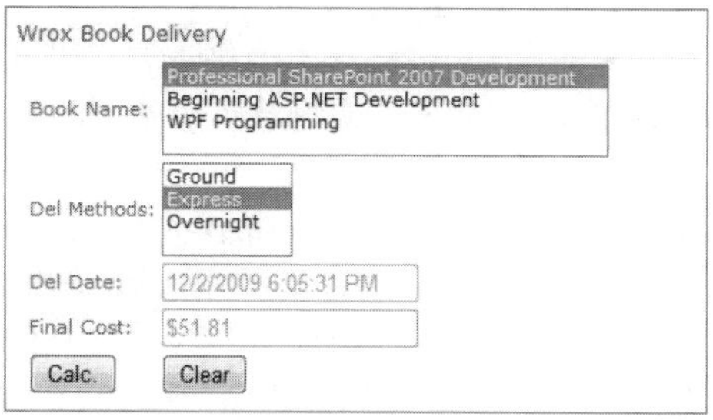

FIGURE 3-31 Custom Web part rendering in browser

How It Works

This was a more elaborate example than the others that you've walked through in this chapter, so let's talk through some of the key parts of the custom solution.

First, you used the core SharePoint project file, and then added a Web part to that empty project. The nice thing about using the SharePoint project file is that you can add multiple SharePoint elements to the solution, and Visual Studio understands how to handle these — it builds, packages, and deploys them in the right place in the SharePoint Root.

Second, the Web part is a standard ASP.NET server control and can, therefore, contain other nested ASP.NET controls. Because of this, you can leverage all of the different controls and framework power that derives from this inheritance. In this example, you used a number of controls (for example, Label, Textbox, and Button) to create the main user interface. In the Web part, you created these controls and then used the Add method to add each control (after you set the properties of the control) to the Controls collection — which enables you to build out and format the UI with specific ASP.NET controls. Within the CreateChildControls event, many of the controls that are added as class-level objects are assigned values. For example, items are added to each of the listboxes as mock data, and text properties are set for the different UI objects. Also, in the CreateChildControls method, each of the controls is added to the Controls collection (after the properties are set), which enables the controls to be displayed in the Web part.

You'll also note that the literalcontrol object directly writes the object into the HTML stream (built out using the StringBuilder object) to create a table that provides some formatting for the UI. Otherwise, the UI controls will display in an unorganized way.

The literalcontrol is not the only object to emit HTML to SharePoint in this manner. You could also use StringWriter and HTMLTextWriter objects to write HTML to the Web part as well. For example, the following code creates a simple StringBuilder object, then writes that through using the StringWriter and HtmlTextWriter objects:

```
StringBuilder sb = new StringBuilder();
sb.AppendLine("<table border='0'><tr><td>");
StringWriter spStrWriter = new StringWriter(sb);
HtmlTextWriter htmlTxtWriter = new HtmlTextWriter(spStrWriter);
Page.RenderControl(htmlTxtWriter);
```

Admittedly, the use of multiple literalcontrol objects is not the most elegant of ways to emit HTML when rendering Web parts. ASP.NET provides a rich framework for writing HTML out to the page, which includes the HtmlTextWriter class.

Third, you tied a specific event to the controls that enabled you to interact with the controls on the page and then acted on that interaction — this was the btnCalc_Click event. This event will take information from the data selected in the two listboxes and calculate the final cost of the book given a specific book selection and the type of delivery the user wants. Note that the btnCalc_Click event also rounds the final cost of the book, and then converts it to a string. It sets the Text property of the txtbxFinal-Cost object — which is set to be disabled, as is txtbxDelDate.

Based on what the user has selected, the btnCalc_Click method runs a number of conditional if statements to assign specific book costs and delivery costs to help calculate the final cost of the book. This method also takes the number of days associated with the delivery method specified by the user, and adds that number of days to the current date, to provide the user with an estimated delivery date for the book.

Lastly, Visual Studio deployed the Web part to the appropriate places in SharePoint, and the appropriate files were created so that the Web part would be displayed in the Custom Web Part Gallery. This capability to build and deploy custom solutions for SharePoint is an immense improvement over SharePoint 2007, where you would have had to use one of a handful of methods to build and deploy a Web part to a SharePoint site.

One thing about the Web part you just built is that it was self-contained. It didn't rely on any other part of SharePoint or an external system. While you can build some very powerful Web parts using this design, you will often want to integrate the SharePoint element you're building with some other part of either SharePoint or an external system (such as a database, Web service, or even a Web 2.0 technology).

You'll see a number of service-based and database integration examples throughout the book that discuss how to integrate with external systems. Next, you will walk through a Web 2.0 example that shows how you can leverage some community code to integrate a custom Visual Web part with Twitter.

TRY IT OUT   Creating a Custom Twitter Visual Web Part

Code files [MyTwitterFeedWebPart.zip and Twitterizer.Framework-1.0.1.129.zip] available for download at Wrox.com.

You can integrate many Web 2.0 applications with SharePoint, one of which is Twitter. To create a custom Twitter Web part, follow these steps:

1. Open Visual Studio and click File ⇨ New ⇨ Project. Navigate to SharePoint 2010, and select the Visual Web Part project template. Provide a name for your project (for example, `MyTwitterFeedWebPart`), and click OK. Visual Studio creates a SharePoint project for you and then adds a Visual Web part to the solution.

2. If you want to rename the Visual Web part to something more intuitive (as opposed to the default `VisualWebPart1`), then right-click the visual Web part and rename it (for example, `TwitterWebPart`). Note that you may need to click Edit, click Find and Replace, and then select Quick Replace to replace all instances of `VisualWebPart1` with your new Web part name.

3. Right-click the user control file (for example, `TwitterWebPartUserControl.ascx`), and select View in Designer.

4. Create a user interface that includes three textboxes and two buttons all structured within a table, as shown in Figure 3-32.

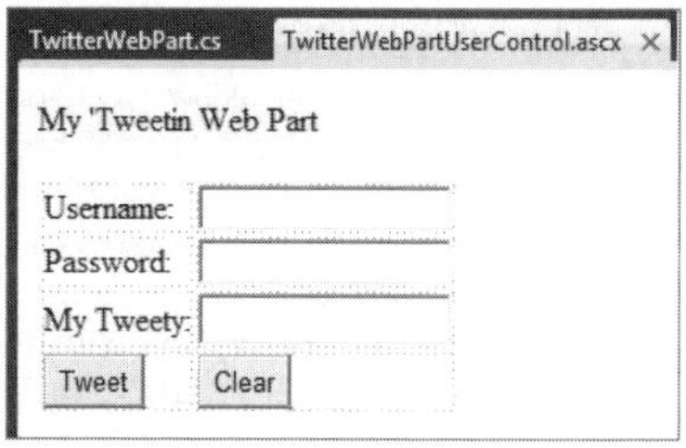

FIGURE 3-32 Twitter Web part in Visual Web Part Designer

Table 3-1 provides a summary of the names and control types for the application

TABLE 3-1 Control Types and Names

CONTROL TYPES	CONTROL NAMES
Textbox	`txtbxUsername, txtbxPassword, txtbxTweet`
Button	`btnTweet, btnClear`

5. The code for this UI looks like the following. Note that to auto-generate the two events associated with the buttons, you double-click on each of the buttons, and the method stubs in the code behind will be generated for you.

```
<%@ Assembly Name="$SharePoint.Project.AssemblyFullName$" %>
<%@ Assembly Name="Microsoft.Web.CommandUI, Version=14.0.0.0,
    Culture=neutral, PublicKeyToken=71e9bce111e9429c" %>
<%@ Register Tagprefix="SharePoint" Namespace=
    "Microsoft.SharePoint.WebControls"
    Assembly="Microsoft.SharePoint, Version=14.0.0.0,
    Culture=neutral, PublicKeyToken=71e9bce111e9429c" %>
<%@ Register Tagprefix="Utilities" Namespace="Microsoft.
    SharePoint.Utilities" Assembly=
    "Microsoft.SharePoint, Version=14.0.0.0,
    Culture=neutral, PublicKeyToken=71e9bce111e9429c" %>
<%@ Register Tagprefix="asp" Namespace="System.Web.UI"
    Assembly="System.Web.Extensions,
    Version=3.5.0.0, Culture=neutral,
    PublicKeyToken=31bf3856ad364e35" %>
<%@ Import Namespace="Microsoft.SharePoint" %>
<%@ Register Tagprefix="WebPartPages" Namespace=
    "Microsoft.SharePoint.WebPartPages"
    Assembly="Microsoft.SharePoint, Version=14.0.0.0,
    Culture=neutral, PublicKeyToken=71e9bce111e9429c" %>
<%@ Control Language="C#" AutoEventWireup="true"
    CodeBehind="TwitterWebPartUserControl.ascx.cs"
    Inherits="MyTwitterFeedWebPart.TwitterWebPart.
    TwitterWebPartUserControl" %>
<p>My &#39;Tweetin Web part</p>
<table border="0">
<tr><td>Username:</td><td>
    <asp:TextBox ID="txtbxUsername" runat="server"></asp:TextBox>
</td></tr><tr>
<td>Password:</td><td>
    <asp:TextBox ID="txtbxPassword" runat="server"></asp:TextBox>
</td></tr><tr><td>My Tweety:</td><td>
    <asp:TextBox ID="txtbxTweet" Height="25" runat="server">
        </asp:TextBox>
</td></tr><tr><td>
    <asp:Button ID="btnTweet" runat="server" Text="Tweet"
        onclick="btnTweet_Click" /></td><td>
    <asp:Button ID="btnClear" runat="server" Text="Clear"
        onclick="btnClear_Click" />
</td></tr></table>
```

6. When you've created the new UI, you're now ready to create the code for the capability to submit a "tweet" from your SharePoint Web part. To do this, you're going to leverage a community .NET wrapper for the Twitter API, called the Twitterizer. To get the API, go to the following link and download the zipped DLL to your local development machine: `http://twitterizer.googlecode.com/files/Twitterizer.Framework-1.0.1.130.zip`. Unzip the zipped file in a readily accessible folder.

7. You now want to add the `Twitterizer.Framework` DLL to your Web part project, which will enable you to very easily call the Twitter API using .NET code. To do this, right-click References and select Add Reference. Choose Browse, and then navigate to where you unzipped the `Twitterizer.Framework` DLL file.

8. Now, go to your code-behind file (for example, `TwitterWebPartUserPartControl.ascx.cs`) and add the following boldfaced code to this file. You can see that you need two `using` statements to reference the added DLL, and that you're going to set three class-level string variables (the text that the user enters). You can also see an instance of the `Twitter` object, which "tweets" the message that the user enters into the "My Tweety" textbox. The Clear button resets all of the textboxes to `null`.

```csharp
using System;
using System.Web.UI;
using System.Web.UI.WebControls;
using System.Web.UI.WebControls.WebParts;

using Twitterizer;
using Twitterizer.Framework;

namespace MyTwitterFeedWebPart.TwitterWebPart
{
    public partial class TwitterWebPartUserControl : UserControl
    {
        string strTweet = "";
        string myTweetUsername = "";
        string myTweetPassword = "";

        protected void Page_Load(object sender, EventArgs e)
        {

        }

        protected void btnTweet_Click(object sender, EventArgs e)
        {
            myTweetUsername = txtbxUsername.Text;
            myTweetPassword = txtbxPassword.Text;
            strTweet = txtbxTweet.Text;

            Twitter myTweet = new Twitter(myTweetUsername,
            myTweetPassword);
            myTweet.Status.Update(strTweet);
        }

        protected void btnClear_Click(object sender, EventArgs e)
        {
            txtbxTweet.Text = "";
            txtbxPassword.Text = "";
            txtbxUsername.Text = "";
        }
    }
}
```

9. When you're finished adding the code, press F5 to build and debug the application. This builds, deploys, and attaches the Visual Studio debug process to the relevant worker processes.

10. After you press F5, Visual Studio invokes Internet Explorer and opens SharePoint at the Create Web Part page. Here you can provide a name for the Web part page and click Create. Then, click "Add a web part" to add the new Tweet Visual Web part, as shown in Figure 3-33.

11. SharePoint now exposes the Web Part Gallery, so navigate to the Custom category, as shown in Figure 3-34, and you will see the new Tweety Bird Web part. Click Add to add it to the new Web part page.

12. After you've added the Tweety Bird Web part, enter your username and password and add a tweet. Click Tweet to update your Twitter account with your new message, as shown in Figure 3-35. (Note that you need Internet connectivity and a Twitter account for this example to work.)

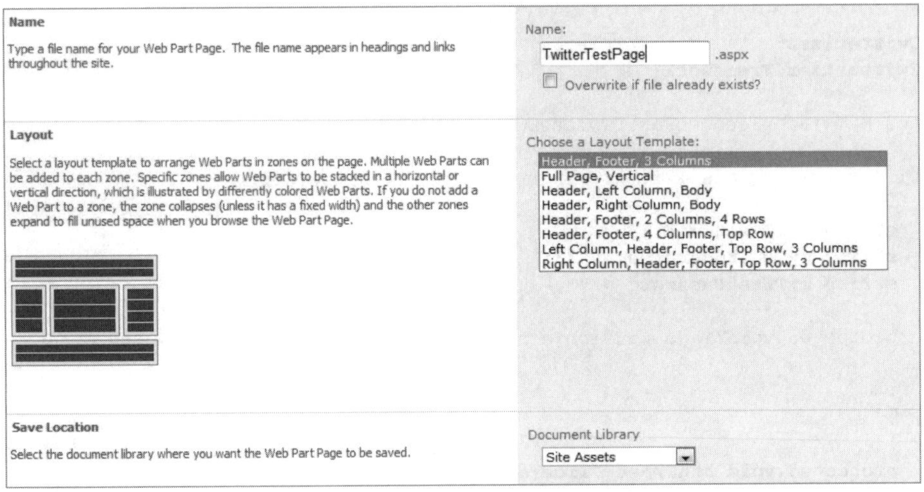

FIGURE 3-33 Creating a new Web part page for the Twitter Web part

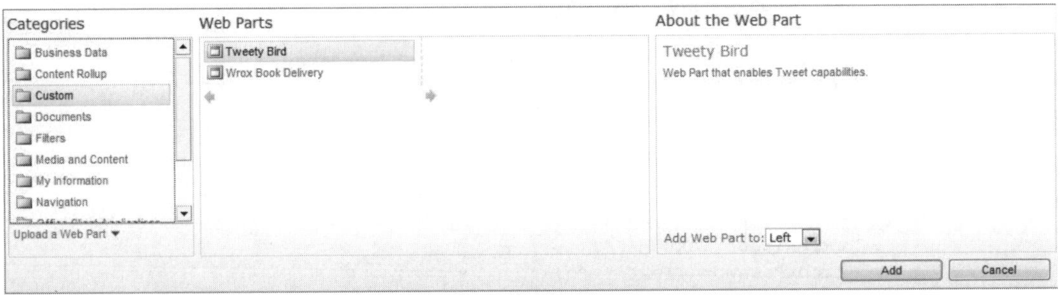

FIGURE 3-34 Adding the Web part to the page

13. When you are done, navigate to your Twitter page to test if your tweet was posted, as shown in Figure 3-36.

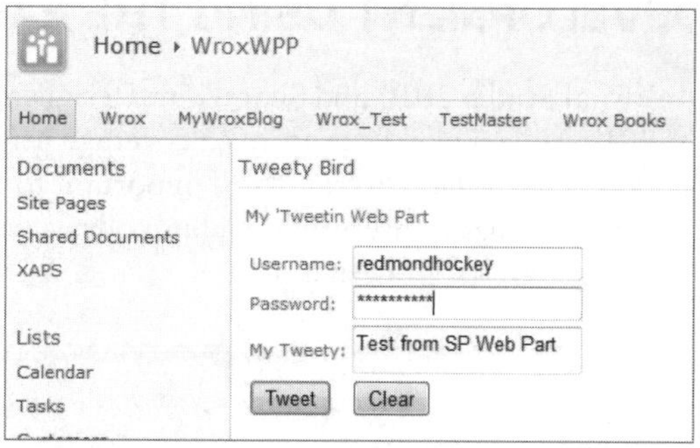

How It Works

The Visual Web part is a new type of Web part for SharePoint 2010 that provides the developer with the capability to create ASP.NET user controls using a WYSIWYG design surface. This user control is then wrapped by Visual Studio in a class that implements the user control as a Web part. In this example, you used the Twitter .NET wrapper that provides a lot of the core functionality to interact with Twitter from remote .NET client applications — such as the one you created here. The nice thing about the .NET wrapper for Twitter is that you don't have to manage the REST calls to Twitter; they are handled through the .NET APIs.

FIGURE 3-35 Visual Web part rendered on the page

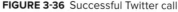

FIGURE 3-36 Successful Twitter call

REST (Representation State Transfer) is a lightweight way to interact with Web-based data using an HTTP protocol. You will learn more about REST in Chapter 5 and Chapter 10.

In this simple example, you built the ASP.NET UI to accept some limited user input — that is, the username, password, and the tweet. The key lines of code that enabled the communication with Twitter were the two lines of code within the `btnTweet_Click` event, which are bolded in the following code snippet.

```
protected void btnTweet_Click(object sender, EventArgs e)
{
    …

    Twitter myTweet = new Twitter(myTweetUsername,
    myTweetPassword);
    myTweet.Status.Update(strTweet);
}
```

Here, an instance of the Twitter object (`myTweet`) is created using the user-entered password and username as parameters. `myTweet` then uses the `Update` method on that object, passing it the tweet message. This is a super-simple way to message tweets to Twitter from your UI (albeit with very little error-checking code).

In general, Visual Studio 2010 has evolved tremendously in the support for SharePoint 2010 development. If you're new to SharePoint development, your thinking may be that this is just the way it should be. However, if you're a returning SharePoint developer, you should be having a "hallelujah" moment right now, given the disparate ways in which development was done in the past using Visual Studio. With this in mind, as you move through the book, know that you will continue to walk through exercises where Visual Studio is at the core of the development experience.

Now that you've learned a little bit about Visual Studio 2010, let's move on to Expression Blend.

DEVELOPMENT USING THE EXPRESSION BLEND SUITE

Visual Studio 2010 and SharePoint Designer 2010 are your two core developer tools for SharePoint 2010, so you won't see as much coverage here for Expression Blend as you did for the aforementioned tools. However, it's still important to at least get an introduction to Expression Blend. The reason is that Expression Blend provides a great suite of applications that support dynamic and more complex UI design.

> **NOTE** *You can download and try Expression Blend for 30 days. For more information, go to* www.microsoft.com/expression/products/Blend_Overview.aspx.

One of the main reasons for introducing it here is that Expression Blend offers a great way to design WPF, Silverlight, and Deep Zoom applications. Silverlight, as you will see later in the book, is a great way to create very dynamic applications — and this dynamic user experience begins with the use of Expression Blend. Further, Deep Zoom can also provide some interesting media experiences with images. For example, the Hard Rock Memorabilia site (http://memorabilia.hardrock.com) leverages the Deep Zoom capabilities within a Silverlight application embedded within an HTML page, as shown in Figure 3-37.

FIGURE 3-37 Hard Rock Cafe Memorabilia site

The type of experience on the site is one that enables you to zoom in to the different images on the page — with remarkable clarity of the images because the application refocuses each time it zooms in to an image. For example, when you zoom in to the center of the Silverlight application on the Hard Rock Cafe site, as shown in Figure 3-38, one of the many images is displayed, along with some metadata about that particular image — in this case a Keith Moon robe.

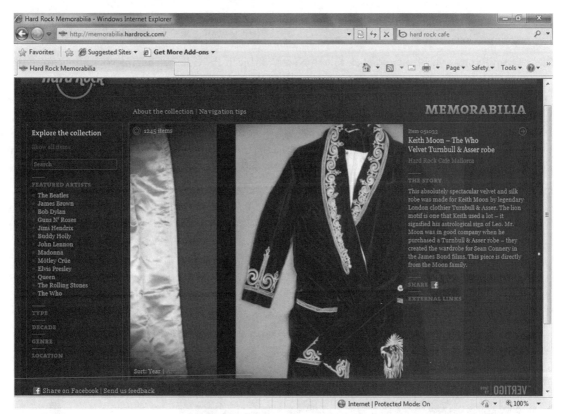

FIGURE 3-38 Zooming in on memorabilia

While you can create Deep Zoom applications like the one shown here, you can also create more every-day business applications using Silverlight. For example, much as you'd create a WinForm application using Visual Studio 2010, you could equally create a Silverlight application using Expression Blend. The added value is that you get more functionality built into Expression Blend, which provides support for animation, behaviors, action triggers, gradient design, and so on — so it truly provides much more of a design experience than the "Cider" UI designer that ships with Visual Studio 2010.

> **NOTE** Note that Expression Blend 3 and Visual Studio 2010 are conversant. So, when you build a Silverlight application in Expression Blend, it actually builds it as a Visual Studio–compatible solution. You can try this by right-clicking the MainPage.xaml in Visual Studio and selecting Open in Expression Blend.

Let's create a simple application using Expression Blend.

Creating a Silverlight Application Using Expression Blend

Code file [MyFirstSilverlightApp.zip] available for download at Wrox.com.

Expression Blend can be used to create UI elements for SharePoint. To create an application using Expression, follow these steps:

1. Open Expression Blend and click File ➪ New ➪ Project. Provide a name for your application (for example, `MyFirstSilverlightApp`), and click OK.

2. After Expression Blend creates your project, you will see that the main view is of the `MainPage.xaml` file. This is the main UI of your application. To keep things simple, click the chevron toward the bottom of the left-hand controls. This opens a fly-out menu that lists eight options, one of which is Controls. Click the Controls link to see the different controls available to you, as shown in Figure 3-39. Drag two labels, a button, a textbox, and a calendar control onto the design surface.

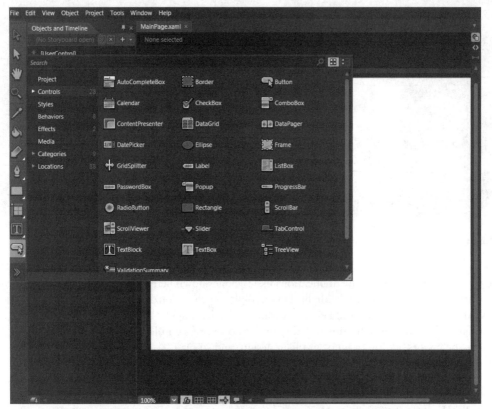

FIGURE 3-39 Expression Blend visual IDE

Table 3-2 provides a summary of the names and control types for the application.

TABLE 3-2 Control Types and Names

CONTROL TYPES	CONTROL NAMES
Label	lblTitle, lblDate
Textbox	txtbxDate
Button	btnDate
Calendar	clndrControl

3. Arrange the controls so that they look like Figure 3-40. Note that you can add some gradient to the control by clicking the control and then clicking different areas of the color palette in the Properties window.

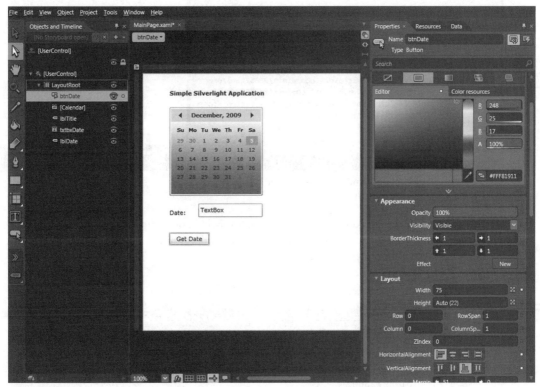

FIGURE 3-40 Designing controls in Expression Blend

4. You could add more sophisticated behaviors, but, for now, save the application and close Expression Blend. You'll add some event handlers for the application — but you're going to do this using Visual Studio.

5. Open Visual Studio 2010 and then open the Silverlight project. Note that when you open it, the project structure will look like Figure 3-41. However, the look and feel of the UI that you designed in Expression remains intact.

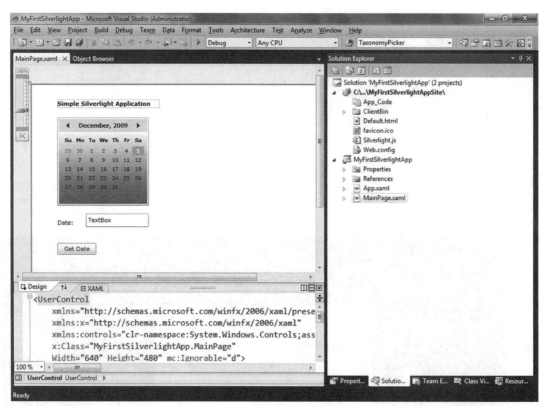

FIGURE 3-41 Silverlight application in Visual Studio

6. Inspect the XAML that makes up the UI (see the following code snippet). Note the gradient elements that provide the richer brush strokes for the calendar and button controls. This was a result of your clicking within the color palette.

```
<UserControl
    xmlns="http://schemas.microsoft.com/winfx/2006/xaml/
        presentation"
    xmlns:x="http://schemas.microsoft.com/winfx/2006/xaml"
    xmlns:controls="clr-namespace:
        System.Windows.Controls;assembly=
        System.Windows.Controls"
        xmlns:d="http://schemas.microsoft.com/expression/
            blend/2008"
        xmlns:mc="http://schemas.openxmlformats.org/
            markup-compatibility/2006"
        xmlns:dataInput="clr-namespace:System.Windows.Controls;
        assembly=System.Windows.Controls.Data.Input"
    x:Class="MyFirstSilverlightApp.MainPage"
    Width="640" Height="480" mc:Ignorable="d">

    <Grid x:Name="LayoutRoot" Background="White">
```

```
            <Button
x:Name="btnDate"
HorizontalAlignment="Left"
Margin="51,0,0,160"
VerticalAlignment="Bottom"
Width="75"
Content="Get Date"
Background="#FFF81911"/>
            <controls:Calendar
x:Name="clndrControl"
HorizontalAlignment="Left"
Margin="51,61,0,0"
VerticalAlignment="Top">
                <controls:Calendar.Background>
                    <LinearGradientBrush
EndPoint="0.5,1"
StartPoint="0.5,0">
                    <GradientStop Color="#FFD3DEE8" Offset="0"/>
                    <GradientStop Color="#FFD3DEE8" Offset="0.16"/>
                    <GradientStop Color="#FFFCFCFD" Offset="0.16"/>
                    <GradientStop Color="#FFE01A1A" Offset="1"/>
            </LinearGradientBrush>
                </controls:Calendar.Background>
            </controls:Calendar>
            <dataInput:Label
x:Name="lblTitle"
HorizontalAlignment="Left"
Margin="51,29,0,0"
VerticalAlignment="Top"
Width="200"
Content="Simple Silverlight Application" FontWeight="Bold"/>
            <TextBox
x:Name="txtbxDate"
Margin="106,0,0,212"
TextWrapping="Wrap"
HorizontalAlignment="Left"
VerticalAlignment="Bottom"
Height="25"
Width="124"/>
            <dataInput:Label
x:Name="lblDate"
HorizontalAlignment="Left"
Margin="51,0,0,212"
VerticalAlignment="Bottom"
Width="51"
Content="Date: "/>
        </Grid>
</UserControl>
```

7. You currently have no events tied to the UI that you created in Expression Blend. So, navigate to the button element and place your cursor right before the end of the element. Press the space bar.

This will invoke the IntelliSense. Find the Click event and then click and accept the default event handler name to add a Click event to the application, as shown in Figure 3-42.

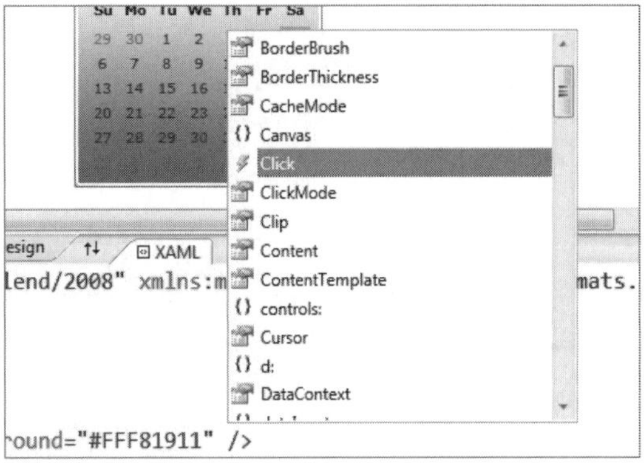

FIGURE 3-42 Adding Click event to Button control

The resulting XAML will be amended as shown in the following bolded addition:

```
...
<Button
x:Name="btnDate"
HorizontalAlignment="Left"
Margin="51,0,0,160"
VerticalAlignment="Bottom"
Width="75"
Content="Get Date"
Background="#FFF81911"
Click="btnDate_Click"/>
...
```

8. Right-click `MainPage.xaml` and select View Code. This opens the code-behind view — much the same experience you went through earlier in this chapter when creating the banner ad for use within SharePoint Designer. Add the following bolded code in the code behind:

```
using System;
using System.Windows;
using System.Windows.Controls;
using System.Windows.Documents;
using System.Windows.Ink;
using System.Windows.Input;
using System.Windows.Media;
using System.Windows.Media.Animation;
using System.Windows.Shapes;

namespace MyFirstSilverlightApp
{
    public partial class MainPage : UserControl
    {
        string strSelectedDate = "";
        DateTime userSelectedDate = new DateTime();

        public MainPage()
```

```
        {
            // Required to initialize variables
            InitializeComponent();
                txtbxDate.IsEnabled = false;
        }

    private void btnDate_Click(object sender, RoutedEventArgs e)
        {
            userSelectedDate = (DateTime)clndrControl.SelectedDate;
            strSelectedDate = userSelectedDate.ToString();

            if (strSelectedDate.Contains("12/25/2009"))
            {
                MessageBox.Show("Voice of Reason:
                You shouldn't be working!");
            }
            else
            {
                txtbxDate.Text = strSelectedDate;
            }
        }
    }
}
```

9. After you've added the code, press F5 to debug the application in your default browser. The result should look similar to Figure 3-43.

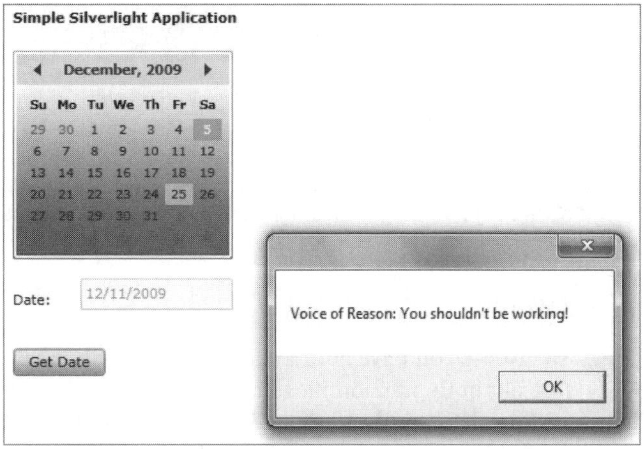

10. After you've successfully tested the application, click Build ➪ Build Solution to build the application one last time.

11. In the Solution Explorer, click the Show All Files button to show all of the solution files in the Solution Explorer.

12. Navigate to the Bin/Debug folder and right-click. Select Open Folder in Windows Explorer.

FIGURE 3-43 Testing the Silverlight application

13. Copy the file path, and then open SharePoint.

14. Navigate to the XAPS document library you created earlier in the chapter. (If you didn't create a document library called XAPS, you can do that now.) Click Add Document and then click Browse.

15. Paste the folder path to your Silverlight application, and then select the .xap file that is in that folder (for example, MyFirstSilverlightApp.xap) and click OK. When the file has been added to the folder, right-click and select Copy Shortcut.

16. Click All Site Content and then click Create. Select the Pages option along the left-hand side, and then select Web Part Page.

17. Provide a name for the page (for example, `BlendTest`), and click Create.

18. Click Site Actions ➪ Edit Page, and in one of the Web part zones, click "Add a web part."

19. Select the Media Content Web part, and then select Silverlight Web Part and click Add. SharePoint will prompt you for a URL to the `.xap` file, so paste the shortcut to the `.xap` file you added to the `XAPS` directory.

20. Click Stop Editing to test your new Silverlight application in SharePoint. The result should look similar to Figure 3-44.

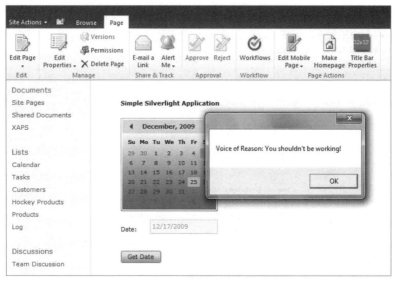

FIGURE 3-44 Adding a Silverlight application to SharePoint

How It Works

Congratulations! You have built another Silverlight application, but you added a little design to it by starting out in Expression Blend and providing some enhancements to the UI. You next opened that same Silverlight application in Visual Studio and added some code behind. You then added the Silverlight application, using SharePoint's built-in Silverlight Web part — a native Web part that acts as a container for Silverlight applications.

Expression Blend 3 is compatible with Visual Studio 2010, which is one of the nice integrations for designers and developers working together on Silverlight projects. However, with the new project templates in Visual Studio 2010, the integration across these two developer tools is even more important.

The integration in this exercise was illustrated through the creation of a Silverlight application using the more feature-rich design environment of Expression Blend, and then opening that application in Visual Studio (you can right-click the `.xaml` file and select Open in Expression Blend from Visual Studio or, alternatively, as you did in this walkthrough, open the project in Visual Studio 2010). You created the XAML-based UI using Expression Blend, and then added the code behind for the XAML in Visual Studio.

The `btnDate` button is associated with an event handler called `btnDate_Click`. The event handler is triggered, or "fires," when the button is clicked.

In the code behind, you set two class-level variables called `strSelectedDate` and `userSelectedDate`. These variables were used to store a string representation of the date that the user selected on the calendar control and a `DateTime` object that would also be used to store the date the user selected (casting the return variable from the selection to a `DateTime` object). Finally, the code behind asserts a conditional statement (the `if` statement) to see if you're working on Christmas day. Note that the `Contains` method is used because the complete string that is returned from selecting the date in the calendar control includes a time element as well (so a direct string comparison would not work in this case).

```
...

namespace MyFirstSilverlightApp
{
    public partial class MainPage : UserControl
    {
        string strSelectedDate = "";
        DateTime selectedDate = new DateTime();

        public MainPage()
        {
            InitializeComponent();
            txtbxDate.IsEnabled = false;
        }

        private void btnDate_Click(object sender,
            RoutedEventArgs e)
        {
            userSelectedDate = (DateTime)clndrControl.SelectedDate;
            strSelectedDate = userSelectedDate.ToString();

            if (strSelectedDate.Contains("12/25/2009"))
            {
                MessageBox.Show("Voice of Reason:
                You shouldn't be working!");
            }
            else
            {
                txtbxDate.Text = strSelectedDate;
            }
        }
    }
}
```

And, if you did select December 25, 2009, then a message would be issued to you via the `MessageBox.Show` event.

Expression Blend enables you to tap into your design and creative juices to begin to build out a compelling and rich UI for SharePoint. It can be applied to WPF applications that run on the client, or it can be used (as was shown here) in the context of Silverlight applications. In Chapter 9, you will have an opportunity to explore Expression Blend a little more. You should spend some time with this tool, because it can dramatically enhance the design of your UI.

SUMMARY

This chapter provided an overview of the major development environments that you will work in as a SharePoint developer. You saw Web-based development (or what some might call "developer configuration" or "power-user tasks"), development within SharePoint Designer 2010, development using Visual Studio 2010, and then development integrating Expression Blend with Visual Studio 2010. You'll see more of each of these as you make your way through the book, but at this point, you should have a baseline understanding of the *types* of things that you can do within each of the environments.

Also, hopefully you're beginning to see how much power there is with the new tooling with SharePoint 2010 — much more than ever before. And, given the evolution in the design tools as well, there are great opportunities here, not only for the designers and developers to work together but also for generating some dynamic and rich Silverlight experiences for SharePoint.

In this chapter, you were introduced to the different ways of developing for SharePoint. You also had a chance to get some coding practice in with these different tools. In Chapter 4, you will learn about some common developer tasks to further put these tools into practice.

EXERCISES

1. What are the types of developer tasks you might manage through the browser?

2. What are the major differences in the way you would use SharePoint Designer over Visual Studio? Can you think of places where they might be complementary?

3. In what ways can you see Expression Blend contributing to your overall solution design experience?

▶ WHAT YOU LEARNED IN THIS CHAPTER

ITEM	DESCRIPTION
Ways to develop for SharePoint	You will typically use tools such as SharePoint Designer and Visual Studio to develop for SharePoint. However, there are also some higher-level development tools built into the Web-based experience (for example, inline text, HTML and script editing, and developer dashboard).
SharePoint Designer 2010	SharePoint Designer is a free tool that enables developers to edit site pages, create master pages, workflows, and all sorts of SharePoint objects such as lists or content types.
Visual Studio 2010	Visual Studio is a professional-grade developer tool that provides a number of in-box project and item templates with a full F5 experience.
Expression Blend	Expression Blend is a suite of tools that can be used to design and customize the user experience. For SharePoint, you can build advanced and custom Silverlight UIs.

RECOMMENDED READING

➤ SharePoint Development Center on MSDN at `http://msdn.microsoft.com/en-us/sharepoint/default.aspx`

➤ Channel 9 SharePoint Developer Learning Center at `http://channel9.msdn.com/learn/courses/SharePoint2010Developer/`

➤ SharePoint Designer Home Page at `http://sharepoint2010.microsoft.com/product/related-technologies/Pages/SharePoint-Designer-2010.aspx`

➤ Visual Studio 2010 Home Page at `http://www.microsoft.com/visualstudio/en-us/products/2010/default.mspx`

➤ Expression Blend Home Page at `http://www.microsoft.com/expression/products/Blend_Overview.aspx`

4

Common Developer Tasks in SharePoint 2010

WHAT YOU'LL LEARN IN THIS CHAPTER:

- ➤ Creating different types of Web parts, including standard, Visual, and Data View Web parts

- ➤ Understanding site columns and content types, and how you can use them when creating lists

- ➤ Understanding how to interact with SharePoint and data in SharePoint using the native APIs

- ➤ Creating and editing site pages and master pages using SharePoint Designer

So far, you've become familiar with SharePoint and learned how to get started with installation and setting up your development environment. Now that you have a sense of what SharePoint is all about, you're no doubt hungrily awaiting some coding exercises.

This chapter discusses a set of common development tasks for beginning SharePoint developers. Although this examination will not be comprehensive, it will get you started and introduce you to a set of key tasks that you will likely do over and over again in your SharePoint development career.

The discussions in this chapter have been included as the result of first thinking about common developer tasks and then culling information from community conversations with SharePoint MVP friends. This has resulted in the following set of developer tasks that will be addressed in this chapter:

- ➤ Creating Web parts

- ➤ Creating site columns, content types, and lists

- ➤ Accessing and managing data

➤ Creating Event receivers

➤ Creating `aspx` pages

➤ Creating master pages

This chapter explores each of these developer tasks through a high-level description, or simple, straightforward walkthroughs. In many cases, you will see a lot of these tasks showing up in greater detail in other walkthroughs throughout the book. The goal of this chapter, then, is to introduce you to a common set of developer tasks for SharePoint and to get you started down the path of beginning SharePoint development.

CREATING WEB PARTS

One of the most common developer tasks you'll likely engage in is the creation and deployment of a Web part. You've seen this already and have, hopefully, worked through the walkthroughs to get a sense for how to do this. Web parts will be covered in detail in Chapter 6, so you should think of this section as an early introduction to what will be covered in detail later in the book.

Standard and Visual Web Parts

SharePoint 2010 includes primarily two different Web parts you will be working with: Standard and Visual. The *standard Web part* provides the core infrastructure that enables you to create and deploy a Web part into SharePoint. Because SharePoint is built on ASP.NET, you can apply many of the same coding techniques that you may have learned through ASP.NET to the creation of a standard Web part.

For example, you can create and apply many of the same objects and events when building out a standard Web part that you may have used when building out an ASP.NET Web part. The following is a short code snippet that includes a `Textbox`, `Label`, and `Button` control that are being instantiated and properties set, as well as a `Click` event that corresponds to the `Button` control:

```
...

namespace MyFirstDevTask.TaskOneWebPart
{
    [ToolboxItemAttribute(false)]
    public class TaskOneWebPart : WebPart
    {
        Label myLabel = new Label();
        TextBox myTextbox = new TextBox();
        Label myResponse = new Label();
        Button myButton = new Button();

        protected override void CreateChildControls()
        {
            myLabel.Text = "Enter Text:";
            myResponse.Text = "";
            myTextbox.Enabled = true;
```

```
        myTextbox.Text = "";
        myButton.Text = "Click Me";
        this.Controls.Add(myLabel);
        this.Controls.Add(myTextbox);
        this.Controls.Add(new LiteralControl("<br/>"));
        this.Controls.Add(myResponse);
        this.Controls.Add(new LiteralControl("<br/>"));
        this.Controls.Add(myButton);

        myButton.Click += new EventHandler(myButton_Click);
    }

    void myButton_Click(object sender, EventArgs e)
    {
        string userResponse = myTextbox.Text;
        myResponse.Text = userResponse;
    }
  }
 }
...
```

In this code snippet, you can see that the four controls are declared at the class level. Then, in the `CreateChildControls` method, the properties for those objects are set. The `Add` method is called to add the controls to the `Controls` collection (to display them in the Web part), and the `myButton_Click` event is called to render the user's entry as text in one of the labels. Figure 4-1 shows this code in action.

FIGURE 4-1 Deployed Web part

If you have not coded Web parts before, this is pretty standard — that is, creating the controls, setting the properties for those controls, adding the controls to the `Controls` collection, and also adding any event handlers for those controls.

The standard Web part is an item-level template in Visual Studio 2010, so you can only add this to a parent project such as an Empty SharePoint project template. It is, though, a standard template available in Visual Studio, so creating and deploying your Web parts is very easy.

The *Visual Web part* is different from the standard Web part in that you have a designer experience you can use to create the user interface (UI) for the Web part (as opposed to what you did in the previous example where you were manually creating the controls that make up your UI). Furthermore, the Visual Web part has both project-level and item-level templates in Visual Studio 2010, so you can have both a parent and a child project that are Visual Web parts.

Using the Designer experience in Visual Studio 2010 to create the Web part UI, you can drag and drop a wide array of library controls from the Toolbox onto the Designer surface. Unlike with the standard Web part where you would manually code and use IntelliSense to create controls or events, with the Visual Web part, you would double-click the control in the Designer, and then jump to the code behind to add your events.

For example, in the Visual Web part, if you were to implement the same code as shown in the discussion of the standard Web part, then you would have an ASP.NET user control (`ascx` file) that represents the UI with a code-behind file. (ascx is the file extension for the ASP.NET user control file.) The ascx user control code would look like the following:

```
...
<asp:Label ID="myLabel" runat="server" Text="Enter Text:"></asp:Label>
 <asp:TextBox ID="myTextbox" runat="server"></asp:TextBox>
<p>
    <asp:Label ID="myResponse" runat="server" Text="Label"></asp:Label>
</p>
<asp:Button ID="myButton" runat="server" onclick="myButton_Click"
    Text="Click Me" />
...
```

The code behind for the ascx user control would look like the following:

```
using System;
using System.Web.UI;
using System.Web.UI.WebControls;
using System.Web.UI.WebControls.WebParts;

namespace MyFirstDevTask.TaskTwoWebPart
{
    public partial class TaskTwoWebPartUserControl : UserControl
    {
        protected void Page_Load(object sender, EventArgs e)
        {
        }

        protected void myButton_Click(object sender, EventArgs e)
        {
            string userResponse = myTextbox.Text;
            myResponse.Text = userResponse;
        }

    }
}
```

Note that the control declarations do not appear in this specific ascx code behind. However, there is a reference to the ascx control in the core Web part class that loads the user control you build with the Designer experience at runtime. The following shows the code that represents this reference inside of the core Web part class. Note that the _ascxPath object simply represents a file-system path to the location of the ascx file you created using the Designer.

```
...
public class TaskTwoWebPart : WebPart
    {
        private const string _ascxPath =
            @"~/_CONTROLTEMPLATES/MyFirstDevTask/TaskTwoWebPart/
            TaskTwoWebPartUserControl.ascx";

        protected override void CreateChildControls()
        {
```

```
        Control control = Page.LoadControl(_ascxPath);
        Controls.Add(control);
    }
}
...
```

Code file [MyFirstDevTask.zip] available for download at Wrox.com.

Although you have the same functionality built into the Web part, you have now seen two slightly different ways of building out the Web part.

Data View Web Parts

While the Data View Web part is not discussed in great detail in this book, it is worth mentioning in this chapter. This is because the Data View Web part is not only accessible to developers but also can be useful for power users or even information workers. Part of the problem, however, is that many times, nondevelopers feel that data-centric work should be left to the developer. With the advance in tools for SharePoint, this trend is starting to wane. Information workers are working more and more with data.

The Data View Web part is interesting in that it is capable of retrieving data from various data sources in the form of Extensible Markup Language (XML). However, the format of the data does not necessarily have to exist as XML, because this Web part understands the data set and transforms it using Extensible Stylesheet Language Transformations (XSLT). XSLT is a supported standard in SharePoint 2010 and enables you to transform well-formed XML into an HTML-rendered format.

The Data View Web part is also versatile. It can consume data, share it, define the formatting of the data in SharePoint, and enable editing against the data. For example, create a new SharePoint list called `Sales` and add three columns to the list — `Customer` (of type `"Single line of text"`), `Total Sales` (of type `Number`), and `Ranking` (of type `Number`). Add some data to the list, so the list looks similar to Figure 4-2.

	Customer	Total Sales	Ranking
	Wingtip ☑ NEW	$5,290,490,109.00	1
	Acme ☑ NEW	$903,209.00	3
	Blue Yonder ☑ NEW	$290,029,129.00	2
	Fabrikam ☑ NEW	$2,090,129,899.00	1
⊕ Add new item			

FIGURE 4-2 Sample sales list

The list will serve as a way for you to rank the top accounts based on the amount of total sales. The Data View Web part will come into play when you use SharePoint Designer to create a Web part that is essentially a view into the list. The major difference, though, is when you create some automatic formatting based on the values in the list.

Using the list you just created, let's walk through how you create the Data View Web part.

TRY IT OUT **Creating a Data View Web Part**

A Data View Web part can be a great way for both developers and end users to provide some automatic and dynamic formatting for a list. To create a Data View Web part, follow these steps:

1. Open your SharePoint site and click Site Actions ➪ Edit in SharePoint Designer.

2. After SharePoint Designer 2010 opens, click Site Pages.

3. You now want to create a new Web part page. To do this, click the Web part page down-arrow on the ribbon and then select one of the predefined templates. Replace the default filename (for example Untitled_1.aspx) with your own filename (for example, WroxWebPartPage.aspx). Press Enter when done.

4. To edit the file, first click the file and then click Edit File in the main Web part page properties window.

5. Click one of the Web part zones, and then click the Insert tab on the ribbon and select Data View. Then, as shown in Figure 4-3, select the Sales list (which is the list you created earlier in this chapter).

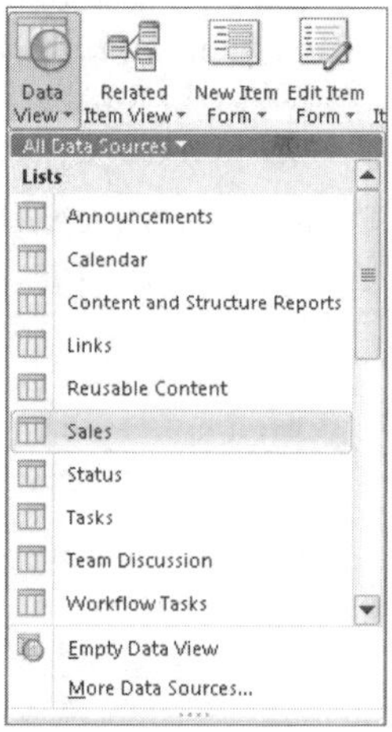

6. After SharePoint Designer updates the view with the most recent data in the list, you can add some automatic formatting.

7. To keep things simple, you'll change the background color of the Ranking column, according to the value of the ranking. To do this, select the first <div> in the Ranking column. (Be sure that you select the full cell.)

8. Under Conditional Formatting, select Format Column and under the Field Name, select Ranking. Make the Comparison value Equals. Then, add the value of 1 in the Value field. Click the Set Style button to change the background of the cell to be green. Do this for all of the Ranking fields using different colors for different Ranking numbers (for example, green for 1, yellow for 2, and red for 3). When you are finished, you should have something similar to Figure 4-4.

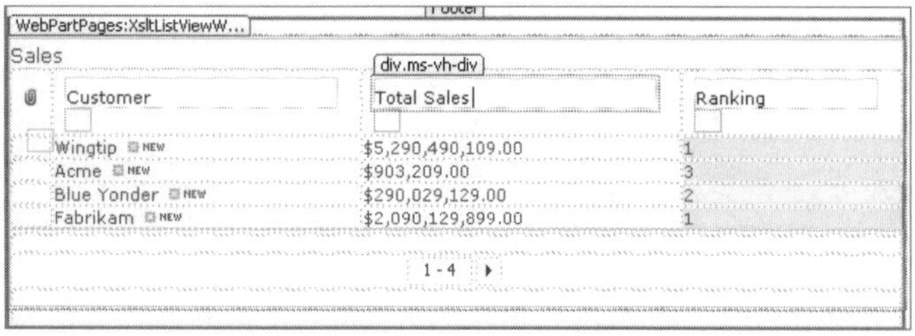

FIGURE 4-3 Selecting the Sales list

FIGURE 4-4 Data View of list in SharePoint Designer

9. Save the Web part page.

10. Open SharePoint, and navigate to the Web part page. The list should look similar to Figure 4-5.

Sales			
☐ 📎 Customer		Total Sales	Ranking
Wingtip ✦ NEW		$5,290,490,109.00	1
Acme ✦ NEW		$903,209.00	3
Blue Yonder ✦ NEW		$290,029,129.00	2
Fabrikam ✦ NEW		$2,090,129,899.00	1
➕ Add new item			

FIGURE 4-5 Completed Data View Web part

11. To test the conditional formatting, open the `Sales` list and change the ranking to another number. Navigate back to the Data View Web part. For example, change the Fabrikam ranking from 1 to 2. The background should now change to yellow.

How It Works

A list is the most common structure for data in SharePoint, which the Data View Web part uses as the primary way it reformats the list. For example, in this walkthrough, SharePoint Designer provided a way for you to reformat the background setting of the cell based on the value of the number in that cell. To accomplish this, the Data View Web part uses HTML and ASP.NET formatting capabilities.

The reformatting of the background was also a simple illustration of what could be accomplished. You can also build more complex, calculated formatted views through SharePoint Designer.

This example was fairly straightforward, and there are many more interesting conditions that you could set against a Data View Web part with more complex calculations that render different types of conditional formatting. While you saw some Web part coding already in this book, you'll see more in-depth coding for standard and Visual Web parts in Chapter 6.

CREATING LISTS, SITE COLUMNS, AND CONTENT TYPES

You'll often find yourself creating different objects in SharePoint, such as lists, site columns, and content types. As you'll see in Chapter 5, *lists* are a core part of SharePoint, and they have a rich object model that you can use to code against them.

As a potential part of lists, *site columns* are reusable column definitions that can be created and then repurposed across the SharePoint site. For example, if you need a very specific site column called `Tax Rate` that has a calculation embedded within it, you can use that site column to enforce some level of consistency across your lists and sites.

Content types are also reusable objects that can be repurposed across your SharePoint site. Content types can come in different shapes and sizes. For example, you might define a content type as a set of columns, or you might define it as a custom document template. One common use of content types is to create custom documents (for example, a legal contract with boilerplate text), and then create the content type and bind that content type to a document library. You'll see how to do this in Chapter 9.

You can create site columns, content types, and lists in a variety of ways. For example, you can create each one of these objects through the SharePoint Web interface. You can also leverage SharePoint Designer 2010 to create all of these objects, or even use Visual Studio 2010 to create content types and list definitions. Using Visual Studio 2010 makes it possible to begin integrating list definitions into other applications, or redeploying a custom list definition across multiple SharePoint sites.

Let's take a look at how you can use SharePoint Designer and Visual Studio to build custom site columns for lists.

TRY IT OUT   Creating a Site Column and List

Site columns are reusable columns that you can customize and leverage to build lists. To create a custom site column and use it in a list, follow these steps:

1. Open SharePoint and then click Site Actions ⇨ Edit in SharePoint Designer.

2. Click Site Columns in the navigation pane.

3. Click New Column.

4. Select Choice as the type of column, and then provide a name (for example, `State`) and description. Click New Group and provide a name for the new group (for example, `Customer_By_State`) and click OK, as shown in Figure 4-6.

5. Add the choices to the Column Editor dialog (for example, WA, IL, and CA) and select Radio Button in the "Display as format" drop-down list. Update the Default value field to map to one of the choices you entered, and leave the rest of the options at their defaults and click OK. Click the Save button to save the new site column to SharePoint.

6. You should now have an entry as a custom category that looks similar to Figure 4-7.

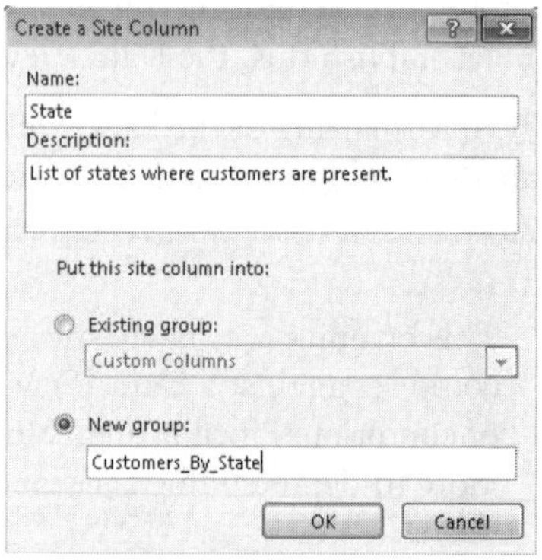

FIGURE 4-6 Creating a site column

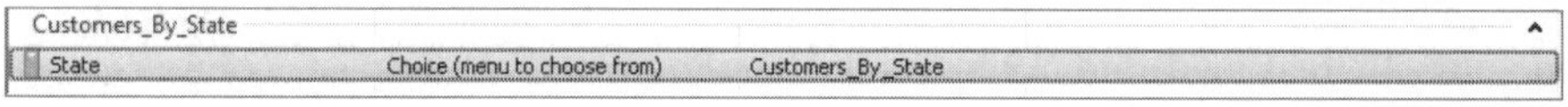

FIGURE 4-7 Entry in Site Columns Gallery

7. Navigate in SharePoint to the list you created earlier (that is, `Sales`).

8. Click the List tab and then List Settings.

9. Click "Add from existing site columns."

10. In the Groups drop-down, select the custom group (for example, `Customers_By_State`). Then, select the site column you created (for example, `State`) and click Add (to add to the "Columns to add" view) and then click OK. This adds the site column to your list.

11. Return to the list view and edit each of the records to include a different state for each of the customers, as shown in Figure 4-8.

Customer	Total Sales	Ranking	State
Wingtip	$5,290,490,109.00	1	WA
Acme	$903,209.00	3	NY
Blue Yonder	$290,029,129.00	2	PA
Fabrikam	$2,090,129,899.00	2	CA

✛ Add new item

FIGURE 4-8 List with newly added site column

How It Works

A site column is the constituent part of a list and is composed of one or more columns. Site columns are created and stored at the site level and, thus, can be reused across your SharePoint site. In this example, you created a site column and added that site column to the `Sales` list. You could also leverage this type of column in other lists across your site — thus, this is a primary factor distinguishing the normal columns from site columns.

While you can create lists in SharePoint Designer 2010, you may have the need to create a site column, list definition, or content type using Visual Studio (for example, if you want to package and distribute a content type with a larger solution). Using the new built-in project templates, this is much easier to create than in past versions of SharePoint.

When you do create objects such as site columns, list definitions, or content types using Visual Studio, though, you will need to be familiar with the Collaborative Application Markup Language (CAML) syntax and structure for the objects you're trying to create. (CAML is an XML syntax that is specific to SharePoint.)

For example, the following XML defines a site column that can be deployed to a SharePoint site and then reused across the site. The site column defines a reusable list of customer types for a program a company is running. Note that there are a number of properties that are set. These are the same properties that SharePoint created for you when you used SharePoint Designer earlier in the section.

```
<?xml version="1.0" encoding="utf-8"?>
<Elements xmlns="http://schemas.microsoft.com/sharepoint/">
    <Field ID="{5644d23d-325f-4882-8fd2-09d455f4910e}"
    Type= "Choice" AllowDeletion="FALSE" Description="Type of program."
    FillInChoice="TRUE"
    Name="CustomerType"
    DisplayName="Customer Type"
    Group="Customers">
    <CHOICES>
        <CHOICE>Premier</CHOICE>
        <CHOICE>Gold</CHOICE>
        <CHOICE>Silver</CHOICE>
```

```
            <CHOICE>Bronze</CHOICE>
            <CHOICE>Non-Affiliated</CHOICE>
      </CHOICES>
      <Default>Bronze</Default>
      </Field>
  </Elements>
```

Let's use Visual Studio 2010 to create this site column and deploy it to SharePoint.

TRY IT OUT   Creating a Site Column using Visual Studio 2010

Code file [MyFirstListDefinition.zip] available for download at Wrox.com.

The project templates in Visual Studio 2010 make it convenient for you to create site columns, content types, and lists. To create a custom site column using Visual Studio, follow these steps:

1. Open Visual Studio 2010 and click File ⇨ New ⇨ Project.

2. Select the Empty SharePoint Project in the SharePoint 2010 project node. Provide a name (for example, `MyFirstListDefinition`) for the project and click OK.

3. In the Project Creation Wizard, ensure that your SharePoint site is typed in correctly and then select the Farm-Level solution for the level of trust. Click Finish.

4. Visual Studio creates an empty SharePoint project for you. When it's completed, right-click the top-level project node and select Add ⇨ New Item.

5. Select the Empty Element template, as shown in Figure 4-9. Provide a name (for example, `CustomerType`) for the file and click Add.

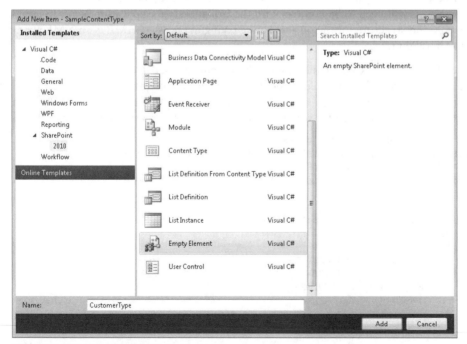

FIGURE 4-9 Empty Element project template

6. Add the following bolded code to the `Elements.xml` file that is created in the default project:

```
<?xml version="1.0" encoding="utf-8"?>
<Elements xmlns="http://schemas.microsoft.com/sharepoint/">
    <Field ID="{5644d23d-325f-4882-8fd2-09d455f4910e}"
    Type= "Choice" AllowDeletion="FALSE" Description="Type of program."
    FillInChoice="TRUE"
    Name="CustomerType"
    DisplayName="Customer Type"
    Group="Customers">
    <CHOICES>
        <CHOICE>Premier</CHOICE>
        <CHOICE>Gold</CHOICE>
        <CHOICE>Silver</CHOICE>
        <CHOICE>Bronze</CHOICE>
        <CHOICE>Non-Affiliated</CHOICE>
    </CHOICES>
    <Default>Bronze</Default>
    </Field>
</Elements>
```

7. After you've completed this, press F6 to build the project. When the project successfully builds, click Build ➪ Deploy Solution to deploy the site column to SharePoint.

8. Navigate to your SharePoint site and click Site Actions ➪ Site Settings. Under Galleries, click Site Columns. You should now see a Customers group with a `Customer Type` site column, as shown in Figure 4-10.

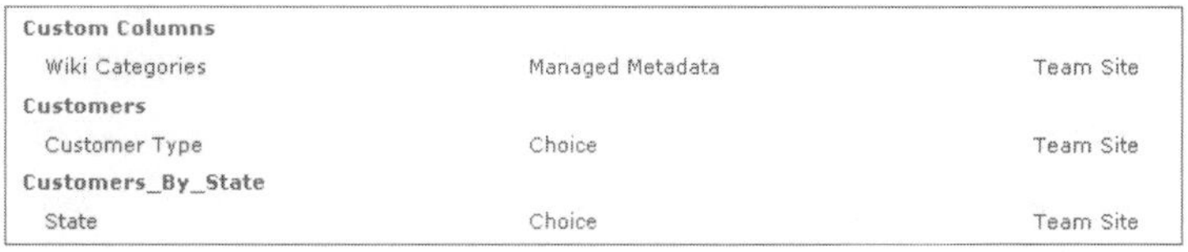

Custom Columns		
Wiki Categories	Managed Metadata	Team Site
Customers		
Customer Type	Choice	Team Site
Customers_By_State		
State	Choice	Team Site

FIGURE 4-10 Customers group in Site Columns Gallery

9. Navigate to the `Sales` list you created earlier.

10. Click the List tab and then select List Settings.

11. Click the "Add from existing site columns" link.

12. In the Groups drop-down menu, select Customers and then select `Customer Type`. Click Add.

13. Click OK to add the new site column you created to the list.

14. Edit each of the list items and add a new customer type to each one of the customer entries, as shown in Figure 4-11.

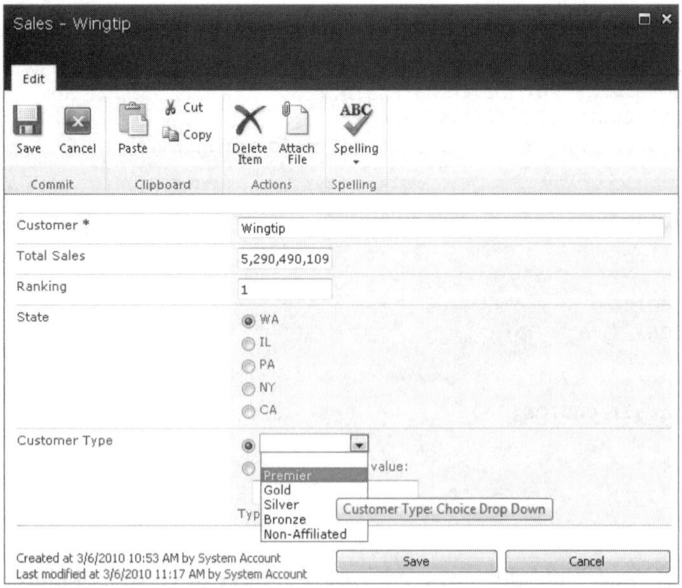

FIGURE 4-11 Leveraging the custom site column in Sales list

15. Your newly amended list should now look similar to Figure 4-12.

FIGURE 4-12 Final list with new Customer Type site column

How It Works

In much the same way that you created a site column with SharePoint Designer, you created a site column using Visual Studio. However, the way in which you did it was quite a bit different — even though the end result was very similar.

Whereas SharePoint Designer abstracts the XML configuration files and deploys the site column to the appropriate place within SharePoint. Visual Studio treats the site column like any other SharePoint project. It creates a *feature* and then deploys the XML elements file (which represents the definition of the site column) to the appropriate place within SharePoint.

WORKING WITH SHAREPOINT DATA

One of the most common tasks when working with SharePoint is interacting with the various data sources such as lists or document libraries. The great thing about SharePoint 2010 is that you have a number of different options to do that. For example, you have the server object model (which carries forward a lot of the 2007 APIs), the client object model (which is a new API to interact with lists), the RESTful service (which leverages WCF Data services to treat lists as entities), ASP.NET Web services (which ship in-box and cover a wide array of scenarios), and Business Connectivity Services (which provide a rich set of APIs for working with external data systems such as SAP, Microsoft Dynamics CRM, and PeopleSoft).

You will see each of these methods of working with data discussed throughout the book. However, this section provides some select examples of tasks that you'll likely do on a daily basis across some of these services and APIs.

Before you can do anything with SharePoint programmatically, however, you must establish a connection and context with your SharePoint site. For the most part, this means adding a reference to your project (for example, a reference to `Microsoft.SharePoint.dll`, `Microsoft.SharePoint.Client.dll`, or a Web service reference such as `http://<server>/_vti_bin/Lists.asmx`). With the appropriate references added to your project, you can begin to set the context (or implement the service), and then code within that site context.

For example, you can set the context for a SharePoint site using the server object model by adding the `Microsoft.SharePoint.dll` to your project reference and then use the following `using` statements to wrap your code. In this code snippet, you set the site collection context and can call the `OpenWeb` method on that site context or use the `RootWeb` property to set the context of the `SPSite` object (that is, `mySiteCollection`). You would then add your code where the comment indicates.

```
...
using (SPSite mySiteCollection = new SPSite(mySiteUrl))
    {
            using (SPWeb mySPSite = mySiteCollection.RootWeb)
                {
                    //Code here.
                }
    }
...
```

One of the innovations in SharePoint 2010 is the SharePoint client object model, which is a more performance-oriented way to read and write data from SharePoint lists. After adding the `Microsoft.SharePoint.Client.Runtime.dll` and `Microsoft.SharePoint.Client.dll` references, you can use the following code to set the context with your SharePoint site. Then, when you've created your application code, you call the `ExecuteQuery` method to batch-process that code. The final statement (that is, the `Close` method) disposes of the context from memory.

```
...
String mySiteUrl = "http://fabrikamhockey/acme";
```

```
ClientContext mySPSiteContext = new ClientContext(mySiteUrl);

//Code here.

mySPSiteContext.ExecuteQuery();
mySPSiteContext.Close();
...
```

You will find yourself using both the server object model and client object model in different scenarios. For server-side only applications, you can use the server object model. For remote client applications, you can use the SharePoint client object model.

Another way to program against SharePoint is by using the native Web services. This is a great way to interact with SharePoint because the services already have context, and they are deployed to SharePoint. To use the Web services, you add a Web reference to your Visual Studio project and then implement the service in your code.

One of the most commonly used Web services is the Lists Web service. Following is a code snippet that shows the instantiation of the Lists Web service proxy (called wsProxy) and the setting of the credentials. (SharePoint must trust the call from the code through an authenticated user.) You must also set the URL of the Web service.

```
...
MySPListWSRefernce.Lists wsProxy = new MySPListWSRefernce.Lists();
wsProxy.Credentials = System.Net.CredentialCache.DefaultCredentials;
wsProxy.Url = "http://fabrikamhockey/_vti_bin/Lists.asmx";
 //Code here
wsProxy.Dispose();
...
```

One of the things you'll need to understand is the way in which SharePoint passes data using the ASP.NET Web services — through *XML payloads*. To query SharePoint using these services often requires CAML constructs, which can get a bit hairy. You'll see coverage of Web services throughout the book, and you most certainly will learn about some of the basics of CAML. Specifically, Chapter 10 provides more information on Web services.

After you've obtained context with the SharePoint object model, you can then interact with data that resides on SharePoint. For example, you can iterate over every list in SharePoint and get the title of the list. You can retrieve views of specific lists, or you can update properties or list items in lists programmatically.

In the following code snippet, you can see that the server object model is used to get the SharePoint site context. Now, however, it iterates through the lists (see bolded code) on the SharePoint site and adds each list title to a listbox.

```
...
string mySiteUrl = "http://intranet.contoso.com/acme/";
string myListItemInfo = "";

using (SPSite mySiteCollection = new SPSite(mySiteUrl))
    {
         using (SPWeb mySPSite = mySiteCollection.RootWeb)
```

```
        {
            foreach (SPList mySPList in mySPSite.Lists)
            {
                myListItemInfo = mySPList.Title.ToString();
                lstbxListTitles.Items.Add(myListItemInfo);
            }
        }
    }
    ...
```

Again, you can do similar types of list interaction by using the SharePoint client object model. In the following code snippet, you can see that the site context is set, but the bolded code shows that a list called Inventory is retrieved from SharePoint, and then loaded with a query to filter on the Salmon field.

```
...
String spURL = "http://fabrikamhockey/acme";
ClientContext spSiteContext = new ClientContext(spURL);
List myProducts = spSiteContext.Web.Lists.GetByTitle("Inventory");
spSiteContext.Load(spSiteContext.Web);
spSiteContext.Load(myProducts, list => list.Fields.Where(field =>
    field.Title == "Salmon"));
spSiteContext.ExecuteQuery();
spSiteContext.Close();
...
```

When updating list data, you can again use one of the different options discussed in this section (that is, server object model, client object model, or native ASP.NET Web services). One example is to use the server object model and then call the Update method to update items on a SharePoint list.

The following code takes the same site context code shown earlier and then, instead of iterating through the list, it creates an instance of a specific list and then adds a record, comprising two fields, to the list: Product_Name and Product_SKU. In this case, you can see that the final call is to the Update method to add the new item (newListItem) to the SharePoint site.

```
...
using (SPSite mySPSite = new SPSite("http://fabrikamhockey/acme"))
    {
        using (SPWeb mySPWeb = mySPSite.OpenWeb())
            {
        SPList productsList = mySPWeb.Lists["Products"];
        SPListItem newListItem = productsList.Items.Add();
        newListItem["Product_Name"] = "Salmon";
        newListItem["Product_SKU"] = "SLM-30989";
        newListItem.Update();
            }
    }
    ...
```

Another task you might find yourself doing quite a bit is querying SharePoint data. This book outlines a few ways to do this, such as CAML queries, conditionals, and Language Integrated Query (LINQ) statements. LINQ is a very effective way to query data, which is supported in SharePoint 2010.

The following LINQ statement is a simple statement that retrieves the list item (from a list represented through the `myCustomerList` object) where the customer name (represented as `c`) is Acme:

```
...
var customers =
        from c in myCustomerList
        where c == "Acme"
        select c;
...
```

One LINQ technique that you'll use in SharePoint is to create a list collection and class, and then populate that object with data (you'll see this used throughout this book). The class is a custom class you create, and the list collection is a collection of those custom class instances. In the preceding code snippet, `myCustomerList` is the list collection. Another technique, though, is to use a tool called SPMetal to transform your lists into an entity model that can be queried directly using LINQ statements.

Let's check out an example of using LINQ.

TRY IT OUT Using LINQ in SharePoint

Code file [MyFirstSPLinqProject.zip] available for download at Wrox.com.

LINQ is a very effective and efficient way to query data. You can prepare your SharePoint lists for LINQ by using SPMetal. To prepare your list and create an application that uses LINQ, follow these steps:

1. Open a command prompt (running as administrator).

2. Navigate to the folder `c:\Program Files\Common Files\Microsoft Shared\web server extensions\14\bin` and enter the following command (ensure that you replace the `<servername>` with your SharePoint URL, for example `http://fabrikamhockey`):

```
spmetal.exe /web:http://<servername> /code:SPEntityModel.cs /language:csharp
```

3. The SPMetal command tool will create a C# file called `SPEntityModel.cs` that you can then use in an application to issue LINQ queries against a modeling of the SharePoint lists (SPMetal essentially translates all of the lists in your SharePoint site into an entity model that is strongly typed).

4. To leverage this entity model in a SharePoint project, open Visual Studio 2010.

5. Click File ➪ New ➪ Project. Select Empty SharePoint Project. Provide a name (for example, `MyFirstSPLinqProject`) and click OK. Set the trust for the solution to be farm level and click Finish.

6. Right-click the project and select Add ➪ Existing Item. Then, navigate to the previously described folder (where you created `SPEntityModel.cs`) and add the file that SPMetal created (that is `SPEntityModel.cs`) to the project.

7. Right-click the project and select Add ➪ New Item. Select the Web Part item template, provide a name (for example, `MySPLinqWebPart`), and click Add.

8. Right-click the References and select Add Reference. Click Browse and navigate to the folder `c:\Program Files\Common Files\Microsoft Shared\web server extensions\14\ISAPI`. Select `Microsoft.SharePoint.Linq.dll` and click OK.

9. Right-click the core Web part class file (for example, `MySPLinqWebPart.cs`), and select View Code.

10. Add the following bolded code to the core Web part class file:

```
using System;
using System.ComponentModel;
using System.Web;
using System.Web.UI;
using System.Web.UI.WebControls;
using System.Web.UI.WebControls.WebParts;
using Microsoft.SharePoint;
using Microsoft.SharePoint.WebControls;
using Microsoft.SharePoint.Linq;
using System.Linq;

namespace MyFirstSPLinqProject.MySPLinqWebPart
{
    [ToolboxItemAttribute(false)]
    public class MySPLinqWebPart : WebPart
    {
        Label myLabel = new Label();
        ListBox listTitles = new ListBox();
        Button myButton = new Button();

        protected override void CreateChildControls()
        {
            myLabel.Text = "Lists:";
            myButton.Text = "Get Lists";

            this.Controls.Add(myLabel);
            this.Controls.Add(listTitles);
            this.Controls.Add(new LiteralControl("<br/>"));
            this.Controls.Add(myButton);

            myButton.Click += new EventHandler(myButton_Click);
        }

void myButton_Click(object sender, EventArgs e)
        {
            //Be sure to update the server reference
            //below to point to your server.
            using (SPEntityModelDataContext dataContext =
                new SPEntityModelDataContext
                ("http://intranet.contoso.com"))
            {
                var salesInfo = from data in dataContext.Sales
                                select data;

                foreach (var salesItem in salesInfo)
                {
                    listTitles.Items.Add(salesItem.Title.ToString() + " | " +
                        salesItem.CustomerType.ToString());
                }
            }
        }
    }
}
```

11. Edit the `.webpart` file to include the following bolded code:

```xml
<?xml version="1.0" encoding="utf-8"?>
<webParts>
  <webPart xmlns="http://schemas.microsoft.com/WebPart/v3">
    <metaData>
      <type name="MyFirstSPLinqProject.MySPLinqWebPart.MySPLinqWebPart,
          $SharePoint.Project.AssemblyFullName$" />
      <importErrorMessage>$Resources:core,ImportErrorMessage;</importErrorMessage>
    </metaData>
    <data>
      <properties>
        <property name="Title" type="string">Customer Types</property>
        <property name="Description" type="string">Web Part that lists customers
            and customer types (using SP LINQ).</property>
      </properties>
    </data>
  </webPart>
</webParts>
```

12. When finished, click Build ⇨ Deploy Solution.

13. After the Web part successfully builds and deploys, navigate to the home site on your team site and click Site Actions ⇨ Edit Page. Click on the wiki portion of the page, and click Insert ⇨ Web Part.

14. Click the Custom category. Select the Customer Types Web part and click Add.

15. When the Web part is added to the page and you click Get Lists, it should look similar to Figure 4-13.

FIGURE 4-13 Finished Web part

How It Works

You used the standard Web part in this walkthrough, which, as discussed earlier in the chapter, is the most common, baseline Web part you can create and deploy to SharePoint. However, one of the key elements in this exercise was the fact that you ran SPMetal against your SharePoint site. Doing this creates an entity model of all of the lists in your site — which essentially means that you now have strongly typed objects that you can query using LINQ. One optimization you gain by running SPMetal against your site is the capability to query a strongly types object with LINQ, as opposed to populating a list collection of custom items first, and running LINQ against that list collection.

The key lines of code in the sample application are those within the `using` statement, which set the context for the application code to use the `dataContext` object (which SPMetal generated for you). The bolded code within the following `using` statement issued the LINQ query (the equivalent of a `SELECT *` SQL statement) against the `Sales` list, and then iterated through each record in the returned data (`sales-Info`) and added the `Title` and `CustomerType` to the list.

```
...
using (SPEntityModelDataContext dataContext =
    new SPEntityModelDataContext
    ("http://intranet.contoso.com"))
        {
```

```
                    var salesInfo = from data in dataContext.Sales
                                select data;

                    foreach (var salesItem in salesInfo)
                    {
                        listTitles.Items.Add(salesItem.Title.ToString() + " | " +
                            salesItem.CustomerType.ToString());
                    }
        ...


            }
        ...
```

The nice thing about using SPMetal is that you can generate an entity model for your SharePoint lists and, even if the data changes within your list, the entity model can still apply. If you do add lists to SharePoint, though, you'll want to regenerate the entity model using SPMetal.

CREATING EVENT RECEIVERS

SharePoint supports a wide array of event receivers. *Event receivers* are events that are triggered through a system or user action, such as updating a list or adding a new document to a document library. You can create event receivers for a wide variety of objects, such as lists, list items, sites, and so on.

For example, say that you want to load external data as additional company metadata (for example, company or national holidays) when a user creates a new calendar item. You can use an event receiver to load additional metadata into the calendar when the user creates a new calendar list item. You might also want to log a transaction when certain lists are updated, which is another effective way to use event receivers.

You can also build event receivers against feature activations or deactivations if you want. This can be particularly handy when you need to clean up dependent features or assemblies when a feature is activated or deactivated. The event receiver can help remove any ancillary files or dependent Web parts from the Web Part Gallery or the file system.

Event receivers are very easy to build and deploy to SharePoint. You create event receivers using a Visual Studio 2010 Event Receiver project or item template.

Let's create a simple event receiver to get you familiar with the process.

TRY IT OUT   Creating a Simple Event Receiver

Code file [SimpleEventReceiver.zip] available for download at Wrox.com.

Event receivers are effective ways to add triggers into your SharePoint solutions. To create a simple event receiver, follow these steps:

1. Open your SharePoint site and create a new list called `TestList`. Leave the new list with only the default `Title` column.

2. Open Visual Studio 2010 and click File ⇨ New Project. Select Event Receiver in the SharePoint 2010 project template folder.

3. Provide a name for your project (for example, `SimpleEventReceiver`), and click OK. Set the project security level to farm level by selecting "Deploy as farm solution" and then click Next.

4. When prompted in the wizard, select the List Item Events option under the type of event receiver you want to associate your event with. Select the `Announcements` list under the event source and "An Item is being added" as the specific event.

5. Click Finish.

6. In the `SimpleEventReceiver.cs` file, add the following bolded code. This will apply some of the code discussed thus far and add a new list item in another list.

```csharp
using System;
using System.Security.Permissions;
using Microsoft.SharePoint;
using Microsoft.SharePoint.Security;
using Microsoft.SharePoint.Utilities;
using Microsoft.SharePoint.Workflow;

namespace SimpleEventReceiver.EventReceiver1
{
    public class EventReceiver1 : SPItemEventReceiver
    {
        public override void ItemAdding(SPItemEventProperties properties)
        {
            string eventName = "Event List: ";
            base.ItemAdding(properties);
            logAnAnnouncement(properties, eventName);
        }

        private void logAnAnnouncement(SPItemEventProperties properties,
            string eventName)
        {
            string listTitle = properties.List.Title;
            //Be sure to replace the URL reference below with your
            //SharePoint server URL.
            string mySiteURL = "http://intranet.contoso.com";
            DateTime currentDate = DateTime.Now;

            using (SPSite mySiteCollection = new SPSite(mySiteURL))
            {
                using (SPWeb mySPSite = mySiteCollection.RootWeb)
                {
                    SPList mySPList = mySPSite.Lists["TestList"];
                    SPListItem newListItem = mySPList.Items.Add();
                    newListItem["Title"] = eventName + listTitle + " @ " +
                        currentDate.ToLongTimeString();
                    newListItem.Update();
                }
            }
        }
    }
}
```

7. Click Build ⇨ Deploy Solution to build and deploy the event receiver project to your SharePoint site.

8. Navigate to the `Announcements` list, and click Add Item to add a new announcement. When you are finished, click Save.

9. Navigate to the `TestList` list, and you will see a new list item.

How It Works

An event receiver is, in essence, a custom DLL that is deployed to the global assembly cache (GAC) on your SharePoint server. Using the project template, Visual Studio creates a feature that then references the custom assembly in the GAC when the action that triggers the event occurs.

In this example, you added an event that is triggered whenever someone adds an event to the `Announcements` list. Specifically, the `ItemAdding` event was a default event handler that was created. It is here that you can add your code. For example, in the following snippet, the bolded method (`logAnAnnouncementEvent`) is a method you added that will contain your event handler code. You'll note that you're passing the properties of the event, which you can use when building out your event handler code, and the string `eventName`.

```
...
        public override void ItemAdding(SPItemEventProperties properties)
        {
            string eventName = "Event List: ";
            base.ItemAdding(properties);
            logAnAnnouncement(properties, eventName);
        }
...
```

Within the `logAnAnnouncementEvent` page, you can see that the one property used is the `Title` of the `List`, which is then stored in the `listTitle` object. You're also adding a date-stamp, and then converting that to a long string when adding the list item to the `TestList` list.

```
        private void logAnAnnouncement(SPItemEventProperties properties,
            string eventName)
        {
            string listTitle = properties.List.Title;
            //Be sure to replace the URL reference below with your
            //SharePoint server URL.
            string mySiteURL = "http://intranet.contoso.com";
            DateTime currentDate = DateTime.Now;

            using (SPSite mySiteCollection = new SPSite(mySiteURL))
            {
                using (SPWeb mySPSite = mySiteCollection.RootWeb)
                {
                    SPList mySPList = mySPSite.Lists["TestList"];
                    SPListItem newListItem = mySPList.Items.Add();
                    newListItem["Title"] = eventName + listTitle + " @ " +
                        currentDate.ToLongTimeString();
```

```
                         newListItem.Update();
              }
         }
   }
```

Most of the other code should now be familiar to you, since you've already seen how you add an item to a list. As you explore event receivers, be sure to try out some other types of events that are more complex and involve other parts of the SharePoint site — or external data that can be leveraged within your SharePoint site.

CREATING ASPX PAGES

For those who are familiar with ASP.NET, you'll recognize the `.aspx` file extension. This is an ASP.NET Web page. Because SharePoint is built on ASP.NET, you'll find the individual pages within SharePoint are this specific type.

What sets SharePoint `aspx` pages apart from other ASP.NET sites is that you get more capabilities built into a SharePoint page when you create it. For example, SharePoint ships with a number of capabilities such as edit functionality and Web part capabilities. When you create a new `aspx` page, it inherits features, and loads and registers dependent assemblies that are required to render the page (and controls on that page) correctly.

For example, if you examine the code in the following default Web part `aspx` page, you'll see that there exists a number of directives that register specific assemblies to the page. SharePoint requires that these directives exist. Now, don't worry. You won't have to memorize what all of these are. SharePoint Designer creates a lot of these for you by default, so that you can focus on page creation and customization.

```
<%-- _lcid="1033" _version="14.0.4736" _dal="1" --%>
<%-- _LocalBinding --%>
<%@ Page language="C#" MasterPageFile="~masterurl/default.master"
     Inherits="Microsoft.SharePoint.WebPartPages.WebPartPage,
     Microsoft.SharePoint,Version=14.0.0.0,Culture=neutral,PublicKeyToken
     =71e9bce111e9429c" meta:webpartpageexpansion="full"
     meta:progid="SharePoint.WebPartPage.Document"  %>
<%@ Register Tagprefix="SharePoint" Namespace="Microsoft.SharePoint.WebControls"
     Assembly="Microsoft.SharePoint, Version=14.0.0.0, Culture=neutral,
     PublicKeyToken=71e9bce111e9429c" %>
<%@ Register Tagprefix="Utilities" Namespace="Microsoft.SharePoint.Utilities"
     Assembly="Microsoft.SharePoint, Version=14.0.0.0, Culture=neutral,
     PublicKeyToken=71e9bce111e9429c" %>
<%@ Import Namespace="Microsoft.SharePoint" %>
<%@ Assembly Name="Microsoft.Web.CommandUI, Version=14.0.0.0, Culture=neutral,
     PublicKeyToken=71e9bce111e9429c" %>
<%@ Register Tagprefix="WebPartPages" Namespace=
     "Microsoft.SharePoint.WebPartPages"
     Assembly="Microsoft.SharePoint, Version=14.0.0.0, Culture=neutral,
     PublicKeyToken=71e9bce111e9429c" %>
...
```

You can create a simple `aspx` page for SharePoint without any of the frills that the Web part pages deliver. The code for this type of page looks more readable, as the following snippet shows. However, note that it does not contain any of the standard SharePoint controls and does not inherit the structure and style that is laid out by the master page.

```
<!DOCTYPE html PUBLIC "-//W3C//DTD XHTML 1.0 Strict//EN"
      "http://www.w3.org/TR/xhtml1/DTD/xhtml1-strict.dtd">
<%@ Page Language="C#" %>
<html dir="ltr" xmlns="http://www.w3.org/1999/xhtml">
<head runat="server">
<meta name="WebPartPageExpansion" content="full" />
<meta http-equiv="Content-Type" content="text/html; charset=utf-8" />
<title>Untitled 1</title>
</head>
<body>
<form id="form1" runat="server">
</form>
</body>
</html>
```

While there are a couple of different paths to creating `aspx` pages for SharePoint, using SharePoint Designer 2010 is a straightforward way to create and edit them. This is because not only is code like this created for you, but there are also templates that you can use to create *Web part pages* — a special type of `aspx` page that have Web parts located in specific ways on the page (using different Web part zone layouts). You could alternatively use Visual Studio 2010 to create `aspx` pages, but you'd have to ensure that you added the previously indicated namespace registration directives manually, and then manually add the pages to the appropriate page on the site. By default, SharePoint Designer can save the `aspx` pages you create in a number of places (for example, the Site Assets library).

Beyond the assemblies that are registered through the directives, you also have HTML markup interlaced with `ContentPlaceHolder` controls and ASP.NET controls. Again, if you're familiar with ASP.NET, these concepts won't be new to you. If you're not, using `ContentPlaceHolder` controls and ASP.NET controls is how you render functional controls or applications on the `aspx` page.

For example, one of the default `ContentPlaceHolder` controls is the search control, which is expressed in the following code:

```
...
<asp:Content ContentPlaceHolderId="PlaceHolderSearchArea" runat="server">
    <SharePoint:DelegateControl runat="server" ControlId="SmallSearchInputBox"/>
</asp:Content>
...
```

Depending on the level of complexity of your `aspx` page, you might have more or fewer of these controls — some that work independently of one another and others that work hand in glove with one another.

SharePoint Designer 2010 provides quite a bit of control over your `aspx` pages. For example, Figure 4-14 shows the default view of the `aspx` page (also called a *site page*) in SharePoint Designer. You can see here that you can edit the permissions of the page. (SharePoint automatically inherits the permissions from the parent site when you create the page.) You can see the version history of the page, you can view and manage the properties of the page, and you can edit the page. Editing the `aspx` page provides you with a Design, Source, and Split view (which shows both the source code and design view), and you also have a Toolbox experience, where you can drag and drop controls onto the Designer as you create your `aspx` page.

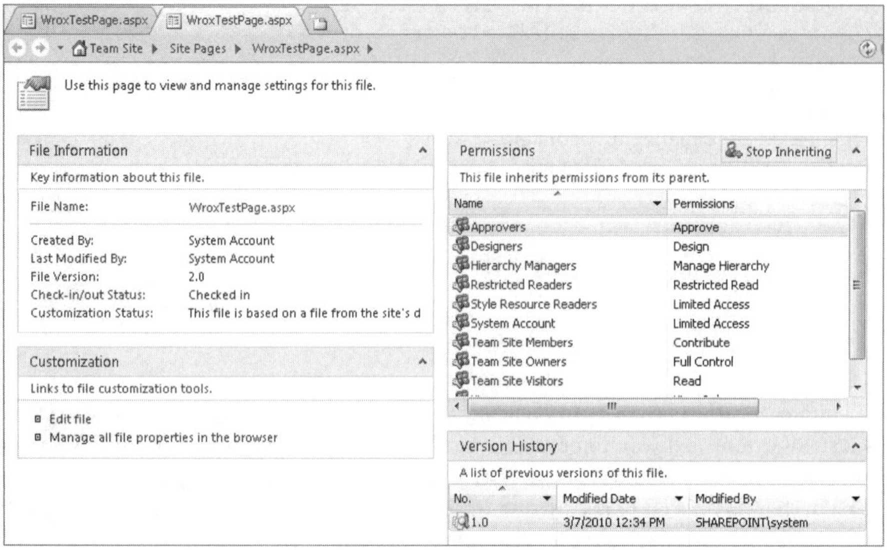

FIGURE 4-14 Creating a site page in SharePoint Designer

To get you started, let's create a simple `aspx` Web part page using SharePoint Designer 2010.

TRY IT OUT   Creating a Simple Web Part Page

Web part pages are a great way to create a predefined `aspx` page template that you can then customize. To create one, follow these steps:

1. Open your SharePoint site and click Site Actions ⇨ Edit with SharePoint Designer.

2. SharePoint Designer opens your SharePoint site and loads all of the options into the navigation pane.

3. Click the Site Pages link in the navigation pane.

4. Right-click the default file and select Rename. Provide a name for the page (for example, `WroxTestPage.aspx`).

5. Click Edit the File in the main window, and then change the view to Split view.

6. Click the View tab. Click Task Panes and select Toolbox. This opens the Toolbox, where you have some default controls to use. Inspect the different controls in the Toolbox. Note that the Page Fields and Content Fields are only accessible if you're creating a SharePoint site that is of type Publishing (that is, a WCM site).

7. Under the ASP.NET Standard controls, drag a drop-down list to one of the Web part zones. Click Edit Items, then add some sample items (for example, `Item_One`, `Item_Two`, and `Item_Three`) to the drop-down list.

8. When you are finished, click the Save icon in the upper-left hand corner, and then click Preview in Browser on the SharePoint Designer ribbon. Your simple `aspx` page should now look similar to Figure 4-15.

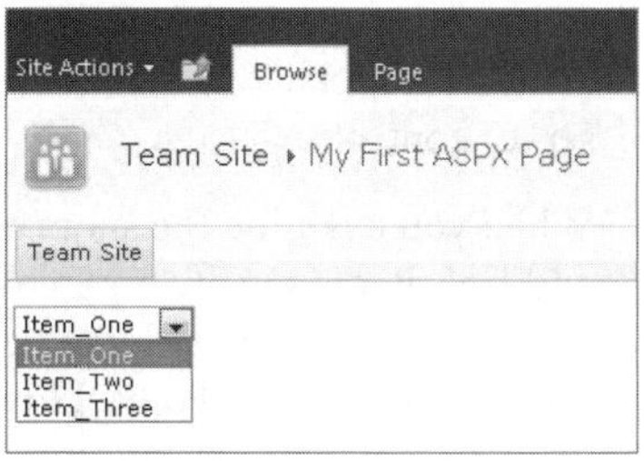

FIGURE 4-15 Simple Web part page with control

How It Works

ASP.NET implicitly understands how to handle and render `aspx` pages. You can also create and render a wide array of controls on an `aspx` page. In this example, you used a simple drop-down list control and added some hard-coded controls to the drop-down list. You then added that control to the `aspx` page. You could similarly add other types of controls to the `aspx` page.

CREATING MASTER PAGES

Master pages are an ASP.NET creation that SharePoint inherits from being built on ASP.NET. SharePoint uses master pages to provide a consistent structure and layout for each of the pages in a SharePoint site. Similar to a single CSS file providing structure for many Web pages, a single master page can serve multiple sites, and define the look, feel, and behavior that you want for all of the pages of that site. Using the master page as the structural foundation of your site, you can then add other content, custom applications, or Web parts to your SharePoint site.

When you install SharePoint, it installs a small set of master pages to your SharePoint site by default. You can then create a copy of the `default.master` master page and customize it to your liking, or add a new, custom master page that provides the branding and behavior you want for your SharePoint site. SharePoint Designer 2010 provides some great capabilities for managing, creating, and editing master pages. For example, you can edit and view your changes from within SharePoint Designer and then check the page in for approval to your SharePoint site.

When a user navigates to a SharePoint site, the site or content page references a master page, which is then merged with the site page. This produces an output that combines the layout of the master page with the content from the site page. If you remember the discussion earlier in the chapter on site pages, the master page was included as a part of the page directives. The following bolded code shows a token reference (the token being `~masterurl/default.master`) to the master page that was used for that site:

```
...
<%@ Page language="C#" MasterPageFile="~masterurl/default.master"
    Inherits="Microsoft.SharePoint.WebPartPages.WebPartPage,
    Microsoft.SharePoint,Version=14.0.0.0,Culture=neutral,
    PublicKeyToken=71e9bce111e9429c" meta:webpartpageexpansion="full"
    meta:progid="SharePoint.WebPartPage.Document"  %>
...
```

A master page is characterized by the `.master` file extension. The master page itself can contain an array of objects. For example, the master page can contain HTML, JavaScript, CSS, and ASP.NET server controls.

When you examine the syntax of the master page, you'll see text and controls that will render a look and feel that is specific to SharePoint. This is especially true when you look at the `default.master` master page, which includes all of the breadcrumbs and default menu and navigation options that are specific to SharePoint. However, you'll also see a series of `ContentPlaceHolder` objects (which were discussed earlier) within a master page, which define regions where content or controls can appear.

When you're customizing SharePoint master pages, there is a set of `ContentPlaceHolder` controls that you need to have on the page (for example, global breadcrumb, top-level navigation, search, and title). You can add more `ContentPlaceHolder` controls than are required by default. However, you cannot remove the ones that are required, or else your content or site pages may fail to render.

> **NOTE** *For the complete list of required controls, go to the MSDN article at* `http://msdn.microsoft.com/en-us/library/ms467402.aspx.`

The following code snippet shows some of the different items that you can embed within a SharePoint master page. Note that these are taken from the `default.master`, which ships with all versions of SharePoint 2010. You can explore the full set of code and controls that ship with this master page by reviewing the file from within SharePoint Designer.

```
<%@ Master Language="C#" %>
<%@ Register Tagprefix="SharePoint" Namespace="Microsoft.SharePoint.WebControls"
    Assembly="Microsoft.SharePoint, Version=14.0.0.0, Culture=neutral,
    PublicKeyToken=71e9bce111e9429c" %> <%@ Register Tagprefix="Utilities"
    Namespace="Microsoft.SharePoint.Utilities" Assembly="Microsoft.SharePoint,
    Version=14.0.0.0, Culture=neutral, PublicKeyToken=71e9bce111e9429c" %>
...
<title id="onetidTitle"><asp:ContentPlaceHolder id="PlaceHolderPageTitle"
    runat="server"/>
</title>
<SharePoint:CssLink runat="server" Alternate="true"/>
<SharePoint:Theme runat="server"/>
<SharePoint:CssRegistration Name="minimalv4.css" runat="server"/>
<SharePoint:CssRegistration Name="layouts.css" runat="server"/>
<SharePoint:ULSClientConfig runat="server"/>
...
<span class="s4-notdlg">
<a href="javascript:;" onclick="javascript:this.href='#mainContent';" class="ms-
    SkiptoMainContent" accesskey="<%$Resources:wss,
    maincontent_accesskey%>" runat="server">
<SharePoint:EncodedLiteral runat="server" text="<%$Resources:wss,
    mainContentLink%>" EncodeMethod="HtmlEncode"/>
```

```
</a>
</span>
…
<asp:ContentPlaceHolder id="PlaceHolderWelcomeMenu" runat="server">
<div class="lb ms-mini-trcMenu">
<wssuc:Welcome id="IdWelcome" runat="server" EnableViewState="false">
</wssuc:Welcome>
<wssuc:MUISelector runat="server"/>
</div>
</asp:ContentPlaceHolder>
…
<div>
<asp:ContentPlaceHolder id="PlaceHolderTitleBreadcrumb" runat="server" />
</div>
…
<div id="DeveloperDashboard" class="ms-developerdashboard">
<SharePoint:DeveloperDashboard runat="server"/>
</div>
…
</body>
</html>
```

When managing your master pages, you'll want to be very mindful of any changes you make to the existing master pages. In fact, at all costs, avoid editing any of the default master pages that ship with SharePoint. Always copy and edit renamed copies so that you never lose a snapshot to which you can safely return. Also, if you will be doing a lot of master page customization in the future, start with a minimal master page (which contains the bare minimum set of controls necessary for a SharePoint site), and add onto that as practice to get familiar with how they work.

Let's check out how to edit a master page.

TRY IT OUT **Editing a Custom Master Page**

Master pages provide a great way to structure and brand your SharePoint site. To edit a custom master page, follow these steps:

1. Open your SharePoint site.

2. Click Site Settings ⇨ "Edit in SharePoint Designer."

3. After SharePoint Designer opens, click the Master Pages link to view all of the master pages that are saved to SharePoint.

4. Click the v4.master master page, and then select Edit File. Do not check out the file.

5. Select all of the text in v4.master, and then copy it to your clipboard. Close the file without saving it.

6. Click the Blank Master Page button on the main ribbon. Select all of the default code and delete it. Copy the v4.master code from your clipboard to the new master page file.

7. Save the file and provide a name you'll remember (for example, MyNewMasterPage.master).

8. Somewhere after the `body` element, add some arbitrary text. For example, add a short message in between the `<H1>` tags, as shown in the following bolded code snippet:

```
...
<a id="HiddenAnchor" href="javascript:;" style="display:none;"></a>
<SharePoint:DelegateControl runat="server" ControlId="GlobalNavigation"/>
<h1>Hello there!</h1>
<div id="s4-ribbonrow" class="s4-pr s4-ribbonrowhidetitle">
...
```

9. Save your new master page, then right-click the master page in the navigation pane and select Check In.

10. Select "Publish a major version," as shown in Figure 4-16. When prompted to approve the master page, click Yes. This automatically invokes a SharePoint master page approval page, where you will find your new master page listed at the top of the page.

11. Click the drop-down menu beside the master page. Select Approve and select the Approved radio button. Click OK. Your master page is now saved and approved in SharePoint.

12. Navigate to your top-level site collection, and click Site Actions ⇨ Site Settings.

13. Under Look and Feel, select the Master Pages link. For both the Site and System Master Page settings, select your new master page from the drop-down menu.

14. Click OK.

15. When you navigate back to the master page, you will see whatever text you entered on the page rendered, as shown in Figure 4-17. Any site that you create using this master page will have this text on it.

FIGURE 4-16 Publishing a master page

FIGURE 4-17 New master page rendered in SharePoint

How It Works

The master page can be a tricky part of SharePoint. Understanding what `ContentPlaceHolder` controls are required, the structure and layout, and how to add code takes a little practice. Furthermore, you may find yourself needing to brush up on some design elements as you build CSS into your master page. However, the resulting master page can be very compelling and useful as you apply structure and branding across your site.

In this example, you created a simple amendment to an existing master page and then applied that master page using the options within SharePoint. Thus, when SharePoint rendered the page, it changed the master page token to point to your newly amended master page.

The text amendment (that is, "Hello There!") used as an example here is vaguely interesting; a more interesting amendment would be the addition of an image or even some JavaScript to enhance the page. You'll be amazed at what you can do to alter the branding of a page by using some of the native themes that ship with SharePoint and some artistic images such as logos or photos.

SUMMARY

This chapter presented a few of the more common developer tasks that you'll find yourself doing in SharePoint 2010. The chapter covered standard and visual Web parts (you'll see detailed coverage of these two types of Web parts in Chapter 6), as well as Data View Web parts, to provide some discussion of customizing your Web parts. This chapter also covered customizing lists by using site columns and content types, and discussed how you can leverage the SharePoint object model and Web services to interact with SharePoint data. The chapter also provided some coverage of event receivers and showed you how you can create a custom `aspx` page and master page.

As you move throughout this book, you'll see many of the topics covered in this chapter resurface as you write more code and explore more of the programmatic capabilities that SharePoint has to offer. For example, in Chapter 5, you'll see more coverage on how you interact with lists, and you'll learn about the client object model, ASP.NET Web services, server object model, and custom Web services in greater detail.

EXERCISES

1. Using Visual Studio 2010, create a simple standard Web part and Visual Web part using the code snippets in this chapter.

2. Create a calculated site column for the `Sales` list that leverages the `Total Sales` column to calculate tax based on a 7 percent state tax for all states.

3. Create a custom `aspx` page that leverages two or more controls from the ASP.NET Toolbox, and publish it to SharePoint.

4. Create a simple master page that has a logo and some header text. Use the minimal master page that ships with SharePoint.

▶ **WHAT YOU LEARNED IN THIS CHAPTER**

ITEM	DESCRIPTION
Web Part	SharePoint is built on the ASP.NET framework and provides different types of Web parts to use when building solutions. This chapter introduced the standard Web part (baseline Web part available in SharePoint), Visual Web part (adds a Designer experience for the UI to standard Web parts), and Data View Web parts (expose list data in a custom-formatted way).
Site Column	Custom column that can be reused across a SharePoint site.
Content Type	Custom object with metadata that can range from predefined columns to custom documents that can be reused across a SharePoint site.
List	Standard way of representing data in SharePoint.
Event Receiver	An event that is triggered when the system or user performs an action.
aspx Page	The standard page in SharePoint. Built on ASP.NET, SharePoint supports simple aspx pages (no controls) or more complex pages that come predefined with controls and layouts (for example, a Web part page).
Master Page	A master page provides a single point of branding and structure that can be leveraged across a SharePoint site.

RECOMMENDED READING

➤ Channel 9 Learning Course on Lists and Events at `http://channel9.msdn.com/learn/courses/SharePoint2010Developer/ListsAndSchemas/`

➤ ASP.NET master pages overview at `http://msdn.microsoft.com/en-us/library/wtxbf3hh.aspx`

➤ SharePoint master page article at `http://msdn.microsoft.com/en-us/library/ms467402.aspx`

5

Programming Against SharePoint 2010 Lists

WHAT YOU'LL LEARN IN THIS CHAPTER:

➤ Understanding the structure and function of a SharePoint 2010 list

➤ Programming against SharePoint lists through client- and server-side object models, ASP.NET Web services, WCF, and RESTful services

➤ Understanding when to use one method over the other

➤ Developing against SharePoint 2010 lists

In Chapter 2, you were introduced to the SharePoint list from both the end-user perspective and the developer perspective. You were also introduced to a simple application that interacted with a list programmatically.

This chapter dives into more detail about the list and will provide you with some additional information about the different ways in which you can programmatically interact with a list (specifically, reading and writing items). You will learn about different application programming interfaces (APIs) and ways to develop against a list. This chapter also provides you with an introduction to list events and teaches you how to create and exploit them.

OVERVIEW OF SHAREPOINT LISTS

In addition to the Web part, the list will be one of the more common objects you code against in SharePoint (and one of the most commonly used artifacts by end users). A *list* is essentially a type of data structure in SharePoint. A list represents a collection of items comprising objects of similar types. Similar in structure and behavior to a database, a SharePoint list contains rows, columns, and fields. It can react to events you customize and deploy into SharePoint.

The data in a list is referred to as a *list item*. A list item comprises a field, and fields contain specific data. Each field within a list item has a specific field type, such as "Single line of text" or Choice. For example, Figure 5-1 shows the default options that are available to you when you create a list and then add columns to that list from the SharePoint Web interface.

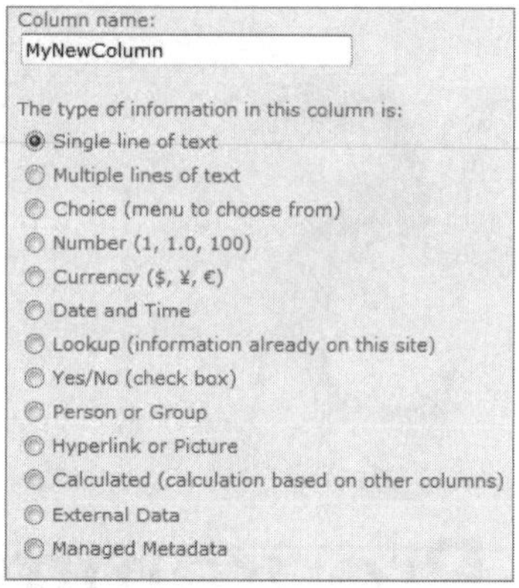

You can create a list through the Internet browser interface, programmatically through an array of APIs, through a Web service, or through defining the list by an XML schema, and then deploying to your SharePoint site. (The out-of-the-box lists are essentially list templates that have a predefined schema.)

There are many types of lists in SharePoint. For example, there is a Calendar list that supports calendar functionality (and

FIGURE 5-1 Column field types

synchronizes with Outlook), an Announcements list that stores announcements you'd like to display on your site, and a Tasks list that enables you to create tasks and delegate to people in your organization. Lists also include *document libraries*, which is where you store files and metadata. Furthermore, you can map workflow and event receivers to lists or even list items (as you'll see later in this chapter) that react to actions such as creating, deleting, or updating items. You can also customize filters for lists and create views that are specific to your liking.

While many of the out-of-the-box lists ship as a predefined structures, you can also customize a list. You did this in Chapter 4 when you created a content type, site column, and custom column, which you then used to create the list. This list, known as the Custom list, is a versatile list because you define it however you want.

A Custom list can be as simple or as complex as you want. For example, Table 5-1 shows the structure of a simple Custom list structure called `Customers` that contains a set of list items. The list items are made up of `Customer Name` and `Customer Email`. Each of the fields within the list items are of the "Single line of text" data type, and each field within the list item contains data (for example, `John Doe` and `John.doe@acme.com`). Table 5-1 illustrates what the `Customers` list might look like with three mock records.

TABLE 5-1 Sample List — Customers

CUSTOMER NAME	CUSTOMER EMAIL
John Doe	John.doe@acme.com
Jane Doe	Jane.doe@acme.com
Jim Doe	Jim.doe@acme.com

Another (more advanced) type of Custom list is the External list. The External list dynamically loads data from external data sources into a SharePoint list. It can connect to different service connections such as Windows Communication Foundation (WCF) or ASP.NET, and can also be programmed against using a standard set of APIs. External lists are covered in greater detail in Chapter 8.

Regardless of whether a list is a custom or standard list, you can program against a list. And, as mentioned earlier, SharePoint offers multiple points of entry for the developer to program against a list. When programming against lists, you can think of the data as living within a specific object within the list. For example, Figure 5-2 shows you a simple taxonomy of how you might conceptually get at the specific data within a list.

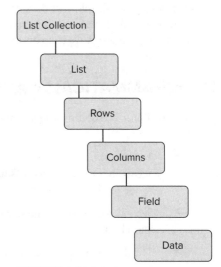

While the structure of lists may look like databases, they are quite a bit different. For example, you would expect to find much more transactional and referential integrity in a SQL Server database than in a list, as well as tools-specific support for database administrators and a richer query model. However, lists can be very useful when displaying data in SharePoint, and, as you'll see, have a straightforward method for extensibility.

FIGURE 5-2 List structure

While Figure 5-2 illustrates the conceptual structure of a list, the way in which you programmatically interact with the list is a little different. For example, while the list collection comprises one or more lists, the column is one of the constituent components of the list, and the rows are just instances of the different columns that make up that list. Further, the data lives in the field within the column. For example, let's say you want to traverse a list. Using a specific set of objects within the SharePoint object model, you can access methods and properties to iterate through a SharePoint Web site to get all of the lists in that site, or iterate through a list to get all of the rows (or `SPListItems`) in that list, among many other programmatic activities.

Figure 5-3 shows an example of the SharePoint object model hierarchy starting with the `SPSite` object as your point of entry.

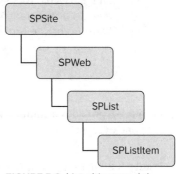

To put the object model hierarchy shown in Figure 5-3 to practice, the following code snippet sets the `SPSite` object to the current SharePoint site collection, sets the list to a specific list, and then creates a CAML query to query against that list to get all results in the list that are greater than 10. (CAML, which stands for Collaborative Application Markup Language, is the XML query structure that you use when querying SharePoint data.) As illustrated in the following code snippet, you build CAML constructs, and then use the SharePoint API to interact with the list.

FIGURE 5-3 List object model

```
...
SPSite mySPSiteCollection = SPContext.Current.Site;
SPList mySPList = mySPSiteCollection.AllWebs["Sales"].Lists["Products"];

SPQuery myCAMLQuery = new SPQuery();
myCAMLQuery.Query = "<Where><Gt><FieldRef Name='Price'/>" +
    "<Value Type='Number'>10</Value></Gt></Where>";
SPListItemCollection mySPListCollection = mySPList.GetItems(myCAMLQuery);
...
```

This example is simple, but illustrative, of one way in which you can interact with SharePoint list data. As you'll see throughout this chapter, lists are versatile data structures in SharePoint, and there are many different ways to program against them as well. So, let's get started!

PROGRAMMATICALLY ACCESSING LISTS

In SharePoint 2010 you programmatically access and code against lists in a number of different ways:

➤ You use the `Microsoft.SharePoint` namespace (that is, the server-side object model) to access lists on the server. What this means, though, is that any application you build must reside (or be consumed) on the server that it is accessing.

➤ Second, you can use the Lists Web service — an ASP.NET Web service that ships with SharePoint.

➤ Third, you can build a custom ASP.NET Web service that you deploy to Internet Information Services (IIS), or deploy into the SharePoint file system (for example, into the `ISAPI` folder).

➤ Fourth, you can build a custom WCF service that you deploy to IIS or to the SharePoint root.

➤ Fifth, you can also use the SharePoint client object model, which supports remote programmatic access to lists from Silverlight, .NET, and JavaScript applications.

➤ Lastly, you can use REST APIs that provide lightweight access to SharePoint list data.

> **NOTE** *SharePoint is flexible in that you can deploy a custom ASP.NET or WCF Web service directly into the SharePoint root to interact with your list. While this is a convenient way to take advantage of being a "trusted" service within SharePoint, the drawback is that if you ever upgrade your SharePoint server, you run the risk of having your custom Web services deleted from the* `vti_bin` *or* `layouts` *folder.*

Table 5-2 provides a summary of each of the options available to you and indicates when you might use one over the other.

TABLE 5-2 SharePoint List APIs/Services

TYPE OF SERVICE/API	WHEN TO USE
Server-side object model	Core SharePoint DLL that is used for building applications that are deployed to or reside (or consumed) on the server.
Client object model	Client-based DLL used for coding against SharePoint on remote clients. It is supported in .NET, Silverlight, and JavaScript applications.

TYPE OF SERVICE/API	WHEN TO USE
WCF Data Services	REST-based service that provides lightweight GET and POST functionality against a SharePoint list. You use this service to interact with Excel spreadsheets. (Note that the WCF Data Services were formerly called ADO.NET Data Services.)
Lists Web service	ASP.NET Web service that provides legacy service functionality for interacting with lists. Good for rapid development and deployment, as well as service-based applications.
Custom WCF service	Option where you design a custom WCF service application and deploy into the SharePoint hive or IIS. This is useful when you require a custom service because the functionality does not exist within SharePoint.
Custom ASP.NET service	Option where you design a custom ASP.NET service application and deploy it in the SharePoint hive or IIS. This is useful when you require a custom service because the functionality does not exist within SharePoint.

After you programmatically access a SharePoint list using any one of the methods shown in Table 5-2, you can then begin to write solutions that leverage the list in different ways. For example, you can use the different methods to issue, create, read, update, and delete capabilities, or you can add more complex events that interact with other parts of the SharePoint object model, or even initiate a workflow that manages business processes through system or user interaction with the list.

Let's examine each of the methods introduced in Table 5-2 and discuss how you can use each method to program against SharePoint lists.

Programming Against Lists Using the Server-Side Object Model

One way to develop applications against a SharePoint list is to leverage the `Microsoft .SharePoint` namespace (the server-side object model). Using the `Microsoft.SharePoint` namespace is relatively easy. However, it is predominantly used for applications that reside on the server.

Before you start the walkthrough, you'll need to create a simple list in your SharePoint site called `Products`. You can create this manually by navigating to your SharePoint site and clicking Site Actions ➪ View All Site Content. Then click Create ➪ Lists ➪ Custom List. Enter **Products** as the name of the list and click Create. After the site is created, you'll want to add two more columns beyond the `Title` column. To add two columns, click the List tab, and then List Settings ➪ Create Column. Add a column named `Product_SKU` and another column named `Price`. You can leave both columns with the default "Single line of text" type. After you create the list, you are now ready to begin the walkthrough.

> **NOTE** *In this first walkthrough, you'll create a very simple WPF application that interacts with a SharePoint list. The goal of the walkthrough is less about the application and more about you learning how to use the SharePoint server-side object model. You saw the server object model being used in Chapter 4, so think of this as another way to leverage the object model.*

TRY IT OUT Programming Against Lists Using the Server-Side Object Model

Code file [SPListApp.zip] available for download at Wrox.com.

The list is a core artifact in SharePoint. The server-side object model is one way of interacting with a list. You can build different types of applications that live on the server and interact with the server object model, such as WinForm or WPF utility tools, Web parts, or event receivers. To build a WPF application that interacts with a list using the server-side object model, follow these steps:

1. Open Visual Studio and click File ➪ New ➪ Project ➪ WPF Application. Ensure that you select .NET Framework 3.5 in the drop-down menu at the top of the New Project dialog, or else you will have compilation issues when building your application.

2. Give your project a name (for example, `WPFSPTestApp`), and click OK.

3. When your solution is set up, right-click the project and select Add Reference. Select the Browse tab and then browse to `c:\Program Files\Common Files\Microsoft Shared\Web Server Extensions\14\ISAPI`. Select the `Microsoft.SharePoint.dll` and click OK.

4. Right-click the `MainWindow.xaml` and select View Designer. Add five labels, five textboxes, and three buttons. Arrange the controls on the designer as shown in Figure 5-4.

Table 5-3 shows the control type and the name of the controls that you should add to the WPF designer.

TABLE 5-3 Control Types for WPF Application

CONTROL TYPE	CONTROL NAME
Label	`lblSPUrl, lblListName, lblProductSKU, lblProdName, lblProductPrice`
Textbox	`txtbxSPURL, txtbxListName, txtbxProductSku, txtbxProductPrice`
Button	`btnLoad, btnClear, btnExit`

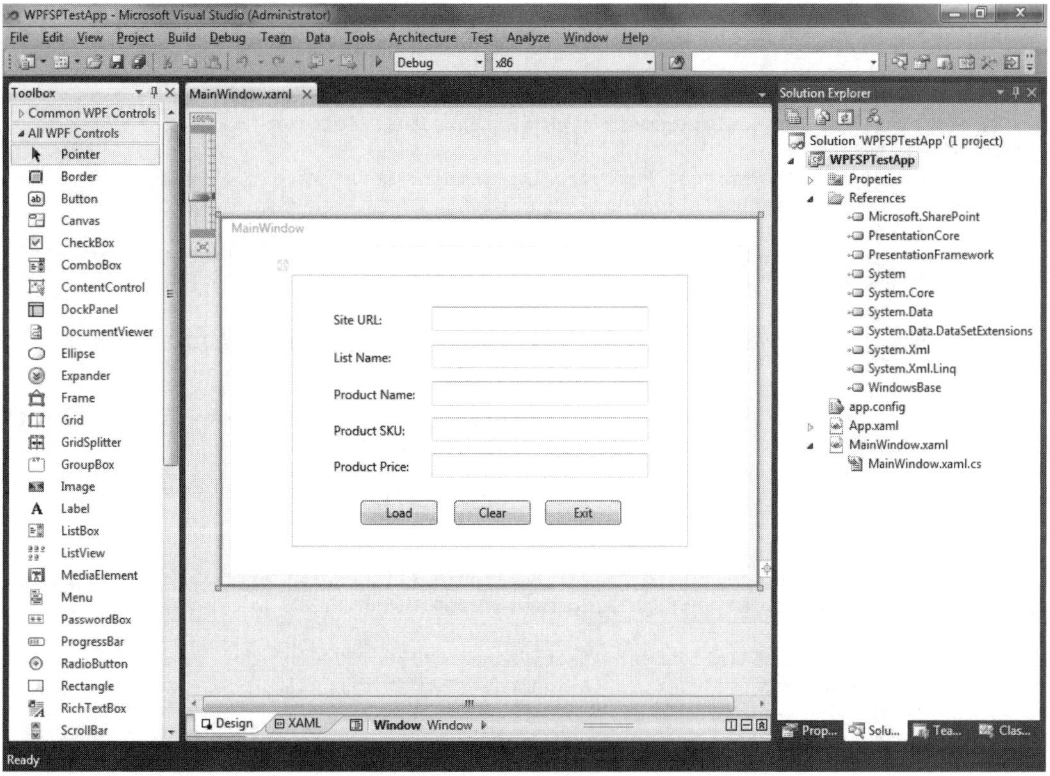

FIGURE 5-4 WPF Client UI for server-side object model list call

The XAML that corresponds to this UI is as follows:

```xaml
<Window x:Class="WPFSPTestApp.MainWindow"
        xmlns="http://schemas.microsoft.com/winfx/2006/xaml/presentation"
        xmlns:x="http://schemas.microsoft.com/winfx/2006/xaml"
        Title="MainWindow" Height="350" Width="525">
<Grid Width="387" Height="258">
        <Label
Content="Site URL:"  Height="28" HorizontalAlignment="Left" Margin="36,30,0,0"
Name="lblSPURL" VerticalAlignment="Top" Width="94" />
        <TextBox
Height="23" HorizontalAlignment="Left" Margin="136,30,0,0"
Name="txtbxSPURL" VerticalAlignment="Top" Width="212" />
        <Label
Content="List Name:"Height="28" HorizontalAlignment="Left" Margin="36,66,0,0"
Name="lblListName" VerticalAlignment="Top" Width="94" />
        <TextBox
Height="23" HorizontalAlignment="Left" Margin="136,66,0,0"
Name="txtbxListName" VerticalAlignment="Top" Width="212" />
        <Label
Content="Product Name:"Height="28" HorizontalAlignment="Left" Margin="590,230,0,0"
Name="lblProductSKU" VerticalAlignment="Top" Width="94" />
        <TextBox
```

```
Height="23" Margin="0,101,39,0" Name="txtbxProdName"
VerticalAlignment="Top" HorizontalAlignment="Right" Width="212" />
        <Button
Content="Load" Height="23" HorizontalAlignment="Left" Margin="67,214,0,0"
Name="btnLoad" VerticalAlignment="Top" Width="75" Click="btnLoad_Click" />
        <Button
Content="Clear" Height="23" HorizontalAlignment="Left" Margin="158,214,0,0"
Name="btnClear" VerticalAlignment="Top" Width="75" Click="btnClear_Click" />
        <Button
Content="Exit" Height="23" HorizontalAlignment="Left" Margin="247,214,0,0"
Name="btnExit" VerticalAlignment="Top" Width="75" Click="btnExit_Click" />
        <Label
Content="Product Name:"Height="28" HorizontalAlignment="Left" Margin="36,101,0,0"
Name="lblProdName" VerticalAlignment="Top" Width="120" />
        <Label
Content="Product SKU:" Height="28" HorizontalAlignment="Left" Margin="36,135,0,0"
Name="lblProductSku" VerticalAlignment="Top" Width="120" />
        <TextBox
Height="23" HorizontalAlignment="Left" Margin="136,135,0,0"
Name="txtbxProductSku"VerticalAlignment="Top" Width="212" />
        <Label
Content="Product Price:" Height="28" HorizontalAlignment="Left" Margin="36,169,0,0"
Name="lblProductPrice" VerticalAlignment="Top" Width="120" />
        <TextBox
Height="23" HorizontalAlignment="Left" Margin="136,169,0,0"
Name="txtbxProductPrice" VerticalAlignment="Top" Width="212" />
    </Grid>
</Window>
```

5. Double-click the Exit button and add the following code to exit the application:

    ```
    ...
    private void btnExit_Click(object sender, RoutedEventArgs e)
        {
            Application.Current.Shutdown();
        }
    ...
    ```

6. Double-click the Clear button and add the following code to clear the fields:

    ```
    ...
    private void btnClear_Click(object sender, RoutedEventArgs e)
        {
            txtbxListName.Text = "";
            txtbxSPURL.Text = "";
            txtbxProdName.Text = "";
            txtbxProductSku.Text = "";
            txtbxProductPrice.Text = "";

        }
    ...
    ```

7. While still in the `Windows.xaml.cs` code behind, add the following `using` statement at the top of the application:

    ```
    using Microsoft.SharePoint;
    ```

8. Add the following five class-level variables (boldfaced in the following code), which represent the user input, and then navigate back to the Designer view:

...

```
public partial class MainWindow : Window
{

    string strSPSiteURL = "";
    string strSPListName = "";
    string strProductName = "";
    string strProductSKU = "";
    string strProductPrice = "";


}
```
...

9. Double-click the Load button and add the following code to add a new record to a SharePoint list:

```
...
private void btnLoad_Click(object sender, RoutedEventArgs e)
    {
        strSPSiteURL = txtbxSPURL.Text;
        strSPListName = txtbxListName.Text;
        strProductName = txtbxProdName.Text;
        strProductSKU = txtbxProductSku.Text;
        strProductPrice = txtbxProductPrice.Text;

        using (SPSite site = new SPSite(strSPSiteURL))
        {
            using (SPWeb web = site.OpenWeb())
            {
                web.AllowUnsafeUpdates = true;

                SPList list = web.Lists[strSPListName];
                SPListItem Item = list.Items.Add();
                Item["Title"] = strProductName;
                Item["Product_SKU"] = strProductSKU;
                Item["Price"] = strProductPrice;
                Item.Update();

                web.AllowUnsafeUpdates = false;
            }
        }

    }
...
```

10. The full application code listing (with the code you added listed in bold) for the code behind is as follows:

```
using System;
using System.Collections.Generic;
using System.Linq;
using System.Text;
using System.Windows;
```

```
using System.Windows.Controls;
using System.Windows.Data;
using System.Windows.Documents;
using System.Windows.Input;
using System.Windows.Media;
using System.Windows.Media.Imaging;
using System.Windows.Navigation;
using System.Windows.Shapes;
using Microsoft.SharePoint;

namespace WPFSPTestApp
{

    public partial class MainWindow : Window
    {
        string strSPSiteURL = "";
        string strSPListName = "";
        string strProductName = "";
        string strProductSKU = "";
        string strProductPrice = "";

        public MainWindow()
        {
            InitializeComponent();
        }

        private void btnExit_Click(object sender, RoutedEventArgs e)
        {
            Application.Current.Shutdown();
        }

        private void btnClear_Click(object sender, RoutedEventArgs e)
        {
            txtbxListName.Text = "";
            txtbxSPURL.Text = "";
            txtbxProdName.Text = "";
            txtbxProductSku.Text = "";
            txtbxProductPrice.Text = "";

        }

        private void btnLoad_Click(object sender, RoutedEventArgs e)
        {
            strSPSiteURL = txtbxSPURL.Text;
            strSPListName = txtbxListName.Text;
            strProductName = txtbxProdName.Text;
            strProductSKU = txtbxProductSku.Text;
            strProductPrice = txtbxProductPrice.Text;

            using (SPSite site = new SPSite(strSPSiteURL))
            {
                using (SPWeb web = site.OpenWeb())
                {
```

```
            web.AllowUnsafeUpdates = true;

            SPList list = web.Lists[strSPListName];
            SPListItem Item = list.Items.Add();
            Item["Title"] = strProductName;
            Item["Product_SKU"] = strProductSKU;
            Item["Price"] = strProductPrice;
            Item.Update();

              web.AllowUnsafeUpdates = false;
            }
          }

        }

      }
}
```

11. When you're finished adding the code, press F5 to debug the application. When prompted by the UI, enter some product information into the dialog, as shown in Figure 5-5.

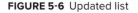

FIGURE 5-5 Compiled WPF application using server-side object model

12. Now, open your SharePoint site and navigate to the list you updated (for example, Products list). You will find that the application has updated the SharePoint list, as shown in Figure 5-6.

	Title	Product_SKU	Price
	Bauer XXXX	BR-XXXX-901	389.99
	CCM Tacks	CM-TCKS-021	309.00
	Nike Air	NK-AIR-788	389.99
	Bauer XXVI ⊕ NEW	BR-XXVI-090	279.99

FIGURE 5-6 Updated list

How It Works

When you're developing applications that are running on the server, you can leverage the server-side object model that is exposed using the `Microsoft SharePoint.dll`. For example, in this walkthrough, you built a simple WPF-based application that was running on the server (assuming that you were building and deploying it on your server machine). Very simply, the application took a number of string inputs from the WPF UI and used the server-side object model to add this input to a list on your SharePoint site. The five `string` variables were declared as follows:

```
...
string strSPSiteURL = "";
string strSPListName = "";
string strProductName = "";
string strProductSKU = "";
string strProductPrice = "";
...
```

You'll note that, per the earlier example, the code leverages the `using` statements to set the context for the SharePoint site and then sets the Web to allow updates, creates an `SPList` object and `SPListItem` object, and then proceeds to set the specific column fields with the data that was entered by the users. Finally, the `Update` method is called to add the data to the list.

```
...
using (SPSite site = new SPSite(strSPSiteURL))
{
    using (SPWeb web = site.OpenWeb())
    {
        web.AllowUnsafeUpdates = true;

        SPList list = web.Lists[strSPListName];
        SPListItem Item = list.Items.Add();
        Item["Title"] = strProductName;
        Item["Product_SKU"] = strProductSKU;
        Item["Price"] = strProductPrice;
        Item.Update();

        web.AllowUnsafeUpdates = false;
    }
}
...
```

> **NOTE** *The preceding walkthrough showed you how to use the server-side object model using a Windows client application. You can also use the server-side object model on the server. To help you see what the project structure of a Web part application looks like, this chapter also provides an additional code sample where a Web part issues the same update action that the WPF application does. This Web part code sample (`ServerSideObjectModel.zip`) is available for download for you at the companion download site (`www.Wrox.com`).*

Programming Against Lists Using ASP.NET Web Services

The second way to interact with lists programmatically is to use the Lists ASP.NET Web service that ships with SharePoint 2010. You might think of this as being not only a convenient service-based way of coding against SharePoint, but also as support for legacy code that may be based on the set of Web methods within the Lists service.

To develop using the ASP.NET service, you create a new application, set a reference to the ASP.NET Web service, and then program against the Web reference (or more accurately, the service proxy you add to the application code). For example, following is a code snippet that creates an instance of the Lists Web service, sets the credentials of the service call as the default credentials, and then sets the absolute URL to the service:

```
…
MySharePointData.SPListGetData.Lists proxy = new
     MySharePointData.SPListGetData.Lists();
proxy.Credentials = System.Net.CredentialCache.DefaultCredentials.
proxy.URL = "http://fabrikamhockey/_vti_bin/lists.asmx";
…
```

Within the Lists Web service, there are a number of Web methods that you can use when programming against SharePoint lists, content types, list items, and files. To access the Web service, you set your Web reference to `http://<server name>/_vti_bin/Lists.asmx` and then use the reference to the service in your code to manage data sent to and from SharePoint.

Table 5-4 provides a sampling of the list of the Web methods that are available in the Lists Web service, along with a description of what the Web method does.

TABLE 5-4 Sample Lists Web Service Members

METHOD NAME	DESCRIPTION
AddAttachment	Adds an attachment to a specific list item in a list
AddList	Creates a list in a SharePoint site based on specific name, description, and list template ID
CheckInFile	Allows documents to be checked in to a SharePoint document library remotely
CheckOutFile	Allows documents in a SharePoint document library to be checked out remotely
DeleteAttachment	Removes the attachment from the specified list item
DeleteList	Deletes a specified list
GetList	Returns the schema for a specified list
GetListAndView	Returns list and view schemas for the specified list

continues

TABLE 5-4 *(continued)*

METHOD NAME	DESCRIPTION
GetListCollection	Returns the names and globally unique identifiers (GUIDs) for all lists in the site
GetListContentType	Returns the content type definition schema for the specified list content type
GetListItemChanges	Returns any changes made to a list since a specified date and time
GetListItems	Returns information about items in a list based on a specified query
UndoCheckOut	Undoes the check-out of a given document in a SharePoint document library
UpdateList	Updates a list based on a specified field definition and list properties
UpdateListItems	Adds, deletes, or updates specified items in a list on a SharePoint site

> **NOTE** *You can find more information about the Lists Web service members at* `http://msdn.microsoft.com/en-us/library/lists.lists_members.aspx`*.*

You've walked through an exercise how to program against lists using the server-side object model, so let's try out another example using the Lists Web service. In this example, you'll create an Office add-in that will read and write data from the document to the SharePoint list, and vice versa. (Note that if you completed the first walkthrough, you can use the same Products list in this example as well.)

TRY IT OUT   **Programming Against Lists Using the Lists Web Service**

Code file [ProductsList.zip] available for download at Wrox.com.

The ASP.NET Web services are a great way to leverage the out-of-the-box capabilities when programming against lists. To programmatically interact with a list using the Lists Web service, follow these steps:

1.   Create a new Custom list and call it Products. Leave the default Title field and add two more fields called Product_SKU and Price. All fields should be of type "Single line of text." Add some data to the list, as shown in Figure 5-7.

	Title	Product_SKU	Price
	Bauer XXXX	BR-XXXX-901	389.99
	CCM Tacks	CM-TCKS-021	309.00
	Nike Air	NK-AIR-788	389.99

FIGURE 5-7 Sample data in list

2. After you've created the list, open Visual Studio 2010 (as Administrator).

3. Select File ➪ New ➪ Project. Be sure to select the .NET Framework 3.5 in the drop-down list in the New Project dialog.

4. Select Office in the Installed Templates, and then select the Excel 2010 Add-In project template.

5. Provide a name (for example, `ProductsList`) and a location for your project, as shown in Figure 5-8. Click OK.

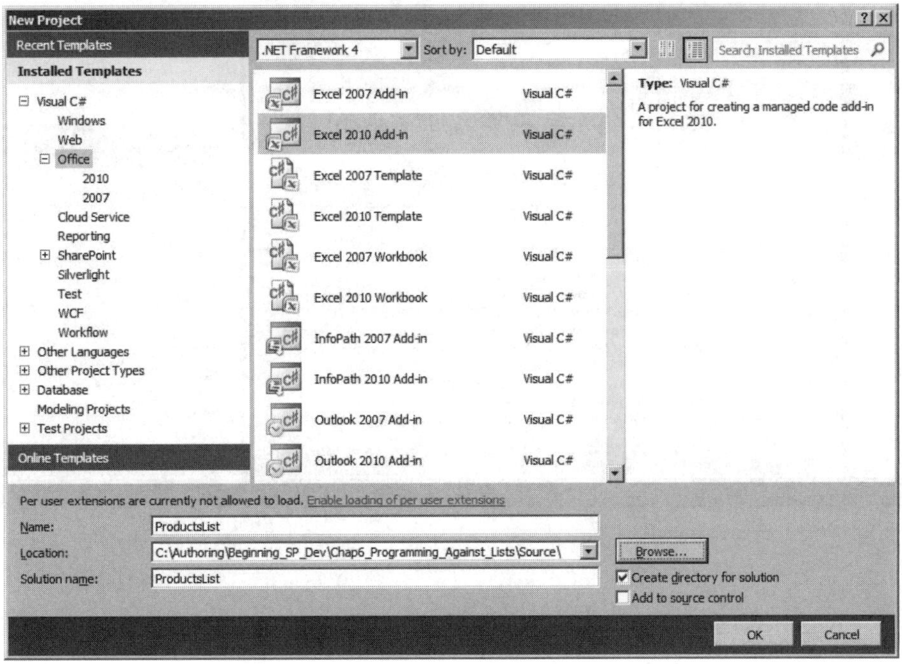

FIGURE 5-8 Office Excel project template

6. Visual Studio 2010 creates a solution structure for you, which includes a number of default files. Right-click the main project file and select Add ➪ New Item. Navigate to the WPF node and select WPF User Control.

7. Provide a name for your user control (for example, `ProductsUserControl.xaml`), and click OK. Visual Studio adds a WPF-based control to your project.

8. Right-click the new control in the Solution Explorer and select View in Designer.

9. Use the Toolbox to drag four labels — a listbox, two textboxes, and two buttons — onto the designer surface. When done, arrange the user interface controls as shown in Figure 5-9.

Table 5-5 shows the control type and the name of the controls that you should add to the WPF user control.

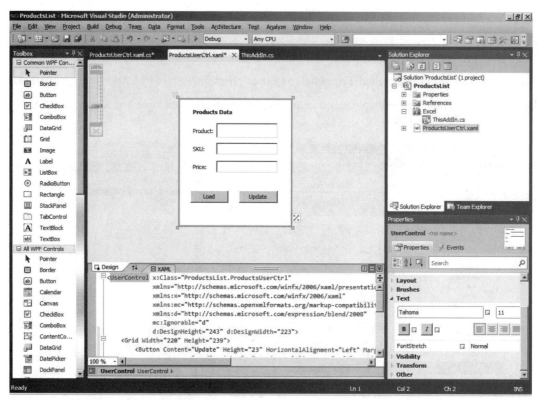

FIGURE 5-9 WPF custom task pane UI

TABLE 5-5 Control Types for WPF User Control

CONTROL TYPE	CONTROL NAME
Label	lblProduct, lblSku, LblPrice, lblTitle
Textbox	txtBxSku, txtbxPrice
Listbox	lstBxProducts
Button	btnUpdate, btnLoadData

Adding controls to the designer surface auto-generates XAML code (the XML mark-up that defines the UI for the application). If you explore the XAML code for the UI, it will look very close to the following code sample. Note that you can edit the properties of the UI either directly from the XAML or by using the Properties window in Visual Studio.

```
<UserControl x:Class="ProductsList.ProductsUserCtrl"
        xmlns="http://schemas.microsoft.com/winfx/2006/xaml/presentation"
```

```
                xmlns:x="http://schemas.microsoft.com/winfx/2006/xaml"
                xmlns:mc="http://schemas.openxmlformats.org/markup-compatibility/2006"
                xmlns:d="http://schemas.microsoft.com/expression/blend/2008"
                mc:Ignorable="d"
                d:DesignHeight="243" d:DesignWidth="223">
    <Grid Width="220" Height="239">
        <Button
Content="Update" Height="23" HorizontalAlignment="Left" Margin="118,173,0,0"
Name="btnUpdate" VerticalAlignment="Top" Width="75" />
        <Button
Content="Load" Height="23" HorizontalAlignment="Left" Margin="22,173,0,0"
Name="btnLoadData" VerticalAlignment="Top" Width="75" />
        <Label
Content="Product:" Height="28" HorizontalAlignment="Left" Margin="22,48,0,0"
Name="lblProduct" VerticalAlignment="Top" Width="55" />
        <Label
Content="SKU:" Height="28" HorizontalAlignment="Left" Margin="22,82,0,0"
Name="lblSku" VerticalAlignment="Top" Width="55" />
        <Label
Content="Price:" Height="28" HorizontalAlignment="Left" Margin="22,116,0,0"
Name="lblPrice" VerticalAlignment="Top" Width="55" />
        <Label
Content="Products Data" Height="28" HorizontalAlignment="Left" Margin="22,12,0,0"
Name="lblTitle" VerticalAlignment="Top" Width="120" FontWeight="Bold" />
        <TextBox
Height="23" HorizontalAlignment="Left" Margin="73,82,0,0"
Name="txtBxSku" VerticalAlignment="Top" Width="120" />
        <TextBox
Height="23" HorizontalAlignment="Left" Margin="73,116,0,0"
Name="txtBxPrice" VerticalAlignment="Top" Width="120" />
        <ListBox
Height="28" HorizontalAlignment="Left" Margin="73,45,0,0"
Name="lstBxProducts" VerticalAlignment="Top" Width="120" />
    </Grid>
</UserControl>
```

10. Double-click each of the buttons to add event handlers for each of them in the code behind. (Note that this will update the XAML, so be sure to inspect the XAML to see these changes.)

11. Next, add a reference to the Lists Web service. To do this, right-click the project and select Add Service Reference. Click the Advanced button in the Add Service Reference dialog, and then click Add Web Reference in the Service Reference Settings dialog.

12. If you're developing on the same machine as your SharePoint site, you can click "Web services on local machine" to discover the services on your development machine. (Otherwise, you'll need to add the service URL into the URL field.)

13. Visual Studio loads all of the available services on the local machine, one of which should be the SharePoint Lists service, as shown in Figure 5-10.

14. When you click the Lists service, you will see a list showing all of the available Web methods.

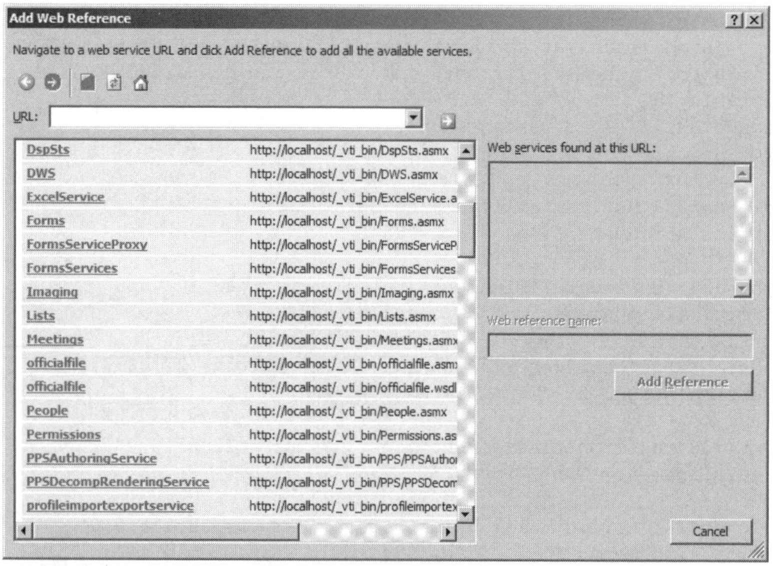

FIGURE 5-10 Add Web Reference dialog

15. Provide a name for the service reference (for example, `SPListWS`) in the Web reference name field, and then click Add Reference. You can now begin leveraging the Lists Web service in your application. After you finish adding the Web service reference, add the following `using` statements at the top of the class:

```
using Excel = Microsoft.Office.Interop.Excel;
using System.Web.Services.Protocols;
```

16. Right-click the WPF-based user control, and select View Code.

17. In the code behind, you're going to add some code to handle reading data from the SharePoint list into the active Excel document and then some to handle writing back to the SharePoint list from the Excel worksheet. The first set of code you'll need is the code that defines your in-memory data object. To add a class to the project and provide a name (for example, `Product`), right-click the project and select Add ➪ Class. The `Product` class contains three public string properties, which are shown in boldface in the following code sample:

```
using System;
using System.Collections.Generic;
using System.Linq;
using System.Text;

namespace ProductsList
{
    class Product
    {
        public string productTitle { get; set; }
        public string productSKU { get; set; }
        public string productPrice { get; set; }
    }
}
```

18. Data is managed in the application through the use of a list collection called `myProducts` (which appears in bold in the following code snippet). Using an in-memory object that is of type `IEnumerable` or a `List` collection makes it easier to query and bind data to controls in your applications.

```
namespace ProductsList
{

    public partial class ProductsUserCtrl : UserControl
    {
        List<Product> myProducts = new List<Product>();

        public ProductsUserCtrl()
        {
            InitializeComponent();
        }
        …

    }
}
```

19. After you've added the code for your class, you must handle the two button events and the changed event for the listbox. The following code snippet represents the event that is triggered when the user clicks the Load button (that is, the `btnLoadData_Click` event). Within the `btnLoadData_Click` event, the application implements the Lists Web service and then, through the use of the `GetListItems` method, within the Lists Web service. Much of the code within the `try` block essentially builds out an XML document using the returned data from the Web service call. It next looks for specific XML elements (that is, `ows_Title`, `ows_Product_SKU`, and `ows_Price`). It then iterates through each record in the XML document and populates the `Product` list collection (as well as adds the names of the products that are being returned to the listbox in the UI).

```
private void btnLoadData_Click(object sender, RoutedEventArgs e)
        {
            SPListWS.Lists myListReadProxy = new SPListWS.Lists();
            myListReadProxy.Credentials =
                System.Net.CredentialCache.DefaultCredentials;
            myListReadProxy.Url = "http://fabrikamhockey/_vti_bin/Lists.asmx";

            try
            {
                XmlNode myListItems = myListReadProxy.GetListItems
                    ("Products", null, null, null, null, null, null);
                XElement newRootElement = new XElement("ProductData");

                foreach (XmlNode outerNode in myListItems.ChildNodes)
                {
                    if (outerNode.NodeType.Equals(System.Xml.XmlNodeType.Element))
                    {
                        foreach (XmlNode node in outerNode.ChildNodes)
                        {
                            if (node.NodeType.Equals(System.Xml.
                                XmlNodeType.Element))
                            {
                                XmlNode listFieldTitle = node.Attributes.
```

```
                              GetNamedItem("ows_Title");
                    XmlNode listFieldProductSKU = node.Attributes.
                              GetNamedItem("ows_Product_SKU");
                    XmlNode listFieldPrice = node.Attributes.
                              GetNamedItem("ows_Price");

                    Product tempProduct = new Product();
                    tempProduct.productTitle = listFieldTitle.InnerText;
                    tempProduct.productSKU =
                              listFieldProductSKU.InnerText;
                    tempProduct.productPrice = listFieldPrice.InnerText;

                    myProducts.Add(tempProduct);
                    lstBxProducts.Items.Add(tempProduct.productTitle);
                }
            }
        }
    }
}
catch (SoapException ex)
{
    MessageBox.Show(ex.Message);
}
}
```

20. The following code provides the methods that handle the `btnUpdate_Click` event. In this code, you create an instance of the Excel worksheet so that you can inject the data coming from the SharePoint list into a specific set of cells. The code does not format the cells, but you could assert some formatting for the worksheet programmatically if you chose. Then, depending on the product name in the cell, the code sets an integer variable called `index`, which is the specific row of data that you will update if you make any changes to the data in the spreadsheet. Then, similar to the `btnLoadData_Click` event, you create an instance of the Lists Web service. However, this time, you call the `UpdateListItems` method. You'll notice the CAML construct that is created and passed with the `UpdateListItems` method. This construct defines the command (`Update`) and then provides the specific index to be updated through the aforementioned `index` variable.

```
...
private void btnUpdate_Click(object sender, RoutedEventArgs e)
    {
        Excel.Worksheet myProductWorksheet = Globals.ThisAddIn.
            Application.ActiveSheet as Excel.Worksheet;
        int index = 0;
        string strProductUpdate = myProductWorksheet.
            Cells[2, 1].Value2.ToString();
        string strProductSkuUpdate = myProductWorksheet.
            Cells[2, 2].Value2.ToString();
        string strProductPriceUpdate = myProductWorksheet.
            Cells[2, 3].Value2.ToString();

        if (strProductUpdate == "Bauer XXXX")
        {
            index = 1;
        }
        else if (strProductUpdate == "CCM Tacks")
        {
```

```
              index = 2;
        }
        else if (strProductUpdate == "Nike Air")
        {
              index = 3;
        }

        SPListWS.Lists myListUpdateProxy = new SPListWS.Lists();
        myListUpdateProxy.Credentials =
              System.Net.CredentialCache.DefaultCredentials;
        myListUpdateProxy.Url = "http://fabrikamhockey/_vti_bin/Lists.asmx";

        System.Xml.XmlNode xmlListView =
              myListUpdateProxy.GetListAndView("Products", "");
        string strListID = xmlListView.ChildNodes[0].Attributes["Name"].Value;
        string strViewID = xmlListView.ChildNodes[1].Attributes["Name"].Value;

        XmlDocument xmlDoc = new XmlDocument();
        XmlElement xmlBatchElement = xmlDoc.CreateElement("Batch");
        xmlBatchElement.SetAttribute("OnError", "Continue");
        xmlBatchElement.SetAttribute("ListVersion", "1");
        xmlBatchElement.SetAttribute("ViewName", strViewID);

        xmlBatchElement.InnerXml = "<Method ID='1' Cmd='Update'>"+
              "<Field Name='ID'>" + index + "</Field>"+"<Field Name='Title'>"
              + strProductUpdate + "</Field><Field Name='Product_SKU'>" +
              strProductSkuUpdate + "</Field><Field Name='Price'>" +
              strProductPriceUpdate + "</Field>" + "</Method>";
        try
        {
              XmlNode xmlReturn = myListUpdateProxy.UpdateListItems
                    ("Products", xmlBatchElement);
              System.Windows.MessageBox.Show("Product Information Added!");
        }
        catch (SoapException ex)
        {
              MessageBox.Show(ex.Message);
        }
    }
...
```

21. The last event that is handled is the lstBxProducts_SelectionChanged event, which updates the worksheet. To create the lstBxProducts_SelectionChanged event double-click the listbox. In the following code, the in-memory list collection, myProducts, is being queried using a LiNQ statement. The results can then be mapped to the textboxes and then added to the spreadsheet.

```
...
private void lstBxProducts_SelectionChanged
      (object sender, SelectionChangedEventArgs e)
          {
              string strSelectedProd = lstBxProducts.SelectedItem.ToString();

              var products = from p in myProducts
                          .Where(p => p.productTitle == strSelectedProd)
```

```
                            select new {p.productSKU, p.productPrice};

              foreach (var d in products)
              {
                  txtBxSku.Text = d.productSKU;
                  txtBxPrice.Text = d.productPrice;
              }

              Excel.Worksheet myProductWorksheet =
                  Globals.ThisAddIn.Application.ActiveSheet as Excel.Worksheet;
              myProductWorksheet.Cells[1, 1].Value2 = "Product";
              myProductWorksheet.Cells[1, 2].Value2 = "SKU";
              myProductWorksheet.Cells[1, 3].Value2 = "Price";
              myProductWorksheet.Cells[2, 1].Value2 = strSelectedProd;
              myProductWorksheet.Cells[2, 2].Value2 = txtBxSku.Text;
              myProductWorksheet.Cells[2, 3].Value2 = txtBxPrice.Text;

          }

      }
}
...
```

22. While the three methods were split out for your reference, the following listing includes the full code for the solution described earlier. You'll note that, as you work through other examples in the chapter, many of the generic .NET features can equally apply to different ways of retrieving data from SharePoint. For example, you can equally use LINQ and in-memory objects to query and filter data while using the client object model, which is discussed later in this chapter.

```
using System;
using System.Collections.Generic;
using System.Linq;
using System.Text;
using System.Windows;
using System.Windows.Controls;
using System.Windows.Data;
using System.Windows.Documents;
using System.Windows.Input;
using System.Windows.Media;
using System.Windows.Media.Imaging;
using System.Windows.Navigation;
using System.Windows.Shapes;
using System.Xaml;
using System.Xml;
using System.Xml.Linq;
using Excel = Microsoft.Office.Interop.Excel;
using System.Web.Services.Protocols;

namespace ProductsList
{

    public partial class ProductsUserCtrl : UserControl
    {
        List<Product> myProducts = new List<Product>();

        public ProductsUserCtrl()
```

```csharp
{
    InitializeComponent();
}
private void btnLoadData_Click(object sender, RoutedEventArgs e)
{
    SPListWS.Lists myListReadProxy = new SPListWS.Lists();
    myListReadProxy.Credentials =
        System.Net.CredentialCache.DefaultCredentials;
    //Be sure to replace the URL below with your SharePoint server name.
    myListReadProxy.Url = "http://fabrikamhockey/_vti_bin/Lists.asmx";

    try
    {
        XmlNode myListItems = myListReadProxy.GetListItems("Products",
            null,
            null, null, null, null, null);
        XElement newRootElement = new XElement("ProductData");

        foreach (XmlNode outerNode in myListItems.ChildNodes)
        {
            if (outerNode.NodeType.Equals(System.Xml.XmlNodeType.Element))
            {
                foreach (XmlNode node in outerNode.ChildNodes)
                {
                    if (node.NodeType.Equals
                        (System.Xml.XmlNodeType.Element))
                    {
                        XmlNode listFieldTitle = node.Attributes.
                            GetNamedItem("ows_Title");
                        XmlNode listFieldProductSKU = node.Attributes.
                            GetNamedItem("ows_Product_SKU");
                        XmlNode listFieldPrice = node.Attributes.
                            GetNamedItem("ows_Price");

                        Product tempProduct = new Product();
                        tempProduct.productTitle = listFieldTitle.InnerText;
                        tempProduct.productSKU =
                            listFieldProductSKU.InnerText;
                        tempProduct.productPrice = listFieldPrice.InnerText;

                        myProducts.Add(tempProduct);
                        lstBxProducts.Items.Add(tempProduct.productTitle);
                    }
                }
            }
        }
    }
    catch (SoapException ex)
    {
        MessageBox.Show(ex.Message);
    }
}

private void btnUpdate_Click(object sender, RoutedEventArgs e)
{
    Excel.Worksheet myProductWorksheet = Globals.ThisAddIn.
```

```csharp
        Application.ActiveSheet as Excel.Worksheet;
int index = 0;
string strProductUpdate = myProductWorksheet.Cells[2, 1].
    Value2.ToString();
string strProductSkuUpdate = myProductWorksheet.Cells[2, 2].
    Value2.ToString();
string strProductPriceUpdate = myProductWorksheet.Cells[2, 3].
    Value2.ToString();

if (strProductUpdate == "Bauer XXXX")
{
    index = 1;
}
else if (strProductUpdate == "CCM Tacks")
{
    index = 2;
}
else if (strProductUpdate == "Nike Air")
{
    index = 3;
}

SPListWS.Lists myListUpdateProxy = new SPListWS.Lists();
myListUpdateProxy.Credentials =
    System.Net.CredentialCache.DefaultCredentials;
myListUpdateProxy.Url = "http://fabrikamhockey/_vti_bin/Lists.asmx";

System.Xml.XmlNode xmlListView =
    myListUpdateProxy.GetListAndView("Products", "");
string strListID = xmlListView.ChildNodes[0].Attributes["Name"].Value;
string strViewID = xmlListView.ChildNodes[1].Attributes["Name"].Value;

XmlDocument xmlDoc = new XmlDocument();
XmlElement xmlBatchElement = xmlDoc.CreateElement("Batch");
xmlBatchElement.SetAttribute("OnError", "Continue");
xmlBatchElement.SetAttribute("ListVersion", "1");
xmlBatchElement.SetAttribute("ViewName", strViewID);

xmlBatchElement.InnerXml = "<Method ID='1' Cmd='Update'>"+
    "<Field Name='ID'>" + index + "</Field>"+"<Field Name='Title'>"
    + strProductUpdate + "</Field><Field Name='Product_SKU'>" +
    strProductSkuUpdate + "</Field><Field Name='Price'>" +
    strProductPriceUpdate + "</Field>" + "</Method>";
try
{
    XmlNode xmlReturn = myListUpdateProxy.UpdateListItems
        ("Products", xmlBatchElement);
    System.Windows.MessageBox.Show("Product Information Added!");
}
catch (SoapException ex)
{
    MessageBox.Show(ex.Message);
}
}

private void lstBxProducts_SelectionChanged(object sender,
```

```
        SelectionChangedEventArgs e)
{
    string strSelectedProd = lstBxProducts.SelectedItem.ToString();

    var products = from p in myProducts
                   .Where(p => p.productTitle == strSelectedProd)
                   select new {p.productSKU, p.productPrice};

    foreach (var d in products)
    {
        txtBxSku.Text = d.productSKU;
        txtBxPrice.Text = d.productPrice;
    }

    Excel.Worksheet myProductWorksheet = Globals.ThisAddIn.
        Application.ActiveSheet as Excel.Worksheet;
    myProductWorksheet.Cells[1, 1].Value2 = "Product";
    myProductWorksheet.Cells[1, 2].Value2 = "SKU";
    myProductWorksheet.Cells[1, 3].Value2 = "Price";
    myProductWorksheet.Cells[2, 1].Value2 = strSelectedProd;
    myProductWorksheet.Cells[2, 2].Value2 = txtBxSku.Text;
    myProductWorksheet.Cells[2, 3].Value2 = txtBxPrice.Text;

    }

  }
}
```

23. Although you have your UI working now, you should not press F5 to debug the application just yet. You've only set up what will be the UI for your custom task pane. To ensure that, when Excel starts, your custom task pane is displayed, you must add a user control to your application and then add some code in the ThisAddIn_StartUp method. To do this, right-click your project and click Add. Then select User Control (WPF). Give the user control a name (for example, XAMLHost) and make the height 800 and the width 350. Press F6 to build the project.

24. When you build the project, your WPF control will display in the Toolbox. Open the user control you just created. Drag and drop the WPF control onto the user control. You can resize the WPF control until all of the controls are visible.

25. Now, right-click on the ThisAddIn class and amend the code in that class with the following bold-faced code. This code creates an instance of the WinForm user control you just created (which is now hosting the XAML control), creates an instance of the custom task pane object, and creates a title variable that you'll need for the custom task pane. The code leverages the Add method to add the user control and title to the CustomTaskPanes collection, which is then set to be visible and docked to the right of the document.

```
using System;
using System.Collections.Generic;
using System.Linq;
using System.Text;
using System.Xml.Linq;
using Excel = Microsoft.Office.Interop.Excel;
using Office = Microsoft.Office.Tools;
using Microsoft.Office.Tools.Excel;
```

```
using System.Windows.Forms;

namespace ProductsList
{
    public partial class ThisAddIn
    {
        XAMLHost ctrl = new XAMLHost();
        string ctrlTitle = "Product Data";
        Office.CustomTaskPane ctp;

        private void ThisAddIn_Startup(object sender, System.EventArgs e)
        {
            ctp = this.CustomTaskPanes.Add(ctrl, ctrlTitle);
            ctp.Visible = true;
            ctp.DockPosition = Microsoft.Office.Core.MsoCTPDockPosition.
                msoCTPDockPositionRight;
        }

        private void ThisAddIn_Shutdown(object sender, System.EventArgs e)
        {
        }

        private void InternalStartup()
        {
            this.Startup += new System.EventHandler(ThisAddIn_Startup);
            this.Shutdown += new System.EventHandler(ThisAddIn_Shutdown);
        }

    }
}
```

26. At this point, you can press F5 to build and debug the application. You should see something similar to Figure 5-11. Click Load to load the data from SharePoint. Select an item within the Product listbox to populate the SKU and Price fields, and then add data into the Excel worksheet. You can then make some changes in one of the cells and click Update. That will update your SharePoint list.

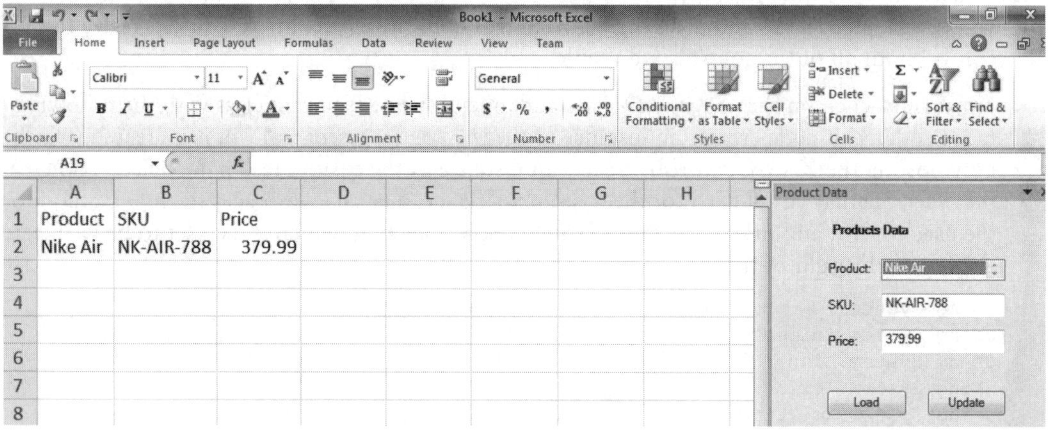

FIGURE 5-11 Excel application leveraging Lists Web service

How It Works

You can call the Lists Web service from a variety of client applications, and the code will more often than not look very similar to the way it was used here. What could be different would be how the data is consumed after the client application retrieves it. For example, in this exercise, you added the data from SharePoint to the spreadsheet by using the Office object model. Per the following code, you created an instance of the worksheet and then mapped the data to hard-coded cells:

```
...
        Excel.Worksheet myProductWorksheet = Globals.ThisAddIn.
            Application.ActiveSheet as Excel.Worksheet;
    myProductWorksheet.Cells[1, 1].Value2 = "Product";
    myProductWorksheet.Cells[1, 2].Value2 = "SKU";
    myProductWorksheet.Cells[1, 3].Value2 = "Price";
    myProductWorksheet.Cells[2, 1].Value2 = strSelectedProd;
    myProductWorksheet.Cells[2, 2].Value2 = txtBxSku.Text;
    myProductWorksheet.Cells[2, 3].Value2 = txtBxPrice.Text;
...
```

The Lists Web service works by relaying XML documents (or *data payloads*) back from the server to the calling application. Depending on the payload, the XML can be quite lengthy to parse. For example, in this exercise, you called the GetListItems method and then walked through an XML document and built out your in-memory object, as reflected in the following code snippet:

```
...
XmlNode myListItems = myListReadProxy.GetListItems("Products", null, null,
    null, null, null, null);
            XElement newRootElement = new XElement("ProductData");

        foreach (XmlNode outerNode in myListItems.ChildNodes)
        {
            if (outerNode.NodeType.Equals(System.Xml.XmlNodeType.Element))
            {
                foreach (XmlNode node in outerNode.ChildNodes)
                {
                    if (node.NodeType.Equals(System.Xml.
                      XmlNodeType.Element))
                    {
                        XmlNode listFieldTitle = node.Attributes.
                            GetNamedItem("ows_Title");
                        XmlNode listFieldProductSKU = node.Attributes.
                            GetNamedItem("ows_Product_SKU");
                        XmlNode listFieldPrice = node.Attributes.
                            GetNamedItem("ows_Price");

                        Product tempProduct = new Product();
                        tempProduct.productTitle = listFieldTitle.InnerText;
                        tempProduct.productSKU =
                            listFieldProductSKU.InnerText;
                        tempProduct.productPrice = listFieldPrice.InnerText;

                        myProducts.Add(tempProduct);
```

```
                             lstBxProducts.Items.Add(tempProduct.productTitle);
                    }
                }
            }
        }
    ...
```

This might be perceived as a lot of programmatic moving parts and, depending on your payload, could affect performance. It is, though, a proven and accepted way of interacting with SharePoint data.

With that said, you can optimize the previous code in any number of ways. For example, you could move the Excel header row to be added on startup, or assert LINQ directly against your XML documents to increase performance and sanitize your code.

As you refine your applications, you'll certainly craft your applications with better designs in mind. However, one way to optimize the calling code into SharePoint is to leverage the SharePoint client-side object model, instead of using the native Lists Web service.

Programming Against Lists Using the Client Object Model

The client object model is a new feature in SharePoint 2010, and enables developers to program against SharePoint lists using remote clients. For example, you can create a WinForm or WPF application, a Silverlight application, or a JavaScript application that all can use the client object model to manage data sent in and out of SharePoint through that remote client.

Depending on what you're trying to do with SharePoint, you'll find the syntax of your code is somewhat cleaner than the earlier Web service example. For example, if you want to issue a SELECT * type query against a SharePoint list, the client object model, in some cases, auto-generates CAML for you. Also, it's easier to manage data in in-memory data objects, with which you can then use LINQ, enumerables, collections, and so on, to quickly and efficiently query and filter that data into your applications.

Let's try an example where you read data from a SharePoint list, and display it within a Windows Form application. In this example, you'll again leverage the Products list you created earlier.

TRY IT OUT   Using the Client-Side Object Model to Programmatically Read List Data

The client object model provides a powerful way to program against lists from a remote client application. To use the client object model when programming against lists, follow these steps:

1. Open Visual Studio 2010 and click File ➪ New Project ➪ Windows Forms application. Provide a name for your project (for example, ReadSPListData). Be sure to select the .NET Framework 3.5 in the drop-down list in the New Project dialog.

2. Add a label, textbox, datagrid view, and two buttons to the Windows form in the Designer view, as shown in Figure 5-12.

Table 5-6 shows the control type and the name of the controls that you should add to the Windows Form designer.

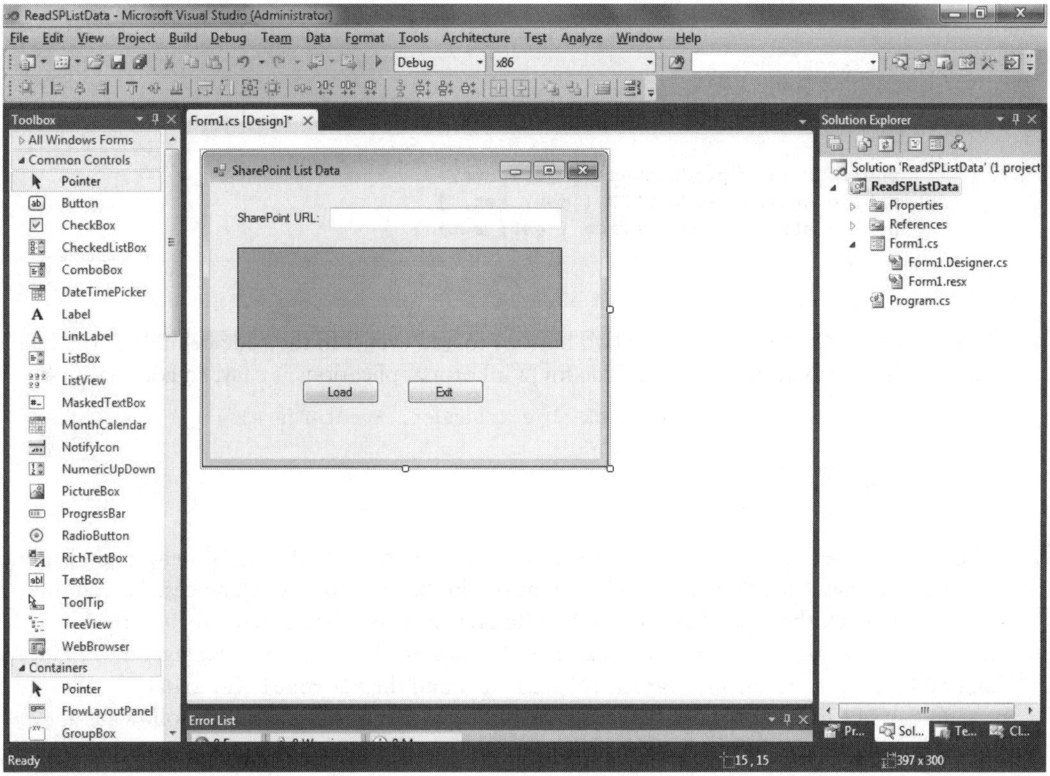

FIGURE 5-12 WinForm UI

TABLE 5-6 Control Types for Windows Form Application

CONTROL TYPE	CONTROL NAME
Label	lblSPURL
Textbox	txtbxSPURL
Datagrid View	dtgrdSPListData
Button	btnLoadData, btnExit

3. You must add a class to the project, so right-click the project name and select Add ➪ Class. Provide a name (for example, `ProductInfo`). Add three properties to the class that map to the same `Products` class you created earlier in the chapter. The code for this will look like the bold-faced code in the following code snippet:

```
using System;
using System.Collections.Generic;
using System.Linq;
```

```
using System.Text;

namespace ReadSPListData
{
    class ProductInfo
    {
        public string productName { get; set; }
        public string productSKU { get; set; }
        public string productPrice { get; set; }
    }
}
```

4. Next, you want to double-click the two buttons to add events in the code behind for the Load button and the Exit button. The Exit code for WinForm applications is easy, so add that first:

```
private void btnExit_Click(object sender, EventArgs e)
{
    Application.Exit();
}
```

5. The btnLoadData_Click event is a little more complex, but add that next. Before you begin coding using the new client object model, you must add the appropriate references. To add these references, right-click the project and select Add Reference. Select the Browse tab, and then browse to
c:\Program Files\Common Files\Microsoft Shared\Web Server Extensions\14\ISAPI
and add the Microsoft.SharePoint.Client.dll and the Microsoft.SharePoint.Client
.Runtime.dll to your project. After you've added these references, add the following using
statements at the top of your main application:

```
using ClientOM = Microsoft.SharePoint.Client;
using Microsoft.SharePoint.Client;
```

When using the client object model, you may run into namespace conflicts (for example, with the
Form class in Windows Forms applications). To get around this, you can add the following line of
code to your application:

```
using ClientOM = Microsoft.SharePoint.Client;
```

This gives you a "custom" namespace reference that enables you to avoid namespace conflicts.

6. You'll next add some code to handle the loading of the data from the SharePoint list using this
feature. You'll note that the syntax for retrieving the data from SharePoint in this case is slightly
different from that of the Lists Web service. You are still achieving pretty much the same function,
but doing it in a more syntactically clean way.

In the following code sample, note that the application uses the string variable entered into the textbox as the SharePoint site context (that is, the URL). It then uses a number of in-memory objects to
manage the data coming from SharePoint (for example, myListItems and myProducts). However,
the key differentiating code is where you begin to set the context by using the ClientContext object.
This is one of the key features of the client object model — the process of setting context and then
calling ExecuteQuery (a batch query method) when interacting with the SharePoint list. You will
again use LINQ to populate an object and iterate through the contents of that object to get the data

into a bindable object that can be mapped directly to the datagrid. One key item within the `foreach` loop is that you'll see values are assigned using the `ElementAt` property. This is the specific element index where the data lives within the SharePoint list. If you were to set a breakpoint right after the LINQ statement and inspect the values within the `returnedListData` object, you could see all of the different values that are returned and the correlating index value.

```
...
private void btnLoad_Click(object sender, EventArgs e)
       {
             string SPUrl = txtbxSPURL.Text;
             IEnumerable<ClientOM.ListItem> myListItems;
             List<ProductInfo> myProducts = new List<ProductInfo>();

             ClientOM.ClientContext SPContext = new ClientOM.ClientContext(SPUrl);
             ClientOM.Web mySPSite = SPContext.Web;
             ClientOM.ListCollection myListCollection = mySPSite.Lists;
             var productsList = SPContext.Web.Lists.GetByTitle("Products");
             ClientOM.CamlQuery myCamlQuery = new CamlQuery();
             IQueryable<ClientOM.ListItem> myList = productsList.
                   GetItems(myCamlQuery);
             myListItems = SPContext.LoadQuery(myList);
             SPContext.ExecuteQuery();

             var returnedListData = from prod in myListItems
                                    select prod;

             foreach (ClientOM.ListItem tempListItem in returnedListData)
             {
                 ProductInfo tempProd = new ProductInfo();
                 tempProd.productName = tempListItem.FieldValues.
                     Values.ElementAt(1).ToString();
                 tempProd.productSKU = tempListItem.FieldValues.
                     Values.ElementAt(4).ToString();
                 tempProd.productPrice = tempListItem.FieldValues.
                     Values.ElementAt(5).ToString();
                 myProducts.Add(tempProd);
             }

             dtgrdSPListData.DataSource = myProducts;
       }
...
```

Taken together, the full code sample for the WinForm code behind is as follows:

```
using System;
using System.Collections.Generic;
using System.ComponentModel;
using System.Data;
using System.Drawing;
using System.Linq;
using System.Text;
using System.Windows.Forms;
```

```
//Be sure to add this along with your other using statements.
using ClientOM = Microsoft.SharePoint.Client;
using Microsoft.SharePoint.Client;

namespace ReadSPListData
{
    public partial class Form1 : System.Windows.Forms.Form
    {
        public Form1()
        {
            InitializeComponent();
        }

        private void btnExit_Click(object sender, EventArgs e)
        {
            Application.Exit();
        }

        private void btnLoad_Click(object sender, EventArgs e)
        {
            string SPUrl = txtbxSPURL.Text;

            IEnumerable<ClientOM.ListItem> myListItems;
            List<ProductInfo> myProducts = new List<ProductInfo>();

            ClientOM.ClientContext SPContext = new ClientOM.ClientContext(SPUrl);
            ClientOM.Web mySPSite = SPContext.Web;
            ClientOM.ListCollection myListCollection = mySPSite.Lists;
            var productsList = SPContext.Web.Lists.GetByTitle("Products");
            ClientOM.CamlQuery myCamlQuery = new CamlQuery();
            IQueryable<ClientOM.ListItem> myList = productsList.
                GetItems(myCamlQuery);
            myListItems = SPContext.LoadQuery(myList);
            SPContext.ExecuteQuery();

            var returnedListData = from prod in myListItems
                                   select prod;

            foreach (ClientOM.ListItem tempListItem in returnedListData)
            {
                ProductInfo tempProd = new ProductInfo();
                tempProd.productName = tempListItem.FieldValues.
                    Values.ElementAt(1).ToString();
                tempProd.productSKU = tempListItem.FieldValues.
                    Values.ElementAt(4).ToString();
                tempProd.productPrice = tempListItem.FieldValues.
                    Values.ElementAt(5).ToString();
                myProducts.Add(tempProd);
            }

            dtgrdSPListData.DataSource = myProducts;
        }
    }
}
```

When you run the application and provide the URL to the SharePoint site (for example, `http://fabrikamhockey`), the application displays the data within the datagrid after you click the Load button, as shown in Figure 5-13.

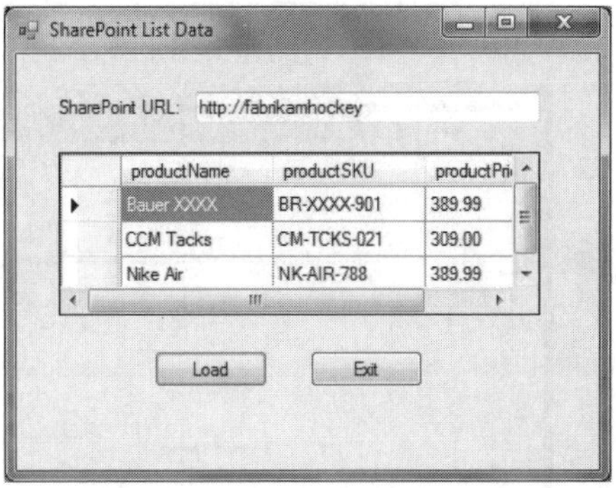

FIGURE 5-13 WinForm application running against a list

The SharePoint client object model is not only useful for reading data from a SharePoint list, but it's also very useful for writing to that list. And again, you have the opportunity to clean up the syntax of your code by not having to use CAML as a part of your call to push data back into SharePoint.

To put this into practice, the next example continues to leverage the `Products` list but, this time, uses a WPF client application that leverages the client object model to submit data back to the SharePoint list.

TRY IT OUT   Using the Client Object Model to Programmatically Write List Data

Code file [SPWriteListApp.zip] available for download at Wrox.com.

The client object model is an effective way to write back to a SharePoint list programmatically. To create a simple application that writes to a list using the client object model, follow these steps:

1. Open Visual Studio. Click File ➪ New ➪ Project ➪ WPF Application (under the Windows category). Be sure to select the .NET Framework 3.5 in the drop-down list in the New Project dialog. Also, provide a name for your project (for example, `SPWriteListApp`) and click OK.

2. Add four labels and textboxes to your WPF Designer surface, and then add three buttons. When finished, the layout of your UI should look similar to Figure 5-14.

Table 5-7 shows the control type and the name of the controls that you should add to the WPF application.

TABLE 5-7 Control Types for WPF Application

CONTROL TYPE	CONTROL NAME
Label	`lblSPUrl, lblProdName, lblProdSku, lblProdPrice`
Textbox	`txtbxURL, txtbxProdName, txtbxProdPrice, txtbxProdSKU`
Button	`btnAdd, btnClear, btnExit`

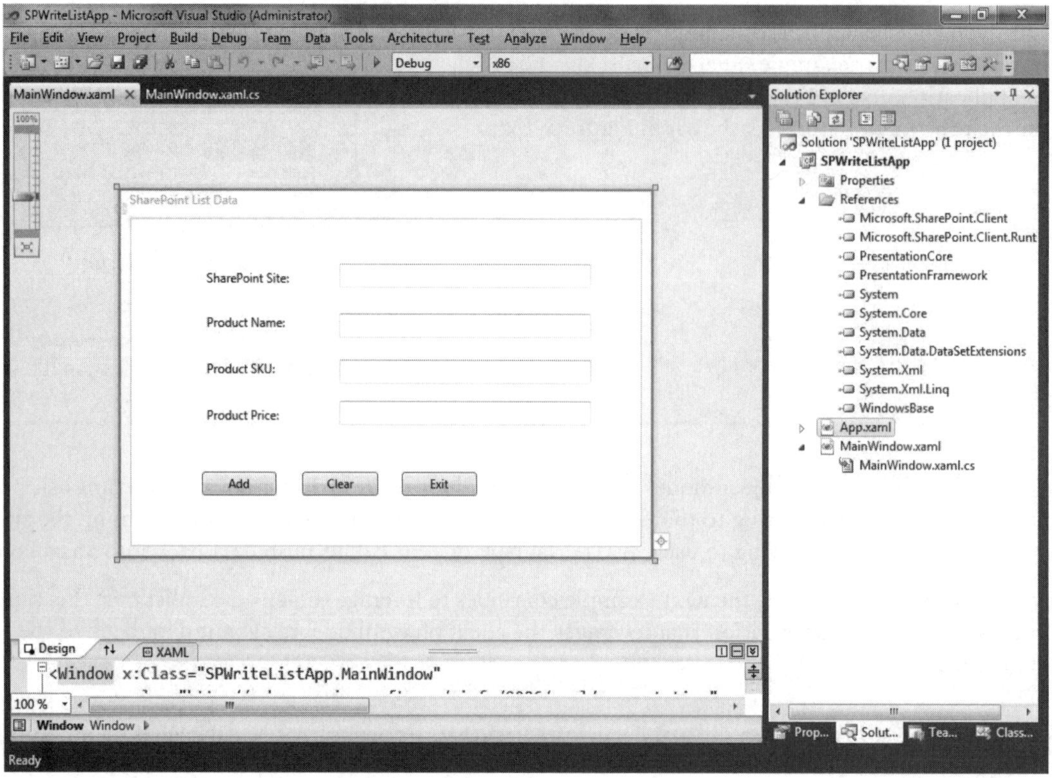

FIGURE 5-14 WPF UI for writing data to list

The XAML code that maps to this UI will look like the following code snippet:

```
<Window x:Class="SPWriteListApp.MainWindow"
        xmlns="http://schemas.microsoft.com/winfx/2006/xaml/presentation"
        xmlns:x="http://schemas.microsoft.com/winfx/2006/xaml"
        Title="SharePoint List Data" Height="350" Width="525">
    <Grid>
        <Button
Content="Add" Height="23" HorizontalAlignment="Left" Margin=
    "70,240,0,0"
Name="btnAdd" VerticalAlignment="Top" Width="75" Click="btnAdd_Click" />
        <Button
Content="Clear" Height="23" HorizontalAlignment="Right" Margin=
    "0,240,258,0"
Name="btnClear" VerticalAlignment="Top" Width="75" Click="btnClear_Click" />
        <Label
Content="SharePoint Site:" Height="28" HorizontalAlignment="Left" Margin=
    "70,43,0,0"
Name="lblSPUrl" VerticalAlignment="Top" Width="120" />
        <Label
Content="Product Name:" Height="28" HorizontalAlignment="Left" Margin=
```

```
            "70,85,0,0"
Name="lblProdName" VerticalAlignment="Top" Width="120" />
            <Label
Content="Product SKU:" Height="28" HorizontalAlignment="Left" Margin=
            "70,129,0,0"
Name="lblProdSku" VerticalAlignment="Top" Width="120" />
            <Label
Content="Product Price:" Height="28" HorizontalAlignment="Left" Margin=
            "70,173,0,0"
Name="lblProdPrice" VerticalAlignment="Top" Width="120" />
            <TextBox
Height="23" HorizontalAlignment="Left" Margin="206,43,0,0"
Name="txtbxURL" VerticalAlignment="Top" Width="248" />
            <TextBox
Height="23" HorizontalAlignment="Left" Margin="206,90,0,0"
Name="txtbxProdName" VerticalAlignment="Top" Width="248" />
            <TextBox
Height="23" HorizontalAlignment="Left" Margin="206,134,0,0"
Name="txtbxProdSKU" VerticalAlignment="Top" Width="248" />
            <TextBox
Height="23" HorizontalAlignment="Left" Margin="206,173,0,0"
Name="txtbxProdPrice" VerticalAlignment="Top" Width="248" />
            <Button
Content="Exit" Height="23" HorizontalAlignment="Left" Margin="268,240,0,0"
Name="btnExit" VerticalAlignment="Top" Width="75" Click="btnExit_Click" />
        </Grid>
</Window>
```

3. Before you begin coding using the new client object model, you must add the appropriate references. To add these references, right-click the project and select Add Reference. Select the Browse tab, and then browse to `c:\Program Files\Common Files\Microsoft Shared\Web Server Extensions\14\ISAPI` and add the `Microsoft.SharePoint.Client.dll` and the `Microsoft.SharePoint.Client.Runtime.dll` to your project. After you've added these references, add the following `using` statements to your application:

```
using ClientOM = Microsoft.SharePoint.Client;
using Microsoft.SharePoint.Client;
```

4. After you've created the UI, you'll want to add the event handlers to each of the buttons you've added to the Designer surface. For the Clear and Exit buttons, this code is similar to earlier examples in this chapter. But the new code that you may not have seen before is the client object model code that adds a new record to a list. This corresponds to the Add button in the WPF UI and is shown here. You'll first note that this code snippet is a slight improvement over the use of CAML constructs to push data back into SharePoint. Note that it's not because CAML goes away; it's because in this example SharePoint abstracts it away — it is now created dynamically.

In the following code snippet, the updating of the list leverages class-level variables that are set via the data that users enter via the textboxes. Then, you use the `ClientContext` object to set the context of the SharePoint site (again leveraging the user entry from the `txtbxURL` textbox). The code then gets the list by name (that is, `Products`) and loads the list in memory. After the list is in memory, you can then create a new `ListItem` object and set the values of this new item through the data that was entered into the textboxes. To update the list, you must call the `ExecuteQuery` method again.

```
...
private void btnAdd_Click(object sender, RoutedEventArgs e)
        {
            strSPURL = txtbxURL.Text;
            strProdName = txtbxProdName.Text;
            strProdSKU = txtbxProdSKU.Text;
            strProdPrice = txtbxProdPrice.Text;

            ClientOM.ClientContext mySPContext = new ClientContext(strSPURL);
            ClientOM.List productsList = mySPContext.Web.Lists.GetByTitle
                ("Products");
            mySPContext.Load(mySPContext.Web);
            mySPContext.Load(productsList);
            mySPContext.ExecuteQuery();

            ListItemCreationInformation newProdRecord =
                new ListItemCreationInformation();
            ClientOM.ListItem newProdItem = productsList.AddItem(newProdRecord);

            newProdItem["Title"] = strProdName;
            newProdItem["Product_SKU"] = strProdSKU;
            newProdItem["Price"] = strProdPrice;
            newProdItem.Update();

            mySPContext.ExecuteQuery();

        }
...
```

The full code listing for the UI code behind is as follows.

```
using System;
using System.Collections.Generic;
using System.Linq;
using System.Text;
using System.Windows;
using System.Windows.Controls;
using System.Windows.Data;
using System.Windows.Documents;
using System.Windows.Input;
using System.Windows.Media;
using System.Windows.Media.Imaging;
using System.Windows.Navigation;
using System.Windows.Shapes;
using Microsoft.SharePoint.Client;
using ClientOM = Microsoft.SharePoint.Client;

namespace SPWriteListApp
{
    public partial class MainWindow : Window
    {
```

```csharp
        string strSPURL = "";
        string strProdName = "";
        string strProdSKU = "";
        string strProdPrice = "";

        public MainWindow()
        {
            InitializeComponent();
        }

        private void btnExit_Click(object sender, RoutedEventArgs e)
        {
            Application.Current.Shutdown();
        }

        private void btnClear_Click(object sender, RoutedEventArgs e)
        {
            txtbxURL.Text = "";
            txtbxProdName.Text = "";
            txtbxProdSKU.Text = "";
            txtbxProdPrice.Text = "";
        }

        private void btnAdd_Click(object sender, RoutedEventArgs e)
        {
            strSPURL = txtbxURL.Text;
            strProdName = txtbxProdName.Text;
            strProdSKU = txtbxProdSKU.Text;
            strProdPrice = txtbxProdPrice.Text;

            ClientOM.ClientContext mySPContext = new ClientContext(strSPURL);
            ClientOM.List productsList = mySPContext.Web.Lists.GetByTitle
                ("Products");
            mySPContext.Load(mySPContext.Web);
            mySPContext.Load(productsList);
            mySPContext.ExecuteQuery();

            ListItemCreationInformation newProdRecord =
                new ListItemCreationInformation();
            ClientOM.ListItem newProdItem = productsList.AddItem(newProdRecord);

            newProdItem["Title"] = strProdName;
            newProdItem["Product_SKU"] = strProdSKU;
            newProdItem["Price"] = strProdPrice;
            newProdItem.Update();

            mySPContext.ExecuteQuery();

        }
    }
}
```

5. When you run the application, it will invoke the WPF interface and you can enter information, as shown in Figure 5-15.

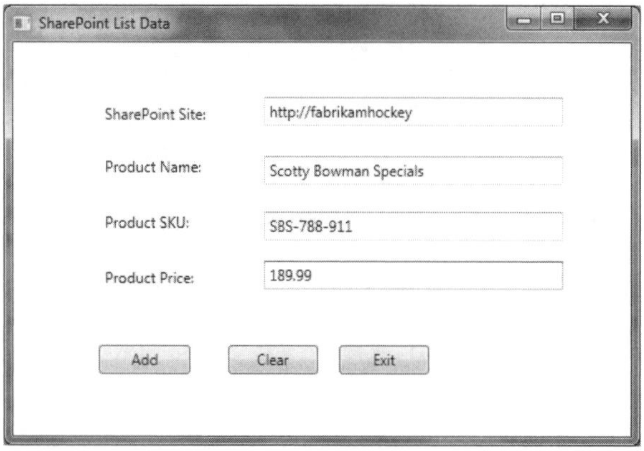
SharePoint List Data
SharePoint Site:
http://fabrikamhockey
Product Name:
Scotty Bowman Specials
Product SKU:
SBS-788-911
Product Price:
189.99
Add
Clear
Exit

FIGURE 5-15 Running the WPF application

6. When you enter the data and click Add, this will execute the client object model code, and add a new record to the SharePoint list, as shown in Figure 5-16.

Title
Product_SKU
Price
Bauer XXXX
BR-XXXX-901
389.99
CCM Tacks
CM-TCKS-021
309.00
Nike Air
NK-AIR-788
389.99
Bauer XXVI NEW
BR-XXVI-090
279.99
Scotty Bowman Specials NEW
SBS-788-911
189.99

FIGURE 5-16 Updated list data

How It Works

For both of the previous exercises, you used the client-side object model to read data from a SharePoint list and write data back to that same list. In many ways, the underlying calls for SharePoint don't necessarily change. For example, the client object model leverages the services that are native to SharePoint beneath the covers to make the call into SharePoint. However, this is abstracted away from you.

What this means is that the client object model essentially represents a layer that translates object-model calls (through object instantiation, property setting, and batch method execution) into LINQ queries that dynamically create CAML queries. (Note that where you require more complex queries, you would still need to use CAML to interact with SharePoint using the client object model.) Thus, the XML is handled for you within the inner workings of the client object model. For the developer, this can result in cleaner syntax.

Another option beyond leveraging the client-side object model is the creation of custom WCF services. These are ideal when you want to host your own service or Web application in IIS, or make the code reusable across multiple clients. (Custom WCF services can be leveraged from a broad array of client applications, including all of the ones you've seen in this chapter.)

Programming Against Lists Using a Custom WCF Service

While Chapter 10 provides more coverage on service-oriented application development in SharePoint, it should be mentioned here because it's also a viable option when developing applications that interact with lists.

Earlier in this chapter, you saw an ASP.NET example of the Lists Web service being leveraged to code against a SharePoint list. However, ASP.NET Web services are not the only type of service-based application you can develop for SharePoint. In SharePoint 2010, you can also build WCF-based applications. While WCF applications can range in size, shape, and functionality, you can leverage them for developing and deploying applications that interact with SharePoint lists.

There are two primary types of WCF applications that you can build that will interact with SharePoint lists:

➤ The first is a standard WCF service application that is deployed to either IIS or to the SharePoint 2010 root.

➤ The second is the new REST-based service that is accessible natively through the ISAPI folder.

When you choose the standard WCF option, you can leverage, say, the native SharePoint object model, and deploy a service to the SharePoint server. For example, if you take the earlier server-side list update code that you ran against the Products list and create a WCF service from it, you can test how you can develop against SharePoint using WCF.

To leverage WCF, you follow these primary steps:

1. Create the service code.

2. Publish and deploy the service code.

3. Consume the service code in a client application.

Let's discuss each of these in the context of updating the Products list using the same code you used in the WPF application you created earlier.

First, to create the service code, you use the standard Visual Studio 2010 project templates (for example, the WCF Service Application). Similar to the earlier exercises in this chapter, you must target .NET Framework 3.5 if you're going to be using the SharePoint object model. If you want to leverage the SharePoint object model within a service, you create a new service and add the Microsoft. SharePoint.dll to the project. You can then access the SharePoint object model within the service.

If you were to create a simple service, you would need to create a *contract* as well as *service code* that handles the interaction with SharePoint — these are standard structural elements of a WCF service. The contract that you might build for the service could look like the following (the boldfaced code represents code you would add to the service):

```
using System;
using System.Collections.Generic;
using System.Linq;
using System.Runtime.Serialization;
using System.ServiceModel;
using System.ServiceModel.Web;
```

```
using System.Text;

namespace UpdateSPList
{
    [ServiceContract]
    public interface IService1
    {
        [OperationContract]
        void updateProduct(string SPSite, string prodName,
            string prodSKU, string prodPrice);
    }

}
```

Note that, in this service, there is only one method that you expose to calling applications that will handle four parameters: the URL of the site (for example, `http://fabrikamhockey`), product name, product SKU, and product price (three fields within the `Products` list). Following is the service code (with the boldfaced code that you would add to the solution) that corresponds to this service contract:

```
using System;
using System.Collections.Generic;
using System.Linq;
using System.Runtime.Serialization;
using System.ServiceModel;
using System.ServiceModel.Web;
using System.Text;
using Microsoft.SharePoint;

namespace UpdateSPList
{
    public class Service1 : IService1
    {
        public void updateProduct(string SPSite, string prodName,
            string prodSKU, string prodPrice)
        {
            string strDashListRoot = SPSite;
            using (SPSite site = new SPSite(strDashListRoot))
            {
                using (SPWeb web = site.OpenWeb())
                {
                    web.AllowUnsafeUpdates = true;
                    SPList list = web.Lists["Products"];
                    SPListItem Item = list.Items.Add();
                    Item["Title"] = prodName;
                    Item["Product_SKU"] = prodSKU;
                    Item["Price"] = prodPrice;
                    Item.Update();
                    web.AllowUnsafeUpdates = false;
                }
            }
        }
    }
}
```

After you've created a WCF service application, you can deploy the service code to IIS. Deploying to IIS requires that you first create a folder on your server file system, publish your code to your folder, and then map that folder (as a virtual directory) to your IIS Web site. You may also need to add information from your `web.config` file (an XML file that contains configuration information specific to your service) to the SharePoint `web.config` file (which is also an XML-based configuration file, but this file lives in `c:\Inetpub\wwwroot\wss\VirtualDirectories\<Site Name>`) to ensure that your WCF service will run properly on the SharePoint server. Figure 5-17 illustrates where you select the virtual directory from within IIS.

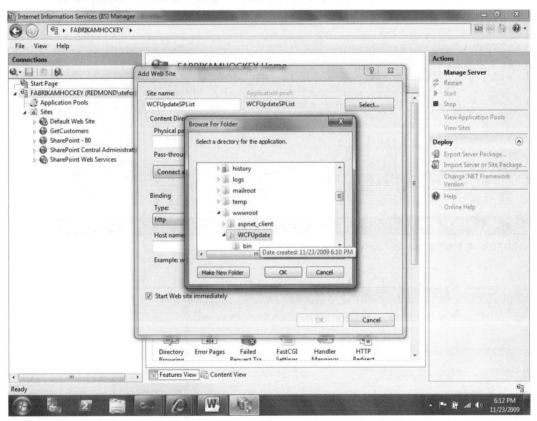

FIGURE 5-17 Publishing the WCF service to IIS

After you create your Web site in IIS, you can test out the service by right-clicking Browse in IIS. Figure 5-18 illustrates what the result of this test looks like. You should note that the URL in Figure 5-18 is the service reference that you would then use when creating a client application and mapping the service to the client.

After you've tested the service, you can then create a client (or server-based) application that will consume your WCF service. Doing this is similar to what you did when adding a reference to the ASP.NET Web service — you right-click Reference in Visual Studio 2010, click Add Service Reference, and then add the URL that was exposed by the earlier test. Figure 5-19 shows the Add Reference dialog where you add the WCF service endpoint.

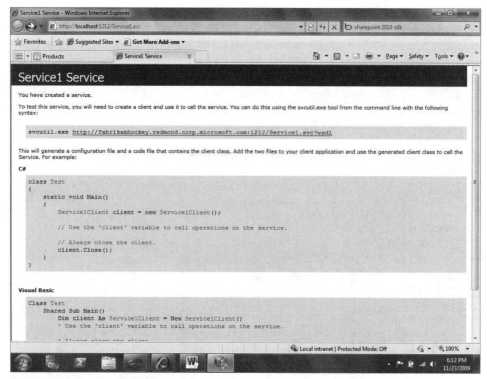

FIGURE 5-18 Testing the WCF service

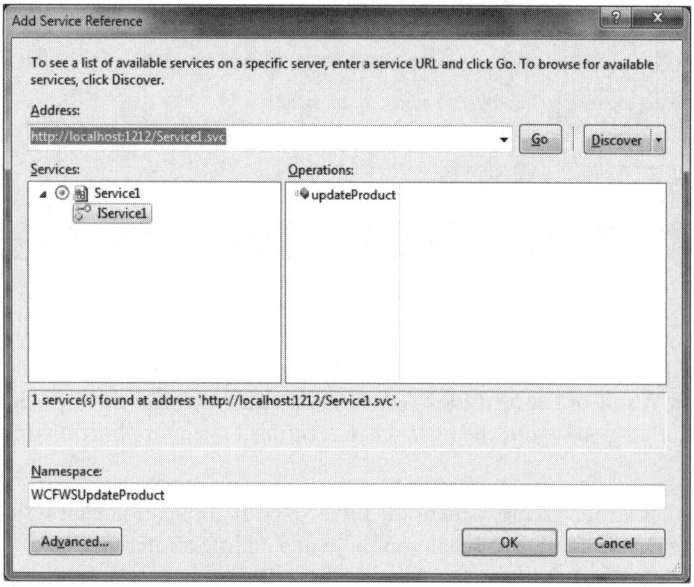

FIGURE 5-19 Adding service reference

After you add the service, you can now code against the service reference. For example, you can create the same WPF application interface you used earlier in the chapter, and then hook up the service code to the Add button, as shown in Figure 5-20.

The following boldfaced code displays how you can implement the service you created and deployed to IIS. This is the code that is mapped to the Add button (btnAdd).

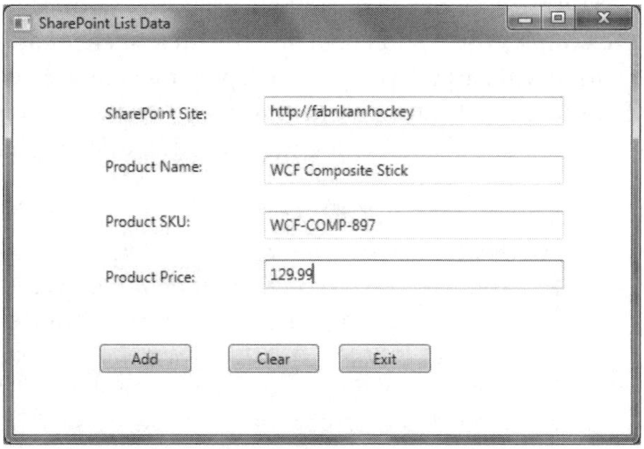

FIGURE 5-20 Testing the WCF service

```
...
    private void btnAdd_Click(object sender, RoutedEventArgs e)
        {
            strSPURL = txtbxURL.Text;
            strProdName = txtbxProdName.Text;
            strProdSKU = txtbxProdSKU.Text;
            strProdPrice = txtbxProdPrice.Text;

            SPWriteListApp.WCFWSUpdateProduct.Service1Client myWCFProxy =
                new WCFWSUpdateProduct.Service1Client();
            myWCFProxy.updateProduct(strSPURL, strProdName, strProdSKU,
                strProdPrice);
            myWCFProxy.Close();
        }
...
```

Once you've implemented the service in your client code, the result of the WCF service call would be similar to the other applications you built in this chapter — they can read or write to a SharePoint list. In this case, the code updates a SharePoint list with new information. Figure 5-21 shows how this code successfully updated the list.

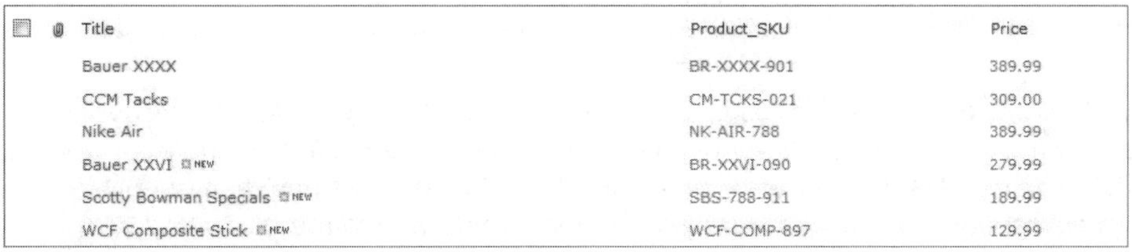

	Title	Product_SKU	Price
	Bauer XXXX	BR-XXXX-901	389.99
	CCM Tacks	CM-TCKS-021	309.00
	Nike Air	NK-AIR-788	389.99
	Bauer XXVI ⊡ NEW	BR-XXVI-090	279.99
	Scotty Bowman Specials ⊡ NEW	SBS-788-911	189.99
	WCF Composite Stick ⊡ NEW	WCF-COMP-897	129.99

FIGURE 5-21 Successfully updating the list

The WCF service code shown earlier leverages the server-side object model. However, one of the key differentiating factors between the WCF framework and the client object model is that you're creating a service that can be consumed remotely and is deployed for use across multiple clients. For example, you could create many different client applications that consume the same list service code discussed earlier. You're also deploying your service to IIS. Both of these sit on top of the server-side object model and, if needed, not only provide a more scalable and portable solution, but also provide remote clients with a way to call into SharePoint.

> **NOTE** *There are a number of discrete (and sometimes tricky) steps that are required when you build and deploy WCF services. It is recommended that at each of the three steps mentioned earlier, you test your code to ensure that it works. Chapter 10 includes a complete exercise on how to create and deploy custom WCF services for SharePoint. Specifically, you will deploy a WCF service, and then consume that service within a Visual Web part.*

The last method of interacting with lists you'll see in this chapter is the RESTful service, which is a WCF Data service.

REST-Based Services and List Development

Beyond building a custom WCF service, you can also leverage the new REST (Representational State Transfer)–based WCF Data services as well. For example, in SharePoint 2010, there is a new service called `ListData.svc` that resides in the `ISAPI` folder. This is a special REST-based service that returns Atom feeds and enables you to interact with your SharePoint site.

This service leverages WCF Data services to enable applications to expose data as a data service, which can then be consumed by client applications, such as Web clients, .NET clients, and so on. The REST Web service not only works with SharePoint list data, but it also works with other data sources (for example, it also works with Excel data and Windows Azure cloud data).

The WCF Data service is reachable via a regular HTTP request, and uses standard HTTP verbs such as `GET`, `POST`, `PUT`, and `DELETE` to perform CRUD (Create, Read, Update, and Delete) operations against the services and sources of data. To leverage the REST APIs in SharePoint 2010, you must have the latest WCF Data services installed in your environment.

> **NOTE** *To use REST in SharePoint 2010, you must install the WCF Data Services separately after you have SharePoint installed and configured. It is a simple installation process that requires you to first install the services and then do a system reboot. You can get more information and download the WCF Data Services bits from* `http://msdn.microsoft.com/en-us/data/bb931106.aspx.`

After you install WCF Data services (and reboot your machine), the quickest way to test the REST-based list service is to reference the service in your browser's URL; for example:

```
http://<your_server>/_vti_bin/ListData.svc/
```

This uses the WCF Data services and REST-based protocols (for example, Atom, AtomPub, and RSS) to return an XML-based Atom feed of the lists in your SharePoint site. The return feed will look similar to the following XML sample, which has been trimmed to include a couple of lists and the Products list that has run through the examples in this chapter:

> **NOTE** *You can return data in two different views in your Internet browser: one has feed reading turned on (formatted view of return XML data) and the other has feed reading turned off (raw XML view). To turn off the RSS Feed to get the raw XML view of output from the REST call for Internet Explorer, you click Tools ➪ Internet Options. Click the Content tab, and click Settings under "Feeds and Web Slices." Uncheck "Turn on feed reading view."*

```xml
<?xml version="1.0" encoding="utf8" standalone="yes" ?>
 <service xml:base="http://fabrikamhockey/_vti_bin/ListData.svc/"
     xmlns:atom="http://www.w3.org/2005/Atom" xmlns:app=
     "http://www.w3.org/2007/app" xmlns="http://www.w3.org/2007/app">
 <workspace>
  <atom:title>Default</atom:title>
 <collection href="Announcements">
  <atom:title>Announcements</atom:title>
  </collection>
…
 <collection href="Products">
  <atom:title>Products</atom:title>
  </collection>
…
<collection href="XAPS">
  <atom:title>XAPS</atom:title>
  </collection>
  </workspace>
  </service>
```

To query and filter on specific lists or list items, you can append additional commands to the REST URL. Following is the generic syntax for these commands:

```
…/_vti_bin/ListData.svc/{Entity}[({identifier})]/[{Property}].
```

If you apply the REST command syntax to the Products list you've been using throughout the chapter, you can see the Products list through an Atom feed by typing the following in the URL address bar:

```
http://<your_ server>/_vti_bin/ListData.svc/Products
```

Within the REST URL syntax, there exist a number of parameters that can be used to query and filter the returned data. These parameters are known as QueryString parameters. Following are the more commonly used QueryString parameters for REST:

➤ $filter

➤ $expand

> ➤ `$orderby`

> ➤ `$skip`

> ➤ `$top`

> ➤ `$metadata` (which will bring back all the XML metadata about the object)

If you apply the `$filter QueryString` filter to the data that the REST returns from the call to the list of `Products` by the price of a product, you can use the following command:

```
http://fabrikamhockey/_vti_bin/ListData.svc/Products?$filter=(Price eq '389.99').
```

The results returned from this query are displayed as shown in Figure 5-22 (which now has feed reading view turned on).

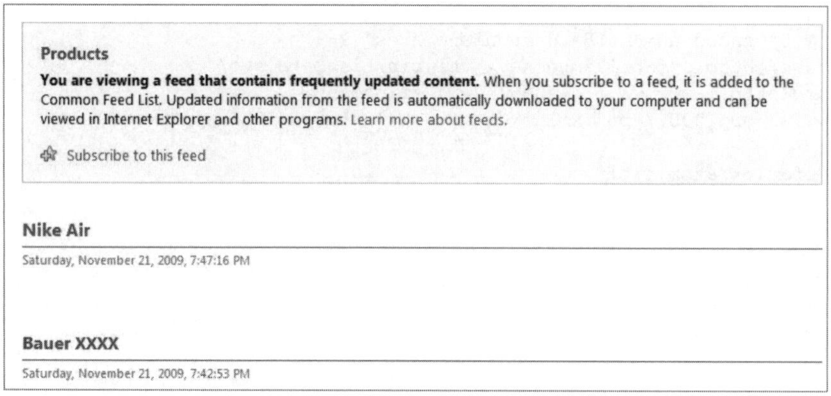

```
Products
You are viewing a feed that contains frequently updated content. When you subscribe to a feed, it is added to the
Common Feed List. Updated information from the feed is automatically downloaded to your computer and can be
viewed in Internet Explorer and other programs. Learn more about feeds.

    Subscribe to this feed

Nike Air
Saturday, November 21, 2009, 7:47:16 PM


Bauer XXXX
Saturday, November 21, 2009, 7:42:53 PM
```

FIGURE 5-22 Returned data from RESTful service call

Another example for the `Products` list would be querying a specific list item in the list. For example, the following REST command returns the third list item:

```
http://fabrikamhockey/_vti_bin/ListData.svc/Products(3).
```

The return data for this query (where the reader feed has now been turned off) is as follows:

```xml
<?xml version="1.0" encoding="utf8" standalone="yes" ?>
 <entry xml:base="http://fabrikamhockey/_vti_bin/ListData.svc/"
     xmlns:d="http://schemas.microsoft.com/ado/2007/08/dataservices"
     xmlns:m="http://schemas.microsoft.com/ado/2007/08/dataservices/metadata"
     m:etag="W/"3"" xmlns="http://www.w3.org/2005/Atom">
  <id>http://fabrikamhockey/_vti_bin/ListData.svc/Products(3)</id>
  <title type="text">Nike Air</title>
  <updated>20091121T19:47:1608:00</updated>
 <author>
  <name />
  </author>
  <link rel="edit" title="ProductsItem" href="Products(3)" />
  <link rel="http://schemas.microsoft.com/ado/2007/08/dataservices/related/
```

```
        Attachments" type="application/atom+xml;type=feed" title=
        "Attachments" href="Products(3)/Attachments" />
    <category term="Microsoft.SharePoint.DataService.ProductsItem"
        scheme="http://schemas.microsoft.com/ado/2007/08/dataservices/scheme" />
    <content type="application/xml">
    <m:properties>
    <d:ContentTypeID>0x0100E03B378FDA26EF44AA88B2A3D4CD3E8F</d:ContentTypeID>
    <d:Title>Nike Air</d:Title>
    <d:Product_SKU>NKAIR788</d:Product_SKU>
    <d:Price>389.99</d:Price>
    <d:ID m:type="Edm.Int32">3</d:ID>
    <d:ContentType>Item</d:ContentType>
    <d:Modified m:type="Edm.DateTime">20091121T19:47:16</d:Modified>
    <d:Created m:type="Edm.DateTime">20091121T11:06:40</d:Created>
    <d:CreatedByID m:type="Edm.Int32">1</d:CreatedByID>
    <d:ModifiedByID m:type="Edm.Int32">1</d:ModifiedByID>
    <d:Owshiddenversion m:type="Edm.Int32">3</d:Owshiddenversion>
    <d:Version>1.0</d:Version>
    <d:Path>/Lists/Products</d:Path>
    </m:properties>
    </content>
    </entry>
```

REST-based development is not just about submitting commands via a URL. You can also create applications using the WCF Data services. For example, what if you want to leverage the SharePoint list data and surface that data inside of a .NET client application using the REST service? You can do this simply by creating a new client application that leverages the REST service. When you add the service, it creates the data context for you (similar to creating other WCF Data services in Visual Studio), and then you can develop against SharePoint using this context.

TRY IT OUT   **Using RESTful Services to Program Against Lists**

> *Code file [RESTSPListExample.zip] available for download at Wrox.com.*

Using the built-in REST support is an efficient and lightweight approach to programming against lists. To leverage REST when programmatically interacting with lists, follow these steps:

1. Open Visual Studio. Click File ⇨ New ⇨ Project ⇨ Windows Form Application. Provide a name for the project (for example, `RESTSPListExample`) and click OK.

2. After Visual Studio creates the project for you, right-click the References node and select Add Service Reference. Type your SharePoint site URL into the Address field and click Go, as shown in Figure 5-23. Visual Studio will discover the `ListData.svc` service for you, and it will also expose the lists that belong to your site.

3. Provide a namespace for the service reference (for example, `SPSiteRestService`), and then click OK.

4. Visual Studio adds a number of objects to the solution, including a service reference and entities that are pulled from the SharePoint site through the REST service context. To view the entities within your site in Visual Studio, click Data ⇨ Show Data Sources. This will open the Data Sources pane in Visual Studio.

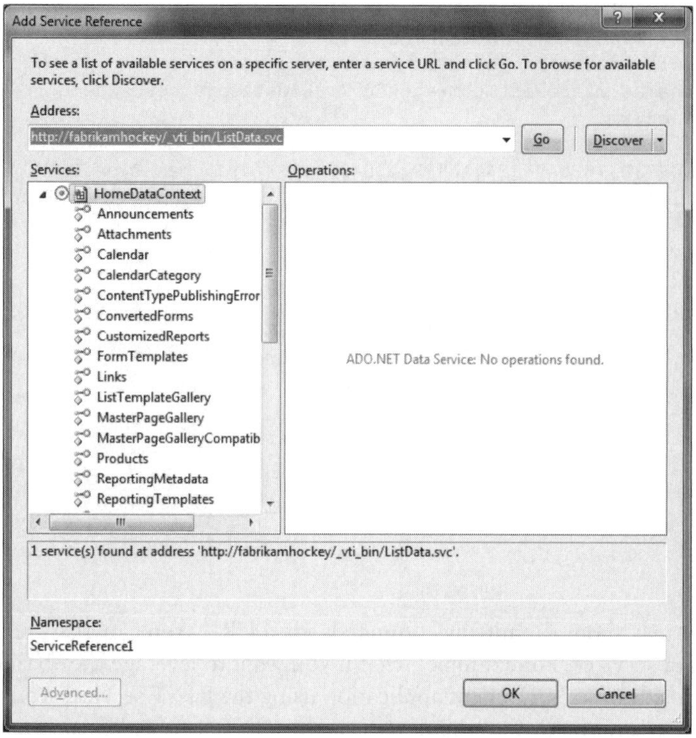

FIGURE 5-23 Add Service Reference dialog

5. Select the `Products` list that you've been using throughout the chapter in the Data Sources pane, and drag it onto the Designer surface.

6. You can now edit the look and feel of the datagrid in the designer (for example, lock it to the Designer surface and select which columns you want to display in the application). Right-click the datagrid and select Edit Columns to add and remove columns as you desire.

7. To load the data using the REST service, you must add some code to the form. Double-click the top portion of the form to generate a `Form1_Load` event, where you'll add your code.

8. You'll need to add a couple of `using` statements, a service proxy, and some binding code to load the data — all of which appears in boldface in the following code snippet. For example, in the following code snippet you'll add two `using` statements, one for the WCF Data services and the other for the REST service, that were added to the project. Also note that you will create a service proxy called `myRestSvc` and pass an explicit reference to the `ListData.svc` endpoint URL. This is done at the class level. After this, there are three lines of code you can add in the `Form1_Load` event to manage the credentials to call into SharePoint by using the `DefaultNetworkCredentials`, create a LINQ query (which essentially selects all items from the list), and bind the return data from the LINQ query to the `Products` list binding source (`productsBindingSource`), which will automatically display the data from the SharePoint list.

```
using System;
using System.Collections.Generic;
using System.ComponentModel;
using System.Data;
```

```
using System.Drawing;
using System.Linq;
using System.Text;
using System.Windows.Forms;
using System.Data.Services.Client;
using RESTSPListExample.SPSiteRestService;
using System.Net;


namespace RESTSPListExample
{
    public partial class Form1 : Form
    {
        //Be sure to replace the URL in the code below
            with your SharePoint site URL.
        TeamSiteDataContext mySPContext = new TeamSiteDataContext (
            new Uri("http://fabrikamhockey/_vti_bin/listdata.svc/"));

        public Form1()
        {
            InitializeComponent();
        }

        private void Form1_Load(object sender, EventArgs e)
        {
            mySPContext.Credentials =
                System.Net.CredentialCache.DefaultNetworkCredentials;

            var q = from p in myRestSvc.Products
                    select p;

            this.productsBindingSource.DataSource = q;

        }
    }
}
```

9. After you've completed the code additions, press F5. The data from the SharePoint list will be automatically populated within the datagrid, as shown in Figure 5-24.

10. You can adjust the LINQ query to filter on specific data from your SharePoint list. For example, if you add the following (boldfaced) where clause to your LINQ statement, this will return only those results where the price is listed as 389.99, as shown in Figure 5-25.

FIGURE 5-24 Querying data in WinForm application

```
...
var q = from p in myRestSvc.Products
                    .Where(p => (p.Price == "389.99"))
                    select p;
...
```

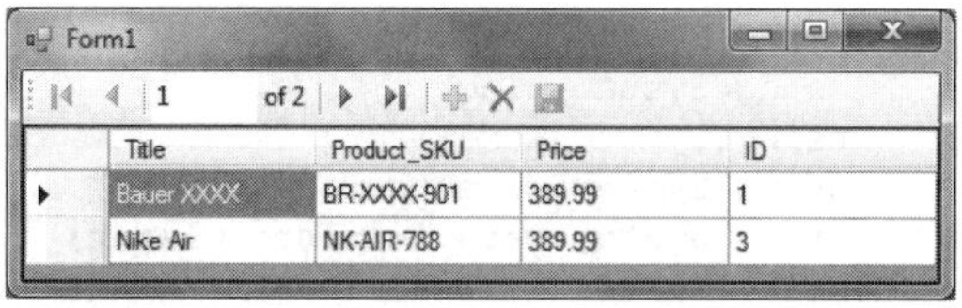

11. The REST APIs also enable updates to your
SharePoint list. To test this, add three labels,
three textboxes, and two buttons to your
Designer surface beneath the datagrid, as shown
in Figure 5-26. Double-click the Refresh button and add the same code you have in the

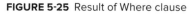

FIGURE 5-25 Result of Where clause

`Form1_Load` event (or create a helper method, and reference that method from both the `btnRe-fresh_Click` event and the `Form1_Load` event).

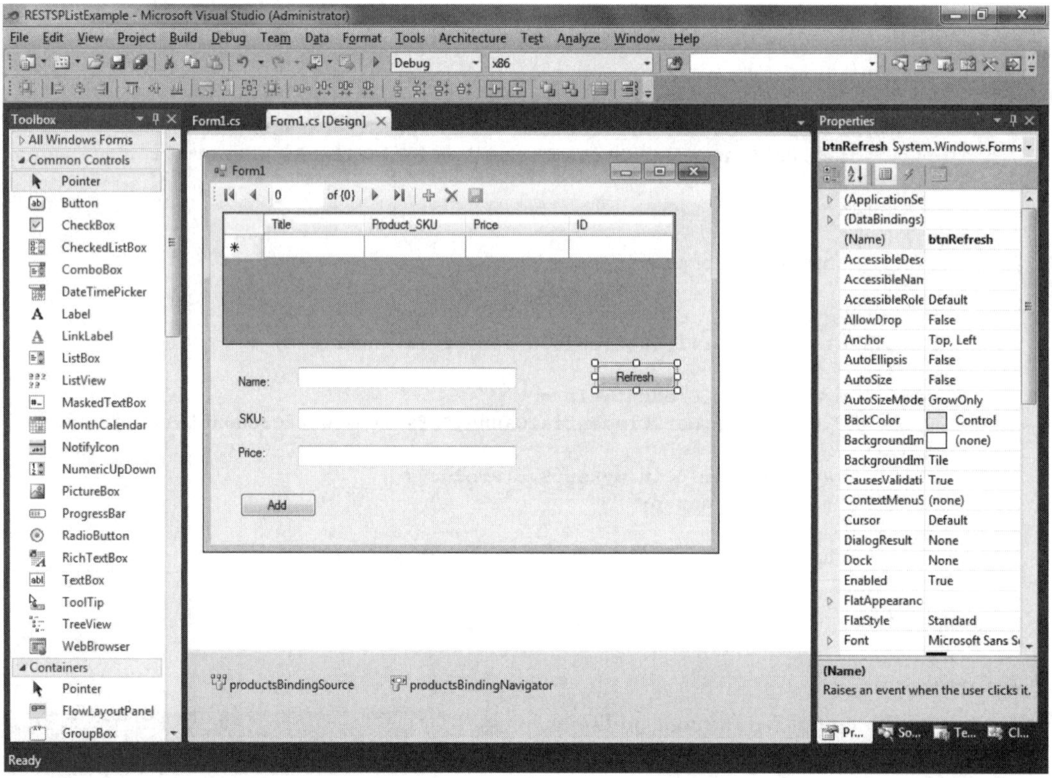

FIGURE 5-26 Extending the WinForm UI

Table 5-8 shows the control type and the name of the controls that you should add to the WPF
application.

TABLE 5-8 Control Types for WPF Application

CONTROL TYPE	CONTROL NAME
Label	`lblName, lblSKU, lblPrice`
Textbox	`txtbxName, txtbxSku, txtbxPrice`
Button	`btnRefresh, btnAdd`

12. Next, double-click the Add button to add some code behind, and add the following code to the `btnAdd_Click` event. This code will take the user entries, create a new `ProductsItem` (which has been set up for you via the REST Data service), and assign the user entries to the three fields (that is, `Title`, `Product`, and `Price`). It then calls the `AddToProducts` method and the `SaveChanges` method to add the data as a new record to the SharePoint list.

```
...
private void btnAdd_Click(object sender, EventArgs e)
        {
            string prodName = txtbxName.Text;
            string prodSKU = txtbxSku.Text;
            string prodPrice = txtbxPrice.Text;

            ProductsItem newItem = new ProductsItem();
            newItem.Title = prodName;
            newItem.Product_SKU = prodSKU;
            newItem.Price = prodPrice;

            mySPContext.AddToProducts(newItem);
            mySPContext.SaveChanges();

        }
...
```

13. To test the new additions, press F5, add some data, click the Add button, and then click the Refresh button. You should see the new data appear in the datagrid, which is issuing the query to the SharePoint list, as shown in Figure 5-27.

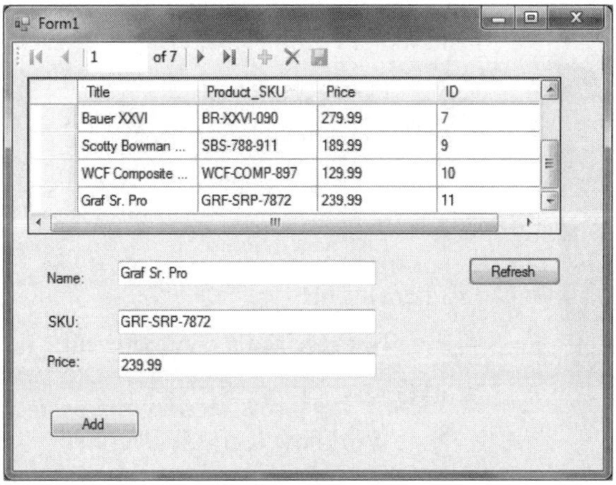

How It Works

The RESTful services work in a slightly different way than the other ways you've seen in this chapter. Specifically, they leverage the `Listdata.svc` service and Data services to treat SharePoint lists as data constructs. The querying against the list works similarly to other ways in which you query entities. You use LINQ as the standard way to query and filter the data, and then manipulate that data into your application.

FIGURE 5-27 Successful data query

At this point, you've seen a number of different ways to programmatically interact with SharePoint lists. According to your needs, you may find yourself choosing one method over another. For example, if you're looking for a clean syntax and you want to code using Silverlight, then perhaps using the client object model would be your choice. On the server, you might find yourself building utility tools or Web parts, so you will want to use the server-side object model as opposed to the client object model. Alternatively, if you wanted to have a more portable solution that multiple applications could call simultaneously, then perhaps the service-oriented architecture is more along your design. Either way, you have options as a SharePoint developer — in fact, more options than you've ever had before.

Let's now discuss event receivers for SharePoint lists.

CREATING EVENT RECEIVERS FOR A SHAREPOINT LIST

A powerful feature that has evolved across SharePoint versions is the *event receiver*. The event receiver is in essence a managed-code assembly that is deployed to SharePoint and reacts to an event, such as adding an item to a list, creating a new list item, provisioning a new SharePoint site, and so on. The fact that you can create custom managed code to execute against events provides quite a bit of power over your lists and any events attached to the lists. The managed-code assembly is strongly typed and signed, and, using Visual Studio 2010, is deployed as a feature into the global assembly cache (GAC), where it's instantiated when the corresponding event is fired.

In earlier versions of SharePoint, you could create an event receiver to document libraries. Then, SharePoint 2007 added a host of event receivers that were supported across the different lists in SharePoint. Further, there were a number of out-of-the-box event receivers that developers could use when developing against lists. These event receivers ranged from list events and list items to feature and Web events.

In SharePoint 2010, the following dozen new event receivers have been added:

- List events:
    - List is being added.
    - List is being deleted.
    - List was added.
    - List was deleted.
- List Item events:
    - List received a context event.
- Workflow:
    - Workflow is starting.
    - Workflow has started.
    - Workflow has completed.
    - Workflow was postponed.
- List Email:
    - List received an email message.
- Web:
    - Site is being provisioned.
    - Site was provisioned.

Not only does SharePoint 2010 support a wide variety of event receivers, but the tooling also supports quickly creating and deploying event receivers against SharePoint objects. This means that, if you were, for example, manually building classes to implement the SPListEventReceiver class to build and deploy event receivers, you can now use the native project templates within Visual Studio 2010 to build your event receivers.

TRY IT OUT Creating an Event Receiver for a List

Code file [SPListEventReceiver.zip] available for download at Wrox.com.

List event receivers come in many different shapes and sizes. To create a simple event receiver that writes a log entry to your local file system, follow these steps:

1. Open Visual Studio. Click File ⇨ New ⇨ Project ⇨ Event Receivers (in the SharePoint 2010 template category). Provide a name for your new project (for example, AnnouncementListEvent), and click OK.

2. Select Deploy as Farm Solution, and click Next. In the next step, select List Item Events for the type of event receiver and Announcements for the item to be the event receiver. Click the checkbox beside "An item is being added," as shown in Figure 5-28. Click Finish. This will create a project that will enable you to create some custom code that is tied to the Announcements list that will fire every time an item is added to the list.

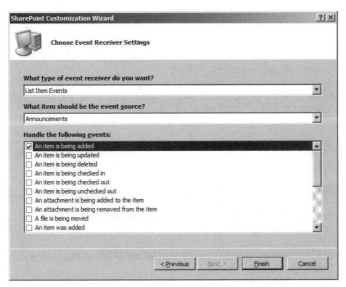

FIGURE 5-28 List event receivers

3. In the EventReceiver1.cs class, you'll see the main event handler for the Announcements list. This is the ItemAdding event.

```
namespace AnnouncementListEvent.EventReceiver1
{
    public class EventReceiver1 : SPItemEventReceiver
```

```
        {
            public override void ItemAdding(SPItemEventProperties properties)
            {
                base.ItemAdding(properties);
            }


        }
    }
    ...
```

4. Add the following two `using` statements at the top of the application code:

```
using System.IO;
using System.Text;
```

5. In the `ItemAdding` event, add some code (that is, the bolded code in the snippet that follows) that will call a method to log some data to a log file. For example, in the following code sample, the `writeDataToLogFile` passes the `SPItemEventProperties` and a string that represents the item event. So, when a user adds a new announcement, the event receiver will add an entry to a log file (that is, `mySPLog.txt`). Note that the method also sets the permissions to access the file system (although this may not be necessary if you're accessing the system as an administrator).

```
...
namespace AnnouncementListEvent.EventReceiver1
{

    public class EventReceiver1 : SPItemEventReceiver
    {

        public override void ItemAdding(SPItemEventProperties properties)
        {
            base.ItemAdding(properties);
            writeDataToLogFile(properties, "An Event");
        }

        private void writeDataToLogFile(SPItemEventProperties properties,
            string eventName)
        {
            FileIOPermission myPermissions = new
                FileIOPermission(PermissionState.Unrestricted);
            myPermissions.AddPathList(FileIOPermissionAccess.AllAccess,
                "c:\\Authoring");

            StreamWriter sw = File.AppendText(@"C:\Authoring\mySPLog.txt");
            StringBuilder sb = new StringBuilder();
                sb.AppendFormat("Date, Event and List:\n {0} {1} {2} ",
                    DateTime.Now.ToString(), eventName, properties.
                    ListTitle);
            sw.WriteLine(sb.ToString());
            sw.Close();
        }

    }
}
...
```

6. When you've finished adding the code, select the Build menu and select Deploy Solution.

7. Open the Announcements list in your SharePoint site, and add a new Announcement, as shown in Figure 5-29.

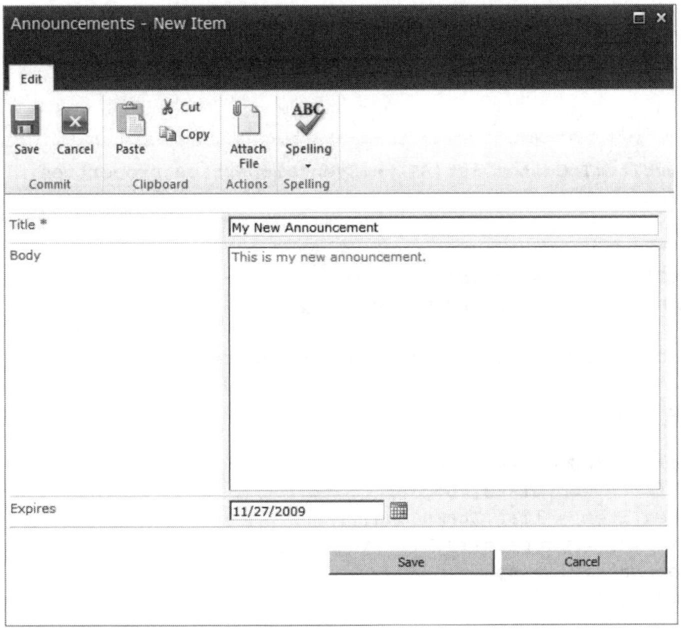

FIGURE 5-29 Triggering the event

8. Once you've added a new item to the Announcement list, navigate back to the place where your log file exists (for example, `c:\Authoring`), as shown in Figure 5-30.

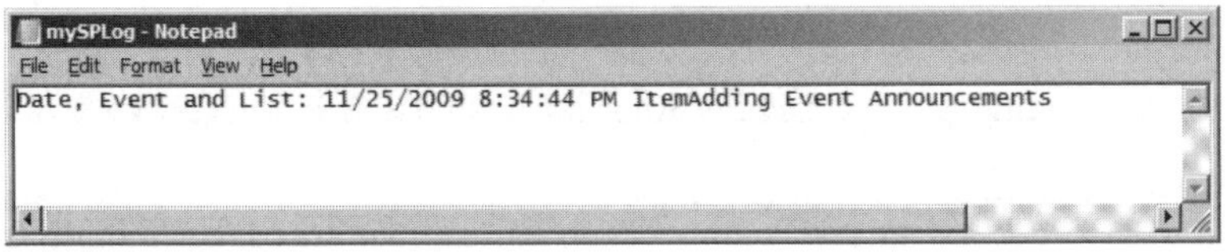

FIGURE 5-30 Log file created

9. You can also add events that interact with other parts of the SharePoint site. For example, let's add another event that writes an entry into a separate list called `Log`. To do this, add the following boldfaced code to your event receiver application:

```
...
namespace AnnouncementListEvent.EventReceiver1
{

    public class EventReceiver1 : SPItemEventReceiver
```

```
    {
        public override void ItemAdding(SPItemEventProperties properties)
        {
            base.ItemAdding(properties);
            writeDataToLogFile(properties, "ItemAdding Event");
            writeListItemToCustomList(properties, "ItemAdding Event");
        }

        ...

        private void writeListItemToCustomList(SPItemEventProperties properties,
            string eventName)
        {
            string spLog = "";
            DateTime currentTime = DateTime.Now;
            spLog = eventName + " " + currentTime.ToString();

            using (SPSite site = new SPSite("http://fabrikamhockey"))
            {
                using (SPWeb web = site.OpenWeb())
                {
                    web.AllowUnsafeUpdates = true;
                    SPList list = web.Lists["Log"];
                    SPListItem Item = list.Items.Add();
                    Item["Title"] = properties.ListTitle.ToString();
                    Item["Log Entry"] = spLog;
                    Item.Update();
                }
            }

        }

    }
}
...
```

10. Redeploy the application by clicking Build ⇨ Deploy Solution. Visual Studio retracts your old solution and replaces it with your new one.

11. Create a Log list with a Title and Log Entry column. Then add an item to your Announcements list. The event receiver code will create another entry to your file system log, and also create an entry in your SharePoint list, as shown in Figure 5-31.

FIGURE 5-31 Log entry in list

How It Works

When you're creating event receivers, you're essentially writing code that fires when a particular event occurs in your SharePoint site. For example, in this example, whenever someone created a new `Announcement`, it would fire an event that would add a log entry in a file on the system and on the list. While you repurposed some of the server-side list and updated a file on the system, you can literally tie any number of events to, for example, list updates such as workflow, custom timer jobs, and so on.

SUMMARY

This chapter provided an overview of the different ways in which you can develop against SharePoint lists. The chapter started with a glimpse into the use of the server-side object model (that is, using `Microsoft.SharePoint.dll`), which provided a brief look into the types of things that you could do by leveraging the `Microsoft.SharePoint` namespace. However, when you move beyond server-side applications, you often need service-based applications, and SharePoint 2010 provides you with a number of native ASP.NET Web services that you can leverage.

One key Web service is the Lists service, which has a number of members that are very useful. The Lists Web service is good in that it provides interactivity with SharePoint lists, but it does require some heavy syntax and XML serialization — which is often achieved through CAML constructs.

As you saw, leveraging the new client object model and the RESTful service can move you "somewhat" beyond the need for CAML queries, and provide a very powerful platform for interacting with lists. This statement is qualified with "somewhat" because CAML never entirely disappears. In some cases, it just gets abstracted away from your view. For example, a general query (`</View>`) auto-generates CAML queries that are then issued against the SharePoint list. So, while you don't see CAML, it is still there behind the scenes.

At the end of the day, one of the most commonly coded objects in SharePoint is the list. And, in SharePoint 2010, you have quite a few more choices that really begin to open up (and provide choice) to the way you develop against lists.

As you move on to Chapter 6, you'll see more ways to code against one of the other, more commonly coded against objects in SharePoint — the Web part. So, hang tight. The journey to becoming a SharePoint developer continues!

EXERCISES

1. What are the different ways in which you can program against lists?

2. Can you generally classify when to use one over the other?

3. How is using RESTful services and the new SharePoint client object model different from the other ways? What do they abstract away from the development process?

4. What are the different event receivers for lists? What user or system action might you map these events to?

▶ **WHAT YOU LEARNED IN THIS CHAPTER**

ITEM	DESCRIPTION
List structure and function	A list is one of the fundamental artifacts in SharePoint.
List Object Model	You programmatically interact with a list using a specific object model. This object model can be accessed using different APIs.
Ways to program against a list	There are a number of ways to program against a list, including the Lists Web service, client object model, server-side object model, REST, and custom WCF services.

RECOMMENDED READING

➤ SharePoint 2010 SDK: `http://msdn.microsoft.com/en-us/library/ee557253(office.14).aspx`

➤ Lists Web Service Members: `http://msdn.microsoft.com/en-us/library/lists.lists_members.aspx`.

➤ Channel 9 Lists and Schema Module: `http://channel9.msdn.com/learn/courses/SharePoint2010Developer/ListsAndSchemas/WCF Data Services on MSDN: http://msdn.microsoft.com/en-us/data/bb931106.aspx`

6

Building and Deploying SharePoint Web Parts

WHAT YOU'LL LEARN IN THIS CHAPTER:

➤ Understanding Web parts and how you can create one

➤ Understanding the difference between a standard and Visual Web part

➤ Using Visual Studio to build and deploy Web parts to SharePoint

In Chapter 5, you learned about the different ways you can program against one of the primary SharePoint artifacts — lists. In this chapter, you'll learn about another core building block in SharePoint — the Web part. The Web part is not unique to SharePoint. It is a set of integrated ASP.NET server controls. Because SharePoint is built on ASP.NET, it inherits the capabilities that are native to ASP.NET Web parts.

Developers can use Web parts to create Web sites, and, once rendered on a SharePoint site, users can then modify the content, behavior, or appearance of the Web part page using their Internet browser to personalize their experiences with the Web site.

SharePoint 2010 offers a wide array of out-of-the-box Web parts and, especially relevant to this chapter, an easier way to build and deploy Web parts into a SharePoint site. With that in mind, this chapter provides a high-level overview of Web parts, discusses the differences between standard and Visual Web parts, and walks through some ways to create custom Web parts for a SharePoint site.

UNDERSTANDING WEB PARTS

Similar to lists, Web parts are some of the most commonly customized objects in SharePoint. Web parts also provide a great opportunity for developers to leverage some very powerful capabilities that are native to ASP.NET.

Developers work with Web parts in a couple of different ways. For example, you might create a Web part as an individual server control that you deploy to your SharePoint site. You can also create SharePoint Web part pages that leverage existing Web parts (whether those Web parts are custom or native to SharePoint), or integrated through a Web part connection (that is, connected Web parts).

As you build out server controls or pages to host your Web parts, you can use tools such as Visual Studio 2010 or SharePoint Designer 2010. If you have a more dynamic UI for your Web parts (for example, a Silverlight-based UI), then you may opt for Expression Blend as well. In Visual Studio 2010, you'll find an enhanced designer experience with the Visual Web part project template that makes it much easier to drag and drop controls onto the designer surface to create custom Web parts. You can also use Visual Studio to leverage the ASP.NET Web part framework — using all of the ASP.NET controls (for example, calendar, textbox, datagrid, and so on) to create your custom Web part.

While, in this chapter, you'll be only leveraging the ASP.NET Web part namespace (`System.Web .UI.WebControls.WebParts`), it is worth mentioning that there is also a Web part namespace for SharePoint as well (`Microsoft.SharePoint.WebPartPages.WebPart`). However, it is generally recommended that, when you create Web parts for SharePoint, you stick to using the ASP.NET Web part namespace. The ASP.NET Web part namespace provides a more popular and comprehensive set of controls and classes for developers. Web parts also require a framework to work on the ASP. NET page. Because SharePoint is built on top of ASP.NET, it leverages the Web part framework.

After you've built and deployed Web parts to a SharePoint site, end users can then modify a SharePoint site depending on the following:

➤ The level of permissions they have in SharePoint

➤ The different out-of-the-box Web parts that are available to them (which would depend on the version of SharePoint they're using)

➤ The type of custom Web parts you have deployed to that SharePoint site

The more permissions users have for a site, the more they can customize and design the site for the users of that site.

Once a Web part is on a page, users can configure the Web part(s) on that page. For example, users can minimize, remove, or hide the Web part. They can also drag the Web part to a different part of the Web part page (into a different *Web part zone*), alter the properties of the Web part (to change the look, feel, or appearance), or even export/import the Web part for use in other pages or sites.

When you deploy a Web Part to SharePoint, it shows up in the Web Part Gallery. The Web Part Gallery is a management application that provides a way to manage Web parts for a site collection. With the Web Part Gallery, you can do things like view, edit, upload, delete, and manage permissions against Web parts. You access the Web Part Gallery within a site collection by clicking Site Actions ➪ Site Settings, and, under Galleries, select Web Parts.

What helps users integrate Web parts into a SharePoint site is the in-context ribbon experience that surfaces the different Web parts that live in the Web Part Gallery and makes them available for users to add to a Web part page. For example, if you click Site Actions ➪ Edit Page, this exposes the Insert tab. If you click the Web part ribbon control, this exposes all of the available Web parts for the SharePoint site — which includes custom Web parts you have built and deployed to your site.

> **NOTE** *If you use Visual Studio 2010 to create a custom Web part, it is automatically deployed to the Web Part Gallery. You can use a "manual" command to deploy a Web part assembly, in which you case, you would need to manually add it to the Web Part Gallery.*

The in-context ribbon experience is a great productivity improvement over the 2007 experience (which was a gallery you invoked as a separate window, and scrolled to find your Web part) and makes it easier to interact with Web parts.

When you navigate to the Web Part Gallery, you are presented with two views:

➤ One view enables you to see all of the Web parts in the site collection.

➤ The other view provides you with a more detailed view of the Web part (and its metadata).

The top-level view of the Web Part Gallery is shown in Figure 6-1, and in it you can see an enumeration of the available Web parts in SharePoint, along with properties for those Web parts.

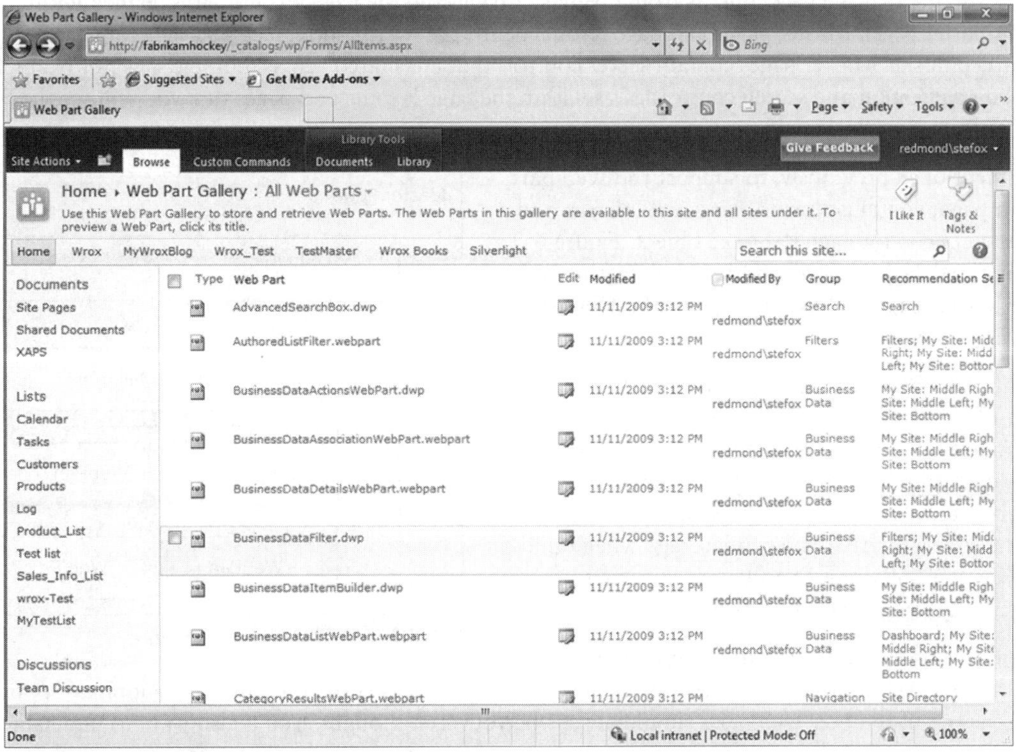

FIGURE 6-1 Web Part Gallery

> **NOTE** *If you click on the Web part link (for example,* `AdvancedSearchBox.dwp`*), SharePoint launches and renders the Web part in a separate Web part page.*

WEB PART ARCHITECTURE

The architecture of an .aspx Web page integrates a number of different zones, configurations, and objects that are associated with those zones. Core to the Web part architecture is the `WebPartManager` object, which manages all of the Web parts on a page. The `WebPartManager` control is the central command center for the Web parts on a page. There is only one `WebPartManager` control instance on a SharePoint Web part page, and it works only with authenticated site users.

The `WebPartManager` also holds a reference to the collection of *Web part zones* (that is, the `WebZone` class), which are containers for Web parts. Depending on the site or Web page template, Web part zones can be positioned differently on the page. Any page using one or more Web parts must have an instance of the `WebPartManager` and a Web part zone to put the part in. The `WebPartManager` is also declared in the SharePoint master page, so the out-of-the-box master pages will already have the `WebPartManager` declaration included.

Within each Web part zone, you have the Web parts. These are the server controls/applications you will build and deploy to SharePoint in this chapter.

It is important to think not just about the single SharePoint Web part page, but also think about the structure that the page inherits from the master page (and the page layout that is defined within that master page). Master pages and page layouts define the overall look, feel, and structure for the SharePoint site. Master pages contain server controls that are shared across multiple sites (for example, ribbon navigation and search controls). It is within the page layouts and pages that you will see the Web parts.

As mentioned previously, to support the Web part on a page, you must have a `WebPartManager` and a `WebPartZone` for each `WebPart` object. Figure 6-2 illustrates the high-level architecture starting from the master page and extending into the Web part on an ASPX page.

SharePoint 2010 provides a number of Web parts out-of-the-box. (The number and type of Web parts available will depend on the SharePoint version.) For example, you have the Chart Web part, Excel Web Access Web part, Business Data Catalog Web part, and so on, that you can leverage when building custom solutions. SharePoint also offers you the capability to create custom Web parts.

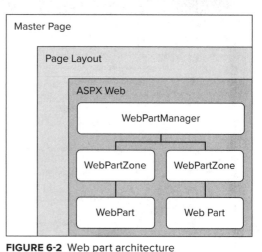

FIGURE 6-2 Web part architecture

As a developer, you'll want to understand the out-of-the-box Web parts so that you don't replicate this functionality in your custom solutions — evaluating the out-of-the-box Web parts should always be your first thought. You'll also want to understand this native functionality so that you can complement your custom Web parts with those that ship with SharePoint.

Adding an out-of-the-box or custom Web part is straightforward. You click Edit Page ⇨ "Add a web part" (or, if you're on a wiki page, you click the Insert tab and then click Web Part), and then select the Web part you want to add to your site. However, you must have a site or Web part page that will play host to the native or custom Web parts.

In the following exercise, you'll create a Web part page that you'll use throughout this chapter for both native and custom Web parts. The first exercise will require you to create a new list in your SharePoint site. Name the list `Sales`, then rename the `Title` column to `Customer` and add a `Sales` column (of type `Number`). Add some data resembling what is shown in Figure 6-3.

Customer	Sales
Fabrikam ☐ NEW	1,203,900.00
Acme ☐ NEW	2,019,200.00
Contoso ☐ NEW	2,039,010.00
Wingtip ☐ NEW	3,029,109.00

FIGURE 6-3 Customer list

After you've created the list, you are ready for the first exercise in this chapter.

TRY IT OUT   **Creating a Web Part Page and Chart Web Part**

A Web part page is a type of `.aspx` page in SharePoint that provides you with some predefined structure. After you create a Web part page, you can insert either native or custom Web parts to that page. To create a Web part page, follow these steps:

1. Navigate to your SharePoint site, and click All Site Content.

2. Click Create.

3. In the Create dialog, navigate to the Page option and click Web Part Page, as shown in Figure 6-4. Click the Create button on the right side of the screen.

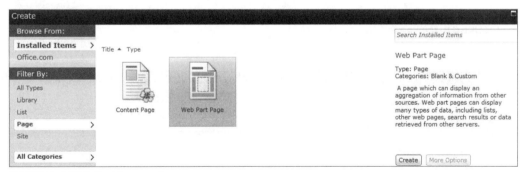

FIGURE 6-4 Web Part Page option

4. This invokes a separate page where you can provide a name for the page and select the structure of the page from a set of predefined layout templates. Provide a name for the page (for example, `Wrox_Web_Page.aspx`), and select one of the layout templates (for example, "Header, Footer, 3 Columns").

5. You can also choose to save the Web part page in a specific location — such as the Shared Documents or Site Assets document library. Leave the default option set to Site Assets, as shown in Figure 6-5, and click OK.

6. The result of this is a new Web part page that is structured using the "Header, Footer, 3 Columns" layout template, as shown in Figure 6-6. The page is also rendered in Edit mode by default.

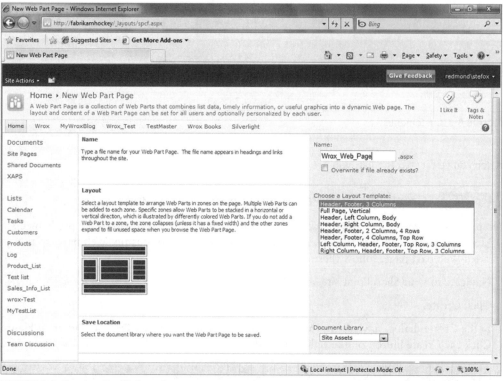

FIGURE 6-5 Naming the Web part page

FIGURE 6-6 Adding a Web part

7. Click "Add a web part" and then navigate to the Miscellaneous category. Select Chart Web Part. Click Add to add the out-of-the-box Web part to the new Web part page.

8. After the Web part is added to the Web part zone, click the Chart Web Part Menu and click Connect to Data, as shown in Figure 6-7.

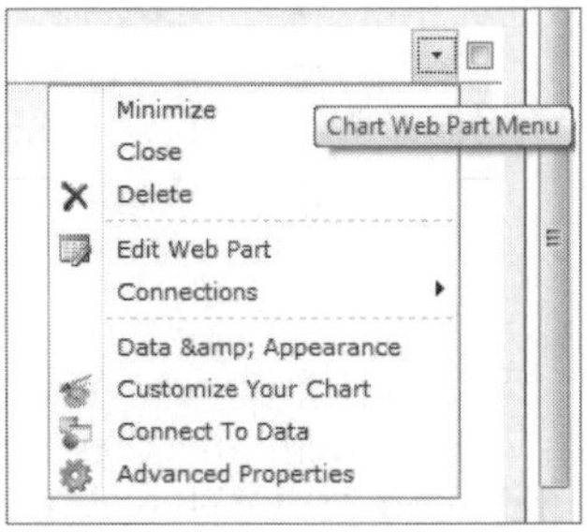

9. Follow the wizard to connect the Chart Web part to your newly created `Sales` list. Accept the default options as you work through the wizard, and then click Finish to complete the connecting of the data to the Chart Web part. When you're finished, your new Chart Web part will look like Figure 6-8.

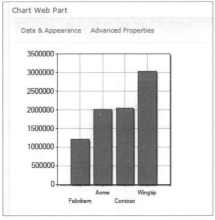

FIGURE 6-7 Connect Web part to data

How It Works

The Chart Web part is a new addition to SharePoint 2010 and provides you with a number of options to display data in SharePoint from different sources. You saw in this walk-through how the native functionality of the Chart Web part used the SharePoint list you created as a data source and then displayed that data graphically as a bar chart.

As you saw in the walkthrough, this is a great way to expose list data in Web parts to create a relationship across different parts of your SharePoint site. Note that you can create different types of charts when linking the Chart Web part to data sources, and you can customize the chart in different ways.

FIGURE 6-8 Chart Web part

It's important to understand the out-of-the-box Web part functionality. However, this book is geared toward developers, the remainder of this chapter discusses how you can create custom Web parts.

CUSTOM WEB PARTS

In SharePoint, you can build sites using the out-of-the-box Web parts without the need to do any coding. Or, you can develop custom Web parts.

Custom Web parts leverage the ASP.NET server controls and can be deployed as individual Web parts (that is, no interaction or connectivity with other Web parts), or you can create connected Web parts (that is, Web parts that can have a summary and detail view of data). Your custom Web parts can also be very simple (for example, leveraging one to two controls), or they can be complex (multiple controls and connected).

One of the key aspects of custom Web parts to remember is that, while you leverage the ASP.NET controls to create the Web parts, the Web part namespace provides the personalization capabilities discussed earlier — that is, the capability for users to configure the Web part the way they want to.

> **NOTE** *You can find a good article on MSDN at* `http://msdn.microsoft.com/en-us/library/ms469765.aspx` *that walks you through how to create a connected Web part.*

There are great tools available for you to create custom Web parts for SharePoint in Visual Studio 2010. Specifically, there are two types of templates that you can use to build the custom Web parts: the standard Web part and the Visual Web part. At the end of the day, the Web part capabilities for each of the templates are the same — they both derive from the same namespace. The difference, though, is in the ways of creating the custom Web parts using the templates.

For the standard Web part template, you must manually create the UI. With the Visual Web part, there is a designer experience that enables you to drag and drop controls onto a designer surface to create your Web part UI. However, the functionality that you can build into the Web parts (that is, your code behind) is the same.

When you create and deploy a custom Web part to SharePoint using Visual Studio 2010, a folder that contains a set of project files is created in your project. In Chapter 3, you saw that Visual Studio deploys Web parts as a feature. To be able to create a feature, Visual Studio creates a project structure with a number of project files — which include feature files, solution package, class files, and so on.

As you get started with Web part development in Visual Studio using the standard Web part template, you will find yourself interacting with the following three primary files:

➤ `elements.xml` — This provides configuration information that is used by the feature definition file.

➤ `foo.webpart` — This configuration file provides information that SharePoint needs to display the Web part (such as title and description).

➤ `foo.cs` — This core Web part class file that contains all of the custom code you create as the core functionality of your Web part application.

The following code snippet provides a snapshot of the default code that is generated when you create a standard Web part in Visual Studio 2010:

```
...
namespace WroxWebPartProject.CustomerInformation
{
    [ToolboxItemAttribute(false)]
    public class CustomerInformation : WebPart
    {

        public CustomerInformation()
        {
        }

        protected override void CreateChildControls()
        {
                base.CreateChildControls();
...
```

```
        }

        protected override void RenderContents(HtmlTextWriter writer)
        {
            base.RenderContents(writer);
        }
    }
}
...
```

Next, you will create a standard Web part using the Web part item template available within Visual Studio 2010. This means that you must have a parent SharePoint project (that implements a feature) to which you would add this item-level template.

Let's create a standard Web part using Visual Studio 2010.

TRY IT OUT   Creating a Simple Standard Web Part

Code file [WroxWebPartProject.zip] available for download at Wrox.com.

Standard Web parts can be very powerful and perform any number of functions. To create a standard Web part, follow these steps:

1.   Open Visual Studio 2010 and click File ⇨ New ⇨ Project.

2.   Navigate to the `SharePoint` folder and select the Empty SharePoint Project template. Provide a name for your project (for example, `WroxWebPartProject`) and click OK. When prompted, select "Deploy as farm solution." Click Finish. This creates the skeletal structure of a SharePoint project.

3.   Right-click the project and click Add ⇨ New Item.

4.   From the SharePoint 2010 Item templates, select Web Part.

5.   Provide a name for the Web part (for example, `CustomerInformation`), and click Add. Visual Studio adds the core elements of the Web part files to the empty SharePoint project.

6.   You'll now want to add a class to the Web part project, so right-click the new Web part project and select Add ⇨ Class. Provide a name for the class (for example, `CustomerData`), and click OK.

7.   In the new class, add the following bolded code:

```
using System;
using System.Collections.Generic;
using System.Linq;
using System.Text;

namespace WroxWebPartProject
{
    class CustomerData
    {
        public string companyName {get; set;}
        public string contactName {get; set;}
        public string contactEmail {get; set;}
        public string companyFY08Sales {get; set;}
```

```
        public string companyFY09Sales {get; set;}
    }
}
```

8. Right-click the core Web part code file (for example, `CustomerInformation.cs`), and select View Code.

9. Add the following bolded code into that core Web part class:

```
using System;
using System.ComponentModel;
using System.Web;
using System.Web.UI;
using System.Web.UI.WebControls;
using System.Web.UI.WebControls.WebParts;
using Microsoft.SharePoint;
using Microsoft.SharePoint.WebControls;
using System.Collections.Generic;

namespace WroxWebPartProject.CustomerInformation
{
    [ToolboxItemAttribute(false)]
    public class CustomerInformation : WebPart
    {

        DataGrid myCustomers = new DataGrid();
        List<CustomerData> myCustomerDataList = new List<CustomerData>();

        protected override void OnPreRender(EventArgs e)
        {
            CustomerData cust1 = new CustomerData();
            CustomerData cust2 = new CustomerData();
            CustomerData cust3 = new CustomerData();
            CustomerData cust4 = new CustomerData();

            cust1.companyName = "Fabrikam";
            cust1.contactName = "Harvey Kitell";
            cust1.contactEmail = "mrpink@fabrikam.com";
            cust1.companyFY08Sales = "$530,002.00";
            cust1.companyFY09Sales = "$650,102.00";
            myCustomerDataList.Add(cust1);

            cust2.companyName = "Contoso";
            cust2.contactName = "Ahmed Kroll";
            cust2.contactEmail = "ahemd@contoso.com";
            cust2.companyFY08Sales = "$1,577,044.00";
            cust2.companyFY09Sales = "$1,653,112.00";
            myCustomerDataList.Add(cust2);

            cust3.companyName = "Acme";
            cust3.contactName = "Jansen Terrace";
            cust3.contactEmail = "jansen@acme.com";
            cust3.companyFY08Sales = "$3,270,000.00";
            cust3.companyFY09Sales = "$2,953,100.00";
            myCustomerDataList.Add(cust3);

            cust4.companyName = "Wingtip";
```

```
                    cust4.contactName = "Hally Cantrall";
                    cust4.contactEmail = "hally@wingtip.com";
                    cust4.companyFY08Sales = "$578,982.00";
                    cust4.companyFY09Sales = "$620,100.00";
                    myCustomerDataList.Add(cust4);

                    myCustomers.DataSource = myCustomerDataList;
                    myCustomers.DataBind();
                }

                protected override void CreateChildControls()
                {
                    this.Controls.Add(myCustomers);
                }
            }
        }
```

10. Next, double-click the `.webpart` file (for example, `CustomerInformation.webpart`), and amend the title and description of the Web part, as shown in the following bolded code:

```
<?xml version="1.0" encoding="utf-8"?>
<webParts>
  <webPart xmlns="http://schemas.microsoft.com/WebPart/v3">
    <metaData>
      <type name="WroxWebPartProject.CustomerInformation.CustomerInformation,
            $SharePoint.Project.AssemblyFullName$" />
      <importErrorMessage>$Resources:core,ImportErrorMessage;</importErrorMessage>
    </metaData>
    <data>
    <properties>
        <property name="Title" type="string">Customer Info Web Part</property>
        <property name="Description" type="string">A Web Part that displays
            customer information.</property>
    </properties>Web Part
    </data>
  </webPart>
</webParts>
```

11. You can now build the standard Web part and deploy it to your SharePoint site. To do this, click Build ➪ Deploy Solution.

12. After you've deployed the Web part to your SharePoint site, navigate to your SharePoint site and to the new Web part page you created earlier. Click Site Actions ➪ Edit Page ➪ "Add a web part" to add the newly created standard Web part to the page.

13. Navigate to the Custom category. You should see the `CustomerInformation` Web part you just deployed (assuming that you named your Web part `CustomerInformation`). Click Add to add it to your SharePoint Web part page. You should have something similar to Figure 6-9 added to your SharePoint site.

Customer Data Web Part				
companyName	contactName	contactEmail	companyFY08Sales	companyFY09Sales
Fabrikam	Harvey Kitell	mrpink@fabrikam.com	$530,002.00	$650,102.00
Contoso	Ahmed Kroll	ahmed@contoso.com	$1,577,044.00	$1,653,112.00
Acme	Jansen Terrace	jansen@acme.com	$3,270,000.00	$2,953,100.00
Wingtip	Hally Cantrall	hal@wingtip.com	$578,982.00	$620,100.00

FIGURE 6-9 Rendered datagrid

How It Works

This walkthrough was fairly straightforward. You first created a standard Web part using the Visual Studio 2010 template, which added the core class and configuration files to the empty SharePoint project. You then created a simple class, which defined five properties of a customer object. You then used an in-memory object to generate some data that was then data-bound to a datagrid control. The application created the in-memory object using a list collection of the custom `CustomerData` object (`myCustomerDataList`), which was instantiated in the following line of code:

```
List<CustomerData> myCustomerDataList = new List<CustomerData>();
```

The application then created four `CustomerData` objects (`cust1`, `cust2`, `cust3`, and `cust4`) and added them to the list collection, which was then bound as a data source to the datagrid control.

You'll notice that there was no special formatting that you created for the datagrid, and the header row took the individual property names as the field data. However, you could add some formatting to the datagrid to improve the look and feel of it. For example, if you added the following bolded code to the `OnPreRender` method, you could alter the look and feel of your datagrid:

```
myCustomers.Width = Unit.Percentage(100);
myCustomers.CellPadding = 1;
myCustomers.HeaderStyle.Font.Bold = true;
myCustomers.HeaderStyle.HorizontalAlign = HorizontalAlign.Left;
myCustomers.HeaderStyle.CssClass = "ms-vh1";
myCustomers.GridLines = GridLines.Horizontal;
myCustomers.BorderWidth = Unit.Pixel(3);
myCustomers.DataSource = myCustomerDataList;
myCustomers.DataBind();
```

Using this styling, the table that you deploy into SharePoint takes on a slightly different look and feel, as shown in Figure 6-10.

Customer Data Web Part

companyName	contactName	contactEmail	companyFY08Sales	companyFY09Sales
Fabrikam	Harvey Kitell	mrpink@fabrikam.com	$530,002.00	$650,102.00
Contoso	Ahmed Kroll	ahmed@contoso.com	$1,577,044.00	$1,653,112.00
Acme	Jansen Terrace	jansen@acme.com	$3,270,000.00	$2,953,100.00
Wingtip	Hally Cantrall	hal@wingtip.com	$578,982.00	$620,100.00

FIGURE 6-10 Formatted datagrid

When you build and deploy the standard Web part to SharePoint, you create a feature using the three core Web part files (discussed earlier in the chapter). The Web part DLL, which is the core functionality for the Web part, is deployed into the global assembly cache (GAC).

While, in this case, you created a simple Web part that leveraged an in-memory object, you can also load data from an external data source (and, more often than not, you will want to do this). This data could be in the form of a Web service, a SharePoint list, an XML packet or file, or other Web 2.0 service that draws data from other non-SharePoint Web assets.

For example, say that you created an XML file that looks like the following XML code snippet and saved it to your local drive (for example, in a folder called `c:/XML_Data`). You could very easily map that XML file to a dataset, and then bind the dataset to the datagrid — and repurpose some of the code you've already written.

```xml
<?xml version="1.0" encoding="utf-8" ?>
<Customers>
  <Customer>
    <CompanyName>Fabrikam</CompanyName>
    <Contact>John Kelly</Contact>
    <ContactEmail>jkelly@fabrikam.com</ContactEmail>
    <FY08Sales>$3,500,398.00</FY08Sales>
    <FY09Sales>$3,750,302.00</FY09Sales>
  </Customer>
  <Customer>
    <CompanyName>Contoso</CompanyName>
    <Contact>Ahmed Zain</Contact>
    <ContactEmail>ahmed@contoso.com</ContactEmail>
    <FY08Sales>$50,980,990.00</FY08Sales>
    <FY09Sales>$52,880,980.00</FY09Sales>
  </Customer>
  <Customer>
    <CompanyName>Acme</CompanyName>
    <Contact>Jane Doe</Contact>
    <ContactEmail>jane.doe@acme.com</ContactEmail>
    <FY08Sales>$7,099,289.00</FY08Sales>
    <FY09Sales>$7,029,001.00</FY09Sales>
  </Customer>
  <Customer>
    <CompanyName>Wingtip</CompanyName>
    <Contact>Janice Wang</Contact>
    <ContactEmail>janice@wingtip.com</ContactEmail>
    <FY08Sales>$980,298.00</FY08Sales>
    <FY09Sales>$1,209,109.00</FY09Sales>
  </Customer>
  <Customer>
    <CompanyName>Metro</CompanyName>
    <Contact>Steve James</Contact>
    <ContactEmail>stevej@metro.com</ContactEmail>
    <FY08Sales>$1,090,989.00</FY08Sales>
    <FY09Sales>$1,300,092.00</FY09Sales>
  </Customer>
  <Customer>
    <CompanyName>Standard</CompanyName>
    <Contact>John McLean</Contact>
    <ContactEmail>johnm@standard.com</ContactEmail>
    <FY08Sales>$45,092,981.00</FY08Sales>
    <FY09Sales>$47,200,189.00</FY09Sales>
  </Customer>
</Customers>
```

If you used the same project that you created in the last walkthrough, instead of using the list collection, you would simply create a new class-level instance of a `DataSet` object and path to the XML file.

```csharp
DataSet myCustomerDataset = new DataSet();
string xmlCustomerFilePath = "c:/XML_Data/Customers.xml";
```

You'd then substitute all of the code within the `OnPreRender` method with the following code snippet to bind the data.

```
myCustomerDataset.ReadXml(xmlCustomerFilePath, XmlReadMode.InferSchema);
myCustomers.DataSource = dataset;
myCustomers.DataBind();
```

You can then add the `myCustomers` list collection to the `Controls` collection in the `CreateChildControls` method, as in the following line of code:

```
this.Controls.Add(myCustomers);
```

The net effect is very similar to the way in which the previous data looked in the datagrid using the list collection. However, in this case, you are now using an external data source to populate the datagrid in your custom Web part. The result of this code is shown in Figure 6-11.

Customer Data Web Part				
CompanyName	**Contact**	**ContactEmail**	**FY08Sales**	**FY09Sales**
Fabrikam	John Kelly	jkelly@fabrikam.com	$3,500,398.00	$3,750,302.00
Contoso	Ahmed Zain	ahmed@contoso.com	$50,980,990.00	$52,880,980.00
Acme	Jane Doe	jane.doe@acme.com	$7,099,289.00	$7,029,001.00
Wingtip	Janice Wang	janice@wingtip.com	$980,298.00	$1,209,109.00
Metro	Steve James	stevej@metro.com	$1,090,989.00	$1,300,092.00
Standard	John McLean	johnm@standard.com	$45,092,981.00	$47,200,189.00

FIGURE 6-11 Datagrid using external data

As you build more complex Web parts, you'll want to add event handlers that map to the controls (for example, buttons or listboxes) — that is, events that are tied to users interacting with controls within your Web parts. For example, let's assume that you want to build out a UI that loads some data from a SharePoint list, and then displays that data in a listbox. Let's walk through an example.

TRY IT OUT   Creating Event Handlers in Standard Web Parts

Code file [SPWebPartEvent.zip] available for download at Wrox.com.

Creating events for a Web part is a core part of building Web parts. To create an event handler using the standard Web part project template, follow these steps:

1.   Open Visual Studio 2010 and create a new Empty SharePoint project. Provide a name for the project (for example, `SPWebPartEvent`) and click OK. When prompted, select "Deploy as farm solution" and click Finish.

2.   Right-click the project and add a new Web part to the project by clicking Add ➪ New Item, and then selecting the Web part item template. Provide a name for the Web part (for example, `SampleEventWebPart`) and click OK.

3.   Open the `.webpart` file (for example, `SPCOMWebPart.webpart`) and amend the `Title` and `Description` properties as shown in the following bolded code snippet.

```
...
        <properties>
          <property name="Title" type="string">SP Site Lists Web Part</property>
```

```
            <property name="Description" type="string">List of lists from
                SharePoint site.</property>
        </properties>
    …
```

4. Open the core Web part class file (for example, `SPCOMWebPart.cs`) and amend the code as shown in the following bolded code. Replace the string `mySiteURL` (`http://intranet.contoso.com`) with the name of your SharePoint server.

```csharp
using System;
using System.ComponentModel;
using System.Web;
using System.Web.UI;
using System.Web.UI.WebControls;
using System.Web.UI.WebControls.WebParts;
using Microsoft.SharePoint;
using Microsoft.SharePoint.WebControls;

namespace SPWebPartEvent.SampleEventWebPart
{
    [ToolboxItemAttribute(false)]
    public class SampleEventWebPart : WebPart
    {
        //Be sure to replace mySiteURL with your server URL.
        string mySiteURL = "http://intranet.contoso.com";
        Button getLists = new Button();
        ListBox mySPLists = new ListBox();
        string listInfo = "";

        protected override void OnPreRender(EventArgs e)
        {
            getLists.Text = "Click";
        }
        protected override void CreateChildControls()
        {
            this.Controls.Add(getLists);
            this.Controls.Add(mySPLists);
            getLists.Click += new EventHandler(getLists_Click);

        }

        void getLists_Click(object sender, EventArgs e)
        {
            using (SPSite mySiteCollection = new SPSite(mySiteURL))
            {
                using (SPWeb mySPSite = mySiteCollection.RootWeb)
                {
                    foreach (SPList myList in mySPSite.Lists)
                    {
                        listInfo = myList.Title.ToString();
                        mySPLists.Items.Add(listInfo);
                    }
                }
            }
```

```
            }

        }

    }
```

5. You can now build and deploy the new Web part by clicking Build ⇨ Deploy Solution.

6. After the Web part project successfully deploys, open your SharePoint site and navigate to the Web part page you created earlier in the chapter. Click "Add a web part," and then navigate to the Custom category. Then select the SP Site Lists Web part and click Add.

7. The resulting Web part will look similar to the one in Figure 6-12. Click the Get Lists button, and this will invoke the `myButton_Click` event, which will populate the listbox with all of the lists from the SharePoint site.

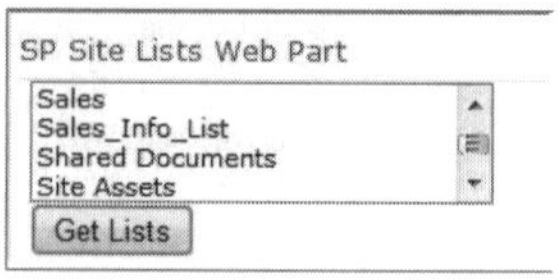

FIGURE 6-12 Site list

How It Works

To start with, the controls used in this custom Web part were declared at the class level. Also, you used the `onPreRender` method to set the `Text` property of the button. This is because you don't typically want to perform your UI processing in the `CreateChildControls` method. There was only one property to set in this method, but you could imagine that, as you use more controls in your Web parts, you perform more processing within the `OnPreRender` method.

```
protected override void OnPreRender(EventArgs e)
{
    getLists.Text = "Click";
}
```

As you've seen before, the controls were then added to the `Controls` collection in the `CreateChildControls` method, and the `getLists_Click` event was added here as well.

```
protected override void CreateChildControls()
{

    this.Controls.Add(getLists);
    this.Controls.Add(mySPLists);
    getLists.Click += new EventHandler(getLists_Click);

}
```

In Chapter 4, you saw a number of common developer tasks — one of which was leveraging the server-side object model. In this example, the `getLists_Click` event uses the server-side object model to provide an enumeration of all the lists in the site. The server-side object model is an efficient way to program Web parts because you are processing server-side code, as opposed to calling Web services (for example, using the Lists Web service).

By creating a button and a listbox, it's possible to tie these two controls together through the `getLists_Click` event. Given that this is the key event in the example, the code (using the server-side object model) sets the site context with the first `using` statement (which gets the site reference from the string variable mySiteURL). You can see that the string listInfo then gets the title of each list, which is then added to the listbox (mySPLists).

```
void getLists_Click(object sender, EventArgs e)
{
    using (SPSite mySiteCollection = new SPSite(mySiteURL))
    {
        using (SPWeb mySPSite = mySiteCollection.RootWeb)
        {
            foreach (SPList myList in mySPSite.Lists)
            {
                listInfo = myList.Title.ToString();
                mySPLists.Items.Add(listInfo);
            }
        }
    }
}
```

VISUAL WEB PARTS

Building custom Web parts using the standard project template is effective, but you may want to quickly design a UI for your Web part without having to build it out manually. This is where you can use Visual Web parts. Visual Web parts are different from standard Web parts in that they include an additional user control, which represents the UI for your Web part.

When you build and deploy your custom Web part using the Visual Web part template, the user control is deployed to the SharePoint root — specifically to the CONTROLTEMPLATES folder (that is, c:\Program Files\Common Files\Microsoft Shared\Web Server Extensions\14\TEMPLATE\ CONTROLTEMPLATES). A new folder will be created as a subdirectory in the CONTROLTEMPLATES for your custom user control UI (.ascx file).

There are some differences when you create a new Visual Studio project using the Visual Web part project template as opposed to the Web part item template.

When you look at the core Web part class, you'll see some additional code that is added by default, which is displayed as bolded code in the following snippet:

```
...

namespace WroxVisualWPProject.CustomerData
{
    [ToolboxItemAttribute(false)]
    public class CustomerData : WebPart
    {
        private const string _ascxPath =
            @"~/_CONTROLTEMPLATES/WroxVisualWPProject/
            CustomerData/CustomerDataUserControl.ascx";

        public CustomerData()
```

```
        {
        }

        protected override void CreateChildControls()
        {
            Control control = this.Page.LoadControl(_ascxPath);
            Controls.Add(control);
            base.CreateChildControls();
        }

        protected override void RenderContents(HtmlTextWriter writer)
        {
            base.RenderContents(writer);
        }
    }
}
```

This code manages the user control that you build and design using the Visual Web Part Designer. For example, you can see that there is a string variable called _ascxPath, which points to the .ascx (that is, the user control) where the UI portion of the Web part will be stored. Then, using the path to the UI as a parameter, the code creates an instance of a Control and then adds this one control to the Controls collection.

> **NOTE** *The Visual Web part described here has the inherent limitation of not being able to be deployed at the sandboxed level, because of the file system reference to retrieve the* .ascx *control. However, as of this writing, there is a community project on Codeplex that provides a Visual Web part that enables farm-level trust. For more information, go to* http://sharepointdevtools.codeplex.com/.

When using a standard Web part, you were building and adding your own individual controls and adding each instance of the control to the Controls collection. In this case, you're using only the Control object, which loads your entire UI at once.

The Designer experience can save you some time when developing the UI for your Web part applications. Let's put this into practice.

To complete the next walkthrough, you'll create a new list that looks like Figure 6-13. Name the list Stats, which will represent a list of players with some associated game stats (all fields of type "Single line of text"). Change the Title column to be Name, and then add four more columns that will replicate a simple stats list (Goals, Assists, PIM, and Games Played).

		Name	Goals	Assists	PIM	Games Played
		John Doe ☐ NEW	2	1	4	6
		Kenneth Krane ☐ NEW	1	1	6	6
		Steve Tries ☐ NEW	0	1	0	6
		Jason Goody ☐ NEW	8	1	0	6
		Alyme Zarin ☐ NEW	7	2	2	6
		Jamie Speedster ☐ NEW	4	5	4	6
		Boris Goon ☐ NEW	0	0	20	6

FIGURE 6-13 Stats list

The list shown in Figure 6-13 contains a number of players with their goals, assists, penalties in minutes (PIM), and the number of games played. You'll create a Visual Web part that pulls this data into a control, then provides an aggregated stat for each player, and also enables you to edit the statistics from within the Visual Web part.

Also, one of the controls you'll use in this exercise is the `UpdatePanel` control. The `UpdatePanel` is an Ajax server control that reduces full-page postbacks by enabling partial-page rendering. This provides a better experience for the user by mitigating the need for the entire page to refresh and update when you're executing an event within one Web part on the page.

With the list created, let's walk through the exercise.

TRY IT OUT   Creating a Visual Web Part

Code file [AjaxVWP.zip] available for download at Wrox.com.

Visual Web parts are very powerful Web parts that provide a built-in Designer to create your UI. To create a Visual Web part, follow these steps:

1. Click File ➪ New Project ➪ Empty SharePoint Project. Provide a name for your project (for example, `AjaxVWP`), and click OK. When prompted, select "Deploy as farm solution," and click Finish.

2. When the project has been created, right-click the project and click Add ➪ New Item. From the `SharePoint 2010` template folder, select the "Visual Web item" template. Provide a name for the new Web part (`AjaxVisualWebPart`), and click OK.

3. You're going to add a custom object to the project, so right-click the project and click Add ➪ Class. Provide a name for the class (for example, `PlayerStat`), and click OK. The class will have six properties, which you can set as string variables, as shown in the following (bolded) code snippet:

```
using System;
using System.Collections.Generic;
using System.Linq;
using System.Text;

namespace AjaxVWP
{
    class PlayerStat
    {
        public string playerName { get; set; }
        public string gamesPlayed { get; set; }
        public string numOfGoals { get; set; }
        public string numOfAssists { get; set; }
        public string numOfPIM { get; set; }
        public string playerAVG { get; set; }
    }
}
```

4. At this point, your project should contain a number of files that look similar to the project structure shown in Figure 6-14.

FIGURE 6-14 Project structure

5. With the project created, since you already have your data source (the SharePoint list), you'll now want to create the UI for the Visual Web part. To do this, right-click the `.ascx` node (for example, `AjaxVisualWebPartUserControl.ascx` node) and then click View Designer. Click View ⇨ Toolbox to see the controls that you can drag and drop onto the Designer.

6. Drag and drop an `UpdatePanel` control onto the Designer and provide a new ID (for example, `viewDataUpdatePanel`). Switch to source view, and then add a `ContentTemplate` element to the `UpdatePanel` object as shown in the following code snippet:

```
...
<asp:UpdatePanel ID="viewDataUpdatePanel" runat="server">
  <ContentTemplate>
  </ContentTemplate>
</asp:UpdatePanel>
...
```

7. Now, add eight labels, one datagrid, three buttons, and four textboxes to the Designer's surface — the datagrid and one button should be added to the `UpdatePanel`. When you're finished, the controls will likely be arranged similarly to those shown in Figure 6-15.

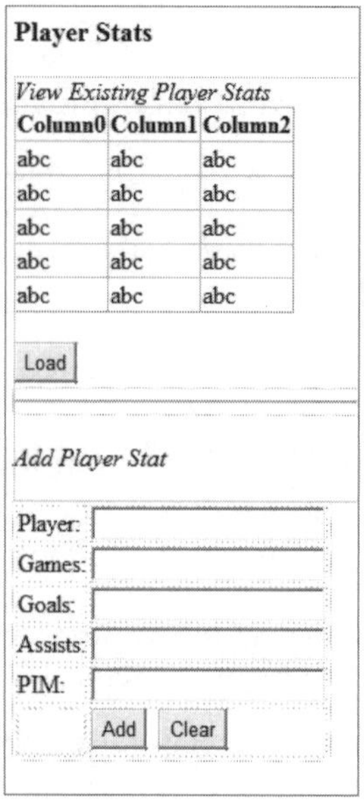

FIGURE 6-15 Visual Web part UI layout

Table 6-1 provides a summary of the control type and names that you'll add to the Visual Web part.

TABLE 6-1 Control Type and Names

TYPE	NAME
UpdatePanel	`viewDataUpdatePanel`
Label	`lblTitle, lblRead, lblWrite, lblPlayer, lblGames, lblGoals, lblAssists, lblPIM`
Datagrid	`statDataGrid`
Button	`btnDataGridLoad, btnAdd, btnClear`
Textbox	`txtbxGames, txtbxGoals, txtbxPIM`

8. Click the Source tab in the Visual Studio IDE, and you'll see the source that makes up the user control that you'll load as a part of this Web part. The code should look similar to the following code snippet when you're done adding the controls to the Designer. Note that, in the following code, the part of the application that reads data will be rendered within the Ajax control, and the part of the application that writes data will render outside of the Ajax `UpdatePanel` control. Also note a table has been used to amend the Visual Web part UI to be more structured. This is not the `Table` server-side control in the Toolbox, but rather a regular HTML table.

```
<%@ Assembly Name="$SharePoint.Project.AssemblyFullName$" %>
<%@ Assembly Name="Microsoft.Web.CommandUI, Version=14.0.0.0, Culture=neutral,
```

```
       PublicKeyToken=71e9bce111e9429c" %>
<%@ Register Tagprefix="SharePoint" Namespace="Microsoft.SharePoint.WebControls"
       Assembly="Microsoft.SharePoint, Version=14.0.0.0, Culture=neutral,
       PublicKeyToken=71e9bce111e9429c" %>
<%@ Register Tagprefix="Utilities" Namespace="Microsoft.SharePoint.Utilities"
       Assembly="Microsoft.SharePoint, Version=14.0.0.0, Culture=neutral,
       PublicKeyToken=71e9bce111e9429c" %>
<%@ Register Tagprefix="asp" Namespace="System.Web.UI" Assembly=
       "System.Web.Extensions, Version=3.5.0.0, Culture=neutral,
        PublicKeyToken=31bf3856ad364e35" %>
<%@ Import Namespace="Microsoft.SharePoint" %>
<%@ Register Tagprefix="WebPartPages" Namespace="Microsoft.SharePoint.WebPartPages"
       Assembly="Microsoft.SharePoint, Version=14.0.0.0, Culture=neutral,
       PublicKeyToken=71e9bce111e9429c" %>
<%@ Control Language="C#" AutoEventWireup="true"
       CodeBehind="AjaxVisualWebPartUserControl.ascx.cs"
       Inherits="AjaxVWP.AjaxVisualWebPart.AjaxVisualWebPartUserControl" %>
<asp:Label ID="lblTitle" runat="server" Text="Player Stats" Font-Size="Large"
    Font-Bold="True"></asp:Label>
<br />
<br />
<asp:UpdatePanel ID="viewDataUpdatePanel" runat="server">
  <ContentTemplate>
      <asp:Label ID="lblRead" runat="server" Text="View Existing Player Stats"
          Font-Italic="True"></asp:Label>
      <br />
      <asp:GridView ID="statDataGrid" runat="server"
          Height="69px">
      </asp:GridView>
      <br />
      <asp:Button ID="btnDataGridLoad" runat="server"
          Text="Load" />
       <br />
      <hr />
      <br />
      <asp:Label ID="lblWrite" runat="server" Text="Add Player Stat"
          Font-Italic="True"></asp:Label>
      <br />
      <br />
  </ContentTemplate>
</asp:UpdatePanel>
<table border="0" width="25%"><tr>
<td><asp:Label ID="lblPlayer" runat="server" Text="Player:"></asp:Label></td>
<td><asp:TextBox ID="txtbxName" runat="server" Width="157px"></asp:TextBox>
</td></tr><tr>
<td><asp:Label ID="lblGames" runat="server" Text="Games:"></asp:Label></td>
<td><asp:TextBox ID="txtbxGames" runat="server" Width="157px"></asp:TextBox>
</td></tr><tr>
<td><asp:Label ID="lblGoals" runat="server" Text="Goals:"></asp:Label></td>
<td><asp:TextBox ID="txtbxGoals" runat="server" Width="157px"></asp:TextBox></td>
</tr><tr>
<td><asp:Label ID="lblAssists" runat="server" Text="Assists:"></asp:Label></td>
<td><asp:TextBox ID="txtbxAssists" runat="server" Width="157px"></asp:TextBox></td>
</tr><tr>
<td><asp:Label ID="lblPIM" runat="server" Text="PIM:"></asp:Label></td>
<td><asp:TextBox ID="txtbxPIM" runat="server" Width="157px"></asp:TextBox></td>
```

```
</tr><tr><td></td>
<td><asp:Button ID="btnAdd" runat="server" Text="Add"/>
  <asp:Button ID="btnClear" runat="server" Text="Clear"
        />
 </td></tr></table>
```

9. With the UI now complete, you'll add some events to the application. Double-click each of the buttons to generate the placeholder events in your code behind.

10. After you do this, if you right-click the `.ascx` file and select View Code, you should see something similar to the following code snippet.

```
using System;
using System.Web.UI;
using System.Web.UI.WebControls;
using System.Web.UI.WebControls.WebParts;
using SPClientOM = Microsoft.SharePoint.Client;
using Microsoft.SharePoint.Client;
using System.Collections.Generic;
using System.Linq;
using System.Data;

namespace AjaxVWP.AjaxVisualWebPart
{
    public partial class AjaxVisualWebPartUserControl : UserControl
    {

        protected void Page_Load(object sender, EventArgs e)
        {

        }

        protected void btnDataGridLoad_Click(object sender, EventArgs e)
        {

        }

        protected void btnEdit_Click(object sender, EventArgs e)
        {

        }

        protected void btnAdd_Click(object sender, EventArgs e)
        {

        }
    }
}
```

11. Switch to the code view of the Visual Web part, and then add the following bolded code to your code behind. Note that you will want to set the `mySiteURL` string variable to your own SharePoint server URL.

```
using System;
using System.Web.UI;
using System.Web.UI.WebControls;
```

```
using System.Web.UI.WebControls.WebParts;
using System.Collections.Generic;
using Microsoft.SharePoint;

namespace AjaxVWP.AjaxVisualWebPart
{
    public partial class AjaxVisualWebPartUserControl : UserControl
    {

        List<PlayerStat> listOfPlayerStats = new List<PlayerStat>();
        //Set this string to your own SharePoint site URL.
        string mySiteURL = "http://intranet.contoso.com";

        protected void Page_Load(object sender, EventArgs e)
        {
        }

        protected void btnDataGridLoad_Click(object sender, EventArgs e)
        {
            statDataGrid.Width = Unit.Percentage(100);
            statDataGrid.CellPadding = 1;
            statDataGrid.HeaderStyle.Font.Bold = true;
            statDataGrid.HeaderStyle.CssClass = "ms-vh1";
            statDataGrid.GridLines = GridLines.Horizontal;
            statDataGrid.BorderWidth = Unit.Pixel(3);
            statDataGrid.HeaderStyle.HorizontalAlign = HorizontalAlign.Left;

            using (SPSite mySiteCollection = new SPSite(mySiteURL))
            {
                using (SPWeb web = mySiteCollection.OpenWeb())
                {
                    SPList myList = web.Lists["Stats"];

                    foreach (SPListItem tempListItem in myList.Items)
                    {
                        PlayerStat tempStat = new PlayerStat();
                        tempStat.playerName = tempListItem["Title"].ToString();
                        tempStat.numOfGoals = tempListItem["Goals"].ToString();
                        tempStat.numOfAssists = tempListItem["Assists"].ToString();
                        tempStat.numOfPIM = tempListItem["PIM"].ToString();
                        tempStat.gamesPlayed = tempListItem["Games"].ToString();
                        tempStat.playerAVG = calcPlayerAverage(tempStat.gamesPlayed,
                        tempStat.numOfGoals, tempStat.numOfAssists);
                        listOfPlayerStats.Add(tempStat);
                    }
                }
            }

            statDataGrid.DataSource = listOfPlayerStats;
            statDataGrid.DataBind();

        }

        protected void btnAdd_Click(object sender, EventArgs e)
        {
            using (SPSite mySiteCollection = new SPSite(mySiteURL))
```

```
            {
                using (SPWeb web = mySiteCollection.OpenWeb())
                {
                    web.AllowUnsafeUpdates = true;

                    SPList list = web.Lists["Stats"];
                    SPListItem newStat = list.Items.Add();

                    newStat["Title"] = txtbxName.Text;
                    newStat["Goals"] = txtbxGoals.Text;
                    newStat["Assists"] = txtbxAssists.Text;
                    newStat["PIM"] = txtbxPIM.Text;
                    newStat["Games"] = txtbxGoals.Text;
                    newStat.Update();

                    web.AllowUnsafeUpdates = false;
                }
            }
        }

        protected void btnEdit_Click(object sender, EventArgs e)
        {
            txtbxName.Text = "";
            txtbxGames.Text = "";
            txtbxGoals.Text = "";
            txtbxAssists.Text = "";
            txtbxPIM.Text = "";
        }

        private string calcPlayerAverage(string games, string goals,
            string assists)
        {
            int numGames = Int32.Parse(games);
            int numGoals = Int32.Parse(goals);
            int numAssists = Int32.Parse(assists);
            double avgStat = 0.00;

            avgStat = (numGoals * 2) + (numAssists * 1) / numGames;

            return avgStat.ToString();
        }
    }
}
```

12. Click Build ⇨ Deploy Solution, which will build and deploy the visual Web part to your SharePoint server. (You can alternatively press F5 to debug your Web part.)

13. Once it is successfully deployed, navigate to your SharePoint site and to the Web part page you created earlier in the chapter.

14. Click Site Actions ⇨ Edit Page ⇨ "Add a web part."

15. Select the Custom Web Part category, and then click the newly deployed Visual Web part. Click Add. Click the Load button to load the current data from the SharePoint Stats list. Note that, when you load the data from the SharePoint list, a new column is added, and a calculated value is added to the column based on data from the other columns in the list. The results should look similar to Figure 6-16.

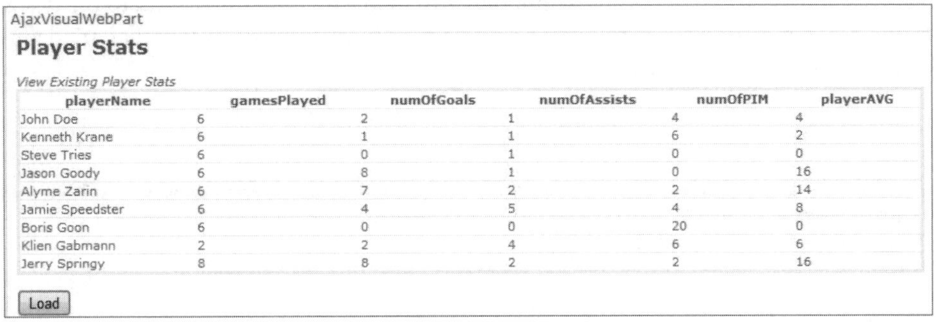

AjaxVisualWebPart					

Player Stats

View Existing Player Stats

playerName	gamesPlayed	numOfGoals	numOfAssists	numOfPIM	playerAVG
John Doe	6	2	1	4	4
Kenneth Krane	6	1	1	6	2
Steve Tries	6	0	1	0	0
Jason Goody	6	8	1	0	16
Alyme Zarin	6	7	2	2	14
Jamie Speedster	6	4	5	4	8
Boris Goon	6	0	0	20	0
Klien Gabmann	2	2	4	6	6
Jerry Springy	8	8	2	2	16

Load

FIGURE 6-16 Visual Web part (read portion)

16. To add a player and some stats for that player, enter some data in the fields and click Add. Then click Load again to reload and view the newly added data. The new record should then be displayed with "Ken Staahl," as shown in Figure 6-17.

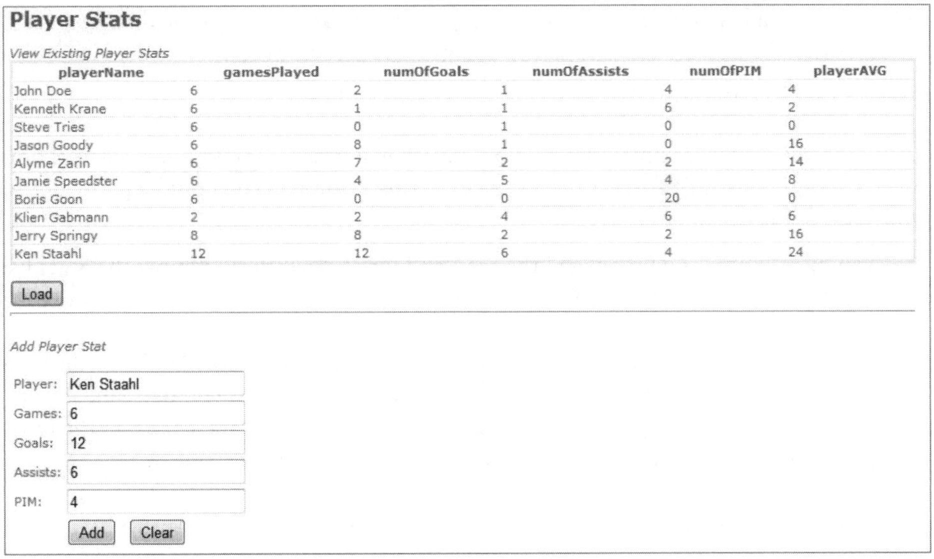

Player Stats

View Existing Player Stats

playerName	gamesPlayed	numOfGoals	numOfAssists	numOfPIM	playerAVG
John Doe	6	2	1	4	4
Kenneth Krane	6	1	1	6	2
Steve Tries	6	0	1	0	0
Jason Goody	6	8	1	0	16
Alyme Zarin	6	7	2	2	14
Jamie Speedster	6	4	5	4	8
Boris Goon	6	0	0	20	0
Klien Gabmann	2	2	4	6	6
Jerry Springy	8	8	2	2	16
Ken Staahl	12	12	6	4	24

Load

Add Player Stat

Player: Ken Staahl

Games: 6

Goals: 12

Assists: 6

PIM: 4

Add   Clear

FIGURE 6-17 Visual Web part (read and write)

How It Works

The Visual Web part is the result of your creating and designing a user control via the designer experience, then integrating the user controls with the Web part code behind, and then deploying the UI and the corresponding code behind as an integrated whole to SharePoint. In this example, you built your UI around a read operation and a write operation.

The read operation was wrapped with an Ajax `UpdatePanel` object, which eliminated the postback on the page when you used that part of the Web part. You did not, however, wrap the write operation with the `UpdatePanel` object. So, when you add the new player to the list, you'll see the page reload when the update to the SharePoint list is in process.

Note that, in the UI source, you require an event handler to map the controls you add to the designer to your code-behind file. For example, the following two buttons have `onClick` events that are defined in the UI source code as shown in the bolded code:

```
...
<tr>
<td></td>
<td><asp:Button ID="btnAdd" runat="server" Text="Add" onclick="btnAdd_Click"/>
  <asp:Button ID="btnClear" runat="server" Text="Clear"
        onclick="btnEdit_Click" />
 </td>
</tr>
...
```

With regard to the code behind, you'll note that you are again using the server-side object model. You could use other ways of interacting with the list within this custom Web part, such as the Lists Web service. But, again, the server-side object model is the best option for server-side applications, and is the most performant compared to the other options.

Within the code, you used a list collection object (`listOfPlayerStats`) to hold the data you get from the Stats list. This is also the object you bind to the datagrid (`statDataGrid`).

```
List<PlayerStat> listOfPlayerStats = new List<PlayerStat>();
```

Even though you used the designer experience to drag and drop a datagrid onto the surface of your Web part UI, you programmatically format the datagrid in this example. You could equally do this by editing the properties in the designer view.

The key server-side object model code managed the read and write operations against the Stats list. For example, the `btnDataGridLoad_Click` event leverages the `using` statements to set context for the SharePoint site, get the Stats list, and then enumerate through each of the list items — mapping each list item to a property in the `PlayerStat` object. You iterate through each of the list items until you've populated the `PlayerStat` object with all of the data from the list. Note that you dynamically call the `calcPlayerAverage` helper function, which dynamically calculates the average based on the information from the list, and adds that average as the last column in the `PlayerStat` object.

```
...
            using (SPSite mySiteCollection = new SPSite(mySiteURL))
            {
                using (SPWeb web = mySiteCollection.OpenWeb())
                {
                    SPList myList = web.Lists["Stats"];

                    foreach (SPListItem tempListItem in myList.Items)
                    {
                        PlayerStat tempStat = new PlayerStat();
                        tempStat.playerName = tempListItem["Title"].ToString();
                        tempStat.numOfGoals = tempListItem["Goals"].ToString();
                        tempStat.numOfAssists = tempListItem["Assists"].ToString();
                        tempStat.numOfPIM = tempListItem["PIM"].ToString();
```

```
                    tempStat.gamesPlayed = tempListItem["Games"].ToString();
                    tempStat.playerAVG = calcPlayerAverage(tempStat.gamesPlayed,
                    tempStat.numOfGoals, tempStat.numOfAssists);
                    listOfPlayerStats.Add(tempStat);
                }
            }
        }
    ...
```

The write function is the btnAdd_Click event, which again leverages the using statements to set context. In this using block, though, you create a new list item (newItem), set the properties of the list item, and then call the Update method to add the new record to the list.

```
    ...
            using (SPSite mySiteCollection = new SPSite(mySiteURL))
            {
                using (SPWeb web = mySiteCollection.OpenWeb())
                {
                    web.AllowUnsafeUpdates = true;

                    SPList list = web.Lists["Stats"];
                    SPListItem newStat = list.Items.Add();

                    newStat["Title"] = txtbxName.Text;
                    newStat["Goals"] = txtbxGoals.Text;
                    newStat["Assists"] = txtbxAssists.Text;
                    newStat["PIM"] = txtbxPIM.Text;
                    newStat["Games"] = txtbxGoals.Text;
                    newStat.Update();

                    web.AllowUnsafeUpdates = false;
                }
            }
    ...
```

The Visual Web part provides a great way to quickly design a UI for your Web part using the designer experience. You can, however, create equally compelling custom Web parts regardless of what type of Web part template you use. As you saw in this exercise, adding Ajax controls to your Web part can enhance the design of your Web part. For example, in this section, you saw how you could use the UpdatePanel to mitigate postback page flickers.

> **NOTE** The UpdatePanel *can be a very effective way to manage the postback page behavior. However, if the processing on the server is protracted, you may also want to design around this, or provide the application consumer with some progress indicator. Otherwise, your user could be left wondering when the process you are developing will finish.*

CUSTOM WEB PART PROPERTIES

After you've created your custom Web part, you can also add custom properties to the Web part class. Custom properties allow you to add custom settings for your Web part that provide additional functionality to consumers of your Web part.

You create Web part properties much like you create other properties in .NET. However, the syntax of a Web part class includes some attributes specific to a Web part. For example, the following code snippet shows an example of custom attributes that are associated with the custom Web part. These attributes define the level of personalization for the Web part, designate the property to be displayed in the property pane (specifically displaying it within a `PropertyGridEditorPart` object), and provides a name and description for the custom property.

```
[Personalizable(PersonalizationScope.User),
WebBrowsable,
WebDisplayName("Name"),
WebDescription("Description")]
```

You can create any number of custom properties for a Web part. To show you how you can create a custom property, let's walk through a simple example. This example will add a list (an `enum` object) as a custom property.

TRY IT OUT   Creating a Simple Custom Web Part Property

Code file [CustomWebPartProperties.zip] available for download at Wrox.com.

Custom properties are great for extending your Web parts with additional options and settings that are specific to a Web part. To create a custom Web part property, follow these steps:

1. Open Visual Studio 2010, and click File ➪ New ➪ Project. Select the SharePoint node and then select Empty SharePoint Project. Provide a name for the project (for example, `CustomWPProperties`) and click OK. When prompted, select "Deploy as farm solution" and click Finish.

2. Right-click the project, select Add ➪ New Item, and select Web Part in the SharePoint node. Provide a name for the Web part (for example, `WPPropertyExample`) and click Add.

3. Right-click the main Web part class file (for example, `WPPropertyExample.cs`) and click View Code.

4. In the main Web part class file, add the following bolded code:

```
using System;
using System.ComponentModel;
using System.Web;
using System.Web.UI;
using System.Web.UI.WebControls;
using System.Web.UI.WebControls.WebParts;
using Microsoft.SharePoint;
using Microsoft.SharePoint.WebControls;
using System.Xml.Serialization;

namespace CustomWPProperties.WPPropertyExample
{
    public class WPPropertyExample : WebPart
```

```
        {
            Label lblTitle = new Label();
            public enum SharePointLists
            {
                Stats,
                Players,
                Customers,
                Sales,
                Budget
            };

            protected SharePointLists listOfList;

            [Personalizable(PersonalizationScope.User),
            WebBrowsable,
            WebDisplayName("Available Lists"),
            WebDescription("Available Lists in SharePoint Site.")]

            public SharePointLists MySticks
            {
                get { return listOfList; }
                set { listOfList = value; }
            }

            protected override void CreateChildControls()
            {
                lblTitle.Text = "Web Part with Property";
                this.Controls.Add(lblTitle);
            }
        }
    }
}
```

5. When you have finished, select Build ➪ Deploy Solution to deploy the Web part class to SharePoint.

6. When the Web part deploys successfully, navigate to the top-level site and click Site Actions ➪ Edit Page. Click on the wiki page. Click the Insert tab and then select Web Part.

7. Add the custom Web part.

8. After you've added the Web part, click the down arrow to expose the Web part menu. Select Edit Web Part.

9. Navigate to the Miscellaneous section in the Property Editor, and you'll see the custom property you added earlier. Figure 6-18 shows what the simple custom property looks like.

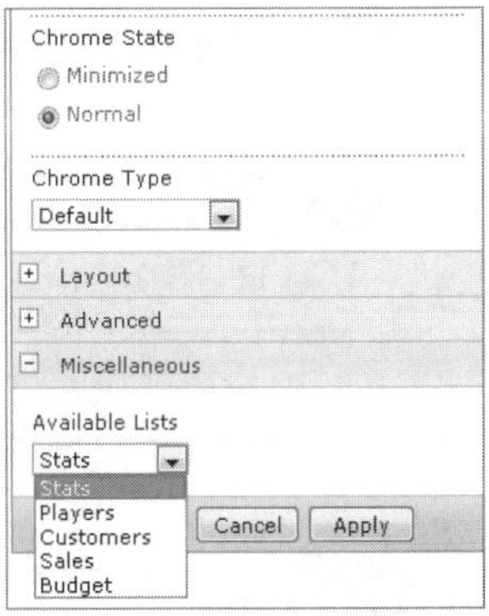

FIGURE 6-18 Custom Web part properties

How It Works

This exercise walked you through how to create a custom property for a Web part. The Web part base class exposes properties that you can programmatically set to display custom settings to users. In this example, you defined an `enum` (`SharePointLists`) that contained five mock SharePoint lists, and then created an instance of the `enum`.

```
public enum SharePointLists
{
    Stats,
    Players,
    Customers,
    Sales,
    Budget
};


protected SharePointLists listOfList;
```

The property is exposed when you decorate the property declaration with the property attributes. For example, in this walkthrough, you set the personalization scope to `User` (as opposed to `Shared`), displayed the properties in the property pane, and then set the name and description of the custom property.

```
[Personalizable(PersonalizationScope.User),
WebBrowsable,
WebDisplayName("Available Lists"),
WebDescription("Available Lists in SharePoint Site.")]

public SharePointLists MySticks
{
    get { return listOfList; }
    set { listOfList = value; }
}
```

By default, the custom property targets the property pane to expose the additional functionality to the user. If the custom property is not rich enough, you can create a custom tool part to manage your custom properties.

> **NOTE** *For more information on how to create a custom tool part to manage custom properties, see* `http://msdn.microsoft.com/en-us/library/dd584178(v=office.11).aspx`.

SUMMARY

Web parts are very versatile artifacts and act as core building blocks for your SharePoint site. You got a taste of what you can do in this chapter. However, you have really only touched the tip of the iceberg.

As you'll see later in the book, you can also integrate Silverlight into your Web parts to add another dimension to your user experience. Thus, your Web parts can be simple designs incorporating a small set of user controls, or they can be elaborate applications that contain multiple, integrated pieces, or even connect with other Web parts on the Web part page.

Through the last couple of chapters, you have learned how to interact with lists and Web parts. In Chapter 7, you will apply that knowledge and build a small sales dashboard solution.

EXERCISES

1. What is the architectural foundation for Web parts in SharePoint?

2. What are some out-of-the-box SharePoint Web parts?

3. What are the levels of scope for configuring Web parts?

4. What are the two types of Web part templates that are available in Visual Studio 2010? How are they different? What would you do with one versus the other (in terms of the types of applications you build)?

5. Create a custom property using a custom tool part.

▶ WHAT YOU LEARNED IN THIS CHAPTER

ITEM	DESCRIPTION
Web Parts	Web parts in SharePoint come in different flavors. There are also native and custom Web parts available for your use.
Web Part Architecture	Web parts are contained within a Web part zone, which is further managed by a Web Part Manager.
Standard Web Part	The standard Web part is a specific type of Web part that is created using the Visual Studio 2010 tools. You must manually create the UI, but you can create some compelling Web parts with this template.
Visual Web Part	The Visual Web part shares the baseline Web part programmability capabilities, but provides a more advanced UI designer experience than the standard Web part.

RECOMMENDED READING

➤ Additional community developer tools at `http://sharepointdevtools.codeplex.com/`

➤ SharePoint Development Center on MSDN at `http://msdn.microsoft.com/sharepoint/`

➤ Channel 9 SharePoint Developer Learning Center at `http://channel9.msdn.com/learn/courses/SharePoint2010Developer/`

7

Creating Your First SharePoint 2010 Application

WHAT YOU'LL LEARN IN THIS CHAPTER:

➤ Creating a solution that reads and writes data to and from a list using the server-side object model and Visual Web parts

➤ Building and deploying the solution using Visual Studio 2010

➤ Using the Chart Web part to render list data

➤ Integrating the different Visual Web parts in the solution on a Web part page

In this chapter, you'll work through the software design lifecycle with the end goal of building a SharePoint application. You've already built a number of smaller applications over the past few chapters, so you should think of this chapter as bringing some of this learning together into one application. However, in this chapter, what you will do is use a subset of the things you've learned over the past few chapters and apply them to the software design process. That is, you'll start out with a relatively simple set of requirements and, from there, design and deploy an application that will satisfy those requirements. For the most part, you'll be sticking to things you've learned thus far.

You'll first get a sense for the set of requirements for what will eventually be a simple sales reporting solution. Next, you'll create an architecture that will satisfy the design of the application. You'll use lists as the data source, and Web parts as the point of entry for the user. And finally, you'll traverse the major design components of your application. There will be three parts to the solution in total, including custom lists, custom Web parts, and leveraging the Chart Web part.

So, let's get started!

REQUIREMENTS

The software design process involves an iterative approach to building and deploying software. The process involves a number of core steps, which, at a high level, include the following:

➤ Defining the problem

➤ Defining a set of requirements that address the problem

➤ Designing a software solution around the requirements

➤ Developing the software solution

➤ Testing the software solution

➤ Deploying the software into a production environment

➤ Revving the software

Depending on the solution you're building, this process can be very complex, and involve many people ranging from project and product managers to developers and testers. It is, though, an exciting and creative process that involves negotiation (for example, on the priorities of the requirements) and rigor (for example, ensuring that you're making the right design choices for the software).

This process is called a *cycle* because after you complete one successful release of a product, you then start back at the top and "rev" the software to include new requirements or design elements that require incremental deployments of the software into the production environment. While the process is somewhat simplified, this is essentially the process you would go through when developing software.

The environment within which you build, test, and deploy software is varied, and for SharePoint, you should ideally have a development environment, as well as both a staging and production environment, where you can build and test your solutions. Further, depending on the size of your organization, you'll find that the process and environment just described may be spread across multiple staging environments and managed by multiple people. Or, it may be very agile, where only one to two developers manage the development and testing process, and the development, staging, and production environments are more collapsed.

To get started in any software design, you must address a problem. In this chapter, the problem can be stated as follows:

> *I'm a Litware account manager, and right now, I don't have visibility into the sales for my accounts.*

The solution you'll build in this chapter will be a sales dashboard and will provide a view into the quarter-by-quarter sales of a set of select companies.

The requirements to satisfy this problem are as follows:

➤ The solution will use lists as the source for the company data.

➤ There must be multiple views into the data.

➤ There must be a quick way to enter customer records close to the data view and have it reflected in the list.

➤ The list view should be displayed in a datagrid for easy viewing.

➤ The solution must have a way to aggregate sales into a FY10 quarterly total.

➤ A simple chart must show a fiscal comparison.

➤ The solution only requires current (that is, FY10) fiscal data to be displayed — but the chart must provide a comparison of FY10 versus past fiscal data.

➤ All of the core constituents of the solution must be visible on one SharePoint site or page.

You're probably grinning to yourself now, because, for those who have had experience with requirements, the list is typically long and egregious — and often involves countless hours of discussions and bargaining for priorities across multiple stakeholders. For illustrative purposes, it will be kept simple here.

So, now you have the requirements. The questions now are how will you architect the solution and what are the design choices you'll make when creating your sales dashboard?

SOLUTION DESIGN

With any architectural decisions, there will again be some back and forth discussion. Often, during this stage, you'll create a specification and review this document (which will outline a design, architecture, user experience, and sometimes APIs) with the key stakeholders in the project. In some organizations, these documents are broken out into different documents — one for the user experience, another for design or APIs, another for test, and so on.

To address the theoretical problem and create the sales solution, you propose a solution where you have the following:

➤ Two lists that will store information about each customer and their FY10 quarterly sales data, as well as a separate list that will contain information about the aggregate sales per fiscal year

➤ Three Visual Web parts that enable you to surface sales data in a datagrid, and also leverage the designer to build a simple data-entry form

➤ A Chart Web part that will reflect the most recent sales tallies, and provide a graphical FY09-to-FY10 comparison

With these decisions in hand, you can now create a high-level design architecture of how these pieces work together. Figure 7-1 provides an overview of how you might sketch out this design.

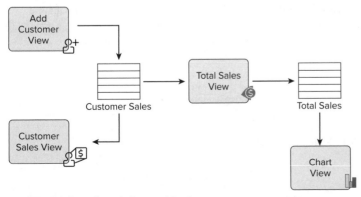

FIGURE 7-1 Sample solution architecture

In Figure 7-1, you can see that there are two main data sources: the Customer Sales list and the Total Sales list. For this application, you'll use the native SharePoint lists as the data source. However, as you increase your SharePoint knowledge, pay some attention to the integrations with Web services, SQL, and through the Business Connectivity Services (BCS). These represent other valid ways to integrate with external data sources.

> **NOTE** BCS is discussed in more detail in Chapter 8, and Web services are discussed in Chapter 10.

The two data lists have four associated views that together will satisfy the requirements. The Add Customer View will enable the user to add records to the Customer Sales list. The Customer Sales View will provide a view of the quarterly totals for each of the customers in the Customer Sales list. The Total Sales View will provide an aggregate view of all sales across all quarters and customers for FY10, which will be stored in the Total Sales list. And the Chart View will render the data in the Total Sales list.

As you work through this architecture, the question you may be asking yourself is, "How do you implement this design?" And, while the answers in this chapter may be based on the past couple of chapters (for example, using custom Web parts), your answers later in the book may be different (for example, using InfoPath or Silverlight). You may make design, security, or performance trade-offs, depending on your eventual solution (and the intended audience for that solution). However, this process is expected, and you should expect to decide across different options when trying to figure out a design. That is, you should have options that could take you toward resolving the same issue.

At this point, depending on how much branding and design you want to exert across the site, you may make some mock-ups of the site. For larger applications, you would certainly do this; for an application of this size, you may simply create a prototype as a starting point.

CUSTOMER SALES AND TOTAL SALES LISTS

With the architecture complete, you'll now want to get down to creating the prerequisite lists — that is the Customer Sales and Total Sales lists. Within the design, you have two lists. The first list will store information about the company and the quarterly sales for FY10. For example, Figure 7-2 provides an overview of what your first list might look like. It has a Company column (of type "Single line of text") and four columns (one for each quarter) entitled Q1, Q2, Q3, and Q4 (also of type "Single line of text"). You'll want to create a list that looks like this one.

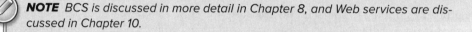

	Company	Q1	Q2	Q3	Q4
	Contoso ⊠ NEW	5678099	6589229	7009019	6980109
	Fabrikam ⊠ NEW	3879200	4083009	3908299	4209189
✚ Add new item					

FIGURE 7-2 Quarterly fiscal data in list (Customer Sales)

The second list (shown in Figure 7-3) is a simple list comprising two columns — one called `Year` (for the fiscal year) and another called `Sales` for total aggregate sales. You could leave this blank with data, or, to have a more meaningful chart, you could add some information so that it looks like the data in Figure 7-3. The `Year` column should be of type `"Single line of text,"` and the `Sales` field should be of type `Number`.

	Year	Sales
	FY 08	46,400,079
	FY 09	50,300,209
⊕ Add new item		

FIGURE 7-3 Aggregate sales list (Total Sales)

> **NOTE** *In this exercise, you create the lists manually. However, you can deploy a list definition and list instance with your solution so that you can package and deploy your solution as a self-contained* WSP *without worry for a user having to create the lists. This is possible by creating a SharePoint project, and then adding a list definition and instance of that list. Figure 7-4 shows the Visual Studio 2010 project template that is available for this purpose.*

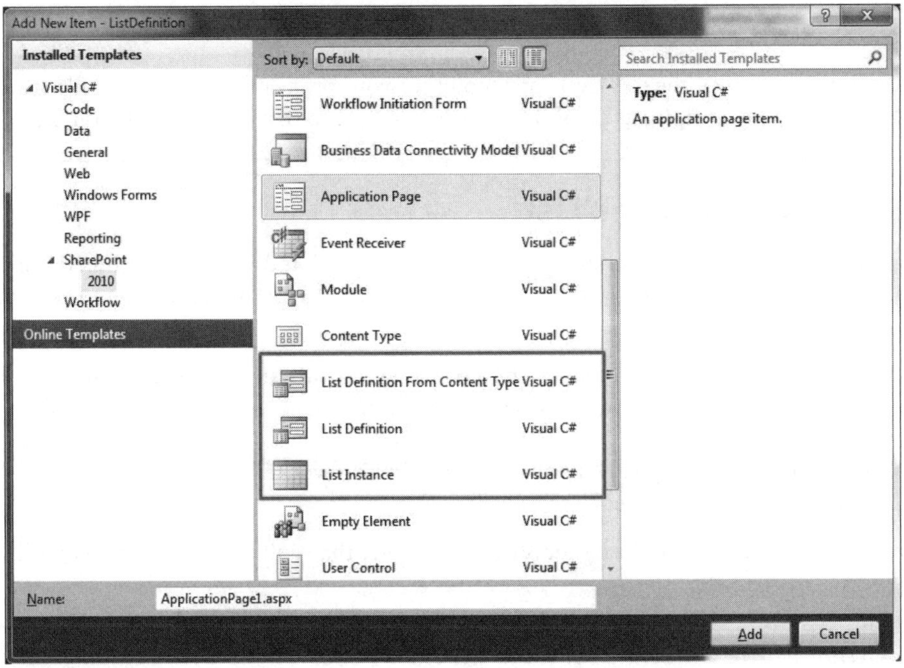

FIGURE 7-4 List Definition template

Now that you've built the `Customer Sales` and `Total Sales` lists, you can now move on to the second phase of the solution: building the Web part interfaces for your dashboard.

BUILDING THE APPLICATION

There are four phases to the development of the application. For this solution, it makes sense to develop the capability to add a record to the `Customer Sales` list first, and then build the other components around that. The other components will read and present data that has been entered into the SharePoint lists.

To get started, create a new solution that will be the main solution for all of your SharePoint projects.

TRY IT OUT Creating Your Solution

Creating a blank solution will enable you to add shell projects to the solution, and to provide a starting point for your solution development. To create a blank solution, follow these steps:

1. Open Visual Studio 2010.

2. Click File ➪ New ➪ Project.

3. Navigate to Other Project Types and select Visual Studio Solutions.

4. Click Blank Solution, and provide a name for your top-level solution (for example, `MyFirstSPSolution`).

How It Works

Visual Studio 2010 solutions provide the top-level entry point for your project files. A solution file is simply a reference file that, when invoked, loads all of the projects you add to that top-level solution file.

Adding a Record to the Sales List

The main interface for this part of the solution is a Visual Web part, and you've seen something similar to this in Chapter 6. Essentially, you'll create a Visual Web part that accepts data from the user and then adds this data to the SharePoint list.

You'll remember from Chapter 5 that there are a number of ways you can develop against a list. For example, you could use the native Web services, server object model, client object model, custom WCF service, or even RESTful services. In this example, you'll use the server-side object model. However, you can try other ways if you want as well, since you've worked through a number of examples in Chapter 5 that could be used here as well.

In the following walkthrough, you'll create the Visual Web part that will add sales records to the `Sales` list.

TRY IT OUT Creating the Sales Record Visual Web Part

Code file [MyFirstSPSolution.zip] available for download at Wrox.com.

A Visual Web part is a convenient way to create ASP.NET interfaces that integrate with SharePoint 2010. To create the Sales Record Visual Web part, follow these steps:

1. Open the solution you created earlier in the chapter and right-click the solution. Select Add ➪ New Project.

2. Navigate to the SharePoint 2010 node and select Empty SharePoint Project. Provide a name for the project (for example, `CustomerSalesWebPart`) and click OK. When prompted, select "Deploy as a farm solution" and click Finish. Visual Studio adds a number of project files to the solution.

3. Add a Visual Web part to the empty SharePoint project by right-clicking the project and selecting Add ➪ New Item. In the SharePoint item template node, select Visual Web part. Provide a name (for example, `CustSalesVWP`) and click Add.

4. Right-click the `.ascx` file (for example `CustSalesVWP.ascx`) and select "View in Designer." This view may be open by default, and to change to Design view, click the Design tab (or Split tab to show both the Design and Code view together).

5. Build a user interface that looks like Figure 7-5, which contains six labels, five textboxes, and two link buttons. To do this, drag and drop controls from the Toolbox onto the designer surface.

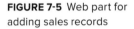

FIGURE 7-5 Web part for adding sales records

Table 7-1 provides an overview of the control types and the corresponding names.

TABLE 7-1 Control Types and Names

CONTROL TYPE	CONTROL NAME
Label	`lblSalesTitle, lblCompany, lblQ1, lblQ2, lblQ3, lblQ4`
Textbox	`txtbxCompanyName, txtbxQ1, txtbxQ2, txtbxQ3, txtbxQ4`
Link button	`lnkbtnAdd, lnkbtnClear`

6. To provide some structure for the controls, you can also use an HTML `Table` object. Double-click the two link-buttons to add event handlers in the code behind.

If you switch to Source view in the Designer, your code will look something like the following. (Note that the directives that Visual Studio adds by default at the top of the page have been removed in this code sample.)

```
...
<asp:Label ID="lblSalesTitle" runat="server" Text="Add Sales Data"
    Font-Bold="True" Font-Size="Small" ForeColor="#000066"></asp:Label>
<table border="0" width="25%"><tr><td>
<asp:Label ID="lblCompany" runat="server" Text="Company:"
    ForeColor="#000066"></asp:Label>
</td><td>
<asp:TextBox ID="txtbxCompanyName" runat="server" Width="157px"></asp:TextBox>
</td></tr><tr><td>
<asp:Label ID="lblQ1" runat="server" Text="Q1:" ForeColor="#000066"></asp:Label>
</td><td>
<asp:TextBox ID="txtbxQ1" runat="server" Width="157px"></asp:TextBox>
</td></tr><tr><td>
<asp:Label ID="lblQ2" runat="server" Text="Q2:" ForeColor="#000066"></asp:Label>
</td><td>
<asp:TextBox ID="txtbxQ2" runat="server" Width="157px"></asp:TextBox>
</td></tr><tr><td>
```

```
<asp:Label ID="lblQ3" runat="server" Text="Q3:" ForeColor="#000066"></asp:Label>
</td><td>
<asp:TextBox ID="txtbxQ3" runat="server" Width="157px"></asp:TextBox>
</td></tr><tr><td>
<asp:Label ID="lblQ4" runat="server" Text="Q4:" ForeColor="#000066"></asp:Label>
</td><td>
<asp:TextBox ID="txtbxQ4" runat="server" Width="157px"></asp:TextBox>
</td></tr><tr><td></td><td>
<asp:LinkButton ID="lnkbtnAdd" runat="server"
    onclick="lnkbtnAdd_Click">Add</asp:LinkButton>
<asp:LinkButton ID="lnkbtnClear" runat="server"
    onclick="lnkbtnClear_Click">Clear</asp:LinkButton>
</td></tr></table>
```

7. Switch to the code behind by right-clicking the `.ascx` (for example `CustSalesVWP.ascx`) file and selecting View Code.

8. Add the following `using` statement at the top of the project file:

    ```
    using Microsoft.SharePoint;
    ```

9. Next, add the following boldfaced code into the `.ascx` code behind (for example, `CustSalesVWP.ascx`). Note that, in the code, you'll want to change the current SharePoint site reference (`http://fabrikamhockey`) to your SharePoint site URL.

    ```
    using System;
    using System.Web.UI;
    using System.Web.UI.WebControls;
    using System.Web.UI.WebControls.WebParts;
    using Microsoft.SharePoint;

    namespace AddDataToSales.SalesDataEntry
    {
        public partial class SalesDataEntryUserControl : UserControl
        {
            protected void Page_Load(object sender, EventArgs e)
            {
            }

            protected void lnkbtnAdd_Click(object sender, EventArgs e)
            {
                //Be sure to update the SharePoint site to your server name.
                using (SPSite site = new SPSite("http://fabrikamhockey"))
                {
                    using (SPWeb web = site.OpenWeb())
                    {
                        web.AllowUnsafeUpdates = true;

                        SPList list = web.Lists["Customer Sales"];
                        SPListItem newItem = list.Items.Add();
                        newItem["Title"] = txtbxCompanyName.Text;
                        newItem["_x0051_1"] = txtbxQ1.Text;
    ```

```
                        newItem["_x0051_2"] = txtbxQ2.Text;
                        newItem["_x0051_3"] = txtbxQ3.Text;
                        newItem["_x0051_4"] = txtbxQ4.Text;
                        newItem.Update();

                        web.AllowUnsafeUpdates = false;
                    }
                }
            }

        protected void lnkbtnClear_Click(object sender, EventArgs e)
        {
            txtbxCompanyName.Text = "";
            txtbxQ1.Text = "";
            txtbxQ2.Text = "";
            txtbxQ3.Text = "";
            txtbxQ4.Text = "";
        }
    }
}
```

10. When you've finished adding the code, right-click the project and select Build. When the project successfully builds, right-click the project again and select Deploy. (Note that you can also edit the `.webpart` file (for example `CustSalesVWP.webpart`) to provide an intuitive description and title for your Web part.)

11. Navigate to your SharePoint site, and create a new Web part page using the Silverlight-enabled Create gallery. Click View All Site Content ⇨ Create ⇨ Page ⇨ "Web Part page." Click Create and provide a name for the page (for example, Sales Dashboard).

12. When the new page is loaded, click "Add a web part." Select the new Web part in the Custom category, and click Add. Your Web part should look somewhat similar to Figure 7-6. (Note that the name of the Web part listed in the gallery will reflect the `Title` property you amended in the `.webpart` file.)

Add Sales Data	
Company:	Acme
Q1:	3874992
Q2:	3409922
Q3:	3489912
Q4:	3289100
	Add Clear

FIGURE 7-6 Web part for adding sales records deployed

Test the Visual Web part to make sure it works. Add some data in the fields and then click Add to add the record into the `Customer Sales` list you created. You can validate that the data has been added by navigating to the Customer Sales list in your SharePoint site.

How It Works

You worked with this type of Visual Web part earlier in the book, and this application implements a similar pattern against the list. Specifically, you're using the SharePoint server-side object model to add a new item to the list. The code sets the context, creates a new item to be added to the `Customer Sales` list, loads them, and then calls the `Update` method to process the commands against SharePoint. Note that you'll want to ensure that you update the SharePoint site reference in this code (`http://fabrikam-hockey`) with the name of your SharePoint site.

As discussed earlier in the book, you could also access the list programmatically through the Lists Web service, client object model (the Visual Web part is deployed to the server, so the client object model is not well-suited for this scenario, but it does work), or a custom WCF service.

The creation of the `newStat` object enables you to update the fields in the list. But notice that, in this sample, you're accessing them by using the hexadecimal value of Q. This is because SharePoint can sometimes interpret some string variants as Excel formulas, so, for these field references, you can either use the specific string, or you can use the field GUID (in which case, you would not have to worry about the field-level hexadecimal reference).

```
SPList list = web.Lists["Customer Sales"];
SPListItem newStat = list.Items.Add();

newStat["Title"] = txtbxCompanyName.Text;
newStat["_x0051_1"] = txtbxQ1.Text;
newStat["_x0051_2"] = txtbxQ2.Text;
newStat["_x0051_3"] = txtbxQ3.Text;
newStat["_x0051_4"] = txtbxQ4.Text;
newStat.Update();

mySPSiteContext.ExecuteQuery();
```

As you learn SharePoint, you'll find that there are other ways to integrate data-entry forms to add data to lists. For example, you might use InfoPath or Silverlight as different data-entry forms. Each of these options has pros and cons, and both will be covered later in this book.

Viewing the Customer Sales

The Customer Sales Web part is a read-only Web part that is designed to simply load and display the data in the `Customer Sales` list. For this part of the solution, you'll use a Visual Web part with a datagrid as the main data display control. Let's get started building this control.

TRY IT OUT   Creating the Customer Sales Web PartCode file

Code file [MyFirstSPSolution.zip] available for download at Wrox.com.

The datagrid is an effective way to bind and display data in any ASP.NET application. In this Web part, you'll create the capability to load and refresh data using the `DataGrid` control. To create the Visual Web part, follow these steps:

1.   Select File ⇨ New ⇨ Project.

2.   Navigate to the SharePoint 2010 node and select Empty SharePoint Project. Provide a name for the new project (for example, `CustomerSalesList`). In the Solution drop-down list, click "Add to Solution."

3.   When prompted, click "Deploy as farm solution," and click Finish.

4.   After the shell project has been created, right-click the project and select Add ⇨ New Item.

5. Select the Visual Web part, provide a name (for example `SalesVWP`), and click Add.

6. Right-click the `.ascx` file (for example, `SalesVWP.ascx`) and select View Designer. Click View ⇨ Toolbox.

7. Drag and drop two labels, one datagrid, one link button, and one Update Panel onto the designer surface. Your UI should look similar to Figure 7-7. Note that you can provide some coloring for the datagrid through the properties in the Properties window. Table 7-2 shows the control types and names.

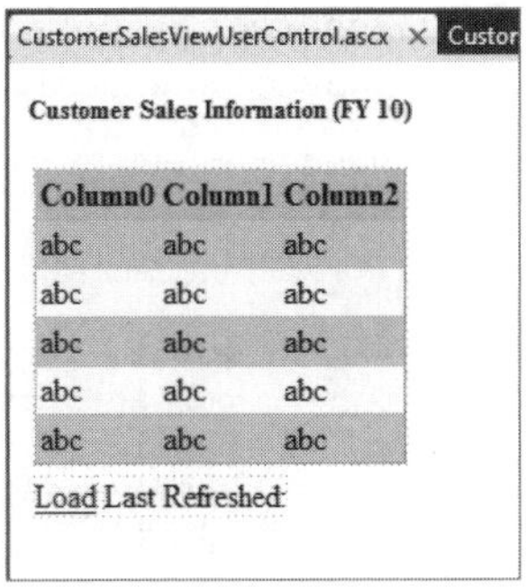

FIGURE 7-7 Visual Web part design for Customer Sales

TABLE 7-2 Control Types and Names

CONTROL TYPE	CONTROL NAME
Label	lblTitle, lblRefreshTime
Update panel	dataUpdatePanel
Datagrid	custDataGrid
Link button	lnkbtnLoadData

If you click the Source tab in the Designer view, the `.ascx` code behind should look similar to the following code snippet. Note that the directives have been removed for brevity. Also note that, in the following code snippet, the boldfaced code indicates the code that must be added to enable the Ajax `UpdatePanel` control. This prevents the postback page flicker.

```
...
<p>
    <asp:Label ID="lblTitle" Font-Size="Small" Font-Bold="True" runat="server"
        Text="Customer Sales Information (FY 10)" ForeColor=
            "#000066"></asp:Label>
</p>
<asp:UpdatePanel ID="dataUpdatePanel" runat="server">
<ContentTemplate>
<table><tr><td>
<asp:GridView ID="custDataGrid" runat="server" BackColor="#CCCCCC" CellPadding="2"
        GridLines="Horizontal" ToolTip="Customer Sales Information (FY 10)"
        Width="100%" ForeColor="#000066">
    <AlternatingRowStyle BackColor="#FFFFCC" />
    <HeaderStyle BackColor="#99CCFF" Width="100%" />
    </asp:GridView>
</td></tr></table>
<table><tr><td>
<asp:LinkButton ID="lnkbtnLoadData" runat="server"
    onclick="lnkbtnLoadData_Click">Load</asp:LinkButton>
</td><td>
<asp:Label ID="lblRefreshTime" runat="server" Text="Last Refreshed:"></asp:Label>
</td></tr></table>
</ContentTemplate>
</asp:UpdatePanel>
```

8.   Right-click the project and select Add ➪ Class. Name the class `CustomerSales` and then add the following boldfaced code to the default code.

```
namespace CustomerSalesList
{
    class CustomerSales
    {
        public string Company { get; set; }
        public string Q1 { get; set; }
        public string Q2 { get; set; }
        public string Q3 { get; set; }
        public string Q4 { get; set; }
    }
}
```

9.   After you've added the references, right-click the `.ascx` file (for example, `SalesVWP.ascx`) and select View Code. This opens the code-behind view for the Web part.

10.   At the top of the project file, add the following `using` statements:

```
using System.Collections.Generic;
using Microsoft.SharePoint;
```

11.   In the code behind, add the following boldfaced code. Note that you'll need to replace the current SharePoint site reference (`http://fabrikamhockey`) with your SharePoint site URL.

```
using System;
using System.Linq;
using System.Text;
using System;
using System.Web.UI;
using System.Web.UI.WebControls;
using System.Web.UI.WebControls.WebParts;

using System.Collections.Generic;
using Microsoft.SharePoint;

namespace CustomerSalesList.CustomerSalesView
{
    public partial class CustomerSalesViewUserControl : UserControl
    {
        List<CustomerSales> listOfCustomerSales = new List<CustomerSales>();

        protected void Page_Load(object sender, EventArgs e)
        {

        }

        private void updateRefreshTime()
        {
            DateTime currentTime = DateTime.Now;
            string refreshMessage = "Last Refreshed: ";
            lblRefreshTime.Text = refreshMessage + currentTime.ToLongTimeString();
        }

        protected void lnkbtnLoadData_Click(object sender, EventArgs e)
```

```
            {
//Be sure to replace the SharePoint site reference here.
        using (SPSite site = new SPSite("http://fabrikamhockey"))
            {
                using (SPWeb web = site.OpenWeb())
                {
                    SPList custSalesDataList = web.Lists["Customer Sales"];
                    SPQuery myCAMLQuery = new SPQuery();
                    myCAMLQuery.Query = "<View/>";
                    SPListItemCollection mySalesListItems =
                        custSalesDataList.GetItems(myCAMLQuery);

                    foreach (SPListItem tempListItem in mySalesListItems)
                    {
                        CustomerSales custSaleInfo = new CustomerSales();
                        custSaleInfo.Company = tempListItem["Title"].ToString();
                        custSaleInfo.Q1 = "$ " + tempListItem["_x0051_1"].
                            ToString() + ".00";
                        custSaleInfo.Q2 = "$ " + tempListItem["_x0051_2"].
                            ToString() + ".00";
                        custSaleInfo.Q3 = "$ " + tempListItem["_x0051_3"].
                            ToString() + ".00";
                        custSaleInfo.Q4 = "$ " + tempListItem["_x0051_4"].
                            ToString() + ".00";
                        listOfCustomerSales.Add(custSaleInfo);
                    }
                }
            }
            custDataGrid.DataSource = listOfCustomerSales;
            custDataGrid.DataBind();
            updateRefreshTime();
            lnkbtnLoadData.Text = "Refresh";
        }
    }
}
```

12. After you've added the boldfaced code, right-click the project and select Build, and then select Deploy Solution from the Build menu after the project successfully builds.

13. Navigate to the same SharePoint page where you deployed the Add Sales Web part, and then click Site Actions ⇨ Edit ⇨ "Add a web part."

14. Click Insert and then select Custom. Find the Web part you just built and deployed.

15. When the Web part loads, it will contain no data. Click the Load link button to load the data from the Customer Sales list. After you've done this, use the Add Sales Web part to add a customer programmatically to the list, and then click Refresh. Note that the Last Refreshed time is updated each time you click the Refresh link button. The results should look similar to Figure 7-8.

Customer Sales Information (FY 10)			
Company	**Q1**	**Q2**	**Q3**	**Q4**
Contoso	$ 5678099.00	$ 6589229.00	$ 7009019.00	$ 6980109.00
Fabrikam	$ 3879200.00	$ 4083009.00	$ 3908299.00	$ 4209189.00
Acme	$ 3874992.00	$ 3409922.00	$ 3489912.00	$ 3289100.00
Refresh Last Refreshed: 8:45:33 PM			

FIGURE 7-8 Customer Sales Information Web part

How It Works

Again, you have worked with this pattern before. That is, you're using a list collection object and then using the return data from the SharePoint list. You are iterating through the results, populating the list collection, and then binding the collection to the datagrid. However, there are a couple of new code excerpts in this Web part that you have not seen before.

The first is a helper function that provides the capability to refresh the data load time. For example, in the following code snippet, you create a `DateTime` object, which is set to the current time, and then set the `Text` property of the `lblRefreshTime` to be the current time you just set.

```
private void updateRefreshTime()
  {
      DateTime currentTime = DateTime.Now;
      string refreshMessage = "Last Refreshed: ";
      lblRefreshTime.Text = refreshMessage + currentTime.ToLongTimeString();
  }
```

While you've seen how to iterate through a set of return data and populate the data, note that, in this case, you're providing some additional formatting for the data by adding a currency symbol and decimal places. You can do this in other ways programmatically in .NET, but this is a straightforward way to hard-code some formatting into the returned data. For example, one way that you can do this is by using the `String.Format` method, which supports passing in a string parameter and the amended string format. Following is sample code:

```
String.Format(tempListItem["_x0051_1"].ToString(), ".00");
foreach (SPListItem tempListItem in mySalesListItems)
  {
      …
      custSaleInfo.Q1 = "$ " + tempListItem["_x0051_1"].ToString() + ".00";
      …
  }
```

> **NOTE** For more information on the `String.Format` method, go to: `http://msdn.microsoft.com/en-us/library/system.string.format.aspx`.

Up to this point, you've created two Web parts. Now let's create the last one to round out your programming tasks.

Viewing the Total Sales

You now have a view of all of the customers and a way to add new customers into the `Customer Sales` list. However, the way in which you want to satisfy the requirement of having an FY10 aggregated view of the sales is to create another Web part that automatically tallies the quarterly values and then exposes those in another datagrid. You'll again leverage a pattern that you've learned about earlier in this book. This time, though, you'll also add some helper code to calculate the total sales.

TRY IT OUT   Creating the Aggregate Sales Web Part

Code file [MyFirstSPSolution.zip] available for download at Wrox.com.

This Web part will contain only one row of data within the datagrid. However, you want to use the same type of color scheme and design, so you'll create a Web part with two labels, a link button, and a datagrid. Follow these steps:

1. Right-click the solution and select Add ⇨ New Project.

2. Navigate to SharePoint 2010 and then select Empty SharePoint Project. Provide a name for the project (for example, `TotalSalesVisualWebPart`) and then click OK. Select Deploy as farm solution and click Finish.

3. After the project has been created, right-click the project and select Add ⇨ New Item. Navigate to the SharePoint 2010 node and select Visual Web Part. Provide a name for the item (for example, `TotalSalesVWP`) and click Add. When the item has been added, right-click the `.ascx` file (for example, `TotalSalesVWP.ascx`) and click View Designer.

4. Click View ⇨ Toolbox.

5. Drag and drop two labels, one datagrid, and one link button, onto the designer surface. Figure 7-9 provides an overview of what the design of the Web part should look like. Table 7-3 shows the control types and names.

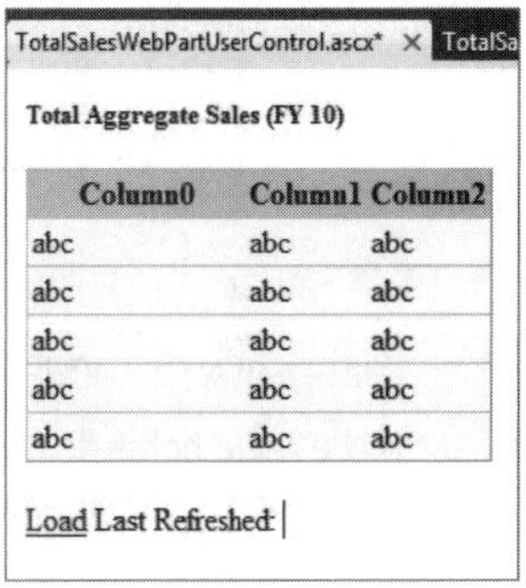

FIGURE 7-9 Total Aggregate Sales Web part

TABLE 7-3 Control Types and Names

CONTROL TYPE	CONTROL NAME
Label	`lblTitleTotalSales, lblRefreshMessage`
Datagrid	`totalSalesDataView`
Link button	`linkbtnLoad`

If you click the Source tab in the Designer view, the `.ascx` code behind should look similar to the following. Note that the directives have been removed for brevity.

```
...
<asp:Label ID="lblTitleTotalSales" runat="server"
    Text="Total Aggregate Sales (FY 10)" Font-Bold="True" Font-Size="Small"
    ForeColor="#000066"></asp:Label>
<p>
<asp:GridView ID="totalSalesDataView" runat="server" BackColor="#FFFFCC"
        CellPadding="2" ForeColor="#000066" GridLines="Horizontal"
        ToolTip="Total Aggregate Sales (FY 10)" Width="38%">
        <HeaderStyle BackColor="#99CCFF" Font-Bold="True" HorizontalAlign=
            "Center" Width="100%" /></asp:GridView>
</p>
<asp:LinkButton ID="linkbtnLoad" runat="server"
    onclick="linkbtnLoad_Click">Load</asp:LinkButton>
 <asp:Label ID="lblRefreshMessage" runat="server" Text="Last Refreshed: ">
</asp:Label>
```

6.   Right-click the project and select Add ➪ Class. Call the class `SalesTotals`, and then add the following boldfaced code to the default code:

```
using System;
using System.Collections.Generic;
using System.Linq;
using System.Text;

namespace TotalSalesVisualWebPart
{
    class SalesTotals
    {
        public string compName { get; set; }
        public string Q1 { get; set; }
        public string Q2 { get; set; }
        public string Q3 { get; set; }
        public string Q4 { get; set; }
    }
}
```

7.   Right-click the project and select View Code. This opens the code behind view for the Web part.

8.   In the code behind, add the following boldfaced code. Note that you will need to replace the SharePoint site reference in the code (`http://fabrikamhockey`) with your own SharePoint site URL.

```
using System;
using System.Web.UI;
using System.Web.UI.WebControls;
using System.Web.UI.WebControls.WebParts;
using System.Collections.Generic;
using System.Data;
using Microsoft.SharePoint;

namespace TotalSalesVisualWebPart.TotalSalesWebPart
{
    public partial class TotalSalesWebPartUserControl : UserControl
    {
        int numOfCompanies = 0;
        int totalQ1 = 0;
        int totalQ2 = 0;
        int totalQ3 = 0;
        int totalQ4 = 0;
        int aggSales = 0;
        string[] totalSales = new string[4];
        DataTable salesTable = new DataTable();

        protected void Page_Load(object sender, EventArgs e)
        {
        }

        protected void linkbtnLoad_Click(object sender, EventArgs e)
        {
//Be sure to replace the SharePoint site reference here.
            using (SPSite site = new SPSite("http://fabrikamhockey"))
            {
```

```
    using (SPWeb web = site.OpenWeb())
    {
        SPList custSalesDataList = web.Lists["Customer Sales"];
        SPQuery myCAMLQuery = new SPQuery();
        myCAMLQuery.Query = "<View/>";
        SPListItemCollection mySalesListItems =
            custSalesDataList.GetItems(myCAMLQuery);

        foreach (SPListItem tempListItem in mySalesListItems)
        {
            SalesTotals tempSalesObject = new SalesTotals();
            numOfCompanies += 1;
            tempSalesObject.compName = tempListItem["Title"].ToString();
            tempSalesObject.Q1 = tempListItem["_x0051_1"].ToString();
            totalQ1 = totalQ1 + Int32.Parse(tempSalesObject.Q1);
            tempSalesObject.Q2 = tempListItem["_x0051_2"].ToString();
            totalQ2 = totalQ2 + Int32.Parse(tempSalesObject.Q2);
            tempSalesObject.Q3 = tempListItem["_x0051_3"].ToString();
            totalQ3 = totalQ3 + Int32.Parse(tempSalesObject.Q3);
            tempSalesObject.Q4 = tempListItem["_x0051_4"].ToString();
            totalQ4 = totalQ4 + Int32.Parse(tempSalesObject.Q4);
        }
    }
}

totalSales[0] = totalQ1.ToString();
totalSales[1] = totalQ2.ToString();
totalSales[2] = totalQ3.ToString();
totalSales[3] = totalQ4.ToString();

DataColumn salesColumnQ1 = new DataColumn("Q1");
salesTable.Columns.Add(salesColumnQ1);
DataColumn salesColumnQ2 = new DataColumn("Q2");
salesTable.Columns.Add(salesColumnQ2);
DataColumn salesColumnQ3 = new DataColumn("Q3");
salesTable.Columns.Add(salesColumnQ3);
DataColumn salesColumnQ4 = new DataColumn("Q4");
salesTable.Columns.Add(salesColumnQ4);

DataRow salesTotalRow = salesTable.NewRow();

salesTotalRow[0] = "$ " + totalSales[0] + ".00";
salesTotalRow[1] = "$ " + totalSales[1] + ".00";
salesTotalRow[2] = "$ " + totalSales[2] + ".00";
salesTotalRow[3] = "$ " + totalSales[3] + ".00";

salesTable.Rows.Add(salesTotalRow);

totalSalesDataView.DataSource = salesTable;
totalSalesDataView.DataBind();

mySPSiteContext.Dispose();
updateRefreshTime();
linkbtnLoad.Text = "Refresh";

aggSales = totalQ1 + totalQ2 + totalQ3 + totalQ4;
```

```
                    updateAggSales(aggSales);

            }

            private void updateAggSales(int aggSales)
            {
string fiscalYear = "FY 10";

                using (SPSite site = new SPSite("http://fabrikamhockey"))
                  {
                    using (SPWeb web = site.OpenWeb())
                      {
                          web.AllowUnsafeUpdates = true;

                          SPList totalSales = web.Lists["Total Sales"];
                          SPListItem newStat = totalSales.Items.Add();
                          newStat["Title"] = fiscalYear;
                          newStat["Sales"] = aggSales;
                          newStat.Update();

                          web.AllowUnsafeUpdates = false;
                      }
                  }

            }

            private void updateRefreshTime()
            {
                DateTime currentTime = DateTime.Now;
                string refreshMessage = "Last Refreshed: ";
                lblRefreshMessage.Text = refreshMessage + currentTime.
                    ToLongTimeString();
            }
        }
}
```

9. After you've added the boldfaced code, right-click the project and select Build, and then right-click the project again and select Deploy after the project successfully builds.

10. Navigate to the same SharePoint page where you deployed the other Web parts, and then click Site Actions ➪ Edit ➪ "Add a web part."

11. Click Insert and then select Custom. Find the Web part you just built and deployed.

12. When the Web part loads, it will contain no data. Click the Load link-button to load the data from the Customer Sales list. After you've done this, use the Add Sales Web Part to add a customer programmatically to the list, and then click Refresh. Note that the Last Refreshed time will update each time you click the Refresh link button, as shown in Figure 7-10. Now you can click the Load button, and the totals will be calculated and displayed. A row will be added into the Sales table.

Total Aggregate Sales (FY 10)			
Q1	Q2	Q3	Q4
$ 13432291.00	$ 14082160.00	$ 14407230.00	$ 14478398.00
Refresh Last Refreshed: 8:45:55 PM			

FIGURE 7-10 Total Aggregate Sales Web part

13. After you've done this, navigate to the `Sales` table and delete the `FY10` list item that was just generated. While you could extend the application to check for a `FY10` record, you will not build this capability into the application in the scope of this chapter.

How It Works

You've seen the pattern in the `Aggregate Sales` application before (that is, the way in which you use the server-side object model to interact with SharePoint data). However, there are a couple of new items that are included in this code sample that you may not have seen before. To begin, you set some class-level variables as follows:

```
int totalQ1 = 0;
int totalQ2 = 0;
int totalQ3 = 0;
int totalQ4 = 0;
int aggSales = 0;

string[] totalSales = new string[4];
DataTable salesTable = new DataTable();
```

These variables enable you to add all of the quarterly sales, and provide an aggregate total for each quarter. For example, `totalQ1` is the total sales of all of the Q1 sales across all of the companies listed in the `Customer Sales` list. Also, `totalSales` represents the array within which you'll store this information. And, lastly, the `DataTable` is another data construct that is used here to show you how to dynamically create an in-memory data object that can also be bound to a `DataGrid` control.

You assigned values to the `totalSales` array through the following statements:

```
totalSales[0] = totalQ1.ToString();
totalSales[1] = totalQ2.ToString();
totalSales[2] = totalQ3.ToString();
totalSales[3] = totalQ4.ToString();
```

Note that, here again, you might use the `String.Format` method to provide additional formatting to your string variables.

You then created a column for each of the quarters, created a row for the `salesTable` object, and assigned the array values to the column values, as shown in the following code:

```
DataColumn salesColumnQ1 = new DataColumn("Q1");
salesTable.Columns.Add(salesColumnQ1);
DataColumn salesColumnQ2 = new DataColumn("Q2");
salesTable.Columns.Add(salesColumnQ2);
DataColumn salesColumnQ3 = new DataColumn("Q3");
salesTable.Columns.Add(salesColumnQ3);
DataColumn salesColumnQ4 = new DataColumn("Q4");
salesTable.Columns.Add(salesColumnQ4);

DataRow salesTotalRow = salesTable.NewRow();

salesTotalRow[0] = "$ " + totalSales[0] + ".00";
salesTotalRow[1] = "$ " + totalSales[1] + ".00";
```

```
salesTotalRow[2] = "$ " + totalSales[2] + ".00";
salesTotalRow[3] = "$ " + totalSales[3] + ".00";

salesTable.Rows.Add(salesTotalRow);
```

One of the benefits of using the `DataTable` object is that you can provide some structure and formatting for the table, and then have access to other methods and properties for that object. Further, you may have noticed with the examples in earlier chapters that, when you bound the list collection object to a datagrid, it inherited the object names. By creating explicit columns, you can control the column headings for a more descriptive table.

The binding of the `DataTable` was the same as when you assigned the list collection to be the data source for the datagrid. For example, the following code sample shows binding the `DataTable` object to the datagrid. You can see that the syntax is very similar, and only the object being bound is different.

```
totalSalesDataView.DataSource = salesTable;
totalSalesDataView.DataBind();
```

The two helper functions you created in the example, `updateRefreshTime` and `updateAggregate-Sales`, simply updated the data-refresh time in the label property to be the current time, and added the new aggregate sales as a row in the `Total Sales` table. However, as discussed earlier, there is no check in the `updateAggregateSales` method to see if the `FY10` row already exists. This may be something you'd want to add to the code so that you don't end up with multiple `FY10` list items.

Adding a Chart Web Part

The last item to add in this application is the out-of-the-box Chart Web part, which will provide a comparative chart view of the data that you have in the `Total Sales` list. For example, if you added entries for `FY08` and `FY09`, when you deploy and run all of the previous applications, you'll have a comparative bar-chart view across three fiscal years. The key takeaway here for you, though, should be that you don't always need to rely on custom components when creating your SharePoint applications. You can integrate out-of-the-box features within your application (and with your custom code).

TRY IT OUT   Adding the Chart Web Part

The Chart Web part can provide some interesting pivots on data. You'll use it here to show a comparative view across your sales quarters. Follow these steps:

1. Open SharePoint and navigate to where you've added the other three Web parts.

2. Click Site Actions ⇨ Edit Page.

3. Click "Add a web part" and navigate to the Business Data category. Select Chart Web Part and click Add.

4. Click the drop-down arrow in the Web part, and select Customize your Chart. Use this wizard to select a particular type of bar chart.

5. In Step 1 of the wizard, select the Column chart, as shown in Figure 7-11. Accept the default options for Step 2 of the wizard and click Next.

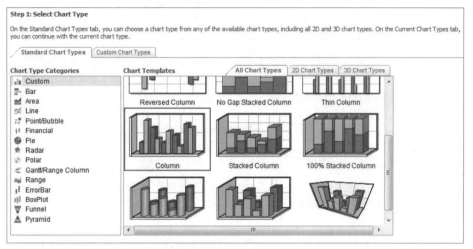

FIGURE 7-11 Standard Chart Types Categories dialog

6. For Step 3 of the wizard, check the Show Chart Title checkbox and provide a title for your chart (for example, FY 10 Sales, as shown in Figure 7-12) and click Auto Preview to see a rendering of the chart. Click Finish to complete the custom chart configuration.

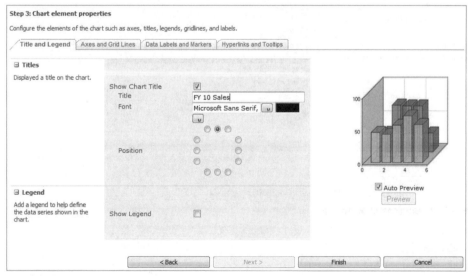

FIGURE 7-12 Adding a chart title and viewing a preview

7. Right-click the drop-down arrow again and select Connect To Data, as shown in Figure 7-13.

8. Select "Connect to a List" and click Next, as shown in Figure 7-14.

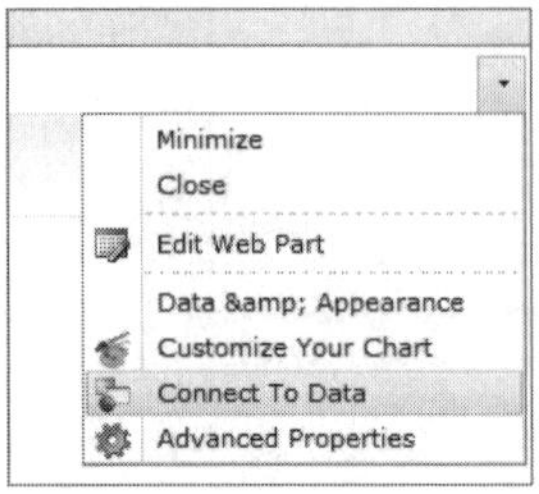

FIGURE 7-13 Connecting Chart Web part to data

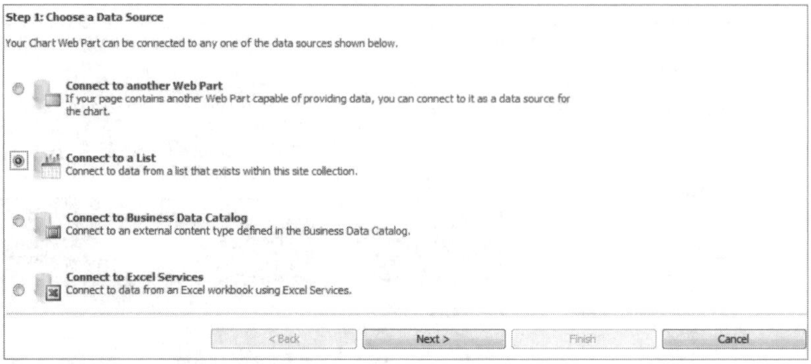

FIGURE 7-14 Connecting to a list

9. Select the list to which you want to bind your Chart map and click Next, as shown in Figure 7-15.

10. If your mapping was successful, you will see a tabular rendering of the data as shown in Figure 7-16. Click Next to move to the next step in the wizard.

11. You can provide some customizations to change how the chart will look in this step. Accept the default options and click Finish to complete the wizard, as shown in Figure 7-17.

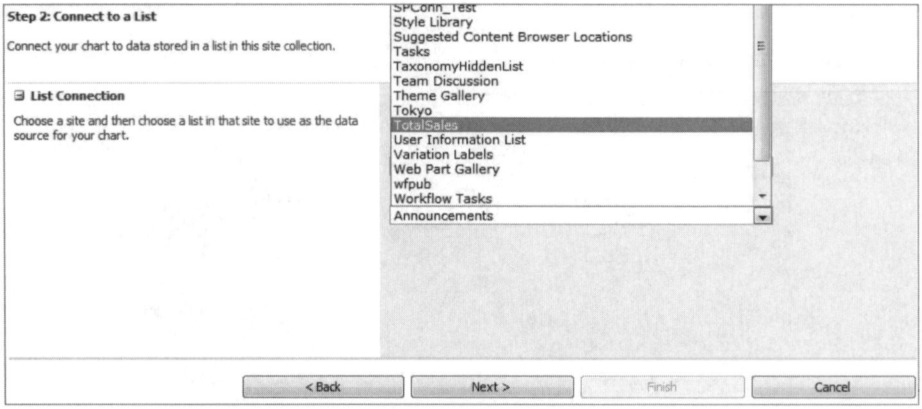

FIGURE 7-15 Binding the chart to a list

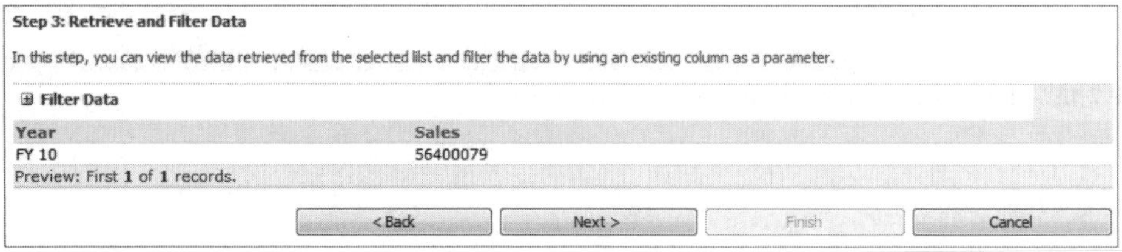

FIGURE 7-16 Retrieving and filtering data

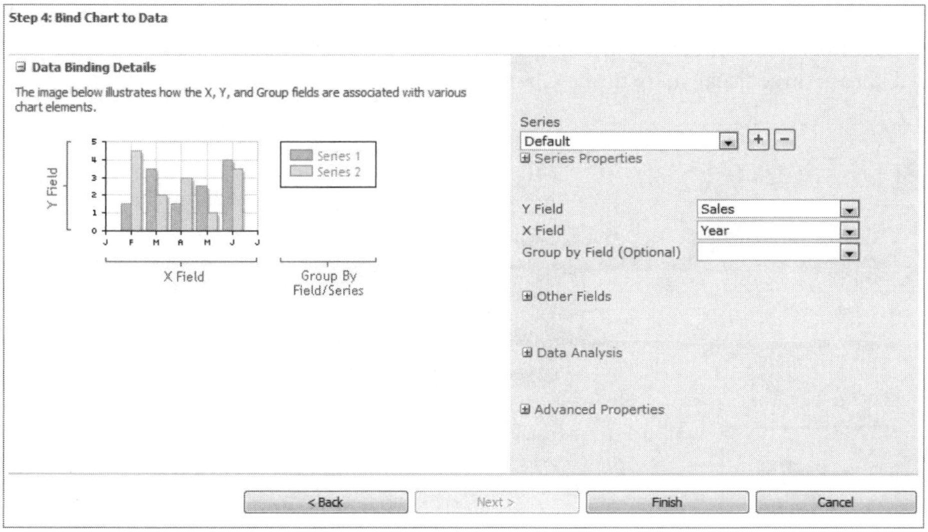

Step 4: Bind Chart to Data
Data Binding Details
The image below illustrates how the X, Y, and Group fields are associated with various chart elements.
Y Field
X Field
Series 1
Series 2
Group By Field/Series
Series
Default
Series Properties
Y Field
Sales
X Field
Year
Group by Field (Optional)
Other Fields
Data Analysis
Advanced Properties
< Back
Next >
Finish
Cancel

FIGURE 7-17 Binding the chart to data

At this point, SharePoint will render the Chart Web part and expose a columnar chart view of the data in the `Total Sales` list. Figure 7-18 provides an example of this. One thing worth mentioning is that, when you update the list, the Chart Web part is updated automatically, so you don't need to worry about your user having to explicitly click a Refresh button anywhere. Once the data is updated from the Aggregate Sales Web part, the changes will be graphically reflected in the Chart Web part.

Data & Appearance
Advanced Properties
Total FY10 Sales
60000000
40000000
20000000
0
FY 08
FY 09

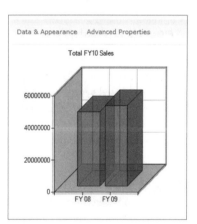

FIGURE 7-18 Displaying data in the Chart Web part

Final Dashboard

Using the site themes, you can very easily provide some branding for the site where you're going to insert all of the Web parts. Alternatively, you could add a simple graphic (such as a company or group logo) to light up the out-of-the-box themes as well. Or, you could go so far as to create a custom master page for your site.

You'll note that, in Figure 7-19, there is a custom logo that is used (the fictional Litware company logo). This was added by using the Image Viewer Web part (Site Actions ➪ Edit Page ➪ "Add a web part" ➪ Insert ➪ "Media and Content," and select the Image Viewer Web part), which simply exposes (using a URL reference) a graphic file you've added to a SharePoint library. However, the effects of including even a simple graphic can be transformative for your site. So, be sure to think about these small enhancements when building your SharePoint sites.

Figure 7-19 shows the final sales dashboard. You can see here that a number of companies have been added to the Customer Sales Information Web part, the sales have been tallied, and the data has been rendered across three fiscal years in the Chart Web part.

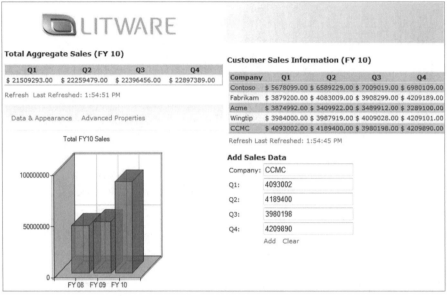

FIGURE 7-19 Rendering the Final Sales dashboard

Congratulations! Now that you've created all of the Web parts that made up the Sales dashboard, you've created your first end-to-end solution. You did apply many of the things you've already seen in the book — with a few new items thrown in — so this should have been pulling practice together. As you become more familiar with the SharePoint object model and APIs, you'll think of other ways that you can creatively integrate data and .NET applications with SharePoint.

SUMMARY

The great thing about SharePoint is that you can create simple or more complex solutions — depending on what you're trying to achieve. For example, you'll learn later in this book that you can use InfoPath as a data-entry form, or the list itself can be exposed as a Web part and, thus, be an artifact of your dashboard. Further, key performance indicators (KPIs) or Excel Services could also be used. And all of this is okay, because, in the real world, you would make choices against all of these features within SharePoint. In this chapter, things have been kept simple, and your design was aligned with what was learned in previous chapters.

You'll want to explore the different ways in which you can build and integrate applications with and into SharePoint 2010. In this chapter (and very much in the past few chapters), you've learned that lists and Web parts are the core building blocks of a SharePoint site, and there are many different ways to code against them and leverage them. As you move into the next few chapters of the book, you'll go beyond the list and Web part to explore other, more advanced programmatic aspects of SharePoint.

Chapter 8 starts that exploration with an examination of the integration of line-of-business (LOB) data using Business Connectivity Services (BCS).

EXERCISES

1. Review other features of SharePoint and write down different ways that you might design the solution, assuming that the requirements do not change. For example, instead of using the server-side object model, use the Lists Web service.

2. Add the capability to check to see if the FY10 list item exists before adding a new record. If it does, then replace the old data with newly updated aggregates calculated using an extended helper function.

3. Create a new list definition and list instance programmatically. Deploy the code into SharePoint and manually add some data to the list to test the functionality.

▶ WHAT YOU LEARNED IN THIS CHAPTER

ITEMS	DESCRIPTION
Design	Designing SharePoint solutions can encompass multiple features or SharePoint artifacts (for example, list, Web part, and so on).
Server-Side Object Model	This chapter put the server-side object model into practice as one of the central list APIs in SharePoint 2010.
Visual Web Parts	Visual Web parts enable many different types of customization. In this chapter, you learned how to use these types of Web parts with datagrids and read/write list programmability.
Lists as a data source	You learned that you can use lists as data sources, which can be manually created or deployed as list definitions/instances with your solution files.

RECOMMENDED READING

➤ Microsoft SharePoint 2010 SDK at `http://msdn.microsoft.com/en-us/library/ee557253(office.14).aspx`

➤ SharePoint 2010 Web Services SDK at `http://msdn.microsoft.com/en-us/library/ee705814(office.14).aspx`

➤ MSDN content on `String.Format` method at `http://msdn.microsoft.com/en-us/library/system.string.format.aspx`

PART III
Advanced Topics for SharePoint 2010 Development

8

Integrating Line-of-Business Data Using Business Connectivity Services

WHAT YOU'LL LEARN IN THIS CHAPTER:

➤ Getting to Know Office business applications (OBAs)

➤ Understanding the Business Connectivity Services (BCS) and how you can build OBAs using them

➤ Working with SharePoint and Office integration techniques using BCS

One of the key innovations in SharePoint 2007 was the Business Data Catalog (BDC), which was a set of services and Web parts that enabled read-access to ADO.NET and Web service-based connections to line-of-business (LOB) systems. However, there were limitations with the BDC (for example, it was read-only), so, SharePoint 2010 introduced the Business Connectivity Services (BCS) as an evolution to the BDC.

BCS evolved the BDC to be read/write, more programmable, and to look and feel like other lists in SharePoint. BCS is important because many companies want to integrate LOB data with SharePoint, and they want read/write access to that data from SharePoint and Microsoft Office. Because these applications integrate LOB systems with SharePoint and Microsoft Office, they are called *Office Business Applications (OBAs)*.

This chapter introduces you to the concept of OBAs and discusses SharePoint's new BCS functionality that provides great integration with LOB systems. This chapter also walks you through some practical examples of how you can integrate ADO.NET-based and Web service-based connections with SharePoint and Microsoft Office to create an OBA.

UNDERSTANDING OFFICE BUSINESS APPLICATIONS (OBAS)

One of the key issues faced by many organizations is unlocking critical business data that resides in large, enterprise systems. This might be seen as a data issue — that is, getting the right data out of a back-end system and into the hands of information workers to help them in their day-to-day jobs. However, many business and IT managers will also tell you that there is a significant monetary and productivity gain in extracting this data, and in creating the connection to those who need it the most.

Take the example of sales forecasting, which typically needs to happen at the summary level on a quarterly basis. Often, you'll find that companies track this information on a daily or weekly basis to ensure that pressure is constantly applied toward tracking and achieving the revenue goals of the company. If the sales data resides in a system that is not easily accessible, then unlocking this information becomes critical to the enterprise.

Let's imagine that a fictional company called Acme has an SAP system in which they store all customer and sales information. Today, accessing data in SAP is difficult, because you may need to interact with an IT professional who has SAP-specific knowledge and access to get you that information.

The sales team wants this information in the tools that they use everyday: Microsoft Excel and SharePoint. This enables them to view and manage the data in the way in which they're most comfortable.

To achieve this, the SAP IT professional copies the data into a spreadsheet, perhaps formats it, and then sends it on to the team via email. The team then uses that spreadsheet in the course of their forecasting exercises.

Now, this may seem acceptable for a quarterly process. However, when you begin to think about this process from the monthly, weekly, daily, or even on-demand perspective, creating a dependency like this on the SAP specialist gets a bit hairy. Furthermore, once you have a snapshot of the data, you may want to leverage it across other applications (for example, pull it into PowerPoint to automatically create sales presentations). Thus, the question becomes why not customize the Office or SharePoint interface, and have a direct link to the LOB data so that information workers don't have to focus on the process of getting the data? The information workers could instead focus on working with the data. Enter Office business applications (OBAs).

Simply defined, an OBA is *a solution that integrates SharePoint and/or Microsoft Office and LOB data*. It was created as a result of companies using Office and SharePoint as a targeted interface into specific LOB data (also called *external system* or *external data source*). OBAs can be very powerful when fully realized.

The power of OBAs derives from the capability to leverage many of the different features of the SharePoint and Office platforms — as well as wider Microsoft and non-Microsoft technologies. For example, OBAs can integrate customizations that you build into the Office client (such as custom Word templates), integrate LOB data into the documents, and then tie the document to an organizational process using SharePoint workflow. You can also create a simple SharePoint list that provides a read/write view into a back-end LOB system. You might also leverage Silverlight to create a more dynamic experience with the LOB data (something you'll learn in Chapter 9), and deploy the Silverlight-enabled application in SharePoint. And the possibilities go on.

The point is that OBAs represent an expansive and versatile way to leverage many different parts of the Office and SharePoint platform to get LOB data into the hands of information workers. And, at the heart of the OBA is the use of SharePoint and Microsoft Office to manage a business process. For example, if you take the sales forecast with SAP, Table 8-1 shows a part of the sales forecast process that an OBA would enable.

TABLE 8-1 OBA Process

PERSON	PROCESS	TECHNOLOGY
Stan (Account Manager)	Navigates to a SharePoint list that is populated with sales data from SAP. He updates his quarterly numbers for his key accounts.	• SharePoint external list (BCS) • SAP (LOB system)
Stan (Account Manager)	Navigates to a SharePoint document library and clicks New to create a new document. SharePoint automatically opens a new Excel template that has a custom ribbon in it. He uses the custom ribbon to access and filter data from the external list, and then to input sales data into the spreadsheet. He pivots and creates forecasting table/charts. When he completes the sales forecast, he saves the document to SharePoint, and an approval workflow is kicked off.	• SharePoint document library • Custom Excel document • Custom content type • SharePoint client object model leveraging external list • Native Excel functionality • Approval workflow
Amy (Stan's Manager)	Opens mail that is generated from SharePoint workflow and clicks a link to Stan's forecast. She approves the document, and an approval email is sent to Stan.	• Approval workflow • SharePoint/Outlook integration

The process outlined in Table 8-1 is a simplified version of what happens in reality. For example, there could be many more turns in the business process, or the process could involve more levels of management and more people. However, the key take-away is that various parts of the SharePoint and Microsoft Office platforms can come together to create an OBA.

> **NOTE** One of Microsoft's flagship OBAs is a partnership product of SAP and Microsoft called Duet Enterprise. In practice it demonstrates many of the benefits just described. For more information, go to `http://office.microsoft.com/en-us/duet/FX101686211033.aspx?ofcresset=1`.

The high-level architecture of an OBA is fairly straightforward: you have a client that consumes a connection, which enables communication with the external LOB system.

For example, Figure 8-1 shows the presentation layer across SharePoint and Office — where you have multiple options for building out your presentation layer, ranging, for example, from Silverlight, custom Web parts, and external lists on the SharePoint side to custom documents/add-ins and Open XML on the Office side. Furthermore, the types of services that you will typically use within an OBA are ASP.NET (`.asmx`), WCF, SQL (generally, ADO.NET), and BCS. These service-oriented designs facilitate the connection to the external system.

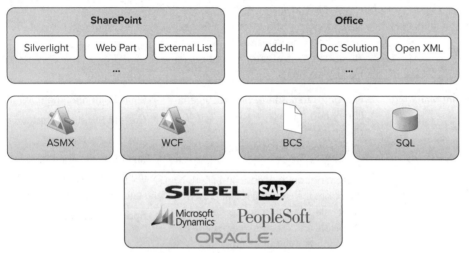

FIGURE 8-1 High-level OBA architecture

The 2010 releases of SharePoint and Microsoft Office include a number of developer entry points for building OBAs. For example, on the client, you can extend the Office user interface (UI) to build custom task panes, extend the Office ribbon, add a SharePoint workflow to a document, or leverage Open XML in your design to manage LOB data passed into and out of your documents. You can further tie these extensions to a service-oriented architecture, such as Windows Communication Foundation (WCF) or REST, and begin to bridge the back end to your presentation layer. This back end could be SharePoint data or it could be LOB data.

On the SharePoint side, you can build Silverlight-enabled applications that bring LOB data into the Silverlight application (and further integrate with the SharePoint object model, such as pushing data to a SharePoint list). You could also create custom Web parts that also integrate with these back-end systems. And you can also leverage BCS to drive that integration to the back-end LOB system.

OBAS AND BCS

OBA and BCS intersect where there is the need for information workers to get at data that lives in external systems, which includes structured data that may live in — for example, SQL Server, enterprise resource planning (ERP) systems, and customer resource management (CRM) systems — and unstructured data that live in, for example, Office documents, SharePoint, and Internet blogs and wikis. This was illustrated in Figure 8-1.

In its simplest form, BCS represents a way to integrate external data systems with both SharePoint and Office. In the process, BCS provides a way for developers to do the following:

➤ Surface external data in both SharePoint and Office

➤ Map external data to Office *types* (such as Contacts or Tasks in Outlook)

➤ Surface LOB data in Microsoft Access, SharePoint Workspace, and Microsoft Outlook

➤ Reuse data connectors across the server and client

➤ Bridge the world of structured/unstructured data with the information worker through BCS solutions

Although characterizing the BCS as a "connector" may seem simple, there are a few key things that exist within the BCS infrastructure that you'll want to be aware of. For example, the BCS architecture shown in Figure 8-2 drills into the OBA architecture shown in Figure 8-1 and provides a snapshot of some of the key pieces in BCS.

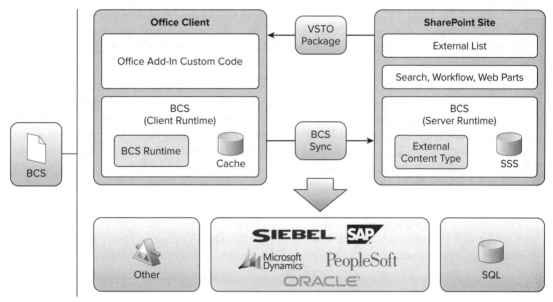

FIGURE 8-2 BCS architecture

You can think of BCS as starting from the bottom of the diagram and moving up, with the "connectors" to the external data. These can be custom connectors that you build using a pure .NET code approach, ADO.NET connections, or service connections. The great thing about supporting services is that you can literally plug into any service endpoint, and then define the data structures that you want to deploy into SharePoint.

On the right-hand side of Figure 8-2, SharePoint 2010 contains a BCS runtime that supports the BCS APIs and the execution of any code you write against BCS. It also contains the external content type, which is the main way that SharePoint understands how to communicate with the external data system.

BCS requires a security infrastructure to mediate the connections between specific users and the data from those external data sources — you do not want sensitive data getting into the wrong hands. There are a number of ways in which developers can mediate this connection — for example, pass-through, leveraging the application pool account security, or creating a custom username and password database. You can manage this security from the Secure Store Service (SSS) from the SharePoint Central Administration site.

Above the security layer, you'll also note that there exists a layer for search, workflow, and Web parts. BCS is a primary way of extending search into your LOB system. So, when SharePoint executes a search, it indexes data and information from the external data source with your other search results. Furthermore, you can tie the workflow to Office documents, and manage this workflow through the out-of-the-box workflow or custom workflow you build and deploy to SharePoint. Finally, the Web parts represent the BDC Web parts that ship with SharePoint 2010.

The top layer contains the external list, which represents a new addition to SharePoint Foundation 2010 that enables the reading and writing of data to and from an external data source. The external list looks and feels much like a normal list. However, the data does not live in the SharePoint list, because it is referenced and loaded into the list via an external content type. The major differences from the SharePoint 2007 BDC Web parts that were used in MOSS 2007 to connect to external systems is that the external data is accessed using the external content type and it now supports read/write integration with your external data sources.

Figure 8-3 shows an external list that is connected to an `AdventureWorks` SQL Server database (which, in this case, is the external data source). Notice how it looks and acts like a "standard" SharePoint list. It includes customer information, and you can see that, when you select one item in the list, you have the capability to view, edit, or delete the item (or the record) from the SQL Server instance of the `Customer` database. Thus, when BCS enables a view of the data within this external list within SharePoint, it can facilitate these operations. (When creating the connection to the external data system, you configure these operations.)

Figure 8-4 shows another example of leveraging BCS. This figure illustrates SAP data that is being consumed within a Silverlight application that is hosted within SharePoint. In this application, Silverlight controls enable you to filter SAP data in the Silverlight UI. The Silverlight application uses the client object model to communicate with an external list and then displays the data with a more dynamic UI.

	CustomerID	NameStyle	Title	FirstName	MiddleName	LastName	Suffix	CompanyName	SalesPerson
☐	1	No	Mr.	Orlando	N.	Gee		A Bike Store	adventure-works\pamela
	View Item	No	Mr.	Keith		Harris		Progressive Sports	adventure-works\david8
	Edit Item								
✕	Delete Item	No	Ms.	Donna	F.	Carreras		Advanced Bike Components	adventure-works\jillian0
	4	No	Ms.	Janet	M.	Gates		Modular Cycle Systems	adventure-works\jillian0
	5	No	Mr.	Lucy		Harrington		Metropolitan Sports Supply	adventure-works\shu0
	6	No	Ms.	Rosmarie	J.	Carroll		Aerobic Exercise Company	adventure-works\linda3
	7	No	Mr.	Dominic	P.	Gash		Associated Bikes	adventure-works\shu0
	10	No	Ms.	Kathleen	M.	Garza		Rural Cycle Emporium	adventure-works\josé1
	11	No	Ms.	Katherine		Harding		Sharp Bikes	adventure-works\josé1
	12	No	Mr.	Johnny	A.	Caprio	Jr.	Bikes and Motorbikes	adventure-works\garrett
	16	No	Mr.	Christopher	R.	Beck	Jr.	Bulk Discount Store	adventure-works\jae0

FIGURE 8-3 External list

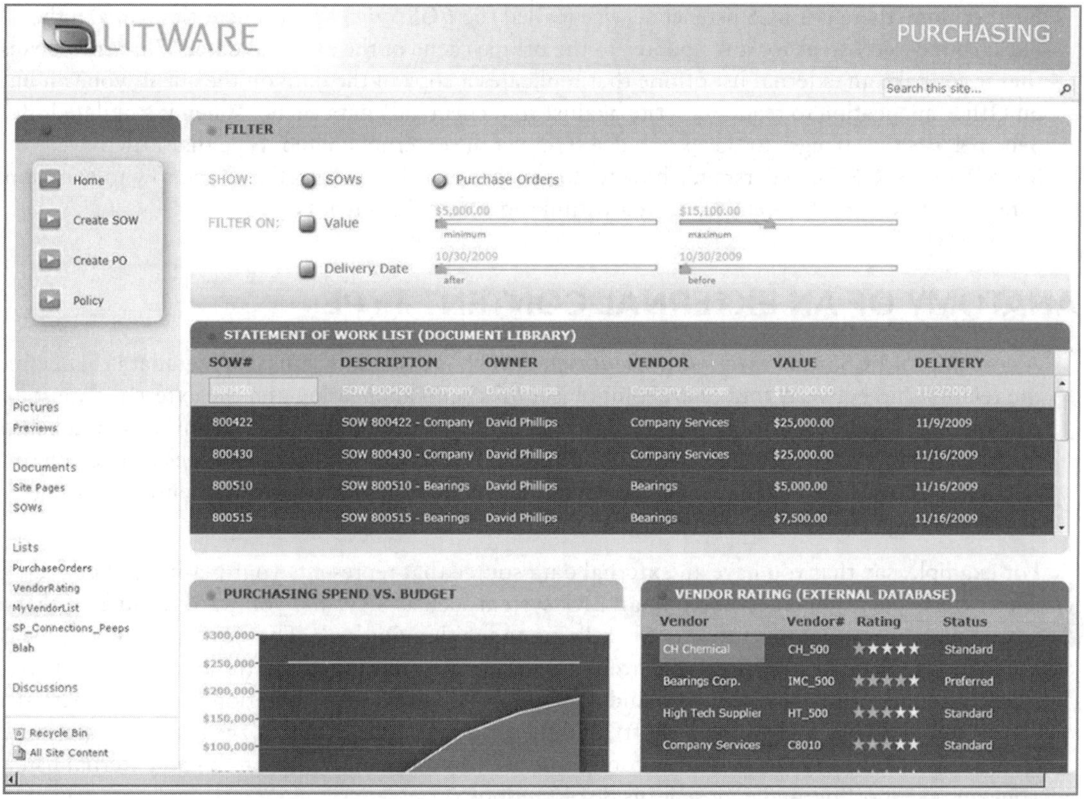

FIGURE 8-4 SAP, Silverlight, and BCS

You'll also note that Figure 8-2 includes a Visual Studio Tools for Office (VSTO) package, which is the way in which you build smart-client applications (for example, Office custom task panes connected to LOB data) within Visual Studio. The VSTO acronym is a throwback to the days when VSTO shipped as a separate product in the Visual Studio family.

However, in Visual Studio 2008 and Visual Studio 2010, the separate tools are subsumed within the Professional (and above) Visual Studio SKU. Specifically, this package represents the way in which Microsoft takes a "snapshot" of the external data and installs it on the client, where it can be used by SharePoint Workspace, Access, and Outlook to surface the external data within those applications. Furthermore, you can also use the metadata cache on the client (which is a database on the client that is a copy of the external data on the client) in combination with a client-side object model to program against the data, and surface that data within the Office client.

When the client-side metadata cache and VSTO package are installed on a client machine, you can use the BCS client object model to program applications that leverage this data. For example, you can build Office applications (application-level add-ins, or document-level solutions) to leverage that offline cache of the external data source. The client-side BCS runtime is installed with Office Professional 2010. Note that while you do have the capability to code directly against the BCS client API, you can also use the SharePoint client object model to create Office add-ins that communicate with an external list.

Furthermore, there is a BCS listener service (called the *BCS Sync*) on the client that runs in the background and listens for any updates to the offline cache of the external data. What this means is that if you take an external list offline that replicates a copy of the data on the client, you can build an Office application to read and write against that client-side data cache. When it's updated, BCS Sync persists the changes to the external system via the external content type that is deployed to SharePoint. BCS Sync understands how to do this because the "instructions" on how to communicate with the external system are stored within the external content type.

ANATOMY OF AN EXTERNAL CONTENT TYPE

A core part of BCS is the *external content type,* which is essentially reusable metadata that defines the relationship between your SharePoint object (or client) application and the external data source. The metadata contains information such as connectivity information, data definitions, and behaviors (or operations) you want to apply to the external data. External content types enable you to manage and reuse the metadata and the operations of a business entity from a central location, and also enable users to interact with that data in a meaningful way.

For example, say that you have an external data source that represents your main set of `Customers`. This external data source is stored in an ERP system such as SAP, and you want to surface (that is, issue a read operation) this inside of SharePoint and within Outlook. The external content type is the metadata that sits between the SharePoint and client application, and the external data source. You create the external content type and configure it to have a read operation from the external data source (for example, SAP or PeopleSoft), and then map the entities within the external data source to the Outlook data types. With this configuration, you can surface the data as an external list, and you can take it offline and expose it inside of Outlook.

External content types offer some great benefits to developers:

➤ You can reuse external content types across the client and server, and across server instances.

➤ You can program against the BCS APIs and create some very compelling applications (for example, using Silverlight and BCS integrations for SharePoint, as you saw earlier).

➤ You can ensure secure access and appropriate discrete permissions against the BCS operations.

➤ You can facilitate searching against your LOB systems and indexing that data within your SharePoint search results.

➤ You can simplify the management of the external data sources through external content types.

For those who are familiar with the BDC Web parts in SharePoint 2007, the external content type is an evolution of the application definition file (ADF), or the XML file that defined the relationship between the external data system and SharePoint. The evolution from ADF to the external content type represents an extension of the ADF to include more operations that can be defined against the external data system, and the fact that it's now used with the external list and with client applications.

Figure 8-5 shows a horizontal overview of the key elements for metadata modeling of the external content type. The specific elements within the model are defined as follows:

➤ `LobSystem` — This represents an external data source, service, or software system.

➤ `LobSystemInstance` — This is a specific implementation of the `LobSystem`.

➤ `Entity` — This describes the structure of the business entity or object. It contains one or more `Methods`, fields (or `TypeDescriptors`) and a unique `Identifier`, and is made up of specific data types.

➤ `Method` — This describes the back-end APIs, with a `MethodInstance` being the specific implementation of a `Method`. `Methods` can also contain filters (defined through the `FilterDescriptor`).

➤ `Parameter` — This is defined through a `TypeDescriptor` and `DefaultValue`.

➤ `AssociationGroup` — This defines relationships across back-end systems.

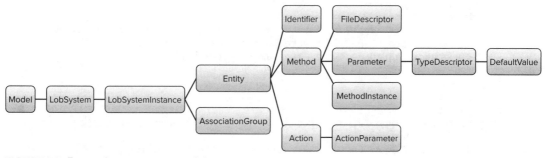

FIGURE 8-5 External content type model

>  **NOTE** You can find more information on the Business Connectivity Services (BCS) metadata and SDK at `http://msdn.microsoft.com/en-us/library/ee556826(office.14).aspx`.

The following code sample shows what the external content type metadata looks like:

```xml
<?xml version="1.0" encoding="utf-8"?>
<Model xmlns:xsi="http://www.w3.org/2001/XMLSchema-instance"
    xmlns:xsd="http://www.w3.org/2001/XMLSchema"
    xmlns="http://schemas.microsoft.com/windows/2007/BusinessDataCatalog"
    Name="BusinessDataCatalog1">
<LobSystems>
 <LobSystem Name="BusinessDataCatalog1LobSystem1" Type="DotNetAssembly">
<LobSystemInstances>
 <LobSystemInstance Name="BusinessDataCatalog1LobSystem1Instance1" />
</LobSystemInstances>
<Entities>
 <Entity Name="Product" Namespace="ProductModel.BusinessDataCatalog1"
```

```
            EstimatedInstanceCount="1000" Version="1.0.0.13">
   <Properties>
    <Property Name="Class" Type="System.String">
        ProductModel.BusinessDataCatalog1.ProductService,
      BusinessDataCatalog1LobSystem1</Property>
   </Properties>
   <Identifiers>
    <Identifier Name="ID" TypeName="System.String" />
   </Identifiers>
   <Methods>
    <Method Name="FindAllEntities">
 <Parameters>
  <Parameter Direction="Return" Name="returnParameter">
   <TypeDescriptor TypeName="System.Collections.Generic.IEnumerable1[[ProductModel.
       BusinessDataCatalog1.Entity1, BusinessDataCatalog1LobSystem1]]"
       IsCollection="true" Name="Entity1List">
     <TypeDescriptors>
      <TypeDescriptor TypeName="ProductModel.BusinessDataCatalog1.Entity1,
          BusinessDataCatalog1LobSystem1" Name="Entity1">
       <TypeDescriptors>
        <TypeDescriptor TypeName="System.String" IdentifierName="ID" Name="ID" />
        <TypeDescriptor TypeName="System.String" Name="Manufacturer" />
        <TypeDescriptor Name="Name" TypeName="System.String" />
       </TypeDescriptors>
    </Parameter>
   </Parameters>
   <MethodInstances>
    <MethodInstance Type="Finder" ReturnParameterName="returnParameter"
         Default="true"
       Name="FindAllEntities" DefaultDisplayName="Entity1 List" />
   </MethodInstances>
   </Method>
   </Methods>
   </Entity>
   </Entities>
   </LobSystem>
   </LobSystems>
   </Model>
```

Note that, in this external content type, there is one LOB system (the external data source) defined, which is called `BusinessDataCatalog1LobSystem1`. This external content type was created using Visual Studio 2010, hence the type being `DotNetAssembly`. You'll also notice that there is one entity defined as well, called `Product` — this is a custom object in the Visual Studio 2010 project.

> **NOTE** *The discussion in this chapter predominantly uses SharePoint Designer for creating the external content types. However, in Chapter 10, you will walk through an example where you use Visual Studio 2010 to create an external list that is integrated with a custom Web service.*

Another important element you'll see defined here is one method instance called `FindAllEntities`, which you could think of as equivalent to a `SELECT *` statement in SQL used to get all of the entities in the data source. Thus, if you were to create an external list from this external content type, the result would be all of the records being returned from the external data source.

One last thing to mention here is that the specific records within the external data source are also defined here as `TypeDescriptors`. (The `TypeDescriptor` is an object that defines the parameter data type.) If you look within this section of the external content type, you'll see that there is a very simple data source that comprises three types:

➤ An `ID` record that is of type `string`

➤ A `Manufacturer` record that is of type `string`

➤ A `Name` record that is also of type `string`

When you start working with external content types, you should be familiar enough with the model metadata to understand the major elements. You may have to troubleshoot or review the XML to ensure that the metadata in your external content type matches that of your external data source, or at least need to inspect it for errors.

As you'll see later in this chapter, a good starting point is using SharePoint Designer 2010 when creating your external content types. Using this tool will abstract a lot of the XML metadata for you, and get you accustomed to working with the external content types and understanding the different operations that are supported and how they are represented in the metadata.

CONNECTIVITY OPTIONS WITH BCS

BCS supports a number of different connectivity options, including the following:

➤ ADO.NET connection to a database (for example a SQL Server database)

➤ Web service connection (includes support for either a WCF or ASP.NET Web endpoint)

➤ .NET assembly (which is one that you build using the Visual Studio BDC Metadata project template)

➤ Custom connector (which is a much more code-intensive process, where you build the connector and external content type metadata from scratch)

Each of these connectors is supported within the same external content type metadata shown earlier. However, there will be slight differences that you may notice as you begin to build them. For example, an ADO.NET database would have the following `LobSystem Type` property:

```
<LobSystem Name="DBConnection" Type="Database">
```

Compare this to a Web service connection, whose `Type` property would be set as follows:

```
<LobSystem Name="WSConnection" Type="Webservice">
```

Another example of the difference between models based on the connection type is the different ways in which methods are defined through the common external content type schema. For example, the following represents a Web service external content type with a method that maps to a Web method within the Web service, called `GetCustomers`. (Note that the `TypeDescriptors` here map to parameters within the Web service.)

```
<Methods>
 <Method Name="GetCustomers">
  <Parameters>
   <Parameter Name="CustomerId" Direction="In">
    <TypeDescriptor Name="Id" TypeName="System.Int32" IdentifierName=
        "CustomerIdentifier" />
   </Parameter>
   <Parameter Name="Customers" Direction="Return">
    <TypeDescriptor Name="CustomerArray" TypeName=
        "ExampleCrmNamespace.Customer[], ExampleCRM" IsCollection="true">
    <TypeDescriptors>
    <TypeDescriptor Name="Customer" TypeName="ExampleCrmNamespace.Customer,
        ExampleCRM">
   <TypeDescriptors>
    <TypeDescriptor Name="Id" TypeName="System.Int32" IdentifierName=
        "CustomerIdentifier" />
    <TypeDescriptor Name="FirstName" TypeName="System.String" />
    <TypeDescriptor Name="LastName" TypeName="System.String" />
   </TypeDescriptors>
  </TypeDescriptor>
 </TypeDescriptors>
</TypeDescriptor>
</Parameter>
</Parameters>
<MethodInstances>
<MethodInstance Name="GetCustomer" Type="SpecificFinder" ReturnParameterName=
    "Customers" ReturnTypeDescriptorName="Customer" />
</MethodInstances>
</Method>
```

Compare the Web service external content type to that of a database method definition (which leverages a stored procedure in this case). The methods in this case look a little different, but they still follow the same metadata taxonomy as the Web service.

```
<Methods>
 <Method Name="GetCustomers">
 <Properties>
  <Property Name="RdbCommandText" Type="System.String">sp_GetCustomers</Property>
  <Property Name="RdbCommandType" Type="System.Data.CommandType, System.Data,
      Version=2.0.0.0, Culture=neutral,
      PublicKeyToken=b77a5c561934e089">StoredProcedure</Property>
 </Properties>
 <Parameters>
  <Parameter Name="@CustomerId" Direction="In">
   <TypeDescriptor Name="Id" TypeName="System.Int32" IdentifierName=
       "CustomerIdentifier" />
  </Parameter>
  <Parameter Name="Customers" Direction="Return">
   <TypeDescriptor Name="CustomerDataReader"
       TypeName="System.Data.SqlClient.SqlDataReader, System.Data,
       Version=2.0.0.0, Culture=neutral,
       PublicKeyToken=b77a5c561934e089" IsCollection="true">
```

```
<TypeDescriptors>
 <TypeDescriptor Name="Customer" TypeName="System.Data.IDataRecord,
      System.Data, Version=2.0.0.0, Culture=neutral,
      PublicKeyToken=b77a5c561934e089">
 <TypeDescriptors>
  <TypeDescriptor Name="Id" TypeName="System.Int32" IdentifierName=
      "CustomerIdentifier" />
  <TypeDescriptor Name="FirstName" TypeName="System.String" />
  <TypeDescriptor Name="LastName" TypeName="System.String" />
 </TypeDescriptors>
 </TypeDescriptor>
</TypeDescriptors>
</TypeDescriptor>
</Parameter>
</Parameters>
<MethodInstances>
 <MethodInstance Name="GetCustomer" Type="SpecificFinder"
      ReturnParameterName="Customers" ReturnTypeDescriptorName
      viswar ="Customer" />
 </MethodInstances>
</Method>
</Methods>
```

Thus, the underlying schema for the external content type metadata remains similar. It's just that the attributes would be different.

DEVELOPING YOUR FIRST APPLICATION USING BCS

Now that you have some background on OBAs, BCS, and the external content type metadata structure, let's walk through the process that you use to create an OBA with BCS. Figure 8-6 shows a high-level process by which you would create an OBA using BCS. It includes five categorized steps that take you from the creation of the data source, all the way to deploying the add-in on the client. The assumption is that you'd be creating an OBA that could cut across the server and the client. Note that if you wanted to create an OBA that lived only on the server, you would stop at the third step in this figure.

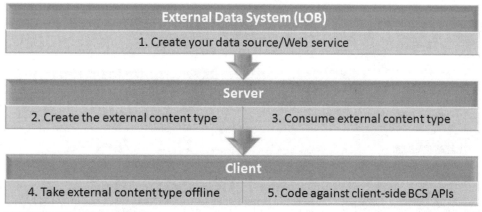

FIGURE 8-6 Creating an OBA

Also, these steps can vary in complexity, depending on what you're trying to do. For example, a simple example could be creating a Web service connection to a LOB system, and then using SharePoint Designer to create an external content type and external list. A more complex process would be creating the business object in SAP, creating a Web service wrapper, building the BCS solution using Visual Studio, and then replicating the external content type on the client for a client-side Word add-in. Either of these examples would fit the definition of an OBA.

In some cases, some of the steps in Figure 8-6 may already be complete (for example, a Web service may already exist, or the back-end data source may have already been created by another developer or database administrator). If you were to build an OBA from scratch, however, this would be the high-level process that you would follow to deploy it on the server and on the client.

The remainder of this chapter will walk through how you create your OBA using the BCS with these five steps in mind.

Creating the External Data Source

The first step represents the creation of the data source — in this case, an external data source. In some cases, the external data source already exists (such as leveraging the sales forecast numbers from the earlier SAP example), or you may need to create one. Either way, this step is where you create or discover an external data source.

If the external data source is a system such as SAP, Oracle e-Business Suite, or Microsoft Dynamics CRM, then you'll need some way of interacting with that data. You typically cannot just interact across a system without some sort of intermediary service. Thus, one of the key work items in this first step is to create a Web service against that external data source. To do this, you might have to create a service within the native toolset (for example, the Web Service Wizard within the SAP tools), or you could leverage existing adaptors (such as BizTalk LOB Adaptors — which are essentially WCF service connections to external systems).

For the purposes of this chapter, let's start with the `AdventureWorksLT2008` SQL Server database as the external data source. This example will be based on using SQL Server 2008 in the development environment, but you could equally use other versions of SQL Server if you choose. As shown in Figure 8-7, in the `AdventureWorksLT2008` database is a table called `SalesLT.Customer`, which is the specific table you'll use in creating your OBA.

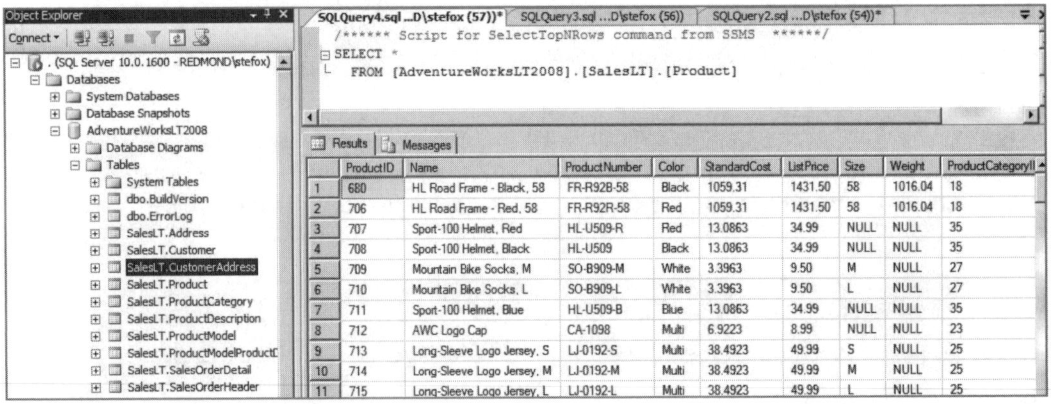

FIGURE 8-7 SQL Server (AdventureWorksLT2008)

The `AdventureWorksLT2008` data required for this walkthrough is available for download at this book's companion download site (`www.wrox.com`). The filename is `SQL2008.AdventureWorksLT2008_Only_Database.zip`. You can download the `AdventureWorksLT2008` database from `http://msftdbprodsamples.codeplex.com/releases/view/37109`.

After you've downloaded the `AdventureWorksLT2008_Only_Database.zip` file, unzip the two files (`AdventureWorksLT2008_Data.mdf` and `AdventureWorksLT2008_Log.ldf`) into the following folder: `c:\Program Files (x86)\Microsoft SQL Server\MSSQL.1\MSSQL\Data`. To attach the `AdventureWorks` database, open SQL Server Management Studio, right-click the Databases node, and click Attach. In the Attach Databases dialog, click Add and browse to the previously described directory. Then select the `AdventureWorksLT2008_Data` file.

After you've attached the `AdventureWorksLT2008` database, you can browse to the `Customer` table to see the data that exists in the database. You can now create an external content type that integrates directly with SQL Server to expose the customer data in an external list. As you've seen, the external content type is the XML file that defines the relationship with your external data source that will map to the `Customer` table in the `AdventureWorksLT2008` database.

Creating the External Content Type

You can create this external content type in three different ways:

➤ You can hand-code the XML in Notepad (which is not recommended).

➤ You can use SharePoint Designer 2010 to create it (which, if you're just starting out with BCS, is recommended).

➤ You can use Visual Studio 2010 (which is geared more toward a heavier coding experience).

If you use SharePoint Designer to create an external content type, it automatically saves the XML metadata in the Business Data Connectivity (BDC) Metadata Store and exposes it within Central Administration — which is where you should start if you're new to BCS. Visual Studio 2010 creates a standard WSP for the BDC Metadata project, so the XML metadata file is deployed into the correct place as a part of the wider project. If you create the XML metadata file outside of SharePoint Designer or Visual Studio, you must import the external content type into Central Administration. To import an external content type, you open the Central Administration site, click Application Management ➪ Managed Service Applications ➪ Business Connectivity Services, and then click the Import button in the SharePoint ribbon. You then browse to the location of the external content type XML file and click Import.

TRY IT OUT   Creating an ADO.NET-Based External Content Type

An external content type is necessary to create the relationship between the external data source and the consuming application. To create an external content type that is integrated with the `AdventureWorksLT2008` Customer table, follow these steps:

1. Open SharePoint Designer 2010.

2. Click File ➪ Open Site and then type the URL of your SharePoint site (for example, `http://fabrikamhockey`).

3. When SharePoint Designer loads the SharePoint site, it will display the current settings for the site. In the left-hand navigation pane, click External Content Types. SharePoint Designer opens a page that displays all of the current external content types listed in the site. Figure 8-8 shows the different external content types registered with this site.

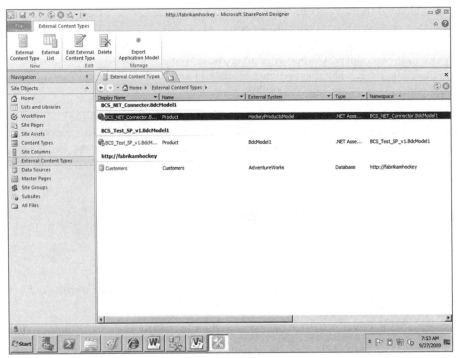

FIGURE 8-8 External content type report in SharePoint Designer

4. To create a new external content type, click the External Content Type button on the ribbon. SharePoint Designer opens the New External Content Type properties window that you can use to create the external content type.

5. Click the New External Content Type link beside Name and Display Name to provide a Name (for example, `MyCustomers`) and Display Name (for example, `Customers`) for your external content type.

6. In the Office Item Type drop-down list, select Contact, as shown in Figure 8-9.

7. Ensure that Offline Sync for External List is set to Enabled.

8. To add a data source, select "Click here to discover external data source."

9. Click Add Connection to add the `AdventureWorksLT2008` database as an external data source. Then, in the Add Connection dialog, select SQL Server and provide the necessary information to load the `AdventureWorksLT2008` database (that is, your "Server name," "AdventureWorksLT2008" as the Database Name, and an optional "Name for the Data Source"). Select the "Connect with User's Identity" radio box to connect to the SQL Server database with your credentials.

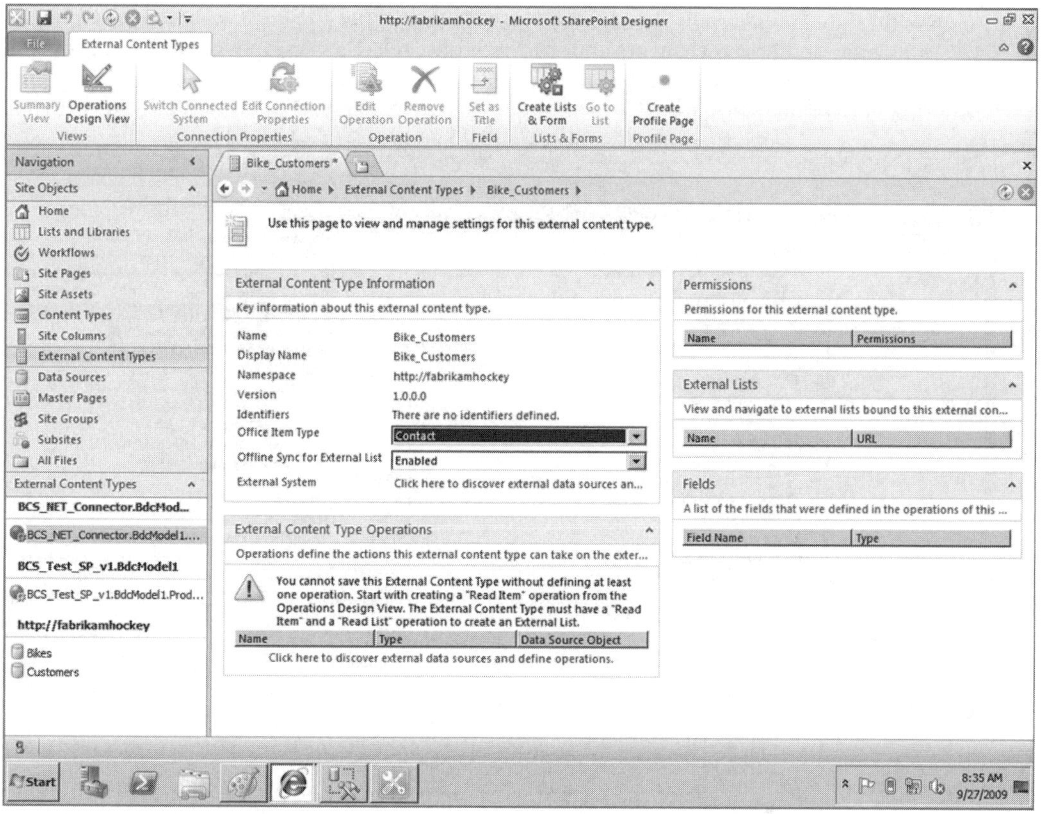

FIGURE 8-9 External content type information

10. After the `AdventureWorksLT2008` database has loaded, browse to the `Customers` table. Right-click and select Create All Operations, as shown in Figure 8-10.

11. This invokes a wizard that enables you to map your columns in your external data source to Office Item types, create filters for your data, and so on.

12. Click Next on the first All Operations page. On the next page of the wizard, you can map some data source elements to Office properties by first selecting the data source elements on the left-hand side of the wizard and then selecting the Office property that most closely aligns to the element (see Figure 8-11). For example, if you click the `LastName` data source element and then select `LastName` from the Office Property drop-down list, you have now

FIGURE 8-10 Available operations

mapped this data source element to Office property. Select the Title, FirstName, CompanyName, EmailAddress, and Phone elements and, for each one, select a corresponding Office property that you feel fits best. (Note that not all of the elements can be mapped. You can set these as Custom Properties in the Office Property list.)

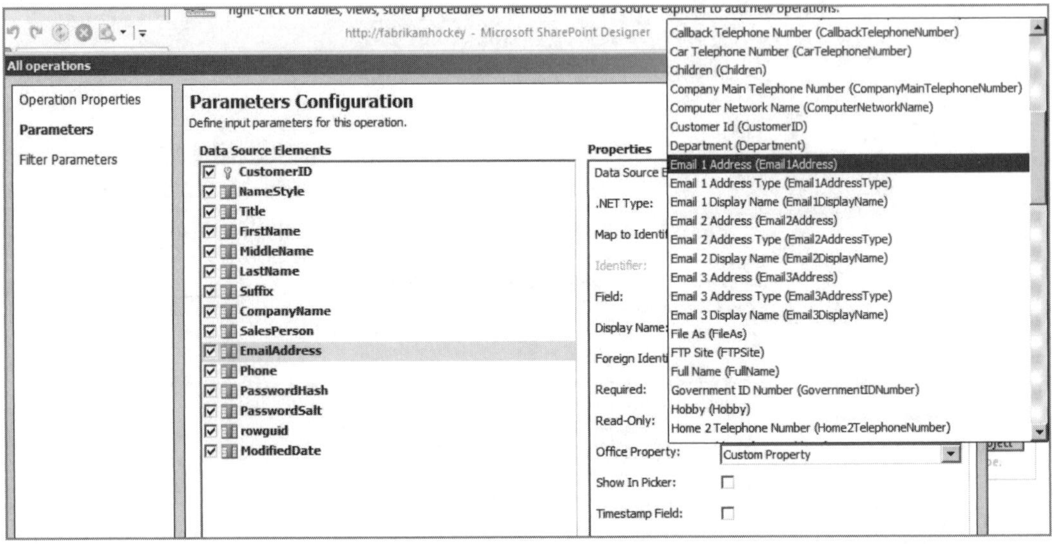

FIGURE 8-11 Parameter configuration

13. Click Next. On the next page of the wizard, you can optionally add a data filter. For this exercise, you will not need a filter, so click Finish to complete the creation of the external content type.

14. Click the Save button (in the upper-left hand region of the screen) to save the external content type. SharePoint Designer will save the external content type to the BDC Metadata Store.

15. The last step is to create an external list from this external content type, which you can also do using SharePoint Designer. To do this, click Create Lists & Form on the ribbon. Provide a name for your list in the List Name field such as My Customers. Leave the other default options as is and leave the Create InfoPath Form check-box unchecked, as shown in Figure 8-12.

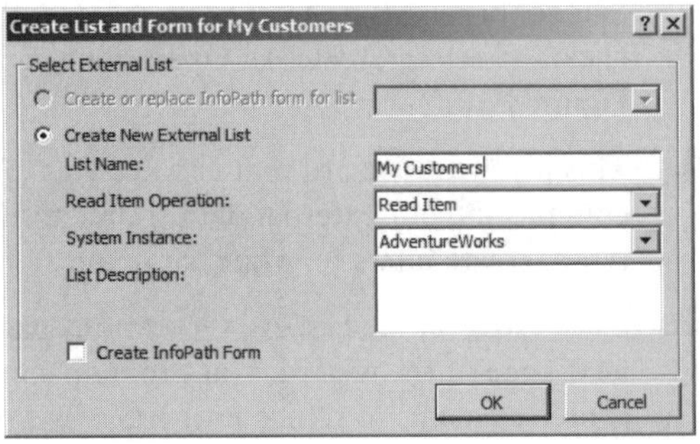

16. SharePoint Designer will now create an external list for you using the external content type you just created. To see the new list, navigate to the home page of the SharePoint site where you created the external list and click on the new list that you created. Note that, with this list, you now have a number of operations against the specific list items (for example, View, Edit, and Delete), as shown in Figure 8-13.

FIGURE 8-12 Create list from external content type

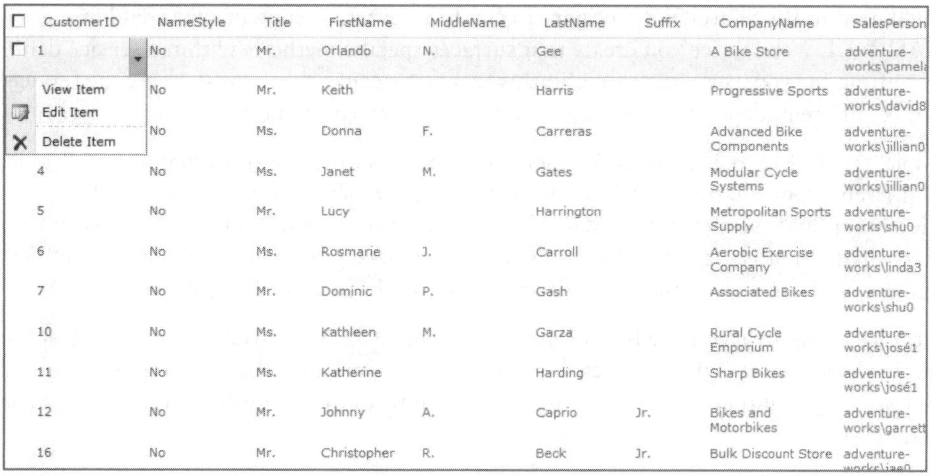

FIGURE 8-13 Complete SharePoint external list with operations

17. You may find that your new list displays an "Accessed denied" message. This is because you've not added any permissions against the external content type. To remedy this, close the SharePoint site and open SharePoint Central Administration. Click Application Management ⇨ "Manage service applications" ⇨ Business Data Connectivity Service. Then, click the new external content type (for example, My Customers) and select Set Object Permissions on the ribbon. In the "Add an account" field, type **All Authenticated Users** and then click Add. When added, check each of the permission checkboxes (that is, Edit, Execute, "Selectable in Clients," and Set Permissions). Click OK to save the changes.

18. Test out these operations by editing one of the list items and then switching back to your SQL Server Management Studio view. Check that the data was updated by refreshing the table view for Customers.

How It Works

In this walkthrough, you used SharePoint Designer 2010 to create an ADO.NET-based external content type. This allowed you to use the native SharePoint Designer tools to build an XML file (similar to the ones discussed earlier in this chapter) that provided information about the relationship SharePoint should expect to have with that back-end system.

Because you assigned all of the operations to the external content type, when you created the list, it exposed these operations as Edit, View, Delete, and, of course, Create (with the capability to create a new list item). If you were to make any of these changes in the external list, the changes would be propagated back to the external data source (in this case, the SQL Server database).

The external content type that you just created was an ADO.NET connection. However, what if you want to create a connection that is integrated using a service connection? For example, in many cases, you'll need to use SharePoint Designer to create an external content type that leverages a WCF or ASP.NET Web service you create that surfaces specific methods within a service definition. The heavy lifting for you as the developer in this scenario occurs if you must create the service, which can be different, depending on what system you're designing the service for.

For example, the toolset to generate a Web service for SAP is different from that within PeopleSoft, which is different from creating a Web service for Oracle e-Business Suite. However, the underlying premise is similar, and the messaging (SOAP) is also a common standard that most services share. Fortunately, SharePoint Designer understands the SOAP messaging structure, can resolve Web service endpoints, and can expose the methods that make up those service definitions.

To keep things straightforward, what follows is a simple ASP.NET Web Service that has a self-contained business object (which represents customer information) that will represent the schema of the external data source. The schema includes a definition for the following customer data called `Customers`:

➤ Customer ID

➤ Title

➤ First Name

➤ Middle Name

➤ Last Name

➤ Email Address

➤ Phone

The following walkthrough uses a Web service that has one method called `GetCustomers` and another called `GetACustomer`. The `GetCustomers` method creates a list collection of `Customers` and then passes the converted list collection as an array back to the calling application. The `GetACustomer` method uses a string parameter to retrieve the specific customer. Let's walk through the creation of the service and then, more importantly, how the Web service is configured using SharePoint Designer.

TRY IT OUT   Creating a Read-Only Web Service-Based External Content Type

Code file [CustWebService.zip] available for download at Wrox.com.

In many cases, you'll want to integrate Web services hosted in Internet Information Services (IIS) with your external lists, which you build using SharePoint Designer. To create the ASP.NET Web service, deploy to IIS, and then create an external content type in SharePoint Designer, follow these steps:

1. Open Visual Studio 2010. Click File ➪ New ➪ Web Site. Select .NET Framework 3.5 in the drop-down list and then select ASP.NET Web Service.

2. Keep the default location as File System and provide a location for the Web service and click OK. After Visual Studio creates the service, leave the default name (that is `Service.asmx`).

3. When the default project is created, navigate to the `App_Code` folder and right-click the `Service.cs` file. Select View Code.

4. Replace the default Hello World service with the following boldfaced code in the `Service` class. This code will create a list collection of `Customers`, and then add three records to the collection. When an application calls the `GetCustomers` method, the return will then be an external data source with three fictional records in it. When the application calls the `GetACustomer` method, based on the input string parameter, it will return one of the three records that is generated dynamically.

```
using System;
using System.Collections.Generic;
using System.Linq;
using System.Web;
using System.Web.Services;

[WebService(Namespace = "http://tempuri.org/")]
[WebServiceBinding(ConformsTo = WsiProfiles.BasicProfile1_1)]

public class Service : System.Web.Services.WebService
{
    public Service () {

    }

    public class Customers
    {
        public string customerID { get; set; }
        public string Title { get; set; }
        public string FirstName { get; set; }
        public string MiddleName { get; set; }
        public string LastName { get; set; }
        public string EmailAddress { get; set; }
        public string Phone { get; set; }
    }

    [WebMethod]
    public Customers[] GetCustomers()
    {
        List<Customers> myCustomers = new List<Customers>();

        Customers customerOne = new Customers();
        customerOne.customerID = "1";
        customerOne.Title = "Dr.";
        customerOne.FirstName = "John";
        customerOne.MiddleName = "Daley";
        customerOne.LastName = "Doe";
        customerOne.EmailAddress = "john.doe@acme.com";
        customerOne.Phone = "(202) 555-1234";

        myCustomers.Add(customerOne);

        Customers customerTwo = new Customers();
        customerTwo.customerID = "2";
        customerTwo.Title = "Ms.";
        customerTwo.FirstName = "Jane";
        customerTwo.MiddleName = "Karen";
        customerTwo.LastName = "Doe";
```

```
        customerTwo.EmailAddress = "jane.doe@acme.com";
        customerTwo.Phone = "(202) 555-1233";

        myCustomers.Add(customerTwo);

        Customers customerThree = new Customers();
        customerThree.customerID = "3";
        customerThree.Title = "Mr.";
        customerThree.FirstName = "Kenneth";
        customerThree.MiddleName = "James";
        customerThree.LastName = "Staple";
        customerThree.EmailAddress = "ken@acme.com";
        customerThree.Phone = "(202) 555-1884";

        myCustomers.Add(customerThree);

        return myCustomers.ToArray();

    }

    [WebMethod]
    public Customers GetACustomer(string customerID)
    {
        Customers returnCust = new Customers();

        if (customerID == "1")
        {

            returnCust.customerID = "1";
            returnCust.Title = "Dr.";
            returnCust.FirstName = "John";
            returnCust.MiddleName = "Daley";
            returnCust.LastName = "Doe";
            returnCust.EmailAddress = "john.doe@acme.com";
            returnCust.Phone = "(202) 555-1234";
        }

        else if (customerID == "2")
        {
            returnCust.customerID = "2";
            returnCust.Title = "Ms.";
            returnCust.FirstName = "Jane";
            returnCust.MiddleName = "Karen";
            returnCust.LastName = "Doe";
            returnCust.EmailAddress = "jane.doe@acme.com";
            returnCust.Phone = "(202) 555-1233";
        }
        else if (customerID == "3")
        {
            returnCust.customerID = "3";
            returnCust.Title = "Mr.";
            returnCust.FirstName = "Kenneth";
            returnCust.MiddleName = "James";
            returnCust.LastName = "Staple";
            returnCust.EmailAddress = "ken@acme.com";
            returnCust.Phone = "(202) 555-1884";
```

```
        }
    return returnCust;
    }

}
```

5. After you've completed this, press F5 to build and test the Web service. (When prompted to enable debugging, accept the default selection, "Modify the Web.config file to enable debugging," and click OK.) Visual Studio will invoke the Web service in debug mode, and you can click either of the Web methods (GetCustomers or GetACustomer) that are listed on the page to invoke a response from the Web method. If you clicked GetCustomers, the response should be similar to Figure 8-14.

FIGURE 8-14 Web method results

6. If this is successful, stop debugging. Right-click the project and select Publish Web Site. Select the File System option and browse to a folder where you want to deploy the Web service (for example, c:\Wrox\GetCustomers). Accept the other default selections and click OK.

7. You'll now want to map the published project (which is published to what will be your virtual path) to IIS. To do this, click Start ➪ Administrative Tools, and open IIS. Right-click the Sites node and add a new Web site called GetCustomerWS. Ensure that the virtual path points to the location where you published the service (for example, c:\Wrox\GetCustomers). You must also provide a port that is not listed as 80 (for example, 1141), and (optionally) you can also provide a host header for the service (for example, fabrikamcustomers). Click Connect As. Select Specific User and Set to add your credentials as the user that the service will use. Click OK when finished. Click Test Settings to test your credentials with the service call.

8. Ensure that Windows authentication is enabled by clicking the Features View tab, double-clicking Authentication ⇨ Windows Authentication, and then clicking Enable.

9. To test the service from within IIS, click the Content View tab, right-click the `Service.asmx` file and select Browse. This opens the Web service and should produce the same results you saw when you pressed F5 from the Visual Studio project. This is just to check that the Web service and methods in that service can be called from within IIS, and that your authentication works properly.

10. Open SharePoint Designer and open your SharePoint site. Click External Content Types in the left-hand navigation menu. When the External Content Types report loads, click External Content Type in the SharePoint Designer ribbon.

11. Walk through the steps to create an external content type as you did with the earlier one you created — that is, click New External Content Type to provide a Name and Display Name (for example, `Customer WS`), select Contact as the Office Item Type, and then click Add Connection to add a data connection. This time, though, select WCF Service.

12. SharePoint Designer will then invoke the Service Connection dialog, where you can add specific information about your service. Add the service endpoint URL (for example, `http://fabrikamhockey:1190/Service.asmx?wsdl`) to the Source Metadata URL field and the service endpoint URL without the `?wsdl` to the Service Endpoint URL field (for example, `http://fabrikamhockey:1190/Service.asmx`), and leave the other options, as shown in Figure 8-15.

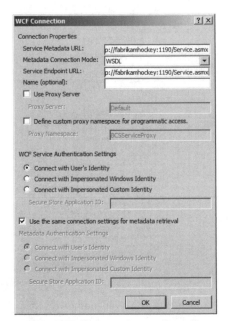

FIGURE 8-15 Web service configuration

13. Click OK to generate the external content type.

14. When the Web service connection is added, you can navigate to the `GetACustomer` method. Right-click the method and select New Read Item Operation. The Read Item wizard opens and will display some information about your Web method operation (for example, Name, Display Name, and Type). Click Next.

15. In the Input Parameters screen, click the `customerID` data source element, and then check the "Map to Identifier" checkbox. Click Next to configure the Return Parameter Configuration data source elements. To do this, click the `customerID` and then check the "Map to Identifier" checkbox. Click `LastName` and in the Office Property drop-down list select `LastName`. You can map the other data source elements to the Office Item types that make the most sense for you. When you are done, click Finish.

16. You must also configure a New Read List operation. To do this, right-click the `GetCustomers` method, and select the New Read List Operation. This opens the configuration wizard. Click Next twice to get to the Return Parameter Configuration page. Click the `customerID` and then check the "Map to Identifier" checkbox. Click Finish to complete the Read List operation.

17.   Click Save to save the external content type in the BDC Metadata Store.

At this point, you can create a new external list as you did in the earlier walkthrough, or you can navigate to your SharePoint site, click All Site Content ➪ Create ➪ External List, provide a list name, and browse for the new service-based external content type to create your external list that way. Whatever road you choose will result in an external list that will look similar to Figure 8-13.

You may have to configure the permissions to the external list. You do this the same way you did in the earlier exercise — go to SharePoint Central Administration, and click Application Management ➪ Manage Service Applications ➪ Business Data Connectivity Service, and select your external content type. Click Set Object Permissions to add users to the list.

How It Works

In much the same way the external content type was created for the ADO.NET connection, you created a similar external content type for the Web service. There are some differences in the way the metadata is described, but in essence, the principle of using the external content type to interact with the external data system is similar. In this case, however, you only created a read-only relationship using the Web service. Thus, your external content type becomes a read-only view of the data.

There must be a read item operation and a read list operation, and you created these in the code. For example, you created a class called `Customers` that was your custom object. You used a list collection to return a blanket call for all customers, and then you passed a `string` parameter to return a (dynamically generated) specific customer. These two Web methods worked together to support the two operations necessary to create an external list.

If you wanted to create both a read and a write relationship with an external system using Web services, this would certainly be possible. To do this, you would follow the same process as you did with the previous walkthrough. Let's give this a try.

TRY IT OUT   **Creating a Read/Write Web Service-Based External Content Type**

Code file [MyNewServiceApplication.zip] available for download at Wrox.com.

You created a read-only BCS application in the last walkthrough. However, you're more than likely going to want to create a read/write external list as well. To do this, follow these steps:

1.   Open Visual Studio and click File ➪ New Project ➪ Web, and select ASP.NET Web Service Application. Provide a name for your project (for example, `MyNewServiceApplication`), a location for the project, and click OK.

2.   Click Data ➪ Add New Data Source. In the Data Source Configuration wizard, click Database ➪ Next ➪ Entity Data Model and click Next. Click "Generate from Database" and then, in the Entity Data Model wizard, click "New Connection." Enter your server name and select the `AdventureWorksLT2008` database and click OK. Click Next and under Tables select the `Customers` table and enter a name for the Model Namespace (for example, `AdventureWorksLT2008Entities`). Click Finish.

3. After you've added the data source, right-click the project and select Add ⇨ Class. Provide a name for the class (for example, `Customers`), and then add the following bolded properties to the class:

```
using System;
using System.Collections.Generic;
using System.Linq;
using System.Web;

namespace MyNewServiceApplication
{
    public class Customers
    {
        public string customerID { get; set; }
        public string firstName { get; set; }
        public string lastName { get; set; }
        public string phoneNum { get; set; }
        public string emailAddress { get; set; }
    }
}
```

4. After you've added the class, right-click the `Service1.cs` file and select View Code.

5. Add the following boldfaced code to the `Service1.cs` file:

```
using System;
using System.Collections.Generic;
using System.Linq;
using System.Web;
using System.Web.Services;

namespace MyNewServiceApplication
{
    [WebService(Namespace = "http://tempuri.org/")]
    [WebServiceBinding(ConformsTo = WsiProfiles.BasicProfile1_1)]
    [System.ComponentModel.ToolboxItem(false)]

    public class Service1 : System.Web.Services.WebService
    {
        AdventureWorksLT2008Entities myCustomerData =
            new AdventureWorksLT2008Entities();
        List<Customers> myCustomerList = new List<Customers>();

        [WebMethod]
        public List<Customers> getCustomers()
        {
            int filter = 100;
            var returnData = (from customer in myCustomerData.Customers
                              select customer).Take(filter).ToArray();

            foreach (var cust in returnData)
            {
                Customers tempCustomer = new Customers();
                tempCustomer.customerID = cust.CustomerID.ToString();
                tempCustomer.firstName = cust.FirstName.ToString();
                tempCustomer.lastName = cust.LastName.ToString();
```

```
                tempCustomer.phoneNum = cust.Phone.ToString();
                tempCustomer.emailAddress = cust.EmailAddress.ToString();
                myCustomerList.Add(tempCustomer);
            }

        return myCustomerList;
    }

    [WebMethod]
    public Customers getACustomer(string custID)
    {
        Customers retCustomer = new Customers();
        int TempCustomerID = Int32.Parse(custID);

        var returnCustData =
            from c in myCustomerData.Customers
            where c.CustomerID == TempCustomerID
            select c;

        foreach (var i in returnCustData)
        {
            retCustomer.customerID = i.CustomerID.ToString();
            retCustomer.firstName = i.FirstName.ToString();
            retCustomer.lastName = i.LastName.ToString();
            retCustomer.phoneNum = i.Phone.ToString();
            retCustomer.emailAddress = i.EmailAddress.ToString();
        }

        return retCustomer;
    }

    [WebMethod]
    public string updateCustomerData(string customerID,
        string firstName, string lastName, string phoneNum,
        string emailAddress)
    {
        string recordUpdate = "record(s) successfully updated.";
        int TempCustomerID = Int32.Parse(customerID);


        Customer myContact = myCustomerData.Customers.First(e =>
            e.CustomerID == TempCustomerID);

        myContact.FirstName = firstName;
        myContact.LastName = lastName;
        myContact.Phone = phoneNum;
        myContact.EmailAddress = emailAddress;

        int numRecordUpdated = myCustomerData.SaveChanges();
        return numRecordUpdated.ToString() + " " + recordUpdate;
    }
  }
}
```

6. To publish your service, you'll first want to create a directory on your local system (for example, `c:\Wrox\NewCustomerWS`). After you've done this, right-click the project and select Publish and then select to File System — using the directory you just created as your publish endpoint. You can now map the published service to IIS.

7. Open IIS. Right-click Sites and select Add Web Site. Provide a Site Name (for example, `NewGetCustomerWS`). Map the physical path to the publish location of your service (for example, `c:\Wrox\NewCustomerWS`). Click Connect As and select Specific User and enter your credentials. Click Test Settings to test the connection to your service using your credentials. Change the Port from 80 to another port number (for example, 8888) and click OK. Click the Content tab, then right-click the `Service1.asmx` file, and select Browse. You should now have a Web page with the three Web methods available for you to test, as shown in Figure 8-16.

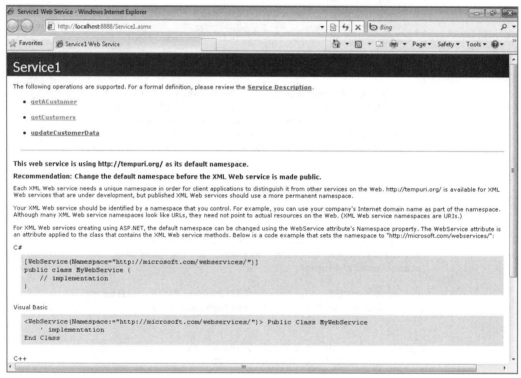

FIGURE 8-16 Testing Service

8. Test out all of the services to ensure that they work. You may get a SQL error when you try to run the Web methods. This is a permissions issue because you are trying to access SQL Server resources. To fix this, click the new Web site you added to IIS, and then click Advanced Settings. You will see an application pool listed in the Advanced Settings dialog (for example, `NewGetCustomersWS`). Click the Application Pools node in IIS, and then find your application pool. Click it, and then select Advanced Settings. In the Advanced Settings dialog, you can change your

Identity to be your machine/domain credentials. To do this, click the ellipsis in the Identity field, and then click Custom accounts. Enter your login information. Click OK to exit the Advanced Settings dialog.

9. Once you've tested the services, open SharePoint Designer 2010 and walk through the exact same process of creating a new external content type. To do this, click External Content Types in the navigation pane, External Content Type in the ribbon, and enter a Name and Display Name (for example, `NewCustService`). Select Contact as the Office Item Type, and then click Add Connection to add a data connection.

10. SharePoint Designer will then invoke the Service Connection dialog, where you can add specific information about your service. Add the service endpoint URL (for example, `http://fabrikam-hockey:8888/Service.asmx?wsdl`) to the Source Metadata URL field, and the service endpoint URL without the `?wsdl` to the Service Endpoint URL field (for example, `http://fabrikam-hockey:8888/Service.asmx`).

11. When the service is added, you can then add the operations for the Web methods. This time, though, you will add three operations. The first will be the New Read Item operation, which you'll add against the `getACustomer` method. The second will be a New Read List operation, which you'll add against the `getCustomers` method. And the third will be a New Update operation, which you'll add against the `updateCustomerData` method.

12. As you walk through the wizard for each Web method, map the data source elements as you did in the earlier walkthrough. For example, ensure that the `custID` is always mapped to the Identifier, and ensure that the `LastName` data source element is always mapped to the `LastName` Office Item type. When you've added the three operations to the three different Web methods, save the external content type and click "Create Lists & Form" to create a new external list. Provide a name for the list (for example, `Updated Customers`) and click OK. When you load the external list and click Edit, the result should look similar to Figure 8-17.

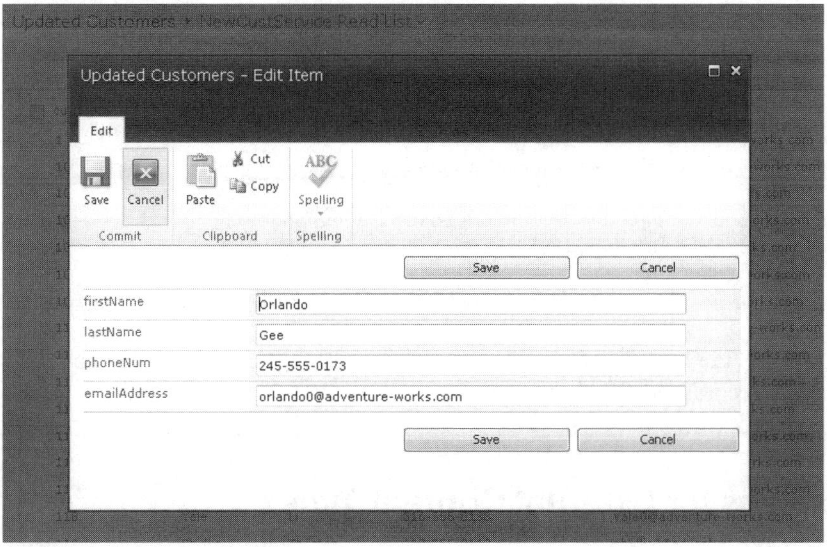

FIGURE 8-17 Read/write external list

13   You may again find that your new list displays an Accessed denied message. To fix this, close the SharePoint site and open SharePoint Central Administration. Click Application Management ➪ Manage service applications ➪ Business Data Connectivity Service. Then click the new external content type and select Set Object Permissions on the ribbon. In the "Add an account" field, type **All Authenticated Users** and then click Add. Check all of the permissions for the added user.

How It Works

From the external content type perspective, you again followed a similar process to create and save it to the metadata store. However, in this example, you used the ADO.NET entity data modeling capabilities built into Visual Studio and .NET that allow you to treat the `Customers` table as a strongly typed object.

Within the code, you enabled three operations: read item, read list, and update list. Each one of these corresponded to the Web method you created in your service (`getACustomer`, `getCustomers`, and `updateCustomerData`, respectively). The read methods used Language Integrated Query (LINQ) to query the entity model for all records, or a specific record based on the string parameter that was passed with the Web method. In the case of the `getCustomers` method, it also had a filter of `100` that it asserted against the data it returned from the Web method.

When the `updateCustomerData` method was called, it leveraged the `myCustomerData` object (which was an instance of `AdventureWorksEntities`).

```
...
AdventureWorksEntities myCustomerData =
    new AdventureWorksEntities();
...
Customer myContact = myCustomerData.Contacts.First(e =>
    e.ContactID == TempCustomerID);
...
```

This provided you with the option to update the records through a variable comparison with those strings that were passed to the Web method, and those that were in the entity model.

```
...
        myContact.FirstName = firstName;
        myContact.LastName = lastName;
        myContact.Phone = phoneNum;
        myContact.EmailAddress = emailAddress;

        int numRecordUpdated = myCustomerData.SaveChanges();
        return numRecordUpdated.ToString() + " " +
            recordUpdate;
...
```

The key method that updated the records was the `SaveChanges` method, which returned an integer value indicating how many records were updated.

Setting Permissions for External Content Types

From the examples in the last section, you have now seen a couple of different ways you can interact with SharePoint Designer to create external content types that integrate with Web services. You also saw that you must have some level of permissions associated with the external content type to support viewing, editing, updating, and deleting list items. Specifically, you saw that after you create an external content type, you can assign specific permissions to it. The administrator of the SharePoint site can restrict or provide these permissions for the external content type that you create. If you are the administrator of your site, then this makes configuring security for the external content type quite easy. However, if you're not the administrator, then you'll need to work with your local administrator to configure the security settings.

As you may have seen if you configured the security for your external lists, the permissions for the external content types are located in the Application Management tab of the SharePoint Central Administration site. You can configure varying levels of permissions against the external content type. These permissions provide discrete permissions against specific external content types for specific users. So, for example, when users are trying to update something when maybe they shouldn't be, it is this permission list that controls access to the external data store.

The way the permissions work is that SharePoint stores users as Active Directory (AD) records. For each identity that has been given permission to a specific site, users can further be allotted discrete privileges against the external content type and the external system. When the user is logged in, the AD identity is passed to SharePoint, and a comparison is done at run-time. The user is then only permitted to act on that data as per the permissions defined for that user.

Note that if you require security to manage a separate set of credentials that are not based on AD, or require a separate username and password not recognized natively by Windows, you may need to use the Secure Store Service (SSS). SSS provides a way to map BCS applications to the username and password that map to an external data source (such as SAP, PeopleSoft, or another LOB system) where permissions are not the same as, for example, your Windows credentials. Thus, SSS represents an authorization service that runs on an application server and supports the shared services infrastructure. SSS provides a database where you can create and store credentials that consist of a user's identity and password, and the application ID that maps to those credentials.

> **NOTE** Chapter 12 provides more information on SSS.

Taking the External List Offline

After you've created and secured your external list, SharePoint supports taking the list offline so that you can program against the cached data on the client from your external data source. BCS also offers a client-side object model to allow you to program against the cached data once you've taken it offline. If you'd like to keep the surfacing of this data low-maintenance, there are also no-code ways to surface this data in the client.

For example, you can use the external content type you created earlier in the chapter to surface the customer data in SharePoint Workspace, Access, and Outlook (with a no-code option). In this next exercise, you'll take the first external list you created in this chapter offline and expose the list in SharePoint Workspace. This external list was the `AdventureWorksLT2008 Customers` table, which you created using SharePoint Designer.

TRY IT OUT   Taking an External List Offline

Taking a list offline enables you to surface LOB data on the client. To take an external list offline, follow these steps:

1.   Open the `My Customers` list you created earlier in the chapter.

2.   Click the List tab on the SharePoint ribbon. Note that in the "Connect & Export" group, you have different options available to you (for example, to sync with Outlook or SharePoint Workspace) to take the external list offline, as shown in Figure 8-18.

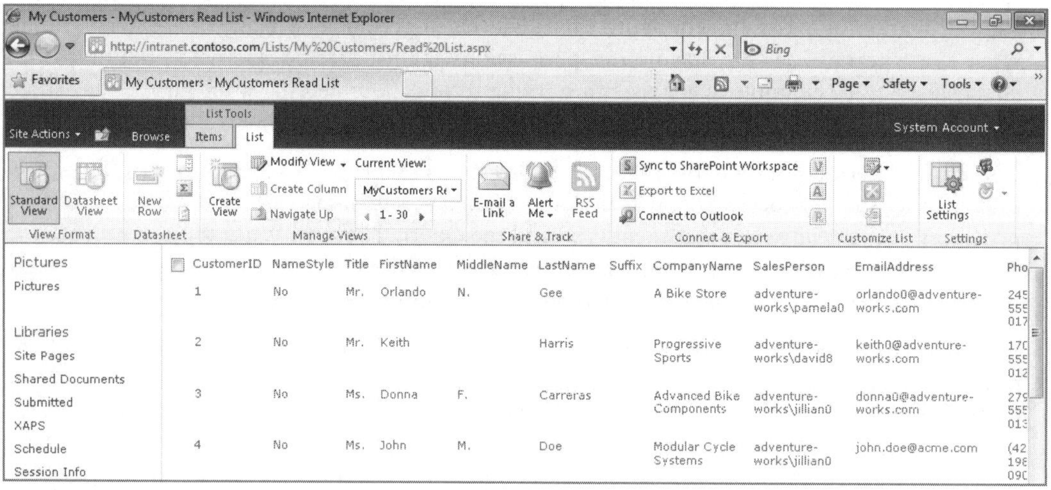

FIGURE 8-18 External list settings

3.   Click the "Sync to SharePoint Workspace" button, and you'll be prompted to accept the Installation of a file to your local machine. Click Install to initiate the VSTO Package installation on your machine.

4.   After the client-side package is installed, you will be prompted with a dialog that indicates the Office Customization was successfully installed. You can then open SharePoint Workspace to view the external list offline in SharePoint Workspace.

How It Works

When you take an external list offline, the VSTO package installs a number of files to the client, including the external content type, a data cache so the external LOB data can be used on the client, and configuration and assembly files that support Office client integration. With the external data source now cached on the client, you can also build applications that use the external data source on the client. For example, having this client-side cache means that you can now quickly build no-code solutions that integrate with Outlook and Access to surface your external data source in the client.

In this next walkthrough, you'll leverage the external list you just took offline in the previous exercise and surface external data in an Access 2010 database.

TRY IT OUT Surfacing External Data in Access

Access 2010 is a great way to integrate LOB data without requiring any code. To surface the client-side cache of the `My Customers` external list in Access, follow these steps:

1. Open Access 2010.

2. Click Blank Database.

3. Select the External Data tab.

4. Click More ➪ Data Services, as shown in Figure 8-19.

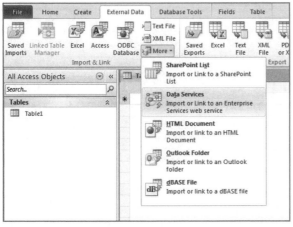

FIGURE 8-19 Integration with Access

5. In the Create Link to Data Services dialog, click Install New Connection.

6. Browse to the BCS client-side install location (for example, the parent install location for the BCS files is typically in the folder `C:\Users\<user>\AppData\Local\Microsoft\BCS`). The separate installs are represented by GUIDs. Select the folder associated with the external content type you just took offline. (Use the folder timestamp if necessary.)

7. Select the `metadata.xml` file and click OK. Then expand and select the external data source listed in the "Create Link to Data Service" dialog (for example, `Customers`).

8. Select "Create Linked Table."

Access creates a linked table for you with a read-only version of the data from your external data source, as shown in Figure 8-20.

How It Works

Access understands the metadata that is generated when SharePoint Designer (and Visual Studio) creates an external content type. Access does not, however, have the capability to read *and* write into the external data system. It can only load and present the data that is based off of the connection metadata in the external content type.

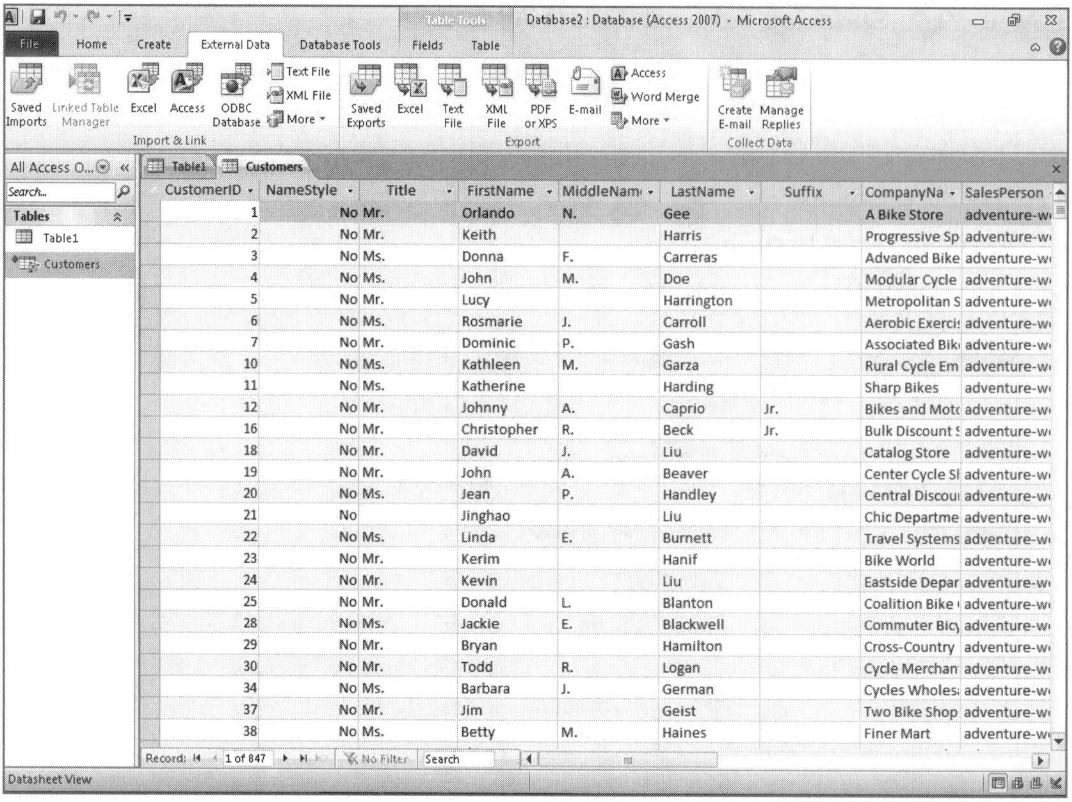

CustomerID	NameStyle	Title	FirstName	MiddleNam	LastName	Suffix	CompanyNa	SalesPerson
1	No	Mr.	Orlando	N.	Gee		A Bike Store	adventure-w
2	No	Mr.	Keith		Harris		Progressive Sp	adventure-w
3	No	Ms.	Donna	F.	Carreras		Advanced Bike	adventure-w
4	No	Ms.	John	M.	Doe		Modular Cycle	adventure-w
5	No	Mr.	Lucy		Harrington		Metropolitan S	adventure-w
6	No	Ms.	Rosmarie	J.	Carroll		Aerobic Exerci	adventure-w
7	No	Mr.	Dominic	P.	Gash		Associated Bik	adventure-w
10	No	Ms.	Kathleen	M.	Garza		Rural Cycle Em	adventure-w
11	No	Ms.	Katherine		Harding		Sharp Bikes	adventure-w
12	No	Mr.	Johnny	A.	Caprio	Jr.	Bikes and Motc	adventure-w
16	No	Mr.	Christopher	R.	Beck	Jr.	Bulk Discount	adventure-w
18	No	Mr.	David	J.	Liu		Catalog Store	adventure-w
19	No	Mr.	John	A.	Beaver		Center Cycle Sl	adventure-w
20	No	Ms.	Jean	P.	Handley		Central Discou	adventure-w
21	No		Jinghao		Liu		Chic Departme	adventure-w
22	No	Ms.	Linda	E.	Burnett		Travel Systems	adventure-w
23	No	Mr.	Kerim		Hanif		Bike World	adventure-w
24	No	Mr.	Kevin		Liu		Eastside Depar	adventure-w
25	No	Mr.	Donald	L.	Blanton		Coalition Bike	adventure-w
28	No	Ms.	Jackie	E.	Blackwell		Commuter Bic	adventure-w
29	No	Mr.	Bryan		Hamilton		Cross-Country	adventure-w
30	No	Mr.	Todd	R.	Logan		Cycle Merchan	adventure-w
34	No	Ms.	Barbara	J.	German		Cycles Wholes	adventure-w
37	No	Mr.	Jim		Geist		Two Bike Shop	adventure-w
38	No	Ms.	Betty	M.	Haines		Finer Mart	adventure-w

FIGURE 8-20 Access-linked table using an external content type

While no-code solutions are interesting, you may find yourself wanting a deeper level of control over custom BCS applications on the client. When you take external lists offline, you can leverage the client-side BCS API to build BCS applications for Microsoft Office 2010. To do this, you create an Office smart-client application and add the appropriate references that provide access to the BCS API. This is a straightforward process.

To do it, you use the Visual Studio 2010 Office templates. (You saw this project earlier in the book in Chapter 5, and you'll see it again in Chapter 11.) Essentially, you create an Office add-in (for example, a Word 2010 add-in), and you can use the Office object model and programmability features such as the custom ribbon and custom task pane to integrate controls with data that you retrieve from LOB systems. For example, let's say you have a listbox control that you want to add to a custom task pane and bind to the external data source you've taken offline (say from the `My Customers` external list). To get the external data from the offline data cache using the BCS API, you would create an event handler like the following code snippet.

```
...
using Microsoft.BusinessData;
using Microsoft.BusinessData.Runtime;
```

```
using Microsoft.BusinessData.MetadataModel;
using Microsoft.BusinessData.MetadataModel.Collections;
using Microsoft.Office.BusinessData.MetadataModel;
using Microsoft.Office.BusinessData.Runtime;
...
private void getLOBData(object sender, EventArgs e)
{
RemoteSharePointFileBackedMetadataCatalog catalog = new
      RemoteSharePointFileBackedMetadataCatalog();
INamespaceEntityDictionaryDictionary entDictAll =
      catalog.GetEntities("*");
foreach (INamedEntityDictionary entDict in entDictAll.Values)
  {
     foreach(IEntity entity om entDict.Values)
       {
           myListBox.Items.Add(entity.Name);
       }
  }
}
...
```

In the code sample, the `getLOBData` method uses the `RemoteSharePointFileBackedMetadataCatalog` object (which provides an entry point to all of the external content types you take offline) and the `InamespaceEntityDictionaryDictionary` object (which is a dictionary of the external content types taken offline) to iterate through all of the external data sources (that is, external content types) you've taken offline and cached to your client machine. The code snippet finds all of the external content types that have been taken offline, and then adds them to a listbox object. Note that when you call the `GetEntities` method, the * parameter returns all of the external content types (or entities) you took offline. However, you could equally add a specific name of an entity if you wanted to retrieve a specific external content type.

Accessing the external content types is the first step in your interaction with the external content type on the client. For example, you may also want to iterate through the records in the external content types (specifically one that the user selects from the previous listbox), and then bind those records to a data grid object. To do this, the following code sample shows you (again) a way to get the data within the external content type bound to a `DataGrid` control. This code sample takes the entity that the user selects in the listbox (that was populated in the earlier code sample), and then walks through the data and populates the `DataGrid` control.

```
...
Private void myListBox_SelectedIndexChanged(object sender,
      EventArgs e)
{
  IEntity entity = entityDictionary[(String)
      this.myListBox.SelectedItem];
  IEntityInstanceEnumerator instanceEnumerator =
      entity.FindFiltered(
      entity.GetDefaultFinderFilters(),
          entity.GetMethodInstances(MethodInstanceType.Finder)[0].
```

```
        Value.Name,
    entity.GetLobSystem().GetLobSysteminstances()[0].Value,
    OperationMode.CacheWithoutRefresh);
    EntityDataTableAdapter adapter = new
        EntityDataTableAdapter(instanceEnumerator);
    entitiesTable = adapter.EntitiesAsDataTable;
    myDataGrid.DataSource = entitiesTable;
}
...
```

Once you have the data from the loaded entity into your application (for example, into a datagrid), then you can either read that data into the application as a report (for example, add the data to content controls inside a document or to cells into a spreadsheet), or have update capabilities built into your application. The following code sample provides an example of how you might deserialize (and materialize) the data from the entity using an entity reference object, iterating through the fields within the selected row in a datagrid, and then calling the Update method to update the client-side cache of the external data system:

```
...
EntityInstanceReference eir = EntityInstanceReference.Deserialize
    (reference, this.catalog);
IEntityInstance instance = eir.Materialize();

        foreach (IField field in instance.
            ViewDefinition.Fields)
        {
            String fieldName = field.Name;
            bool isReadonly = field.TypeDescriptor.
                ContainsReadOnly;
            if (this.dt.Columns.Contains(field.Name))
            {
                if (!field.TypeDescriptor.ContainsReadOnly)
                {
                    instance[field] =
                        this.dataGridCustomers.Rows[index].
                        Cells[this.dt.Columns.
                        IndexOf(field.Name)].Value;
                }
            }
        }
instance.Update();
...
```

Figure 8-21 shows an example of how this code can be applied. In the custom task pane, a listbox and datagrid are used to load in all of the entities (that is, external content types) that have been taken offline. Depending on what the user selects, different data populates the datagrid from the entity. You can further see Load and Update buttons that integrate the data from the external data system (via the DataGrid) into the document, using Word content controls as the point of entry into the document. Any changes that are entered into the content controls are subsequently updated to the client-side data cache when the user clicks the Update button.

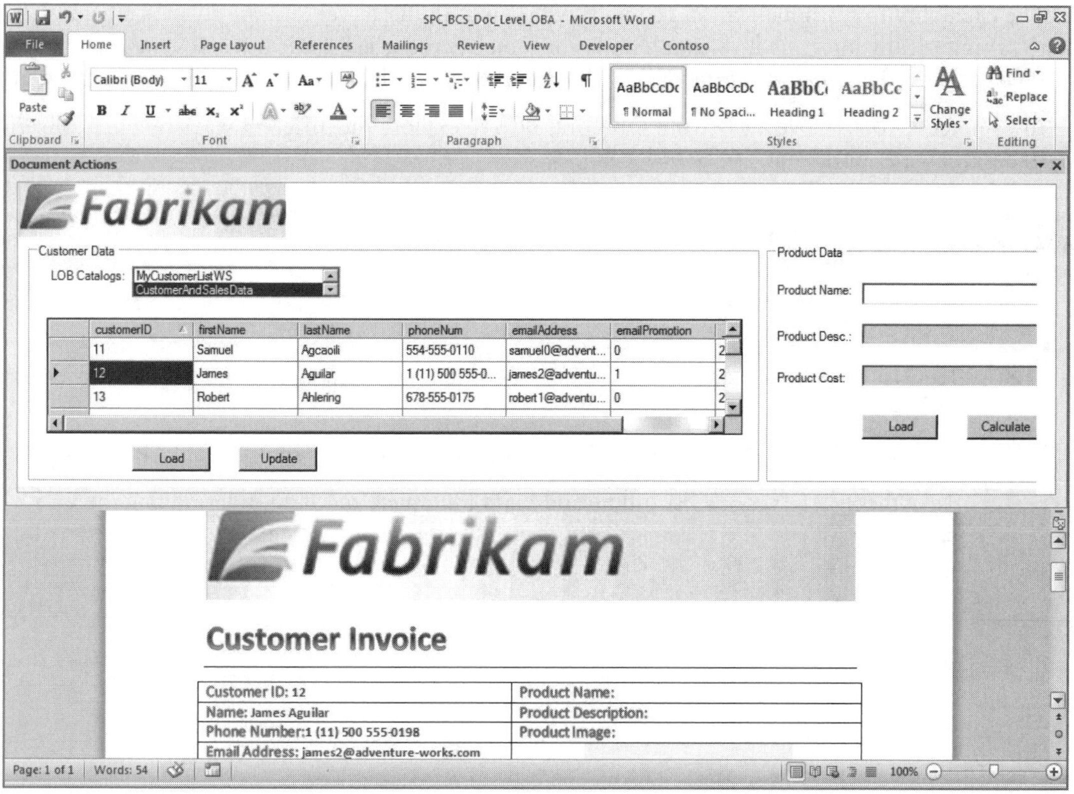

FIGURE 8-21 Custom Office application

After you update the client-side cache, then the BCS Sync service transports your changes to the server. Thus, you can have a symmetrical relationship with applications interacting with your offline data on the client, as well as SharePoint solutions updating that data on the server — in short, an offline story where one (at least not a good one) did not exist before.

SUMMARY

At the heart of BCS is the external content type, which supports connectivity across a variety of external data sources (such as Web services, SQL Server databases, and custom business objects). Furthermore, the capability to create external content types in either SharePoint Designer or Visual Studio provides the developer with some flexibility when first learning how to create them, versus more advanced ways to have more control over the creation and deployment process.

The capability to consume external content types on both the server and the client is a great way to symmetrically integrate how that data is consumed across the two. It increases the capability to repurpose the data, and also provides a rich object model for both server and client programming.

In Chapter 9, you'll move away from OBA and BCS to explore the different ways in which Silverlight integrates with SharePoint.

EXERCISES   Exercises

1. Describe what an OBA is and what types of SharePoint (and Office) features you could use when building one.

2. How is the external content type in SharePoint 2010 different from the ADF in SharePoint 2007?

3. How would you secure an external content type against, for example, an SAP system?

4. Take the `My Customers` list offline and build a simple Office add-in leveraging the BCS client-side API.

▶ **WHAT YOU LEARNED IN THIS CHAPTER**

ITEM	DESCRIPTION
Office Business Application (OBA)	An OBA is an application that integrates LOB data with SharePoint and/or Office. LOB data could include data from systems such as SAP, PeopleSoft, and Microsoft Dynamics CRM.
Business Connectivity Services (BCS)	BCS is the evolution of the BDC Web parts from SharePoint 2007, and provides CRUD capabilities between a SharePoint or client application and an external data system. BCS supports ADO.NET or Web service connections.
External Content Type	An external content type is the metadata file that integrates the LOB system (or external data system) with SharePoint or Office. It is the evolution of the application definition file (ADF) from SharePoint 2007.
SharePoint Designer and BCS	SharePoint Designer 2010 provides a way to simply create an external content type using a wizard experience.
Client-side Options with BCS	Using Visual Studio 2010, you can leverage the client-side BCS API to build and deploy Office add-ins.

RECOMMENDED READING

➤ BCS team blog at `http://blogs.msdn.com/bcs/`

➤ Channel 9 SharePoint Developer Learning Center: `http://channel9.msdn.com/learn/courses/SharePoint2010Developer/`

➤ Channel 9 BCS Module at `http://channel9.msdn.com/learn/courses/SharePoint2010Developer/AccessingExternalData/`

➤ BCS on MSDN at `http://msdn.microsoft.com/en-us/library/ee556826(office.14).aspx`

9

Creating Enhanced User Experiences for SharePoint with Silverlight

WHAT YOU'LL LEARN IN THIS CHAPTER:

➤ Getting to know Silverlight

➤ Understanding why you should integrate Silverlight with SharePoint

➤ Understanding how you can integrate SharePoint and Silverlight

Thus far, you've seen some discussion on Silverlight, but this book really hasn't delved deeply enough into the topic to give you a feeling for its true power. For example, in Chapter 3 you learned how it is possible to embed Silverlight within your master page to improve the look and feel of your site with some advanced branding techniques. You learned how to use Expression Blend as a way to create a more complex Silverlight-based application and user interface (UI) that work in concert with Visual Studio to really evolve your SharePoint 2010 applications. However, you have barely scratched the surface with these topics. There is so much more that is possible with the integration of Silverlight and SharePoint.

This chapter provides an introduction to Silverlight, so you'll begin to see why integrating the two technologies is so compelling. You'll also see that there are three main ways (or classifications) of integrating Silverlight with SharePoint — and it is these three "levels" of integration that will guide how you create the pattern for bringing these two technologies together.

UNDERSTANDING SILVERLIGHT

As of this writing, Silverlight has just been released in version 4. Silverlight 4 has some incredibly rich features that range from Webcam capabilities, rich media, multicasting, evolved controls, and improved developer tooling. However, while Microsoft has recently shipped

Silverlight 4, this chapter tries to avoid an enumeration of version-specific features. Instead, it focuses on some core patterns that you, as a beginning SharePoint developer, can focus on, and then apply with what is a fast-revving product at Microsoft.

Silverlight is a relatively new technology from Microsoft that enables developers to build Rich Internet Applications (RIAs). These RIAs manifest as in- and out-of-browser applications that provide rich, interactive, and dynamic user experiences. Also, because it is Web-based, Silverlight is cross-platform and cross-browser, and, as such, is supported in different browsers such as Internet Explorer, Safari, and FireFox.

To create these applications, Silverlight combines a language called Extensible Application Markup Language (XAML) — pronounced "zammel" — with code behind that is primarily C# or VB.NET, although it can also include dynamic scripting languages (such as JavaScript).

As an extension to what you saw in Chapter 3, the following is a simple example that illustrates a "Hello World" application with a grid block that encapsulates a label, textbox, and a button. Each of the controls has properties associated with it, and you can see that the button has a `btnGreeting_Click` event handler that calls an event that lives in the code behind.

```
<UserControl x:Class="ASimpleSilverlightApplication.MainPage"
    xmlns="http://schemas.microsoft.com/winfx/2006/xaml/presentation"
    xmlns:x="http://schemas.microsoft.com/winfx/2006/xaml"
    xmlns:d="http://schemas.microsoft.com/expression/blend/2008"
    xmlns:mc="http://schemas.openxmlformats.org/markup-compatibility/2006"
    mc:Ignorable="d"
    d:DesignHeight="171" d:DesignWidth="400" xmlns:dataInput=
        "clr-namespace:System.Windows.Controls;
        assembly=System.Windows.Controls.Data.Input">
<Grid x:Name="LayoutRoot" Background="White" Height="167">
<TextBox Height="23" HorizontalAlignment="Left"
Margin="73,57,0,0" Name="txtbxName" VerticalAlignment="Top" Width="144" />
<dataInput:Label Height="22" Content="Name:" HorizontalAlignment="Left"
Margin="12,58,0,0" Name="lblName" VerticalAlignment="Top" Width="55" />
<Button Content="Click" Height="23" HorizontalAlignment="Left"
Margin="38,105,0,0" Name="btnGreeting" Click="btnGreeting_Click"
VerticalAlignment="Top" Width="75" />
</Grid>
</UserControl>
```

> **NOTE** To create a Silverlight application and use this code, you use the Silverlight Application project type in Visual Studio 2010. You do not need to create a Silverlight application that is hosted in a new Web site (which is a choice you have when creating the new project). Drag and drop the controls to the XAML designer to ensure that all of the appropriate references are added to your project (for example, `System.Windows.Controls.Data.Input`).

While the XAML is shown here, the Designer experience in Visual Studio and Expression Blend is such that you don't need to code Silverlight applications by directly authoring the XAML. You can use the designers to create your UI through a drag-and-drop experience in either Visual Studio or Expression Blend. However, it is good to understand and be familiar with the underlying UI syntax.

The code behind for the previous application calls the `btnGreeting_Click` event handler, as you can see by the following bolded code:

```csharp
using System;
using System.Collections.Generic;
using System.Linq;
using System.Net;
using System.Windows;
using System.Windows.Controls;
using System.Windows.Documents;
using System.Windows.Input;
using System.Windows.Media;
using System.Windows.Media.Animation;
using System.Windows.Shapes;

namespace ASimpleSilverlightApplication
{
    public partial class MainPage : UserControl
    {
        public MainPage()
        {
            InitializeComponent();
        }

        private void btnGreeting_Click(object sender, RoutedEventArgs e)
        {
            string yourName = txtbxName.Text;
            MessageBox.Show("Hello " + yourName);
        }
    }
}
```

When you press F5, you can test the Silverlight application from within Visual Studio. Running this sample application in debug mode will result in something similar to Figure 9-1.

Even though Silverlight is a Web-based experience, it is also .NET-based. What this means is that you will use Visual Studio or Expression Blend to build your applications and then deploy them to a Web property where a "light" .NET runtime will enable you to execute the Silverlight applications you build. Specifically, the applications execute within an ActiveX browser plug-in that

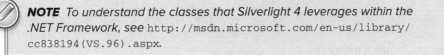

FIGURE 9-1 Simple Silverlight application

runs inside of your browser. This results in dynamic managed-code applications that leverage the strength of the .NET framework. The "light" means that not every class library you have in the standard .NET Framework ships with the .NET Framework that Silverlight leverages.

> **NOTE** *To understand the classes that Silverlight 4 leverages within the .NET Framework, see* http://msdn.microsoft.com/en-us/library/cc838194(VS.96).aspx.

When it comes to developer skills, this also means that those who have programmed using .NET before have the capability to quickly translate those skills into real development. This means leveraging C# or VB.NET, LINQ, WCF, and so on. However, Silverlight is not limited to just .NET. You can also integrate dynamic languages, such as JavaScript, Ajax, Ruby, and Python with Silverlight, along with Web 2.0 technologies, services (for example, ASP.NET Web services, WCF, and REST), and much more. The types of applications you can build with Silverlight vary quite dramatically — from the simple Web banner application to the fully featured business application.

There are countless examples of Silverlight being used on the Web today, and the number of applications is growing daily. For example, Figure 9-2 shows a Netflix movie player that is a Silverlight-enabled way to watch movies over the Web. For those who don't have Netflix, it delivers a Web-based experience for viewing movies, and the Silverlight viewer enables you to load and navigate across a movie you want to watch.

FIGURE 9-2 Netflix Silverlight movie viewer

However, media management is but one example of Silverlight's applications. As it has evolved as a technology, it has become much richer; and with Silverlight 4, the possibility of building business applications that are hosted on the Web is now a reality. Some of the major enhancements to Silverlight 4 include richer media management, a wider set of controls, better business application features, and much, much more.

> **NOTE** *To learn more about Silverlight, see* `http://silverlight.net.`

Let's create a simple Silverlight application.

TRY IT OUT Creating a Simple Silverlight Application

Code file [SilverlightApplication1.zip] available for download at Wrox.com.

Silverlight is a great new way to build dynamic and compelling RIAs. To create a simple Silverlight application, follow these steps:

1. Click File ⇨ New ⇨ Project. In the Silverlight templates, select the Silverlight application template (which provides you with the capability to create a Silverlight application with or without a Web site associated with it).

2. Provide a name for the application and click OK.

3. You'll be prompted with a checkbox to host the Silverlight application in a new Web site, as shown in Figure 9-3. You don't need to do this unless you want to have a separate Web site for your application, where, for example, you might deploy Web services that you want to leverage within your Silverlight application. So, uncheck the box next to "Host the Silverlight application in a new Web site" and then click OK.

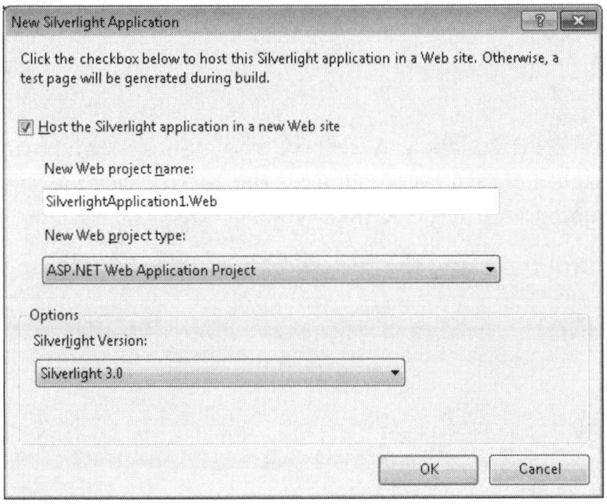

FIGURE 9-3 New Silverlight Application dialog

4. After you create a new Silverlight application, the project structure that Visual Studio creates includes a number of project files in your Solution Explorer, as shown in Figure 9-4.

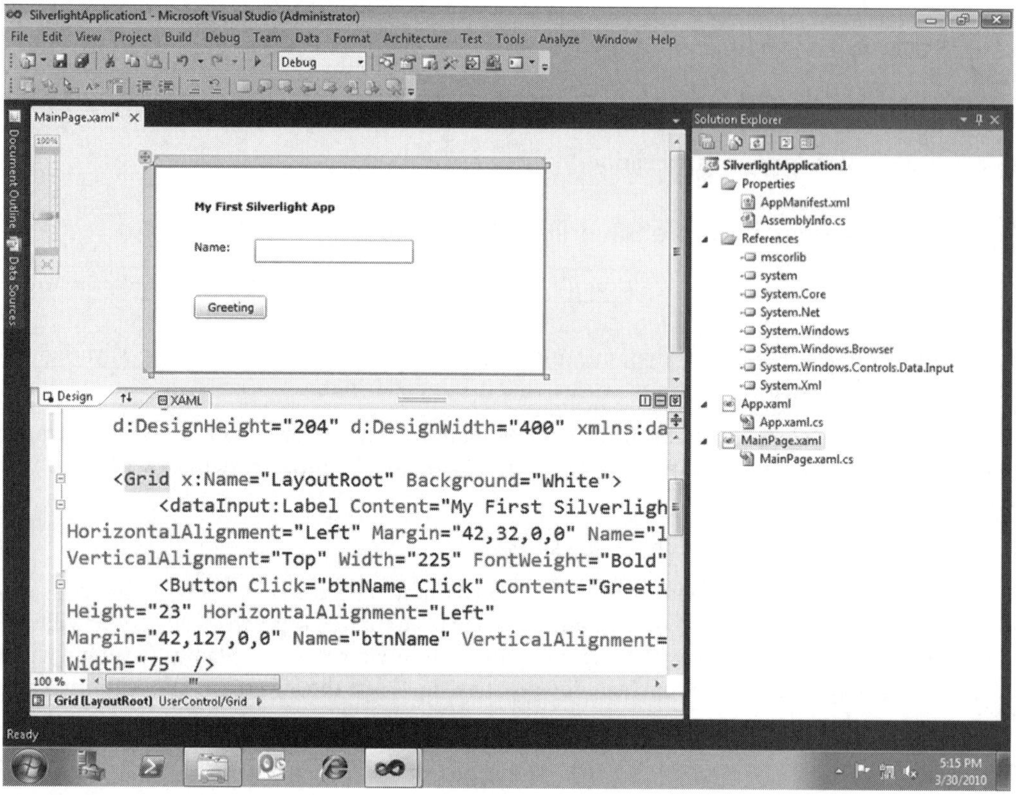

FIGURE 9-4 Simple Silverlight UI

5. Drag and drop four controls from the Toolbox (two labels, a textbox, and a button), and arrange the UI as shown in Figure 9-4. Note that right beneath the Designer is the XAML view; as you add controls to the Designer, the XAML is updated within the XAML view.

Table 9-1 provides an overview of the control types and the corresponding names you'll use in the Silverlight application.

TABLE 9-1 Control Types and Names

CONTROL TYPE	CONTROL NAME
Label	lblName, lblTitle
Textbox	txtbxName
Button	btnName

6. You've worked with XAML before in Chapter 3, but as a refresher, there are some important properties that you'll want to be sure you pay attention to when building out your Silverlight applications. One of the properties is the x:Name property, which represents the name (or ID) of

a Silverlight control. If you want to code against an object within Silverlight, having the name is essential. You can see these properties in the following boldfaced code. Other properties within the XAML are the layout properties, which are updated as you move the controls about on the Designer. Also note that if you have dependent assemblies that you require (for example, leveraging the Silverlight toolkit would require you to have dependent assemblies associated with your Silverlight application), you may need to ensure that there is a namespace reference to these listed within the opening `UserControl` element within the XAML code. Ensure that the XAML in your new application reflects the following bolded code:

```
<UserControl x:Class="SilverlightApplication1.MainPage"
    xmlns="http://schemas.microsoft.com/winfx/2006/xaml/
        presentation"
    xmlns:x="http://schemas.microsoft.com/winfx/2006/xaml"
    xmlns:d="http://schemas.microsoft.com/expression/blend/2008"
    xmlns:mc="http://schemas.openxmlformats.org/
        markup-compatibility/2006"
    mc:Ignorable="d"
    d:DesignHeight="204" d:DesignWidth="400" xmlns:dataInput=
        "clr-namespace:System.Windows.Controls;assembly=
        System.Windows.Controls.Data.Input">

<Grid x:Name="LayoutRoot" Background="White" Height="186">
<dataInput:Label Content="My First Silverlight App" Height="21"
HorizontalAlignment="Left" Margin="42,32,0,0" Name="lblTitle"
VerticalAlignment="Top" Width="225" FontWeight="Bold" />
<Button Click="btnName_Click" Content="Greeting"
Height="23" HorizontalAlignment="Left"
Margin="42,115,0,0" Name="btnName" VerticalAlignment="Top"
Width="75" />
<TextBox Height="23" HorizontalAlignment="Left"
Margin="104,72,0,0" Name="txtbxName" VerticalAlignment="Top"
Width="163" />
<dataInput:Label Content="Name:" Height="21"
HorizontalAlignment="Left" Margin="42,72,0,0" Name="lblName"
VerticalAlignment="Top" Width="56" />
</Grid>
</UserControl>
```

7. Right-click the `MainPage.xaml` file, and select View Code.

8. Add the following bolded code to your Silverlight application:

```
using System;
using System.Collections.Generic;
using System.Linq;
using System.Net;
using System.Windows;
using System.Windows.Controls;
using System.Windows.Documents;
using System.Windows.Input;
using System.Windows.Media;
using System.Windows.Media.Animation;
using System.Windows.Shapes;

namespace SilverlightApplication1
```

```
    {
        public partial class MainPage : UserControl
        {
            public MainPage()
            {
                InitializeComponent();
            }

            private void btnName_Click(object sender,
                RoutedEventArgs e)
            {
                string myNamePrefix = "Length of Name: ";
                string myName = txtbxName.Text;
                int myNameLength = 0;
                myNameLength = myName.Length;
                MessageBox.Show(myNamePrefix +
                    myNameLength.ToString());
                btnName.Content = "Goodbye";
            }
        }
    }
```

9. After you've added the code, press F5 to test out the application. Visual Studio will invoke an instance of your default browser and then launch the Silverlight application, which should look similar to Figure 9-5. The Silverlight application leverages the built-in test harness (there is an HTML page that launches and hosts the Silverlight application) to run the application.

FIGURE 9-5 Debugging the simple Silverlight application

How It Works

You're now likely somewhat familiar with the XAML code, as you've seen a couple of examples. The important takeaway from the XAML discussion is that you create objects with properties you can code against.

For example, when you add code behind in Silverlight, it's much like other .NET experiences. You are building code against the objects that you've created and added to your project. As shown in this example, the objects are UI controls (such as labels and buttons), and examples of the properties of those controls are content, text, height, and width.

So, the code in this example maps to the XAML, calculates the length of the string that is entered into the textbox, and then changes the Content property of the btnName button after you click OK, to say "Goodbye."

...

```
        private void btnName_Click(object sender,
            RoutedEventArgs e)
        {
            string myNamePrefix = "Length of Name: ";
            string myName = txtbxName.Text;
            int myNameLength = 0;
```

```
        myNameLength = myName.Length;
        MessageBox.Show(myNamePrefix +
            myNameLength.ToString());
        btnName.Content = "Goodbye";
    }
...
```

As you move throughout this chapter, you'll see how you can integrate Silverlight with SharePoint. But, for now let's talk briefly about *why* you should integrate the two technologies.

WHY INTEGRATE SILVERLIGHT AND SHAREPOINT?

If you look at the momentum across SharePoint and Silverlight, it is pretty incredible to see the growing center of gravity around each of them. For example, at the 2009 SharePoint Conference in Las Vegas, Steve Ballmer, CEO of Microsoft, announced that the developer community for SharePoint would soon be at "1 million developers." Also, he noted that the business around SharePoint was stable and growing, with more than $1 billion in revenue, 100 million enterprise licenses, a network of more than 4,000 partners, and a strong opportunity for post-deployment customizations. What this means for you (and, more generally, for software development firms) is that there is a great opportunity to build and leverage SharePoint development skills.

With Silverlight, there is similar growth. As mentioned, the product is now in its fourth release, with quicker go-to-market cycles than other products at Microsoft. As of this writing, Silverlight had more than 500 million downloads, 500,000 developers worldwide, many partners using the technology, and thousands of applications being built worldwide.

Also, where developers have used Adobe Flash, they can now use Silverlight within the .NET and Microsoft stack. This translates into vastly improved integration across the different technologies. For example, the tools support and .NET class library support provide great integration across the applications you're trying to build. This support also makes building these applications a much easier proposition. This is evidenced by, for example, the integration between Visual Studio and Expression Blend to more closely tie together the developer and designer experiences.

So, taken separately, these two technologies are doing very well. However, there are some great opportunities when you bring these two technologies together.

For example, they are both Web-based technologies. They are both based on .NET and can support some level of scripting and dynamic language integration. Furthermore, SharePoint is a platform, so naturally it plays host to interoperable technologies such as Silverlight, and, within this light, supports Silverlight out of the box in SharePoint 2010. And, lastly, the developer story is solid. Not only do you have SharePoint project templates out of the box with Visual Studio 2010 (along with the Silverlight templates), but as mentioned earlier you also have a seamless integration with Expression Blend.

All this translates into great things for these two technologies coming together, not only for the end consumer of Silverlight applications in SharePoint, but also for the developers and designers working together to create and deploy them.

The opportunities for applications within the convergence of these two technologies are equally compelling. For example, you can build the following:

➤ Simple self-contained applications, where the code resides within the Silverlight application but doesn't integrate with the SharePoint object model — SharePoint simply plays host to the Silverlight application

➤ Complex business applications, where the Silverlight application pulls in external data sources and integrates them with SharePoint to, for example, update a SharePoint list, or customize the navigation system

➤ Branding applications that leverage the animation and storyboard features of Silverlight, and build counting logic that enable video swapping along timelines and keeping count of click-throughs on advertisements

➤ Multi-touch applications that leverage the Silverlight UI with multi-touch capabilities to browse and view thumbnail representations of the underlying documents in SharePoint document libraries

And the list goes on. Literally, if you look at the opportunity space here, it's as far as it is wide. And, again, the developer and designer story is so complementary and compelling that companies will naturally gravitate toward using these tools.

With that in mind, let's now dig a bit deeper into how SharePoint and Silverlight integrate.

INTEGRATING SILVERLIGHT WITH SHAREPOINT

If you were to think at a very high architectural level about how SharePoint integrates with Silverlight, you might envisage something like what is shown in Figure 9-6. This figure shows that, while SharePoint is built upon a foundation of a server or a client (depending on your OS installation), at the top end of the experience, SharePoint is rendering pages as aspx and HTML pages (and, of course, embedded scripts). SharePoint also supports the integration of Silverlight (in or out of browser) as an enhanced user experience, or a deeper-level integration with the underlying artifacts within SharePoint. Note that, while Silverlight applications are ultimately hosted within the aspx pages within SharePoint, you can also integrate Silverlight applications that are hosted outside of SharePoint — as you will see in one of the exercises later in this chapter.

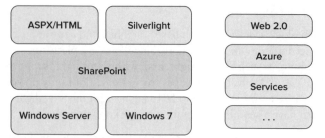

FIGURE 9-6 High-level architectural integration

Furthermore, what Figure 9-6 also represents is the fact that you can integrate other technologies within Silverlight (or directly with SharePoint), such as Web 2.0 technologies, Azure service end-points, third-party services, and so on. Thus, there is a wide berth for the integration that can drive at a superficial level (for example, simply hosting an application) or drive much deeper (for example, a Silverlight application integrating with the underlying SharePoint object model). And, in both of these cases, you could also integrate other Microsoft or non-Microsoft technologies, services, or data sources to further complement the integrated solutions.

You can sensibly classify the integrations with SharePoint in three primary ways, as is illustrated in Figure 9-7. These classifications are not necessarily hard and fast, but they have helped developers in the past quickly distinguish the different types and levels of integration.

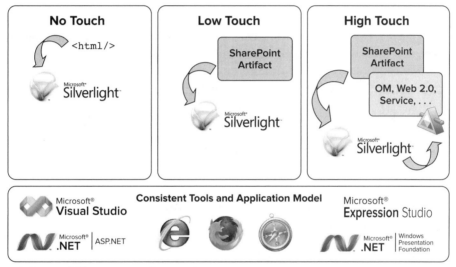

FIGURE 9-7 Different types of integration

The first is essentially a *no-touch* option. What this means is that you have a Silverlight application hosted outside of your SharePoint domain (for example, on the Web), and SharePoint provides a way to host that application. A practical example might be a stock widget that you can simply point to by creating a Content Editor Web part, and then adding an `<iframe>` object to reference the Silverlight application to load on page load.

The second classification, the *low-touch* integration, is where you have code that is executing, but it may either be self-contained or have a light touch with SharePoint. This might be where you've deployed a Web part that is hosting a Silverlight application to SharePoint, or you're leveraging the out-of-the-box Silverlight Web part to host your Silverlight application.

The *high-touch* classification is where you would see integration with the SharePoint object model. This is, for example, where you might leverage the Lists Web service to provide a Silverlight rendering of a list, or where you might leverage the SharePoint client object model to read and update portions of a list. Either way, you are explicitly leveraging the SharePoint object model in some capacity.

For the remainder of this chapter, you'll walk through examples of each of the three types of integration to better understand how to accomplish this integration.

No-Touch Integration

The no-touch integration should simply be the easiest way to integrate Silverlight into your SharePoint site. What's great is that you can integrate anything from community Silverlight widgets to third-party consumer widgets to applications that you leverage within the enterprise, using this type of classification. In fact, with only a few steps, you should be able to set up and render this type of application.

Let's try a couple of examples.

The first example is a community example from Dave LaVigne's blog at `http://franksworld.com/blog/archive/2009/10/07/11739.aspx`. He created a simple Silverlight application that you can reference using some straightforward `<iframe>` code (which he provides for you).

TRY IT OUT   Leveraging Community Hosted Silverlight Applications in SharePoint

1. Navigate to LaVigne's blog and, first, copy the code that he provides in his blog entry:

```
<iframe
    src="http://www.franksworld.com/silverlight/meeting/"
    frameborder="0" style="width: 512px; height: 299px;
        border:0px" ></iframe>
```

2. Next, go to your SharePoint site and select Site Actions ➪ Edit Page.

3. Click "Add a web part," and click the "Media and Content" category.

4. Select the Content Editor Web part and click Add.

5. After the Content Editor Web part has been added (Figure 9-8), click the "Click here to add new content" link.

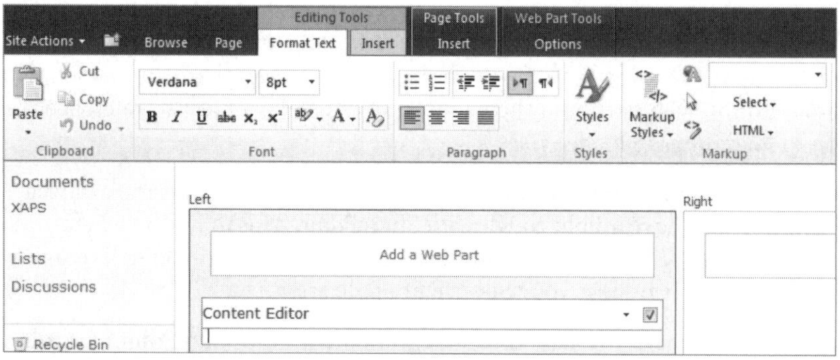

FIGURE 9-8 Using the Content Editor Web part as a host

6. Click the HTML drop-down menu and select Edit HTML Source.

7. In the HTML source window, add the `<iframe>` code you copied from the blog and click OK. Then, click Apply in the Tools pane. The community Silverlight application should now render in your SharePoint site, as shown in Figure 9-9.

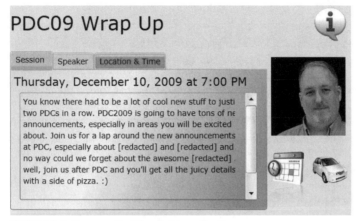

FIGURE 9-9 Community Silverlight application

How It Works

The way this integration works is that LaVigne provides the hosting mechanism for the Silverlight application, and all you're doing is borrowing a link to that hosted application to effectively render it within an out-of-the-box Web part. The Web part, which enables you to infuse HTML source into the page rendering, loads the `<iframe>` code on page load and then displays the Silverlight application.

With this approach, you leveraged mostly a *hosted* community example to integrate a no-touch integration with SharePoint. However, this is just one way of achieving a no-touch example. Another way might be for you to leverage a hosting service that can host a Silverlight application.

One such service is a new Azure offering that hosts Silverlight applications and videos. Using this type of hosted service, you can host Web-based Silverlight applications inside your SharePoint Web parts (using the same `<iframe>` method that you used here). Figure 9-10 shows a weather widget hosted in the "cloud." (You can find out more information about the new Windows Azure offering for Silverlight at `http://silverlight.live .com/quickstart.htm`.)

Similar to the first example, this example also relies on a separate domain to host the Silverlight application. However, what's interesting here is that you can not only host third-party Silverlight applications on hosting services like Azure, but you can also host your own. This bodes well for when you want to reuse the Silverlight application in

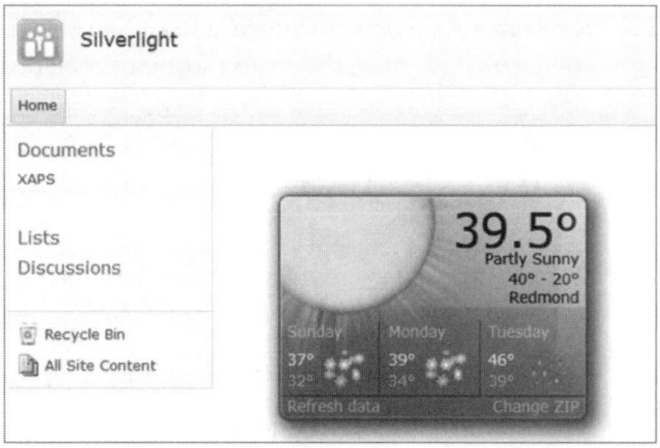

FIGURE 9-10 Third-Party Silverlight application

multiple places within your SharePoint site. For example, think about a scenario where you're surfacing company data within a Silverlight application, and you want to leverage the application across the SharePoint farm. You add the Silverlight application at a farm-level document library and then you can consume this application across multiple site collections.

> **NOTE** *If for some reason you cannot load Dave LaVigne's blog and you are unable to complete the previous exercise, you can also use the* `<iframe>` *code approach with other types of hosted Silverlight applications that you build (for example, replace the reference to LaVigne's blog with a reference to test the HTML page you build and deploy to your local machine), or use the* `<object>` *tag to reference a Silverlight application that you host in a document library in SharePoint. While the code is slightly different, the concept of referencing an external Silverlight application using the Content Editor Web part is consistent across these approaches. You'll see an exercise that uses the* `<object>` *tag reference later in this chapter.*

Note that, as an example of adding your own Silverlight application for *local* hosting, you could take the Silverlight application you created in the earlier walkthrough and add that to SharePoint. You could then add code within `<object>` tags to the Content Editor Web part. The difference is the fact that you're now using code within an `<object>` tag and the domain that hosts the Silverlight application is *your* SharePoint domain, as opposed to an external, Web-facing domain.

Let's take a look at an example of this.

TRY IT OUT Hosting the Silverlight Application Locally

Hosting your Silverlight application locally is also a lightweight option. To host the application locally, follow these steps:

1. Navigate to your SharePoint site, and click All Site Content ➪ Create.

2. In the Create options, select Document Library. Provide a name for your document library (for example, XAPS), and click Create.

3. Navigate to the new document library, and then click "Add new document." Upload the `.xap` file you created in the earlier walkthrough to the document library, as shown in Figure 9-11.

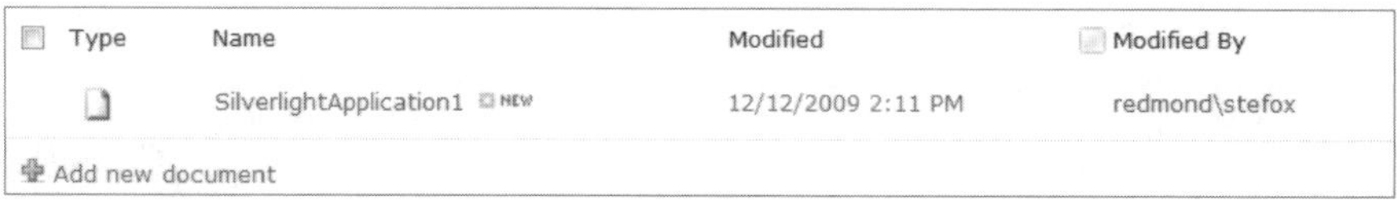

	Type	Name	Modified	Modified By
☐	▯	SilverlightApplication1 ▭ NEW	12/12/2009 2:11 PM	redmond\stefox
✛ Add new document				

FIGURE 9-11 Adding the XAP to a document library

4. Right-click the `.xap` file and select Copy Shortcut.

5. Now navigate to a site collection or Web part page and click Site Actions ➪ Edit Page, and then click "Add a web part" in one of the Web part zones.

6. Select the Media and Content category, and click Content Editor Web Part.

7. Select "Click here to add new content." Select the HTML drop-down menu, and click Edit HTML Source.

8. Add the following snippet of JavaScript code to the HTML Source window. Add the shortcut you copied to the value property, and click OK.

```
<div id="mySLApp" />
<script type="text/javascript">
var slDivObj = document.getElementById('mySLApp');
slDivObj.appendChild(slDivObj);
slDivObj.innerHTML = '<object data="data:application/x-silverlight,"
    type="application/x-silverlight" width="400" height="400">
    <param name="source" value=" http://fabrikamhockey/sl/
    XAPS/SilverlightApplication1.xap "/></object>';
</script>
```

(When you add this code, ensure that you have no line breaks with the line of code that begins with `slDivObj.innerHTML`. You may find that this will cause your Silverlight application to not load properly.)

9. Click Stop Editing to exit Edit mode. Your `Hello World` Silverlight application will be rendered dynamically as a part of the HTML source in the SharePoint site, as shown in Figure 9-12.

FIGURE 9-12 Silverlight application hosted locally

Thus far, you have learned a couple of different ways to host Silverlight applications in SharePoint within a *no-touch classification*. One of the ways leveraged remote hosting, and the other leveraged SharePoint (that is, hosting the Silverlight application in a SharePoint document library) and JavaScript — but both used the Content Editor Web part as the way in which the application was dynamically loaded on page load.

There are also other ways to host a Silverlight application in SharePoint. Let's now take a look at the low-touch integration classification as you begin to leverage the out-of-the-box SharePoint Web part.

Low-Touch Integration

Having worked with the no-touch integration, you'll see that the low-touch integration is a little more involved. In some cases, you won't need to write code. (Think back to Chapter 3, where you created a wiki site collection and then integrated a WMV video with the Silverlight Media Web part.) However, there are other cases where you will write some code — as you will in the walk-through in this section. The writing code part, though, will mainly execute code within the context of the Silverlight application and not reach into the SharePoint infrastructure to, for example, get or put data into a SharePoint artifact such as a list.

In this section, you'll walk through an example that will leverage an in-memory data source, and then use Language Integrated Query (LINQ) to manage that data across a set of Silverlight controls. The scenario is loading a person's employee review scores from an external data structure. When the data is loaded, you can then see what the person's employee review scores are, as well as what the ultimate reward and promotion potential is going to be. Based on the level of rewards, the Silverlight application will then change the thermometer graphic to indicate the level of reward.

TRY IT OUT   Creating a Low-Touch Integration

Code file [LowIntegrationSLApp.zip] available for download at Wrox.com.

You can create self-contained, low-touch integrations with SharePoint. To do this, follow these steps:

1. Open Visual Studio 2010. Click File ➪ New ➪ Project. Select the Silverlight Application template and provide a name for your project (for example, `LowIntegrationSLApp`) and click OK.

2. When prompted, uncheck the "Host the Silverlight application in a new Web site" checkbox.

3. After Visual Studio creates the new solution, right-click the project and click Add ➪ New Item.

4. Select Data ➪ XML File.

5. Provide a name for the XML file (for example, `Employee.xml`), as shown at the bottom of Figure 9-13.

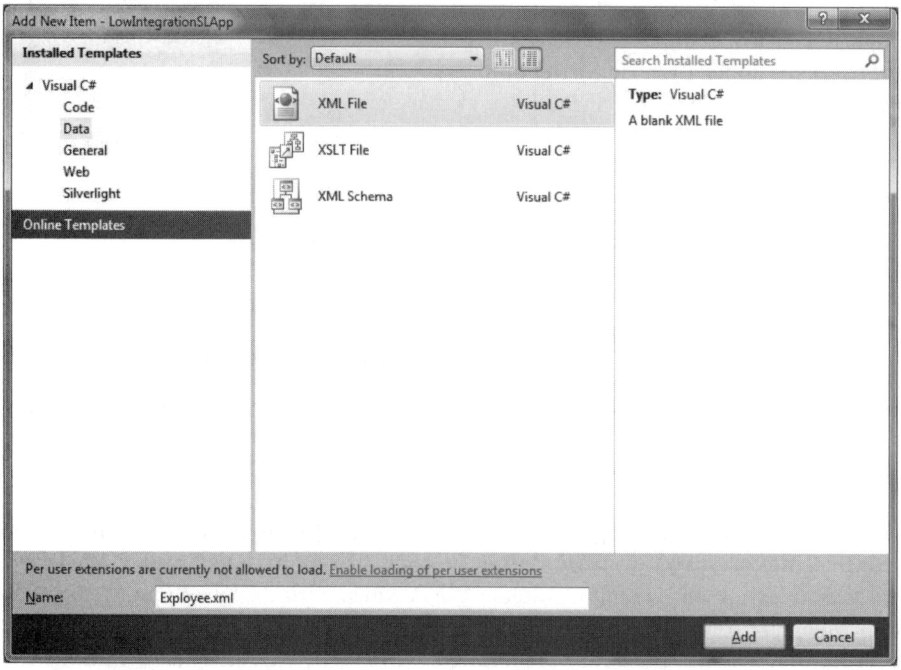

FIGURE 9-13 XML data object

6. After the new XML file has been added to the project, add the following XML code to the new file. This code represents the data records that you'll load into the Silverlight application.

```xml
<?xml version="1.0" encoding="utf-8" ?>
<Employees>
  <Employee>
    <Name>John Doe</Name>
    <EmpID>837901</EmpID>
    <FY08>3.2</FY08>
    <FY09>3.4</FY09>
    <FY10>3.8</FY10>
  </Employee>
  <Employee>
    <Name>Kelly Jackson</Name>
    <EmpID>983011</EmpID>
    <FY08>2.8</FY08>
    <FY09>2.9</FY09>
    <FY10>3.0</FY10>
  </Employee>
  <Employee>
    <Name>Sam Sheppard</Name>
    <EmpID>10290</EmpID>
    <FY08>4.2</FY08>
    <FY09>4.3</FY09>
    <FY10>4.5</FY10>
  </Employee>
  <Employee>
    <Name>Lamont Smyth</Name>
    <EmpID>129775</EmpID>
    <FY08>3.8</FY08>
    <FY09>3.6</FY09>
    <FY10>3.2</FY10>
  </Employee>
  <Employee>
    <Name>Beth Canyon</Name>
    <EmpID>38921</EmpID>
    <FY08>2.1</FY08>
    <FY09>2.2</FY09>
    <FY10>2.0</FY10>
  </Employee>
  <Employee>
    <Name>Barry McCathry</Name>
    <EmpID>201982</EmpID>
    <FY08>3.3</FY08>
    <FY09>2.9</FY09>
    <FY10>3.7</FY10>
  </Employee>
  <Employee>
    <Name>Steve Denn</Name>
    <EmpID>290122</EmpID>
    <FY08>4.5</FY08>
    <FY09>4.6</FY09>
    <FY10>4.5</FY10>
```

```
    </Employee>
    <Employee>
      <Name>Ahmed Habul</Name>
      <EmpID>0992812</EmpID>
      <FY08>3.9</FY08>
      <FY09>3.8</FY09>
      <FY10>3.9</FY10>
    </Employee>
</Employees>
```

7.   With the XML file complete, you'll now want to add a custom class to the project. To do this, right-click the project and select Add ➪ Class. Provide a name for the class (for example, `Employees.cs`), and click OK, as shown at the bottom of Figure 9-14.

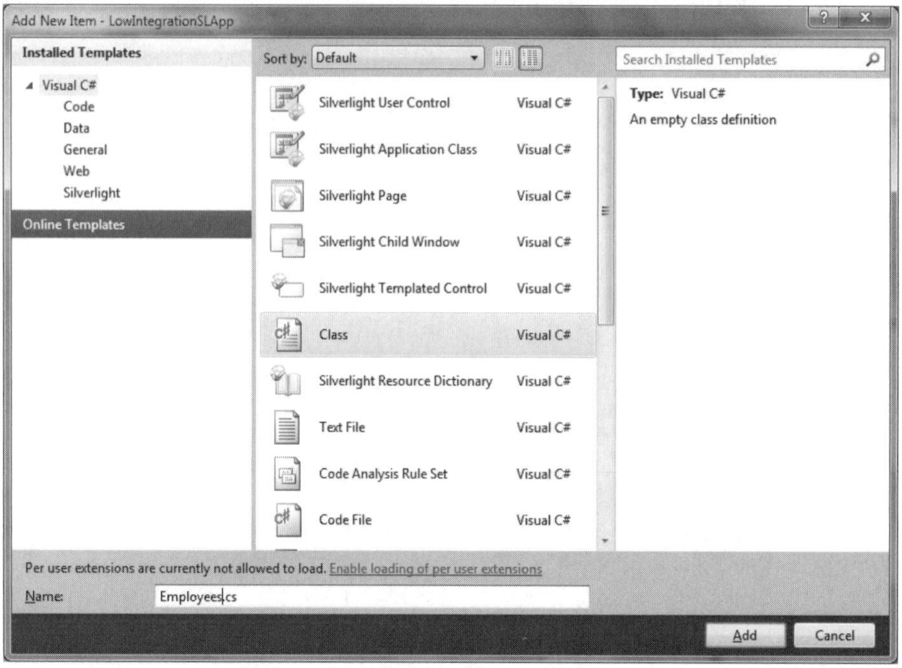

FIGURE 9-14 Adding a class to Silverlight

8.   Add the following bolded code to the new class, which you'll use to load the XML data and then use LINQ to populate the properties in this object:

```
using System;
using System.Net;
using System.Windows;
using System.Windows.Controls;
using System.Windows.Documents;
using System.Windows.Ink;
using System.Windows.Input;
using System.Windows.Media;
using System.Windows.Media.Animation;
```

```
using System.Windows.Shapes;

namespace LowIntegrationSLApp
{
    public class Employees
    {
        public string empName { get; set; }
        public string empID { get; set; }
        public string empFY08 { get; set; }
        public string empFY09 { get; set; }
        public string empFy10 { get; set; }
    }
}
```

9. At this point, the data portions of your application are complete. You will now work on the UI for the application. To do this, right-click the `MainPage.xaml` file and select View Designer.

10. Add ten labels, two buttons, one listbox, one image, three rectangles, and seven textboxes to the Designer surface and arrange them, as shown in Figure 9-15.

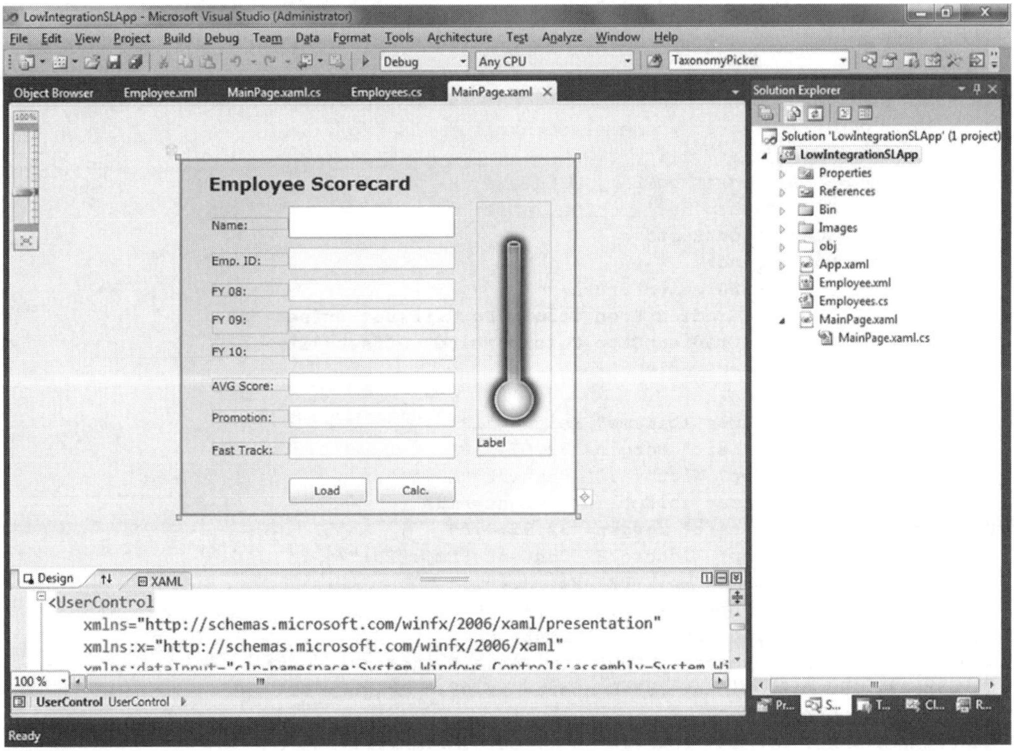

FIGURE 9-15 Employee Scorecard application in Visual Studio

Table 9-2 provides an overview of the control types and the corresponding names you'll use in the Silverlight application.

TABLE 9-2 Control Types and Names

CONTROL TYPE	CONTROL NAME
Label	lblTitle, lblName, lblEmplID, lblFY08, lblFY09, lblFY10, lblSummary, lblFastTrack, lblPromotion, lblMessage
Listbox	lstbxEmployeeNames
Button	btnCalc, btnRefresh
Textbox	txtbxEmplID, txtbxFY08, txtbxFY09, txtbxFY10, txtbxAVGScore, txtbxPromo, txtbxFastTrack,

11. You can either choose to build out the UI yourself, or you can leverage the following bolded XAML code:

```
<UserControl
    xmlns="http://schemas.microsoft.com/winfx/2006/xaml/presentation"
    xmlns:x="http://schemas.microsoft.com/winfx/2006/xaml"
    xmlns:dataInput="clr-namespace:
        System.Windows.Controls;assembly=
        System.Windows.Controls.Data.Input"
    xmlns:d="http://schemas.microsoft.com/expression/blend/2008"
        xmlns:mc="http://schemas.openxmlformats.org/
        markup-compatibility/2006"
    x:Class="LowIntegrationSLApp.MainPage"
    Width="400" Height="350" mc:Ignorable="d">
    <Grid x:Name="LayoutRoot">
        <Grid.Background>
                <LinearGradientBrush>
                    <GradientStop Color="PowderBlue" Offset="0"/>
                    <GradientStop Color="White" Offset="1"/>
                </LinearGradientBrush>
        </Grid.Background>
<dataInput:Label x:Name="lblName" Height="13"
HorizontalAlignment="Left" Margin="32,57,0,0"
VerticalAlignment="Top" Width="78" Content="Name:"/>
<dataInput:Label x:Name="lblEmplID" Height="13"
HorizontalAlignment="Left" Margin="32,92,0,0"
VerticalAlignment="Top" Width="78" Content="Emp. ID:"/>
<dataInput:Label x:Name="lblFY08" Height="13"
HorizontalAlignment="Left" Margin="32,122,0,0"
VerticalAlignment="Top" Width="78" Content="FY 08:"/>
<dataInput:Label x:Name="lblFY09" HorizontalAlignment="Left"
Margin="32,150,0,0" Width="78" Content="FY 09:" Height="22"
VerticalAlignment="Top"/>
<dataInput:Label x:Name="lblFY10" HorizontalAlignment="Left"
Margin="32,0,0,156" Width="78" Content="FY 10:"
Height="13" VerticalAlignment="Bottom"/>
<dataInput:Label x:Name="lblSummary" Height="13"
```

```
HorizontalAlignment="Left" Margin="32,0,0,122"
VerticalAlignment="Bottom" Width="78" Content="AVG Score:"/>
<dataInput:Label x:Name="lblPromotion" Height="13"
HorizontalAlignment="Left" Margin="32,0,0,91" VerticalAlignment="Bottom"
Width="78" Content="Promotion:"/>
<dataInput:Label x:Name="lblFastTrack" Height="13"
HorizontalAlignment="Left" Margin="32,0,0,59" VerticalAlignment="Bottom"
Width="78" Content="Fast Track:"/>
<TextBox x:Name="txtbxEmplID" IsEnabled="False" Height="22"
Margin="110,87,122,0" VerticalAlignment="Top" TextWrapping="Wrap"/>
<TextBox x:Name="txtbxFY08" IsEnabled="False" Height="22"
Margin="110,118,122,0" VerticalAlignment="Top" TextWrapping="Wrap"/>
<TextBox x:Name="txtbxFY09" IsEnabled="False" Margin="110,147,122,0"
TextWrapping="Wrap" Height="22" VerticalAlignment="Top"/>
<TextBox x:Name="txtbxFY10" IsEnabled="False" Margin="110,0,122,151"
TextWrapping="Wrap" Height="22" VerticalAlignment="Bottom"/>
<TextBox x:Name="txtbxAVGScore" IsEnabled="False"
Height="22" Margin="110,0,122,118" VerticalAlignment="Bottom" TextWrapping="Wrap"/>
<TextBox x:Name="txtbxPromo" IsEnabled="False" Height="22" Margin="110,0,122,86"
VerticalAlignment="Bottom" TextWrapping="Wrap"/>
<TextBox x:Name="txtbxFastTrack" IsEnabled="False" Height="22"
Margin="110,0,122,55" VerticalAlignment="Bottom" TextWrapping="Wrap"/>
<ListBox
Margin="0,46,122,0" Height="32" VerticalAlignment="Top"
x:Name="lstbxEmployeeNames" HorizontalAlignment="Right"
Width="168" SelectionChanged="lstbxEmployeeNames_SelectionChanged" />
<Button x:Name="btnRefresh" Height="25" HorizontalAlignment="Left"
Margin="110,0,0,12" VerticalAlignment="Bottom" Width="79"
Content="Load" Background="#FF0689FA" Click="btnRefresh_Click"/>
<dataInput:Label x:Name="lblTitle" Margin="29,13,130,0"
VerticalAlignment="Top" Content="Employee Scorecard" FontWeight="Bold"
FontSize="18" FontFamily="Verdana"/>
<Button Background="#FF0689FA" Content="Calc." Height="25"
HorizontalAlignment="Left" Margin="199,0,0,12" Name="btnCalc"
VerticalAlignment="Bottom" Width="79" Click="btnCalc_Click" />
<Image x:Name="imgThermo" Source="Images/Thermometer.png"
Margin="300,42,25,58" Height="250" Width="75"/>
<Rectangle Height="0" HorizontalAlignment="Left"
Margin="310,112,0,0" Name="shapeRectanglePromo" Stroke="Green"
StrokeThickness="2" VerticalAlignment="Top" Width="53" />
<Rectangle Height="0" HorizontalAlignment="Left"
Margin="310,177,0,0" Name="shapeRectangleNoPromo" Stroke="Orange"
StrokeThickness="2" VerticalAlignment="Top" Width="53" />
<Rectangle Height="0" HorizontalAlignment="Left"
Margin="310,235,0,0" Name="shapeRectangleLowScore" Stroke="Red"
StrokeThickness="2" VerticalAlignment="Top" Width="53" />
<dataInput:Label Height="22" HorizontalAlignment="Left"
Margin="300,271,0,0" Name="lblMessage" VerticalAlignment="Top" Width="75" />
</Grid>
</UserControl>
```

If you copy and paste the code (or type in the boldfaced code), you'll need to manually add a reference to the System.Windows.Controls.Data.Input DLL. This is because Visual Studio automatically adds this reference when you drag and drop the label control, but it does not add this reference if you simply copy and paste, or type in, the code.

12. With the UI complete, you can now add the code behind. The events that you want to manage within this application map to the user changing a selection in the listbox, and clicking one of the two available buttons. To add the code behind, right-click the `MainPage.xaml` file and then select View Code. Add the following bolded code into the code behind:

```
using System;
using System.Windows;
using System.Windows.Controls;
using System.Windows.Documents;
using System.Windows.Ink;
using System.Windows.Input;
using System.Windows.Media;
using System.Windows.Media.Animation;
using System.Windows.Shapes;
using System.Xml;
using System.Linq;
using System.Collections.Generic;
using System.Xml.Linq;
using System.Windows.Media.Imaging;

namespace LowIntegrationSLApp
{
    public partial class MainPage : UserControl
    {
        string promotion = "";
        string fastTrack = "";
        double avgScore = 0.0;

        List<Employees> myEmployeeList = new List<Employees>();

        public MainPage()
        {
            // Required to initialize variables
            InitializeComponent();
        }

        private void btnRefresh_Click(object sender, RoutedEventArgs e)
        {
            XElement employee = XElement.Load(@"Employee.xml");
            resetThermometer();
            string tempEmpName = "";
            string tempEmpID = "";
            string tempFY08 = "";
            string tempFY09 = "";
            string tempFY10 = "";

            var employees =
```

```
                    from emp in employee.Elements("Employee")
                    select new
                        {
                            tempEmpName = (string)emp.Element("Name"),
                            tempEmpID = (string)emp.Element("EmpID"),
                            tempFY08 = (string)emp.Element("FY08"),
                            tempFY09 = (string)emp.Element("FY09"),
                            tempFY10 = (string)emp.Element("FY10")
                        };

        foreach (var item in employees)
        {
            Employees tempEmployee = new Employees();
            tempEmployee.empName = item.tempEmpName.ToString();
            lstbxEmployeeNames.Items.Add(tempEmployee.empName);
            tempEmployee.empID = item.tempEmpID.ToString();
            tempEmployee.empFY08 = item.tempFY08.ToString();
            tempEmployee.empFY09 = item.tempFY09.ToString();
            tempEmployee.empFy10 = item.tempFY10.ToString();
            myEmployeeList.Add(tempEmployee);
        }
    }

    private void lstbxEmployeeNames_SelectionChanged(object sender,
        SelectionChangedEventArgs e)
    {
        resetThermometer();

        string tempEmpID = "";
        string tempFY08 = "";
        string tempFY09 = "";
        string tempFY10 = "";

        string empFilter = lstbxEmployeeNames.SelectedItem.ToString();

        var expr =
            from emp in myEmployeeList
            select new
                {
                    emp.empName,
                    emp.empID,
                    emp.empFY08,
                    emp.empFY09,
                    emp.empFy10
                };
        foreach (var item in expr)
        {
            if (item.empName == empFilter)
            {
                txtbxEmplID.Text = item.empID;
                txtbxFY08.Text = item.empFY08;
```

```
                txtbxFY09.Text = item.empFY09;
                txtbxFY10.Text = item.empFy10;
            }
        }
    }

    private void btnCalc_Click(object sender, RoutedEventArgs e)
    {
        resetThermometer();
        double rvwFY08 = Double.Parse(txtbxFY08.Text);
        double rvwFY09 = Double.Parse(txtbxFY09.Text);
        double rvwFY10 = Double.Parse(txtbxFY10.Text);

        avgScore = Math.Round(((rvwFY08 + rvwFY09 + rvwFY10) /
            3), 2) * 100 / 100;

        if (avgScore >= 4.5)
        {
            promotion = "Yes";
            fastTrack = "Yes";
            shapeRectanglePromo.Height = 3;
            lblMessage.Content = "High Reward";
        }
        else if (avgScore >= 4.0)
        {
            promotion = "Yes";
            fastTrack = "No";
            shapeRectangleNoPromo.Height = 3;
            lblMessage.Content = "Med. Reward";
        }
        else
        {
            promotion = "No";
            fastTrack = "No";
            shapeRectangleLowScore.Height = 3;
            lblMessage.Content = "Low Reward";
        }

        txtbxPromo.Text = promotion;
        txtbxFastTrack.Text = fastTrack;
        txtbxAVGScore.Text = avgScore.ToString();
    }

    private void resetThermometer()
    {
        shapeRectanglePromo.Height = 0;
        shapeRectangleNoPromo.Height = 0;
        shapeRectangleLowScore.Height = 0;

        txtbxAVGScore.Text = "";
        txtbxFastTrack.Text = "";
```

```
            txtbxPromo.Text = "";

            lblMessage.Content = "";
        }
    }
}
```

13. With the Silverlight application complete, build the project to ensure that it builds successfully.

14. After it builds, click the Show All Files button at the top of the Solution Explorer and navigate to the `Bin` directory. You'll notice that there is an `.xap` file in that folder, which is the built Silverlight application. (To see what's inside of this file, you can copy the `.xap` file to a separate location and then replace the `.xap` file extension with `.zip` and open it to see what's contained inside.)

15. Right-click the `Bin` directory and select "Open Folder in Windows Explorer," as shown in Figure 9-16. Copy the file path to your Clipboard.

16. Open your SharePoint site and click All Site Content.

17. Click Create ➪ Sites to create a new test site for the Silverlight application.

18. Select Blank Site, provide a name and URL, and click Create.

19. With your new site created, select Site Actions ➪ Edit Page.

20. In your site, create a new document library called `XAPS`. Then, click "Add new document" and click Browse.

21. Paste the file path to the `.xap` file into the Browse dialog, and then click OK. This will add your Silverlight application to your document library.

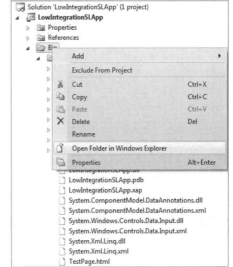

FIGURE 9-16 Opening a folder in Solution Explorer

22. Right-click the `.xap` file and select Copy Shortcut.

23. Navigate to an existing (or create a new) Web part page. Click Site Actions ➪ Edit Page, and then click the "Add a web part" in the top Web part zone.

24. Navigate to the "Media and Content" Web part category, and select Silverlight Web Part.

25. Click Add, and you will be prompted for the link to the `.xap` file. Paste the shortcut to the `.xap` file you added to the `XAPS` document library, and click OK.

26. The Silverlight application is now rendered in the SharePoint page, as shown in Figure 9-17. This figure also shows another example of a Silverlight application that illustrates some charting capabilities (another example of a low-touch integration with SharePoint).

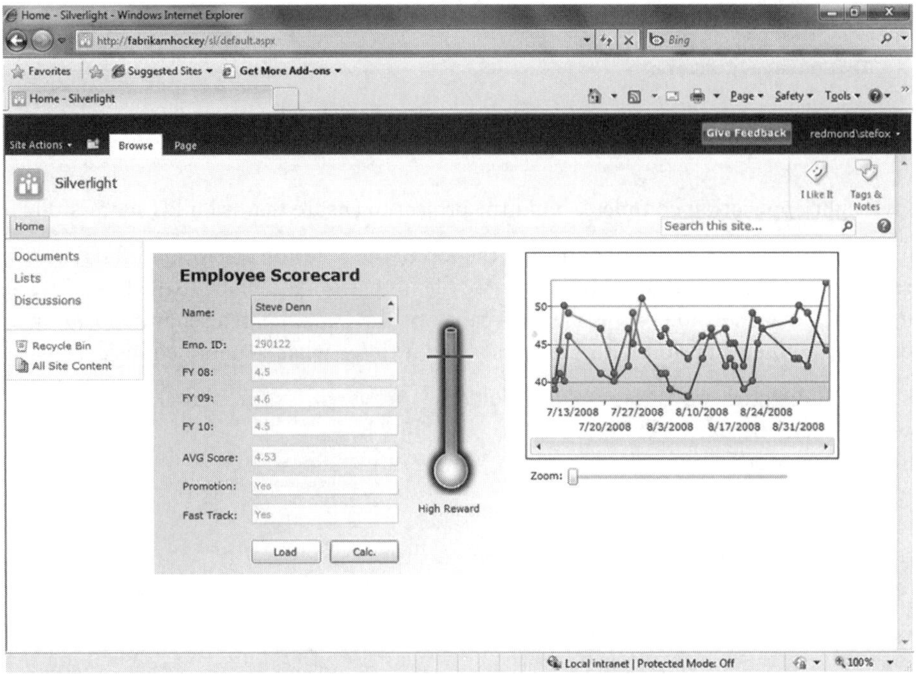

FIGURE 9-17 Employee Scorecard Silverlight application in SharePoint

How It Works

The low-touch walkthrough is a more complex application because it has some processing built into the Scorecard application. For example, three primary events drive the application: two button clicks and a selection changed event on the list. When the user clicks the Load button, it loads the XML data from the `Employee.xml` file and then feeds that into the in-memory list collection.

Again, LINQ is an important aspect of how you query the data. For example, LINQ queries show up in two out of the three events, as is shown in the following bolded code. Interestingly, the queries are issued against two different *types* of objects — one is an XML object, and the other is a list collection.

```
...
        private void btnRefresh_Click(object sender, RoutedEventArgs e)
        {
            XElement employee = XElement.Load(@"Employee.xml");

            var employees =
                    from emp in employee.Elements("Employee")
                    select new
                        {
                            tempEmpName = (string)emp.Element("Name"),
                            tempEmpID = (string)emp.Element("EmpID"),
                            tempFY08 = (string)emp.Element("FY08"),
                            tempFY09 = (string)emp.Element("FY09"),
                            tempFY10 = (string)emp.Element("FY10")
                        };

...
```

```
    }
    private void lstbxEmployeeNames_SelectionChanged(object sender,
        SelectionChangedEventArgs e)
    {
        ...

        string empFilter = lstbxEmployeeNames.SelectedItem.ToString();

        var expr =
            from emp in myEmployeeList
            select new
                {
                    emp.empName,
                    emp.empID,
                    emp.empFY08,
                    emp.empFY09,
                    emp.empFy10
                };
        ...
    }
    ...
```

There is also a straightforward helper function that resets the data fields (the `resetThermometer` method) and, depending on what employee is selected, varied and calculated data will be displayed.

What's interesting about the low-touch scenario is that you can have very powerful applications that may not necessarily reach inside the SharePoint object model but still accomplish quite a lot (especially if SharePoint is your collaboration portal). Think about the opportunity here for employee self-service applications in this context (for example, updating vacation or personal information).

Now that you've seen the no-touch and the low-touch alternatives, let's examine the high-touch classification.

High-Touch Integration

The high-touch integration is more involved than the other two classifications, but it is more powerful and has a deeper relationship with the SharePoint object model. You could think of the high-touch integration as having two major pivots:

➤ How you *integrate with* the SharePoint object model

➤ How you *deploy to* SharePoint

With regard to how you integrate, there are a number of ways to achieve this integration, including the following:

➤ Leveraging the ASP.NET or REST services that ship with SharePoint

➤ Creating a custom Windows Communications Foundation (WCF) service

➤ Using the new SharePoint client object model

Some of the ways in which you can interact with SharePoint are out of the box, and there will be other occasions when you must create some custom code to facilitate that connectivity. One such example is when you want to re-create the navigation system in SharePoint to completely rebrand and redesign the SharePoint UI with Silverlight, as opposed to the native .aspx rendering. You would need to do a lot of custom coding here through custom services, but it is definitely possible, and the opportunity is there for you to exploit.

In terms of deployment, you can integrate with SharePoint on a number of levels. You could, for example, build a Silverlight application that is deployed using the native Silverlight Web part — and for many of your more simple applications, this may be fine. However, there may be other instances where you want to install the Silverlight application as a native object (that is, deploy it as a WSP). This may be because you have other components you want to integrate with the Silverlight application (such as complex Web services or other SharePoint controls), and, in this case, using the out-of-the-box Silverlight Web part may not suffice.

A specific scenario might be when you want to build an integrated Silverlight application that binds SAP data to a Silverlight UI, and then further has some controls integrating the data with a SharePoint list. Testing this in the context of the out-of-the-box Silverlight Web part would be challenging. The out-of-the-box Silverlight Web part has some limitations (for example, programmatically setting properties such as the height and width of the Web part), and you'd likely want to have more control over your integrated code and add more features (for example, event receivers) that would not be possible with the out-of-the-box Silverlight Web part.

Also, if you wanted to leverage the Visual Studio BDC Metadata template, you would be building an external list first, and then coding against that list. So, you would want to keep your Visual Studio 2010 solution intact with all of the proper project files (for example, Web part project, Silverlight project, and BDC Metadata project).

Integrating Using the Native Silverlight Web Part

To get you started, let's walk through a straightforward integration. In this walkthrough, let's use the native Web services that ship with SharePoint and the out-of-the-box Silverlight Web part.

TRY IT OUT **Creating a High-Touch Integration**

Code file [SPSilverlightApplication.zip] available for download at Wrox.com.

The high-touch integration can result in some very dynamic integrations with SharePoint, ranging from business applications that integrate with lists to replacing the navigation system within SharePoint. To create a high-touch integration, follow these steps:

1. Open SharePoint and click All Site Content.

2. Click Create, and, in the Create gallery, click the Custom List.

3. Provide a name for your custom list (for example, `Product_List`), and click Create.

4. Rename the `Title` field to `Product_Name` and then add three additional columns to the list (for example, `Product_SKU`, `Price`, and `Inventory`). All of the columns should be of type "Single line of text."

5. Populate the four columns with some data, as shown in Figure 9-18.

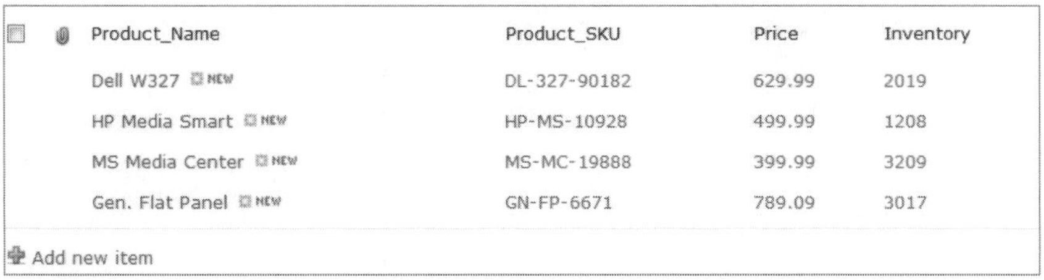

	Product_Name	Product_SKU	Price	Inventory
	Dell W327 ☑ NEW	DL-327-90182	629.99	2019
	HP Media Smart ☑ NEW	HP-MS-10928	499.99	1208
	MS Media Center ☑ NEW	MS-MC-19888	399.99	3209
	Gen. Flat Panel ☑ NEW	GN-FP-6671	789.09	3017

➕ Add new item

FIGURE 9-18 Creating the products List

6. Open Visual Studio 2010. Click File ⇨ New ⇨ Project. Select the Silverlight template and click Silverlight Application.

7. Provide a name for your project (for example, `SPSilverlightApplication`), and click OK.

8. When prompted, uncheck the "Host the Silverlight application in a new Web site" checkbox.

9. You'll require an in-memory object for this exercise. So, right-click the project and click Add ⇨ Class. Provide a name for the class (for example, `SPListRow`), and click OK.

10. The four properties of your custom object should look like the following boldfaced code, which maps to the data in your SharePoint list:

```
...

namespace SPSilverlightApplication
{
    public class SPListRow
    {
        public string productName { get; set; }
        public string productSKU { get; set; }
        public string productPrice { get; set; }
        public string productInventory { get; set; }
    }
}
...
```

11. You'll now want to add a service reference to one of the out-of-the-box ASP.NET Web services. Right-click the References node and select Add Service Reference.

12. In the Add Service Reference dialog, add `http://localhost/_vti_bin/Lists.asmx` to the Address field and click Go. (Note that you can replace `localhost` with your local server name, as shown in Figure 9-19.)

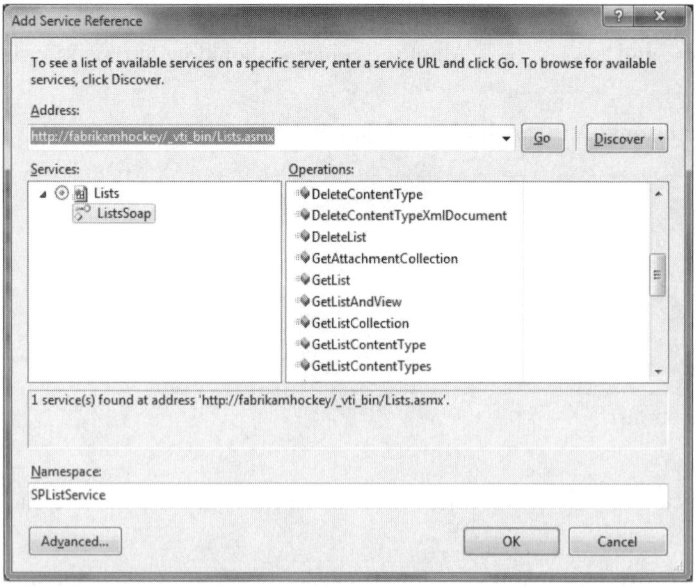

FIGURE 9-19 Adding lists to Web service reference

13. Provide a name for your service reference (for example, `ListService`), and click OK.

14. You'll now want to add five images to your project. To do this, right-click the project and select Add ➪ New Folder. Name the new folder `Images`. Then, right-click the `Images` folder and select Add Existing Item. You can add five of your own images or use the ones that are included with this book's companion source code. When you're finished, your project should look like Figure 9-20.

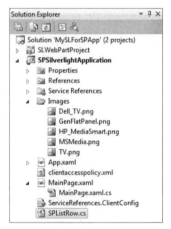

15. The next thing you want to do is build out your UI. So, right-click the `MainPage.xaml` file and select View Designer. This will open the Silverlight application in Designer mode.

FIGURE 9-20 Solution Explorer for Silverlight integration

16. Add the following boldfaced code to your XAML-based UI. This will create a UI that has some gradient styling, as well as a listbox and button control that will leverage the ASP.NET Web service to integrate with SharePoint. Note that there is an event that maps to the button and listbox control.

```
<UserControl x:Class="SPSilverlightApplication.MainPage"
    xmlns="http://schemas.microsoft.com/winfx/2006/xaml/presentation"
    xmlns:x="http://schemas.microsoft.com/winfx/2006/xaml"
    xmlns:d="http://schemas.microsoft.com/expression/blend/2008"
    xmlns:mc="http://schemas.openxmlformats.org/markup-compatibility/2006"
    mc:Ignorable="d"
    d:DesignHeight="300" d:DesignWidth="800" xmlns:dataInput=
```

```xml
                "clr-namespace:System.Windows.Controls;assembly=
                System.Windows.Controls.Data.Input">

<Grid x:Name="LayoutRoot">
    <Rectangle>
        <Rectangle.Fill>
            <LinearGradientBrush StartPoint="0.9, 0.5" EndPoint="0.9, 0.9">
                <LinearGradientBrush.GradientStops>
                    <GradientStopCollection>
                        <GradientStop Color="#FFd3ddab" Offset="0"/>
                        <GradientStop Color="#FF819d35" Offset="0.49"/>
                        <GradientStop Color="#FF739221" Offset="0.49"/>
                        <GradientStop Color="#FF678822" Offset="0.79"/>
                        <GradientStop Color="#FFBBC749" Offset="0.92"/>
                        <GradientStop Color="#FFdbde58" Offset="1"/>
                    </GradientStopCollection>
                </LinearGradientBrush.GradientStops>
            </LinearGradientBrush>
        </Rectangle.Fill>
    </Rectangle>
    <Canvas>
    <dataInput:Label
                    Canvas.Left="20"
                    Canvas.Top="20"
                    Height="34"
                    FontFamily="Arial Black"
                    FontWeight="Bold"
                    FontSize="20"
                    Content="High Definition Media Products"
                    HorizontalAlignment="Left"
                    Name="lblListData"
                    VerticalAlignment="Top"
                    Width="376"/>
        <ListBox
                x:Name="lstbxSharePointListData"
                Height="100"
                Width="350"
                HorizontalAlignment="Left"
                Canvas.Left="20"
                Canvas.Top="70"
                 SelectionChanged="lstbxSharePointListData_SelectionChanged">
        <ListBox.Effect>
            <DropShadowEffect ShadowDepth="0" BlurRadius="20" Opacity="1"
                Color="Black" Direction="315"/>
        </ListBox.Effect>
        <ListBox.ItemTemplate>
            <DataTemplate>
                <StackPanel Orientation="Vertical">
                    <TextBlock FontFamily="Arial"
                            Padding="1"
                            FontSize="10"
                            FontWeight="Bold"
                            Foreground="Black"
                            Text="{Binding productName}"/>
```

```
                      <TextBlock FontFamily="Arial"
                                 Padding="1"
                                 FontSize="8"
                                 Foreground="Gray"
                                 Text="{Binding productSKU}"/>
                      <TextBlock FontFamily="Arial"
                                 Padding="1"
                                 FontSize="8"
                                 Foreground="Gray"
                                 Text="{Binding productPrice}"/>
                      <TextBlock FontFamily="Arial"
                                 Padding="1"
                                 FontSize="8"
                                 Foreground="Gray"
                                 Text="{Binding productInventory}"/>
                </StackPanel>
            </DataTemplate>
        </ListBox.ItemTemplate>
    </ListBox>
    <Button
            Name="btnLoadListData"
            Height="35"
            Width="100"
            Content="Load"
            Canvas.Left="55"
            Canvas.Top="200"
            Click="btnLoadListData_Click">
        <Button.Effect>
            <DropShadowEffect ShadowDepth="0" BlurRadius="20" Opacity="1"
                Color="Black" Direction="315"/>
        </Button.Effect>
    </Button>
    <Rectangle
            Canvas.Left="430"
            Canvas.Top="30"
            Height="191"
            HorizontalAlignment="Left"
            Name="rctnglProduct"
            Stroke="Black"
            StrokeThickness="2"
            VerticalAlignment="Top"
            Width="344" >
        <Rectangle.Effect>
            <DropShadowEffect ShadowDepth="0" BlurRadius="20" Opacity="1"
                Color="Black" Direction="315"/>
        </Rectangle.Effect>
    </Rectangle>

    <Image
        x:Name="imgProduct"
        Height="180"
        Width="300"
        Source="Images/TV.png"
```

```
                Canvas.Left="453"
                Canvas.Top="35"/>
            <dataInput:Label
                            Height="23"
                            HorizontalAlignment="Left"
                            Name="lblModel"
                            VerticalAlignment="Top"
                            Width="137"
                            Content="Model Information"
                            Canvas.Left="546"
                            Canvas.Top="230"
                            FontWeight="Bold" />
        </Canvas>
    </Grid>
</UserControl>
```

If you copy and paste the code (or type in the boldfaced code), you'll need to manually add a reference to the `System.Windows.Controls.Data.Input` DLL. This is because Visual Studio automatically adds this reference when you drag and drop the label control, but it does not add this reference if you simply copy and paste, or type in, the code.

17. At this point, your UI should look similar to Figure 9-21.

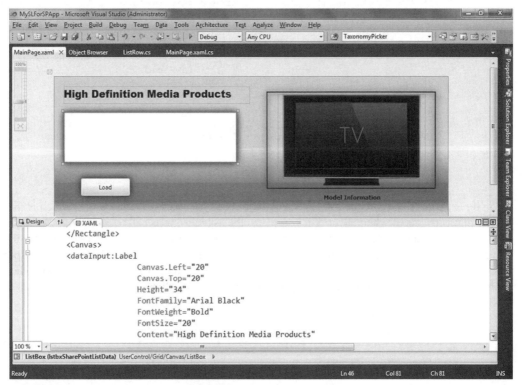

FIGURE 9-21 Silverlight application in Visual Studio

18. With your UI complete, you now want to add some event handlers to the code behind. To do this, right-click the `MainPage.xaml` and select View Code.

19. You're going to add the event code that maps to the button and listbox controls, and also manages the asynchronous calls that are characteristic of Silverlight applications. You'll first want to add the `btnLoadListData` event, which creates an instance of the Web service, creates a query that maps to the structure of the list, and then calls the service to retrieve the returned XML from SharePoint. This code will allow you to do the following: once you've retrieved the data via the XML payload, you can then use LINQ to query the data and map it to the internal object you created earlier.

```
...
private void btnLoadListData_Click(object sender, RoutedEventArgs e)
        {
            ListService.ListsSoapClient SPListService =
                new ListService.ListsSoapClient();
            SPListService.GetListItemsCompleted += new
                EventHandler<ListService.GetListItemsCompletedEventArgs>
                (SPListService_GetListItemsCompleted);

            string listFromSharePoint = "Product_List";
            string listViewName = null;
            XElement query = XElement.Parse(@"<Query />");
            XElement viewFields = XElement.Parse(@"<ViewFields>
                                        <FieldRef Name='Title' />
                                        <FieldRef Name='Product_SKU' />
                                        <FieldRef Name='Price' />
                                        <FieldRef Name='Inventory' />
                                    </ViewFields>");
            string rowLimit = null;
            XElement queryOptions = XElement.Parse(@"<QueryOptions/>");
            string webID = null;

            SPListService.GetListItemsAsync(listFromSharePoint, listViewName,
                query, viewFields, rowLimit, queryOptions, webID);
        }
...
```

20. You'll next want to handle the `SPListService_GetListItemsCompleted` event, which is the event that is triggered when Silverlight completes the asynchronous call to SharePoint. In this example, you create an XML document that will represent the data coming back from SharePoint and then use the LINQ query to map each row and item in the returned XML (at least the specific elements of interest) to a property in the `SPListRow` object. The last thing the following code does is to bind the items (that is, the rows) to the listbox in the Silverlight application.

```
...
        void SPListService_GetListItemsCompleted(object sender,
            ListService.GetListItemsCompletedEventArgs e)
        {
            XDocument listResults = XDocument.Parse(e.Result.ToString());

            var rows = from item in listResults.Descendants(XName.Get("row",
```

```
                 "#RowsetSchema"))
                    select new SPListRow
                    {
                        productName = (string)item.Attribute("ows_Title").Value,
                        productSKU =
                            (string)item.Attribute("ows_Product_SKU").Value,
                        productPrice = (string)item.Attribute("ows_Price").Value,
                        productInventory =
                            (string)item.Attribute("ows_Inventory").Value,
                    };

            lstbxSharePointListData.ItemsSource = rows;
        }

        ...
```

21. The last event to handle is the `lstbxSharePointListData_SelectionChanged` event. This is triggered when the user changes a selection in the listbox. You can see that, in this case, the goal is to swap the image that is loaded into the Silverlight application and also to decorate the new image with an updated product name. The following code uses a hard-coded comparison to the product names from the SharePoint list against the selected item product name, and then loads an image based on that selection:

```
        ...
        private void lstbxSharePointListData_SelectionChanged(object sender,
            SelectionChangedEventArgs e)
        {
            SPListRow tempProdInfo = new SPListRow();
            BitmapImage tempImage = new BitmapImage();
            string selectedProdInfo = "";

            tempProdInfo = (SPListRow)lstbxSharePointListData.SelectedItems[0];
            selectedProdInfo = tempProdInfo.productName;
            lblModel.Content = selectedProdInfo;

            if (selectedProdInfo == "Dell W327")
            {
                Uri tempURI = new Uri("Images/Dell_TV.png", UriKind.Relative);
                tempImage.UriSource = tempURI;
                imgProduct.Source = tempImage;
            }
            else if (selectedProdInfo == "HP Media Smart")
            {
                Uri tempURI = new Uri("Images/HP_MediaSmart.png", UriKind.Relative);
                tempImage.UriSource = tempURI;
                imgProduct.Source = tempImage;
            }
            else if (selectedProdInfo == "MS Media Center")
            {
                Uri tempURI = new Uri("Images/MSMedia.png", UriKind.Relative);
                tempImage.UriSource = tempURI;
                imgProduct.Source = tempImage;
```

```
        }
        else if (selectedProdInfo == "Gen. Flat Panel")
        {
            Uri tempURI = new Uri("Images/GenFlatPanel.png", UriKind.Relative);
            tempImage.UriSource = tempURI;
            imgProduct.Source = tempImage;
        }
        else
        {
            Uri tempURI = new Uri("Images/TV.png", UriKind.Relative);
            tempImage.UriSource = tempURI;
            imgProduct.Source = tempImage;
        }
    }
...
```

The full code behind for this application is as follows:

```
using System;
using System.Collections.Generic;
using System.Linq;
using System.Net;
using System.Windows;
using System.Windows.Controls;
using System.Windows.Documents;
using System.Windows.Input;
using System.Windows.Media;
using System.Windows.Media.Imaging;
using System.Windows.Media.Animation;
using System.Windows.Shapes;
using System.Xml;
using System.Xml.Linq;

namespace SPSilverlightApplication
{
    public partial class MainPage : UserControl
    {
        public MainPage()
        {
            InitializeComponent();
        }

        private void btnLoadListData_Click(object sender, RoutedEventArgs e)
        {
            ListService.ListsSoapClient SPListService = new
                ListService.ListsSoapClient();
            SPListService.GetListItemsCompleted += new
                EventHandler<ListService.GetListItemsCompletedEventArgs>
                (SPListService_GetListItemsCompleted);

            string listFromSharePoint = "Product_List";
            string listViewName = null;
            XElement query = XElement.Parse(@"<Query />");
```

```
        XElement viewFields = XElement.Parse(@"<ViewFields>
                                        <FieldRef Name='Title' />
                                        <FieldRef Name='Product_SKU' />
                                        <FieldRef Name='Price' />
                                        <FieldRef Name='Inventory' />
                                    </ViewFields>");
        string rowLimit = null;
        XElement queryOptions = XElement.Parse(@"<QueryOptions/>");
        string webID = null;

        SPListService.GetListItemsAsync(listFromSharePoint,
            listViewName, query, viewFields, rowLimit,
            queryOptions, webID);
    }

    void SPListService_GetListItemsCompleted(object sender,
        ListService.GetListItemsCompletedEventArgs e)
    {
        XDocument listResults = XDocument.Parse(e.Result.ToString());

        var rows = from item in listResults.Descendants(XName.Get("row",
            "#RowsetSchema"))
                    select new SPListRow
                    {
                        productName = (string)item.Attribute("ows_Title").Value,
                        productSKU =
                            (string)item.Attribute("ows_Product_SKU").Value,
                        productPrice = (string)item.Attribute("ows_Price").Value,
                        productInventory =
                            (string)item.Attribute("ows_Inventory").Value,
                    };

        lstbxSharePointListData.ItemsSource = rows;
    }

    private void lstbxSharePointListData_SelectionChanged(object sender,
        SelectionChangedEventArgs e)
    {
        SPListRow tempProdInfo = new SPListRow();
        BitmapImage tempImage = new BitmapImage();
        string selectedProdInfo = "";

        tempProdInfo = (SPListRow)lstbxSharePointListData.SelectedItems[0];
        selectedProdInfo = tempProdInfo.productName;
        lblModel.Content = selectedProdInfo;

        if (selectedProdInfo == "Dell W327")
        {
            Uri tempURI = new Uri("Images/Dell_TV.png", UriKind.Relative);
            tempImage.UriSource = tempURI;
            imgProduct.Source = tempImage;
        }
```

```
            else if (selectedProdInfo == "HP Media Smart")
            {
                Uri tempURI = new Uri("Images/HP_MediaSmart.png", UriKind.Relative);
                tempImage.UriSource = tempURI;
                imgProduct.Source = tempImage;
            }
            else if (selectedProdInfo == "MS Media Center")
            {
                Uri tempURI = new Uri("Images/MSMedia.png", UriKind.Relative);
                tempImage.UriSource = tempURI;
                imgProduct.Source = tempImage;
            }
            else if (selectedProdInfo == "Gen. Flat Panel")
            {
                Uri tempURI = new Uri("Images/GenFlatPanel.png", UriKind.Relative);
                tempImage.UriSource = tempURI;
                imgProduct.Source = tempImage;
            }
            else
            {
                Uri tempURI = new Uri("Images/TV.png", UriKind.Relative);
                tempImage.UriSource = tempURI;
                imgProduct.Source = tempImage;
            }
        }
    }
}
```

22. After you've added all of the code to the code behind, you can press F5 to test the Silverlight application. When you press F5 to debug, you may receive a warning about a Web service call. You can click Yes to move past this error.

23. However, you may find that the Web service may throw a communication exception error. This is because Silverlight is making a cross-domain call to a SharePoint Web service, but the Silverlight application has not yet been deployed into SharePoint (so it is not a trusted application). To get around this, you can either wait to test the Silverlight application until after you've created the Web part, or you can add a client access policy file in the root of your SharePoint site (for example, `c:\inetpub\wwwroot\wss\VirtualDirectories\80`). The client access policy file then enables cross-domain calls to the SharePoint domain from Silverlight. To create a client access policy file, copy the following code below into a Notepad text file, and then save this into your SharePoint site root directory with the name `clientaccesspolicy.xml`.

```xml
<?xml version="1.0" encoding="utf-8"?>
<access-policy>
  <cross-domain-access>
    <policy>
      <allow-from http-request-headers="*">
        <domain uri="*"/>
      </allow-from>
      <grant-to>
        <resource path="/" include-subpaths="true"/>
```

```
          </grant-to>
        </policy>
    </cross-domain-access>
</access-policy>
```

24. When the Silverlight application loads in your default browser, click the Load button to load the data from SharePoint. Once the data is loaded, you can then click one of the items in the listbox to update the image in the rectangle, and update the product name, which appears as a caption beneath it, as shown in Figure 9-22.

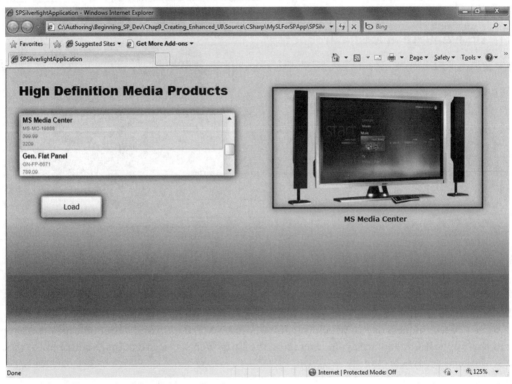

FIGURE 9-22 Testing the Silverlight application

25. At this stage, you are ready to deploy the application to SharePoint. To keep things simple, in this walkthrough, you deploy the code to SharePoint using the out-of-the-box Silverlight Web part. To do this, follow the same steps that you used earlier. That is, upload the .xap file into a SharePoint document library, and right-click the link to the file once it's uploaded. Select Copy Shortcut. Then, click Site Actions ➪ Edit Page, and click "Add a web part." Click the "Content and Media" Web part category, select Silverlight Web part, and click Add. When prompted, paste the shortcut into the URL field and click OK.

26. Your Silverlight application should now look similar to Figure 9-23.

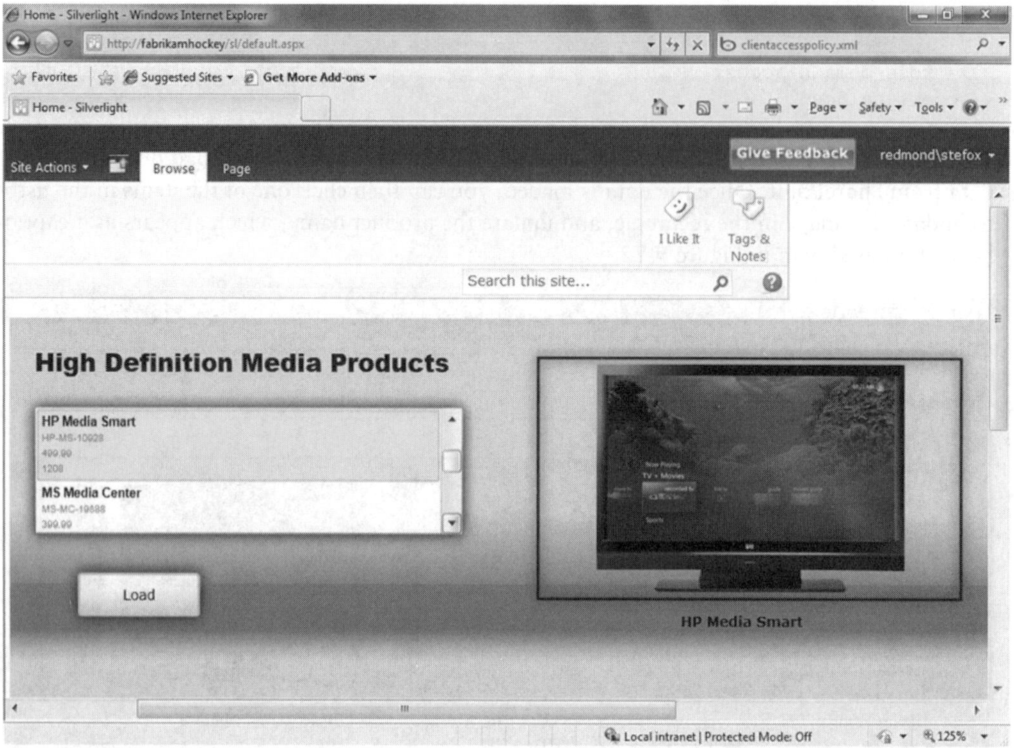

FIGURE 9-23 Silverlight application in SharePoint

How It Works

At this point, you should be seeing a trend. When you work with SharePoint, you may have to program using some key techniques, one of which is manipulating XML data from SharePoint into your application. In this application, you are again leveraging the Lists Web service to manage this, but, in this case, you use the service asynchronously.

The key calls in the application were the GetListItemsAsync method and the SPListService_ GetListItemsCompleted method. The Async event handles the calling of the service once the service instance has been created. The Completed event processes what needs to be done after the Async has successfully called. How this breaks down across the two calls is that the Async retrieves data, and the Completed event processes and binds that data to the listbox.

These calls make this Silverlight integration a high-touch classification because the application is tied to the object model in some way. What is not as deeply tied to SharePoint is the way in which the application is deployed — that is, you could deploy the Silverlight application as a Web part project, and then it becomes a much more deeply integrated part of the SharePoint infrastructure.

Note that you don't always have to manage XML when integrating Silverlight and SharePoint. One of the new features in SharePoint 2010 is the client object model, which you can use to interact with data from a SharePoint list, and then data-bind the resulting list data to a Silverlight control. You saw this in

Chapter 5, where you created a .NET application that used the client-side object model. If you do use Silverlight, your code may be cleaner.

For example, the following bolded code shows the syntax of a call from a Silverlight application that, similarly to the Lists service, would query a specific list and return that data for use in the Silverlight client application. Note the use of the ClientContext object here, which loads a specific site and list and then gets the items within the list by calling the GetByTitle method.

```
...

using Microsoft.SharePoint.Client;
using ClientOM = Microsoft.SharePoint.Client;

namespace OMSilverlightApplication
{
    public partial class Page : UserControl
    {
        ClientOM.List mySPList;

        public Page()
        {
            InitializeComponent();

            ClientContext context =
new ClientContext("http://fabrikamhockey/");
            context.Load(context.Web);
context.Load(context.Web.Lists);
mySPList = context.Web.Lists.GetByTitle("Product_List");
            context.ExecuteQueryAsync(succeededCallback, failedCallback);
        }

        void succeededCallback(object sender, ClientRequestSucceededEventArgs args)
        {
            //Bind data in list to Silverlight control

        }

        void failedCallback(object sender, ClientRequestFailedEventArgs args)
        {
            //Throw error.

        }
    }
}

...
```

This code creates a new connection (or context) with SharePoint, which allows you to set properties and call methods on that context. You then call the ExecuteQueryAsync method in Silverlight applications (and ExecuteQuery for synchronous applications), which then runs one of two different streams of code, depending on whether the callback was successful or the callback failed. In this specific example, the query will get the specific list called Product_List, which you can then, for example, bind to a listbox or other Silverlight control.

Deploying Silverlight Applications to SharePoint as Integrated Web Parts

As mentioned earlier, there may be cases where you want to deploy the Silverlight application as an object that is deployed as a component of a WSP to SharePoint. This way, you can more easily debug and test your integrations, or you can build more complex Silverlight applications. There are a couple of ways that this can be done.

If you remember back to Chapter 3, you were introduced to a small snippet of code that leveraged JavaScript as a way to inject a Silverlight application into a master page. As a refresher, here is the code:

```
<div id="slApp" />
<script language="JavaScript" type="text/javascript">
var slDIV = document.getElementById('slApp');
slSPDIV.appendChild(slSPDIV);
slSPDIV.innerHTML = '<object data="data:application/x-silverlight,
    " type="application/x-silverlight" width="800" height="400">
    <param name="source"
    value="http://fabrikamhockey/sl/XAPS/SPSilverlightApplication.xap"/>
    </object>';
</script>
```

In this code, you can see that you create an HTML `<div>` element that is then used in combination with JavaScript to set the properties and create an HTML `<object>` that hosts the Silverlight application when the page loads. You can use this code by embedding the script in a Visual Studio 2010 Web part (as a `LiteralControl` object), which then is deployed to SharePoint as a feature.

Let's take a look at an example of deploying a Silverlight application as a Web part.

TRY IT OUT   Deploying a Silverlight Application as a Web Part

Code file [MySLForSPApp.zip] available for download at Wrox.com.

A great way to have more control and flexibility (especially if you want to build more complex Web parts using Silverlight and other integrated SharePoint objects) is to deploy the Silverlight application as a Web part. To do this, follow these steps:

1. Open the Visual Studio solution from the previous exercise (for example, `SPSilverlightApplication`). Right-click on the solution and select Add ➪ New ➪ Project. Select the Empty SharePoint Project under the SharePoint 2010 node.

2. When prompted by the wizard, select "Deploy as farm solution" and ensure that your project is being built against the correct SharePoint site. Click Finish.

3. Provide a name for the project (for example, `SLWebPartProject`), and click OK. When managing your projects through one solution, you can create a dependency across the projects, so, when the Web part project builds and deploys, it does so with the latest Silverlight changes. To do this, right-click the new project and select Project Dependencies. Check the Silverlight project name to create a dependency between the Web part project and the Silverlight project.

4. After the project is created, right-click the project and select Add New Item.

5. Navigate to the SharePoint 2010 node and select Web Part.

6. Provide a name for the Web part (for example, SLWebPart), and click OK.

7. In the SLWebPart.cs file, add the following bolded code in the CreateChildControls method. Note that you need to ensure that the value property of the object points to a valid URL for your Silverlight application. (This code writes the script required to add the Silverlight application to the Web page through the use of the LiteralControl object.)

```
using System;
using System.ComponentModel;
using System.Runtime.InteropServices;
using System.Web.UI;
using System.Web.UI.WebControls;
using System.Web.UI.WebControls.WebParts;
using Microsoft.SharePoint;
using Microsoft.SharePoint.WebControls;

namespace SLWebPartProject.SLWebPart
{
    [ToolboxItemAttribute(false)]
    public class SLWebPart : WebPart
    {
        public SLWebPart()
        {
        }

        protected override void CreateChildControls()
        {
            string slStreamCode = "<div id=\"slApp\"/>" +
                    "<script language=\"JavaScript\" type=\"text/javascript\">" +
                    "var slSPDIV = document.getElementById('slApp');" +
                    "slSPDIV.appendChild(slSPDIV);" +
                    "slSPDIV.innerHTML =" +
                    "'<object data=\"data:application/x-silverlight,\" +
                        type=\"application/x-silverlight\" width=\"800\" +
                        height=\"400\"><param name=\"source\ +
                        " value=\"http://fabrikamhockey/sl/XAPS/ +
                        SPSilverlightApplication.xap\"/></object>';" +
                    "</script>";

            this.Controls.Add(new LiteralControl(slStreamCode));

            base.CreateChildControls();
        }

    }
}
```

Note that you can also use an HtmlTextWriter object and the Render method to write this script to the Web page. Following is what this code would look like:

```
protected override void Render(HtmlTextWriter slAppOutput)
{
        slAppOutput.Write("<div id=\"slApp\"/>");
```

```
            slAppOutput.Write("<script language=\"JavaScript\" type=\"text/
javascript\">");
            slAppOutput.Write("var slSPDIV = document.getElementById('slApp');");
            slAppOutput.Write("slSPDIV.appendChild(slSPDIV);");
            slAppOutput.Write("slSPDIV.innerHTML =");
            slAppOutput.Write("'<object data=\"data:application/x-silverlight,\"
type=\"application/x-silverlight\" width=\"800\" height=\"400\"><param name=\"source\"
value=\"http://intranet.contoso.com/XAPS/LowIntegrationSLApp.xap\"/></object>';");
            slAppOutput.Write("</script>");
        }
```

8. Click Build ➪ Deploy Solution. The SharePoint Web part project will build and then be deployed to your SharePoint site.

9. Now you can open SharePoint and navigate to your test site.

10. Click Site Actions ➪ Edit Page, and then click "Add a web part."

11. Select the Custom category, and then select the Web part you deployed (for example, `SLWebPart`), and click Add.

Your Silverlight application will look similar to the way it looked when you used the out-of-the-box Silverlight Web part. However, in this case, the Web part is deployed as an artifact (that is, a feature) of SharePoint.

How It Works

The Silverlight application code didn't change in this walkthrough. What did change was how the Silverlight application was deployed. Because you created a Web part project and deployed that with the code to write the script within the `LiteralControl`, when the Web part renders in SharePoint, it displays the Silverlight application.

Admittedly, the coding for this is not as elegant as, say, creating an instance of the Silverlight control method that was possible in Silverlight 2. And, if you do prefer this method, you can still use it. You just need to deploy the Silverlight 2 SDK alongside your most recent version of Silverlight so that you have the proper DLL in your global assembly cache (GAC). (The earlier version of Silverlight deploys the `System.Web.Silverlight.dll` to your GAC, which can be used to create a control in your Web part project, as opposed to writing script through a `LiteralControl`.)

The difference in the code just described, as opposed to that created by using the Silverlight control method, is shown in boldfaced code in the following example:

```
...
protected override void OnLoad(EventArgs e)
{
base.OnLoad(e);
ScriptManager sm = ScriptManager.GetCurrent(this.Page);
if (sm == null)
{
sm = new ScriptManager();
Controls.AddAt(0, sm);
}
}
```

```
protected override void CreateChildControls()
{
base.CreateChildControls();
System.Web.UI.SilverlightControls.Silverlight ctrl = new
     System.Web.UI.SilverlightControls.Silverlight();
ctrl.ID = "InsertSPListItem";
ctrl.Source = "http://fabrikamhockey/sl/XAPS/SPSilverlightApplication.xap";
ctrl.Width = new Unit(800);
ctrl.Height = new Unit(400);
Controls.Add(ctrl);
}
...
```

SUMMARY

This chapter provided an overview of how you can integrate Silverlight and SharePoint. It started out with a high-level discussion of Silverlight, explored the merits of integrating the two technologies, and then walked through three different classifications of how you could integrate Silverlight and SharePoint.

This is an area where you, as a developer, should pay special attention. If you look at the SharePoint 2010 release, the support for Silverlight out of the box opens up the opportunity to get started quickly with this integration. Furthermore, if you look at the set of features built into SharePoint that are Silverlight-enabled, you might speculate about the growing interest (from a product perspective) in having Silverlight more deeply baked within SharePoint. Beyond this speculation, though, there are a ton of great opportunities — ranging from the small widget to the more complex business application — that will pave the way for these two technologies to continue to converge and mature together.

Silverlight and SharePoint get very powerful when you begin to introduce Web services. Chapter 10 examines Web services in greater detail, and, specifically, you'll see coverage of ASP.NET Web services, WCF services, and REST.

EXERCISES

1. Describe the types of applications that you could build with Silverlight.

2. Describe why integrating Silverlight and SharePoint could be good. Are there cases where it may not make sense?

3. What are the different ways in which you can integrate Silverlight and SharePoint?

4. When would it make sense to deploy a Silverlight application using the Visual Studio 2010 templates?

▶ **WHAT YOU LEARNED IN THIS CHAPTER**

ITEM	DESCRIPTION
Silverlight	Microsoft's technology that enables you to build Rich Internet Applications (RIAs) that can now run in or out of a browser.
No-Touch Integration	Classification of Silverlight and SharePoint integration where the Silverlight application is integrated through `<iframe>` code (or a similar type of mark-up integration).
Low-Touch Integration	Classification of Silverlight and SharePoint integration where the Silverlight application is hosted in SharePoint but has self-contained functionality.
High-Touch Integration	Classification of Silverlight and SharePoint integration where the Silverlight application is interacting with the SharePoint object model.

RECOMMENDED READING

➤ Silverlight home page at `http://Silverlight.net`.

➤ Silverlight on Azure Quick Start Guide at `http://silverlight.live.com/quickstart.htm`

➤ *Professional SharePoint 2007 Developing Using Silverlight 2* (Indianapolis: Wiley, 2009)

➤ Silverlight team blog at `http://team.silverlight.net/`

➤ Tim Heuer's blog at `http://timheuer.com/blog/`

➤ Paul Stubbs' blog at `http://blogs.msdn.com/pstubbs`

10

Developing Service-Oriented Applications for SharePoint 2010

WHAT YOU'LL LEARN IN THIS CHAPTER:

➤ Using Web services that are native to SharePoint

➤ Building custom Web services, including ASP.NET, WCF, REST, and Azure services

➤ Implementing custom Web services using different client solutions in SharePoint 2010

One of the key innovations in the software industry over the past few years has been the growing use of Web services to integrate systems. One of the key undercurrents of this book is that SharePoint 2010 is a platform, and, since it is a platform, it is imperative that you be able to interoperate with Web services.

This chapter is not the first time you're seeing the use of services. For example, in Chapter 5, you saw how to use Web services to interact with a SharePoint list, and, in Chapter 8, you saw BCS solutions that leveraged Web services. However, this chapter is a concerted look at both native and custom Web services, and how you can develop custom solutions that integrate with SharePoint.

Web services enable you to develop applications that can expose or reach out to systems or application programming interfaces (APIs) mediated either by a network or by the Internet. One of the primary benefits of Web services is that they can bridge heterogeneous systems — those systems that, without these services, might exist in isolation. The Web services can be restricted to an enterprise network (for example, multiple applications accessing an Expenses Web service to submit expenses to a common remote SAP system), or you can leverage Web services that can bridge systems across the Internet (for example, accessing stock Web services or weather services).

In Web service parlance, you typically have a *client* and a *server* when consuming a service. The server is where the Web service is built and deployed to (for example, Windows Server 2008 R2). The client is the application that consumes the exposed Web service. (A typical client application within SharePoint could be a Silverlight application or Web part.) It is also very common for Windows, Windows Presentation Foundation (WPF), or even Microsoft Office applications to leverage Web services to interact with SharePoint.

Within this architecture, you will also require something that hosts the Web service, such as Internet Information Services (IIS). In Figure 10-1, note that the client can leverage a number of different service proxies/connections in SharePoint 2010 and subsequently integrate with different types of systems or applications (such as enterprise services, Web 2.0 social services, and even custom Azure services).

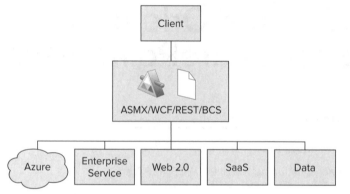

FIGURE 10-1 Service architecture

Web services communicate across the client and the server in a couple of different ways. Using the Hypertext Transfer Protocol (HTTP), you can build services using the Simple Object Access Protocol (SOAP) and Web Services Description Language (WSDL) standards — you'll find that these are the standards that the native SharePoint Web services use. Characteristic of SOAP standards is the passing of XML messages from client to server — for example, a Web service will send back a data packet that is well-formed XML as a return data object.

Beyond Web services that use SOAP, you can also build Representational State Transfer (REST) Web services. RESTful Web services are "lightweight" services (or, more accurately, protocols) that enable you to GET, PUT, POST, or DELETE using HTTP methods. RESTful services do not require the WSDL service-level definitions and often integrate much better into the Web browser experience.

In SharePoint 2007, there were a number of constraints when it came to building Web services. Many of these constraints go away in SharePoint 2010. For example, Windows Communication Foundation (WCF) — a newer type of Web service that was introduced in .NET 3.0 — is supported natively, as is REST. Furthermore, you also get the capability to build and deploy custom ASP.NET services to SharePoint, or leverage the native ASP.NET Web services that ship with SharePoint. You can very easily integrate custom services into SharePoint as well. What this means for developers is that you have an abundance of options when developing service-based applications.

While this chapter does not provide a comprehensive backdrop regarding the history and evolution of Web services, it does arm you with a fundamental treatment of Web services as they are supported in SharePoint 2010. With this in mind, this chapter covers four major areas:

➤ *ASP.NET Web services* — Ironically, many developers consider these services legacy. But you'll find a wealth of native ASP.NET services in SharePoint 2010, and building ASP.NET Web services is a straightforward proposition.

➤ *RESTful services* — You saw these in Chapter 5, but you'll see them in a different light in this chapter (programming against Excel on the server).

➤ *Windows Communication Foundation (WCF)* — Lately, this has been a more common way to build and deploy Web services, given the tighter control that developers have over many elements of the service development and deployment process (for example, security and binding).

➤ *Cloud computing* — SharePoint 2010 is aligned with the cloud computing evolution (given SharePoint Online and its capability to host custom code through sandboxed solutions); thus, you'll see a new cloud platform, called Azure, discussed in the context of SharePoint 2010.

ASP.NET WEB SERVICES

ASP.NET Web services are native to SharePoint 2010. A number of useful services ship out of the box (native), and you can very easily build and deploy ASP.NET Web services either into the SharePoint root, or to IIS. In this section, you'll see coverage of both the native Web services and custom Web services — and how you can leverage both to build your solutions for SharePoint 2010.

As discussed earlier, one of the core characteristics of ASP.NET Web services is the use of the SOAP and WSDL standards. For SharePoint, this means that when you call an ASP.NET Web service, the data package (or *payload*) will be passed across the service using these standards. The XML structure is accessible through a couple of ways.

The first is through the use of Collaborative Application Markup Language (CAML), with which you can issue queries against a service call to, for example, a SharePoint list. You saw this in Chapter 5.

Another way to interact with the data occurs when extracting the data from the XML payload. You use XLinq structures (for example, the XDocument object) to get the data into a format you can query. Because data programmability is now both strongly and loosely typed in SharePoint, you can manage queries against the data using the XDocument object, or you can use Language Integrated Query (LINQ) queries to query and manage the data.

Beyond XML payloads, the WCF Data Services enable you to treat SharePoint data as strongly typed objects. You also saw this in Chapter 5 where REST was used to view and update list data.

> **NOTE** *Another pattern you've seen in this book is the use of custom objects (for example, classes) and the use of* List *collections, which are* IEnumerable *objects that allow you to query and easily bind your resulting queries to controls such as datagrids and listboxes.*

There are many different types of Web services that are native to SharePoint 2010. These services cut across supporting `List` interaction, authentication, Excel Services, meetings management, and so on. To review the full set of services that ship with SharePoint, navigate to `c:\Program Files\Common Files\Microsoft Shared\Web Server Extensions\14\ISAPI`. All of the ASP.NET Web services end with the `.asmx` file extension. You can also open each of these services in the browser by typing **http://<server name>/_vti_bin/<Web Service Name>.asmx** and then browse the different Web methods that each service offers.

> **NOTE** *To get more information on SharePoint 2010 class libraries and Web services, go to* `http://msdn.microsoft.com/en-us/library/ee556847(office.14).aspx.`

Let's first take a look at a native Web service example and then move on to discussing custom ASP.NET Web services.

Native Web Service

As mentioned earlier, there are many different ASP.NET Web services available for you to use when building your SharePoint solutions. There are also a number of amendments to the Web services in SharePoint 2010. Those who are returning to SharePoint 2010 development from SharePoint 2007 may need to test some of the code they built with the SharePoint 2007 Web services to ensure there is no broken code. For the most part, though, you should find a relatively seamless upgrade path from 2007 to 2010.

There are two types of services in SharePoint. The first enables you to access administrative capabilities. A set of non-administrative services is also available. To access the SharePoint Web services, you use the following URL syntax: `http://<site>/_vti_bin/<Web Service Name>.asmx` (for example, `http://intranet.contoso.com/_vti_bin/socialdataservice.asmx`). Note that if you're accessing administrative services, you will need to add the port number, because you would not be accessing the default port 80 (for example, `http://intranet.contoso.com:8080/_vti_bin/diagnostics.asmx`).

There are many new service capabilities that are built into SharePoint 2010. These capabilities range from new administrative services such as `Diagnostics` (a service for managing client reports) to more social-centric services such as `SocialDataService` (a service to manage social features).

Although there are many more services that you can leverage within SharePoint 2010, let's walk through one example to show you how you can use a service to build a service-oriented solution for SharePoint using the `SocialDataService` Web service (that is, `http://<server>/_vti_bin/socialdataservice.asmx`). As a part of the growing support for more social-centric applications, this Web service enables you to work with social metadata such as tags and terms, and insert comments, among other activities centrical to building social applications.

> **NOTE** For more information on the Web services available in SharePoint 2010, see the MSDN technical guidance at http://msdn.microsoft.com/en-us/library/ee556847(office.14).aspx.

Before you walk through the following example, create three different wiki sites in your SharePoint site collection, and then rate each of the sites using the wiki Rating feature. You'll need the URLs of these three wiki sites for this walkthrough.

TRY IT OUT **Leveraging the Social Data Web Service**

Code file [SocialRatingWebPart.zip] available for download at Wrox.com.

The Social Data Web Service provides rich access to a number of key social APIs in SharePoint. To use the service in an application, follow these steps:

1. Open Visual Studio 2010 and click File ➪ New ➪ Project.

2. Select Empty SharePoint Project. Provide a name for your application (for example, `SocialRatingWebPart`), and then click OK. When prompted, select "Deploy as farm solution" and click Finish.

3. When Visual Studio creates the project, right-click the project and select Add ➪ New Item. In the SharePoint 2010 project node, select Visual Web Part. Provide a name for the Web part (for example, `SocialRatingData`) and click Add.

4. Right-click the `.ascx` file and select View Designer. Click the Source tab, and then add the following bolded code below to the `ascx` code behind:

```
<%@ Assembly Name="$SharePoint.Project.AssemblyFullName$" %>
<%@ Assembly Name="Microsoft.Web.CommandUI, Version=14.0.0.0, Culture=neutral,
    PublicKeyToken=71e9bce111e9429c" %>
<%@ Register Tagprefix="SharePoint" Namespace="Microsoft.SharePoint.WebControls"
    Assembly="Microsoft.SharePoint, Version=14.0.0.0, Culture=neutral,
    PublicKeyToken=71e9bce111e9429c" %>
<%@ Register Tagprefix="Utilities" Namespace="Microsoft.SharePoint.Utilities"
    Assembly="Microsoft.SharePoint, Version=14.0.0.0, Culture=neutral,
    PublicKeyToken=71e9bce111e9429c" %>
<%@ Register Tagprefix="asp" Namespace="System.Web.UI" Assembly=
    "System.Web.Extensions, Version=3.5.0.0, Culture=neutral,
    PublicKeyToken=31bf3856ad364e35" %>
<%@ Import Namespace="Microsoft.SharePoint" %>
<%@ Register Tagprefix="WebPartPages" Namespace="Microsoft.SharePoint.WebPartPages"
    Assembly="Microsoft.SharePoint, Version=14.0.0.0, Culture=neutral,
    PublicKeyToken=71e9bce111e9429c" %>
<%@ Control Language="C#" AutoEventWireup="true"
    CodeBehind="SocialRatingDataUserControl.ascx.cs" Inherits=
```

```
"SocialRatingWebPart.SocialRatingData.SocialRatingDataUserControl" %>

<asp:UpdatePanel ID="RatingUpdatePanel" runat="server">
<ContentTemplate>
<asp:Label ID="lblSocialRatingTitle" runat="server" Font-Bold="True"
    ForeColor="#000066" Text="Wiki Rating Data"></asp:Label>
<table>
<tr>
<td><asp:Label ID="lblRatingDataList" runat="server" ForeColor="#000066"
        Text="Rating Data"></asp:Label></td>
<td><asp:ListBox ID="lstbxRatingData" runat="server" Width="172px"></asp:ListBox>
</td></tr><tr><td>
    <asp:Label ID="lblRating" ForeColor="#000066"  runat="server"
        Text="Avg. Rating:"></asp:Label>
</td><td>
    <asp:Label ID="lblData" ForeColor="#000066"  runat="server"
        Text="Data"></asp:Label>
</td></tr></table><table><tr>
<td><asp:Button ID="btnRefresh" runat="server" Text="Refresh"
    ToolTip="Click to refresh." onclick="btnRefresh_Click" /></td>
<td></td></tr></table>
</ContentTemplate>
</asp:UpdatePanel>
```

5. Right-click the References node and select Add Service Reference.

6. Click the Advanced button, and then click the Add Web Reference button. Enter the following URL into the URL field (making sure you replace the server name with your SharePoint server, such as `http://fabrikamhockey/_vti_bin/socialdataservice.asmx`):

    http://<server name>/_vti_bin/socialdataservice.asmx.

7. Click the Design tab to switch into the Designer view and then double-click the `btnRefresh` button.

8. When the code behind opens, add the following bolded code to the code behind:

```
using System;
using System.Web.UI;
using System.Web.UI.WebControls;
using System.Web.UI.WebControls.WebParts;
using SocialRatingWebPart.SocialWS;

namespace SocialRatingWebPart.SocialRatingData
{
    public partial class SocialRatingDataUserControl : UserControl
    {
        protected void Page_Load(object sender, EventArgs e)
        {
        }

        protected void btnRefresh_Click(object sender, EventArgs e)
        {
            // Add the URLs for your three wiki sites here.
            string ratingonConfURL = "http://intranet.contoso.com/conf/
                Pages/Home.aspx";
```

```
            string ratingonProjURL = "http://intranet.contoso.com/projects/
                Pages/Home.aspx";
            string ratingonPlansURL = "http://intranet.contoso.com/plans/
                Pages/Home.aspx";

            SocialDataService mySocialDataService = new SocialDataService();
            mySocialDataService.Credentials =
                System.Net.CredentialCache.DefaultCredentials;
            mySocialDataService.Url = "http://intranet.contoso.com/
                _vti_bin/socialdataservice.asmx";

            SocialRatingDetail confWikiRating =
                mySocialDataService.GetRatingOnUrl(ratingonConfURL);
            SocialRatingDetail projWikiRating =
                mySocialDataService.GetRatingOnUrl(ratingonProjURL);
            SocialRatingDetail plansWikiRating =
                mySocialDataService.GetRatingOnUrl(ratingonPlansURL);

            addRatingsToWebPart(confWikiRating.Rating,
                projWikiRating.Rating, plansWikiRating.Rating);

            mySocialDataService.Dispose();

        }

        private void addRatingsToWebPart(int confRate, int projRate, int plansRate)
        {
            int avgRating = 0;
            string confWiki = "Conference Wiki: " + confRate.ToString();
            string projWiki = "Project Wiki: " + projRate.ToString();
            string plansWiki = "Plans Wiki: " + plansRate.ToString();

            avgRating = (confRate + projRate + plansRate) / 3;

            string avgRatingForWikis = "Average Rating: " + avgRating.ToString();

            lstbxRatingData.Items.Add(confWiki);
            lstbxRatingData.Items.Add(projWiki);
            lstbxRatingData.Items.Add(plansWiki);
            lstbxRatingData.Items.Add(avgRatingForWikis);

            lblData.Text = avgRating.ToString();
        }
    }
}
```

9. Amend the .webpart file to have a more intuitive title and description, such as shown here:

```
    …
        <properties>
          <property name="Title" type="string">Wiki Rating Web Part</property>
          <property name="Description" type="string">Web Part that displays
              wiki rating data.</property>
        </properties>
    …
```

10. Press F6 to build the project. When the project successfully builds, click Build ⇨ Deploy Solution to deploy the new Visual Web part to SharePoint.

11. Navigate to your SharePoint site. Create a new Web part page and then click "Add a new web part."

12. In the Custom category, select your newly created Web part and click Add. When the Web part is added to the page, click the Refresh button. You should see the social data service load information into the Web part, as shown in Figure 10-2.

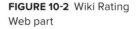

FIGURE 10-2 Wiki Rating Web part

How It Works

The Social Data Web service provides a set of Web methods to interact with SharePoint social data. Note that your first step in using the Web service was creating a proxy, and then you set the credentials and endpoint for the service proxy. In this example, you used the `GetRatingOnURL` method to extract the ratings you'd given your three wiki sites by passing the string URL in with the method call.

```
SocialRatingDetail confWikiRating = mySocialDataService.
    GetRatingOnUrl(ratingonConfURL);
        SocialRatingDetail projWikiRating = mySocialDataService.
    GetRatingOnUrl(ratingonProjURL);
        SocialRatingDetail plansWikiRating = mySocialDataService.
            GetRatingOnUrl(ratingonPlansURL);
```

You also created a helper function to calculate the average ratings for the three different wikis, and passed it the `Rating` property, which is the property that is returned from the call to the `GetratingOnURL` method. Note that you recast the `Rating` properties into integer values before you calculated the average. After you calculated the average rating using the three, you added the information to a listbox (`lstbxRatingData`) and set the `Text` property of a label (`lblData`) so that it would contain the rating.

Custom ASP.NET Services

As a general practice, just as you should generally use the server-side object model for server-side applications, you should equally leverage the services that ship with SharePoint 2010 when designing service-based applications for SharePoint. This is because you don't want to re-create the wheel, so to speak, and it's much easier for you to use the services that SharePoint natively understands. However, there may be times when you want to create your own custom ASP.NET service. For example, you may want to integrate Enterprise Resource Planning (ERP) data from disparate systems, or you may need to create a connection to a legacy data in SQL. The end goal, therefore, would be to surface this data in SharePoint. This is also very possible. Let's take a look at an example.

The example you'll build is a custom Web service that will retrieve data from a SQL database. It will be a straightforward Web service that will illustrate how you can build a custom ASP.NET Web service and then deploy it to IIS. However, what you'll do in this example is also leverage the Business Connectivity Services (BCS), one of the core new capabilities built into SharePoint 2010. You learned about this in Chapter 8. However, in this example, you'll use the BDC Metadata project template in Visual Studio 2010 to call the service.

TRY IT OUT | Integrating a Custom ASP.NET Service with BCS

Code file [SalesBDCModel.zip] available for download at Wrox.com.

The BDC Metadata model is a great way to model external data and create an external list using the new BCS in SharePoint 2010. The process of creating a model is equally compelling when you use a Web service to integrate external data from SharePoint into the external list. To create an external list using a custom Web service, follow these steps:

1. Create a new SQL Server database called `Sales`. To do this, open SQL Server 2008 (or 2005), and right-click the Database node. Select New Database. In design view, create five columns, as shown in Figure 10-3.

2. After you've finished creating the database, save it with the name `Sales`, and then add some sample data to the table, as shown in Figure 10-4.

Column Name	Data Type	Allow Nulls
CompanyID	int	☐
CompanyName	nvarchar(50)	☑
FY08Sales	int	☑
FY09Sales	int	☑
FY10Sales	int	☑

FIGURE 10-3 Creating data in SQL Server

CompanyID	CompanyName	FY08Sales	FY09Sales	FY10Sales
1	Acme	9820901	9792091	9980981
2	Wingtip	10293091	11209301	12238920
3	Fabrikam	2981009	2887290	2789098
4	Blue Yonder	50948903	51888219	52398012

FIGURE 10-4 Sales data

3. With the database complete, open Visual Studio 2010 and select File ⇨ New. Select the Web category. Within the Web category, select ASP.NET Web Service. Provide a name for your service, and then click OK.

4. Click Data ⇨ New Data Source. In the Data options, select Data Model and click OK.

5. In the Data Connection Wizard, select New Connection.

6. When prompted in the Data Connection Wizard, provide your server name information, and then click the `Sales` database you just created. Select the table you created in the wizard, and then click Finish.

7. Visual Studio adds the new entity data model from your database to the solution, which you can then use in your service.

8. Before you start working with the service code, you'll need a custom object. To add this, right-click the project and select Add ⇨ Class. Call the new class `SalesObject`, and then add the following bolded code to the newly added class. Note that, because you allowed nulls in your database, you need to add a ? when declaring each of the class variables.

```
using System;
using System.Collections.Generic;
using System.Linq;
using System.Web;

namespace MySalesService
{
    public class SalesObject
```

```
        {
            public int companyID { get; set; }
            public string companyName { get; set; }
            public int? fy08Sales { get; set; }
            public int? fy09Sales { get; set; }
            public int? fy10Sales { get; set; }
        }
    }
```

9. Right-click the `Service.cs` file and select View Code. Replace the existing `Hello World` service code with the following bolded code in the `Service.cs` file. This will be the core code that will execute when your service is called.

```csharp
using System;
using System.Collections.Generic;
using System.Linq;
using System.Web;
using System.Web.Services;

namespace MySalesService
{
    [WebService(Namespace = "http://tempuri.org/")]
    [WebServiceBinding(ConformsTo = WsiProfiles.BasicProfile1_1)]
    [System.ComponentModel.ToolboxItem(false)]

    public class Service1 : System.Web.Services.WebService
    {
        SalesEntities mySalesData = new SalesEntities();
        List<SalesObject> mySalesList = new List<SalesObject>();

        [WebMethod]
        public List<SalesObject> getAllSalesData()
        {
            var returnSalesData = (from sales in mySalesData.Sales_Data
                                   select sales).ToArray();

            foreach (var s in returnSalesData)
            {
                SalesObject tempSales = new SalesObject();
                tempSales.companyID = s.CompanyID;
                tempSales.companyName = s.CompanyName.ToString();
                tempSales.fy08Sales = s.FY08Sales;
                tempSales.fy09Sales = s.FY09Sales;
                tempSales.fy10Sales = s.FY10Sales;
                mySalesList.Add(tempSales);
            };

            return mySalesList;
        }

        [WebMethod]
        public string[] getSpecificSale(int companyID)
        {
```

```
            string[] mySalesInfo = new string[5];

            var returnSpecificSalesItem = (from sales in mySalesData.Sales_Data
                            .Where(x => x.CompanyID == companyID)
                                select sales);

            foreach (var s in returnSpecificSalesItem)
            {
                mySalesInfo[0] = s.CompanyID.ToString();
                mySalesInfo[1] = s.CompanyName.ToString();
                mySalesInfo[2] = s.FY08Sales.ToString();
                mySalesInfo[3] = s.FY09Sales.ToString();
                mySalesInfo[4] = s.FY10Sales.ToString();
            }

            return mySalesInfo;
        }
    }
}
```

10. At this point, you can press F5 to test the service code.

11. You should now be able to click each of the Web methods in your new service to execute the code, as shown in Figure 10-5. The code will retrieve all of the items (getAllSalesItems), or get one item if you enter an ID (getSpecificSale). Test both of the methods to ensure that they work.

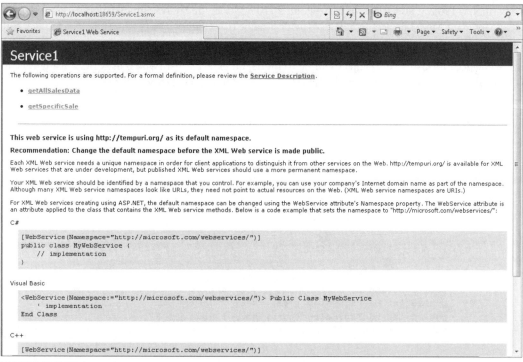

FIGURE 10-5 Web service page

12. You'll now want to deploy the service. To do this, create a new folder on your local drive using a name you'll remember (for example, `SalesService`). Then, right-click the Web service project and select Publish. Select the Local File System option, navigate to the newly created folder, and then click Publish. You are now ready to create a new Web site in IIS, which will use the published Web service to this folder.

13. Open IIS and navigate to the `Sites` folder. Right-click the `Sites` node and select New Web Site. Provide a name for the site (for example, `SPWebService`). Navigate to the new folder you created in Step 12 to map a virtual directory to the new Web site.

14. To test the service, use a local account. To do this, click Connections ➪ Use Custom Account. Provide a local system account that has system-wide access to the machine and SQL Server (for example, `administrator`). Click Test Connection to ensure that you are successfully authenticated when calling the service. (Note that when you deploy the service, you would use another type of account set up by your administrator that enables applications or users to call this service within a specific security protocol.)

15. When you've configured the security, click the Content tab. Then right-click the `Service1.asmx` file and select Browse. You should see the same service definition page as you did when you tested your service from within Visual Studio. However, the URL may be different. This is the URL you will use when implementing the service. Test the service Web methods to ensure that they work properly.

16. Now that you've created, tested, and deployed your Web service to IIS, you are ready to consume the custom ASP.NET Web service in a SharePoint application. To do this, open Visual Studio, click File ➪ New Project, and select the SharePoint 2010 node. In the SharePoint 2010 node, select the BDC Metadata Model project template. Provide a name (for example, `SalesBDCModel`), and click OK.

17. Visual Studio will create a new project for you with a number of default objects in the solution. The goal for using this project will be to model an external list (which uses BCS) using the custom Web service and then deploy the service to SharePoint as an external list.

18. Right-click the `Entity1.cs` file, and select View Code. Using the following bolded code, amend the `Entity1` class to map to the data structure from your database:

```
using System;
using System.Collections.Generic;
using System.Linq;
using System.Text;

namespace SalesBDCModel.BdcModel1
{

    public partial class Entity1
    {
        public int Identifier1 { get; set; }
        public string bdcCompanyName { get; set; }
        public int bdcFY08Sales { get; set; }
        public int bdcFY09Sales { get; set; }
        public int bdcFY10Sales { get; set; }
    }
}
```

19. When you are finished, you'll need to amend the code `Entity1Service` code, which executes the methods for your external list. For example, the `ReadItem` method uses the `id` parameter to load a specific list item, and the `ReadList` method loads all of the list items. The goal, though, is for you to load a specific item or list of items using the custom ASP.NET service. Amend the `Entity1Service.cs` file using the following bolded code:

```
using System;
using System.Collections.Generic;
using System.Linq;
using System.Text;
using SalesBDCModel.SPSalesWebService;

namespace SalesBDCModel.BdcModel1
{
    public class Entity1Service
    {
        public static Entity1 ReadItem(int id)
        {
            SPSalesWebService.Service1 myWSProxy = new Service1();
            string[] returnedData = new string[5];
            returnedData = myWSProxy.getSpecificSale(id).ToArray();

            Entity1 entity1 = new Entity1();

            entity1.Identifier1 = id;
            entity1.bdcCompanyName = returnedData[1];
            entity1.bdcFY08Sales = Int32.Parse(returnedData[2]);
            entity1.bdcFY09Sales = Int32.Parse(returnedData[3]);
            entity1.bdcFY10Sales = Int32.Parse(returnedData[4]);

            myWSProxy.Dispose();

            return entity1;

        }

        public static List<Entity1> ReadList()
        {
            List<Entity1> mySalesInfoList = new List<Entity1>();
            SPSalesWebService.Service1 myWSProxy = new Service1();
            var salesData = myWSProxy.getAllSalesData();

            foreach (var item in salesData)
            {
                Entity1 tempEntity = new Entity1();
                tempEntity.Identifier1 = item.companyID;
                tempEntity.bdcCompanyName = item.companyName.ToString();
                tempEntity.bdcFY08Sales = item.fy08Sales;
                tempEntity.bdcFY09Sales = item.fy09Sales;
                tempEntity.bdcFY10Sales = item.fy10Sales;
                mySalesInfoList.Add(tempEntity);
            }

            myWSProxy.Dispose();

            return mySalesInfoList;
```

```
            }
        }
    }
```

20. The final step in this custom solution is to ensure that the BDC model (the `.bdml` file) maps to the data that will be returned from the Web service call — essentially the properties in the `Entity1` object. To do this, double-click the BDC Explorer in the Solution Explorer and then amend the `TyepDescriptors` (think of these as the individual data elements within your model — for example, `Identifier1`, `bdcCompanyName`, and so on) within the BDC model under the `Entity1` node.

Specifically, ensure that, under the `ReadItem` node, the `id` includes a `TypeDescriptor` called `Identifier1` (`System.Int32`), and the `Entity1` node under the `returnParameter` node includes `bdcCompanyName` (`System.String`), `bdcFY08Sales` (`System.Int32`), `bdcFY09Sales` (`System.Int32`), `bdcFY10Sales` (`System.Int32`), and `Identifer1` (`System.Int32`). Table 10-1 summarizes the `TypeDescriptors` and type names for the `ReadItem` method.

TABLE 10-1 TypeDescriptor and Type Name

TYPEDESCRIPTOR	TYPE NAME
Identifer1 (id)	System.Int32
bdcCompanyName (Entity1)	System.String
FY08Sales (Entity1)	System.Int32
FY09Sales (Entity1)	System.Int32
FY10Sales (Entity1)	System.Int32
Identifier1 (Entity1)	System.Int32

Then, under the `ReadList` node, ensure that the `Entity1` node (under the `EntityList` and `returnParameter` nodes) includes the same `TypeDescriptors` as you had under the `returnParameter` in the `ReadItem` method. In fact, you can copy and paste the `Entity1` node from the `ReadItem` method to the `ReadList` method. Table 10-2 summarizes the `TypeDescriptors` and type names for the `ReadList` method.

TABLE 10-2 TypeDescriptor and Type Name

TYPEDESCRIPTOR	TYPE NAME
bdcCompanyName (Entity1)	System.String
FY08Sales (Entity1)	System.Int32
FY09Sales (Entity1)	System.Int32
FY10Sales (Entity1)	System.Int32
Identifier1 (Entity1)	System.Int32

When you've finished amending the structure of the BDC model, it should look like Figure 10-6. It is important that you model these correctly or else the external list will not be created properly because the data and data types will be incorrectly mapped.

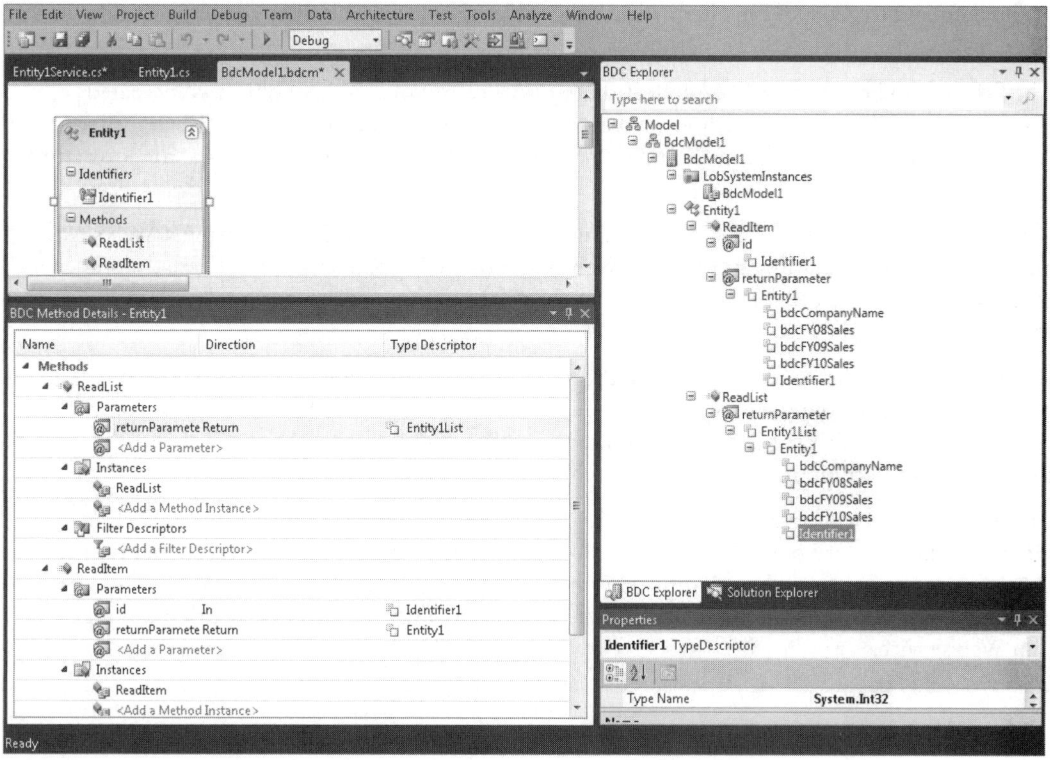

FIGURE 10-6 Amending the BDC Explorer

21. You can now save and build your project. When the project successfully builds, click Build ➪ Deploy to deploy the new external list to SharePoint.

22. When deployed, open SharePoint and click Site Actions ➪ View All Site Content.

23. Click Create ➪ Lists ➪ External List. Click Create and then provide a name and description. Because Visual Studio deployed the BDC Metadata model to SharePoint, you can click the Browse button and then select the model you just deployed to SharePoint. When finished, click OK.

24. By default, SharePoint opens the external list after you click OK, as shown in Figure 10-7.

Identifier1	bdcCompanyName	bdcFY08Sales	bdcFY09Sales	bdcFY10Sales
1	Acme	9820901	9792091	9980981
2	Wingtip	10293091	11209301	12238920
3	Fabrikam	2981009	2887290	2789098
4	Blue Yonder	50948903	51888219	52398012
5	Contoso	874930	889092	998012

FIGURE 10-7 External list using the Web service

How It Works

In this walkthrough, you did a number of things. First, you created your data object (that is, the `Sales` database in SQL Server). Second, you created a service to interact with that data in two ways: to get all of the data and to get a specific item within the table. To accomplish this, you created a method called `getAllSalesData` and another method called `getSpecificSale`.

The first method returned a `List` collection (`mySalesList`) of a custom object you created (`SalesObject`). The second method used an integer input parameter (`companyID`) as a filter to find the specific record within the database and then converted that to an array (`mySalesInfo`) to return to any client application.

After you finished creating the service, you deployed the service to IIS by creating a Web site in IIS and pointing the virtual directory of the Web site to the published Web service. Lastly, you created a SharePoint application that then called the Web service to populate an external list and display one of the records.

When the external list loads, it is calling the `ReadList` method, which, in turn, calls your Web service and loads the data from the external data system (in this case, it was SQL Server). If you click a particular item, this calls the `ReadItem` method and retrieves the specific list item using the `id` (which is the `Identifier1` column).

The walkthrough was an advanced example of how you can integrate Web services with BCS. However, this is a very powerful integration, because, once you get the external data into your external list, you can then use the SharePoint client object model to further interact with that data. This means creating dynamic Silverlight applications, for example, against the external list that leverages the custom Web service.

WCF WEB SERVICES

WCF is another type of Web service that is supported in SharePoint 2010. Used more frequently these days, WCF was designed to a set of standards that enables developers to build service-oriented applications to support distributed computing.

WCF follows architectural principles similar to those of ASP.NET Web services — that is, there is a client and server, and the service is hosted. Client applications can consume one or more WCF services, and services will typically have a WSDL interface. WCF also implements a number of more advanced service standards, such as WS-Addressing, WS-Security, and WS-ReliableMessaging — which makes it a more robust, flexible and secure option than its ASP. NET counterpart.

A WCF service has three main parts:

➤ A *service class*, which is the core code that executes the service

➤ The *hosting mechanism*

➤ The *endpoint* to the service to which the client application will connect

The endpoints specify a contract that defines the methods of the service class. They also define a binding that specifies how a client will communicate with the service, and the address where the endpoint is hosted. Thus, while a service in WCF may (from an execution perspective) perform the exact same function as its ASP.NET counterpart, there are a number of syntactical and structural differences between them that make them slightly more complex to write, but, overall, more robust, flexible, and secure.

One of the key innovations in SharePoint 2010 is that it offers native support for WCF. This means that you can either deploy a custom WCF service to IIS, or you can deploy it into the SharePoint root. You should note that you can also self-host WCF services using the `ServiceHost` class. When a client application connects to the hosted WCF service, it does so using the endpoint that is defined within the service — essentially a URL specifying where the methods of the service can be accessed.

> **NOTE** *For more general information on WCF, go to* `http://msdn.microsoft.com/en-us/library/ms735119.aspx`.

SharePoint 2010 offers a number of new WCF services. For example, one WCF service that was discussed earlier in the book was the `Listdata.svc` service — a WCF service that provides WCF Data Services–based interaction with list data. There have also been some other additions to SharePoint, including administrative services (`BdcAdminService.svc`), BDC services (`BdcRemoteExecutionService.svc` and `BDCResolverPickerService.svc`), and other storage, client accessibility, and security services (for example, `CellStorage.svc`, `Client.svc`, and `spclaimproviderwebservice.svc`). (See the "SharePoint 2010 Class Libraries and Web Services" MSDN site mentioned earlier to get more information.)

Of specific interest in this section is the use of custom WCF services for SharePoint 2010. To illustrate how you can create and implement a WCF service, you will leverage the database you created earlier in the chapter and build a WCF service that reads and writes data to the SQL database using a custom WCF service.

TRY IT OUT   Integrating a Custom WCF Service with SharePoint

Code files [GetSPSalesRecord.zip and AddSalesRecordWebPart.zip] available for download at Wrox.com.

WCF services can be used in many different ways. To create a custom WCF service and leverage that service in SharePoint, follow these steps:

1. Open Visual Studio 2010 and click File ⇨ New. Under WCF, click WCF Service Application. Provide a name for the project (for example, `GetSPSalesData`) and click OK.

2. Click Data ⇨ Add a New Data Source. Use the same process that you did earlier in the chapter to add the `Sales` database as an entity data model to the Visual Studio solution.

3. After you finish adding the `Sales` database, right-click the project and select Add ⇨ Class. Call the class `SalesObject`, and then add the following bolded code to the new class:

```
using System;
using System.Collections.Generic;
```

```
using System.Linq;
using System.Text;

namespace AddSalesRecordWebPart
{
    class SalesObject
    {
        public int companyID { get; set; }
        public string companyName { get; set; }
        public int? fy08Sales { get; set; }
        public int? fy09Sales { get; set; }
        public int? fy10Sales { get; set; }
    }
}
```

4. Open the `Service1.svc` file and amend the file, using the following bolded code:

```
using System;
using System.Collections.Generic;
using System.Linq;
using System.Runtime.Serialization;
using System.ServiceModel;
using System.ServiceModel.Web;
using System.Text;

namespace GetSPSalesData
{
    public class Service1 : IService1
    {
        SalesEntities mySalesData = new SalesEntities();
        List<SalesObject> mySalesList = new List<SalesObject>();

        public List<SalesObject> getAllSalesData()
        {
            var returnSalesData = (from sales in mySalesData.Sales_Data
                                   select sales).ToArray();

            foreach (var s in returnSalesData)
            {
                SalesObject tempSales = new SalesObject();
                tempSales.companyID = s.CompanyID;
                tempSales.companyName = s.CompanyName.ToString();
                tempSales.fy08Sales = s.FY08Sales;
                tempSales.fy09Sales = s.FY09Sales;
                tempSales.fy10Sales = s.FY10Sales;
                mySalesList.Add(tempSales);
            };

            return mySalesList;
        }

        public void addSalesRecord(int paramCompanyID, string paramCompanyName,
            int paramFY08Sales, int paramFY09Sales, int paramFY10Sales)
        {
            SalesObject newRecord = new SalesObject()
            {
```

```
                    companyID = paramCompanyID,
                    companyName = paramCompanyName,
                    fy08Sales = paramFY08Sales,
                    fy09Sales = paramFY09Sales,
                    fy10Sales = paramFY10Sales,
                };

                Sales_Data myNewSalesRecord = new Sales_Data();

                using (SalesEntities dataContext = new SalesEntities())
                {
                    myNewSalesRecord.CompanyID = newRecord.companyID;
                    myNewSalesRecord.CompanyName = newRecord.companyName;
                    myNewSalesRecord.FY08Sales = newRecord.fy08Sales;
                    myNewSalesRecord.FY09Sales = newRecord.fy09Sales;
                    myNewSalesRecord.FY10Sales = newRecord.fy10Sales;

                    dataContext.AddToSales_Data(myNewSalesRecord);
                    dataContext.SaveChanges();
                }

            }
        }
    }
```

5. Open the `IService1.cs` file and ensure that the following bolded code replaces the default code. (This is your service contract that must map to the two methods you have in your service code.)

```
using System;
using System.Collections.Generic;
using System.Linq;
using System.Runtime.Serialization;
using System.ServiceModel;
using System.ServiceModel.Web;
using System.Text;

namespace GetSPSalesData
{
    [ServiceContract]
    public interface IService1
    {
        [OperationContract]
        List<SalesObject> getAllSalesData();

        [OperationContract]
        void addSalesRecord(
            int paramCompanyID,
            string paramCompanyName,
            int paramFY08Sales,
            int paramFY09Sales,
            int paramFY10Sales);
    }
}
```

6. You have now completed the custom WCF service. Press F5 to build and test the service.

7. After the test page invokes, you can now deploy the service to IIS the same way you published and deployed the ASP.NET service to IIS. To do this, create a new folder on your local server drive (for example, `c:\Wrox\MyWCFService`), publish the solution to that folder, create a new Web site in IIS, and then point the virtual directory to that newly published folder and code.

8. Before you can use the WCF service in SharePoint, however, there is another configuration step that is required. If you open the WCF service project, you'll see a `web.config` file, which contains all of your WCF service configurations. WCF provides more granular and flexible control over your Web service settings, and you can use the `web.config` file to configure many service settings. To enable the service in SharePoint, you must copy and paste the Service Model settings in your `web.config` file into your SharePoint site's `web.config` file. This way, when SharePoint uses the endpoint URL, it understands the bindings and other properties defined in the `config` file it needs to use to properly handle the WCF service.

To find the specific elements you need to copy, double-click the `web.config` file in the Visual Studio project, and then copy all of the code between the `system.serviceModel` tags from the `web.config` file in the Visual Studio project and add it to the appropriate places in the SharePoint `web.config` file. You can typically find the SharePoint `web.config` file in the following directory: `c:\inetpub\wwwroot\wss\VirtualDirectories\<SharePoint_Server>\`. The following code snippet shows the copied `system.serviceModel` elements within the SharePoint `web.config` file.

```
...
<system.serviceModel>
    <serviceHostingEnvironment aspNetCompatibilityEnabled="true" />
    <bindings>
      <basicHttpBinding>
        <binding name="projectBasicHttpConf" closeTimeout="00:01:00"
            openTimeout="00:01:00" receiveTimeout="00:10:00"
            sendTimeout="00:01:00" allowCookies="true"
            maxBufferSize="4194304" maxReceivedMessageSize="500000000"
            messageEncoding="Text" transferMode="StreamedResponse">
          <security mode="TransportCredentialOnly">
            <transport clientCredentialType="Windows"
                proxyCredentialType="Windows" realm="" />
          </security>
        </binding>
      </basicHttpBinding>

      <wsHttpBinding>
            <binding name="WSHttpBinding_IService1" closeTimeout="00:01:00"
                openTimeout="00:01:00" receiveTimeout="00:10:00"
                    sendTimeout="00:01:00"
                bypassProxyOnLocal="false" transactionFlow="false"
                    hostNameComparisonMode="StrongWildcard"
                maxBufferPoolSize="524288" maxReceivedMessageSize="65536"
                messageEncoding="Text" textEncoding="utf-8"
                    useDefaultWebProxy="true"
                allowCookies="false">
                <readerQuotas maxDepth="32" maxStringContentLength="8192"
                    maxArrayLength="16384"
                    maxBytesPerRead="4096" maxNameTableCharCount="16384" />
                <reliableSession ordered="true" inactivityTimeout="00:10:00"
                    enabled="false" />
                <security mode="Message">
```

```
                              <transport clientCredentialType="Windows"
                                  proxyCredentialType="None"
                                  realm="" />
                              <message clientCredentialType="Windows"
                                  negotiateServiceCredential="true"
                                  algorithmSuite="Default" />
                          </security>
                      </binding>
                  </wsHttpBinding>
          </bindings>

          <client>
              <endpoint address="http://demo2010a.contoso.com:1122/Service1.svc"
                  binding="wsHttpBinding" bindingConfiguration=
                      "WSHttpBinding_IService1"
                  contract="SalesWCFService.IService1" name="WSHttpBinding_IService1">
                  <identity>
                      <dns value="localhost" />
                  </identity>
              </endpoint>
          </client>
      </system.serviceModel>
  ...
```

9. With the service deployed and SharePoint's `web.config` file now configured, you are ready to use the service in a SharePoint application. To test the service from IIS, right-click the service in Content view, and then select Browse. When the service page loads, navigate to `Service1.svc` and copy the URL from the Internet browser.

10. Open Visual Studio, create a new Empty SharePoint project, provide a name for it (for example, `AddSalesDataRecordWebPart`) and click OK. Right-click the project when created, then click Add ➪ New Item, and add a Web Part project to it. Provide a name for the Web part (for example, `SalesRecordWebPart`) and click Add.

11. Add a reference to the URL by right-clicking the References node and clicking Add Service Reference. Copy the IIS URL into the URL field, and click Go. When the endpoint is loaded into the Service Reference dialog, provide a name for the service and click Add.

12. Right-click the main Web part class file and click View Code. Add the following bolded code to the main Web part class file:

```
using System;
using System.ComponentModel;
using System.Web;
using System.Web.UI;
using System.Web.UI.WebControls;
using System.Web.UI.WebControls.WebParts;
using Microsoft.SharePoint;
using Microsoft.SharePoint.WebControls;
using System.Text;

namespace AddSalesRecordWebPart.SalesRecordWebPart
{
    [ToolboxItemAttribute(false)]
    public class SalesRecordWebPart : WebPart
```

```
    {
        DataGrid datagrdSalesView = new DataGrid();
        TextBox txtbxCompanyID = new TextBox();
        TextBox txtbxCompanyName = new TextBox();
        TextBox txtbxFY08Sales = new TextBox();
        TextBox txtbxFY09Sales = new TextBox();
        TextBox txtbxFY10Sales = new TextBox();
        Button btnLoad = new Button();
        Button btnGet = new Button();

        protected override void Render(HtmlTextWriter writer)
        {
            txtbxCompanyID.Enabled = true;
            txtbxCompanyName.Enabled = true;
            txtbxFY08Sales.Enabled = true;
            txtbxFY09Sales.Enabled = true;
            txtbxFY10Sales.Enabled = true;
            btnLoad.Text = "Add";
            btnGet.Text = "Get";

            writer.Write("<table><tr>");
            writer.Write("<td><b>Sales Information</b></td><td></td></tr>");
            writer.Write("<tr><td>Sales Data:</td><td>");
            datagrdSalesView.RenderControl(writer);
            writer.Write("</td></tr><tr><td>Company ID:</td><td>");
            txtbxCompanyID.RenderControl(writer);
            writer.Write("</td></tr><tr><td>Company Name:</td><td>");
            txtbxCompanyName.RenderControl(writer);
            writer.Write("</td></tr><tr><td>FY 08 Sales:</td><td>");
            txtbxFY08Sales.RenderControl(writer);
            writer.Write("</td></tr><tr><td>FY 09 Sales:</td><td>");
            txtbxFY09Sales.RenderControl(writer);
            writer.Write("</td></tr><tr><td>FY 10 Sales:</td><td>");
            txtbxFY10Sales.RenderControl(writer);
            writer.Write("</td></tr><tr><td>");
            btnGet.RenderControl(writer);
            writer.Write("</td><td>");
            btnLoad.RenderControl(writer);
            writer.Write("</td></tr></table>");

            btnLoad.Click += new EventHandler(btnLoad_Click);
            btnGet.Click += new EventHandler(btnGet_Click);

        }


        void btnGet_Click(object sender, EventArgs e)
        {
            SalesWCFService.Service1Client proxy =
                new SalesWCFService.Service1Client();
            var salesData = proxy.getAllSalesData();

            List<SalesObject> mySalesInfoList = new List<SalesObject>();

            foreach (var item in salesData)
```

```
        {
            SalesObject tempEntity = new SalesObject();
            tempEntity.companyID = item.companyID;
            tempEntity.companyName = item.companyName.ToString();
            tempEntity.fy08Sales = item.fy08Sales;
            tempEntity.fy09Sales = item.fy09Sales;
            tempEntity.fy10Sales = item.fy10Sales;
            mySalesInfoList.Add(tempEntity);
        }

        datagrdSalesView.DataSource = mySalesInfoList;
        datagrdSalesView.DataBind();
    }

    void btnLoad_Click(object sender, EventArgs e)
    {
        int companyID = Int32.Parse(txtbxCompanyID.Text);
        string companyName = txtbxCompanyName.Text;
        int fy08Sales = Int32.Parse(txtbxFY08Sales.Text);
        int fy09Sales = Int32.Parse(txtbxFY09Sales.Text);
        int fy10Sales = Int32.Parse(txtbxFY10Sales.Text);

        SalesWCFService.Service1Client proxy =
            new SalesWCFService.Service1Client();
        proxy.addSalesRecord(companyID, companyName, fy08Sales,
            fy09Sales, fy10Sales);
    }
}
}
```

13. When finished, click Build ➪ Deploy to deploy the Web part to SharePoint.

14. After the Web part successfully builds, navigate to SharePoint and either use an existing page or create a new Web part page, and click "Add a new Web part."

15. Select the Custom category, and add the new Web part you just created. Click Get to invoke the one Web method within your custom WCF service. Then, add some data and click Add to add some data to the SQL database via your WCF service. The result should look similar to Figure 10-8.

FIGURE 10-8 Sales Web part

How It Works

In much the same way that you created an ASP.NET Web service and then consumed it in an application, you walked through a similar process here using a custom WCF service. However, there were some differences this time, even though you used the same database in your service code.

First, your service code included the capability to add a record this time, as opposed to just retrieving data (addSalesRecord). In this method, you passed a number of parameters that you would eventually insert as a record. To do this, you created a new object, and then, using the database data context, you added an instance of the object to the database and saved the changes by calling the SaveChanges method.

```
public void addSalesRecord(int paramCompanyID, string paramCompanyName,
    int paramFY08Sales, int paramFY09Sales, int paramFY10Sales)
{
    SalesObject newRecord = new SalesObject()
    {
        companyID = paramCompanyID,
        companyName = paramCompanyName,
        fy08Sales = paramFY08Sales,
        fy09Sales = paramFY09Sales,
        fy10Sales = paramFY10Sales,
    };

    Sales_Data myNewSalesRecord = new Sales_Data();

    using (SalesEntities dataContext = new SalesEntities())
    {
        myNewSalesRecord.CompanyID = newRecord.companyID;
        myNewSalesRecord.CompanyName = newRecord.companyName;
        myNewSalesRecord.FY08Sales = newRecord.fy08Sales;
        myNewSalesRecord.FY09Sales = newRecord.fy09Sales;
        myNewSalesRecord.FY10Sales = newRecord.fy10Sales;

        dataContext.AddToSales_Data(myNewSalesRecord);
        dataContext.SaveChanges();
    }

}
```

Second, you added some configuration information to the SharePoint web.config file after deploying the WCF service. While this does make for an extra step in the development and deployment process, it does provide more granular control over the security and bindings for your services — and is very much typical of a WCF service. However, remember that what you need is typically created in your web.config file (unless you want to further customize the configuration settings).

Lastly, instead of using BCS (and the BDC Metadata model), you used the Visual Web part as your client application. In this case, implementing the service was fairly straightforward and only required that you call the addSalesRecord method and pass in a number of variables — which the user entered into the textboxes.

```
void btnLoad_Click(object sender, EventArgs e)
{
    int companyID = Int32.Parse(txtbxCompanyID.Text);
    string companyName = txtbxCompanyName.Text;
    int fy08Sales = Int32.Parse(txtbxFY08Sales.Text);
    int fy09Sales = Int32.Parse(txtbxFY09Sales.Text);
    int fy10Sales = Int32.Parse(txtbxFY10Sales.Text);

    SalesWCFService.Service1Client proxy =
        new SalesWCFService.Service1Client();
    proxy.addSalesRecord(companyID, companyName, fy08Sales,
        fy09Sales, fy10Sales);
}
```

The example in this exercise deployed the WCF service to IIS, so when you created your client application, it was calling the service from IIS. However, in SharePoint 2010, you can equally deploy a WCF service to the SharePoint root (that is, the ISAPI folder). The way in which you would deploy to the SharePoint root would be as follows:

1. Create an Empty SharePoint Project and set it to "Deploy as farm solution."

2. Add a WCF Service Library to the solution.

3. Copy the IService.cs and Service.cs files to the SharePoint project.

4. Add your service operations and contracts to the two service files.

5. Create a mapped SharePoint folder to the ISAPI folder.

6. Add a .svc file to the ISAPI mapped folder, and add the service registration information.

7. Deploy the SharePoint project to your SharePoint site.

Once you deploy the WCF service to SharePoint, you can consume the service either server-side or client-side through Windows Form, WPF, or even Silverlight applications.

> **NOTE** *While there is no walkthrough presented in this discussion for a WCF solution deployed to the SharePoint root, there is a code accompaniment (*WCFServiceApp.zip*) that is available for you to download for you at this book's companion download site (*www.wrox.com*). You can review the project to see how it is structured, as well as the way in which a client application calls the WCF service.*

You can build many more interesting and complex applications using WCF, so you should explore it more as you sharpen your SharePoint development skills.

RESTFUL WEB SERVICES

You can also use the Representational State Transfer (REST) services in SharePoint 2010. While REST is less of a service and more of a communications protocol, SharePoint 2010 supports REST to give you better data access and programmability.

In some cases, the REST capabilities are surfaced using WCF services. For example, in Chapter 5, you leveraged the WCF Data services and REST capabilities by using the Listdata service (listdata.svc).

What this functionality provides to the developer is a way to interact with SharePoint data in a strongly typed way. However, the strongly typed interaction with SharePoint data is not the only benefit provided by the REST APIs. They also provide a way to interact with other types of data within SharePoint, such as Excel data. You accomplish this through the REST protocols, which are Atom, AtomPub, and RSS.

In this section, you'll see more of the REST protocols at work (as opposed to the WCF Data services, which you already saw in Chapter 5) to interact with Excel data in SharePoint.

The REST protocols enable you to access data in Excel documents in various read/write ways. For the following example, create an Excel 2010 spreadsheet, add some data to a workbook (as shown in Figure 10-9), and create a named range called `Sales`. Next, create a chart from the named range by selecting all of the data in the table, clicking Insert ➪ Chart, and then selecting the Bar Chart to add the chart into the workbook. Note that the chart is called `Chart 1` by default.

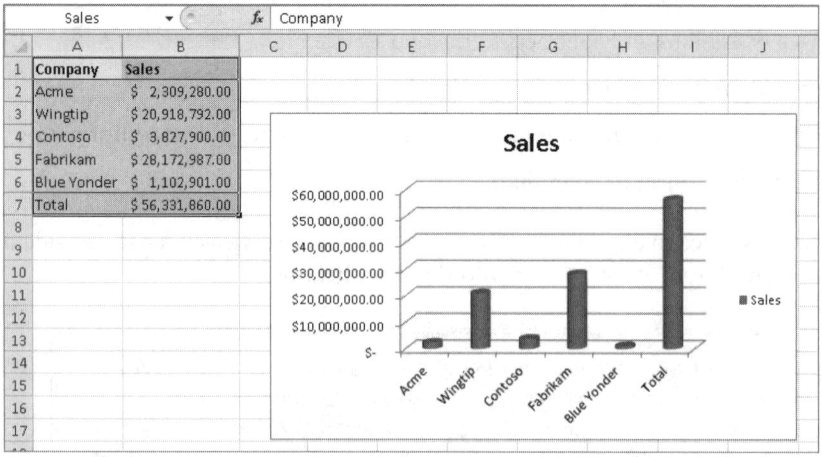

FIGURE 10-9 Creating a Sales spreadsheet

After you've created the workbook, save and upload the spreadsheet into SharePoint — for example, into the Shared Documents document library with the name `RestExample.xlsx`. With the Excel document in SharePoint, you can now use REST to retrieve or insert data.

Let's walk through an example where you retrieve the data using the REST protocols.

TRY IT OUT Using REST to Interact with Data in Excel

Code file [RestExample.xlsx] available for download at Wrox.com.

REST is a lightweight set of protocols to interact with data in various ways, one of which is retrieving data from Excel. To retrieve data from an Excel spreadsheet using REST, follow these steps:

1. Open your Internet browser and navigate to your SharePoint instance to ensure that you have connectivity to your server.

2. Type the following URI into your Internet browser:

```
http://<server name>/_vti_bin/ExcelRest.aspx/Shared%20Documents/
    RestExample.xlsx/Model
```

3. In your Internet browser, you should now see something similar to Figure 10-10. What you're seeing is an ATOM feed of the types of items in your workbook that are accessible using the REST protocols.

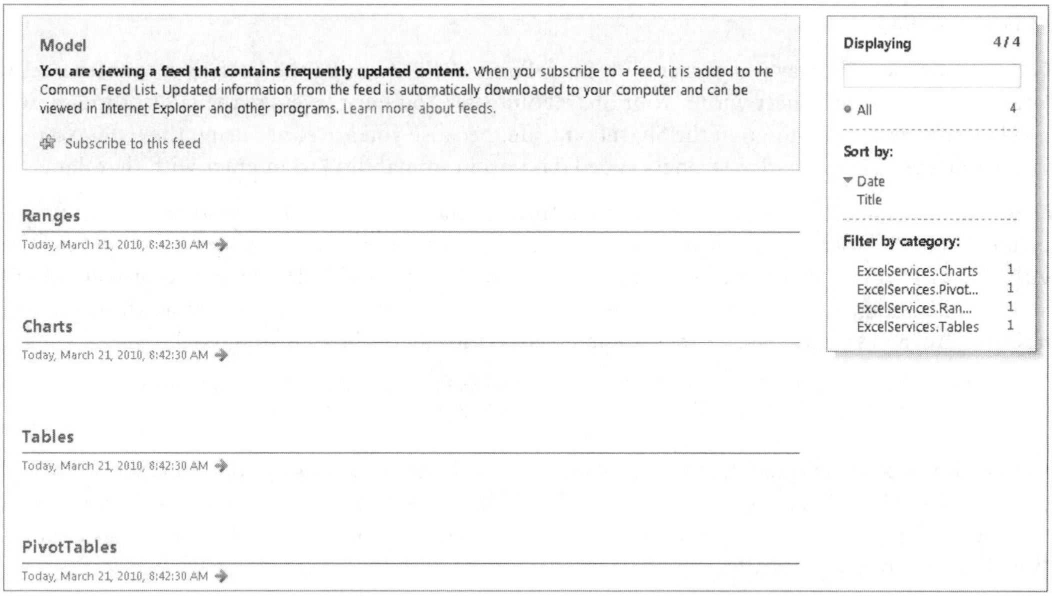

FIGURE 10-10 Atom feed of available item types

4. Because you created a named range in the spreadsheet, you can access the named range using the Atom feed. To do so, type the following URI into the Internet browser:

```
http://intranet.contoso.com/_vti_bin/ExcelRest.aspx/Shared%20Documents/
    RestExample.xlsx/Model/Ranges('Sales')?$format=html
```

5. You should now see something similar to Figure 10-11, which shows the result of the Atom feed — the table that you made the named range in your Excel spreadsheet.

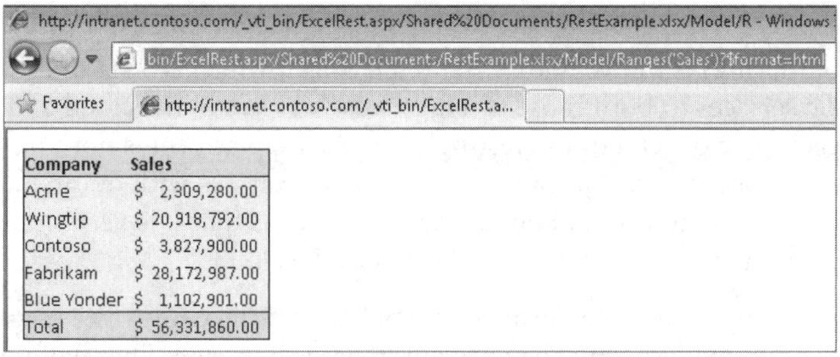

FIGURE 10-11 Surfacing a named range in the browser

6. Lastly, type the following URI into your Internet browser to expose the chart you also created in the spreadsheet:

```
http://intranet.contoso.com/_vti_bin/ExcelRest.aspx/Shared%20Documents/
    RestExample.xlsx/Model/Charts('Chart%201')
```

How It Works

REST is a lightweight way to interact with SharePoint 2010. By using the URIs, you can interact with data in an Excel spreadsheet within your SharePoint site. You must leverage the URIs, though, with an Excel document that is stored in the SharePoint site, because you are either using the `ExcelRest.aspx` redirect or `Listdata.svc` (for strongly typed data programmability) to interact with that data.

There are also a number of supported REST return formats. For example, supported return formats include HTML, Atom, image, or workbook. To enable this return data, you append the REST URI with `?$format=html` to return, for example, the named range as HTML. This is what you did with the `Sales` named range in the walkthrough. Note that you could also return the data as an Atom feed as is indicated by the `?$format=atom` that is appended to the end of the following URI:

```
http://intranet.contoso.com/_vti_bin/ExcelRest.aspx/Shared%20Documents/
     RestExample.xlsx/Model/Ranges('Sales')?$format=atom
```

You saw one way to leverage the `Listdata` service in Chapter 5 (where you developed a client application to talk to SharePoint lists), and here you should be thinking how you can develop applications that leverage the lightweight REST protocol to get and put data into SharePoint lists, or access data in Excel spreadsheets programmatically.

AZURE AND SHAREPOINT

A growing trend in software development is cloud computing. *Cloud computing* is where code and data live in the cloud so that organizations can both consume and deploy services in an Internet-based data center for hosting. The business mechanics of cloud computing can make a lot of sense when thinking about things like hardware, upgrading, administration, and software maintenance. Cloud computing offsets these costs by moving the management and maintenance of applications to companies like Microsoft.

One of the key Microsoft cloud offerings is the Windows Azure platform, which is a set of cloud capabilities that provides specific services to both those trying to host services in the cloud and those trying to develop and deploy services in the cloud. Interestingly, the Azure platform is not limited to being consumed by cloud-only applications. You can integrate Azure services with on-premises applications as well. In fact, the easy way to think about an Azure service is that it is very similar to any other service endpoint — except that it is deployed and hosted in the cloud.

The demand for cloud computing is big, and, in the near term, you'll see many companies trying to integrate more with the Windows Azure platform. The question, then, is how does SharePoint integrate with the cloud?

At present, SharePoint can integrate with Windows Azure services; again, it is just another endpoint. Thus, you build and deploy a service in the cloud and, as long as you have connectivity to the service, you can integrate and run it with SharePoint. While this book mainly focuses on SharePoint on-premises (that is, SharePoint Server 2010), there is no reason why you cannot integrate Azure-based services with SharePoint does make for an extra step in the development and deployment process, Online (for example, using sandboxed solutions as your point of integration) when it is released later in 2010.

Integrating SharePoint with Azure services or data primarily means two things at present. The first is that you can integrate with services that are already hosted on Azure. Or, you can build your own Azure services (or applications), deploy these services in the cloud, and then integrate these services with SharePoint. The Windows Azure platform provides a set of developer tools and a replicated developer environment where you can test any services you will deploy to the cloud.

> **NOTE** *For more information on how to get started using Windows Azure, go to* `http://www.microsoft.com/windowsazure/`.

An interesting data service that is built on Azure is a technology codenamed "Dallas," where companies are hosting large quantities of public data on Azure, and then, through a subscription model, you can build applications that leverage that data in some capacity. While the technology is currently limited, in the future it is sure to grow in use and popularity, because the data will grow to include census, crime, and news data — and other types of data that can prove interesting when mined and analyzed in different ways.

In this section, you'll see how you can integrate Dallas data hosted on Azure integrated with SharePoint. To complete the exercise that follows, you'll need to have a Live ID and a developer key to access the Dallas data and services.

To get a developer key, navigate to `https://www.sqlazureservices.com` and then sign in with your Live ID. Click Home and follow the instructions to get your developer key sent to you via email. It's a very simple process and will only take you a couple of minutes. After you have your developer key, click Catalog, and then subscribe to one or more of the data catalogs. When you subscribe to a catalog, it is then added to your Subscriptions. For this walkthrough, use the `infogroup` data catalog that is hosted on Azure.

TRY IT OUT   Creating a Web Part Integrated with Azure

Code file [AzureProject.zip] available for download at Wrox.com.

Azure is a very powerful cloud-based platform that hosts services and data. To integrate Azure with SharePoint, follow these steps:

1.   Navigate to your Dallas Azure Catalog page and then click the link that reads, "Click here to explore the dataset," as shown in Figure 10-12.

FIGURE 10-12 infogroup data catalog

2. Explore the catalog using the Web-based filters to get a better sense for what public data is returned from your filtering.

3. Copy the Account Key, Unique User ID, and link feed to the catalog (for example, `https://api.sqlazureservices.com/InfoUsaService.svc/businessAnalytics/canada?$format=atom10`) to a text document and save them to your desktop.

4. Open Visual Studio 2010 and create an Empty SharePoint project and provide a name for the project (for example, `AzureProject`). Add the Web part item-level template to the Empty SharePoint project.

5. Right-click the project and click Add ➪ Class. Call the class `Customer` and add the following bolded code to the class:

```
using System;
using System.Collections.Generic;
using System.Linq;
using System.Text;

namespace AzureProject
{
    class Customer
    {
        public string contactName { get; set; }
        public string companyName { get; set; }
        public string companyAddress { get; set; }
        public string companyCity { get; set; }
        public string companyProvince { get; set; }
        public string companyPostalCode { get; set; }
        public string companyPhone { get; set; }
    }
}
```

6. Amend the `.webpart` file so that it has a more intuitive title and description.

```
...
        <properties>
          <property name="Title" type="string">Azure Dallas Web Part</property>
          <property name="Description" type="string">Web Part that displays
              Dallas data from Azure.</property>
        </properties>
...
```

7. In the main Web part class, add the following bolded code. Where noted in the code, add your account key, unique user ID, and the link to the data catalog.

```
using System;
using System.ComponentModel;
using System.Web;
using System.Web.UI;
using System.Web.UI.WebControls;
using System.Web.UI.WebControls.WebParts;
using Microsoft.SharePoint;
using Microsoft.SharePoint.WebControls;
using Microsoft.Dallas.Services;
using System.Net;
using System.IO;
```

```csharp
using System.Xml.Linq;
using System.Collections.Generic;
using System.Linq;

namespace AzureProject.AzureWebPart
{
    [ToolboxItemAttribute(false)]
    public class AzureWebPart : WebPart
    {
        Button btnGetAzureData = new Button();
        DataGrid datagrdAzureData = new DataGrid();
        Label lblData = new Label();

        string myAccountKey = "<your account key>"
        string myUniqueUserId = "<your user ID>";
        string myDallasURL = "<your Dallas URL>";

        protected override void CreateChildControls()
        {
            btnGetAzureData.Text = "Load Azure Data";
            lblData.Text = "Azure Data: ";

            this.Controls.Add(new LiteralControl("<table><tr><td>"));
            this.Controls.Add(lblData);
            this.Controls.Add(new LiteralControl("</td><td>"));
            this.Controls.Add(datagrdAzureData);
            this.Controls.Add(new LiteralControl("</td><tr><td></td<td>"));
            this.Controls.Add(btnGetAzureData);
            this.Controls.Add(new LiteralControl("</td></tr></table>"));

            btnGetAzureData.Click += new EventHandler(btnGetAzureData_Click);
        }

        void btnGetAzureData_Click(object sender, EventArgs e)
        {
            List<Customer> customerSalesLeads = new List<Customer>();
            WebRequest azureWebRequest = WebRequest.Create(myDallasURL);
            azureWebRequest.Headers.Add("$accountKey", myAccountKey);
            azureWebRequest.Headers.Add("$uniqueUserID", myUniqueUserId);
            HttpWebResponse azureWebResponse = (HttpWebResponse)azureWebRequest.
                GetResponse();
            Stream AzureDataStream = azureWebResponse.GetResponseStream();
            StreamReader reader = new StreamReader(AzureDataStream);
            string responseFromAzure = reader.ReadToEnd();
            XDocument xmlAzureResultData = XDocument.Parse(responseFromAzure);

            XNamespace nsContent = "http://www.w3.org/2005/Atom";
            XNamespace nsProperties = "http://schemas.microsoft.com/ado/2007/
                08/dataservices/metadata";
            XNamespace nsValue = "http://schemas.microsoft.com/ado/2007/
                08/dataservices";

            var result = (from q in xmlAzureResultData.Descendants(nsContent +
                "entry")
                            where q.Element(nsContent + "content").
                                Element(nsProperties + "properties").
```

```
                               Element(nsValue + "City").Value == "SOOKE"
                       select new Customer
                       {
                           contactName = q.Element(nsContent +
                               "content").Element(nsProperties +
                               "properties").Element(nsValue +
                               "ContactName").Value.ToString(),
                           companyCity = q.Element(nsContent +
                               "content").Element(nsProperties +
                               "properties").Element(nsValue +
                               "CompanyName").Value.ToString(),
                           companyAddress = q.Element(nsContent +
                               "content").Element(nsProperties +
                               "properties").Element(nsValue +
                               "Address").Value.ToString(),
                           companyName = q.Element(nsContent +
                               "content").Element(nsProperties +
                               "properties").Element(nsValue +
                               "City").Value.ToString(),
                           companyProvince = q.Element(nsContent +
                               "content").Element(nsProperties +
                               "properties").Element(nsValue +
                               "Province").Value.ToString(),
                           companyPostalCode = q.Element(nsContent +
                               "content").Element(nsProperties +
                               "properties").Element(nsValue +
                               "PostalCode").Value.ToString(),
                           companyPhone = q.Element(nsContent +
                               "content").Element(nsProperties +
                               "properties").Element(nsValue +
                               "Phone").Value.ToString()
                       });
               foreach (var c in result)
               {
                   Customer tempCustomer = new Customer();
                   tempCustomer.contactName = c.contactName;
                   tempCustomer.companyCity = c.companyCity;
                   tempCustomer.companyAddress = c.companyAddress;
                   tempCustomer.companyName = c.companyName;
                   tempCustomer.companyProvince = c.companyProvince;
                   tempCustomer.companyPostalCode = c.companyPostalCode;
                   tempCustomer.companyPhone = c.companyPhone;
                   customerSalesLeads.Add(tempCustomer);
               }

               datagrdAzureData.DataSource = customerSalesLeads;
               datagrdAzureData.DataBind();

               reader.Close();
               AzureDataStream.Close();
               azureWebResponse.Close();
           }
       }
   }
```

8. When you've added the code, click Build to build the project. After the project has successfully built, click Build ⇨ Deploy Solution to deploy the Web part to SharePoint.

9. Once the Web part has deployed, navigate to your SharePoint site and either create a new Web part page or use an existing one. Click "Add a web part," and then navigate to the Custom category. Add your newly created Azure Web part.

10. Click the Load Azure Data to invoke the Web request to the Azure service and load the Dallas data. The results should look similar to Figure 10-13.

Azure Dallas Web Part								
		contactName	companyName	companyAddress	companyCity	companyProvince	companyPostalCode	companyPhone
Azure Data:		RON WHITE	SOOKE	7228 WRIGHT RD	ABSOLUTE TOWING	BC	V9Z 0S5	2508810961
		JAY MC GHEE	SOOKE	PO BOX 761 STN MAIN	BIGFOOT DANGER TREE SVC	BC	V9Z 1H7	2506422463
		PAM BLACKSTONE	SOOKE	2277 POND PL	BLACKSTONE MARKETING AND COMMS	BC	V9Z 0V9	2506420868
		GRAHAM STALLARD	SOOKE	2205 OTTER POINT RD	CAPITAL REGIONAL ELECTORAL	BC	V9Z 1J2	2506421620
Load Azure Data								

FIGURE 10-13 Rendered Azure data in Web part

How It Works

This example opens up the opportunity for you to begin to code against Azure-based services that live in the cloud. However, you shouldn't think of these services as any different from other types of services. These are simply a different endpoint.

In this walkthrough, rather than using the service proxies as you did in the ASP.NET and WCF examples, you used the WebRequest object to interact with the Azure data. The WebRequest object is a .NET class that represents a request/response model for working with data that lives in the cloud. Using this class, the request was sent from the client application using a specific URI (in this case, the Dallas data URL), and the response was handled by reading the response stream into an XDocument object.

(For more information on the WebRequest class, go to http://msdn.microsoft.com/en-us/library/system.net.webrequest.aspx.)

In the walkthrough, the bulk of the code was invoked when you clicked the button in the Web part (btnGetAzureData). This invoked the Click event, which then created a new WebRequest object, made the request to the specific Dallas URL (myDallasURL), and then added your account key and unique user ID as values within the request.

```
...
WebRequest azureWebRequest = WebRequest.Create(myDallasURL);
azureWebRequest.Headers.Add("$accountKey", myAccountKey);
azureWebRequest.Headers.Add("$uniqueUserID", myUniqueUserId);
HttpWebResponse azureWebResponse = (HttpWebResponse)azureWebRequest.GetResponse();
Stream AzureDataStream = azureWebResponse.GetResponseStream();
StreamReader reader = new StreamReader(AzureDataStream);
string responseFromAzure = reader.ReadToEnd();
XDocument xmlAzureResultData = XDocument.Parse(responseFromAzure);

XNamespace nsContent = "http://www.w3.org/2005/Atom";
```

```
XNamespace nsProperties = "http://schemas.microsoft.com/ado/2007/
     08/dataservices/metadata";
XNamespace nsValue = "http://schemas.microsoft.com/ado/2007/08/dataservices";

…
datagrdAzureData.DataSource = customerSalesLeads;
datagrdAzureData.DataBind();
reader.Close();
AzureDataStream.Close();
azureWebResponse.Close();
```

After making the request, a good portion of the code within the `Click` event constructed a query that could be used to get the specific information you wanted. (You can certainly optimize this code with LINQ to get a more concise query against the returned data set, and you would likely want to emit the HTML formatting using the `HtmlTextWriter` class, as you've seen throughout the book.) In this case, you created a query that parsed all records from the response stream that were located in the city of Sooke, British Columbia. After you bound the returned data to the datagrid (`datagrdAzureData`), you then disposed all of the objects associated with the `WebRequest`.

SUMMARY

Service-based applications open up a vast amount of potential for building interesting applications that span heterogeneous systems. In this chapter, you saw the increased support for services of all kinds in SharePoint 2010. Specifically, you learned about native and custom ASP.NET Web services, custom WCF services, the REST protocols, and Azure services. All of these provide you with different capabilities and levels of functionality that can extend out into the enterprise, or out into the wider cloud.

As a beginning developer, your first option should always be to see if the service exists already before creating a custom service. SharePoint 2010 has a rich set of native Web services, and you'll find that these will often fit the bill. However, if the functionality does not exist in the native SharePoint Web services, then custom services may be the option. WCF services are being used more these days, as they offer more flexibility and power over security. However, that's not to say that you could not use custom ASP.NET services as well. Many organizations still leverage ASP.NET for their custom services.

With either ASP.NET or WCF, you also have the option to deploy to IIS, or to deploy to the SharePoint root. Deploying to IIS provides you with a higher level of scalability, but leveraging the SharePoint root deploys your services as a "trusted" context with SharePoint. The flip side is that any services deployed to the `ISAPI` folder can get deleted through routine maintenance and upgrades.

If you're looking for more lightweight services, then REST would be the option to use to interact with SharePoint data. As you've seen, combined with WCF Data services, you can do some strongly typed programming against SharePoint lists. And, in this chapter, you have seen how you can very easily use the REST protocols when interacting with Excel documents.

When it comes to the cloud, Microsoft's newest offering is Azure. It will be exciting to see where Azure moves in the future. Cloud computing is a reality, and many companies are moving in this direction.

In Chapter 11, you'll see how you can integrate in different ways with Office 2010.

1. Explore the native ASP.NET Web services in SharePoint 2010 and build some applications using other native Web services.

2. Create either an ASP.NET or WCF Web service, and then deploy it in the SharePoint 2010 root, as opposed to deploying it to IIS.

3. Use the REST URI that points to your `Sales` named range and surface this within a Word document.

4. Create a custom Azure service and then build a SharePoint Web part that implements that service.

▶ WHAT YOU LEARNED IN THIS CHAPTER

ITEM	DESCRIPTION
ASP.NET Services	ASP.NET 2.0 services provide SOAP and WSDL-based services to interact with SharePoint. SharePoint 2010 provides an array of native ASP.NET services that you can leverage, as well as the capability to support custom services.
WCF Services	First supported in .NET 3.0, WCF provides more advanced and flexible management over Web service implementation. This follows similar standards to ASP.NET but expands to support broader settings such as security and bindings.
REST	REST is a set of protocols that are not only supported through WCF services in SharePoint (for example, `Listdata.svc`) but also through lightweight URIs. REST enables you to leverage the power of WCF Data services or issue URI commands to the browser to retrieve Excel data.
Azure	Windows Azure is the platform in the cloud that provides you with the capability to build, deploy, and host services and data on the Internet using a scalable infrastructure.

RECOMMENDED READING

➤ SharePoint 2010 SDK on MSDN at `http://msdn.microsoft.com/en-us/library/ee557253(office.14).aspx`

➤ Azure Getting Started home page at `http://www.microsoft.com/windowsazure`

➤ Channel 9 Azure Learning Center at `http://channel9.msdn.com/learn/courses/Azure/`

➤ Channel 9 Services Module at `http://channel9.msdn.com/learn/courses/SharePoint2010Developer/ServicesArchitecture/`

11

Integrating SharePoint with Microsoft Office

WHAT YOU'LL LEARN IN THIS CHAPTER:

➤ Creating integrated Office 2010 solutions using both no-code and code options

➤ Using content types as documents you can map to your document libraries

➤ Using InfoPath for forms processing and management

➤ Using a workflow to manage your business processes

➤ Using Office 2010 server-side services to augment your SharePoint solutions

It's almost impossible to talk about SharePoint without discussing Office, because they are so tightly integrated in a number of ways. For the end user, many of the Office 2010 features provide improved features for integrating with SharePoint — such as the Office Web Application view and editing capabilities, publish to SharePoint, and many document management capabilities. For the developer, the bar has been raised even more in 2010. For example, you have a wide array of possibilities to integrate your Office 2010 solutions with SharePoint. The great thing is that you also have a choice that takes you from many no-code options for integrating with Office to more code-heavy solutions so that you can customize your solutions.

In this chapter, you'll see both no-code and code solutions that will cut across technologies such as content types, InfoPath, SharePoint workflow, server-side services (that is, Visio Services, Excel Services, Access Services, and Word Services), and Visual Studio Tools for Office (VSTO) customizations that integrate with SharePoint lists. Each of these options illustrates the strong integration possibilities with SharePoint 2010, so be sure (as you would when thinking about out-of-the-box features versus custom features) that you evaluate the different options when thinking about integrating Office with SharePoint — and, more generally, how you can augment your SharePoint 2010 solutions using Office.

CONTENT TYPE AS A DOCUMENT TEMPLATE

Content types are interesting and useful artifacts in SharePoint. They are reusable objects, settings, and metadata that can be applied to specific types of content in SharePoint. They enable you to create predictable and manageable behaviors for a document or item within SharePoint. For example, say that you want to create a specific content type called Legal Contract that can be repurposed across your SharePoint farm. You can assign the Legal Contract content type a set of columns (for example, `Customer Name`, `Contract ID`, and `Active Date`) and metadata, and then register it as such within SharePoint. It can then be reused across your site.

Content types, however, are not just about columns. You can create a specific document template and have that template be your content type. You apply the Legal frame to a custom Legal Word template, which has boilerplate legalese in it. You don't want people in an organization constantly re-creating the same document, so you can create the legal template in Word and create a content type to be reused across the SharePoint site (or within a specific document library).

Thus, one way to integrate Office with SharePoint is by using content types. They could be used in two ways. First, you can simply expose an Office document to be used as the default document in a document library. Thus, when the user clicks New in the document library, the specific document you want to act as the content type for that document library will appear.

Second, you can do the same thing, but with a *custom* document. This is a little more involved, because it means that you will have created a document-level customization (for example, a custom task pane that integrates line-of-business data), which involves managed code customization. Chapter 5 and Chapter 8 showed you how to perform Office customizations. Mapping a customized document to a content type means that when the user clicks New, the custom document appears as the default document selection. If you apply the Legal Contract, the custom document may apply a specific set of ribbon customizations to apply boilerplate legalese, depending on what type of contract you're trying to create. Thus, by using a content type in this manner, you can cut down on retyping by associating the custom legal template with a document library.

You create content types in the "Site content types" Gallery, which you can find by clicking Site Actions ⇨ Site Settings, as shown in Figure 11-1.

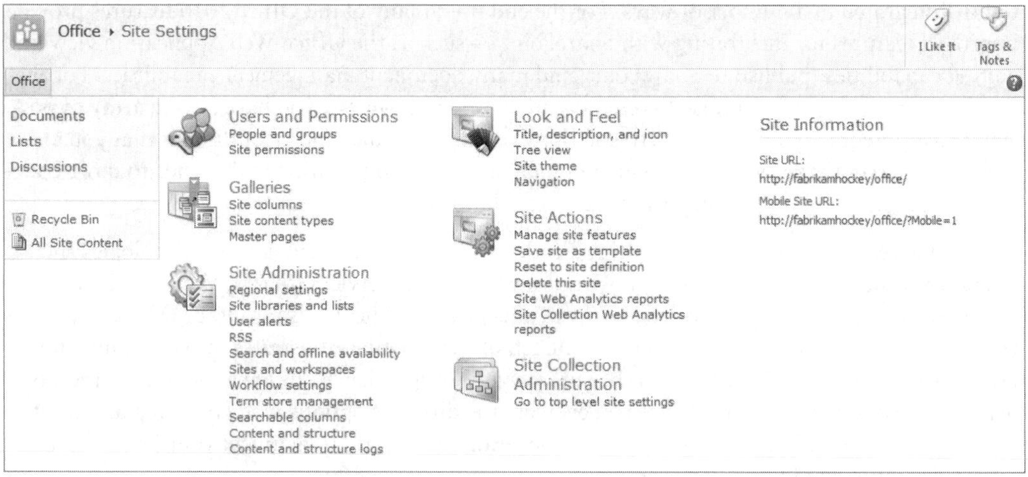

FIGURE 11-1 "Site content types" in Site Settings

Let's create a content type. To complete this exercise, open Microsoft PowerPoint and create a simple deck that has some boilerplate text in a slide. What's in the PowerPoint deck is less important than the fact that you'll use a content type to map it to a document library so that, if it were a real document, everyone in an organization could use it.

TRY IT OUT   Creating a Content Type

Content types are very versatile, and creating a content type is fairly straightforward. To create one, follow these steps:

1. Click Site Actions ⇨ Site Settings.

2. Click "Site content types" and then click Create.

3. Provide a Name (for example, Beginning_SharePoint_PPT) and Description (for example, "Template for PPT decks") for the content type, and then select the parent content type (Document Content Types and Document). You can also choose to create a new category for your content type, as shown in Figure 11-2. Click OK to create the new content type.

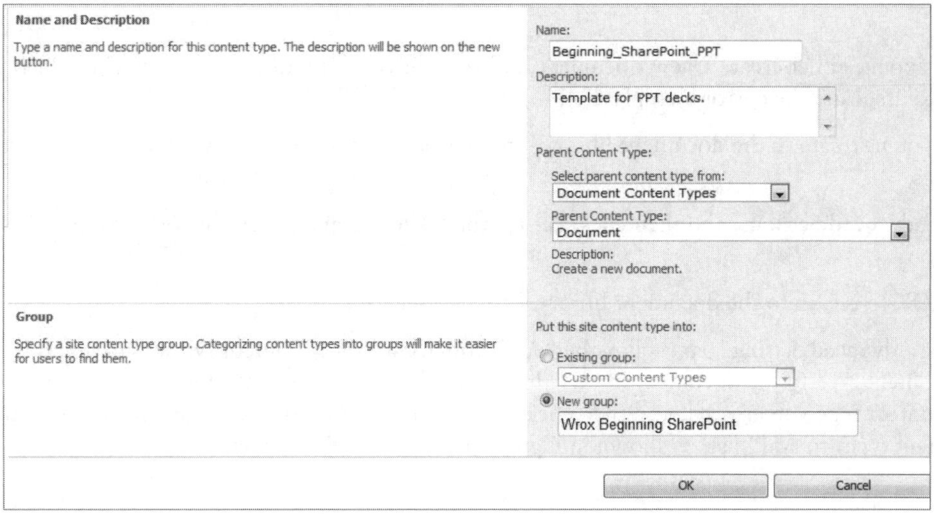

Name and Description
Type a name and description for this content type. The description will be shown on the new button.

Name:
Beginning_SharePoint_PPT

Description:
Template for PPT decks.

Parent Content Type:
Select parent content type from:
Document Content Types

Parent Content Type:
Document

Description:
Create a new document.

Group
Specify a site content type group. Categorizing content types into groups will make it easier for users to find them.

Put this site content type into:
◯ Existing group:
Custom Content Types

◉ New group:
Wrox Beginning SharePoint

OK   Cancel

FIGURE 11-2 Creating a content type

4. When the content type is created, click Advanced Settings on the Site Content Type Information page. Here you can upload a specific template for the content type, or you can provide a link to the document if you've uploaded into SharePoint already (Figure 11-3). The document you will upload (or point to) is the document you created earlier in this chapter. Note that you can upload the document into a document library, and then add that URL into the appropriate field. When finished, click OK.

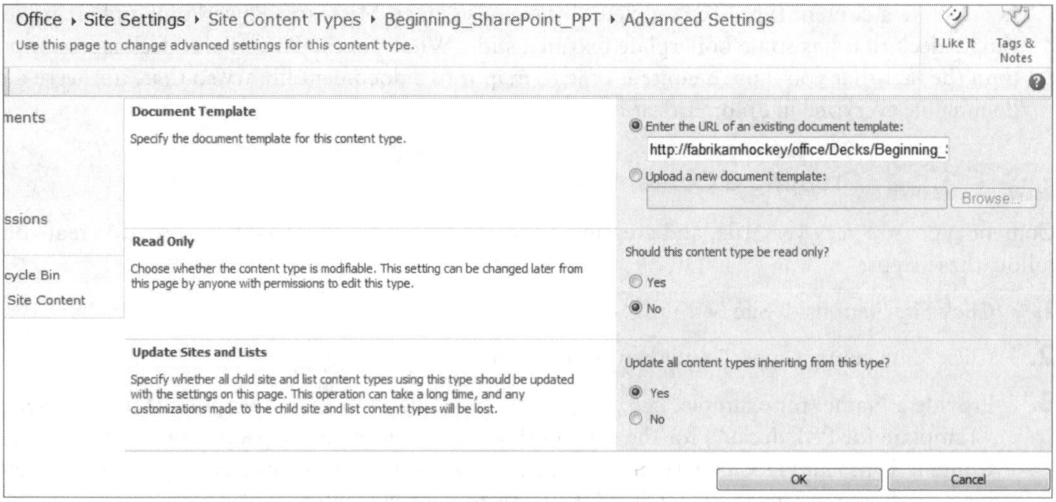

Office ▸ Site Settings ▸ Site Content Types ▸ Beginning_SharePoint_PPT ▸ Advanced Settings

Use this page to change advanced settings for this content type.

I Like It   Tags & Notes

Document Template

Specify the document template for this content type.

◉ Enter the URL of an existing document template:

http://fabrikamhockey/office/Decks/Beginning_:

◯ Upload a new document template:

Browse...

Read Only

Choose whether the content type is modifiable. This setting can be changed later from this page by anyone with permissions to edit this type.

Should this content type be read only?

◯ Yes
◉ No

Update Sites and Lists

Specify whether all child site and list content types using this type should be updated with the settings on this page. This operation can take a long time, and any customizations made to the child site and list content types will be lost.

Update all content types inheriting from this type?

◉ Yes
◯ No

OK   Cancel

FIGURE 11-3 Uploading a custom document for your content type

5. At this point, either create a new document library or navigate to an existing one with which you want to associate the custom template.

6. After you navigate to the document library, on the ribbon click the Library tab and then Library Settings.

7. Click Advanced Settings, and then click Yes for the "Allow management of content types?" checkbox.

8. Click OK to return to the document library settings page.

9. On the Advanced Settings page, click the "Add from existing site content types" link to add your new content type to the document library. In the Available Site Content Types list, find the custom content type you created, and then click the Add button to move that content type into the "Content types to add" list, as shown in Figure 11-4. Click OK to finish.

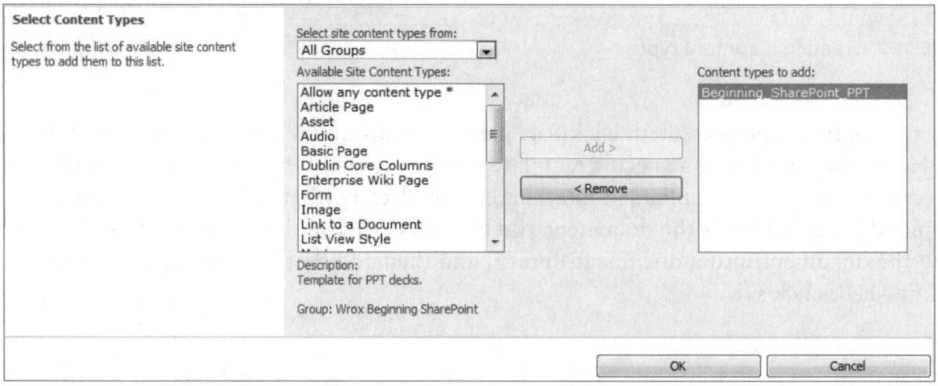

Select Content Types

Select from the list of available site content types to add them to this list.

Select site content types from:

All Groups

Available Site Content Types:

Allow any content type *
Article Page
Asset
Audio
Basic Page
Dublin Core Columns
Enterprise Wiki Page
Form
Image
Link to a Document
List View Style

Description:
Template for PPT decks.

Group: Wrox Beginning SharePoint

Content types to add:

Beginning_SharePoint_PPT

Add >
< Remove

OK   Cancel

FIGURE 11-4 Adding new content type to document library

10. You can also choose to not display other content types, so only your content type will show up. To do this, click Change New Button Order and Default Content Type and unclick the Visible checkbox for the Document content type, and ensure that your content type is checked, as shown in Figure 11-5.

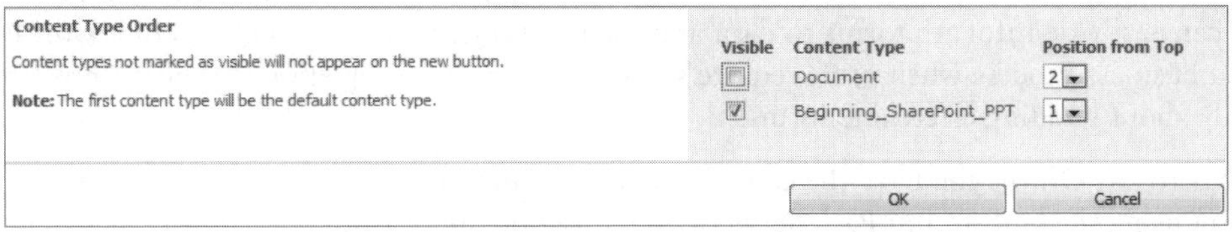

FIGURE 11-5 Making your content type visible

11. Now you can navigate to your document library and click New Document. Your custom Microsoft PowerPoint deck will be the one to appear to the end user, as shown in Figure 11-6.

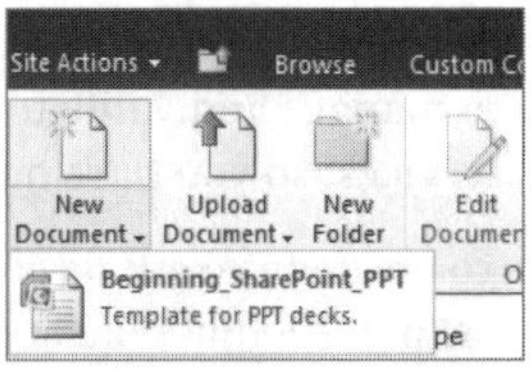

FIGURE 11-6 Custom content type in document library

How It Works

The content type in this example is fairly straightforward. You simply used the Document content type category and then mapped a specific document (in this case, a Microsoft PowerPoint deck) to that Document content type.

In the case of this example, though, you uploaded the document where SharePoint stores the document in a special location. When the user clicks the New Document button, SharePoint loads the document from that location. Then, the user can add specific content and then save the document back to SharePoint.

You can leverage content types all across SharePoint and integrate them with Office documents as well. For example, the document information panel is one way that you can integrate content types within the document itself. Furthermore, you're not relegated to just PowerPoint documents when creating and mapping content types to document libraries. You can also map, for example, Word templates or Excel templates as a content type.

You can also map *custom* documents that have code built into them. In Chapter 5, you built a VSTO document-level solution that read and wrote data in an Excel spreadsheet. If you wanted, this could be the template that you could use to deploy and map as the content type to your document library.

The point is that you have a variety of options when creating content types. So, leverage their reusable nature to build structure around your SharePoint site.

> **NOTE** There is a useful MSDN article that walks you through how you can create a custom VSTO document-level solution and then map that to a content type in SharePoint. It applies to SharePoint 2007, but it can still be used as a reference. You can find the article at http://msdn.microsoft.com/en-us/magazine/cc507632.aspx. You can also find a new extensibility project template for deploying Office Business Applications to SharePoint at http://code.msdn.microsoft.com/vsixforsp.

USING INFOPATH IN YOUR SHAREPOINT SOLUTIONS

Another way to integrate Office into your SharePoint solutions is by using *InfoPath forms*. InfoPath forms are templates that overlay XML but are very versatile in the way you can use them. For example, you can easily tie InfoPath forms to data and then integrate them with a SharePoint workflow to manage a business process when users require some level of form completion. In short, InfoPath is essentially about building electronic forms.

Within Microsoft Office, you have the capability to build and publish forms quickly and easily into SharePoint using the built-in InfoPath Services. What's good about InfoPath forms is that they are accessible across a wide audience, and they fit into a good number of scenarios — that is, wherever you want to enter data or have a form within a workflow, you can use an InfoPath form.

With this in mind, you can customize SharePoint list forms, as well as add custom layouts and rules to manage and validate data. InfoPath is great in that it also works well against ADO.NET or Web services, so you have built-in flexibility to interact with different types of data.

To create InfoPath forms, you use the InfoPath client application to create the forms, and then leverage the publish functionality built into InfoPath to push the forms into SharePoint. InfoPath provides some out-of-the-box templates that enable you to create forms that map directly to objects within SharePoint.

For example, Figure 11-7 shows the SharePoint List and SharePoint Form Library templates, which are two templates that enable you to create a direct connection to SharePoint. Many other templates exist for you to use against SharePoint, and, in many cases, these are easy to configure or build a UI for (for example, creating a form to load data from a Web service).

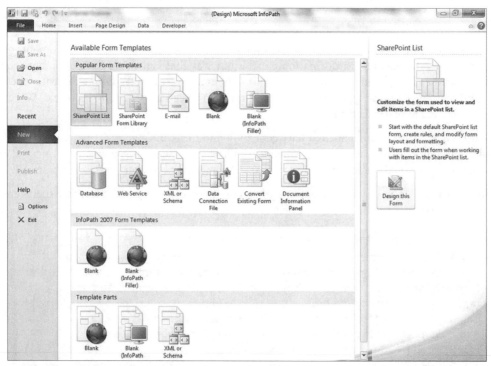

FIGURE 11-7 InfoPath form templates

Let's walk through a simple InfoPath example.

TRY IT OUT   Creating an InfoPath Form for SharePoint

InfoPath forms are easy to create and deploy to SharePoint. To create an InfoPath form, follow these steps:

1. Create a Custom list called `Customers` in your SharePoint site. Create three columns entitled `Contact Name`, `Email`, and `Phone Number`. Make all of the fields of type `"Single line of text."`

2. Open InfoPath 2010 and click File.

3. Double-click the SharePoint List template.

4. In the Data Connection Wizard, enter the URL for the SharePoint site and click Next.

5. Click the Customize an Existing SharePoint List radio button, and then select the `Customers` list.

6. Accept the default name for the connection on the next step of the wizard, and click Finish.

7. When complete, InfoPath will generate a form that maps to the fields you created in your `Customers` list, as shown in Figure 11-8.

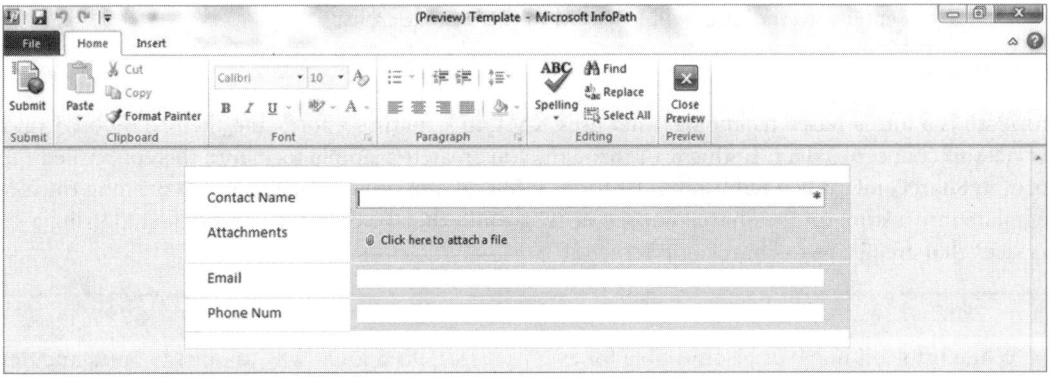

FIGURE 11-8 Contacts form

8. You can click Preview to preview the form, or you can click the Quick Publish button (to the right of the Save icon) to publish the form to SharePoint. When it is published, InfoPath will prompt you with a successful publish message.

9. To use the form in SharePoint, navigate to your SharePoint site and click Site Actions ⇨ Edit Page.

10. Click "Add a web part." Click the Office Client Applications category, and select InfoPath Form Web Part. Click Add.

11. SharePoint exposes the default InfoPath capabilities, but you need to map it to a particular form. To do this, select "Click here to open the tool pane."

12. In the "Lists or Library" drop-down, select the `Customers` list and leave all of the other default options. Click OK. SharePoint renders the InfoPath form you created in the SharePoint Web part, as shown in Figure 11-9.

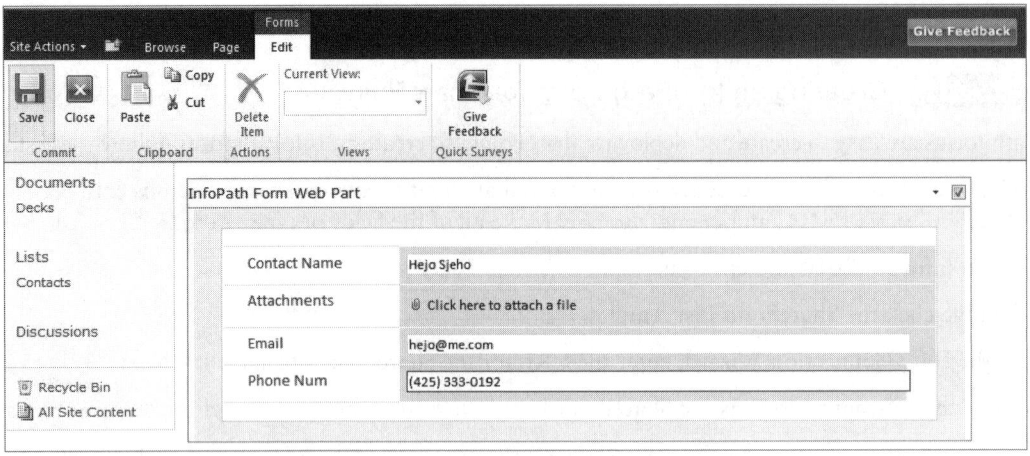

FIGURE 11-9 Rendered InfoPath form for Customers list

13. To use the InfoPath form, click the Forms Edit tab. Add some data to the form and click Save. The data you enter into the form will be saved in the `Contacts` list.

How It Works

InfoPath is a forms-based technology that uses XML to structure a form and then ADO.NET or Web services to connect to data. In this walkthrough, you created a simple form and then published the form to SharePoint. When publishing the form to SharePoint, you were essentially pushing the XML template into a store on the SharePoint server that could then be displayed and rendered using a set of services that are native to SharePoint Server 2010.

While InfoPath may not be amenable for every project, it's a great way to quickly build and deploy forms-based applications for SharePoint. You can also tie InfoPath forms (as well as other types of documents) to a SharePoint workflow, which is examined next.

MANAGING OFFICE DOCUMENTS THROUGH A SHAREPOINT WORKFLOW

Workflow is all about managing business processes. For example, let's say you're the content track owner for a major conference. You have 10 speakers who are reporting into your track, and each speaker must move documents through a review process. You can use the document libraries in SharePoint, along with either an in-box workflow or a custom workflow to manage the review and submission process.

The process might be as follows:

1.   Anu, a speaker, submits the PowerPoint deck to the document library.

2.   This kicks off the workflow that emails Jane, who is the reviewer of all decks.

3.   She opens the mail and clicks a link in the mail that takes her to Anu's deck.

4.   She reviews the deck, and either makes comments and rejects the submission, or approves it. If she approves the deck, the workflow terminates. If she rejects the deck, Anu must make the changes and then resubmit it.

This process continues until the workflow is complete — in essence until Jane approves the deck.

When you break down this workflow, each *turn* in the workflow marshals an activity through the business process, and you can build different types of activities. The in-box workflows for SharePoint are simple and generic enough that you can use them for many different scenarios — for example, feedback collection, approval, and so on. The in-box workflows are also sequential workflows. They continue to run through a set of activities in a sequential manner.

> **NOTE** *You'll note that you can also build a more complex workflow called a* state workflow, *which moves forward based on the state of an activity. You build these workflows using the Visual Studio workflow templates that leverage the Windows Workflow Foundation (WF) capabilities built into .NET. These are beyond the scope of this book.*

Let's take a look at the in-box functionality for SharePoint workflow.

TRY IT OUT   Leveraging the In-Box Workflow Capabilities

In this scenario, let's assume that you've created a contract and you want to route the contract through the native SharePoint approval workflow. To do this, follow these steps:

1.   Create a mock-up document that you can use for the workflow. Figure 11-10 provides an overview of a sample mock document.

2.   Create a new document library called Contracts, but don't add the Contracts document just yet.

3.   Click the Library tab, and then, on the far-right of the ribbon, click the Workflow settings drop-down menu. Select Add a Workflow, as shown in Figure 11-11.

4.   Select the Approval – SharePoint 2010 workflow. Provide a name for the workflow, and then click the "Start this workflow when a new item is created" and "Start this workflow when an item is changed" options, as shown in Figure 11-12.

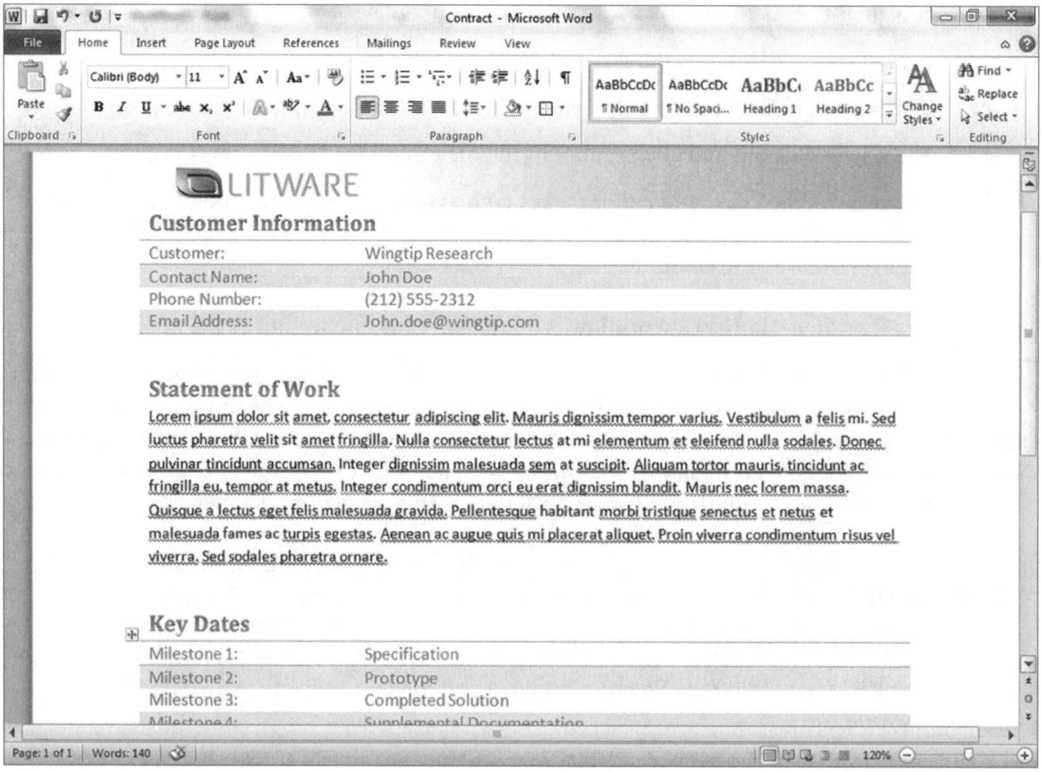

FIGURE 11-10 Contract document

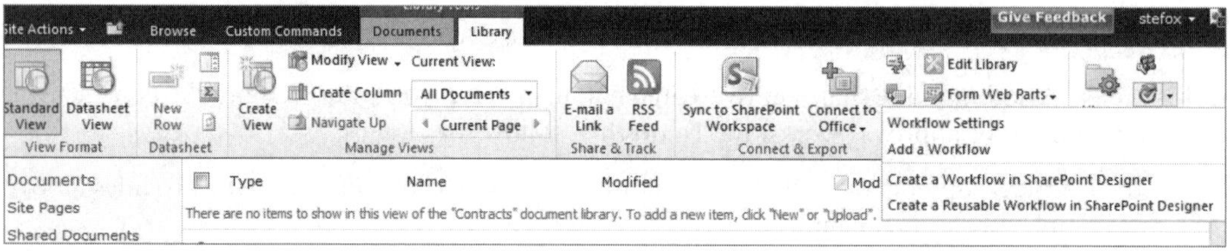

FIGURE 11-11 Add a Workflow option

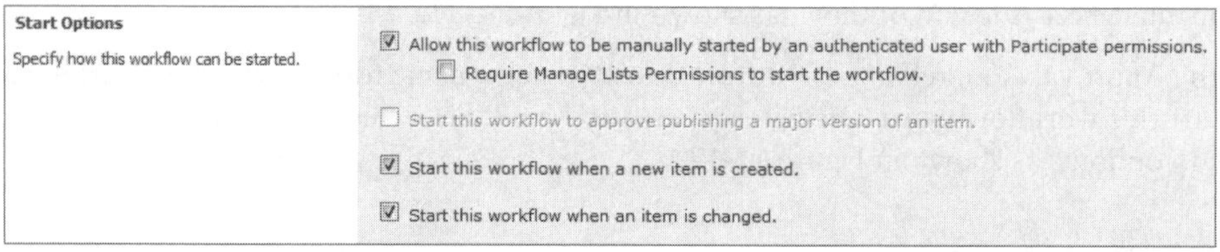

FIGURE 11-12 Configuring the workflow

5. Click Next.
6. Add the person you want to assign the workflow to (for example, the approver), write a simple notification message (which will be included in the default email message that is routed to the approver), provide a due date for the task and a task duration. Click Finish.
7. Return to the document library, and click "Add new document" to add the document to the document library.
8. After the document has been added to the document library, you'll see a new column appear in your document library. This is the workflow, and you can see that, because you marked the workflow to start when a new item is created, it is now in progress. If you click on the In Progress link, you'll note that the workflow is rendered as a flowchart using Visio Services, as shown in Figure 11-13.

Started: 2/13/2010 2:33 PM
Status: In Progress
Last run: 2/13/2010 2:34 PM
Workflow Visualization
Open in Visio
40%

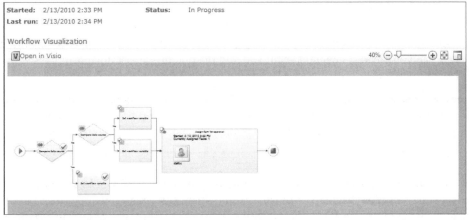

FIGURE 11-13 Workflow rendering using Visio Services

9. You can click the Tasks list in your SharePoint site, and you will see a new task that has been created by the workflow. If you click the drop-down menu, you can View or Edit the item.
10. Select Edit in the task and, when the workflow task opens, click Approve to complete the workflow.
11. Return to the document library. Your workflow should now be marked as Approved, as shown in Figure 11-14.

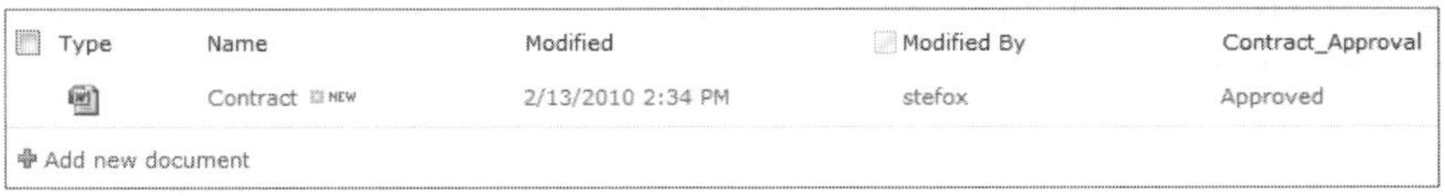

Type
Name
Modified
Modified By
Contract_Approval
Contract NEW
2/13/2010 2:34 PM
stefox
Approved
Add new document

FIGURE 11-14 Approved workflow

How It Works

The in-box workflow in SharePoint provides a number of different workflow options. In SharePoint 2010, the workflow available to you in the document library settings includes the following:

➤ *Disposition* — This supports records management and manages the document expiration and retention process by enabling participants to decide whether to retain or delete expired documents.

➤ *Three-state* — This is designed to track the status of a list item through three states (phases).

➤ *Approval* — This routes a document or item that is saved to a list or library to a group of people for approval.

➤ *Collect Signatures* — This enables you to collect signatures from an individual or group of individuals.

➤ *Collect Feedback* — This enables you to collect feedback from an individual or group of individuals.

These in-box workflow options enable application logic in your SharePoint site to execute against a list or a library. So, when you create a new document and add the document to a document library, the workflow will begin to execute.

The great thing about the in-box workflow is that it cuts across the most common scenarios (for example, feedback and approval), and the activities that are built into the in-box workflow are predefined and leverage existing lists (for example, the Tasks list) and communication channels (for example, email).

You can build a lower-level workflow for SharePoint, and, to do this, you would use the Sequential and State Machine workflow templates in Visual Studio 2010. Information workers also have the capability to define workflow in Visio, the capability to export workflow to SharePoint Designer 2010, or the capability to further export the SharePoint Designer workflow to Visual Studio 2010.

> **NOTE** For more information on how to create and deploy custom workflow using the Windows Workflow Foundation for SharePoint, see `http://channel9.msdn.com/learn/courses/SharePoint2010Developer/Workflow/`.

INTEGRATING OFFICE DOCUMENTS WITH SHAREPOINT LIST DATA

So far, you've seen many no-code solutions to integrating Office with SharePoint. However, there are many custom solutions you can build that leverage managed code solutions to integrate the two.

For example, in Chapter 5, you saw an example where you created an Excel add-in that integrated list data with spreadsheet cells. In this section, you'll create a document-level solution using Visual

Studio to integrate SharePoint list data with a Microsoft Word 2010 document — specifically, to integrate data from the list to appear in content controls.

The capability built into Visual Studio 2010 is a throwback to the VSTO functionality that was, at one point, a separate product. In Visual Studio 2008, though, VSTO became a native part of the Visual Studio developer experience. This capability enables you to build managed code solutions (that is, C# or VB.NET) against Office documents.

Not all Office documents are supported within the tools, but the most common ones are, such as Excel, Word, Outlook, and PowerPoint. In fact, when you look at the developer ecosystem around Office development, developers are coding against Excel the most, then Outlook, and then Word. Other Office applications such as PowerPoint and InfoPath are also on the list.

The way the Office development tools work is that they provide a .NET wrapper to access the Component Object Model (COM) interfaces that are native to Office. There is a very rich set of interfaces that you can code against when building Office add-ins and document-level solutions (add-ins execute at the application level, and document-level solutions execute at the document or template level). Once they are built, you publish the custom assemblies to a CD/DVD, Web share, or file share. End users can then install the assembly on their client desktops from these shares.

So, let's get started with building a custom document-level solution.

TRY IT OUT   Creating a Document-Level Solution for Word

Code file [OfficeSPIntegration.zip] available for download at Wrox.com.

You can build and deploy document-level solutions for Microsoft Office applications, which appear in the custom document when you open that document. To create a document-level solution, follow these steps:

1. Open Visual Studio 2010 and click File ⇨ New Project.

2. Navigate to Office 2010 and then select Word 2010 Document as the project template in Visual Studio 2010.

3. Provide a name (for example, `ContractsTemplate`) and location for the project, as shown in Figure 11-15, and click OK.

4. In the project wizard, you can either choose a new document or you can leverage an existing document or template in your project. For this walkthrough, use the document you created in the earlier workflow walkthrough (that is, the Contracts document). To do this, select Copy an Existing Document, then browse to the location of the document, and click OK.

5. After this step, you may be prompted with a VBA security prompt. Accept the dialog and move on.

6. Visual Studio will then create the project infrastructure for you.

7. You'll notice that the Word document itself is part of a Designer experience within Visual Studio (Figure 11-16). You'll also notice that there is a core class that marshals the startup and shutdown events for the document customization. If you click View ⇨ Toolbox, you'll see Word controls that can be dragged and dropped onto the document surface.

FIGURE 11-15 Word 2010 template

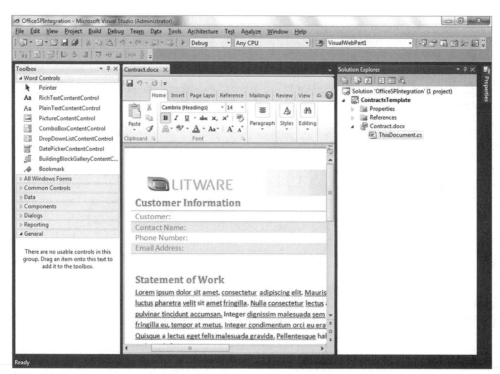

FIGURE 11-16 Word document in Visual Studio

8. Now that you have created a project, jump over to your SharePoint site and create a new Custom list called `Contracts`. Add four columns to the list called `Customer`, `Contact_Name`, `Phone_Number`, and `Email_Address` (all of type `Text` to keep things simple). After you complete the list, add some data. Your list should look similar to Figure 11-17.

	Customer	Contact_Name	Phone_Number	Email_Address
	Fabrikam ☑ NEW	John Doe	(425) 555-1234	johndoe@fabrikam.com
	Contoso ☑ NEW	Jane Smyth	(212) 555-3091	jane.smyth@contoso.com
	Acme ☑ NEW	Ahmed Patel	(344) 398-0019	ahmed@acme.com
	Wingtip ☑ NEW	LaSean Smythe	(553) 298-4455	lasean@wingtip.com

✦ Add new item

FIGURE 11-17 Custom list

9. Where you have the `Customer` Information table in your document, drag four `RichTextContentControls` onto the document surface. Each `Content` control will be placed beside the four elements in the table — that is, one for `Customer`, `Contact Name`, `Phone Number`, and `Email Address`.

10. You can click the `Content` control to expose the properties of the control. In the Properties window, name the controls as follows: (1) `wccCustomer`, (2) `wccContactName`, (3) `wccPhoneNum`, and (4) `wccEmailAddress`.

11. Now right-click the project and select Add ➪ Class. Name the class `Customers` and click OK.

12. Add the following bolded code to the default class code that is created for you. These are four properties of the class that map to the list you created in SharePoint.

```
using System;
using System.Collections.Generic;
using System.Linq;
using System.Text;

namespace ContractsTemplate
{
    class Customers
    {
        public string custName { get; set; }
        public string contactName { get; set; }
        public string contactNum { get; set; }
        public string contactEmail { get; set; }
    }
}
```

13. After you've added the `Customers` class, right-click the project and select Add References. Select the Recent tab (or browse) and add the `Microsoft.SharePoint.Client.dll` and `Microsoft.SharePoint.Client.Runtime.dll` to the References folder. Using these references, you will leverage the client object model to interact with the data in the SharePoint list.

14. After you add the references, right-click the project and click Add ➪ New Item. Select Ribbon (Designer). Provide a name for the ribbon (for example, `CustomerRibon`) and click OK.

15. In the Visual Ribbon Designer, drag a combo box control into the first group, and then add a button alongside in the first group. You can rename the group control by clicking the outside edge of the control and changing the `Name` property in the Properties window. You can also change the `Label` text. You can do the same thing for the combo box control (for example, `cmbobxCustomers`) and the button control (for example, `btnLoad`).

16. Click the combo box and then, in the Properties window, click the Collection ellipsis to add four items that map to the names of the companies you added in your SharePoint list (for example, Fabrikam, Contoso, Acme, and Wingtip).

17. Double-click the button to get to the code behind.

18. In the code behind, add the following bolded code to the existing default code. Note that you will need to update the server URL referenced in the `mySPSite` string to reflect your SharePoint server.

```
using System;
using System.Collections.Generic;
using System.Linq;
using System.Text;
using Microsoft.Office.Tools.Ribbon;

using Microsoft.SharePoint.Client;
using ClientOM = Microsoft.SharePoint.Client;

namespace ContractsTemplate
{
    public partial class CustomerRibbon
    {
        IEnumerable<ClientOM.ListItem> myListItems;
        List<Customers> myCustomers = new List<Customers>();
        //Be sure to update this URL to reflect your SharePoint server.
        string mySPSite = "http://fabrikamhockey";
        string custFilter = "";

        private void CustomerRibbon_Load(object sender, RibbonUIEventArgs e)
        {

        private void btnLoad_Click(object sender, RibbonControlEventArgs e)
        {
            custFilter = cmbobxCustomers.Text;

            ClientOM.ClientContext SPContext = new ClientOM.ClientContext(mySPSite);
            ClientOM.Web mySPWeb = SPContext.Web;
            ClientOM.ListCollection myListCollection = mySPWeb.Lists;
            var productsList = SPContext.Web.Lists.GetByTitle("Contracts");
            ClientOM.CamlQuery myCamlQuery = new CamlQuery();
            IQueryable<ClientOM.ListItem> myList = productsList.
                GetItems(myCamlQuery);
            myListItems = SPContext.LoadQuery(myList);
            SPContext.ExecuteQuery();

            var returnCustomerData = from cust in myListItems
                                     select cust;

            foreach (ClientOM.ListItem tempListItem in returnCustomerData)
```

```
        {
            Customers tempCustomer = new Customers();
            tempCustomer.custName =
                tempListItem.FieldValues.Values.ElementAt(1).ToString();
            tempCustomer.contactName =
                tempListItem.FieldValues.Values.ElementAt(4).ToString();
            tempCustomer.contactNum =
                tempListItem.FieldValues.Values.ElementAt(5).ToString();
            tempCustomer.contactEmail =
                tempListItem.FieldValues.Values.ElementAt(6).ToString();
            myCustomers.Add(tempCustomer);
        }

        if (custFilter == "Fabrikam")
        {
            Globals.ThisDocument.wccCustomer.Text =
                myCustomers[0].custName.ToString();
            Globals.ThisDocument.wccContactName.Text =
                myCustomers[0].contactName.ToString();
            Globals.ThisDocument.wccPhoneNum.Text =
                myCustomers[0].contactNum.ToString();
            Globals.ThisDocument.wccEmailAddress.Text =
                myCustomers[0].contactEmail.ToString();
        }
        else if (custFilter == "Contoso")
        {
            Globals.ThisDocument.wccCustomer.Text =
                myCustomers[1].custName.ToString();
            Globals.ThisDocument.wccContactName.Text =
                myCustomers[1].contactName.ToString();
            Globals.ThisDocument.wccPhoneNum.Text =
                myCustomers[1].contactNum.ToString();
            Globals.ThisDocument.wccEmailAddress.Text =
                myCustomers[1].contactEmail.ToString();
        }
        else if (custFilter == "Acme")
        {
            Globals.ThisDocument.wccCustomer.Text =
                myCustomers[2].custName.ToString();
            Globals.ThisDocument.wccContactName.Text =
                myCustomers[2].contactName.ToString();
            Globals.ThisDocument.wccPhoneNum.Text =
                myCustomers[2].contactNum.ToString();
            Globals.ThisDocument.wccEmailAddress.Text =
                myCustomers[2].contactEmail.ToString();
        }
        else if (custFilter == "Wingtip")
        {
            Globals.ThisDocument.wccCustomer.Text =
                myCustomers[3].custName.ToString();
            Globals.ThisDocument.wccContactName.Text =
                myCustomers[3].contactName.ToString();
            Globals.ThisDocument.wccPhoneNum.Text =
                myCustomers[3].contactNum.ToString();
            Globals.ThisDocument.wccEmailAddress.Text =
```

```
                                  myCustomers[3].contactEmail.ToString();
                         }
                     }
                 }
         }
```

19. After you've added all of this code, press F5 to run the application.

20. Microsoft Word will invoke the custom assembly, and you'll see a new tab added to the Word ribbon. In the combo box, select one of the four companies that is listed in the combo box.

21. Click the Load button.

Your custom Word assembly will call the client object model code and then load the specific information that maps to the selection in the combo box you selected. Change selections to test out other companies loading into the content controls in the document. The final integration should look similar to Figure 11-18.

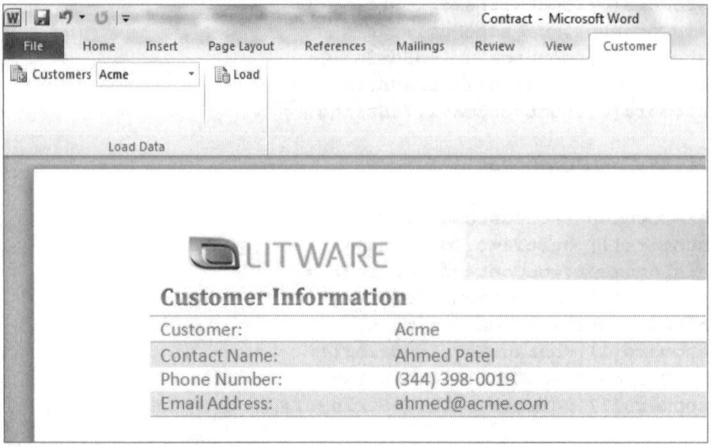

FIGURE 11-18 Content controls loaded in Word document

How It Works

As mentioned earlier, the Office development tools provide a set of APIs that enable you to code against the Office object model — which is fairly extensive. In this example, the core object you used in the Office object model was the content control, which is a way to programmatically surface data within a Word document. The content control is an object that can be explicitly data-bound, or, as you did in the walkthrough, you can dynamically set properties (in this case the Text property) of the content control at run-time.

Thus, while you've seen some of the code before (that is, where you leverage the client object model to get list data from SharePoint), the one thing that was new was leveraging the Globals API to get at the specific content control (for example, wccCustomer) to assign the Text property with a specific index value from the list collection you created.

Following is a code snippet where you were assigning the specific field values (custName, contactName, contactNum, and contactEmail) from the fourth index position in the list collection (marked as 3 in the index because the starting index point is 0).

```
Globals.ThisDocument.wccCustomer.Text = myCustomers[3].custName.ToString();
Globals.ThisDocument.wccContactName.Text = myCustomers[3].contactName.ToString();
Globals.ThisDocument.wccPhoneNum.Text = myCustomers[3].contactNum.ToString();
Globals.ThisDocument.wccEmailAddress.Text = myCustomers[3].contactEmail.ToString();
```

While you didn't deploy the application, you can do this by right-clicking your project and then selecting Properties. Select the Publish tab in your Properties, and you'll see a number of items that you can specify. In Figure 11-19, you can see that a specific publishing folder and installation folder (which don't have to be the same) have been specified. You can configure other options, but if you simply want to deploy the custom Word document to a specific folder, just set those options and click Publish Now.

After you publish the application, you can navigate to the folder, and you'll find a folder with all of the published application files, the document you customized, a deployment manifest (which tracks the version and other assembly information), and then, finally, the setup file, as shown in Figure 11-20. If you double-click the setup.exe file, this will install the custom application onto your client machine. If you published your application to a file share or Web site, then other people could also install the application. Note that if they were to install the application, they would require access to the SharePoint site you built the application against in order to run the application.

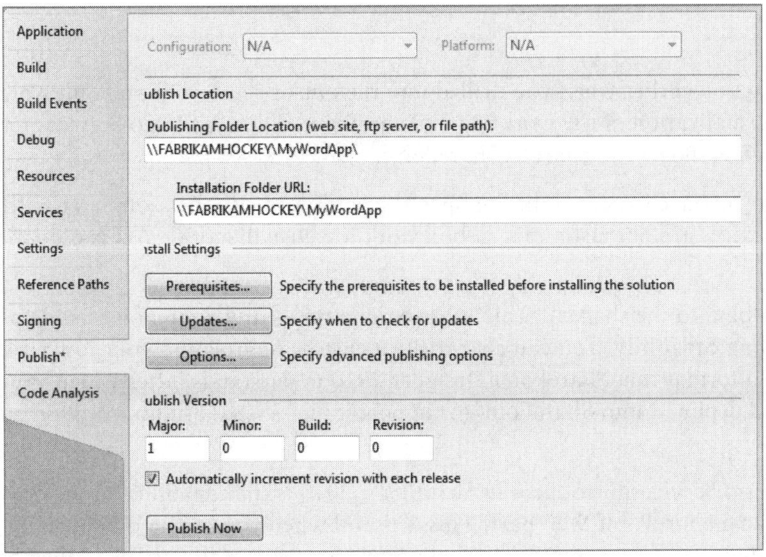

FIGURE 11-19 Publish tab in project Properties

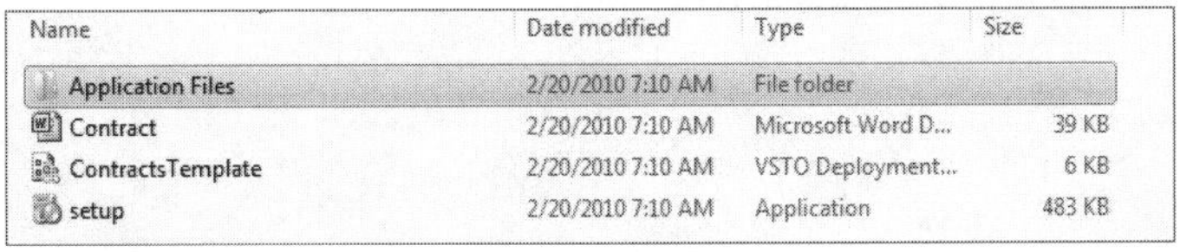

FIGURE 11-20 Final publishing of files

With regard to Office development, there are many more types of applications that you can build. The Office object model is vast, and given that so many people use Office on a daily basis, there is a great opportunity for developers to engage and deploy their SharePoint integrations in this space.

SERVER-SIDE SERVICES

The Office server-side services are another Office integration that is new to SharePoint 2010. While some of these services existed in SharePoint 2007 (for example, Excel Services), they have been augmented in some fashion or are new to the services stack. Of interest to this chapter are four main server-side services:

➤   Visio Services

➤   Excel Services

➤   Word Services

➤   Access Services

The remainder of this chapter briefly examines each one of these services.

Visio Services

You saw Visio Services in action earlier when you drilled into the out-of-the-box SharePoint workflow and saw a flowchart visualization of the workflow in SharePoint. This was Visio Services rendering the workflow as a server-side Visio chart in SharePoint.

You may have noticed that you have the capability to open the workflow visualization in Visio from the server as well. Visio Services are not just about in-box workflow visualization. You can do much more using these services.

For example, you can data-bind to the shapes within a Visio diagram — and SharePoint list data is supported within this binding capability. You can also create a custom SharePoint workflow within Visio and then save this in a format that SharePoint Designer 2010 understands, after which you can flesh out that workflow and deploy it into SharePoint (or import it into Visual Studio 2010 for further customization).

Another innovation that Visio Services introduces in SharePoint 2010 is the capability to surface a Visio diagram from within a SharePoint Web part. This is useful when you have a dynamically changing and data-bound diagram (for example, data bound to a SharePoint list) that can then be rendered within a Web part on the server.

Let's walk through a simple example to show how this can be done.

TRY IT OUT   Creating a Simple Visio Web Part Diagram

Visio has some great "mash-up" capabilities, which enable it to easily be integrated into SharePoint 2010. To create a simple Visio Web part diagram, follow these steps:

1.   Open Visio 2010. Click File ⇨ New and then select the ITIL Diagram.

2.   Create a diagram that looks similar to Figure 11-21.

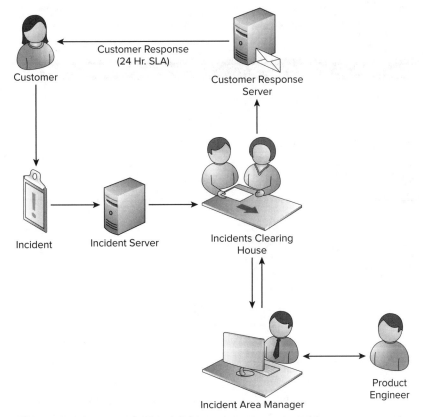

FIGURE 11-21 Incident process definition

3.   When you finish building the diagram, click the Backstage tab (the tab on the upper-left part of the Visio document) and then click Share. At the bottom of the Backstage view, select Web Diagram. Note that, after you've finished, when you click Save As, there is an Options button that you can click to see what pages (if you have multiple pages in your Visio diagram) will be published to Visio Services.

4.   Next, upload the Visio diagram to a document library.

5.   Click the drop-down menu beside the uploaded document and select View Properties.

6.   Select Copy Shortcut.

7.   Navigate to the location where you want to add the diagram on your SharePoint site, and then click Site Actions ⇨ Edit Page.

8. Click "Add a web part" (or, if you're on a wiki page, click the Insert tab and select Web Part).

9. Navigate to the Office Client Applications, and select Visio Web Access Web part.

10. Once it is added, you can edit the Web part using the tool pane. Specifically, you want to copy the shortcut to the Visio diagram into the Web Drawing URL file and then click Apply. The Visio Web drawing will now be rendered in your SharePoint site, as shown in Figure 11-22.

FIGURE 11-22 Visio Web drawing in SharePoint

When you interact with the drawing in SharePoint, you can adjust the size of the Web part, or you can move the diagram around within the Web part. As mentioned earlier, you could bind lists (or other data sources) to the shapes within the diagram to add another dimension to your Web diagrams. This is a trivial task, which involves your clicking on a particular shape when you have the diagram open, clicking the Data tab, and then walking through a wizard to link that shape to a specific data source.

Excel Services

Excel Services are yet another set of shared services that you can use on the server side in a number of ways. For example, with Excel Services, three pieces work together:

➤ Excel Web Access (for exposing Excel data and objects in Web parts)

➤ Excel Calculation Services (which you can leverage on the server)

➤ Excel Web Services (which provide an API to programmatically interact with your Excel documents)

You can use Excel Services to expose data from an Excel spreadsheet and surface this data in a Web part. You can leverage the REST APIs (similarly to what you did in Chapter 5 with a SharePoint list). Or, you can leverage the Open XML SDK and access the underlying XML structure and data within an Excel document. Interestingly, the Open XML SDK does not relegate you to just coding against an Excel document. You can also move data from within Word documents to Excel documents, or to other documents (for example, PowerPoint documents), where you can programmatically access the underlying data within the document. Lastly, Excel Services also exposes a native ASP.NET API through the Excel Services Web service. This API has a number of members that enable you to also programmatically interact with documents on the server.

Let's keep things relatively straightforward in this section and show you how you can integrate data from an Excel spreadsheet with an Excel Web Access Web part.

TRY IT OUT Integrating Excel Data with an Excel Web Access Web Part

Excel Web Access Web parts expose data in an Excel spreadsheet in SharePoint. To create an Excel Web Access Web part, follow these steps:

1. Open Microsoft Excel 2010. Click File ➪ New ➪ Blank Workbook.

2. Add some data in the spreadsheet, and then create a simple chart using the native chart capabilities. To do this, select the data from which you want to create a chart, and then select Insert. Then select a particular chart type. Figure 11-23 shows the Bar chart graphically representing the data.

3. At this point, save the Excel document to a document library on your SharePoint site.

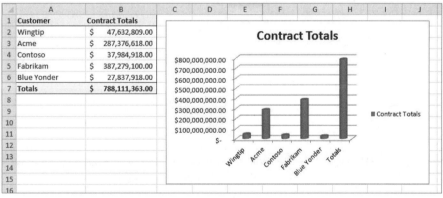

FIGURE 11-23 Excel workbook data

4. When saved, right-click the document and select "Edit in Microsoft Excel."

5. In the Backstage view, click Share ➪ Publish to Excel Services.

6. When the Save As dialog prompts you, click the Options button, and then select the parts of the workbook you want to publish to Excel Services. In this example, you'll only expose the chart.

7. Save the Excel document. Navigate to a separate SharePoint site or Web page, and click Site Actions ➪ Edit Page.

8. Click "Add a web part" (or Insert ⇨ web part), and then navigate to the Office Client Applications category.

9. Select Excel Web Access and click Add.

10. SharePoint adds the Web part, but you still must configure it. Open the tools pane and enter the URL to the spreadsheet in the Workbook field (or navigate to the spreadsheet). Enter the object you want to expose in the Excel Web Access Web part (Chart 1).

11. Click OK. Figure 11-24 shows what the example data would look like rendered in the Web part.

FIGURE 11-24 Excel Web Access rendering Excel data

How It Works

This walkthrough was fairly straightforward. It leveraged many of the native features that ship in-box with SharePoint. Essentially, the Excel Services provide built-in capabilities to render specific parts of an Excel workbook, and, in this example, you simply tapped into that functionality.

You exposed the chart (which is named Chart 1 by default) as the object to be rendered within the Excel Web Access Web part. Note that the Excel Web Access Web part does not refresh on page load. Rather, it provides you with the capability to refresh changes from your workbook through an explicit call you can make by clicking Data ⇨ Refresh All Connections.

Another way to leverage native APIs that ship with SharePoint is the Excel Services Web services. To browse the methods that are available to you, open your Internet browser and type in the following URL:

```
http://<your_server_name>/_vti_bin/ExcelService.asmx
```

You'll see that there are a variety of methods that you can use. For example, what if you wanted to create a simple Windows Form application that retrieves the `Customer` and `Contract Totals` from the spreadsheet from the earlier walkthrough? You could use the Excel Services Web service to do that.

Specifically, you have four options (`GetCell`, `GetCellA1`, `GetRange`, `GetRangeA1`), but one option is to use the `GetRangeA1` method. By using the `GetRangeA1` method, you can pass in a number of parameters (such as session ID, the name of the spreadsheet, the range of the cells you'd like to retrieve, formatting information, and alert information), and the values from the range will be returned to you.

Let's walk through an example.

TRY IT OUT Leveraging the Excel Services Web Service

Code file [ExcelServices.zip] available for download at Wrox.com.

The Excel Services Web service provides a number of methods to interact with data on the server from a spreadsheet. To retrieve data from a spreadsheet programmatically using the Excel services API, follow these steps:

1. Open the `Contracts` Excel spreadsheet you added to SharePoint in Edit mode, and select all of the `Customer` and `Contract Totals`. Create a named range by typing `ContractTotals` in the Name box (in the upper left-hand corner of the spreadsheet) and then pressing Enter.

2. Save and close the spreadsheet.

3. Open Visual Studio 2010. Click File ➪ New ➪ Windows ➪ Windows Form Application.

4. Add a data grid and two buttons to your Windows Form application. Name the data grid `datagrdExcelData`, one button `btnLoad`, and the other button `btnExit`. The `Text` property for `btnLoad` should be `Load`, and the `Text` property for `btnExit` should be `Exit`.

5. Right-click References, and click Add Service Reference. Then, in the Service Reference Settings dialog, click Advanced ➪ Add Web Reference. Type in the URL to the Excel Services Web service:

```
http://<server_name>/_vti_bin/ExcelService.asmx.
```

6. Provide a name for the Web service reference (for example, `XLWebService`) and click Add Reference.

7. Double-click the Exit button and add the following bolded code:

```
private void btnExit_Click(object sender, EventArgs e)
{
    Application.Exit();
}
```

8. Double-click the Load button and add the following bolded code:

```
private void btnLoad_Click(object sender, EventArgs e)
  {
    XLWebService.ExcelService proxy = new XLWebService.ExcelService();
    proxy.Credentials = new System.Net.NetworkCredentials
        ("Administrator", "pass@word1");
```

```
XLWebService.Status[] wsStatus;

string sheetName = "Sheet1";
string namedRange = "ContractTotals";

DataTable contractData = new DataTable("Contract Totals");
DataColumn compName = contracData.Columns.Add("Customer",
    Type.GetType("System.String"));
DataColumn contractTotal = contractData.Columns.Add("Contract Totals",
    Type.GetType("System.String"));
DataRow newRow;

string sessionID = proxy.OpenWorkbook
    ("http://fabrikamhockey/Contracts/Contract_Totals.xlsx", "en-US",
    "en-US", out wsStatus);

object[] returnData = proxy.GetRangeA1(sessionID, sheetName, namedRange, false,
    out wsStatus);

for (int I = 11 I < returnData.Length; i++)
  {
    newRow = contractData.NewRow();
    newRow["Customer"] = ((object[])(returnData[i]))[0].ToString();
    newRow["Contract Totals"] = "$ " + ((object[])(returnData[i]))[1].
        ToString() + ".00";
    contractData.Rows.Add(newRow);
  }
datagrdExcelData.DataSource = contractData;
}
}
```

9. When finished adding the code, press F6 to build the project, and then press F5 to run it.

10. When the application launches, click Load to run the Excel Web Service and load the data from the spreadsheet. The result should look similar to Figure 11-25.

How It Works

In the walkthrough, you're using the built-in capabilities of the Excel Web Services — specifically, using the GetRangeA1 method to retrieve data from your Contracts spreadsheet. However, you are specifically using a named range to target a group of cells that you can then retrieve using this method. You assigned this named range to a string variable and then passed this in as one of the key parameters.

FIGURE 11-25 Retrieved data from Excel spreadsheet

```
String namedRange = "ContractTotals";
```

In the code, you first needed to create a service proxy (`proxy`), which you then used to call the `OpenWorkbook` method and `GetRangeA1` method.

```
…
XLWebService.ExcelService proxy = new XLWebService.ExcelService();
proxy.Credentials = new System.Net.NetworkCredentials("Administrator",
    "pass@word1");
…
string sessionID = proxy.OpenWorkbook
    ("http://fabrikamhockey/Contracts/Contract_Totals.xlsx", "en-US",
    "en-US", out wsStatus);
object[] returnData = proxy.GetRangeA1(sessionID, sheetName, namedRange, false,
    out wsStatus);
…
```

You'll also note that you used a `DataTable` object. This was to get the data into a more structured data object that would directly data-bind to the datagrid. The following code shows an instantiation of the `DataTable`, along with two columns and the creation of a new row, that you used inside the `for` loop to populate the table:

```
…
DataTable contractData = new DataTable("Contract Totals");
DataColumn compName = contracData.Columns.Add("Customer",
    Type.GetType("System.String"));
DataColumn contractTotal = contractData.Columns.Add("Contract Totals",
    Type.GetType("System.String"));
DataRow newRow;
…
```

You used a tricky expression to retrieve the values from the `returnData` object. In the `for` loop, you used `((object[])(returnData[i]))[0].ToString()` as the expression to get at the specific field data in the `returnData` object. You'll note that you needed an `object[]` cast, and then used the `i` variable to get data from a specific index. Because, within the array, the first position had data from the first column, and the second data from the second column, you had to use `[0]` and `[1]`, respectively, to retrieve the data from those elements in the array.

```
…
for (int i = 11 I < returnData.Length; i++)
 {
     newRow = contractData.NewRow();
newRow["Customer"] = ((object[])(returnData[i]))[0].ToString();
newRow["Contract Totals"] = "$ " + ((object[])(returnData[i]))[1].
    ToString() + ".00";
contractData.Rows.Add(newRow);
 }
…
```

Once you did this, you could then data-bind the results to the datagrid.

```
datagrdExcelData.DataSource = contractData;
```

Beyond the native Web services, there are many ways to leverage Excel Services — especially when you begin to integrate them with other client applications and technologies. Beyond leveraging the native Excel Services capabilities, or exposing them in WinForm, WPF, or Silverlight applications, Open XML is a very powerful standard, and, given that some of the more common Office documents (such as Word, Excel, and PowerPoint) leverage this underlying standard, you can create some very powerful applications.

> **NOTE** *To download the Open XML SDK, go to* http://www.microsoft
> .com/downloads/details.aspx?FamilyID=c6e744e5-36e9-45f5-8d8c-
> 331df206e0d0&DisplayLang=en

Word Services

The server-side Word Services provide some enhanced capabilities. Where Excel Services provide you with a set of ASP.NET services that are native to SharePoint, Word Services represent an API that you can leverage to accomplish a number of tasks. Primarily, you can use the automation services to automate the conversion of .docx files into other file types such as PDF or XPS. While this may not sound exciting, it's actually very compelling, given the speed with which you can execute this automation against documents living on the server.

Think of the scenario (for example, invoices, itineraries, expense claims, sales proposals, and so on) where you operate on those items on a daily basis in Microsoft Office. This scenario requires a batch process to translate those documents into PDF format, then save them to the server and distribute them to a customer for review/approval.

One of the core reference assemblies you'll use to automate Word tasks is the Microsoft.Office. Word.Server.dll. This is where you'll find many of the APIs you need to do the conversions mentioned previously.

For instance, the following code snippet provides an example of an event receiver that has been built and deployed against a specific list so that any .docx document added to the list will be automatically converted into PDF. Note that, in this code, the ItemAdded event is an auto-generated event when you use the Visual Studio EventReceiver class. The bolded code is the code that you would write to manage the conversion, of which the bulk lies within the if statement. The if condition checks to see if the document ends with the .docx extension. If it does, by using the SPWeb context as it runs through the process of setting the OutputFormat (that is, the .pdf extension), you establish a path to the document library where the file is stored, and then create a ConversionJob object to set specific properties for the conversion. You then start the conversion by calling the Start method.

```
...
public class MyEventReceiver : SPItemEventReceiver
{
public override void ItemAdded(SPItemEventProperties properties)
{
```

```
    string fileToConvert = properties.AfterURL;

if(fileToConvert.EndsWith(".docx");
    {
        using (SPWeb web = properties.OpenWeb())
        {
          ConversionjobSettings myJobSettings = new ConversionJobSettings();
        {
            OutputFormat = SaveFormat.PDF;
        }
        string filePath = http://fabrikamhockey/myDocs/ + fileToConvert;
        ConversionJob myJob = new ConversionJob("DOCX Automation",
        myJobSettings)
        myJob.UserToken = web.CurrentUser.UserToken;
        myJob.AddFile(filePath, filePath.Replace(".docx", ".pdf"));
        myJob.Start();
          }
    }
Base.ItemAdded(properties);
}
}
...
```

Word Services are a native component of SharePoint Server 2010 and allow you to perform the previously described batch operations on the server, which historically required you to automate the desktop implementation of Word. And you're not just limited to converting docx files to PDF ones; you can also automate the conversion of docx files to doc (for example, Word 97) or update fields or even use in combination with the Open XML SDK to integrate the power of working with the underlying data structures within documents to then move that data across documents and convert those documents.

For example, you can use the combination of the Word Services and the Open XML SDK to handle tasks that don't necessarily require custom application logic — such as inserting data from other documents, or deleting or amending content in documents, and then batch processing the conversion of these changes into a customer-ready format on the server. The end result is that you can use these two technologies together on the server without having to automate client-side tasks (that is, build VSTO add-ins to do the same work), which can save you time and effort in the area of deployment and configuration of individual client desktops with an Office add-in that does something similar. Instead, you deploy your code to the server and run the code on the back end.

Access Services

The last server-side service to discuss in this chapter is Access Services. Access 2010 is an interesting shift away from the integration that was introduced in SharePoint 2007. With Access 2010, SharePoint 2010 becomes a more powerful endpoint for Access databases.

What this means is that you can create Access databases using the client installation of Access and then publish the databases to SharePoint 2010. The publishing process creates a dashboard that renders all of the tables, macros, and links you create in Access within a SharePoint site. During the publishing process, the structure of the Access database (as it exists within Access) is translated into a list structure and queries that SharePoint understands. However, the experience is bidirectional — meaning that you don't just end up with a read-only view of the data, but you get a read/write view of the data from within a dashboard in SharePoint with forms that let you customize the way in which your data is presented.

Let's walk through an example.

TRY IT OUT Creating an Access Database for SharePoint

Access 2010 has tighter integration with SharePoint 2010 than it did with SharePoint 2007 (where you created views with Access databases). To create and publish an Access database to SharePoint, follow these steps:

1. Open Access. Click File ➪ New ➪ Blank Web Database.

2. Access will create a table, by default called `Table_1`. Right-click the table and rename it something else (for example, `Inventory`).

3. Right-click the newly named table (or select the Views drop-down menu), and then select Design View.

4. Add some columns and then switch back to Datasheet view. Add some data into the fields, as shown in Figure 11-26.

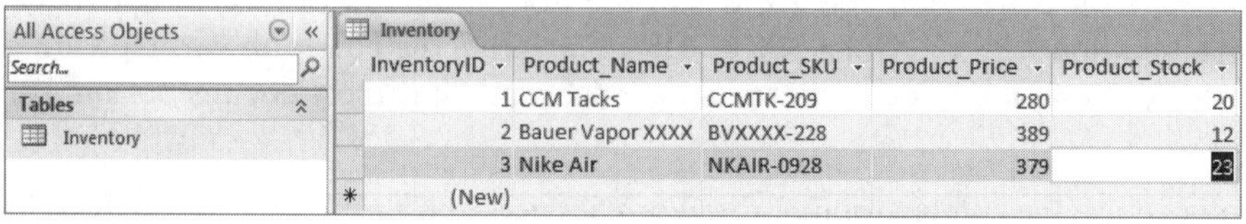

FIGURE 11-26 Simple Access database

5. When you've finished adding values into the fields, save the database.

6. Because you're building an Access database for SharePoint, you'll want to provide a form for your database. You can create simple forms using the native theming that Access provides in-box. To create a form, select the Create tab and then click Form. You can add controls, graphics, or other types of branding. In this walkthrough, simply click Themes and select one of the native themes. When you are finished, click Views and then Form View to see what the final form will look like.

7. When you have finished, click the Save button.

8. Now that you've created the database and form, you are ready to publish the Access database to SharePoint. To do this, click the Backstage tab and select Share. In the Share options, click the Publish to Access Services option.

9. You'll first want to run the compatibility checker to ensure that your database is compatible with the Web. If it is, Access will provide a message that reads, "Access database is compatible with the Web" in the Backstage view.

10. Add the Server URL for your site (for example, `http://fabrikamhockey`) and then the Site Name (for example, `Inventory`).

11. After you've done this, click Publish to Access Services, and Access will publish your database to your SharePoint site.

12. When the site has been published successfully, you'll be prompted with a success dialog that contains the URL that points to the new Access database that has been published to SharePoint.

13. Click the `Inventory_DB` form. Your Access database form will be rendered, as shown in Figure 11-27, enabling you to walk through the data and change it as necessary.

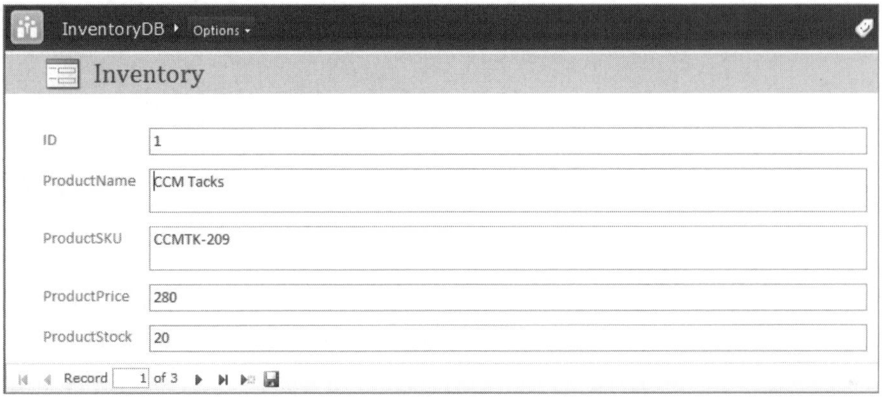

FIGURE 11-27 Newly published Access database

SUMMARY

There is tremendous potential for developers that stretches across the relationship between Office and SharePoint. They have been designed to work hand in glove. This chapter only scratched the surface of what's possible for you to do — with both no-code and code solutions. Specifically, you saw some simple integrations using content types, InfoPath, in-box workflows, and server-side services. You also saw some more code-centric solutions using the Office development templates in Visual Studio 2010, the Excel Web services on the server, and the Word services API.

You can leverage many of the areas discussed in this chapter to very easily augment your SharePoint solutions with preexisting functionality and technologies that are very widely understood in the market.

You've come a long way from the start of the book, and now there's only one more chapter to go. In Chapter 12, you'll see a high-level discussion on some of the different security aspects of SharePoint.

1. Create a custom document-level solution. Then deploy this as a content type into SharePoint so that whenever a user clicks the New Document button in a document library, it will load your custom document.

2. Create an InfoPath form that loads data from an external Web service (for example, to populate a listbox), and then use the InfoPath form to push the data into a SharePoint list.

3. Use Excel to create a document-level solution and tie a custom ribbon to cells in a spreadsheet instead of tying a custom ribbon to content controls for Word.

4. Create an event receiver for a document library so that when a document (that is, a `.docx` file) is added, it is converted to an older Word 97 document (`doc`).

▶ **WHAT YOU LEARNED IN THIS CHAPTER**

ITEM	DESCRIPTION
Content Type	A reusable object (such as a set of columns or a document) that can be used across a SharePoint site.
InfoPath Forms	InfoPath is a forms-based technology that provides a great way to build robust, data-driven (ADO.NET or service-driven) forms that can be easily published to SharePoint.
Workflow	SharePoint provides some in-box workflows but also provides the capability for you to build more a complex, custom workflow. You can use Visual Studio 2010 to build out this workflow for SharePoint.
Custom Add-Ins/ Doc-Level Solutions	You can build code-centric, smart-client Office applications that are rendered whenever a specific document is opened (document-level solution) or whenever a specific Office application is opened (application-level add-in).
Office Server-Side Services	A set of services that provides you with ASP.NET services and APIs to programmatically interact with documents on the server.

RECOMMENDED READING

➤ Visio team blog at `http://blogs.msdn.com/visio`

➤ Channel 9 Office Developer Learning Center at `http://channel9.msdn.com/learn/courses/Office2010/`

➤ Channel 9 SharePoint Developer Learning Center at `http://channel9.msdn.com/learn/courses/SharePoint2010Developer/`

➤ MSDN Office Developer Center at `http://msdn.microsoft.com/en-us/office/default.aspx`

➤ InfoPath team blog at `http://blogs.msdn.com/infopath`

➤ Office Developer Training Kit download at `http://www.microsoft.com/downloads/details.aspx?displaylang=en&FamilyID=f1599288-a99f-410f-a219-f4375dbe310c`

12

Securing Your SharePoint 2010 Applications

WHAT YOU'LL LEARN IN THIS CHAPTER:

➤   Authenticating users in SharePoint

➤   Understanding the difference between farm-level solutions and sand-boxed solutions

➤   Understanding federated authentication using forms-based authentication and claims-based authentication

SharePoint security is a vast topic that can't be covered fully in a single chapter. You could likely dedicate an entire book to SharePoint security. This is because when you talk about security and SharePoint, you're not just referring to SharePoint. SharePoint is built on ASP. NET, which has its own security architecture and framework. It is deployed to Internet Information Services (IIS), which also has its own framework and configuration. And SharePoint itself has its own security infrastructure that leverages Active Directory (AD), among other security technologies. The goal of this chapter, therefore, is to provide a high-level introduction to a set of SharePoint security topics.

SharePoint 2010 has a flexible security infrastructure that supports a number of different technologies (such as AD, claims-based authentication, forms-based authentication, Kerberos, and many more). The different types of security in SharePoint support different scenarios. For example, if you're trying to grant access for an individual or group to content on a site within your organization, then you would leverage AD, and assign permissions to specific site content to individuals or groups. If you were trying to federate that access to an external system (for example, integrating SAP data within a SharePoint site), then you might use the Secure Store Service (SSS) or claims-based authentication to provision access.

When you're developing for SharePoint, you develop and deploy applications at different security levels. For example, you can build either a farm-level solution or a sandboxed solution for SharePoint 2010. You also need to think about those users who have access to specific service-based applications, such as applications based on Business Connectivity Services (BCS). Exposing augmented permissions to all users could result in unwanted deletions, corruptions, or, worse, data mismanagement or public exposure.

The key take-away here is that you have many different ways in SharePoint to negotiate and configure security.

In this chapter, you'll start by becoming familiar with the authorization fundamentals using AD. You'll then see how you can develop farm-level and sandboxed solutions to get a sense for how they're different. You'll also see how you can use SSS to provision access to external systems for BCS applications. And, finally, you'll learn about federated authentication for SharePoint through forms-based and claims-based authentication.

AUTHORIZATION

In Chapter 1, you saw a high-level architecture of a SharePoint farm and walked through an example where you assigned permissions to a specific user in a SharePoint site. Within this architecture, you had one or more servers (constituting the "farm"). You had IIS running on the servers, and then you had Web applications within IIS that hosted the SharePoint site collection and the Central Administration site collection. Within this architecture, there are a couple of fundamental security items to call out.

The first is that, because SharePoint is built on ASP.NET, and IIS supports ASP.NET, IIS is agnostic to the Web application being a SharePoint site. It treats it just as it would any other Web application. Of particular significance is the fact that each Web application runs inside an *application pool*, which is an isolated environment where your Web application runs its worker processes. This is a protective measure to isolate site processes to not bring down all Web applications on IIS by all sites using the same application pool — although you could theoretically connect all of the Web applications to the same application pool, which would increase your failover risk significantly.

The second is that, by default, SharePoint leverages AD to help manage permissions. AD is a Windows-based technology that provides a number of key network and security services, such as directory services, Domain Name System (DNS–)-based naming and network information, network authority management, central identity storage, and so on. The goal with AD is to have one standard approach for the Windows environment that helps manage policies and authorization for a team or organization. Using AD, you can manage authentication that scales across tens of thousands of users, and manage different domains and servers that cut across a global server farm.

One of the fundamental aspects of SharePoint is the management of different permission levels using AD records. A *record* is an individual entry within AD. For example, Figure 12-1 shows a set of Users within Active Directory.

What this means is that site collection administrators can provision access to individuals who have a record in AD. You can also give a user different levels of permissions (such as view, contributor, or full control), or you can add the user to a higher-level security group that you can then use to manage security within your site. (For many administrators, the group is the preferred way to manage security because it provides a more controlled and manageable approach.) For example, in Figure 12-2, you can see that Arlene Huff (one of the records listed in AD from Figure 12-1) is now being added with full control to a SharePoint site.

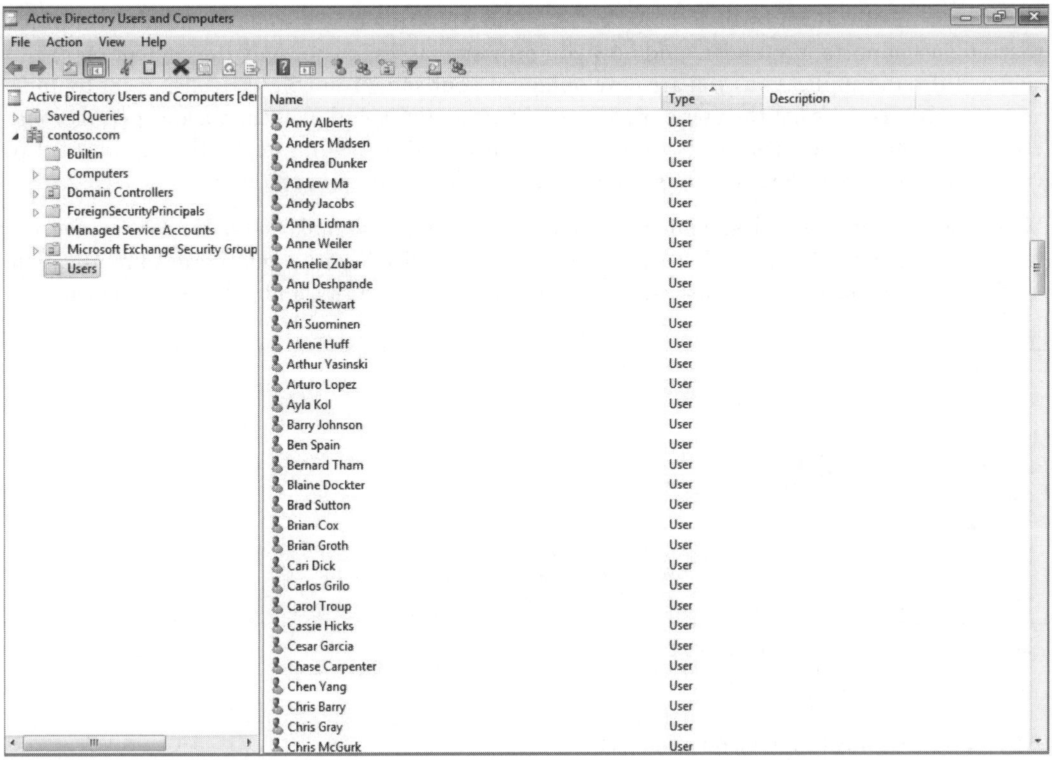

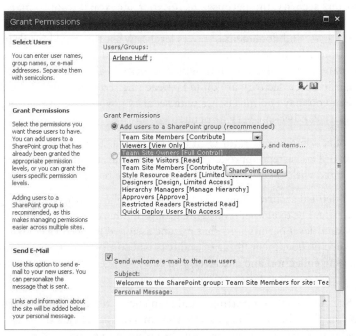

FIGURE 12-1 Active Directory Users group

FIGURE 12-2 Adding a user to a SharePoint site

Because many of you who will develop against a site collection may also be the administrator for that site, it's important to understand how you provision access to not only the content on the site, but also the applications you are developing for your site. (You will likely also want to understand — and test — what the user experience is against your solution at the various permissions levels.) Provisioning access within your organization using AD is the first step in this regard, and you can do this by clicking Site Actions ➪ Site Permissions from your SharePoint site.

Within SharePoint's Central Administration site, you also have a granular set of security management features, as shown in Figure 12-3. To access these features, click Security in Central Administration. You'll then see security features for user management, general security, and policy management.

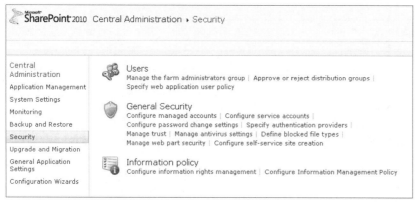

FIGURE 12-3 Security in Central Administration

If you are the person who administers security and permissions for your site, you'll want to manage them carefully. As you might imagine, you can assess permissions on a very discrete level in SharePoint (for example, at the site, lists, and document libraries levels). What this could result in is splintered or disjointed authentication, where security inheritance is broken (that is, a site does not inherit the permissions set by the parent site collection, and overall security is difficult to manage). The implications of mismanaging role-based security are quite far-reaching. For example, if you do "break the inheritance model," then you may run into issues with security governance in your organization, and management of security can become very difficult.

This is where the role of the site collection administrator is an important one. Not only does this person need to ensure a pragmatic and consistent approach to security in SharePoint, but this person also must ensure that it is implemented with governance and the appropriate restrictions in place.

This is where security groups (and defined security policies) can come into play to help you manage authentication for your SharePoint site. For example, leveraging groups in SharePoint can help avoid the management of discrete, individual-level permissions that may be assigned to sites. Users will, of course, want to restrict access to specific document libraries and lists when information should not be widely shared. However, at the site collection and site level, you can leverage security groups to your advantage.

To create a security group, click Site Actions ➪ Site Settings, and then click Create Group from the ribbon. Before clicking Create to complete the creation process, you can complete fields such as name, description, group administrator, level of permissions for the group, and so on.

AD also provides a way to federate security through the use of claims providers. This functionality was introduced with Active Directory Federation Services (ADFS) 2.0. A claims provider issues claims, and then packages those claims into security tokens that are used to authenticate a user. Using a claims-based approach to security can augment credentials from outside systems, and make it possible for you to add these credentials to AD, thus providing access to SharePoint assets and lighting up these users in features such as the People Picker. For more information on claims providers, see `http://msdn.microsoft.com/en-us/library/ee536164(v=office.14).aspx`.

SOLUTION TRUST

Another type of security issue you should be aware of in SharePoint is the use of *farm-level solutions* versus *sandboxed solutions* — that is, setting the specific trust level for your SharePoint solution. This is less about the user accessing SharePoint as a collaborative resource (that is authorization) and more about you deploying the solution into SharePoint with specific levels of access to SharePoint resources.

Farm-level solutions are scoped at the SharePoint farm level, so they have full-trust access to all the resources and functionality in SharePoint. Sandboxed solutions are solutions that run in the context of a site collection. Sandboxed solutions are restricted — for example, they cannot connect to resources that are not on the local server, access a database, call unmanaged code, write to the system disk, or access resources in a different site collection. Sandboxed solutions, though, do have the capability to monitor and shut down applications, should they have any performance issues. The metrics by which you can control and monitor sandboxed solutions are also configurable. (Of note is the fact that sandboxed solutions are one of the key ways in which you build and deploy SharePoint 2010 solutions to SharePoint Online.)

For most of the solutions in this book, you've built and deployed your applications as farm-level solutions. However, there are many interesting types of solutions that can be built using sandboxed solutions. For example, you could have Silverlight-based applications that integrate with Web 2.0, Azure Web services, or other types of Web-based services, and host them in SharePoint. You could build event receivers and workflow against lists, or use lists as data sources, and then code against them (for example, contacts or a vacation list). You can also leverage a growing set of community tools that will push the boundaries of what Visual Studio 2010 ships with (for example, the community Visual Web part created by Wouter van Vugt).

> **NOTE** *You can download Wouter van Vugt's Community Visual Web part mentioned from* `http://sharepointdevtools.codeplex.com.`

Before you start the following exercise, you must create a simple list called `Customers`. Change the `Title` field to be `Customer`, and then add a new column called `Total Sales` (of type `Currency`). Add some data to the list so that it looks like Figure 12-4.

☐ 🔗 Customer	Total Sales
Wingtip	$5,290,490,109.00
Acme	$903,209.00
Blue Yonder	$290,029,129.00
Fabrikam	$2,090,129,899.00

FIGURE 12-4 Customer list

TRY IT OUT   **Creating a Sandboxed Solution**

Code file [SandboxedSolution.zip] available for download at Wrox.com.

Sandboxed solutions are excellent ways to create and deploy solutions that can run within a site collection. To create a sandboxed solution, follow these steps:

1.   Open Visual Studio 2010 and click File ⇨ New ⇨ Project. Navigate to the SharePoint 2010 node and select Empty SharePoint Project. Provide a name for the project (for example, `SandboxedSolution`), and click OK. In the SharePoint Customization Wizard, select "Deploy as Sandboxed Solution" and click Finish.

2.   Right-click the Visual Studio project from the Solution Explorer and select Add ⇨ New Item. In the Add New Item dialog, navigate to the SharePoint 2010 node and select Web Part. Provide a name for the Web part (for example, `SSWebPart`), and click Add.

3.   In the main Web part class file (for example, `SSWebPart.cs`), add the following bolded code to the project:

```
using System;
using System.ComponentModel;
using System.Web;
using System.Web.UI;
using System.Web.UI.WebControls;
using System.Web.UI.WebControls.WebParts;
using Microsoft.SharePoint;
using Microsoft.SharePoint.WebControls;
using System.Text;

namespace SandboxedSolution.SSWebPart
{
    [ToolboxItemAttribute(false)]
    public class SSWebPart : WebPart
    {
        Label lblTitle = new Label();
        DataGrid dtgrdLists = new DataGrid();
        ListBox lstbxCustData = new ListBox();
        Button btnGetData = new Button();

        protected override void CreateChildControls()
        {
            this.Controls.Add(new LiteralControl("</br>"));
            lblTitle.Text = "List Data";
            lblTitle.Font.Bold = true;
            this.Controls.Add(lblTitle);

            this.Controls.Add(new LiteralControl("</br>"));
            this.Controls.Add(lstbxCustData);

            this.Controls.Add(new LiteralControl("</br>"));
            btnGetData.Text = "Get Data";
            this.Controls.Add(btnGetData);

            btnGetData.Click += new EventHandler(btnGetData_Click);
```

```
        }

        void btnGetData_Click(object sender, EventArgs e)
        {
            lstbxCustData.Items.Clear();

            SPSite mySiteCollection = SPContext.Current.Site;
            SPWeb mySPSite = SPContext.Current.Web;
            SPList custList = mySPSite.Lists["Customers"];
            foreach (SPListItem item in custList.Items)
            {
                lstbxCustData.Items.Add(item["Title"].ToString());
                lstbxCustData.Items.Add(item["Total Sales"].ToString());
            }
        }

    }
}
```

4.   In the .webpart file (for example, SSWebPart.webpart), amend the Title and Description properties to be more intuitive for the user, as per the following code snippet.

...

```
    <properties>
      <property name="Title" type="string">SS Web Part</property>
      <property name="Description" type="string">
          Sandboxed Solution Web Part.</property>
    </properties>
```

...

5.   When you've finished, click Build ➪ Deploy Solution. This builds and deploys your sandboxed Web part to SharePoint.

6.   After Visual Studio deploys successfully to SharePoint, click Site Actions ➪ Site Settings at your top-level SharePoint site. Then, under the Galleries section, click Solutions. You will now see the sandboxed solution added to the Solutions Gallery — which is where SharePoint stores all of the sandboxed solutions for your SharePoint site. Note that when the solution is added to the Solutions Gallery, as shown in Figure 12-5, SharePoint activates it for you.

Your resource quota is 300 server resources. Solutions can consume resources and may be temporarily disabled if your resource usage exceeds your quota.				
Current Usage (Today)				
Average Usage (Last 14 days)				

☐ Name	Edit	Modified	Status	Resource Usage
SandboxedSolution ☐ NEW	📝	4/2/2010 2:04 PM	Activated	1.00

FIGURE 12-5 Solutions Gallery

7.   Now, browse to your top-level SharePoint site and click Site Actions ➪ Edit Page. Click anywhere on the page. Then, click the Insert tab and select Web Part. Navigate to the Custom Web Part group and then select your sandboxed solution. It should look similar to Figure 12-6 when you click the Get Data link button.

FIGURE 12-6
Sandboxed
Solution Web part

How It Works

On the SharePoint server, sandboxed solutions run in a separate worker process called `SPUCWorkerProcess.exe` that isolates them. Farm-level solutions are hosted in the IIS worker process (`W3WP.exe`) and have access to all farm resources. Running code within the `SPUCWorkerProcess.exe` runs code that can only affect the site collection where you've deployed the solution.

In this exercise, you created a simple Web part that accessed data in a SharePoint list called `Customers`. And, while the presentation of the Web part wasn't what you'd call advanced design, one of the key pieces was that you were interacting with a list within the site collection. This was done when you called the `btnGetData_Click` event, set the current SharePoint context to `Current.Site`, retrieved the `Customers` list, and then added information from the `Customers` list to the `lstbxCusData` listbox.

```
void lnkbtnGetData_Click(object sender, EventArgs e)
  {
     SPSite mySiteCollection = SPContext.Current.Site;
     SPWeb mySPSite = SPContext.Current.Web;
     SPList custList = mySPSite.Lists["Customers"];
     foreach (SPListItem item in custList.Items)
       {
          lstbxCustData.Items.Add(item["Title"].ToString());
          lstbxCustData.Items.Add(item["Total Sales"].ToString());
       }

  }
```

If you had been trying to access resources outside of the scope of the site collection, this application would not have worked.

SECURE STORE SERVICE

In Chapter 8, you learned about Business Connectivity Services (BCS) and how you could build SharePoint solutions that integrate with external data systems. One of the primary ways to integrate security with the external data systems to BCS is the SSS. These external data systems can use SSS when they do not share a username and password with the AD-based users of SharePoint.

SSS is a shared service that provides the storage and mapping of user credentials from an external system to SharePoint. SSS stores account usernames and passwords, and maps these credentials to solutions (for example, external content types) by way of an *application identity* (*Application ID*) or group of identities.

A real-world example of this security integration is if John Doe has an account that lives in AD, and he has another account that lives in a separate system such as PeopleSoft, SSS can be used to link his external system (that is, the PeopleSoft system) credentials to his Windows credentials. Thus, when he tries to load an external list with data in it, the external content type can rationalize the two sets of credentials, and load the data for John to see. It does this by way of your configuring the external content type to map the Application ID of the SSS to the external data system with the credentials that are stored in it.

Let's say that you've created a new BCS solution (for example, an external list that surfaces CRM data in your SharePoint site) that requires you to map the separate set of user credentials with SharePoint. How do you go about configuring SSS to map the external content type that surfaces that data?

To configure SSS, you must first create a new instance of SSS by clicking Central Administration ➪ Application Management ➪ Manage Service Applications. On the ribbon, when you click the New drop-down arrow, you'll see an option where you can create a new SSS, as shown in Figure 12-7.

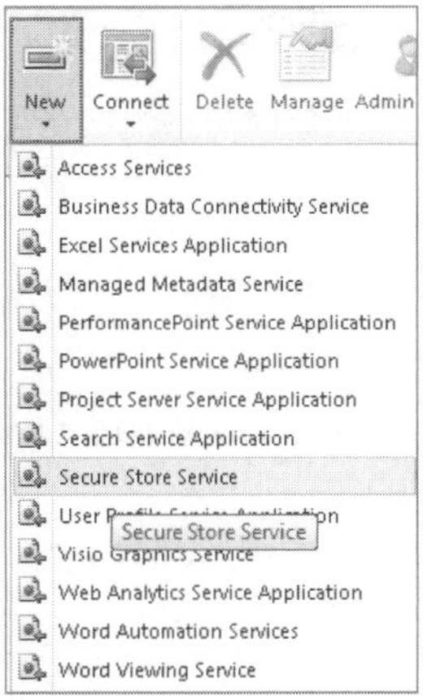

This prompts the Create New Secure Store Service Application dialog shown in Figure 12-8, where you can enter in information about the SSS (for example, Service Application Name, type of credentials to use with the database that stores the external system credentials, application pool to use, and so on).

FIGURE 12-7 Creating a new instance of a Secure Store Service

Because you will be storing sensitive data in the SSS application database, after you've created the new SSS application, you must encrypt it by clicking Generate New Key on the ribbon. You will be prompted for a strong passphrase, after which you can walk through a wizard to create the Application ID — this includes adding the external data system credentials. In Figure 12-9, you can see that the Application ID MyCRMSettings now exists, and you can use it to map John's external credentials to the BCS application.

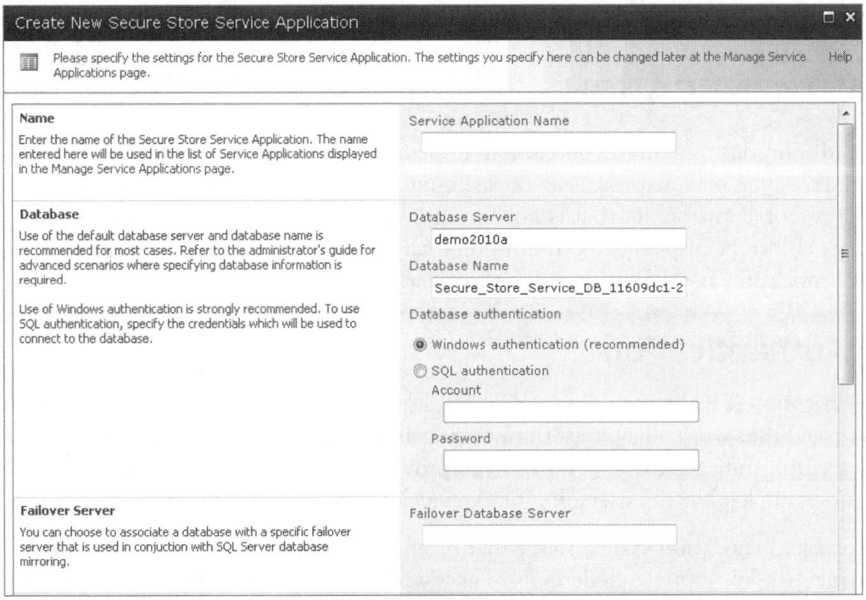

FIGURE 12-8 Creating a new SSS application

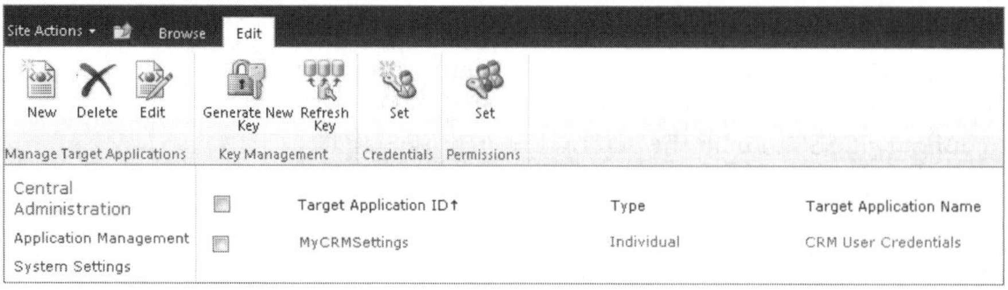

FIGURE 12-9 Target Application ID

With the Application ID created, you can now begin to use it when you are creating new external content types. For example, Figure 12-10 shows a dialog for creating a new connection (when creating an external content type in SharePoint Designer 2010). Note that the SSS Application ID that is being used is the one described earlier. Thus, all user credentials stored in the MyCRMSettings Application ID will now have access to the external list that is surfaced in SharePoint.

FIGURE 12-10 Using the target Application ID

> *NOTE* For more information on how to create and configure SSS, see http:// technet.microsoft.com/en-us/library/ee806866(office.14).aspx.

FEDERATED AUTHENTICATION

While you may build solutions to a SharePoint site that members of your organization use (thus authorized through AD), you may also want to expose content and solutions to those who are not in your domain. To provision connectivity that is not for anonymous access, you must have a "single sign-on" process, which can be implemented in different ways. This section examines the concepts of forms-based authentication and claims-based authentication.

Forms-Based Authentication

Forms-based authentication (FBA) is based on ASP.NET, and provides users access to a system using a prompt (or login page) that will collect a username and password from the user trying to access the system. You'll see this quite a bit when you want to provide access to registered users (to add content to a site, for example), but the users do not exist as a record within AD.

FBA is a cookie-based authentication system that either prompts or redirects users to a login page, where the user provides the appropriate credentials to access a SharePoint site. When the user enters his or her credentials into the login page, there is a comparison with a credential store. If there is a match, then the user is allowed to access the site. If there is not a match, then the user is denied access.

The custom identity store (or *membership provider*) can manifest in a number of ways, such as an XML file, SQL Server database, Access database, and so on — although, SQL Server is the easiest of the these options to set up and use. You store what is referred to as *membership information* in the custom identity store, which includes information about roles, profile, and personalization information.

There are a number of steps when setting up FBA for SharePoint that you'll need to walk through. At a high-level, these steps are as follows:

1. Create an identity store/membership provider.

2. Provision access to the membership provider.

3. Configure IIS to support the new membership provider.

4. Create a new Web application that enables FBA in the Default zone.

Figure 12-11 shows where you enable FBA when you create a new Web application in SharePoint Central Administration. You get here by opening Central Administration and clicking Manage Web Applications and New on the ribbon to create a new Web application. This creates a new Web application in IIS that supports FBA. You click the "Enable Forms Based Authentication (FBA)" checkbox, and then provide a membership provider name and a role manager name.

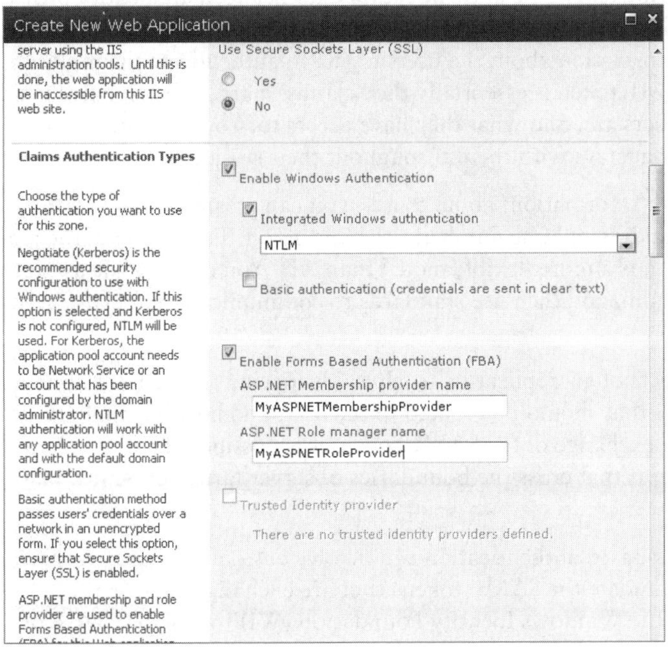

FIGURE 12-11 Enabling FBA

When using FBA, note that you must amend SharePoint's `web.config` file to include information to support. For example, you may need to include the connection string to your membership provider and PeoplePicker wildcards in the `web.config` file.

> **NOTE** *For more detailed information on SharePoint and FBA, see the MSDN article at* `http://msdn.microsoft.com/en-us/library/bb975136.aspx`. *Also, see the "Recommended Reading" section later in this chapter for more links to blogs and MSDN articles on this topic.*

Claims-Based Authentication

SharePoint Server 2010 incorporates a powerful and flexible approach to authenticating users. It works with any organizational identity system, including AD, Lightweight Directory Access Protocol (LDAP), system-specific databases, and more Web-centric models such as LiveID. This approach is known as *claims-based authentication*.

Claims-based authentication was created around the concept of an identity, and is based on accepted industry standards such as WS-* and protocols such as the Security Assertion Markup Language (SAML).

SAML is an XML-based standard for exchanging authentication data between an identity provider and a service provider that live on different domains. At the heart of this data exchange is a SAML token, which essentially provides information about the users trying to authenticate themselves against a particular system. The SAML token is essentially the "claims" part. It provides information that makes a claim as to who users are, and what they have access to. You might think of a token as metadata about the users that stays with them throughout their sessions.

While AD provides limited claims (or information) about a user, you can create an *identity* through information such as a name, email address, phone number, title, and so on. This is one of the reasons why claims-based authentication is a more flexible model than AD. You can provide as much information as you want within a claim, and then use standards to communicate that claim across systems and domains.

The identity delivers important aspects of an application, such as identifying the user who is trying to access the system, the permissions that should be granted to the user, and how the application interacts with the user. Through the exchange of the SAML token, it is possible, then, to federate your identity across systems — systems that cross the boundaries of server farms, domains, platforms, and, of course, networks.

When it comes to SharePoint, claims-based authentication can involve custom code. This is because you must understand how you can validate the SAML tokens that are exchanged across the domains. For example, you can use the Windows Identity Foundation (WIF) with your WCF or ASP.NET applications to manage SAML tokens.

As mentioned earlier in the chapter, leveraging claims-based authentication will also involve having an *issuer* in place, such as Active Directory Federated Services (ADFS) 2.0. The issuer is the service that issues the tokens. With the issuer and the SAML token, you must also ensure that the application is using the token trusts and is aware of the issuer.

> **NOTE** *Microsoft provides a very good exploration of claims-based identity and access control in the form of a downloadable PDF book. To get the book, see* `http://msdn.microsoft.com/en-us/library/ff423674.aspx.`

SUMMARY

There are many different types of security within SharePoint. This chapter provided a high-level view of some of the different types of security that you will come across when developing (and administering) SharePoint.

For example, this chapter discussed authorization and Active Directory (AD), developing solutions that run at different levels of system trust, connecting external data systems to SharePoint using Secure Store Service (SSS), and, finally, federated authentication through forms-based and claims-based authentication. You will definitely want to further explore these and other security topics for SharePoint as you move forward in your SharePoint development activities.

EXERCISES

1. Create a security group in your SharePoint site using members from AD. Provision access to the site as full control to that security group.

2. Create a more complex sandboxed solution that reads and writes data within a site collection.

3. Create a new Application ID in the SSS. Add your credentials as the only set of credentials to the new Application ID, and then use it in a BCS-based application.

4. Set up a SharePoint site to use FBA.

▶ **WHAT YOU LEARNED IN THIS CHAPTER**

ITEMS	DESCRIPTION
Active Directory (AD)	AD is a Windows-based technology that provides key network and security services, such as directory services, Domain Name System (DNS) based naming and network information, network authority management, central identity storage, and so on.
Farm-Level Solution	A solution that runs with full trust and access to farm-level resources in SharePoint.
Sandboxed Solution	A solution that runs in an isolated worker process (SPUCWorkerProcess.exe), and provides access to a restricted set of APIs and objects within SharePoint.
Secure Store Service (SSS)	A service that provisions secure connections between external data systems and BCS applications.
Forms-Based Authentication (FBA)	An ASP.NET method of authentication that prompts the user (through a form) for a username and password.
Claims-Based Authentication	A form of authentication that uses claims (that is, SAML tokens) that contain information about the user.

RECOMMENDED READING

➤ Channel 9 module on sandboxed solutions at `http://channel9.msdn.com/learn/courses/SharePoint2010Developer/SandboxedSolutions/`

➤ Channel 9 module on claims-based security at `http://channel9.msdn.com/learn/courses/SharePoint2010Developer/SharePoint2010Security/`

➤ FBA and SharePoint at the following sites:

   ➤ `http://msdn.microsoft.com/en-us/library/bb975135.aspx`

   ➤ `http://msdn.microsoft.com/en-us/library/bb977430.aspx`

   ➤ `http://blog.summitcloud.com/2009/11/forms-based-authentication-sharepoint-2010-fb/`

➤ TechNet article on SharePoint and authentication at `http://technet.microsoft.com/en-us/library/cc262350%28office.14%29.aspx`

PART IV
Appendix

▶ **APPENDIX:** Where to Go from Here

Where to Go from Here

With what you've learned in this book, you have a good starting point for developing for SharePoint. However, there are a number of things that couldn't be covered in this book that you may want to learn more about. Following are some topics that you may want to learn about as you continue with your SharePoint development:

➤ New innovations in social networking (for example, wikis and blogs)

➤ Customizing the search experience

➤ Enterprise content management (ECM) and records management

➤ PerformancePoint Services and business intelligence (BI) solutions

➤ SharePoint Online

➤ Workflows

You can find information on these topics in a variety of locations. For example, a great starting place would be the MSDN SharePoint Developer Center. Many of the chapters included a reference to this site, but here it is again:

```
http://msdn.microsoft.com/en-us/sharepoint/default.aspx
```

You may also want to check out the MSDN Office Developer Center:

```
http://msdn.microsoft.com/en-us/office/default.aspx
```

Also, Channel 9 offers a number of training kits that you can download and walk through, for both SharePoint and other Microsoft technologies. The Channel 9 Learning Center is located here:

```
http://channel9.msdn.com/learn/
```

With just these three sites, you'll find a ton of developer resources.

In terms of books, I would recommend *Professional SharePoint 2010 Development* (Indianapolis: Wiley, 2010) and *Inside SharePoint 2010* (Redmond, WA: Microsoft Press, publication date to be announced) as two good professional-grade books. The authors are long-time industry professionals in SharePoint and offer a lot with these books.

Lastly, following are a few blogs worth checking out. You'll certainly find more, but these have proven to be useful and informative over the years.

- ➤ SharePoint Team at `http://blogs.msdn.com/sharepoint`
- ➤ Andrew Connell at `www.andrewconnell.com/blog`
- ➤ Arpan Shah at `http://blogs.msdn.com/arpans`
- ➤ Paul Stubb at `http://blogs.msdn.com/pstubbs`
- ➤ Paul Andrew at `http://blogs.msdn.com/pandrew`
- ➤ Scot Hillier at `www.shillier.com/default.aspx`
- ➤ Sahil Malik at `http://blah.winsmarts.com`
- ➤ Wouter van Vugt at `http://blogs.code-counsel.net/Wouter/default.aspx`
- ➤ Todd Baginski at `www.toddbaginski.com/blog`
- ➤ Tim Heuer at `http://timheuer.com/blog`
- ➤ Steve Fox at `http://blogs.msdn.com/steve_fox`

Remember that you are embarking on an exciting journey with SharePoint development, and, with the knowledge gained from reading this book, you can now continue to grow, in passion and in skill, alongside the rest of an expanding SharePoint developer community.

INDEX

INDEX

APIs, uses, 162–163
Calendar list, 160
creating, 50–51, 136–137
Custom list, 160
databases and, 161
document libraries, 160
event receivers, 210–215
events, 160
external, offline, 307–313
External list, 160
Internet browser, 160
items, 160
overview, 159–162
programmatically accessing with, 162–163
programming against, 52–58
    ASP.NET Web services, 171–186
    client object model, 186–191
    custom WCF Service, 197–202
    server-side object model, 163–170
REST-based services and, 202–210
services, uses, 162–163
software design, 252–253
Tasks list, 160
as Web Part, 59–60
workflow, 160
Lists Web service, 52, 142
  members, 171–172
  programming against a list, 52–58, 171–186
LiteralControl, 360
literalcontrol object, 110
LOB (line-of-business)
  data, 4
  systems, 277
LobSystemType property, 287
low-touch integration, 327, 331–343

M

managed code, 10
master pages, 91–92
  creating, 153–156
  customizing, 92–98
  editing, 155–156
MCMS (Microsoft Content Management
    System), 76
membership information, 442
membership providers, 442
metadata
  Access, 309
  external content types, 284, 285–286
methods
  Add, 131
  CreateChildControls, 131, 232
  ExecuteQuery, 141, 357
  ExecuteQueryAsync, 357
  FindAllEntities, 286
  GetACustomer, 296
  getBookInfo, 89–90
  GetByTitle, 357
  GetCustomers, 296
  getCustomers, 306
  GetListAndView, 57
  GetListItems, 185
  GetListItemsAsync, 356
  OnPreRender, 230
  SaveChanges, 306, 386
  updateCustomerData, 306
  UpdateListItems, 58
  Web methods, 305
Microsoft description of SharePoint, 4
Microsoft Office. *See* Office
Microsoft.SharePoint namespace, 162

X–Y–Z